Chiang Mai
& Northern Thailand

Joe Cummings

LONELY PLANET PUBLICATIONS
Melbourne • Oakland • London • Paris

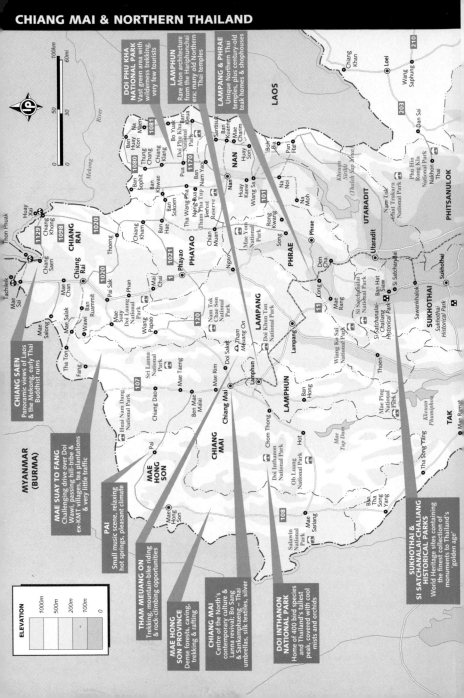

CHIANG MAI & NORTHERN THAILAND

DOI PHU KHA NATIONAL PARK
Vast green area with wilderness trekking, very few tourists

LAMPHUN
Rare Mon architecture from the Hariphunchai era; many old Northern Thai temples

LAMPANG & PHRAE
Unique Northern Thai temples, plus century-old teak homes & shophouses

CHIANG SAEN
Panoramic views of Laos & the Mekong, early Thai Buddhist ruins

MAE SUAY TO FANG
Challenging drive over Doi Wawi, passing hill-tribe & ex-KMT villages, tea plantations & very little traffic

PAI
Small music scene, relaxing hot springs, pleasant climate

THAM MEUANG ON
Trekking, mountain-bike riding & rock-climbing opportunities

MAE HONG SON PROVINCE
Dense forests, caving, trekking & rafting

CHIANG MAI
Centre of the North's contemporary culture & Lanna revival; Bo Sang & Sankamphaeng – Thai umbrellas, silk textiles, silver

DOI INTHANON NATIONAL PARK
Home of 400 bird species and Thailand's highest peak, covered with cool mists and orchids

SUKHOTHAI & SI SATCHANALAI-CHALIANG HISTORICAL PARKS
World Heritage sites containing the finest collection of monuments to Thailand's 'golden age'

MYANMAR (BURMA)

LAOS

ELEVATION
1000m
500m
200m
100m
0

UM PHANG
Rafting, trekking & elephant riding to spectacular waterfalls

Chiang Mai & Northern Thailand
1st edition – April 2002

Published by
Lonely Planet Publications Pty Ltd ABN 36 005 607 983
90 Maribyrnong St, Footscray, Victoria 3011, Australia

Lonely Planet offices
Australia Locked Bag 1, Footscray, Victoria 3011
USA 150 Linden St, Oakland, CA 94607
UK 10a Spring Place, London NW5 3BH
France 1 rue du Dahomey, 75011 Paris

Photographs
Many of the images in this guide are available for licensing from
Lonely Planet Images.
email: lpi@lonelyplanet.com.au
Web site: www.lonelyplanetimages.com

Front cover photograph
Umbrellas from Baw Sang, the 'umbrella village' in Chiang Mai
(Izzet Keribar).

ISBN 1 74059 064 3

Printed through Colorcraft Ltd, Hong Kong
Printed in China

Contents – Text

Contents – Maps

4 Contents – Maps

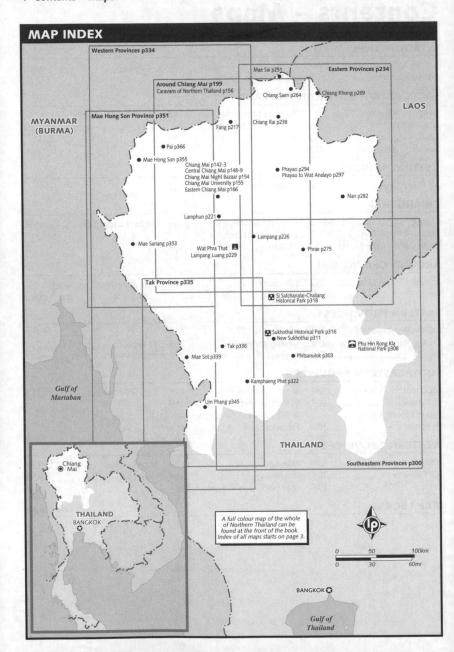

MAP INDEX

Western Provinces p334

Around Chiang Mai p199
Caravans of Northern Thailand p156

Mae Hong Son Province p351

MYANMAR
(BURMA)

Mae Sai p251

Eastern Provinces p234

Chiang Saen p264   Chiang Khong p269

LAOS

Chiang Rai p238

Fang p217

Pai p366

Mae Hong Son p355

Chiang Mai p142-3
Central Chiang Mai p148-9
Chiang Mai Night Bazaar p154
Chiang Mai University p155
Eastern Chiang Mai p166

Phayao p294
Phayao to Wat Analayo p297

Nan p282

Lamphun p221

Lampang p226

Mae Sariang p353

Wat Phra That
Lampang Luang p229

Phrae p275

Tak Province p335

Si Satchanalai-Chaliang
Historical Park p318

Sukhothai Historical Park p316
New Sukhothai p311

Phu Hin Rong Kla
National Park p308

Tak p336

Mae Sot p339

Phitsanulok p303

Gulf of
Martaban

Kamphaeng Phet p322

Um Phang p345

THAILAND

Southeastern Provinces p300

Chiang
Mai

THAILAND
BANGKOK

A full colour map of the whole
of Northern Thailand can be
found at the front of the book.
Index of all maps starts on page 3.

0   50   100km
0   30   60mi

BANGKOK

Gulf of
Thailand

The Author

Joe Cummings

Born in the sub-tropical port of New Orleans, Joe began travelling in Southeast Asia shortly after finishing university. Before writing became a full-time job, he played guitar in a succession of bands, volunteered for the Peace Corps, worked as a movie extra, and taught English in Thailand, Malaysia, Taiwan and the USA. Along the way he earned an MA degree in Thai language and art history.

For Lonely Planet and other publishers he has written over 30 original guidebooks, phrasebooks and atlases for countries in Asia and North America. For Lonely Planet he has authored the *Thai* and *Lao* phrasebooks, *World Food Thailand* and guides to *Bangkok, Thailand, Thailand's Islands & Beaches, Laos* and *Myanmar*, plus parts of *South-East Asia on a shoestring*. Most recently he wrote the text for Lonely Planet's pictorial *Buddhist Stupas in Asia: The Shape of Perfection*.

From the Author

Many people helped during the creation of this guidebook, but I owe special thanks to the following: Mau Travel Service in Chiang Mai for researching intra-Asia air fares; Lynne Cummings for style-checking; Suwanee Emon for her invaluable assistance with Thai language and with fact-checking; Andrew Forbes for creating a walking tour of Chiang Mai's gates and bastions; Dennis Gillman for palmistry under fire; Oliver Hargreave for help with maps; Ajahn Dhamnu Haripitak for discussions on Lanna art; Peter Holmshaw for added history on Mae Salong; Panupong Laohasom for his Lanna mural photography; Karin Madison for tape transcriptions and data organisation; Jeff Petry for his hilltribe expertise; Simon Robson for assistance in Mae Rim and environs; and Claudine Triolo for writing the Lanna-Style Temple Murals special section.

This Book

This first edition of *Chiang Mai & Northern Thailand* was written by long-standing Chiang Mai resident Joe Cummings.

FROM THE PUBLISHER

This book was coordinated in Lonely Planet's Melbourne office by Bruce Evans and Jane Thompson (editing) and Meredith Mail (mapping and layout). Anastasia Safioleas and Jocelyn Harewood assisted with editing and proofing, while Chris Thomas assisted with mapping. Thanks to Mark Germanchis for layout assistance; Leonie Mugavin for checking the Getting There & Away chapter; Shahara Ahmed for looking over the health section; Quentin Frayne for the Language chapter; Clint Curé (CC), Jenny Bowman (JB), Martin Harris (MH) and Simon Borg (SB) for the illustrations; and Katie Butterworth for the chapter end. Glenn Beanland of LPI gave support for colour photos and Jenny Jones designed the cover. Tim Fitzgerald, Chris Love and Kristin Odijk did final checks for the whole book.

THANKS
Many thanks to the travellers who used the last edition and wrote to us with helpful hints, advice and interesting anecdotes. Your names appear in the back of this book.

Foreword

ABOUT LONELY PLANET GUIDEBOOKS

The story begins with a classic travel adventure: Tony and Maureen Wheeler's 1972 journey across Europe and Asia to Australia. There was no useful information about the overland trail then, so Tony and Maureen published the first Lonely Planet guidebook to meet a growing need.

From a kitchen table, Lonely Planet has grown to become the largest independent travel publisher in the world, with offices in Melbourne (Australia), Oakland (USA), London (UK) and Paris (France).

Today Lonely Planet guidebooks cover the globe. There is an ever-growing list of books and information in a variety of media. Some things haven't changed. The main aim is still to make it possible for adventurous travellers to get out there – to explore and better understand the world.

At Lonely Planet we believe travellers can make a positive contribution to the countries they visit – if they respect their host communities and spend their money wisely. Since 1986 a percentage of the income from each book has been donated to aid projects and human rights campaigns, and, more recently, to wildlife conservation.

UPDATES & READER FEEDBACK

Things change – prices go up, schedules change, good places go bad and bad places go bankrupt. Nothing stays the same. So, if you find things better or worse, recently opened or long-since closed, please tell us and help make the next edition even more accurate and useful.

Lonely Planet thoroughly updates each guidebook as often as possible – usually every two years, although for some destinations the gap can be longer. Between editions, up-to-date information is available in our free, quarterly *Planet Talk* newsletter and monthly email bulletin *Comet*. The *Upgrades* section of our website (W www.lonelyplanet.com) is also regularly updated by Lonely Planet authors, and the site's *Scoop* section covers news and current affairs relevant to travellers. Lastly, the *Thorn Tree* bulletin board and *Postcards* section carry unverified, but fascinating, reports from travellers.

Tell us about it! We genuinely value your feedback. A well-travelled team at Lonely Planet reads and acknowledges every email and letter we receive and ensures that every morsel of information finds its way to the relevant authors, editors and cartographers.

Everyone who writes to us will find their name listed in the next edition of the appropriate guidebook, and will receive the latest issue of *Comet* or *Planet Talk*. The very best contributions will be rewarded with a free guidebook.

We may edit, reproduce and incorporate your comments in Lonely Planet products such as guidebooks, websites and digital products, so let us know if you don't want your comments reproduced or your name acknowledged.

How to contact Lonely Planet:
Online: e talk2us@lonelyplanet.com.au, W www.lonelyplanet.com
Australia: Locked Bag 1, Footscray, Victoria 3011
UK: 10a Spring Place, London NW5 3BH
USA: 150 Linden St, Oakland, CA 94607

Introduction

Northern Thailand straddles the most important historical crossroads of northern Southeast Asia, a vast region of mountains, valleys and rivers where peoples from China, Laos, Myanmar and Thailand have long traded goods and ideas in a fusion of cultures. This blend has been further enlivened by the presence of tribal societies – such as the Hmong-Mien, Thai Lü and Phuan – whose ethnic heritage knows no fixed political boundaries.

Long an important trading entrepot due to its position along caravan routes from China's Yunnan province to the port of Mawlamyaing (Moulmein) in Myanmar, Northern Thailand rose to prominence when local Thai princes consolidated power and asserted cultural dominance over the region in the 13th century. Two Northern Thai kingdoms in particular, Lan Na Thai (Lanna) and Sukhothai, came to the fore and are widely recognised by today's Thais as the original sources of Thai nationhood. Lanna's main capital, Chiang Mai, became known as the most important religious and cultural relay point for northern Southeast Asia, especially after the convening of the eighth world synod of Theravada Buddhism in 1477.

Even a half millennium later, whether they come to work, play, or simply observe, Thai and foreign visitors alike find that Chiang Mai has perhaps the strongest sense of place of any city in Thailand. A capital born in pride for things Northern Thai, it's a city that continues to holds fast to its *khon meuang* (people of the principality, ie, Northern Thai) identity. Even modern office buildings may bear stylised *kaalae* (X-crossed, carved gables common to traditional Northern Thai rooflines), and one of the city's plushest shopping centres is referred to as a *kàat*, an old Northern Thai term meaning 'market'.

Northern Thailand's hill tribes, called *chao khǎo* (mountain people) by the Thais, frequently come down from their highland homes to trade in Chiang Mai and other cities of the North, adding another significant element to the region's culture. Even in Chiang Mai's modern Night Bazaar, in a part of the city where the hill tribes have traded with Thais and Yunnanese caravaners for centuries, one still sees their colourful garb and distinctive faces.

Away from the main avenues and tourist districts, the narrow, winding *soi* (lanes) of the moated city will draw the visitor into a semi-private world of humble noodle shops, cobblers and over 30 Lanna-style Buddhist temples.

Outside of the cities Northern Thailand boasts more natural forest area, and more national parks and wildlife sanctuaries, than any other region of the country. River rafting, hiking, bird-watching and camping

CHIANG MAI &
NORTHERN THAILAND

MYANMAR (BURMA)
VIETNAM
Gulf of Tonkin
LAOS
Chiang Mai
Gulf of Martaban
THAILAND
BANGKOK
CAMBODIA
ANDAMAN SEA
VIETNAM
Gulf of Thailand
SOUTH CHINA SEA
MALAYSIA
INDONESIA
SINGAPORE

attract those interested in experiencing Northern Thailand's natural surroundings, while visitors keen on learning more about the region's ethnic minorities can visit semi-remote villages on mountain slopes.

Bus, train and plane travel options are relatively abundant throughout the North, but you can also choose to propel yourself via rented bicycle, motorcycle or car, all easily arranged through rental agencies in towns and cities.

Northern Thai cuisine will keep gourmets busy sorting out the exciting blend of Thai, Lao, Shan and Yunnanese influences. For those who'd like to learn the culinary arts, there are ample opportunities to study Thai cooking in Chiang Mai and other Northern towns.

Northern Thailand boasts its own brand of Thai massage as well, and here again one can begin to master the healing art of *nûat phǎen bohraan* (traditional massage) via local study programs.

Visits to neighbouring Laos and Myanmar, both of which have open land borders with Northern Thailand, offer yet more opportunity for delving into the region's cultural and historical background.

Facts about Northern Thailand

HISTORY
Prehistory

In Phrae and Lampang archaeologists have found stone implements that suggest human habitation in Northern Thailand over 600,000 years ago. Tools dating to around 6000 BC link the region to the Hoa Binh culture associated with northern Vietnam.

Northern Thailand's prehistoric cultures added pottery, rope and basketry to their toolkits during the area's Neolithic period (circa 6000–600 BC) and by 5000 BC these early Northerners had developed art in the form of cave or rock-shelter paintings. Among the more impressive known rock-art sites is Pratu Pha, approximately 45km north of Lampang, where one can still make out more than a hundred drawings of animals, humans and abstract patterns. Around this same time, communities in the North were raising animals for food, and by 3000 BC rice cultivation had begun.

Beginning roughly 800 BC, Northerners were using bronze tools, most of which were probably imported, since the ore deposits necessary for making this metal appear to be relatively limited in Northern Thailand.

Although it's virtually impossible to identify the ethnicity or language of the prehistoric Northern Thais, some scholars speculate that they may have been the Mon-Khmer forebears of the Lawa/Luwa/Wa tribes of the region's present and immediate past.

Arrival of the Mon

Around the 6th century AD, several city-states around Thailand were occupied by Mon-Khmer speaking members of the Austro-Thai ethnolinguistic family, and an important network of agricultural communities was thriving in Central and Southern Thailand. Chief among these was the Mon kingdom of Dvaravati (Sanskrit for 'Place of Gates'). It appears to have been centred on or near present-day Nakhon Pathom in Central Thailand, although the area around what is now Lopburi was also an important Dvaravati locus.

The Mon may have descended from a group of Indian immigrants from Kalinga, an area overlapping the boundaries of the modern Indian states of Orissa and Andhra Pradesh. The Dvaravati Mon produced many works of art, including Buddha images, stucco reliefs on temple walls and in caves, architecture, exquisite terracotta heads, votive tablets and various sculptures. This kingdom in fact may have been a cultural relay point for the pre-Angkor cultures of ancient Cambodia and Champa to the east.

The Dvaravati Mon were apparently the first to establish a relatively sophisticated principality in Northern Thailand. Northern Thai chronicles recount that a hermit named Suthep decided that a riverbank spot near what is today Lamphun was a suitable site for a new kingdom, and so in AD 750 he invited Princess Chama Thewi from Lopburi – then part of Dvaravati – to found Hariphunchai.

DVARAVATI

CHINA
VIETNAM
MYANMAR (BURMA)
LAOS
Mekong River
THAILAND
CAMBODIA
VIETNAM
ANDAMAN SEA
Gulf of Thailand
INDONESIA
MALAYSIA
SINGAPORE

Extents of Dvaravati Kingdom 6th–8th Century AD

Although the story of the hermit and the Lopburi princess has taken on mythical proportions, the idea that the Mon were immigrants to the Lamphun area finds some support in Northern Thai chronicles, which state that the local population at Hariphunchai – the first community in Northern Thailand known to have written records (all of which appear in Mon script) – were originally Lawa.

Chama Thewi reportedly introduced the North to Theravada Buddhism by bringing along learned monks and Buddhist texts from Lopburi. The story implies that the Dvaravati Mon (and their hermit sponsor) were seeking a place in which to transplant their culture. In fact Dvaravati in general, and Lopburi in particular, came to be threatened around that time by the expanding Angkor empire, centred by the east in present-day Cambodia.

During the reign of Angkor king Suryavarman 1 (AD 1002–49) Lopburi became an Angkor vassal state and the Dvaravati Mon watched their art and religion fade under Hindu-Khmer influence. Although Dvaravati declined quickly under Angkor rule, the Hariphunchai kingdom maintained

ANGKOR

CHINA
VIETNAM
MYANMAR (BURMA)
LAOS
Mekong River
THAILAND
CAMBODIA
VIETNAM
ANDAMAN SEA
Gulf of Thailand
INDONESIA
MALAYSIA
SINGAPORE

Extents of Angkor Kingdom 9th–13th Century AD

its religion and customs for another two centuries.

Thai Meuang

Around this same time Northern Thailand began receiving its first Thai immigrants. Most present-day sources agree that before the first millennium AD an identifiably 'Thai' culture, as separate from the Mon-Khmer branch of the Austro-Thai ethnolinguistic family, did not yet exist in Northern Thailand. Early Thai legends suggest that Thai-speaking peoples of Thai-Kadai origin came into the region from the north and/or the east, ie, from the direction of southwestern China and/or northern Vietnam.

These Thai speakers clearly showed a preference for living in river valleys, from the Red River (Hong He) in the south of China and Vietnam to the Brahmaputra River in Assam, India. Originally the two main terminals for movement into what is now Thailand were the 'northern terminal' in the Yuan Jiang and other river areas in China's modern-day Yunnan and Guangxi Provinces, and the 'southern terminal' along Central Thailand's Mae Nam Chao Phraya (Chao Phraya River).

Between these two terminals, river valleys along the Nan, Ping, Kok, Yom and Wang Rivers in Northern Thailand developed sizable settlements, and were linked to various valley communities in Laos and in the Shan State in Myanmar. Arriving in small groups from perhaps as early as the 8th century, and more numerously from the mid-11th century on, these migrant Thais established local administrative plans along traditional social schemata according to *meuang* (principality or city-state), under the rule of chieftains or sovereigns called *jâo meuang*.

Each meuang was based in a river valley or section of a valley. Some meuang were loosely collected under one jâo meuang or more formally allied under powerful rulers known as *pháyaa* (*pha-nyáa* in Northern Thai).

Often called Yuan or Yün by non-Thais, they called themselves Khon Meuang (Meuang People), a label that has endured over the centuries and is today used to refer to Northern Thais in general, especially Thais from Chiang Mai.

In the mid-13th century, the rise to power of the Mongols under Kublai Khan in Song-dynasty China caused a more dramatic southward migration of Thai peoples. Wherever Thais met indigenous populations of Tibeto-Burmans and Mon-Khmers in the move south (into what is now Myanmar, Thailand and Laos), they were somehow able to displace, assimilate or co-opt them without force. The most probable explanation for this relatively smooth assimilation is that there were already smaller numbers of Thai peoples in the area.

Sukhothai & Lan Na Thai

Taking advantage of declining Khmer power in the lower North, a Thai pháyaa named Si Intharathit united several meuang to found a kingdom called Sukhothai – from the Sanskrit *sukhodaya* ('arising of happiness') – in 1238. Although little is really known about this first Thai kingdom, many Thais today have a sentimental, romantic view of the Sukhothai period, seeing it as a 'golden age' of Thai politics, religion and

culture – an egalitarian, noble period when all the people had enough to eat and the kingdom was unconquerable. A passage from Sukhothai's famous Ram Khamhaeng inscription reads:

This land of Sukhothai is thriving. There is fish in the water and rice in the fields…The King has hung a bell in the opening of the gate over there; if any commoner has a grievance which sickens his belly and grips his heart, he goes and strikes the bell; King Ram Khamhaeng questions the man, examines the case and decides it justly for him.

Among other accomplishments, the third Sukhothai king, Phaya Ruang (today more popularly known as Pho Khun Ram Khamhaeng), sponsored a fledgling Thai writing system which became the basis for modern Thai; he also codified the Thai form of Theravada Buddhism, as borrowed from the Singhalese. Under Ram Khamhaeng, the Sukhothai kingdom extended from Nakhon Si Thammarat in the South to the upper Mekong River Valley (Laos), and to Bago (Myanmar).

Meanwhile Phaya Mang Rai, ambitious and charismatic son of the daughter of the Thai Lü pháyaa of Chiang Rung (today

called Jinghong by the Chinese) in southern Yunnan, succeeded his Lao father as the ruler of Ngoen Yang (near present-day Chiang Saen) in 1259. To better defend his kingdom's northern flank from the growing power of Kublai Khan's Mongols, Phaya Mang Rai established the self-named meuang Chiang Rai farther southwest in Northern Thailand in 1262. Around six years later he added Chiang Khong to his dominions, and by the time another decade had passed, he had established a short-lived capital at Fang. Eighteen years later, by means of political intrigue as well as military might, the pháyaa made perhaps the most strategic decision of his career when he annexed Hariphunchai to his kingdom.

Many characteristics of the Mon culture of Hariphunchai, particularly those related to Buddhism and literature, were absorbed into the Thai cultural context during this time. Much as the captive Mon of central Myanmar's Thaton had previously influenced the Burman culture of the Bagan kingdom, and the defeated Angkor court later made significant contributions to Central Thailand's Ayuthaya kingdom, the first Northern Thai kingdoms owe much to their Mon predecessors at Lamphun.

On the fertile plains around the natural lagoon of Kwan Phayao (Lake Phayao), south of Chiang Rai, a Lawa chieftain called Si Jom Thong founded a fledgling Thai-style meuang in AD 1097, probably with the aid of Thai jâo. Originally called Phu Kam Yao, a name which later coalesced into Phayao, the meuang evolved into a Thai kingdom encompassing much of present-day Phayao and Nan Provinces under the reign of Phaya Ngam Meuang in the mid-13th century. Phaya Ngam Meuang was a contemporary of both Phaya Mang Rai of Chiang Rai and Ram Khamhaeng of Sukhothai, and had schooled with the latter in Lopburi.

To better resist expansionist pressures from the Mongols to the north and the Burmese to the west, Phaya Mang Rai and Phaya Ngam Meuang formed an alliance in 1276. This alliance grew when Phaya Mang Rai, Phaya Ngam Meuang and Ram Khamhaeng met together in 1287 and re-

portedly swore eternal friendship. With the support of the Sukhothai kingdom to the south, in 1296 Phaya Mang Rai commenced construction of Chiang Mai (New City).

Chiang Mai became the capital of a new, larger kingdom called Lan Na Thai (Million Thai Rice-Fields), nowadays often known simply as 'Lanna'. In 1327 Phaya Mang Rai's successor Saen Phu founded his own small kingdom, Chiang Saen on the banks of the Mekong River along an important north-south trade route. The linking of Chiang Saen, Chiang Rai, Chiang Mai and Phayao created a strong base from which Lanna could expand.

In 1376, Central Thailand's powerful Ayuthaya rulers annexed Sukhothai, folding it into the sovereign state that was becoming known to the world outside as

Two Kings and a Queen

The famous alliance between Sukhothai's Ram Khamhaeng and the two lords of the upper North, Phaya Ngam Meuang and Phaya Mang Rai, may have been at least partially prompted by a cuckolding.

According to legend, Ram Khamhaeng decided to pay his old schoolmate Phaya Ngam Meuang a visit at his palace in Phayao. Whether his intentions were to forge an alliance or to spy on the rival kingdom, we don't know, but when Ram Khamhaeng saw Phaya Ngam Meuang's queen, he was struck by her beauty. In the middle of the night he entered her chambers, climbed into her bed and, pretending to be her husband, made love to her. Shortly after he had left, Phaya Ngam Meuang came to his queen and when the queen inquired as to why he was making a second visit, they realised what Ram Khamhaeng had done.

Perhaps because Ram Khamhaeng knew that Phaya Ngam Meuang now had just cause to attack the Sukhothai kingdom (or perhaps because he felt strong guilt for having deceived his old friend), so the story goes, he more willingly entered into a triple alliance with Phaya Ngam Meuang and Phaya Mang Rai.

AYUTHAYA

CHINA
VIETNAM
MYANMAR (BURMA)
LAOS
Mekong River
THAILAND
CAMBODIA
VIETNAM
ANDAMAN SEA
Gulf of Thailand
INDONESIA
MALAYSIA
SINGAPORE

Extents of Ayuthaya Kingdom AD 1350–1767

Siam. As its former partner state Sukhothai waned, Lanna grew.

Lanna soon crossed the Mekong River to annex the meuang of Wiang Jan. In the 14th century, Wiang Jan was taken from Lanna by Chao Fah Ngum of Luang Prabang, who made it part of his Lan Chang (Million Elephants; known in modern Lao as Lan Xang) kingdom. Wiang Chan later flourished as an independent kingdom for a short time during the mid-16th century and eventually became the capital of Laos in its royal, French (where it got its more popular international spelling, 'Vientiane') and now socialist incarnations.

Within a century and a half of its founding, Lanna had extended across Northern Thailand to include Nan and Phrae, ascending to the height of its power and influence. Buddhist monks from Lanna travelled to and from India and Sri Lanka to ensure the continuity of the teachings and lineage, and in 1477 Chiang Mai's Wat Jet Yot hosted the 8th *sangayana* (world Buddhist council). Buddhist missionaries from Chiang Mai were sent to such far-flung Thai capitals as Chiang Tung (today Kyaingtong, Myanmar), Chiang Rung (Jinghong, China) and Luang Prabang (Laos).

Perhaps because its rulers became so enamoured with the building of stupas and Buddhist monasteries, and with the exporting of missionaries, Lanna's economy began to weaken towards the beginning of the 16th century. After a period of dynastic decline, Lanna fell to the Burmese in 1558.

Burmese Rule & Cooperation with Siam

Although Lanna residents apparently resented Burmese rule far less than did their Siamese counterparts in Ayuthaya, they did make intermittent attempts to restore independence, to no avail. Around 1600 and again in 1662, Siamese kings temporarily usurped Burmese control over Chiang Mai, but in each case the Burmese regained the city.

The most successful uprising placed a Lan Chang noble, Phra Chao Ong Kham, in charge of Chiang Mai between 1727 and 1759, a period during which Burma itself was in political turmoil. Chiang Mai remained independent until 1763 (four years after Phra Chao Ong Kham's death). When the Burmese retook the capital, they relocated most of the city's residents to Inwa (Ava) near Mandalay to serve as labourers and prisoners of war.

After the Burmese sacking of Ayuthaya in 1767, Lanna resistors reckoned the time was ripe to seek an alliance with the Siamese in order to expel the invaders. Chao Kawila, a Northern Thai from Lampang, convinced Phraya Taksin, a half-Chinese, half-Thai general based at the new Siamese capital of Thonburi, to aid the Lanna resistors in mounting an attack on the Burmese occupation of Chiang Mai. Phraya Taksin and his supporters agreed to a joint offensive on the condition that if the Burmese were expelled, Lanna would afterwards become a vassal state to Siam.

The joint Lanna-Siamese forces successfully reclaimed the northern capital in February 1775, followed by Chiang Saen in 1804. For Lanna the establishment of this Thonburi-Ratanakosin period was the beginning of the end of independence from the Siamese. In 1874 the first royal governor

THONBURI-RATANAKOSIN

CHINA
MYANMAR (BURMA)
VIETNAM
LAOS
Mekong River
THAILAND
ANDAMAN SEA
CAMBODIA
VIETNAM
Gulf of Thailand
INDONESIA
MALAYSIA
SINGAPORE

Extents of Thonburi-Ratanakosin Kingdom AD 1767–Present

from Bangkok arrived and set about creating a new administrative structure. Under the Bangkok-imposed system, all of Siam was classified into *mùu bâan* (villages), *tambon* (collections of villages), *amphoe* (districts), *jangwàt* (provinces) and *monthon* (literally, circle; a designated group of provinces). Chiang Mai, for example, became part of Monthon Phayap.

Postal service between Bangkok and Chiang Mai began in 1883, and telegraph and railway lines constructed between 1888 and 1919 further linked the North with the Siamese capital. In 1927 Rama VII became the first Siamese monarch to visit Chiang Mai. The monthon system was abolished when a bloodless revolution transformed Siam from an absolute monarchy to constitutional monarchy in 1932. From thereon the history of Northern Thailand was tied up with that of the country as a whole.

Military Rule & Communist Insurgency

In 1939 the country officially changed its name from Siam to Thailand – rendered in Thai as *pràthêt thai*. 'Pràthêt' comes from the Sanskrit pradesha or 'country', while 'Thai' is considered to have the connotation of 'free', although in general usage it refers to the Thai, Tai or T'ai peoples, who are found as far east as Tonkin, as far west as Assam, as far north as southern China, and as far south as northern Malaysia. Since Northern Thailand appears to have been the locus of the first Thai kingdoms (at least inside Thailand's historical borders), most Northern Thais welcomed the name change, unlike many of their counterparts in former Siam.

Japanese forces briefly occupied parts of the North following their 1941 invasion of Thailand in WWII, conscripting Northern Thais to build roads intended to take the Japanese invaders deeper into Asia. Some of the roadbeds developed under the Japanese are still in use in the North.

In the aftermath of the war, the development of a right-wing military dictatorship in Bangkok alienated many Northerners as well as many students, farmers and workers throughout Thailand. From 1964 to 1973 the Thai nation was ruled by army officers Thanom Kittikachorn and Praphat Charusathien. During this time Thailand allowed the USA to establish several army bases within its borders in support of the US campaign in Indochina.

Reacting to political repression, in June 1973 10,000 Thai students in Bangkok publicly demanded a civilian constitution. On 14 October of the same year the military brutally suppressed a large demonstration at Thammasat University in Bangkok, but King Bhumibol and General Krit Sivara, who sympathised with the students, refused to support further bloodshed, forcing Thanom and Praphat to leave Thailand. A 14-party coalition government took charge and steered a leftist agenda past a conservative parliament. Among the civilian government's lasting achievements were a national minimum wage, the repeal of harsh anti-communist laws and the ejection of US military forces from Thailand.

This elected government ruled until 6 October 1976, when students demonstrated again, this time protesting against Thanom's return to Thailand as a monk. Thammasat

University again became a battlefield as border patrol police and right-wing, paramilitary civilian groups assaulted a group of 2000 students holding a peaceful sit-in. It is estimated that hundreds of students were killed and injured in the fracas, and more than a thousand were arrested. Using public disorder as an excuse, the military stepped in and installed a new right-wing government.

This bloody incident disillusioned many Thai students and older intellectuals not directly involved with the demonstrations. Numerous idealists 'dropped out' of Thai society and joined the People's Liberation Army of Thailand (PLAT) – armed communist insurgents based in the hills of Northern Thailand. The PLAT, which had been active in Thailand since the 1930s, also operated in parts of Northeastern and Southern Thailand, but the main communist bases were in the North at Phu Hin Rong Kla and Khao Kho.

From their Northern Thai bases the communists were able to maintain intermittent control over large parts of the rural North, particularly in Tak, Sukhothai, Phitsanulok, Nan and Phrae Provinces. Outside the *amphoe meuang* (provincial capitals) it was often considered unsafe to travel, particularly at night, and particularly in government-controlled vehicles (including public buses). Any public works projects, such as new highway development, undertaken by the Thai government became automatic targets of the PLAT.

Meanwhile Thai army patrols seeking PLAT units often mistreated Northern Thai civilians who had no contact with the communists. This served to widen the disaffection between rural Northern Thais and Bangkok. Although in a few cases the Communist Party of Thailand (CPT) sponsored rural schools and clinics, for the most part the conflict between the communists and the government severely hampered rural development in the North.

Shift to Civilian Rule

Shuffles in the military-backed government over the next few years propelled ex-General Prem Tinsulanonda to the helm in 1980. By this time the PLAT had reached a peak force numbering around 10,000 armed insurgents. Prem served as prime minister till 1988 and is credited with the political and economic stabilisation of Thailand in the post–Indochina War years. The major success of the Prem years was a complete dismantling of the CPT and PLAT through an effective combination of a 1982 amnesty program (which brought the students back from the forests) and military action.

With the PLAT out of the picture, Prem's administration began focusing on a gradual democratisation of Thailand that culminated in the 1988 election of his successor, retired general and businessman Chatichai Choonhavan.

Under Chatichai, Thailand enjoyed a brief period of unprecedented popular in government. Thailand seemed to be entering a new era in which the country's double-digit economic boom ran concurrently with democratisation. The North began, for the first time since before WWII, to share in the fruits of Thailand's growth, albeit at a slower pace than Central and Southern Thailand, the nation's economic dynamos.

Another military coup in 1991 reminded Thais that the men in green were still major players. Civilian rule was restored the following year, and in September 1997 Thai parliament voted in a new constitution that guaranteed – at least on paper – more human and civil rights than had hitherto been codified in Thailand. The year 1997 is also memorable because a debt crisis drove the Thai currency into a deflationary tailspin and brought the national economy to a virtual halt from which it has yet to fully recover.

Northern Thais, who continue to feel somewhat independent from Bangkok rule, tend to blame all the country's political and economic woes on *khon tâi* (southern people; ie, Bangkokians). Even during the boom years of the 1980s and early 1990s, when the North's largest city, Chiang Mai, benefited economically, most of the region's population remained among the poorest in Thailand.

GEOGRAPHY

Northern Thailand comprises roughly 25% of the nation's total area of 517,000 sq km, or about 130,000 sq km. Mountain ranges and rivers that ripple across the region have helped preserve the autonomy of Northern Thais and many other ethnic groups for centuries. At the same time this rugged topography offers relatively scant land for easy cultivation. Some peoples adapted better than others to the demanding conditions, and before the advent of road and rail, these features functioned as a sort of natural filter between the North and the outside world.

Representing the southernmost extreme of a series of mountain ranges that extends from the Tibetan Plateau and across northern Myanmar and southwest China, the peaks of Northern Thailand form an important watershed for most of Thailand's major rivers. All but one (the Salawin) of these rivers and their tributaries drain into the Gulf of Thailand via the Chao Phraya Delta near Bangkok; Mae Nam Salawin, which forms a partial border between Thailand and Myanmar, exits into the Indian Ocean via the Gulf of Mottama.

Where these rivers have eroded valleys amid the mountainous terrain, however, the broad alluvial plains have proved to be terrifically fertile. Farming – especially of fruit, vegetables and ornamental plants that require cooler weather than is found in Central or Southern Thailand – plays an important role in the Northern economy.

CLIMATE

Northern Thailand, like all of Thailand, is tropical. More specifically, the region is subject to a 'dry and wet monsoon climate', ruled by monsoons that produce three seasons. The southwest monsoon usually arrives in June or July and lasts into November (the 'rainy season'). A northeast monsoon follows, but it completely bypasses Northern Thailand, creating a dry, 'cool' period (the 'cool season') from November till mid-February. When the northeast monsoon stops, the lull between monsoons means much higher relative temperatures (the 'hot season') from March to June.

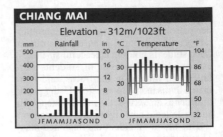

CHIANG MAI

Elevation – 312m/1023ft

Rainfall

As a rule of thumb, the dry season is shorter the farther south you go. From Chiang Mai north, the dry season may last six months (mid-November to May); the lower North, on the other hand, may experience a dry season of five months (December to May). Occasional rains in the dry season are known as 'mango showers' (heralding the mango season). The arrival of the rains brings relief from the hot, dry weather of the preceding months and softens the soil for planting.

In Northern Thailand it tends to rain most during August, although there may be floods in September or October, when the ground has reached full saturation. Travelling in the rainy season is generally not bad, but unsealed roads may be impassable.

Temperature

During the dry half of the year – the 'cool' and 'hot' seasons – Northern Thailand is considerably less humid than Central or Southern Thailand. The hot part of the dry season reaches its hottest in the plains surrounding Lampang and Phitsanulok, where temperatures easily soar to 40°C in the daytime, dropping only a few degrees at night. The temperature can drop to 13°C at night during the cool season in Chiang Mai and even lower in the mountains of Mae Hong Son, Chiang Rai and Nan – if you're visiting during the cooler months, long-sleeved shirts and pullovers are in order.

ECOLOGY & ENVIRONMENT
Environmental Policy

Thailand, like all countries with very high population densities, has put enormous pressure on the ecosystems within its borders. Fifty years ago the countryside was around 70% forest; as of 2000 an estimated 20% of the natural forest cover remained. Much of the total remaining natural forest is found in Northern Thailand, hence the percentage of forest cover in this region is much higher than the national average, perhaps as much as 40%.

Logging and agriculture are mainly to blame for the decline, and the loss of forest cover has been accompanied by dwindling wildlife resources. Species notably extinct in Northern Thailand include the kouprey (a type of wild cattle), Schomburg's deer and the Javan rhino, but innumerable smaller species have also fallen by the wayside.

In response to environmental degradation the Thai government has created a large number of protected parks, reserves and sanctuaries since the 1970s, and has enacted legislation to protect specific plant and animal species. More national parks have been established in Northern Thailand than in any other region, possibly a recognition that there is more to protect in the North.

In 1989 all logging was banned in Thailand following a disaster in which hundreds of tonnes of cut timber washed down deforested slopes in Surat Thani Province, killing more than 100 people and burying a number of villages. It is now illegal to sell timber felled in the country, and all imported timber is theoretically accounted for before going on the market. The illegal timber trade further diminished with Cambodia's ban on all timber exports, along with the termination of all Thai contracts by the Burmese. Laos is now the number-one source of imported timber in Thailand, both legal and illegal.

These days builders even need government permission to use timber salvaged from old houses. Northern Thailand is the primary source and consumer of such recycled timber. This has helped curb illegal logging operations in the interior, but corruption remains a problem.

Corruption impedes government attempts to shelter 'exotic' species from the illicit global wildlife trade and to preserve Thailand's sensitive coastal areas. The Royal Forest Department is currently under pressure to take immediate action in those areas where preservation laws have gone unenforced. A crackdown on restaurants serving 'jungle food' *(aahǎan pàa)*, which consists of exotic and often endangered wildlife species like barking deer, bear, pangolin, civet and gaur, has been fairly successful.

The tiger is one of the most endangered of Thailand's large mammals. Although tiger hunting and trapping is illegal, poachers continue to kill the cats for the lucrative overseas Chinese pharmaceutical market; among the Chinese, the ingestion of tiger penis and bone is thought to have curative effects. Taipei, where at least two-thirds of pharmacies deal in tiger parts (in spite of the fact that such trade is forbidden by Taiwanese law), is the world centre for Thai tiger consumption. Around 200 to 300 wild tigers are thought to be hanging on in seven Thai national parks, of which only Nam Nao is located in the North.

Forestry department efforts are limited by lack of personnel and funds. The average ranger is paid less than 100B (US$2.28) a day (some aren't paid at all but receive only food and lodging) to take on armed poachers backed by the rich and powerful Chinese godfathers who control illicit timber and wildlife businesses.

Compared to Central Thailand, particularly the eastern seaboard stretching from Bangkok to Rayong, Northern Thailand has almost no heavy industry.

Tourism & the Environment

In some instances tourism has had positive effects on environmental conservation in Thailand. Conscious that the country's natural beauty is a major tourist attraction, and that tourism is one of Thailand's major revenue earners, the government has stepped up efforts to protect wilderness areas and to add more acreage to the park system. In the North, where eco-tourism has become a mainstay of the tourism industry, the addition of new national parks and other protected areas has been particularly aggressive.

However, tourism has also made negative contributions. Eager to make fistsful of cash, hotel developers and tour operators have rushed to provide ecologically inappropriate services for visitors in sensitive areas. While this appears to be much more of a problem in coastal areas of Central and Southern Thailand, where hotel development in protected areas in not uncommon, the potential for abuse is present in the North as well if visitor demand ever reaches the proportions it has in the South.

What can visitors to Northern Thailand do to minimise the impact of tourism on the environment? Firstly, they can avoid all restaurants serving 'exotic' wildlife species. The main patrons of this type of cuisine are the Thais themselves, along with visiting Chinese from Hong Kong and Taiwan; fortunately such restaurants have become increasingly rare as Thailand becomes more aware of the importance of preserving biological diversity.

When you're using hired boats along rivers, lakes or reservoirs, volunteer to collect (and later dispose of) rubbish if it's obvious that the usual mode is to throw everything overboard. Remember that anything plastic tossed into an inland waterway may end up in the stomachs or around the necks of aquatic wildlife, and if the debris misses these creatures it may make its way into the Gulf of Thailand to threaten other species.

Obviously, it is ecologically sensitive to refrain from purchasing crafts or souvenirs made from bone, horn, ivory, fur or animal hide that may have come from wildlife. Thai law forbids the collection of many of these items – report any violations in national park areas to the Tourism Authority of Thailand (TAT) and the Royal Forest Department, or in other places to Wildlife Fund Thailand (WFT); see the contact details of these organisations later in this section.

One of the difficulties in dealing with rubbish and sewage problems in tourist areas is that many Thai people don't understand why tourists expect different methods of disposal than are used elsewhere in the country. In urban areas and populated rural areas throughout Thailand, piles of rotting rubbish and open sewage lines are frequently the norm – after all, Thailand is still a 'developing' country.

Thais sensitive to Western paternalism are quick to point out that on a global scale the so-called 'developed' countries contribute far more environmental damage than does Thailand (eg, per capita greenhouse emissions for Australia, Canada and the USA average over five tonnes each while Asean countries on average contribute less than 0.5 tonnes per capita).

Hence, in making complaints or suggestions to Thai people employed in the tourist industry, it's important to emphasise that you want to work with them rather than against them in improving environmental standards.

Wherever you are, refrain from purchasing or accepting drinking water offered in plastic bottles wherever possible. When there's a choice, request glass water bottles, which are recyclable in Thailand. The deposit is refundable when you return the bottle to any vendor who sells drinking water in glass bottles.

For those occasions where only water in plastic bottles is available, you might consider transferring the contents to your own reusable water container, if the vendor or source of the plastic bottle is a more suitable disposal point than your eventual destination. If not, take the bottle with you and dispose of it at a legitimate rubbish collection site.

Some guesthouses offer drinking water from large, reusable plastic water containers. This service is available in most areas of Thailand. Encourage hotel and guesthouse staff to switch from disposable plastic to either glass or reusable plastic.

In outdoor areas where rubbish has accumulated, consider organising an impromptu clean-up crew to collect plastic, Styrofoam and other nonbiodegradables for delivery to a regular rubbish pick-up point.

By expressing your desire to use environmentally friendly materials – and by taking direct action to avoid the use and indiscriminate disposal of plastic – you can provide an example of environmental consciousness not only for the Thais but for other international visitors.

Visitors should consider filing letters of complaint regarding any questionable environmental practices with the TAT, WFT and the Royal Forest Department (see the contact details later). Municipal markets selling endangered species should also be duly noted – consider enclosing photos to support your complaints. For a list of endangered species in Thailand, contact the WFT.

Write to the following organisations to offer your support for stricter environmental policies or to air specific complaints or suggestions:

Asian Society for Environmental Protection
(☎ 025 245 363) c/o CDG-SEAPO, Asian Institute of Technology, Bangkok 10501
Bird Conservation Society of Thailand (☎ 022 943 5965) 69/12 Ramintra Soi 24, Jarakhe-Bua, Lat Phrao, Bangkok 10230
Forest Protection Office (☎ 025 793 004, 025 795 266) Royal Forest Department, 61 Thanon Phahonyothin, Bangkhen, Bangkok 10900
Friends of Nature (☎ 026 424 426) 670/437 Thanon Charansanitwong, Bangkok 10700
Magic Eyes (☎ 022 350 819) 5th floor, Bangkok Bank Bldg, 333 Thanon Silom, Bangkok 10400
Office of the National Environment Board (☎ 022 797 180) 60/1 Soi Prachasamphan 4, Thanon Phra Ram IV (Rama IV), Bangkok 10400
Project for Ecological Recovery (☎ 026 910 718) 77/3 Soi Nomjit, Thanon Naret, Bangkok 10500
Tourism Authority of Thailand (TAT; ☎ 026 641 222, fax 026 941 220/1, e center@tat .or.th) 202 Thanon Ratchadaphisek, Huay Khwang, Bangkok 10310
Wildlife Fund Thailand (WFT; ☎ 025 213 435, fax 025 526 083, e pisitnp@mozart .inet.co.th) 251/88–90 Thanon Phahonyothin, Bangkhen, Bangkok 10220
World Wide Fund for Nature (☎ 025 246 128, e wwfcomms@wwfthai.org, w www.wwfthai .org) WWF Program Office, Asian Institute of Technology, PO Box 4, Khlong Luang, Pathum Thani 12120

FLORA & FAUNA

A large portion of Northern Thailand is flanked by relatively undeveloped zones in frontier Myanmar and Laos. Forested areas of Northern Thailand thus provide wildlife corridors for an astounding variety of flora and fauna.

Flora

All of the indigenous vegetation in Northern Thailand is associated with tropical forest. Most of it is monsoon forest, defined as having a distinct dry season of three months or more (as opposed to rainforest, where rain falls more than nine months per year). Evergreen forests of the coniferous variety can be found in Northern Thailand's higher altitudes.

According to the Thai forestry department's most recent (2000) statistics, Northern Thailand is 43% forested. By comparison Central Thailand bears only 23% forest, Eastern Thailand 20%, Southern Thailand 17% and Northeastern Thailand 12%. The most heavily forested province in all of Thailand is Chiang Mai.

The region boasts an incredible array of fruit trees, bamboo (more species than any country outside China), tropical hardwoods and over 27,000 flowering species, including Thailand's national floral symbol, the orchid.

Fauna

As with plant life, variation in the animal kingdom closely affiliates with geographic and climatic differences. Hence, Northern Thailand's indigenous fauna is mostly of Indochinese origin, which in modern geopolitical terms means species common to northern Vietnam, northern Laos and southwestern China. The lower North is a potential habitat for plants and animals from the Sundaic realm (ie, typical of Peninsular Malaysia, Sumatra, Borneo and Java) as well, and this overlap between the Indochinese and Sundaic realms can be particularly rich in wildlife variation.

Thailand boasts over 1000 recorded resident and migrating bird species – approximately 10% of the world's species. In the North, inland waterways are especially important habitats for Southeast Asian waterfowl. Although hunting, particularly in highland areas, has affected the bird population, loss of habitat due to logging and urban development remains the greatest threat to bird survival in Thailand.

Indigenous mammals, mostly found in dwindling numbers within Northern Thailand's national parks and wildlife sanctuaries, include tigers, leopards, elephants, Asiatic black bears, Malayan sun bears, gaur (Indian bison), banteng (wild cattle), serows (Asiatic goat-antelope), sambar deer, barking deer, mouse deer, pangolins, gibbons, macaques and tapirs. Forty of Thailand's 300 mammal species, including the clouded leopard, Malayan tapir, tiger, Irrawaddy dolphin, goral, jungle cat, dusky langur and pileated gibbon, are on the International Union for Conservation of Nature (IUCN) list of endangered species. Thailand is a signatory to the UN Convention on International Trade in Endangered Species (Cites).

Herpetofauna in Northern Thailand include snake varieties, of which six are venomous: the common cobra (six subspecies), king cobra (hamadryad), banded krait (three species), Malayan viper, green viper and Russell's pit viper. Although the relatively rare king cobra can reach up to 6m in length, the region's largest snake is the reticulated python, which can reach a whopping 10m. The country's many lizard

MH

The king cobra can pack enough venom in a bite to kill 20 people.

species include two commonly seen in homes and older hotels or guesthouses, the túk-kae (a large gecko) and the jîng-jòk (a smaller house lizard).

Insect species number some 6000, while the region's rich inland aquatic environment supports thousands of species.

National Parks, Reserves & Wildlife Sanctuaries

Northern Thailand boasts more national parks than any other region. At the time of writing there were 29 national parks in Northern provinces, and an additional 26 of the 39 national parks scheduled to be gazetted in the future are destined for the North.

The majority of the parks, reserves and sanctuaries are well maintained by the Royal Forest Department. Poaching, illegal logging and shifting cultivation have taken their toll on protected lands, but since 1990 the government has been cracking down with some success. Tourism, so far, has had little deleterious effect on Northern parks.

Most of the national parks are easily accessible, yet only around 5% of the average annual number of visitors is non-Thai. Most parks charge a fee to visit (typically 20B for Thais, 200B for foreigners) and there is usually somewhere to stay for a reasonable price. For more information on staying in national parks, see Accommodation in the Facts for the Visitor chapter.

For a true appreciation of Northern Thailand's geography and natural history, a visit to at least one national park is a must. In Bangkok the reservations office is at the Royal Forest Department's national parks division (☎ 025 614 292), 61 Thanon Phahonyothin, Chatuchak, Bangkok. Any bookings from Bangkok must be paid in advance.

GOVERNMENT & POLITICS

Thailand (officially the 'Kingdom of Thailand') has been an independent nation since AD 1238, and is the only country in South or Southeast Asia never colonised by a foreign power.

Since 1932 the government of Thailand has nominally been a constitutional monarchy inspired by the British model but with a myriad of subtle differences. National polls elect the 500-member lower house (Sapha Phu Thaen Ratsadon – House of Representatives – with four-year terms), 200 senators of the upper house (Wuthisapha – Senate – with six-year terms) and prime minister. In Thailand the Senate votes on constitutional change while the House of Representatives legislates.

Ten political parties field candidates in national elections, but in the current political milieu, five receive the bulk of the votes: the Thai Rak Thai, Democrat, New Aspiration, National Development and Thai Nation Parties.

The king appoints all judges who sit on Thailand's supreme court (sǎan diikaa).

1997 Constitution

Thailand's 16th charter since 1932, the first to be composed and ratified by a civilian government (and thus known as the rát-thammánuun pràchaachon; people's constitution) establishes mechanisms to monitor the conduct of elected officials and political candidates and to protect civil rights.

The document makes voting in elections compulsory; allows public access to information from state agencies; provides free public education for 12 years; permits communities to manage, maintain and use local natural resources; and forces parliament to consider new laws upon receipt of 50,000 or more signatures in a public referendum. It also establishes several watchdog entities, including the constitution court, administrative court, national anticorruption commission, national election commission, human rights commission and parliamentary ombudsmen to support the enforcement of the constitution. Other amendments include: Election candidates must hold at least a bachelor's degree; and any legislators who become prime minister or members of the premier's cabinet must relinquish their MP status.

Administrative Divisions

For administrative purposes, Northern Thailand is divided into 17 jangwàt (provinces), out of the country's total of 76 (although only 14 are covered in this book).

Each province is further subdivided into amphoe (districts), which are then subdivided into kìng-amphoe (subdistricts), tambon (communes or groups of villages), mùu bâan (villages), sùkhǎaphíbaan (sanitation districts) and thêtsàbaan (municipalities). Urban areas with more than 50,000 inhabitants and a population density of over 3000 per sq km, such as Chiang Mai, are designated nákhawn; those with populations of 10,000 to 50,000 with not less than 3000 per sq km are meuang (muang on Roman-script highway signs). The term 'meuang' is also used loosely to mean

NORTHERN THAILAND'S PROVINCES

1 Chiang Rai
2 Mae Hong Son
3 Chiang Mai
4 Lampang
5 Phayao
6 Nan
7 Phrae
8 Lamphun
9 Utaradit
10 Sukhothai
11 Tak
12 Kamphaeng Phet
13 Phitsanulok
14 Phetchabun

'metropolitan area' (as opposed to an area within strict municipal limits).

A provincial capital is an *amphoe meuang*. An amphoe meuang takes the same name as the province of which it is capital, eg, Amphoe Meuang Chiang Mai (often abbreviated as 'meuang Chiang Mai') means the City of Chiang Mai, capital of Chiang Mai Province.

Appointment of Provincial governors *(phûu wâa râatchákaan)* to their four-year terms is made by the Ministry of the Interior – a system that leaves much potential for corruption.

District officers *(nai amphoe)* are also appointed by the Ministry of the Interior but are responsible to their provincial governors. The cities are headed by elected mayors *(naayók thêtsàmontrii)*, tambon by elected commune heads *(kamnan)* and villages by elected village chiefs *(phûu yài bâan)*.

A few districts in Northern Thailand – such as Bo Sang in Chiang Mai Province and Nong Bua in Nan Province, still have honorary jâo meuang. Usually an elder of the community, these jâo meuang typically preside over local festivals and perform other ritual functions.

Monarchy

His Majesty Bhumibol Adulyadej (pronounced 'Phumiphon Adunyadet') is the ninth king of the Chakri dynasty (founded 1782) and, as of 1988, the longest-reigning king in Thai history. Born in 1927 in the USA, where his father Prince Mahidol was studying medicine at Harvard University, and schooled in Bangkok and Switzerland, King Bhumibol was a nephew of Rama VII (King Prajadhipok) as well as the younger brother of Rama VIII (King Ananda Mahidol).

His Majesty ascended the throne in 1946 following the death of Rama VIII, who had reigned as king for only one year before his untimely death in a gun accident. In 1996 Thailand celebrated the king's 50th year of reign. His Majesty is the world's longest-reigning living monarch.

A jazz composer and saxophonist, King Bhumibol has had jam sessions with the likes of jazz greats Woody Herman and Benny Goodman, and his compositions (sounding like 1940s-style big band with bits of Thai melodic phrasing) are often played on Thai radio. He is fluent in English, French, German and Thai.

The king has his own privy council comprising up to 14 royal appointees who assist with the king's formal duties; the president of the privy council serves as interim regent until an heir is throned.

The king and Queen Sirikit have four children: Princess Ubol Ratana (born 1951); Crown Prince Maha Vajiralongkorn (1952); Princess Mahachakri Sirindhorn (1955); and Princess Chulabhorn (1957). A royal decree issued by King Trailok (reigned 1448–88) to standardise succession in a polygamous dynasty makes the king's senior son or full brother his *uparaja* (Thai: *ùpàrâat*; heir apparent). Thus Prince Maha Vajiralongkorn was officially designated as crown prince and heir when he reached 20 years of age in 1972; if he were to decline the crown or be unable to ascend the throne due to incurable illness or death, the senior princess (Ubol Ratana) would ordinarily be next in line. However, King Bhumibol has enacted a decree that will allow for Princess Sirindhorn to ascend the throne if the Crown Prince isn't able to.

Thailand's political system is officially a constitutional monarchy, but the Thai constitution stipulates that the king be 'enthroned in a position of revered worship' and not be exposed 'to any sort of accusation or action'.

With or without legal writ, the vast majority of Thai citizens regard King Bhumibol as a sort of demigod, partly in deference to tradition but also because of his involvement in impressive public works.

Neither the constitution nor the monarchy's high status prevent Thai people from gossiping about the royal family in private, however. Gathered together, the various whisperings and speculations with regard to royal intrigue would make a fine medieval fable. Many Thais, for example, favour Princess Sirindhorn for succession to the Thai throne, although none would say this publicly, nor would this popular sentiment appear in the Thai media.

Among the nation's soothsayers, it has long been prophesied that the Chakri dynasty will end with Rama IX; current political conditions, however, would suggest the contrary. His Majesty's health has faltered in the last two years, and most Thais are preparing themselves for the transfer of kingship to Prince Maha Vajiralongkorn.

It is often repeated that the Thai king has no political power (by law his position is strictly titular and ceremonial), but in times of national political crisis Thais have often looked to the king for leadership. Two attempted coups d'etat in the 1980s may have failed because they received tacit royal disapproval. By implication, the successful military coup of 1991 must have had palace approval, whether post facto or a priori.

Along with nation and religion, the monarchy is very highly regarded in Thai society – negative comment about the king or any member of the royal family is a social as well as legal taboo. See the Society & Conduct section later in this chapter.

ECONOMY
Boom & Bust
During the 1980s Northern Thailand rode the coat-tails of the nation's steady GNP growth rate that by 1988 had reached 13% per annum. Thailand in the early and mid-1990s found itself on the threshold of attaining the exclusive rank of NIC (newly industrialised country). Soon, economic experts said, Thailand would be joining Asia's 'little dragons', also known as the Four Dragons or Tigers – Hong Kong, Singapore, South Korea and Taiwan – in becoming a leader in the Pacific Rim economic boom.

In mid-1997 the 20-year boom went bust throughout Southeast and East Asia, with Thailand leading the way. The economies worst affected by the financial turmoil – Thailand, Indonesia, Malaysia, the Philippines and South Korea – displayed certain common pre-crisis characteristics, including wide current account deficits, lack of government transparency, high levels of external debt and relatively low foreign exchange reserves. For the most part the crisis stemmed from investor panic, with the rush to buy dollars to pay off debts creating a self-fulfilling collapse. Between 30 June and 31 October the baht depreciated roughly 40% against the US dollar, and dollar-backed external debt rose to 52.4% of the country's GDP. Such currency problems echoed the European currency crisis of 1992–93, when sudden, unforeseen drops in the pound, lira and other currencies sounded the death knell for a long period of steady growth and economic stability.

Coincidentally, a recession had already begun in Northern Thailand roughly three years before the 1997 crash, which meant at least that Northerners were a bit better prepared for economic hardship.

Many of Thailand's banks and finance companies were forced to close in 1998, as the government made valiant efforts to restructure the economy and most especially the financial and property sectors. The International Monetary Fund (IMF) provided a US$17.2 billion rescue package in the form of short-term loans, with the stipulation that Thailand follow IMF's prescriptions for recapitalisation and restructuring.

Following the 1997 recession the Thai economy shrank 10% in 1998, then grew 4% to 5% in 1999 and 2000. Exports in 1999 increased 13% over the previous year's, while manufacturing rose 15%. This growth enabled Thailand to take an 'early exit' from the IMF's loan package in 2000.

By the middle of 2001 the economy was healthier than at any time since 1996, according to independent analysts. Despite the IMF bail-out and Thailand's subsequent move out of its recessions, the Thais continue to live in an era of self-imposed austerity and relatively high unemployment (7.5%). Some observers have concluded that this forced cooling-off is the best thing that could have happened to the overheated economy, giving the nation time to focus on infrastructure priorities and offering the Thai citizenry an opportunity to reassess cultural change.

Unfortunately the global crises initiated by the 2001 suicide attacks on New York

City and the Pentagon are slowing recovery in Thailand, particularly in the North which is so dependent on tourism. On the positive side, the economic crisis has precipitated a national discussion about Thailand's role in globalisation.

At the time of writing the inflation rate was a low 2% per annum. As in most countries, prices continue to rise.

The Regional Picture

Northern Thailand relies primarily on agriculture and tourism to sustain itself. Farmers grow mountain or dry rice (as opposed to water rice, the bulk of the crop produced in Thailand) for domestic use, maize, tea, various fruits and flowers. Teak and other lumber were once major products of the North, but since 1989 all logging of primary forest has been banned in Thailand in order to prevent further deforestation. Large teak plantations currently under cultivation may yield profitable lumber in a few more years.

Tourism – both domestic and international – is a major income-earner in the provincial capitals of Chiang Mai, Chiang Rai, Mae Hong Son, Lampang, Phitsanulok and Sukhothai. A few isolated districts also do well from tourism, such as Chiang Khong (crossing point to Huay Xai in Laos), Chiang Saen, Mae Sot and Pai.

Some parts of the North, mainly around Chiang Mai, produce a large quantity of arts and crafts intended for the tourist and/or export market. These enterprises vary from small one-person cottage businesses to warehouses with dozens of employees. Moving up in scale, factories that make clothing and furniture for export can be found here and there, mainly in Chiang Mai and Lamphun Provinces. A sizable industrial estate outside the provincial capital of Lamphun contains the most capital-intensive businesses of this sort.

Outside of the provincial capitals and districts that cater to tourism, many rural areas of the North are in fact quite poor. Hill-tribe groups, who are used to ploughing the slopes to raise corn and mountain rice, carry out much of the cultivation in the highlands, while the lowland Thais are engaged in commerce or less land-intensive kinds of farming such as orchid raising or fruit growing.

Underground Economy

Opium was once Northern Thailand's number-one cash crop, but since the government crackdown of the 1980s and the advent of a royally sponsored crop substitution program, opium production has dropped to an all-time low.

However, the North continues to serve as a major conduit for illicit narcotics from neighbouring Myanmar and Laos, with the largest and financially most significant commodity being *yaa bâa,* crude amphetamine pills manufactured by the millions along the border. The size of this underground drug economy may in fact exceed legal transactions in the North. It is reported that the dealers and middle-persons make more money than they ever did in the old days of opium trafficking, while the hill tribes, traditional opium cultivators, now receive nothing.

POPULATION

According to preliminary results of Thailand's last census, the country's population has reached 60 million and is currently growing at a slow rate of 1% to 1.5% per annum (as opposed to 2.5% in 1979), thanks to a vigorous nationwide family-planning campaign. An estimated 11 million Thai citizens live in Northern Thailand, about 18% of the nation's total population. Of these about half live in or very near provincial capitals.

The population growth rate for the North is 0.71%, the lowest of any region in the country, probably due to high infant mortality rates coupled with migration towards Bangkok. At 67 persons per sq km, the North also has the lowest population density of any region in Thailand. By province, the density ranges from 16.5/sq km in Mae Hong Son to 126/sq km in Phichit.

See the 'People of Northern Thailand' special section for information on the various groups living in the region.

Austro-Thai Migration

The Thai-Kadai is the most significant ethno-linguistic group in all of Southeast Asia, with 72 million speakers in an area extending from the Brahmaputra River in India's Assam state to the Gulf of Tonkin and China's Hainan Island. To the north, there are Thai-Kadai speakers well into the Chinese provinces of Yunnan and Guangxi, and to the south they are found as far as the northern Malaysian state of Kedah. In Thailand and Laos they are the majority populations, and in China, Vietnam and Myanmar (Burma) they are the largest minorities. The major Thai-Kadai groups comprise the Ahom (Assam), the Siamese (Thailand), the Thai Dam (Laos and Thailand), the Thai Yai (Shan; Myanmar and Thailand), the Thai Neua (Laos, Thailand and China), the Thai Lü (Laos, Thailand and China) and the Yuan (Laos and Thailand). All of these groups belong to the Thai half of Thai-Kadai; the Kadai groups are relatively small (less than a million) and include such comparatively obscure languages in southern China as Kelao, Lati, Laha, Laqua and Li.

EDUCATION

Although the literacy rate in Thailand as a whole runs a high 94%, Northern Thailand ranks lowest among all the regions, with an average 88%. School is compulsory for nine years, and in 1997 the government decreed that all citizens were entitled to free public schooling for 12 years, a policy that may help bring the cash-strapped North closer to the national average.

Although high value is placed on education as a way to achieve material success, the system itself tends to favour rote learning at most levels over independent thinking.

Thailand's public school system is organised around six years at the *pràthŏm* (primary) level beginning at age six, followed by either three or six years of *mátháyom* (secondary) education. The three-year track is intended for those planning to follow with three to five years of *wíchaa-chîip* (trade school), while the six-year *mátháyom* track is usually chosen by students planning to attend university.

Chiang Mai University offers the region's best tertiary education, and is especially well regarded for its schools of medicine, medical technology and engineering.

A teaching certificate may be obtained after attending a two- to four-year, post-*mátháyom* program at one of the teachers colleges *(sa-thǎaban râatcha-phát)* found in each province in the region.

The education statistics don't take into account the teaching provided by Buddhist monks at wát (temple-monasteries) in rural areas of Northern Thailand, where monastic schooling is sometimes the only formal education available for the local children. Such schooling tends to more common in the North and Northeast than in the other regions.

For the foreign and local elite, private and international primary and secondary schools, usually modelled after either the American or British education systems, are found in Chiang Mai, Lampang and Chiang Rai.

ARTS

Northern Thailand produced the nation's first identifiably Thai art during the Sukhothai and Lanna periods, as the newly empowered Thais blended their own ideas with the grand religious architecture of the Mon and Khmer cultures. While similar innovations took place in other parts of Thailand in succeeding eras, Thai art historians agree that none distinguished themselves quite as much as those of the North.

Northern Thai art of the past, as well as the present, owes its character to a blending of many influences. Along with the Mon art of Hariphunchai, absorbed when Phaya Mang Rai annexed the kingdom to Lan Na Thai, Northern Thailand benefited from a constant influx of peoples from neighbouring China, Myanmar and Laos, not to mention indigenous groups such as the Lawa. Other Thai-speaking ethnicities, particularly the Thai Lü and Thai Yai (Shan), also affected the development of Northern Thai art.

An excellent book for those with an interest in Northern Thai art and design, both traditional and contemporary, is the coffee-table tome *Lanna Style: Art & Design of Northern Thailand*, by William Warren with photography by Ping Amranand.

Traditional Architecture

Largely due to firmly held animist-Buddhist beliefs, traditional home and temple architecture in Northern Thailand followed strict rules of design that dictated proportion, placement, materials and ornamentation.

Traditional Northern Thai residential architecture consists of single-room wooden houses raised on stilts and of more elaborate structures of interlocking rooms with both indoor and shaded outdoor spaces, all supported at least 2m above the ground on stilts. Since originally all Thai settlements were founded along river or canal banks, the use of stilts protected the house and its inhabitants from flooding during the annual monsoon. Even in areas where flooding wasn't common, the Northern Thais continued to raise their homes on stilts, using the space beneath the house as a cooking area, for tethering animals, or for parking their bicycles and motor vehicles. Teak has always been the material of choice for wooden structures, although with the shortage of teak in Thailand nowadays few houses less than 50 years old are constructed of teak.

Rooflines in Northern Thailand are steeply pitched and often decorated at the corners or along the bargeboards with motifs related to the *naga* (mythical sea serpent), long believed to be a spiritual protector of Thai-speaking cultures throughout Asia. Where bargeboards meet at the roof gable, they often cross to form an 'X' motif called *ka-lae*, one of the most readily recognisable features of the Northern Thai house and one that probably comes from the Lawa tradition. Khon Meuang often carve the ka-lae into elaborate flowing patterns.

Of course, other groups living in Northern Thailand have their own ways of designing and building homes. Among the Hmong-Mien and Mon-Khmer tribes living mostly at well-drained higher elevations, stilts have never been necessary and the

raised wooden floor is forsaken for a dirt floor covered by walls of bamboo and palm thatch. The Jin Haw (Chinese Muslims), meanwhile, traditionally built their houses of air-dried brick, a legacy of rural architecture in Yunnan, China. Nowadays few Jin Haw build their homes in this way, preferring to use modern house plans.

In the larger, older cities such as Chiang Mai, Lampang and Phrae, it is possible to see grander buildings with elaborate multi-room plans, built in the 18th or 19th centuries and often mixing European and Thai design motifs. In neighbouring countries that endured French, Portuguese or British rule, such architecture is often referred to as 'colonial'.

Temple Architecture

Technically speaking, a *wát* (from the Pali-Sanskrit *avasa*, 'dwelling for pupils and ascetics') is a Buddhist compound where men or women can be ordained as monks or nuns. Virtually every Thai-speaking village in Northern Thailand has at least one wát, while in towns and cities wát are quite numerous. Without an ordination area (designated by stone ordination-precinct markers called *sěhmaa*), or a monastic centre where monks or nuns reside is simply a *sǎmnák sǒng* (residence for monks). The latter are often established as meditation retreat facilities in forest areas, sometimes in conjunction with larger *wát pàa* (forest monasteries).

The typical wát compound in Thailand will contain at the very least an *uposatha* (Northern Thai: *sǐm*), a consecrated chapel where monastic ordinations are held, and a *vihara* (Thai: *wíhǎan*), where important Buddha images are housed. Classic Northern Thai wíhǎan and sǐm differ from their Central Thai counterparts in several ways. Firstly, the walls tend to be more solid-looking, mainly because windows tend to be smaller (more suited to the cooler Northern climate). Secondly, the three-tiered roof system tends to be more steeply pitched, and the roof eaves sweep closer to the ground, creating a dramatic effect. Partial fourth and fifth tiers often include shade porticoes at the front of the building. In Northern Thai wát the sǐm will almost always be much smaller than the wíhǎan, while in Central Thailand they are often equal or nearly equal in size.

Decorative motifs inside and outside temple structures are often unique to Northern Thailand. In particular, Northern Thai temple sǐm and wíhǎan tend to feature a mythical serpent-like creature with a dragon's head – called *naga* in Pali-Sanskrit, *nâak* in Thai – on the ends of the bargeboards, at the top of the gables and in stucco reliefs over doors and gateways.

Next to the wíhǎan. stands the compound's principle chedi or *jedi* (from the Pali *chetiya*), also known by the more generic term 'stupa', a solid cone-shaped monument that pays tribute to the enduring stability of Buddhism. The classic Northern Thai–style chedi features an elaborate octagonal base and a geometric dome with reticulated corners. Many chedi are believed to contain 'relics' (*dhatu* in Pali-Sanskrit; pieces of bone or monastic possessions) belonging to the historical Buddha. Such chedi are usually called *thâat,* the Thai pronunciation of 'dhatu'.

Other structures typically found in wát compounds include: one or more *sǎalaa* (open-sided shelters for community meetings and Dhamma lectures); a number of *kùtì* (monastic quarters); a *hǎw trai* (Tripitaka library where Buddhist scriptures are stored); a *hǎw klawng* (drum tower), sometimes with a *hǎw rákhang* (bell tower); various other chedi or stupas (the smaller squarish stupas are *thâat kràdùuk*, bone reliquaries, where the ashes of deceased worshippers are interred); plus various ancillary buildings – such as schools or clinics – that

Thai Art Styles

The following scheme is the latest one used by Thai art historians to categorise historical styles of Thai art:

Mon Art (formerly Dvaravati, 6th to 11th centuries; & Hardphunchai, 11th to 13th centuries) Originating in Central, Northern and Northeastern Thailand, Mon Art is an adaptation of Indian styles, principally Gupta.

Khmer Art (7th to 13th centuries) Centred in Central and Northeastern Thailand, this style is characterised by post-classic Khmer styles accompanying the spread of Khmer empires.

Peninsular Art (formerly Srivijaya period) This style, centred in Chaiya and Nakhon Si Thammarat, exhibits Indian influence in the 3rd to 5th centuries, Mon and local influence in the 5th to 13th centuries and Khmer influence in the 11th to 14th centuries.

Lanna (13th to 15th centuries) Centred in Chiang Mai, Chiang Rai, Phayao, Lamphun and Lampang, Lanna is influenced by Shan/Burmese and Lao traditions.

Sukhothai (13th to 15th centuries) Centred in Sukhothai, Kamphaeng Phet and Phitsanulok, this style is unique to Thailand.

Lopburi (10th to 13th centuries) This Central Thai style is characterised by a mix of Khmer, Pala and local styles.

Suphanburi-Sangkhlaburi (formerly U Thong, 13th to 15th centuries) This Central-Thai style, combining Mon, Khmer and local styles, was a prototype for the later Ayuthaya style.

Ayuthaya A (1350–1488) This Central Thai style is characterised by Khmer influences that were gradually replaced by revived Sukhothai influences.

Ayuthaya B (1488–1630) This style has characteristic ornamentation distinctive of the Ayuthaya style, with, for example, crowns and jewels on Buddha images.

Ayuthaya C (1630–1767) This style is characterised by a baroque stage and then decline.

Ratanakosin (19th century–present) This is the Bangkok style that consists of simpler designs and European influences.

differ from wát to wát according to local community needs. Many wát also have a *hǎw phǐi wát* (spirit house) for the temple's reigning earth spirit.

Historical Parks Since 1981, the Thai government has made the restoration of nine key archaeological sites part of its national economic development plan. As a result, the Fine Arts Department, under the Ministry of Education, has developed nine historical parks *(ùtháyaan pràwàttìsàat)*, which in Northern Thailand include the following: Kamphaeng Phet Historical Park in Kamphaeng Phet Province; Si Thep Historical Park in Phetchabun Province; and Sukhothai Historical Park and Si Satchanalai-Chaliang Historical Park in Sukhothai Province.

These parks are administered by the Fine Arts Department to guard against theft and vandalism. Unesco has declared the ruins at Kamphaeng Phet, Si Satchanalai-Chaliang and Sukhothai as World Heritage Sites, which makes them eligible for UN funds and/or expertise in future restoration projects.

Contemporary Architecture

Modern Northern Thai architects are not nearly as daring as their Bangkok counterparts. Thais began mixing traditional Thai with European forms in the late 19th and early 20th centuries, as exemplified by any number of older residences and shophouses in the North's provincial capitals, particularly Chiang Mai, Nan and Phrae. This style is referred to as 'Ratanakosin', even though that style is often thought of as belonging only to Bangkok.

Shophouses throughout the country, whether they're 100 years or 100 days old, share the basic Chinese shophouse *(hâwng thǎew)* design where the ground floor is reserved for trading purposes while the upper floors contain offices or residences.

During most of the post-WWII era, the trend in modern Thai architecture – inspired by the European Bauhaus movement – was towards a boring functionalism (the average building looked like a giant egg carton turned on its side). The Thai aesthetic, so vibrant in prewar eras, almost entirely disappeared in this characterless style of architecture.

More recently, a handful of rebellious architects have begun reincorporating traditional Thai motifs – mixed with updated Western classics – in new buildings. The Regent Chiang Mai Resort & Spa (see Places to Stay in the Chiang Mai chapter) in Mae Rim is a good example.

Sculpture

Although Northern Thailand as a region hasn't produced any individually world-famous classical or modern sculptors, within the realm of Buddhist art Northern Thai work is well known and well appreciated internationally.

Historically the most commonly sculpted materials have been wood, stone, ivory, clay and metal. Depending on the material, artisans use a variety of techniques – including carving, modelling, construction and casting – to achieve their designs.

Northern Thailand's most famous sculptural output has been its bronze Buddha images, coveted the world over for their originality and grace. Bronze Buddhas from Sukhothai and from Chiang Saen garner special praise. Sukhothai Buddhas, whether sitting, standing, walking or lying, are known for their placid, 'boneless' look. Chiang Saen Buddhas, on the other hand, are stolid and heroic-looking. Nowadays historic bronzes have all but disappeared from the art market in Thailand. Most are zealously protected by temples, museums or private collectors.

Traditional Painting

As with sculpture, Northern Thai painting traditions were mostly confined to religious art, in which the application of natural pigments to temple walls became the favoured medium. Unlike the gold-brocaded, brightly painted and richly detailed murals of Central Thai wíhǎan, the Northern Thai works tend to contain softer, lighter colours, stronger lines and less detail. Always instructional in intent, such painted images ranged from the elaborate depiction of the *jataka* (stories of the Buddha's past lives) to simple scenes of daily life in Northern Thailand. Gold leaf is usually not used in the paintings, although a technique called *laai kham* (gold design) fills in wall space with gold-stencilled patterns.

Since painting lacks the durability of other art forms, there are very few surviving examples of pre–20th century religious painting. However, the study and application of mural painting techniques have been kept very much alive in the North.

See the special section 'Lanna-Style Temple Murals' for further detail on Northern Thai temple paintings.

Contemporary Painting

The beginnings of Thailand's modern art movement are usually attributed to Italian artist Corrado Feroci, who was first invited to Thailand by Rama VI in 1924. Feroci's design of Bangkok's Democracy Monument was inspired by Italy's Fascist art movement of the 1930s. He also created the bronze statue of Rama I that stands at the entry to Memorial Bridge, and several monuments around the city of Bangkok. In 1933 Feroci founded the country's first fine arts institute, a school that eventually developed into Silpakorn University in Bangkok, Thailand's premier training ground for artists. In gratitude, the Thai government gave Feroci the Thai name Silpa Bhirasri.

Today contemporary Thai painting is exhibited at a number of Chiang Mai venues. One of the most important modern movements in Thai art was an updating of Buddhist themes, begun in the 1970s by painters Pichai Nirand, Prateung Emjaroen and Chiang Mai resident Thawan Duchanee. The movement has grown stronger since their early efforts to combine modern Western schemata and Thai motifs.

Other important venues and sources of support for modern art are Northern Thailand's few luxury hotels, such as the Westin Chiang Mai, Regent Chiang Mai, Rim Kok Resort, Dusit Island Resort and Le Meridian Baan Boran.

Literature & Poetry

The first known work of literature to be written in Thai is thought to have been composed by the Sukhothai king Phaya Li Thai in 1345. This work was *Traiphum Phra Ruang,* a treatise describing the three realms of existence according to a Hindu-Buddhist cosmology. Although there is some controversy about the dating of the work (as there is for all pre-Bangkok Thai literature), according to contemporary scholars this work and its symbolism was of considerable influence on Thailand's artistic and cultural universe.

Although other literature was undoubtedly written during the Lanna era, very little remains. A tradition of poetry called *kà-wii láan-naa* (Lanna verse) survives to this day, even though no original written examples of the genre exist. Even today there are several famous Lanna poets, and the city of Chiang Mai holds a Lanna poetry contest annually. To the average non-Thai, even those who speak Northern Thai, Lanna verse can appear rather esoteric, with rigid rules for meter, rhyming and alliteration that disrupt 'normal' syntax.

A few epics and folk tales that circulated among Lanna, Lan Chang and Sipsongpanna (the Tai area of southern Yunnan, called Xishuangbanna in China) have survived. Most were handed down orally and only written down during the past century or so. Two of the better-known, earlier-written examples are *Thao Cheung* (thought to have been composed around the end of the 15th century or beginning of the 16th) and *Lilit Yuan Phai* (between 1427 and 1520). Both are epic stories of Lao/Thai kings who defeated would-be invaders or oppressors in terrific battles.

During the reign of the last Lanna king, Phaya Kaew (reigned 1495–1525), Buddhist scholars in Chiang Mai composed many Pali texts. One of these, *Mangkhalatha Thibani,* by Phra Siri Mangkhalajan, is still used for teaching Pali in Thailand.

During the subsequent era of Burmese rule, Northern Thai literature appears to have been suppressed, or at least nothing of note remains. Once the Burmese were expelled from Northern Thailand in 1775, and Northern Thailand became part of Siam, Bangkok became the focus of Thai literature.

Thus far the region has not produced the likes of Pira Sudham, the famous Northeastern Thai novelist from Buriram Province, and today Northern Thailand is better known for Lanna verse than for prose literature.

Music

Northern Thai music is not very well known outside of Northern Thailand, although Northern Thai melodies are sometimes incorporated into classical compositions performed by the Central Thai *pìi-phâat* ensemble. For the most part, the only time you'll hear authentic Northern Thai music is when small local ensembles – almost always made up of men who have regular day jobs – perform at local dry-season festivals. This tradition is mostly instrumental, with the main instruments being the *phin pía* (a kind of lute made of wood), the *seung* (another wooden lute), the *khlùi* (bamboo flute) and the *sa-láw* (a bowed instrument with a coconut-shell soundbox).

In Chiang Mai, Chiang Rai and Mae Hong Son, you may also hear Northern Thai instrumental music played in the background in large restaurants catering to tour groups, or in tourist hotel lobbies.

Unlike in Northeastern and Central Thailand, where folk traditions have been transformed into a thriving pop genre called *lûuk thûng* (literally, children of the fields), Northern Thai music hasn't yet gone mainstream. However, there is a modest pop tradition, which takes Northern Thai song forms and blends them with *phleng phêua chiiwít* (songs for life; a politically oriented Thai folk form popular since the 1970s) acoustic guitar instrumentation.

Often referred to as *phleng kham meuang*, Northern Thai–style folk-pop is much narrower in range than phleng phêua chiiwít.

The Phin is a traditional musical instrument similar to the lute.

Most songs tend to be of very slow tempo with plaintive singing about lost romance or nostalgia for nature. A recurring song topic is the story of a Northern girl seduced by a rich Bangkokian (whom the Northern Thai refer to as *khon tâi*, 'people from the south') who leaves her with nothing.

Only two Northern Thai singers have enjoyed any fame from performing songs of their own culture. The most famous, Jaran Manopetch, died of a heart attack at his Chiang Mai home in 2001. Soontaree Vechanont, who once sang duets with Jaran, performs regularly at her own restaurant in Chiang Mai (see that chapter for details).

SOCIETY & CONDUCT
Traditional Culture

Much of what is more generally called 'Thai culture' is believed to have originated in the North during the Sukhothai and Lanna years, when the culture forged a national identity for itself. This culture consists of a complex of behavioural modes rooted in the history of Thai migration throughout Southeast Asia, with many commonalities shared by the Lao people of neighbouring Laos, the Shan of northeastern Myanmar, and the numerous tribal Thais found in isolated pockets from Dien Bien Phu (Vietnam) all the way to Assam (India). Nowhere are such norms more generalised than in Thailand, the largest of the Thai homelands, and it could be said that nowhere in Thailand do people act more 'Thai' than in the North.

Aside from the hill tribes, each of which has its own distinctive culture, practically every ethnicity in Northern Thailand, whether of Northern Thai ancestry or not, has adapted to a greater or lesser degree to the regional culture. These cultural underpinnings are evident in virtually every facet of everyday life.

Sanùk/Mûan

The Thai word *sanùk* (*mûan* in Northern Thai) means 'fun'. To the Thais anything worth doing – even work – should have an element of sanùk, otherwise it automatically becomes drudgery. This doesn't mean

Thais don't want to work or strive, just that they tend to approach tasks with a sense of playfulness. Nothing condemns an activity more than the description *mâi sanùk* (not fun). Sit down beside a rice field and watch workers planting, transplanting or harvesting rice: That it's back-breaking labour is obvious, but participants generally inject the activity with lots of sanùk – flirting, singing, trading insults and cracking jokes. The same goes in an office or a bank, or other white-collar work situation – at least when the office is predominantly Thai. (Businesses run by non-Thais don't necessarily exhibit sanùk.) The famous Thai smile comes partially out of this desire to make sanùk.

Face

Like Thais everywhere, the Khon Meuang believe strongly in the concept of saving face, ie, avoiding confrontation and endeavouring not to embarrass yourself or other people (except when it's sanùk to do so). The ideal face-saver doesn't bring up negative topics in conversation, and when they notice stress in another's life they usually won't say anything unless that person complains or asks for help. Laughing at minor accidents – like when someone trips and falls down – may seem callous to outsiders but it's really just an attempt to save face on behalf of the person undergoing the mishap. This is another source of the Thai smile – it's the best possible face for almost any situation.

Status & Obligation

All relationships in traditional Northern Thai society – and virtually all relationships in the modern Thai milieu as well – are governed by connections between *phûu yài* (big person, or senior) and *phûu náwy* (little person, or junior). Phûu náwy are supposed to defer to phûu yài following lines of social rank defined by age, wealth, status and personal and political power. Examples of 'automatic' phûu yài status include: adults (vs children); bosses (vs employees); elder classmates (vs younger classmates); elder siblings (vs younger siblings); teach-ers (vs pupils); military (vs civilian); and Thai (vs non-Thai).

While this tendency towards social ranking is to some degree shared by many societies around the world, the Thai twist lies in the set of mutual obligations linking phûu yài to phûu náwy. Some sociologists have referred to this phenomenon as the 'patron-client relationship'. Phûu náwy are supposed to show a degree of obedience and respect (together these concepts are covered by the single Thai term *kreng jai*) towards phûu yài, but in return phûu yài are obligated to care for or 'sponsor' the phûu náwy they have frequent contact with. In such relationships phûu náwy can, for example, ask phûu yài for favours involving money or job access. Phûu yài reaffirm their rank by granting requests when possible; to refuse would be to risk a loss of face and status.

Age is a large determinant where other factors are absent or weak. In such cases the terms *phîi* (elder sibling) and *náwng* (younger sibling) apply more than phûu yài and phûu náwy, although the intertwined obligations remain the same. Even people unrelated by blood quickly establish who's phîi and who's náwng; this is why one of the first questions Thais ask new acquaintances is 'How old are you?'.

When dining, touring or entertaining, the phûu yài always picks up the tab; if a group is involved, the person with the highest social rank pays the bill for everyone, even if it empties his or her wallet. For a phûu náwy to try and pay would cause loss of face. Money plays a large role in defining phûu yài status in most situations. A person who turned out to be successful in his or her post-school career would never think of allowing an ex-classmate of lesser success – even if he or she were once on an equal social footing – to pay the bill. Likewise, a young, successful executive will pay an older person's way in spite of the age difference.

The implication is that whatever wealth you come into is to be shared – at least partially – with those less fortunate. This doesn't apply to strangers – the average Thai isn't big on charity – but always comes into play with friends and relatives.

Foreigners often feel offended when they encounter such phenomena as two-tiered pricing for hotels or sightseeing attractions – one price for Thais, another for foreigners. But this is just another expression of the traditional patron-client relationship. On the one hand foreigners who can afford to travel to Thailand from abroad are seen to have more wealth than Thai citizens (on average this is self-evident), hence they're expected to help subsidise Thais' enjoyment of these commodities. At the same time, paradoxically, the Thais feel they are due certain special privileges as nationals – what might be termed the 'home-town discount'. Another example: In a post-office line, Thais may get served first as part of their nature-given national privilege.

Comportment

Personal power (*baará-mii*, sometimes mistranslated as 'charisma') also has a bearing on one's social status, and can be gained by cleaving as close as possible to the ideal 'Thai' behaviour. 'Thai-ness' is first and foremost defined, as might be expected, by the ability to speak Thai.

Other hallmarks of the Thai ideal, which has been heavily influenced by Thai Buddhism, include discretion in behaviour towards the opposite sex, modest dress, a neat and clean appearance, and modes of expression and comportment that value the quiet, subtle and indirect rather than the loud, obvious and direct.

The degree to which Thais can conform to these ideals matches the degree of respect they receive from most of their associates. Although high rank – based on age or civil, military or clerical roles – will exempt certain individuals from chastisement by their social 'inferiors', it doesn't exempt them from the way they are perceived by other Thais. This goes for foreigners as well, even though most first-time visitors can hardly be expected to speak idiomatic Thai. But if you do learn some Thai, and you do make an effort to respect Thai social ideals, you'll come closer to enjoying some of the perks awarded for Thai-ness.

Dos & Don'ts

Thais are tolerant of most kinds of behaviour, as long as it doesn't insult the two sacred cows of monarchy and religion.

King & Country The monarchy is held in considerable respect in Thailand and visitors should be respectful too – avoid disparaging remarks about anyone in the royal family. In fact, such remarks about the beloved Thai king could land you in prison – the penalty for lese-majesty is seven years.

While it's OK to criticise the Thai government and even Thai culture openly, it's considered a grave insult to Thai nationhood as well as to the monarchy not to stand when you hear the national or royal anthems. Radio and TV stations in Thailand broadcast the national anthem daily at 8am and 6pm; in towns and villages (even in some Bangkok neighbourhoods) this can be heard over public loudspeakers in the streets. The Thais stop whatever they're doing to stand during the anthem (except in Bangkok, where nobody can hear anything above the street noise) and visitors are expected to do likewise. The royal anthem is played just before films are shown in public cinemas; again, the audience always stands until it's over.

Religion Correct behaviour in temples entails several considerations, the most important of which is to dress neatly and to take your shoes off when you enter any building that contains a Buddha image. Buddha images are sacred objects, so don't pose in front of them for pictures and *definitely* do not clamber upon them.

Shorts and sleeveless shirts are considered improper dress for both men and women when visiting temples. Thai citizens wearing either would be turned away by monastic authorities, but except for the most sacred temples in the country (eg, Wat Phra That Doi Suthep near Chiang Mai), Thais are often too polite to refuse entry to improperly clad foreigners. Some *wát* will offer trousers or long sarongs for rent so that tourists dressed in shorts may enter the compound.

Monks are not supposed to touch, or be touched by, women. If a woman wants to hand something to a monk, the object should be placed within reach of the monk or on the monk's 'receiving cloth', not handed directly to him. When sitting in a religious edifice, keep your feet pointed away from any Buddha images. The usual way to do this is to sit in the 'mermaid' pose *(nâng phá-phîap)* in which your legs are folded to the side, with the feet pointing backwards.

Some larger wát in Bangkok charge entry fees. In other temples, a small donation is appropriate. Usually donation boxes are near the entry of the *bòt* (central sanctuary) or next to the central Buddha image at the rear. In rural wát there may be no donation box available; in these places, it's OK to leave money on the floor next to the central image or even by the doorway, where temple attendants will collect it later.

Social Gestures & Attitudes Traditionally Thais greet each other with a prayer-like palms-together gesture known as a *wâi*. If someone wâi's you, you should wâi back (unless wâi-ed by a child or serviceperson). Most urban Thais are familiar with the international-style handshake and will offer the same to a foreigner, although a wâi is always appreciated.

Thais are often addressed by their first name with the honorific *khun* or other title preceding it. Other formal terms of address include *nai* (Mr) and *naang* (Miss or Mrs). Friends often use nicknames or kinship terms like *phîi* (elder sibling), *náwng* (younger sibling), *phâw* (father) *mâe* (mother) or *lung* (uncle), depending on the age difference. Although you could substitute the Northern Thai equivalents for these kinship terms (in most cases they're practically the same, but there are stark differences in other cases), if you don't really speak *kham meuang* (Northern Thai) it's considered rather insulting to use these terms (see the Language section for more details on kham meuang and its social implications).

A smile and *sawàt-dii khráp/khâ* (the all-purpose Thai greeting) goes a long way towards calming the initial trepidation that

locals may feel upon seeing a foreigner, whether in the city or the countryside.

When handing things to other people you should use both hands or your right hand only, never the left hand (reserved for toilet ablutions). Books and other written materials are given a special status over other secular objects. Hence you shouldn't slide books or documents across a table or counter-top, and never place them on the floor – use a chair if table space isn't available.

When encounters take a turn for the worse, try to refrain from getting angry – it won't help matters, since losing your temper means a loss of face for everyone present. Remember that this is Asia, where keeping your cool is the paramount rule. Talking loudly is perceived as rude by cultured Thais, whatever the situation. See the earlier sections on Face and Comportment regarding the rewards for 'Thai-ness' – the pushy foreigner often gets served last.

Feet & Head The feet are the lowest part of the body (spiritually as well as physically) so don't point your feet at people or point at things with your feet. Don't prop your feet on chairs or tables while sitting. Never touch any part of someone else's body with your foot.

In the same context, the head is regarded as the highest part of the body, so don't touch Thais on the head – or ruffle their hair – either. If you touch someone's head accidentally, offer an immediate apology or you'll be perceived as very rude.

Don't sit on pillows meant for sleeping, as this represents a variant of the taboo against head-touching.

Never step over someone, even on a crowded 3rd-class train where people are sitting or lying on the floor. Instead, squeeze around them or ask them to move.

In rural areas and at temple fairs people often eat food while seated on the floor; stepping over the food is a sure way to embarrass and offend your Thai hosts.

Dress Shorts (except knee-length walking shorts), sleeveless shirts, tank tops (singlets) and other beach-style attire are not considered appropriate dress for men for anything other than sporting events. Such dress is especially counterproductive if worn to government offices (eg, when applying for a visa extension). The attitude of 'This is how I dress at home and no-one is going to stop me' gains nothing but contempt or disrespect from the Thais.

Nowadays many young Thai women wear sleeveless shirts and 'spaghetti-strap' tops, and as long as you're wearing a brassiere, this now seems to be acceptable for foreign women, too. Knee-length shorts and skirts are fine for women as well.

Sandals or slip-on shoes are OK for almost all but the most formal occasions.

Thais would never dream of going abroad and wearing dirty clothes, so they are often shocked to see Westerners travelling around Thailand in clothes that apparently haven't been washed in weeks. If you keep up with your laundry you'll receive much better treatment everywhere you go.

Shoes Shoes are not worn inside people's homes, nor in some guesthouses and shops. If you see a pile of shoes at or near the entrance, you should respect the house custom and remove your shoes before entry.

The Northern Thai Costume

What many Khon Meuang (Northern Thais) today consider 'traditional Northern Thai' costuming is actually derived from traditional Shan or Khün clothing, as early lithographs and photographs of Northern Thailand will attest. These outfits, which often include turban-like headgear and buttoned shirts with mandarin collars, were selected by Chiang Mai University professors of Thai culture in the 1970s, when the demand for 'traditional' costuming for parades and tourist events arose.

These quasi-Northern ensembles are much more suited to the higher elevations and latitudes of the northern and eastern Shan states than to the warmer climates of Chiang Mai, Chiang Rai, Lampang and other provincial capitals where such costuming is most favoured.

Visiting Homes Thais can be very hospitable and it's not unusual to be invited home for a meal or a sociable drink. Even if your visit is very brief, you will be offered something to eat or drink, probably both – a glass of water, a cup of tea, a piece of fruit, a shot of rice liquor, or whatever they have on hand. You are expected to partake of whatever is offered, whether you're thirsty or hungry or not; to refuse at least a taste is considered impolite.

Upcountry When travelling in minority villages, try to find out what the local customs and taboos are, either by asking someone or by taking the time to observe local behaviour. See the 'Trekking' special section for more-specific guidelines on conduct.

Treatment of Animals

Thailand is a signatory to the UN Convention on International Trade in Endangered Species (Cites). Educational levels have risen to the point that many international watchdog groups, such as the World Wide Fund for Nature (e wwfcomms@wwfthai .org, W www.wwfthai.org) and Wildlife Conservation Society, receive much local supp ort. An illicit trade in endangered and threatened wildlife continues but appears to be much smaller than it was even 12 years ago.

In less developed parts of the North, especially among the hill tribes, hunting remains a norm for obtaining animal protein. Harder to understand, at least for some of us, is the taking of monkeys, birds and other animals from the jungle to be kept as pets – usually tied by a rope or chain to a tree, or confined to cages. Several non-governmental organisations (NGOs) are working to educate the public as to the cruelty of such practices, and have initiated wildlife rescue and rehabilitation projects.

Prostitution

Lanna, Sukhothai and other Northern Thai kingdoms apparently had no laws forbidding polygamy – or even a word for this Judaeo-Christian concept – and Siam as a nation passed its first such statute only in

1934. Most men of wealth counted among their retinue at least one *sŏhphenii* (from the Sanskrit term for a woman trained in the *Kamasutra* and other amorous arts), a word that has come to mean 'prostitute' but which was once better translated as 'courtesan'. In addition, the traditional Thai *mia lŭang mia náwy* (major wife, minor wife) system made it socially permissible for a man to keep several mistresses. All Thai kings up to Rama IV had mia náwy (or *sànŏm*, as the royal version was called), as did virtually any Thai male who could afford them until recent times. Even today talk of mia náwy hardly raises an eyebrow in Thailand as the tradition lives on among wealthy businessmen, *jâo phâw* (organised-crime 'godfathers') and politicians.

Prostitution was not declared illegal until the 1950s, when American-supported Field Marshal Phibul bullied his way into the prime minister's seat. The numbers of women working as commercial sex workers (CSWs) increased immediately after prohibition.

Unlike in Bangkok or Pattaya, where there are highly visible areas where Thai CSWs transact business with tourists, prostitution in Northern Thailand is almost exclusively involved with Thai clientele. Today the highest per-capita concentration of sex workers is, in fact, found in the North.

Unlike in the West, there are few pimps in Thailand. Instead, a network of procurers or suppliers and brothel owners controls the trade, taking a high proportion (or all) of the sex service fees. At its worst, the industry takes girls sold or indentured by their families, sometimes even kidnapped, and forces them to work in conditions of virtual slavery.

Most CSWs are uneducated and come from village areas. Researchers estimate they have a maximum working life of 10 years, although the average is two years or less. Many women return to their villages – some with a nest egg for their families, others with nothing – where they are often treated with a measure of respect. Various Thai volunteer groups offer counselling to Thailand's sex workers – helping them to leave the industry or to educate them to the dangers of sexually transmitted infections (STIs), particularly AIDS. Thanks to such efforts, the latest national surveys indicate that condom use among sex workers in Thailand averages 94%. On the negative side, health officials estimate that the HIV infection rate is higher in the North than in any other region, probably because of the steady influx of CSWs from neighbouring Laos, Myanmar and China, where condom use is much lower.

Officially prostitution remains illegal, but the government has been either powerless or unwilling to enforce most laws forbidding the trade. Largely due to international pressure, the Thai government has since 1993 ordered a crackdown on CSWs under 18 years of age, an act that has had quantifiable results but has by no means banished under-18s from the trade.

Under current Thai law, a jail term of four to 20 years and/or a fine of 200,000B to 400,000B can be imposed on anyone caught having sex with prostitutes under 15 years of age (the age of consent in Thailand). If the child is under 13, the sentence can amount to life imprisonment. Many Western countries have also instituted extra-territorial legislation whereby citizens can be charged for child prostitution offences committed abroad. The Thai government is encouraging people to assist in the eradication of child prostitution by reporting child sexual abuses to the relevant authorities. In this instance, travellers visiting Thailand can contact the tourist police (☎ 1155) or Ecpat International (☎ 022 153 388, ℮ ecpatbkk@ksc15.th.com) at 328 Thanon Phayathai, Bangkok 10400.

RELIGION
Theravada Buddhism
Approximately half of the residents of Northern Thailand are Theravada Buddhists. Thai scholars occasionally refer to the religion as Lankavamsa (Singhalese lineage) Buddhism because Thailand originally received this form of Buddhism from Sri Lanka during the Sukhothai period.

Many of the kings of Sukhothai and Lanna were keen sponsors of Buddhism, establishing monasteries throughout their kingdoms and sending monks abroad to study the religion. Since the Sukhothai period, Thailand has maintained an unbroken canonical tradition and 'pure' ordination lineage, the only country among the Theravadin countries to have done so. Ironically, when the ordination lineage in Sri Lanka broke down during the 18th century under Dutch persecution, it was Thailand that restored the *sangha* (Buddhist monastic community) there. To this day the major sect in Sri Lanka is called Siamopalivamsa (Siam-Upali lineage, Upali being the name of the Siamese monk who led the expedition to Sri Lanka), or simply Siam Nikaya (Siamese sect).

Basically, the Theravada (literally, Teaching of the Elders) school of Buddhism is an earlier and, according to its followers, less corrupted form of Buddhism than the Mahayana schools found in East Asia and in the Himalayan lands. It is also called the 'Southern' school, since it took a southern route from India, its place of origin, through Southeast Asia (Sri Lanka, Myanmar, Thailand, Laos and Cambodia in this case), while the 'Northern' school proceeded north into Nepal, Tibet, China, Korea, Mongolia, Vietnam and Japan.

Theravada doctrine stresses the three principal aspects of existence: *dukkha* (stress, unsatisfactoriness, unease), *anicca* (impermanence, transience of all things) and *anatta* (insubstantiality or nonessentiality of reality – no permanent 'soul'). The truth of anicca reveals that no experience, no state of mind, no physical object lasts; trying to hold onto experiences, states of mind and objects that are constantly changing creates dukkha; to understand anatta is to understand that there is no part of the changing world that we can point to and say 'This is me' or 'This is God' or 'This is the soul'. These three concepts, when 'discovered' by Siddhartha Gautama in the 6th century BC, were in direct contrast to the Hindu belief in an eternal, blissful self *(paramatman)*. Hence Buddhism was originally a 'heresy' against India's Brahmanic religion.

Gautama, an Indian prince-turned-ascetic, subjected himself to many years of severe austerity before he realised that this was not the way to reach the end of suffering. He turned his attention to investigating the arising and passing away of the mind and body in the present moment. Seeing that even the most blissful and refined states of mind were subject to decay, he abandoned all desire for those things he now saw as unreliable and unsatisfying. He then became known as Buddha, 'the enlightened' or 'the awakened'. Gautama Buddha spoke of four noble truths that had the power to liberate any human being who could realise them. These four noble truths are:

1. The truth of dukkha: 'All forms of existence are subject to dukkha'.
2. The truth of the cause of dukkha: 'Dukkha is caused by tanha (grasping)'.
3. The truth of the cessation of dukkha: 'Eliminate the cause of dukkha (ie, grasping) and dukkha will cease to arise'.
4. The truth of the path: 'The Eightfold Path is the way to eliminate dukkha.'

The Eightfold Path (Atthangika-Magga) leading to the end of dukkha consists of:

1. Right understanding
2. Right mindedness (right thought)
3. Right speech
4. Right bodily conduct
5. Right livelihood
6. Right effort
7. Right attentiveness
8. Right concentration

These eight limbs belong to three different 'pillars' of practice: wisdom (*pañña;* path factors 1 and 2); morality (*sila;* 3 to 5); and concentration (*samadhi;* 6 to 8). The path is also called the 'Middle Way', since it avoids both the extreme of austerity and the extreme of sensuality. Some Buddhists believe it is to be taken in successive stages, while others say the pillars and/or limbs are interdependent. Another key point is that the word 'right' can also be translated as 'complete' or 'full'.

The ultimate aim of Theravada Buddhism is *nibbana* (Sanskrit: *nirvana*), which literally means the 'blowing out' or extinction of all grasping and thus of all suffering (dukkha). Effectively, it is also an end to the cycle of rebirths (both moment-to-moment and life-to-life) that is existence.

In reality, most Thai Buddhists aim for rebirth in a 'better' existence rather than the supramundane goal of nibbana. By feeding monks, giving donations to temples and performing regular worship at the local wát they hope to improve their lot, acquiring enough merit (Pali: puñña; Thai: bun) to prevent or at least reduce their number of rebirths. Making merit (tham bun) is an important social and religious activity among Northern Thai Buddhists. The concept of rebirth is almost universally accepted in Thailand, even by non-Buddhists, and the Buddhist theory of karma is well expressed in the Thai proverb tham dii, dâi dii; tham chûa, dâi chûa (good actions bring good results; bad actions bring bad results).

The Tiratana (Triple Gems) revered by Thai Buddhists include the Buddha, the Dhamma (the teachings) and the Sangha (the Buddhist community). All are quite visible in Thailand. The Buddha, in his myriad sculptural forms, is found on a high shelf in the lowliest roadside restaurants as well as in the lounges of expensive Bangkok hotels. The Dhamma is chanted morning and evening in every wát and taught to every Thai citizen in primary school. The Sangha is seen everywhere in the presence of orange-robed monks, especially in the early morning hours when they perform their alms-rounds, in what has almost become a travel-guide cliche in motion.

Buddhism has no particular 'Sabbath' or day of the week when the faithful are supposed to make temple visits. Nor is there anything corresponding to a liturgy or mass over which a priest presides. Instead, Thai Buddhists visit the wát whenever they feel like it, most often on wan phrá (literally, excellent days), which occur every 7th or 8th day, depending on phases of the moon. On such visits typical activities include: the traditional offering of lotus buds, incense and candles at various altars and bone reliquaries around the wát compound; the offering of food to the temple Sangha (monks, nuns and lay residents – monks always eat first); meditating (individually or in groups); listening to monks chanting suttas or Buddhist discourse; and attending a thêht (Dhamma talk) by the abbot or some other respected teacher. Visitors may also seek counsel from individual monks or nuns regarding new or ongoing life problems.

Monks Socially, every Buddhist male is expected to become a monk (Pali: bhikkhu; Thai: phrá or phrá phíksù) for a short period in his life, optimally between the time he finishes school and the time he starts a career or marries. Men or boys under 20 years of age may enter the Sangha as novices (Pali: samanera; Thai: nehn) – this is not unusual, since a family earns great merit when one of its sons 'takes robe and bowl'. Traditionally, the length of time spent in the wát is three months, during the Buddhist lent (phansǎa), which usually begins in July and coincides with the rainy season. However, nowadays men may spend as little as a week to accrue merit as monks. Others are ordained for a lifetime. Of these a large percentage become scholars and teachers, while some specialise in healing and/or folk magic.

The Sangha is divided into two sects: the Mahanikai (Great Sect) and the Thammayut (from the Pali dhammayutika or 'dharma-adhering'). The latter is a minority sect (the ratio being one Thammayut to 35 Mahanikai) begun by King Mongkut and patterned after an early Mon form of monastic discipline that he had practised as a monk. Members of both sects must adhere to 227 monastic vows or precepts as laid out in the Vinaya Pitaka – Buddhist scriptures dealing with monastic discipline. Overall discipline for Thammayut monks, however, is generally stricter. Thammayut monks are expected to attain proficiency in meditation as well as Buddhist scholarship or scripture study; the Mahanikai monks typically 'specialise' in one or the other. Other factors may supersede sectarian divisions when it comes to disciplinary disparities. Monks who live in the city, for example, usually emphasise study of the Buddhist scriptures while those living in the forest tend to emphasise meditation.

Nuns At one time the Theravada Buddhist world had a separate Buddhist monastic lineage for females. The female monks were called *bhikkhuni* and observed more vows than monks did – 311 precepts as opposed to the 227 followed by monks. The bhikkhuni sangha travelled from its birthplace in India to Sri Lanka around two centuries after the Buddha's lifetime, taken there by the daughter of King Ashoka, Sanghamitta Theri. However, the tradition died out there following the Hindu Chola invasion in the 13th century. Monks from Siam later travelled to Sri Lanka to restore the male sangha, but because there were no ordained bhikkhuni in Thailand at the time, Sri Lanka's bhikkhuni sangha was never restored.

In Thailand, the modern equivalents are *mâe chii* (nuns) – women who live the monastic life as *atthasila* (eight-precept) nuns. They are outnumbered by male monastics approximately 46 to 1. Thai nuns shave their heads, wear white robes and take vows in an ordination procedure similar to that undergone by monks. Generally speaking, nunhood in Thailand isn't considered as 'prestigious' as monkhood. The average Thai Buddhist makes a great show of offering new robes and household items to the monks at the local wát but pays much less attention to the nuns. This is mainly due to the fact that nuns generally don't perform ceremonies on behalf of lay people, so there is often less incentive for self-interested lay people to make offerings to them. Furthermore, many Thais equate the number of precepts observed with the total merit achieved; hence nunhood is seen as less 'meritorious' than monkhood since mâe chii keep only eight precepts.

This difference in prestige represents social Buddhism, however, and is not how those with a serious interest in Buddhist practice regard the mâe chii. Nuns engage in the same fundamental hermitic activities – meditation and Dhamma study – as monks do, activities that are the core of monastic life. The reality is that wát that draw sizable contingents of mâe chii are highly respected, since women don't choose temples for reasons of clerical status. When more than a few nuns reside at one temple it's usually a sign that the teachings there are particularly strong. The Institute of Thai Mae Chii, headquartered at Wat Bowonniwet, Bangkok, since 1962, publishes a quarterly journal (Thai-language only) devoted to the activities of Thai Buddhist nuns.

A number of foreigners come to Thailand to be ordained as Buddhist monks or nuns, especially to study with meditation masters at *wát wípàtsa-naa* (meditation monasteries) in Northern Thailand.

Further Information If you wish to find out more about Buddhism you can contact the World Fellowship of Buddhists (☎ 026 611 284–89, ✉ wfb_hq@asianet.co.th), 616 Soi 24, Thanon Sukhumvit, Bangkok.

A Buddhist bookshop at Wat Suan Dok in Chiang Mai sells a few English-language books on Buddhism. Suriwong Book Centre and Shaman Books in Chiang Mai carry a good selection of Buddhist literature in English.

For more information on meditation study in Thailand, see the Courses section in the Facts for the Visitor chapter, and also the Meditation Courses section in the Chiang Mai chapter.

Recommended books about Buddhism include:

Buddhism Explained by Phra Khantipalo
Buddhism, Imperialism, & War by Trevor Ling
Good, Evil & Beyond: Kamma in the Buddha's Teaching by PA Payutto
Heartwood from the Bo Tree by Buddhadasa Bhikkhu
In This Very Life: The Liberation Teachings of the Buddha by Sayadaw U Pandita
Living Dharma by Jack Kornfield
Phra Farang: An English Monk in Thailand by Phra Peter Pannapadipo
A Still Forest Pool: The Teaching of Ajahn Chah at Wat Pah Pong compiled by Jack Kornfield & Paul Breiter
Thai Women in Buddhism by Chatsumarn Kabilsingh

The Long View: An Excursion into Buddhist Perspectives by Suratano Bhikkhu (T Magness)

The Mind & the Way by Ajahn Sumedho

Things as They Are by Ajahn Maha Boowa Nyanasampanno

What the Buddha Never Taught by Timothy Ward

What the Buddha Taught by Walpola Rahula

World Conqueror & World Renouncer by Stanley Tambiah

Two good sources of publications on Theravada Buddhism are: the Buddhist Publication Society, PO Box 6154, Sangharaja Mawatha, Kandy, Sri Lanka; and the Barre Center for Buddhist Studies, Lockwood Rd, Barre, MA 01005, USA.

On the Internet, an excellent resource is Access to Insight: Readings in Theravada Buddhism (Ⓦ www.accesstoinsight.org), from which you can freely download many publications (including many English translations from the Pali canon), all cross-indexed by subject, title, author, proper names and even Buddhist similes. Two other recommended Internet sites with lots of material on Theravada Buddhism, as well as links to other sites, are DharmaNet Electronic Files Archive (Ⓦ www.dharmanet.org) and Buddha Net (Ⓦ www.buddhanet.net).

Other Religions

Of the 50% of Northern Thais who are not Theravada Buddhists, perhaps 5% to 10% – mostly Chinese – practice Mahayana Buddhism, Taoism, Confucianism or a combination of all three. Perhaps an equal percentage, again mostly Chinese, practice Islam, a legacy of the Mongol presence in Yunnan centuries ago.

Several million hill-tribe members practice their own religions, usually a type of animism or a localised theism. A small portion of the North's hill tribes have been converted to Christianity via a steady stream of Christian missionaries from the West. Some missionary groups are quite aggressive; in remote areas in the North you may notice yellow and black signs, in Thai script, nailed high up on the trunks of tall dipterocarp trees alongside two-lane highways. These bear slogans such as 'Christ will erase your sins'.

Before entering any temple, sanctuary or mosque you must remove your shoes, and in a mosque your head must be covered.

LANGUAGE

Most non-hill tribe residents of the North speak Northern Thai as their first language. Northern Thai – kham meuang – is very similar to Standard Thai, as spoken in Central Thailand, with a mutual intelligibility rated at greater than 70%.

Standard Thai is taught in public schools through Northern Thailand, and is the official language of all government agencies. Thus most educated Northerners can speak Standard Thai, and will usually do so automatically with anyone they think comes from outside the region.

Northern Thai has its own script, based on a half-millennium-old Mon script that was originally used only for Buddhist scripture. The script became so popular during the Lanna period that it was exported for use by the Thai Lü in China, the Khün in the eastern Shan State and other Thai-Kadai-speaking groups living between Lanna and China. Although very few Northerners nowadays can read the Northern Thai script – often referred to as 'Lanna script' – it is occasionally used in signage to add a Northern Thai cultural flavour. The script is especially common for use on signs at the entrance gates of monasteries in the North, although the name of the wát will also be written in Thai (and occasionally Roman) script. A Web site (Ⓦ www.lanna20.com/lannafont.htm) from which you can download a Northern Thai script font was under reconstruction at the time of writing, but should be operational again by the time you read this.

Very few outsiders bother to learn Northern Thai, since Standard Thai is so widely spoken. Unless you have a very keen interest in learning the Northern dialect it's best to stick to Standard Thai, as many Northerners seem to take offence when outsiders try speaking kham meuang to them. This attitude dates back to a time, perhaps no more than 20 or 25 years ago, when Central Thais considered Northerners to be very backward, and

Some Northern Thai Words & Phrases

Most Northern Thais, particularly city residents, can speak and understand Central Thai, and thus you don't really need to use kam meuang (Northern Thai). On the other hand, it's nice to know a few words and phrases in common use. Here are some you may hear frequently in the streets and markets of Northern Thailand.

English	Northern Thai (Roman script)	Northern Thai (in Central Thai alphabet)
Northern Thai people	khon meuang	คนเมือง
Chiang Mai	jiang mai	เจียงใหม่
Greetings	sawàt-dii khráp/jâo	สวัสดีครับ/เจ้า
Thank you	yin dii	ยินดี
What's your name	jêu a-yăng	จื้ออะหยัง
My name is (men)	phŏm jêu	ผมจื้อ
My name is (women)	khà-jâo jêu	ขะเจ้าจื้อ
How much?	tâo tai	เต้าไต
very much	nák kha-nàat	นักขนาด
I don't know	bàw húu	บ่อฮู้
speak	ûu	อู้
(I) speak Northern Thai	ûu kam meuang	อู้กำเมือง
(I) can't speak Northern Thai	ûu kam meuang bàw jâang	อู้กำเมืองบ่อจ้าง
Is that right?	mâen kàw	แม่นก่อ
No (it isn't right)	bàw mâen	บ่อแม่น
Very beautiful	ngáam tâe	ง้ามแต้
Very delicious	lam tâe-tâe	ลำแต้ๆ

Note: As in Central Thai, you should add a 'politening syllable' to the end of your sentences when speaking to strangers or to people to whom you may want to show an extra measure of respect. Male speakers end their sentences with the word khráp (ครับ), which is the same word used in Central Thai. Women end phrases with jâo (เจ้า).

thus made fun of their language. Thus when Northern Thais hear outsiders speaking Northern Thai, many automatically assume either that they're being made fun of, or that the outsider is presuming that Northern Thais don't know how to speak Central Thai. This is in contrast to Northeastern Thailand (Isan), where many Northeasterners seem happy to chat in Isan dialect with willing outsiders.

The Language chapter of this guide covers only the Standard Thai dialect. If you're one of the very few people in this world interested in learning kham meuang, the only generally available book is *Lanna Language* by Kobkan Thangpijaigul. All materials are written out in Lanna script, International Phonetic Alphabet (IPA), English translation and Thai translation.

Although the book contains English, it is mostly intended for people who are already fluent in, or very familiar with, Central Thai. An optional 90-minute cassette tape is also available to go with the text.

For real diehards who want to understand Northern Thai as spoken a hundred or more years ago, there's *The Northern Thai Dictionary of Palm-Leaf Manuscripts*, avail-able via Silkworm Books in Chiang Mai. Actually, many of the words in this dictionary are still in general use. Definitions of Northern Thai words are given in Central Thai and English.

Each of Northern Thailand's hill tribes has its own unique language. Lonely Planet's *Hill Tribes phrasebook* offers an introduction to the major hill tribe languages of the region.

Facts for the Visitor

HIGHLIGHTS
Historic Art & Architecture
Thailand is rich in astounding temple architecture and World Heritage–listed historical parks. Sukhothai and Si Satchanalai–Chaliang Historical Parks contain the finest collection of monuments to Thailand's 'golden age'. Lampang and Phrae feature unique Northern Thai temples and century-old teak homes and shophouses. Rare Mon architecture from the Hariphunchai era, as well as many old Northern Thai temples, can be found in Lamphun. In Chiang Mai you can visit older Buddhist temples with rare Lanna-style mural paintings (see the special section 'Lanna-Style Temple Murals').

Nature
Those in search of dense forests, spectacular waterfalls and the perfect spot for a wilderness hike will not be disappointed. Doi Inthanon National Park is home to 400 bird species and Thailand's tallest peak. Doi Phu Kha National Park's vast green area is perfect for a long hike with the added bonus of very few visitors. You can visit the dense forests of Mae Hong Son Province, and in Tak raft, hike or take an elephant ride to the spectacular waterfalls near Um Phang. Around Chiang Mai there are a surprising number of hiking, mountain-biking and rock-climbing opportunities.

Culture
Chiang Mai is the centre of the North's contemporary culture and the Lanna revival. It is also the city to study massage, Thai cooking and Buddhist meditation; and there are hill-tribe villages dotted around Chiang Rai and Nan Provinces.

Shopping
Heir to Northern Thailand's international caravan trade is Chiang Mai's Night Bazaar. For Thai umbrellas, silk textiles and silver look no further than Bo Sang and San Kamphaeng. Mae Sai sells goods from Myanmar, as well as gems, while Pasang is the place for cotton clothing and textiles.

Road Trips
There are plenty of side trips to be made around Northern Thailand. The Mae Hong Son Loop is a dramatic mountain circuit that will take you from Chiang Mai to Mae Hong Son via Pai and Mae Sariang. You could also take a cross-border trip from Mae Sai, at the northernmost tip of Thailand, to Kengtung, Myanmar's historic Thai Khěun capital, to see crumbling Buddhas and colonial architecture. A journey from Chom Thong to Mae Chaem will lead the visitor to scenic river valleys, Thailand's highest peak and historic Lanna temples. A challenging but rewarding drive from Mae Suay to Fang will take you over Doi Wawi, passing hill-tribe and ex-KMT villages, as well as tea plantations.

Relaxing
Visit Pai for its small but vibrant music scene, relaxing hot springs and pleasant climate; Chiang Khong for panoramic views of Laos and the Mekong; and inexpensive Soppong for its tranquillity.

SUGGESTED ITINERARIES
Northern Thailand's asymmetric shape doesn't lend itself to simple linear north-south or east-west routes. Depending on your interests and available time you might pick from the following circuits or combine parts of several to create your own travel route.

The following suggested itineraries assume you want to see as much of the country as possible within a given interval. Another approach is to spend more time in a few places rather than less time in many.

Most visitors begin their journey in Chiang Mai or Phitsanulok. Depending on how much time you have available, you might want to save your Chiang Mai explorations until after you've seen other

Onward Travel

At the end of their Northern Thai sojourn, whatever the duration, most people either head to Bangkok for flights home or to other countries in the area, or else they take the ferry from Chiang Khong to Huay Xai in Laos. From Huay Xai one has the option of travelling around northern Laos, then on to China via Boten (for this you'll need a Chinese visa, available in Chiang Mai), or continuing southward in Laos to Vientiane and then either back into Thailand via Nong Khai or on to Vietnam via Cau Treo or Lao Bao. See the Getting There & Away chapter for more detail.

parts of the region. Chiang Mai then won't seem as overwhelming as on first arrival. You'll also understand more about the Thai character after travelling around the country, and in Chiang Mai it pays to be a good judge of character – in order to separate the touts from the genuinely friendly.

One Week

There's plenty to keep you occupied for a full week in Chiang Mai if you're keen to absorb all the sights in or nearby the Northern capital, or on taking courses in Thai cooking, massage or meditation. A day trip to Lamphun could be included for those interested in seeing the two famous Hariphunchai chedi and more old temples.

If you want to see a bit of the countryside, a trip to Doi Inthanon could easily be added to a week's itinerary. Hiring a car or motorcycle, one might even be able to squeeze in a drive to Pai and back. Or substitute a two-day trip to the old capital of Sukhothai to view the historical park.

10 Days

With 10 days you could follow the suggestions for a one-week itinerary and add excursions farther away. One could do the full Mae Hong Son circuit, for example, or visit Chiang Dao and Doi Mae Salong.

As an alternative, start your trip in Phitsanulok and take in the temple ruins of Sukhothai, Si Satchanalai-Chaliang and/or Kamphaeng Phet before continuing to Chiang Mai. Once in Chiang Mai, choose one of the aforementioned options or make up your own itinerary. Lampang and Lamphun could be combined into a trip worth three or four days.

Two Weeks

With two weeks you could extend your itinerary to include Tak Province in the southeast or Phrae and Nan Provinces in the extreme northeastern section of the North. Another suitable choice would be to do the Chiang Dao-Tha Ton-Doi Mae Salong-Doi Tung-Mae Sai circuit, which will take you through diverse geography and cultures and bring you to Thailand's northernmost point.

Three Weeks

Consider extending the Chiang Dao–Mae Sai route described previously to include historic Chiang Saen, laid-back Chiang Khong and Doi Phu Kha National Park. For most people this will leave a few days for Chiang Mai and environs.

One Month

With four weeks at your disposal you can fit in almost everything suggested in previous suggested itineraries. If you have time left over, consider a jaunt to Si Thep Historical Park or Nam Nao National Park, both in rarely visited Phetchabun Province. Of course, you could also spend nearly the entire month attending one of the 26-day meditation courses at Wat Phra That Chom Thong in Chom Thong or Wat Ram Poeng in Chiang Mai.

Six Weeks

If you're lucky enough to have this much time on your hands to explore the North you can choose to move along at a slower pace, or you could take in two of the North's least-visited provinces, Phayao and Utaradit. Although neither province holds sights of great interest for most people, they make good choices if you'd like to expose yourself to Northern Thai towns and villages that most foreigners have never seen.

Don't forget your phrasebook, as very little English is spoken in these two provinces.

PLANNING
When to Go
Climate-wise, the best overall time to visit Northern Thailand is between mid-October and March. During these months it rains least and is not so hot. Between the months of April and June Thailand is miserably hot.

The peak months for tourist visitation are August, November, December, February and March, with secondary peak months in January and July. You should consider travelling during the least crowded months (April, May, June, September and October) if your main objective is to avoid other vacationers and to take advantage of discounted rooms and other low-season rates. On the other hand, it's not difficult to leave the crowds behind, even during peak months, if you simply avoid some of the most popular destinations. In certain places, such as Pai and Chiang Mai, it can be difficult to find a room in December and January. During these months you should try to schedule morning arrivals, if at all possible, as late morning is the best time to catch a room when space is tight.

Maps
Lonely Planet publishes the 1:1,000,000-scale *Thailand, Vietnam, Laos & Cambodia Road Atlas*. This atlas features over 80 pages of detailed maps, with close-ups of popular destinations and city maps (including one of Chiang Mai). It has topographic shading, handy trip maps, distance charts and a complete geographic index. The atlas is readily available at Suriwong Book Centre in Chiang Mai, in many Bangkok bookshops as well as overseas.

Thailand's Highway Department issues a detailed, full-colour road map of the North that costs 150B per sheet. The 1:1,000,000-scale maps include information on 'roads not under control by the Highway Department' – many of the roads you may travel on in the North. Bookshops sometimes sell this set for 250B, including a mailing tube, but the Highway Department, on Thanon Si Ayuthaya in Bangkok, offers the set at a lower price.

Budget Car & Truck Rental puts out a series of superb map guides called *Budget World Class Drives*. An example is the *Chiang Mai Golden Triangle Loop*, which contains around 20 maps showing various driving circuits in the upper North. The booklets are available only when you rent a vehicle through Budget (☎ 053 202 871) in Chiang Mai.

The Lonely Planet atlas or the maps from the Highway Department are more than adequate for most people. Do-it-yourself trekkers, or anyone with a keen interest in geography, may find general survey sheet maps issued by the Thai military to be helpful. These maps are available in several scales, complete with elevations, contour lines, place names (in Thai and Roman script) and roadways. Most trekkers find the 1:250,000-scale maps, of which there are 52 separate sheets costing 60B each, perfectly adequate. Four *(Mae Hong Son, Mae Chan, Tavoy* and *Salavan)* of the 52 aren't available to the public because of ongoing border disputes with Myanmar and Laos – the Thai army doesn't want to be accused of propagating incorrect borders.

Even more detailed are the army's 1:50,000-scale maps (321 sheets at 70B each). The maps can be purchased in Bangkok at the Thai Army Map Department (Krom Phaen Thi Thahan; ☎ 022 228 844, 022 229 196), sometimes referred to as the Royal Survey Department, opposite the Interior Ministry on the western side of Thanon Ratchini in Ko Ratanakosin, very near Wat Ratchabophit. The entrance is on Thanon Kanlayana Maitri. DK Books in Chiang Mai stocks a selection of the Thai Army maps covering various parts of the North and sells them for 100B each.

David Unkovich, motorcycle travel guru of Northern Thailand, publishes the locally available *Mae Hong Son Loop*, a well-researched 1:750,000-scale map suitable for visitors travelling the region's best driving routes.

City Maps Lonely Planet's *Bangkok City Map* is printed on durable laminated paper and is a handy reference for getting your bearings in the big city. The Tourism Authority of Thailand (TAT) issues several good maps of Northern provinces. Some of them contain bus schedules and other travel information; however, the city map insets are not always so good on these maps.

The tourist brochures that the TAT issues for many provinces in Thailand often contain small inset maps of the provincial capital. Like the city insets on the aforementioned province maps, they're useable but not brilliant. See the individual city sections for information on other city maps.

What to Bring

Bring as little as possible – one medium-sized shoulder bag, duffel bag or backpack should do. Pack lightweight clothes as well as a pullover if you expect to be in the North during the cool season. Natural fibres can be cool and comfortable, except when they get soaked with sweat or rain, in which case they quickly become heavy and block air flow. Some lightweight synthetics breathe better than natural fibres, draw sweat away rather than holding it in, and may be more suitable for the mid-rainy season.

Sunglasses can be bought cheaply in Chiang Mai and most provincial capitals. Slip-on shoes or sandals are highly recommended – besides being cooler than lace-ups, they are easily removed before entering a Thai home or temple. Taking a small torch (flashlight) is a good idea, as it makes it easier to find your way back to your bungalow at night if you are staying at a remote guesthouse. A few other handy things include: a compass; a plastic lighter for lighting candles and mosquito coils (lighters, candles and 'mossie' coils are available in Thailand); and foam earplugs for noisy nights.

Toothpaste, soap and most other toiletries can be purchased anywhere in Northern Thailand. Sun block and mosquito repellent are available, although they can be expensive and the quality of both is generally substandard. If you plan to wash your own clothes, bring along a universal sink plug, a few plastic clothes pegs and 3m of plastic cord (or plastic hangers) for hanging wet clothes out to dry.

If you plan on bringing a laptop computer along, see Email and Internet Access later in this chapter for information on using computer modem communications in Thailand.

Tampons etc Most Thai women don't use tampons, but rather sanitary napkins. Thus you'll rarely find tampons for sale. In general only the o.b. brand is available, usually in pharmacies or minimarts that carry toiletries. In Chiang Mai more upscale pharmacies may also carry Tampax-brand tampons. Boots stores in Chiang Mai carry their own brand, which are similar to Tampax tampons. If you're coming for a relatively short interval, it's best to bring your own. Sanitary napkins are widely available from minimarts and supermarkets throughout Thailand.

Many women have found that the Keeper Menstrual Cap – a reusable natural rubber device that is inserted to catch menstrual flow – is a convenient and environmentally friendly alternative to disposable tampons or pads. For information on this product, contact Health Keeper (☎ 800 663 0427, 519-896 8032, fax 896 8031, ⓔ orderinfo@keeper.com, ⓦ www.keeper.com), 83 Stonegate Drive, Kitchener, ON, Canada N2A 2Y8.

Sarong Sense Pick up a *phâakhamáa* (short Thai-style sarong for men) or a *phâa-sîn* (a longer sarong for women) to wear in your room or when bathing outdoors. These can be bought at any local market (different patterns and colours can be found in different parts of the country) and the vendors will show you how to tie them.

The sarong is a very handy item; it can be used to sleep on or as a light bedspread (many Thai guesthouses do not supply top sheets or bedspreads), as a makeshift 'shopping bag', as a turban/scarf to keep off the sun and absorb perspiration, as a towel, as a small hammock and as a device with which to climb coconut palms – to name just a few of its many functions.

An unsewn sarong is not proper street attire. Women can have sarongs sewn into a 'tube' suitable for everyday wear as a skirt.

Hooks and eyes may be added to the waistline for ease of keeping the sarong on, or you can learn to tie them in the traditional way.

TOURIST OFFICES

The Tourism Authority of Thailand (TAT; W www.tat.or.th), a government-operated tourist information and promotion service founded in 1960 and attached to the prime minister's office, maintains 22 offices in Thailand and 16 overseas.

The quality of the printed information that the TAT produces is second to none among Southeast Asian countries, with pamphlets on sightseeing, accommodation and transportation options. The staff is huge; the main office occupies 10 floors of an office building in Bangkok.

In addition to the following offices, you'll also find TAT information counters in the international and domestic terminals of Bangkok's Don Muang airport. The Chiang Mai TAT office is especially good with written information, as well as with answering questions.

Tourist Offices in Northern Thailand

Local TAT offices include:

Chiang Mai (☎ 053 248 604, fax 053 248 605, e tatcnx@samart.co.th) 105/1 Thanon Chiang Mai–Lamphun, Chiang Mai 50000
Chiang Rai (☎ 053 717 433, fax 053 717 434, e tatcei@loxinfo.co.th) 448/16 Thanon Singkhlai, Chiang Rai 57000
Phitsanulok (☎ 055 252 743, 055 259 907, fax 055 252 742, e tatphs@loxinfo.co.th) 209/7–8 Surasi Trade Center, Thanon Borom Trailokanat, Phitsanulok 65000

Tourist Offices Abroad

TAT's international offices include:

Australia
(☎ 02-9247 7549, fax 9251 2465, e info@thailand.net.au) Level 2, 75 Pitt St, Sydney, NSW 2000
France
(☎ 01 53 53 47 00, fax 01 45 63 78 88, e tatpar@wanadoo.fr) 90 Av des Champs Elysées, 75008 Paris

Germany
(☎ 069-138 1390, e tatfra@t-online.de) Bethmannstrasse 58, D-60311 Frankfurt/Main
Hong Kong
(☎ 02-2868 0732, fax 2868 4585, e tathkg@hk.super.net) Room 401, Fairmont House, 8 Cotton Tree Dr, Central
Japan
Osaka: (☎ 06-6543 6654, fax 6543 6660, e tatosa@ca.mbn.or.jp) Technoble Yotsubashi Bldg 3F, 1-6-8 Kitahorie, Nishi-ku, Osaka 550-0014
Tokyo: (☎ 03-3218 0337, fax 3218 0655) Room 259, South Tower 2F, Yurakucho Denki Bldg, 1-7-1 Yurakucho, Chiyoda-ku, Tokyo 100-0006
Laos
(☎ 021-217157, fax 217158) 79/9 Thanon Lan Xang, Vientiane, Lao PDR
Malaysia
(☎ 603-2162 3480, fax 2162 3486, e sawatdi@po.jaring.my) Suite 2201, Level 22, Menara Lion, 165 Jalan Ampang, 50450 Kuala Lumpur
Singapore
(☎ 65-235 7694, fax 733 5653) c/o Royal Thai embassy, 370 Orchard Rd, 238870
Taiwan
(☎ 02-2502 1600, fax 2502 1603, e tattpe@ms3.hinet.net) 13th floor, Boss Tower, 111 Sung Chiang Rd
UK
(☎ 020-7499 7679, e info@tat-uk.demon .co.uk) 49 Albemarle St, London W1X 3FE
USA
(☎ 323-461 9814, fax 461 9814, e tatla@ix.netcom.com) 1st floor, 611 North Larchmont Blvd, Los Angeles, CA 90004

VISAS & DOCUMENTS
Passport

Entry into Thailand requires a passport valid for at least six months from the time of entry. If you anticipate your passport expiring while you're in Thailand, you should obtain a new one before arrival or inquire with your government as to whether your embassy in Thailand (if one exists) can issue a new one after arrival. See Embassies & Consulates later in this chapter for further information.

Visas

Whichever type of visa you have, be sure to check your passport immediately after stamping. Overworked officials sometimes stamp 30 days on arrival even when you hold a longer visa; if you point out the error before you've left the immigration area at your port of entry, officials will make the necessary corrections. If you don't notice this until you've left the port of entry, go to Bangkok and plead your case at the central immigration office.

Once a visa is issued, it must be used (ie, you must enter Thailand) within 90 days. The Thai Department of Foreign Affairs (W www.mfa.go.th) maintains one of the best Internet sites for information about visas for Thailand.

Visa Exceptions Citizens of Brazil, Korea, New Zealand and Peru may enter Thailand without a visa, in accordance with inter-governmental agreements, for a maximum stay of 90 days for purposes of tourism or temporary business only. No extension of stay will be granted, however.

Transit & Tourist Visas The Thai government allows people of 57 different nationalities to enter the country without a visa for 30 days at no charge. People of 17 other nationalities, such as those from smaller European countries like Andorra or Liechtenstein, or from West Africa, South Asia or Latin America, can obtain 15-day Transit Visas on arrival upon payment of a 300B fee.

People of a few nationalities (eg, Hungarians) must obtain a visa in advance of arrival or they'll be turned back. Check with a Thai embassy or consulate in advance to be sure if you plan on arriving without a visa. More information can be found at the Thai Department of Foreign Affairs' Web site.

Without proof of an onward ticket and sufficient funds for the projected stay, any visitor can be denied entry, but in practice your ticket and funds are rarely checked if you're dressed neatly for the immigration check. See Exchange Control in the Money section later in this chapter for the amount of funds required per visa type.

Next in length of validity is the Tourist Visa, which is good for 60 days and costs

US$15. Two passport photos must accompany all applications.

Non-Immigrant Visas This visa is good for 90 days, must be applied for in your home country, costs US$20 and is not difficult to obtain if you can offer a good reason for your visit. Business, study, retirement and extended family visits are among the purposes considered valid. If you want to stay longer than six months, this is the one to get.

The Non-Immigrant Business Visa (usually abbreviated by Thai immigration officials as 'non-B') allows an unlimited number of entries to Thailand for one year. The only hitch is that you must leave the country at least once every 90 days to keep the visa valid.

Visa Extensions & Renewals Sixty-day Tourist Visas may be extended by up to 30 days at the discretion of Thai immigration authorities. The Chiang Mai office (☎ 053 277 510) is next to the airport on Thanon Mahidon, but you can apply at any immigration office in the country – every province that borders a neighbouring country has at least one. The usual fee for extending a Tourist Visa is 500B. Bring along one photo and one copy each of the photo and visa pages of your passport. Normally only one 30-day extension is granted.

The 30-day, no-visa stay can be extended for seven to 10 days (depending on the immigration office) for 500B. You can also leave the country and return immediately to obtain another 30-day stay. There is no limit on the number of times you can do this, nor is there a minimum interval you must spend outside the country.

Extension of the 15-day, on-arrival Transit Visa is only allowed if you hold a passport from a country that has no Thai embassy.

If you overstay your visa, the usual penalty is a fine of 200B each extra day, with a 20,000B limit; fines can be paid at the airport or in advance at the Investigation Unit (☎ 022 873 101–10), Immigration Bureau, Room 416, 4th floor, Old Building, Soi Suan Phlu, Thanon Sathon Tai, Bangkok.

Extension of a Non-Immigrant Visa very much depends on how the officials feel about you – if they like you then they will extend it. Other than the 500B extension fee, money doesn't usually come into it; neat appearance and polite behaviour count for more. Typically, you must collect a number of signatures and go through various interviews, which may result in a 'provisional' extension. You may then have to report to a local immigration office every 10 to 14 days for the next three months until the actual extension comes through.

Becoming a monk doesn't necessarily mean you'll get a longer visa – again, it depends on who you see and how they feel about you. (See also Tax Clearance later in this section.)

Retirees 55 years of age and older may extend the 90-day Non-Immigrant Visa by one year at a time. To do this you will need to bring the following documents to the immigration bureau: a copy of your passport; one photo; a 500B extension fee; and proof of your financial status or pension. The requirement for the latter is that foreigners aged 60 or older must show proof of an income of not less than 200,000B per year (or 20,000B per month for extensions of less than a year); for those who are aged 55 to 59 the minimum is raised to 500,000/50,000B per year/month. According to immigration regulations: 'If the alien is ill, or has weak health and is sensitive to colder climates, or has resided in Thailand for a long period, and is 55 to 59 years of age, special considerations will be granted'.

Foreigners with Non-Immigrant Visas who have resided in Thailand continuously for three years – on one-year extensions – may apply for permanent residency in Bangkok at Section 1 (☎ 022 873 117), Subdivision 1, Immigration Division 1, Room 301, 3rd floor, Immigration Bureau, Soi Suan Phlu, Thanon Sathon Tai; foreigners who receive permanent residence must carry an 'alien identification card' at all times.

The Thai government maintains the One-Stop Visa Centre (☎ 026 939 333, fax 026 939 340), 207 Thanon Ratchadaphisek, Krisda Plaza, Bangkok, where Non-Immi-grant Visas for investors, businesspeople and foreign correspondents (only) can be renewed in less than three hours.

Various law offices in Chiang Mai can assist with visa extensions, renewals and applications – for a fee, of course.

Re-Entry Permits & Multiple-Entry Visas
If you need to leave and re-enter the kingdom before your visa expires, say for a return trip to Laos or the like, you may need to apply for a Re-Entry Permit at a Thai immigration office. The cost is 500B; you'll need to supply one passport photo. There is no limit to the number of Re-Entry Permits you can apply for and use during the validity of your visa.

Thailand does not issue multiple-entry visas other than the Non-Immigrant Business Visa. If you want a visa that enables you to leave the country and then return, the best you can do is to obtain a visa permitting two entries; this will cost double the single-entry visa. For example, a two-entry, 90-day Non-Immigrant Visa will cost US\$40 and will allow you six months in the country, as long as you cross a border with immigration facilities by the end of your first three months. The second half of your visa is validated as soon as you recross the Thai border. All visas acquired in advance of entry are valid for 90 days from the date of issue.

An alternative is to apply for a Re-Entry Permit (or the Multiple Re-Entry Permit, if established as proposed by Thai immigration) after you're already in Thailand, as described previously.

See Non-Immigrant Visas earlier in this section for a description of the multiple-entry Non-Immigrant Business Visa.

Tax Clearance
Anyone who receives income while in Thailand must obtain a tax clearance certificate from the Revenue Department before they'll be permitted to leave the country. There are Revenue Department offices in every provincial capital. The Chiang Mai office (☎ 053 220 626, ext 107) of the Revenue Department is in the Provincial Hall, San Phi Seua.

Onward Tickets

Thai immigration does not seem very concerned if you arrive without proof of onward travel. Legally speaking, all holders of Tourist Visas or the no-visa 30-day stay permit are *supposed* to carry such proof. In all our years of frequent travel in and out of the kingdom, our onward travel documents haven't been checked a single time.

Travel Insurance

A travel insurance policy to cover theft, loss and medical problems is absolutely essential. Some policies offer lower and higher medical-expense options; the higher ones are chiefly for countries, such as the USA, that have extremely high medical costs. There is a wide variety of policies available, so check the small print.

Some policies specifically exclude 'dangerous activities', which can include scuba diving, motorcycling or even trekking. A locally acquired motorcycle licence is not valid under some policies.

You may prefer a policy that pays doctors or hospitals directly rather than you having to pay on the spot and claim later. If you have to claim later make sure you keep all documentation. Some policies ask you to call back (reverse charges) to a centre in your home country where an immediate assessment of your problem is made.

Check that the policy covers ambulances or an emergency flight home.

Driving Licence & Permits

An International Driving Permit is necessary for any visitor who intends to drive a motorised vehicle while in Thailand. These are usually available from motoring organisations, such as the American Automobile Association (AAA) or the Automobile Association (AA), in your home country. If you'd like to obtain a Thai driving licence, see the Driving Permits section in the Getting Around chapter for details.

Hostel Cards

Hostelling International (HI; formerly known as International Youth Hostel Federation) issues a membership card that allows you to stay at Thailand's member hostels. Without such a card or the purchase of a temporary membership you won't be admitted. See the Accommodation section later in this chapter for more information.

Memberships may be purchased at any member hostel worldwide. For information on Thailand's hostels, check out the Web site (W www.tyha.org).

Student Cards

International Student Identity Cards (ISIC) can be used as identification to qualify for the student discount at some museums in Thailand (although these are rare). It's probably not worth getting one just for a visit to Thailand, but if you already have one, or plan to use one elsewhere in Asia, then bring it along.

ISIC cards are issued via student-oriented travel agencies with ISIC agreements around the world. Check W www.istc.org to find the issuing agency closest to you.

Copies

All important documents (passport data page and visa page, credit cards, travel insurance policy, air/bus/train tickets, driving licence etc) should be photocopied before you leave home. Leave one copy with someone at home and keep another with you, separate from the originals.

You can also store details of your vital travel documents in Lonely Planet's free online Travel Vault. See eKno Communication Service under Post & Communications later in this chapter.

EMBASSIES & CONSULATES
Thai Embassies & Consulates

To apply for a visa, contact the Royal Thai embassy (or consulate) in any of the following countries. In many cases, if you apply in person you may receive a Tourist or Non-Immigrant Visa on the day of application; by mail it generally takes anywhere from two to six weeks.

Australia
 Canberra: (☎ 02-6273 1149, 6273 2937) 111 Empire Circuit, Yarralumla, ACT 2600

Sydney: (☎ 02-9241 2542) 8th floor, 131 Macquarie St, Sydney, NSW 2000

Canada
Ottawa: (☎ 613-722 4444) 180 Island Park Dr, Ottawa, ON K1Y OA2
Vancouver: (☎ 604-687 1143) 1040 Burrard St, Vancouver, BC V6Z 2R9

China
Beijing: (☎ 010-6532 1903) 40 Guanghua Lu, Beijing 100600
Guangzhou: (☎ 020-8188 6968, ext 3301–03) White Swan Hotel, Southern St, Shamian Island, Guangzhou, Guangdong Province
Kunming: (☎ 871-316 8916) King World Hotel, 145 Dong Feng Dong Lu, Kunming, Yunnan Province 650051
Shanghai: (☎ 021-6321 9442) 7 Zhongshan Rd, East 1, Shanghai 200002

France
(☎ 01 56 26 50 50) 8 Rue Greuze, 75116 Paris

Germany
(☎ 30-794810) Lepsiusstrasse 64–66, 12162 Berlin

Hong Kong
(☎ 02-2521 6481–5) 8th floor, Fairmont House, 8 Cotton Tree Drive, Central

India
Calcutta: (☎ 033-440 7836, 440 3230/1) 18-B Mandeville Gardens, Ballygunge, Calcutta 700 019
Mumbai: (☎ 022-363 1404, 369 2543) 4th floor, Malabar View, 33 Marine Drive St, Chowpatty Sea Face, Mumbai 400 007
New Delhi: (☎ 021-6321 9442) 56-N Nyaya Marg, Chanakyapuri, New Delhi, 110021

Indonesia
(☎ 021-390 4052–4) Jalan Imam Bonjol 74, Jakarta Pusat 10310

Japan
Osaka: (☎ 06-243 5563, 243 5569) 4th floor, Konoike East Bldg, 3-6-9 Kitakyohoji-machi, Chuo-ku, Osaka 541-0057
Tokyo: (☎ 03-3441 1386/7) 3-14-6 Kami-Osaki, Shinagawa-ku, Tokyo

Laos
(☎ 021-214581–3) Thanon Phonkheng, Vientiane Poste 128

Malaysia
Kota Bharu: (☎ 09-744 5266, 748 2545) 4426 Jalan Pengkalan Chepa, 15400 Kota Bharu, Kelantan
Kuala Lumpur: (☎ 03-248 8222, 248 8350) 206 Jalan Ampang, Kuala Lumpur
Penang: (☎ 04-226 8029, 226 9484) No 1 Jalan Tunku Abdul Rahman, 10350 Penang

Myanmar (Burma)
(☎ 01-512017, 512018) 437 Pyay Rd, 8 Ward, Kamayut township, Yangon

Nepal
(☎ 01-371410, 371411) Ward No 3, Bansbari, PO Box 3333, Kathmandu

Netherlands
(☎ 070-345 9703) Laan Copes van Cattenburch 123, 2585 EZ, The Hague

New Zealand
(☎ 04-476 8618/9) 2 Cook St, Karori, PO Box 17226, Wellington 5

Philippines
(☎ 02-810 3833, 815 4219) 107B Rada St, Legaspi Village, Makati, Metro Manila

Singapore
(☎ 65-737 2644, 737 2158) 370 Orchard Rd, 238870

UK
(☎ 020-7589 0173, 020-7589 2944) 29–30 Queen's Gate, London SW7 5JB

USA
Chicago: (☎ 312-664 3129) 700 N Rush St, Chicago, IL 60611
Los Angeles: (☎ 213-962 9574–7) 2nd floor, 611 N Larchmont Blvd, Los Angeles, CA 90004
New York: (☎ 02-212 754 1770, 212 754 2536–8) 351 East 52nd St, New York, NY 10022
Washington DC: (☎ 202-944 3600) 1024 Wisconsin Ave NW, Washington, DC 20007

Vietnam
Hanoi: (☎ 04-823 5092–4) 63–65 Hoang Dieu St, Hanoi
Ho Chi Minh City: (☎ 08-822 2637/8) 77 Tran Quoc Thao St, District 3, Ho Chi Minh City

Embassies & Consulates in Thailand

Bangkok and, to a more limited extent, Chiang Mai, are good places to collect visas for onward travel. The visa sections of most embassies and consulates are open from around 8.30am to 11.30am weekdays only (call first to be sure, as some are open only two or three days a week).

Visas are necessary for visits to Myanmar and are available direct from the Myanmar embassy in Bangkok or from many travel agencies in Chiang Mai. Lao visas can be acquired from local agencies as well, including a few agencies in Chiang Khong; you can also arrange them on arrival at airports in Vientiane and Luang Prabang.

Your Own Embassy

It's important to realise what your own embassy – the embassy of the country of which you are a citizen – can and can't do to help you if you get into trouble. Generally speaking, it won't be much help in emergencies if the trouble you're in is remotely your own fault. Remember that you are bound by the laws of the country you are in. Your embassy will not be sympathetic if you end up in jail after committing a crime locally, even if such actions are legal in your own country.

In genuine emergencies you might get some assistance, but only if other channels have been exhausted. For example, if you need to get home urgently, a free ticket home is exceedingly unlikely – the embassy would expect you to have insurance. If you have all your money and documents stolen, it might assist with getting a new passport, but a loan for onward travel is out of the question.

Some embassies used to keep letters for travellers or have a small reading room with home newspapers, but these days the mail holding service has usually been stopped and even newspapers tend to be out of date.

Visas are available on arrival in Malaysia, Cambodia and Vietnam.

Bangkok Countries with diplomatic representation in Bangkok include:

Australia (☎ 022 872 680) 37 Thanon Sathon Tai

Austria (☎ 022 873 970–2) 14 Soi Nantha, Thanon Sathon Tai

Bangladesh (☎ 023 929 437) 727 Soi 55, Thanon Sukhumvit

Belgium (☎ 022 360 150) 44 Soi Phipat, Thanon Silom

Cambodia (☎ 022 546 630) 185 Thanon Ratchadamri, Lumphini

Canada (☎ 026 360 540) 15th floor, Abdulrahim Bldg, 990 Thanon Phra Ram IV

China (☎ 022 457 043) 57 Thanon Ratchadaphisek

Denmark (☎ 022 132 021–5) 10 Soi 1, Thanon Sathon Tai

France (☎ 022 668 250–6) 35 Soi 36, Thanon Charoen Krung; Consular section (☎ 022 872 585–7) 29 Thanon Sathon Tai

Germany (☎ 022 879 000) 9 Thanon Sathon Tai

India (☎ 022 580 300–6) 46 Soi Prasanmit (Soi 23), Thanon Sukhumvit

Indonesia (☎ 022 523 135) 600–602 Thanon Phetburi

Israel (☎ 022 604 854–9) 75 Ocean Tower 2, 25th floor, Soi 19, Thanon Sukhumvit

Japan (☎ 022 526 151–9) 1674 Thanon Phetburi Tat Mai

Laos (☎ 025 396 667, 025 397 341) 520/1–3 Soi 39, Thanon Ramkhamhaeng

Malaysia (☎ 026 792 190–9) 33–35 Thanon Sathon Tai

Myanmar (Burma; ☎ 022 332 237, 022 344 698) 132 Thanon Sathon Neua

Nepal (☎ 023 917 240) 189 Soi Phuengsuk (Soi 71), Thanon Sukhumvit

Netherlands (☎ 022 547 701, 022 252 6103–5) 106 Thanon Withayu

New Zealand (☎ 022 542 530–3) 93 Thanon Withayu

Norway (☎ 022 610 230–5) 18th floor, UBC II Bldg, 591 Soi 33, Thanon Sukhumvit

Philippines (☎ 022 590 139) 760 Thanon Sukhumvit

Singapore (☎ 022 862 111, 286 1434) 129 Thanon Sathon Tai

South Africa (☎ 022 538 473) 6th floor, Park Place, 231 Soi Sarasin

South Korea (☎ 022 477 537) 23 Thanon Thiam-Ruammit, Huay Khwang, Sam Sen Nok

Spain (☎ 022 525 132) 701 Diethelm Tower, 7th floor, 93/1 Thanon Withayu

Sri Lanka (☎ 022 611 934–5) 13th floor, Ocean Tower II Bldg, 75/6 Soi 19, Thanon Sukhumvit

Sweden (☎ 022 544 954–5) 20th floor, Pacific Place, 140 Thanon Sukhumvit

Switzerland (☎ 022 530 156–60) 35 Thanon Withayu Neua

UK (☎ 022 530 191–9) 1031 Thanon Withayu

USA (☎ 022 054 000) 120–122 Thanon Withayu

Vietnam (☎ 022 515 836–8) 83/1 Thanon Withayu

Chiang Mai Chiang Mai has several foreign consular posts where you may be able to arrange visas. The Indian and Chinese consulates here are familiar stopping-off points for travellers on their way to India or China; at either consulate it takes about four days to process a visa.

Australia (☎ 053 221 083, fax 053 219 726)
165 Thanon Sirimangkhalajan
Austria (☎ 053 400 231, fax 053 400 232) 15
Mu 1, Thanon Huay Kaew
Canada (☎/fax 053 850 147) 151 Thanon
Chiang Mai–Lampang (Hwy 11)
China (☎ 053 276 125, 053 200 424, fax 053
274 614) 111 Thanon Chang Lo
Finland (☎ 053 234 777, fax 053 251 512)
104–112 Thanon Tha Phae
France (☎ 053 281 466, fax 053 821 039) 138
Thanon Charoen Prathet
India (☎ 053 243 066, 053 242 491, fax 053
247 879) 344 Thanon Faham (Charoen Rat)
Japan (☎ 053 203 367, fax 053 203 373)
104–107 Airport Business Park, 90 Thanon
Mahidon
Sweden (☎ 053 220 844, fax 053 210 877)
YMCA International Hotel, 11 Thanon
Soemsuk
UK (☎ 053 263 015, fax 053 263 016) 198
Thanon Bamrungrat
USA (☎ 053 252 629–31, fax 053 252 633) 387
Thanon Wichayanon

CUSTOMS

Like most countries, Thailand prohibits the importation of illegal drugs, firearms and ammunition (unless registered in advance with the Police Department) and pornographic media. A reasonable amount of clothing for personal use, toiletries and professional instruments are allowed in duty-free, as are one still camera or one movie/video camera with five rolls of still film or three rolls of movie film or videotape. Up to 200 cigarettes can be brought into the country without paying duty, or other smoking materials to a total of up to 250g. One litre of wine or spirits is allowed in duty-free.

Electronic goods like personal stereos, calculators and computers can be a problem if the customs officials have reason to believe you're bringing them in for resale. As long as you don't carry more than one of each, you should be OK.

For information on currency importation or export, see the Money section later in this chapter.

Antiques & Art

Upon leaving Thailand you must obtain an export licence for any antiques or objects of art you want to take with you. An antique is any 'archaic movable property whether produced by man or by nature, any part of ancient structure, human skeleton or animal carcass, which by its age or characteristic of production or historical evidence is useful in the field of art, history or archaeology'. An object of art is a 'thing produced by craftsmanship and appreciated as being valuable in the field of art'. Obviously these are very sweeping definitions, so if in doubt go to the Fine Arts Department for inspection and licensing.

An application can be made by submitting two front-view photos of the object (no more than five objects to a photo) and a photocopy of your passport, along with the object in question, to one of two locations in Thailand: the Bangkok National Museum or the Chiang Mai National Museum. You need to allow three to five days for the application and inspection process to be completed.

Thailand has special regulations for taking a Buddha or other deity image (or any part thereof) out of the country. These require not only a licence from the Fine Arts Department but a permit from the Ministry of Commerce as well. The one exception to this are the small Buddha images (*phrá phim* or *phrá khrêuang*) that are meant to be worn on a chain around the neck; these may be exported without a licence as long as the reported purpose is religious.

Temporary Vehicle Importation

Passenger vehicles (car, van, truck or motorcycle) can be brought into Thailand for tourism purposes for a period of up to six months. Documents needed for the crossing are: a valid International Driving Permit; passport; vehicle registration papers (in the case of a borrowed or hired vehicle, authorisation from the owner); and a cash or bank guarantee equal to the value of the vehicle plus 20%. (For entry through Khlong Toey Port or Bangkok International Airport, this means a letter of bank credit; for overland crossings via Malaysia or Laos, a 'self-guarantee' filled in at the border is sufficient.)

Home Country Customs

Be sure to check the import regulations in your home country before bringing or sending back a large quantity or high-valued Thailand purchases. The limit varies from country to country; the USA, for example, allows US$400 worth of foreign-purchased goods to enter without duty (with no limit on handicrafts and unset gems), while in Australia the total value is limited to A$400.

MONEY
Currency

The basic unit of Thai currency is the baht (bàat). There are 100 satàang in one baht; coins include 25-satàang and 50-satàang pieces and baht in 1B, 5B and 10B coins. Older coins exhibit Thai numerals only, while newer coins have Thai and Arabic numerals. Twenty-five satàang equals one saleung in colloquial Thai, and people still refer to 25-satàang coins as saleung on occasion.

Paper currency comes in denominations of 10B (brown), 20B (green), 50B (blue), 100B (red), 500B (purple) and 1000B (beige). A 10,000B bill was on the way when the 1997 cash crunch came, and has been tabled for the moment. Ten-baht bills are being phased out in favour of the 10B coin and have become rather uncommon. Notes are also sized according to the amount they're worth; the larger the denomination, the larger the note. Large denominations – 500B and especially 1000B bills – can be hard to change in small towns, but banks will always change them.

Exchange Rates

Exchange rates at the time of writing include:

country	unit		baht
Australia	A$1	=	21.8B
Canada	C$1	=	27.8B
Euro zone	€1	=	40.7B
Hong Kong	HK$1	=	5.8B
Japan	¥100	=	36.2B
New Zealand	NZ$1	=	17.7B
Singapore	S$1	=	24.7B
UK	UK£1	=	64.7B
USA	US$1	=	44.3B

Prior to June 1997 the baht was pegged to a basket of currencies heavily weighted towards the US dollar, and for over 20 years its value hardly varied beyond 20B to 26B to US$1. A year after flotation, the baht had slipped approximately 30% against the US dollar. Lately exchange rates seem to have stabilised, but there's always the chance the Thai currency will go for another rollercoaster ride. Hence it's a good idea to stay abreast of exchange rates during your stay in Thailand – changing currencies at the right time could extend your budget significantly. Exchange rates are printed in the Bangkok Post and the Nation every day, and you can walk into any Thai bank and ask to see a daily rate sheet.

Exchanging Money

There is no black-market money exchange for baht, so there's no reason to bring in any Thai currency. The banks and legal moneychangers offer the best exchange rates within the country. For buying baht, US dollars are the most readily acceptable currency and travellers cheques get better rates than cash, except at some moneychangers where it's the opposite. Since banks charge 23B commission and duty for each travellers cheque cashed, you will save on commissions if you use larger cheque denominations (eg, a US$50 cheque will only cost 23B, while five US$10 cheques will cost 115B). British pounds are second to the US dollar in general acceptability.

Note that you can't exchange Malaysian ringgit, Indonesian rupiah, Nepali rupees, Cambodian riel, Lao kip, Vietnamese dong or Myanmar kyat for Thai currency at banks, although some moneychangers along Thanon Charoen Krung and Thanon Silom in Bangkok carry these currencies. In Chiang Mai you can try International Business Center (☎ 053 216 283) on Thanon Tha Phae. At such places the rates are comparable with black-market rates in countries with discrepancies between the 'official' and free-market currency values.

Visa and MasterCard credit-card holders can get cash advances of up to US$500 (in baht only) per day through some branches of the Thai Farmers Bank, Bangkok Bank and Siam Commercial Bank, and also at the night-time exchange windows in Chiang Mai, Mae Hong Son, Chiang Rai and Phitsanulok.

American Express (AmEx) card holders can also get advances, but only in travellers cheques. The AmEx agent in Chiang Mai is SEA Tours (☎ 053 271 441), 2/3 Thanon Prachasampan, off Thanon Chang Khlan near the Night Bazaar area.

Regular bank hours are 8.30am to 3.30pm weekdays. Several banks in Chiang Mai have special foreign-exchange offices in tourist-oriented areas that are open longer (8.30am to 8pm) and every day of the week. Note that all banks are closed on public holidays.

Exchange Control Legally, any traveller arriving in Thailand must have at least the following amounts of money in cash, travellers cheques, bank draft or letter of credit, according to visa category: US$500/1000 per person/family with a Non-Immigrant Visa; US$250/500 per person/family with a Tourist Visa; US$125/250 per person/family with a Transit Visa or no visa. Your funds may be checked by authorities if you arrive on a one-way ticket or if you look as if you're at 'the end of the road'.

There is no limit to the amount of Thai or foreign currency you may bring into the country. Upon leaving Thailand, you're permitted to take no more than 50,000B per person without special authorisation; exportation of foreign currencies is unrestricted. An exception is made if you're going to Cambodia, Laos, Malaysia, Myanmar or Vietnam, where the limit is 500,000B.

It's legal to open a foreign currency account at any commercial bank in Thailand. As long as the funds originate from abroad, there are no restrictions on their maintenance or withdrawal.

ATMs & Credit/Debit Cards Debit cards (also known as cash cards or check cards) issued by a bank in your own country can be used at several Thai banks to withdraw cash (in Thai baht only) directly from your cheque or savings account back home, thus avoiding all commissions and finance charges. You can use MasterCard debit cards to buy baht at foreign exchange booths or desks at the branches of either the Bangkok Bank or Siam Commercial Bank. Visa debit cards can buy cash through the Thai Farmers Bank exchange services.

These cards can also be used at most Northern Thai ATMs, although a surcharge of around US$1 is usually subtracted from your home account each time you complete a machine transaction. Some travellers now use debit or ATM cards in lieu of travellers cheques because they're quicker and more convenient, although it's a good idea to bring along an emergency travellers-cheque fund in case you lose your card. One disadvantage of debit card accounts, as opposed to credit card accounts, is that you can't arrange a 'charge back' for unsatisfactory purchases after the transaction is completed – once the money's drawn from your account it's gone.

Credit cards as well as debit cards can be used for purchases at many shops, hotels and restaurants. The most commonly accepted cards are Visa and MasterCard, followed by AmEx and Japan Card Bureau (JCB). Diner's Club and Carte Blanche are of much more limited use.

Another alternative to carrying around large amounts of cash or travellers cheques is to open an account at a Thai bank and request an ATM card. Major banks in Thailand now have 24-hour ATMs in provincial capitals and in many smaller towns as well. Once you have a card you'll be able to withdraw cash at machines throughout Thailand, whether those machines belong to your bank or another Thai bank. ATM cards issued by Thai Farmers Bank or Bangkok Bank can be used with the ATMs of 14 major Thai banks. A 10B transaction charge is usually deducted for using an ATM belonging to a bank with which you don't have an account. If you plan on making frequent ATM withdrawals, using a Thai ATM card will yield significant savings, in transactions fees, over foreign ATM cards.

Card Problems Occasionally when you try to use a card at upcountry hotels or shops, the staff may try to tell you that only cards issued by Thai Farmers Bank or Siam Commercial Bank are acceptable. With a little patience, you should be able to make them understand that the Thai Farmers Bank will pay the merchant and that your bank will pay the Thai Farmers Bank – and that any Visa or MasterCard issued anywhere in the world is indeed acceptable.

Another problem concerns illegal surcharges on credit-card purchases. It's against Thai law to pass on to the customer the 3% merchant fee charged by banks, but almost all merchants in Thailand do it anyway. Some even ask 4% or 5%! The only exception seems to be hotels (although even a few hotels will hit you with a credit-card surcharge). If you don't agree to the surcharge they'll simply refuse to accept your card. Begging and pleading or pointing out the law doesn't seem to help.

The best way to get around the illegal surcharge is to politely ask that the credit-card receipt be itemised with cost of product or service and the surcharge listed separately. Then when you pay your bill, photocopy all receipts showing the surcharge and request a 'charge back'. Not all banks in all countries will offer such refunds – the banks in the UK, for example, refuse to issue such refunds, while the banks in the USA usually will.

To report a lost or stolen credit/debit card, call the following telephone hotlines: AmEx (☎ 022 730 022); MasterCard (☎ 022 608 572); Visa (☎ 022 567 326); Diners Club (☎ 022 383 660).

See Dangers & Annoyances later in this chapter for important warnings on credit-card theft and fraud.

International Money Transfer If you have a reliable place to take mail in Northern Thailand, one of the safest and cheapest ways to receive money from overseas is to have an international cashier's cheque (or international money order) sent by courier. It usually takes no more than four days for courier mail to reach Thailand from anywhere in the world.

If you have a bank account in Thailand or your home bank has a branch in Chang Mai, you can have money wired direct via a telegraphic transfer. This costs a bit more than having a cheque sent; telegraphic transfers take anywhere from two days to a week to arrive. International banks with branches in Bangkok include Bank of America, Bank of Tokyo, Banque Indosuez, Banque Nationale de Paris, Citibank, Deutsche Bank, Hongkong Bank, Chase Manhattan Bank, Merrill Lynch International Bank, Sakura Bank, Standard Chartered Bank, United Malayan Bank and many others.

Western Union, justifiably claiming to be 'the fastest way to send money worldwide', has an office in Chiang Mai (☎ 053 224 979) at the Central Department Store, 3rd floor, Kad Suan Kaew shopping centre, Thanon Huay Kaew.

Security

Give some thought in advance to how you're going to carry your financial media – whether travellers cheques, cash, credit and debit cards, or some combination of these. Many travellers favour pouches that can be worn hidden beneath clothing. Hip-pocket wallets are easy marks for thieves. Pickpockets work markets and crowded buses throughout the country, so it pays to keep your money concealed. See Dangers & Annoyances later in this chapter for more on petty crime.

It's a good idea not to keep all your money in one place; keep an 'emergency' stash well concealed in a piece of luggage separate from other money. Long-term travellers might even consider renting a safety deposit box at a bank in Chang Mai. Keep your onward tickets, a copy of your passport, a list of all credit-card numbers and some money in the box just in case all your belongings are stolen while you're on the road. It's not common, but it does happen.

Costs

Food and accommodation in Northern Thailand are generally quite inexpensive, especially considering the value compared to other countries in Southeast Asia.

Budget-squeezers should be able to get by on 240B per day if they really keep watch on their expenses, especially if they share rooms with other travellers. This estimate includes basic food, guesthouse accommodation, nonalcoholic beverages and local transport, but not film, souvenirs, tours, long-distance transport or vehicle hire. Add another 60B to 85B per day for every large beer you drink (30B to 55B for small bottles).

Expenses vary, of course, from place to place: Where there are high concentrations of budget travellers, for example, food tends to be more expensive and accommodation cheaper. With experience, you can travel in Northern Thailand for even less money if you live like a Thai of modest means and learn to speak the language.

Someone with more money to spend will find that for around 400B to 500B per day, life can be quite comfortable; cleaner and quieter accommodation is easier to find once you pass the 200B-a-night zone in room rates. Of course, a 100B guesthouse room with a mattress on the floor and responsive management is better than a poorly-maintained 500B room with air-con that won't turn off and a noisy all-night card game next door.

If you can spend 1000B a day for accommodation you'll be able to stay in the best upcountry accommodation Northern Thailand provides, which usually means air-con, hot water, TV and telephone. Those seeking international-class accommodation and food will spend at least 1500B to 2000B a day for a room with all the modern amenities – IDD phone, 24-hour hot water and air-conditioning, carpeting, swimming pool, fitness centre and all-night room service. Such hotels are generally found only in Chiang Mai, Chiang Rai, Mae Hong Son and Phitsanulok.

Tipping & Bargaining

Tipping is not normal practice in Northern Thailand, although they're getting used to it in expensive hotels and restaurants. Elsewhere don't bother. The exception is loose change from a large Thai restaurant bill;

for example if a meal costs 288B and you pay with a 500B note, some Thais and foreign residents will leave the 12B coin change on the change tray. It's not so much a tip as a way of saying 'I'm not so money-grubbing as to grab every last baht'. On the other hand, change from a 50B note for a 44B bill will usually not be left behind.

Good bargaining, which takes practice, is another way to cut costs. Anything bought in a market should be bargained for; prices in department stores and most nontourist shops are fixed. Sometimes accommodation rates can be bargained down. One may need to bargain hard in heavily touristed areas since many visitors often pay whatever is asked, creating an artificial price zone between the local and tourist market that budgeters must deal with.

On the other hand, the Thais aren't always trying to rip you off, so use some discretion when going for the bone on a price. There's a fine line between bargaining and niggling – getting hot under the collar about 5B makes both seller and buyer lose face. Likewise, a frown is a poor bargaining tool. Additional suggestions concerning costs can be found in the Accommodation and Shopping sections of this chapter.

The cost of transportation between cities and within them is very reasonable; again, bargaining (when hiring a vehicle) can save you a lot of baht. See the Getting Around chapter for more details on hiring a vehicle.

Value-Added Tax

Thailand has a 7% value-added tax (VAT). The tax applies only to certain goods and services but unfortunately no-one seems to know what's subject to VAT and what's not, so the whole situation can be rather confusing. Legally the tax is supposed to be applied to a retailer's cost for the product. For example, if a merchant's wholesale price is 100B for an item that retails at 200B, the maximum adjusted retail including VAT should be 207B, not 214B. But this rarely stops Thai merchants from adding 'VAT' surcharges to their sales.

Visitors to Thailand who hold valid tourist visas and who depart Thailand by air may apply for a VAT refund on purchases made at certain designated shops and department stores. However, the labyrinth of rules and restrictions can seem so complicated that relatively few visitors bother to apply. First of all you must have a valid tourist visa and not have been in Thailand for more than 180 days in a calendar year. Secondly, VAT refunds are available only to visitors departing the country by air, and are available only at the departure halls of Thailand's international airports, where you must fill out a VAT refund application and present it to customs officers along with purchased goods and receipts.

Other Consumer Taxes

Tourist hotels will usually add a 10% hotel tax, and sometimes an 8% to 10% service charge as well, to your room bill.

POST & COMMUNICATIONS

Thailand has a very efficient postal service and within the country postage is very cheap. The typical post office in Northern Thai towns is open from 8.30am to 4.30pm weekdays and 9am to noon on Saturday. Larger main post offices in provincial capitals may also be open for a half-day on Sunday.

Postal Rates

Air mail letters weighing 10g or less cost 14B to anywhere in Asia and the Middle East (Zone 1 in Thai postal parlance), 17B to Europe, Africa, Australia and New Zealand (Zone 2), and 19B to the Americas (Zone 3). Each additional 10g costs 5B, 7B and 9B respectively. Aerograms cost 15B regardless of the destination, while postcards are 12B to 15B, depending on size. Printed matter and small packets up to 20g cost 12B, 16B or 18B, depending on the zone.

Letters sent by registered mail cost 25B in addition to the regular air-mail postage. International express mail service (EMS) fees vary according to 15 zones of destination radiating out from Thailand, ranging from 310B for a document sent to Zone 1 to 2050B for a document sent to Zone 15. EMS packages range from 460B to 2400B.

Within Thailand, this service costs only 25B in addition to regular postage.

The rates for parcels shipped by international post vary according to weight (rising in 1kg increments), country of destination and whether they're shipped by surface (takes up to two months) or air (one to two weeks). Sample air rates include: Singapore, 560B for the first kilogram, then 100B for each additional kilogram; UK 990B first kilogram, 400B for each additional kilogram; USA 775B first kilogram and 300B for each additional kilogram.

A service called Economy Air SAL (for Sea, Air, Land) uses a combination of surface and air mail modes with rates beginning at 20B per 50g, plus 7B for each 25g after that. As a comparison, a 2kg parcel sent to the USA by regular air mail costs 1810B, while the same parcel sent via Economy Air SAL costs only 888B. There are a few other wrinkles to all this, depending on what's in the package. Printed matter, for example, can travel by air more cheaply than other goods.

Parcels sent domestically cost 15B for the first kilogram, plus 10B for each additional kilogram.

Most provincial post offices sell do-it-yourself packing boxes (11 sizes) costing from 7B to 35B; tape and string are provided at no charge. Some of these offices even have packing services, which cost from 4B to 10B per parcel, depending on size. Private packing services may also be available in the vicinity of large provincial post offices.

You can insure the contents of a package at the cost of 7B for every US$20 of the value of the goods within, plus an 'operation charge' of 25B.

Receiving Mail

Mail can be sent to poste restante at almost any post office in Northern Thailand. Post offices in *amphoe meuang* (provincial capitals) are the most reliable for this service, but even in smaller towns the staff will take mail on your behalf if you arrange it in advance.

As with many Asian countries, confusion at poste restante offices is most likely to arise over first names and family names.

Ask people who are writing to you to print your family name clearly and to underline it. If you're certain a letter should be waiting for you and it cannot be found, it's always wise to check that it hasn't been filed under your first name.

The AmEx office in Chiang Mai will take mail on behalf of AmEx card holders. The hours are 9am to 5pm Monday to Saturday. AmEx won't accept courier packets that require your signature.

Couriers

Several companies in Northern Thailand offer courier services in provincial capitals, including DHL, UPS and FedEx.

Telephone

The telephone system in Thailand, operated by the government-subsidised Telephone Organization of Thailand (TOT) under the Communications Authority of Thailand (CAT), is quite efficient and you can usually direct-dial most major centres with little difficulty.

The telephone country code for Thailand is 66. See the boxed text for Thailand's area codes. Note that Thailand recently changed its dialling system so that you're supposed to dial the area code with the main number even if calling locally. Eventually the old area codes will simply become part of the number and, supposedly, there will be no area codes in Thailand. However, we were still able to dial locally without using the area code at the time of writing.

Telephone Office Hours Main post-office telephone centres in most provincial capitals are open from 7am to 11pm daily

Thailand's Area Codes

The area codes for Thailand's major cities are presented here. See the relevant destination chapters for the area codes of smaller towns not listed here. Note that zeros aren't needed in area codes when dialling from overseas but they must be included when dialling domestically. To dial a domestic phone number, whether local or long-distance, dial the number preceded by the area code (since 2001 all calls have required the area code, even local calls).

Bangkok, Nonthaburi, Pathum Thani, Samut Prakan, Thonburi	☎ 02
Cha-am, Phetchaburi, Prachuap Khiri Khan, Pranburi, Ratchaburi	☎ 032
Kanchanaburi, Nakhon Pathom, Samut Sakhon, Samut Songkhram	☎ 034
Ang Thong, Ayuthaya, Suphanburi	☎ 035
Lopburi, Saraburi, Singburi	☎ 036
Aranya Prathet, Nakhon Nayok, Prachinburi	☎ 037
Chachoengsao, Chonburi, Pattaya, Rayong, Si Racha	☎ 038
Chanthaburi, Trat	☎ 039
Chiang Khan, Loei, Mukdahan, Nakhon Phanom, Nong Khai, Sakon Nakhon, Udon Thani	☎ 042
Kalasin, Khon Kaen, Mahasarakham, Roi Et	☎ 043
Buriram, Chaiyaphum, Nakhon Ratchasima (Khorat)	☎ 044
Si Saket, Surin, Ubon Ratchathani, Yasothon	☎ 045
Chiang Mai, Chiang Rai, Lamphun, Mae Hong Son	☎ 053
Lampang, Nan, Phayao, Phrae	☎ 054
Kamphaeng Phet, Mae Sot, Phitsanulok, Sukhothai, Tak, Utaradit	☎ 055
Nakhon Sawan, Phetchabun, Phichit, Uthai Thani	☎ 056
Narathiwat, Pattani, Sungai Kolok, Yala	☎ 073
Hat Yai, Phattalung, Satun, Songkhla	☎ 074
Krabi, Nakhon Si Thammarat, Trang	☎ 075
Phang-Nga, Phuket	☎ 076
Chaiya, Chumphon, Ko Samui, Ranong, Surat Thani	☎ 077

(the one in Chiang Mai is open 24 hours); the smaller provincial phone offices may be open from 8am to either 8pm or 10pm. Bangkok's international CAT phone office (now called the Public Telecommunications Service Centre), at the Thanon Charoen Krung main post office, is open 24 hours.

International Calls To direct-dial an international number (other than those in Cambodia, Laos, Malaysia and Myanmar) from a private phone, simply dial ☎ 001 before the number you're calling. For operator-assisted international calls, dial ☎ 100.

Home Country Direct service is available from several public spots in Chiang Mai (see the Post & Communications section in the Chiang Mai chapter). Home Country Direct phones offer easy one-button connection with international operators in some 40 countries around the world. You can also direct-dial Home Country Direct access numbers from any private phone (most hotel phones won't work) in Thailand. For details see the boxed text 'Home Country Direct'.

Hotels generally add surcharges (sometimes as much as 30% over and above the CAT rate) for international long-distance calls; it's always cheaper to call abroad from a CAT telephone office. These offices are almost always attached to a city's main post office, often on the building's 2nd floor, around the side or just behind the main post office. There may also be a TOT office down the road, used only for residential or business service (eg, billing or installation), not public calls; even when public phone services are offered, TOT offices accept only cash payments – reverse-charge (collect) and credit-card calls aren't permitted. Hence the CAT office is generally your best choice.

The procedure for making an international long-distance phone call *(thorásàp ráwàang pràthêt)*, once you've found the proper office and window, begins with filling out a form with details of the call. Except for reverse-charge calls, you must estimate in advance the time you'll be on the phone and pay a deposit equal to the time/distance rate. There is always a minimum three-minute charge,

---

Home Country Direct

For Home Country Direct service, dial ☎ 001-999 followed by:

country	number
Australia (Optus)	61-2000
Australia (OTC)	61-1000
Canada (AT&T)	15-2000
Canada	15-1000
Denmark	45-1000
Finland	358-1000
France	33-1000
Germany	49-1000
Israel	972-1000
Italy	39-1000
Japan	81-0051
Korea	82-1000
Netherlands	31-1035
New Zealand	64-1066
Norway	47-1000
Singapore	65-0000
Sweden (telephone 1)	46-1000
Sweden (telephone 2)	41-2000
Switzerland	41-1000
UK (BT)	44-1066
UK (MCL)	44-2000
USA (AT&T)	11-1111
USA (Hawaii)	14424
USA (MCI)	12001
USA (Sprint)	13877

---

which is refunded if your call doesn't go through. Usually, only cash or international phone credit cards are acceptable for payment at CAT offices; some provincial CAT offices also accept AmEx and a few take Visa and MasterCard.

If the call doesn't go through you must pay a 30B service charge anyway – unless you're calling reverse charges *(kèp plai thaang)*. For reverse-charge calls it's the opposite, ie, you pay the 30B charge only if the call goes through. Depending on where you're calling, reimbursing someone later for a reverse-charge call to your home country may be less expensive than paying CAT/TOT charges – it pays to compare rates at the source and destination. For calls between the USA and Thailand, for example, AT&T's collect rates are less than TOT's direct rates.

Private long-distance telephone offices exist in most towns, but are sometimes only for calls within Thailand. Often these offices are just a desk or a couple of booths in the rear of a retail shop. They typically collect a 10B surcharge for long-distance domestic calls and 50B for international calls, and accept cash only.

Whichever type of phone service you use, the least expensive time of day to make calls is from midnight to 5am (30% discount on standard rates), followed by 9pm to midnight or 5am to 7am (20% discount). You pay full price from 7am to 9pm (this rate is reduced by 20% on Sunday). Some sample rates for a three-minute call during the daytime include: 55B to Africa; 40B to Asia; 34B to Australia; 46B to Europe; and 42B to the UK.

If you're calling from a private phone, you must dial the international access code ☎ 001 before dialling the country code, area code and phone number you wish to reach.

Cambodia, Laos, Malaysia & Myanmar
CAT does not offer long-distance service to Cambodia, Myanmar, Laos or Malaysia. To call these countries you must go through TOT. To call Laos, Myanmar or Cambodia you can direct dial ☎ 007 and the relevant country code (Laos: 856; Myanmar: 95; Cambodia: 855) followed by the area code and number you want to reach. For calls to Laos from Northern Thailand the rate is 18B per minute. Malaysia can be dialled direct by prefixing the code ☎ 09 to the Malaysian number (including area code). The rate is 20B to 30B per minute, depending on time of day.

International Phonecards A CAT-issued, prepaid international calling card, called Thai Card, comes in 300B and 500B denominations and allows calls to many countries at standard CAT rates. You can use the Thai Card codes from either end (eg, for calling the UK from Thailand or calling Thailand from the UK).

Lenso phonecards allow you to make international phone calls from yellow Lenso wall phones. Cards come in 250B and 500B denominations and are sold in various shops. You can also use most major credit cards with Lenso phones and dial AT&T direct-access numbers.

Of course, a wide range of other international 'phonecards' – actually calling card access numbers, not true phonecards – are available outside Thailand.

Internet Phone The cheapest way to call internationally is via the Internet. Some Internet calls – such as those from Thailand to the USA – are free, while others are much less costly than regular phone calls. Many Internet cafes in Thailand allow Internet phone calls. Most charge only the regular per-minute or per-hour fees they charge for any other kind of Internet access if the call itself is a free call, as in the previous example. A few places charge extra for Internet phone calls, and of course if the call isn't free you will pay for both Internet time and the call – but this is still often less expensive than using CAT.

Domestic Calls There are three kinds of public pay phones in Northern Thailand – 'red', 'blue' and 'green'. The red phones are for local city calls, the blue phones are for both local and long-distance calls (within Thailand) and the green ones are for use with phonecards.

Local calls from pay phones cost 1B for 164 seconds (add more coins for more time). Local calls from private phones cost 3B, with no time limit. Some hotels and guesthouses feature private pay phones that cost 5B per call. Long-distance rates within the country vary from 3B to 12B per minute, depending on the distance.

Card phones are available at most airports as well as major shopping centres and other public areas throughout urban Thailand. Phonecards come in 25B, 50B, 100B, 200B and 240B denominations, all roughly the same size as a credit card; they can be purchased at any TOT office. In airports you can usually buy them at the airport information counter or at one of the gift shops.

Another way to pay for domestic calls is to use the Pin Phone 108 system, which allows you to dial ☎ 108 from any phone –

including cellular phones and public pay phones – then enter a PIN code to call any number in Thailand. To use this system, however, you must have your own phone number in Thailand.

Cellular Phones TOT authorises use of private cell phones using two systems, NMT 900MHz (Cellular 900) and GSM, and the older NMT 470MHz. GSM is quickly becoming the standard.

It costs 1000B to register a phone and 500B per month for 'number rental' with the 900MHz and GSM, or 300B for 470MHz. Rates are 3B per minute within the same area code, 8B per minute to adjacent area codes and 12B per minute to other area codes. Cell phone users must pay for incoming as well as outgoing calls. Keep this in mind whenever you consider calling a number that begins with the code 01 – this means you are calling a cell phone number and will therefore be charged accordingly. Please note that you must also dial the zero in '01'.

In Chiang Mai and Chiang Rai we've seen sidewalk tables where you can make cell phone calls anywhere in Thailand for 3B per minute. The vendors are able to do this by repeatedly taking advantage of special promotions on new cell phone accounts.

eKno Communication Service

Lonely Planet's eKno global communication service provides low-cost international calls – for local calls you're usually better off with a local phonecard. eKno also offers free messaging services, email, travel information and an online travel vault, where you can securely store all your important documents. You can join online at W www.ekno.lonelyplanet .com, where you will find the local-access numbers for the 24-hour customer-service centre. Once you have joined, always check the eKno Web site for the latest access numbers for each country and updates on new features.

Fax

Telephone offices in main post offices throughout the North offer fax services in addition to regular phone services. There's no need to bring your own paper, as the post offices supply their own forms. A few TOT offices also offer fax services. International faxes typically cost 100B to 130B for the first page, and 70B to 100B for each subsequent page, depending on the size of the paper and the destination.

Larger hotels with business centres offer fax services but always at higher rates.

Email & Internet Access

The Net continues to expand in Thailand. The scene is changing rapidly and nowadays Thailand's better Internet service providers (ISPs) offer upcountry nodes in a dozen or more towns and cities around Northern Thailand, which means if you are travelling with a laptop you won't necessarily have to pay long-distance charges.

The major limitation in email and Internet access continues to be the CAT, which connects all ISPs via the Thailand Internet Exchange (THIX) at speeds that are relatively low by international standards. The CAT also collects a hefty access charge from local ISPs, which keeps the rates high relative to the local economy.

Many guesthouses and bars/cafes in Chiang Mai now offer email and Internet log-ons at house terminals. For the visitor who only needs to log on once in a while, these are a less expensive alternative to getting your own account – and it certainly beats lugging around a laptop. The going rate is 1B or 2B per on- and off-line minute, although we've seen a few places where slower connections are available at a half-baht per minute, and even less.

Cybercafes are plentiful in any town with a population over 50,000. For that reason we don't list cybercafes in this guide except for towns where they're a rarity, or where the services offered are especially extensive.

Nowadays most ISPs worldwide offer the option of Web-based email, so if you already have an Internet account at home you can check your email anywhere in Thailand simply by logging onto your ISP's Web site using an Internet browser (such as Microsoft Internet Explorer or Netscape). If you have any doubts about whether your home

ISP offers Web-based email, check before you leave home. You may want to register with one of the many free Web-based email services, such as MS Hotmail, Yahoo!, Juno or Lonely Planet's own eKno. You can log onto these services at any cybercafe in Thailand.

Plugging in Your Own Machine In older hotels and guesthouses the phones may still be hard-wired, but in newer hotels RJ11 phone jacks are the standard. For hard-wired phones you'll need to bring an acoustic coupler. Some hotels and guesthouses that feature room phones without RJ11 jacks may have a fax line in the office, and virtually all fax machines in Thailand are connected via RJ11 jacks. Some places will allow guests to use the house fax line for laptop modems, provided online time is kept short.

Longer-term visitors may want to consider opening a monthly Internet account. Local ISPs – of which there were 18 at last count – typically charge around 400B to 500B per month for 20 hours of Net access and 700B to 800B for 40 hours. Low-grade, text-only services are available for as little as 200B a month. With any of these accounts additional per-hour charges are incurred if you exceed your online time.

Temporary Internet accounts are available from several Thai ISPs. One of the better ones is WebNet, offered by Loxinfo (W www.loxinfo.co.th). You can buy a block of 12 hours (160B), 30 hours (380B) or 63 hours (750B), good for up to one year. Purchasers are provided with a user ID, password, Web browser software, local phone access numbers and log-on procedures, all (except the Web browser software) via email. You'll be able to navigate the Internet, check email at your online home address and access any online services you subscribe to.

DIGITAL RESOURCES

The World Wide Web is a rich resource for travellers. You can research your trip, hunt down bargain air fares, book hotels, check on weather conditions or chat with locals and other travellers about the best places to visit (or avoid!).

There's no better place to start your Web explorations than the Lonely Planet Web site (W www.lonelyplanet.com). Here you'll find succinct summaries on travelling to most places on earth, postcards from other travellers and the Thorn Tree bulletin board, where you can ask questions before you go or dispense advice when you get back. You can also find travel news and updates to many of our most popular guidebooks, and the subWWWay section links you to the most useful travel resources elsewhere on the Web.

You can also find travel news and updates on Thailand. Go to W www.lonelyplanet .com.au/dest/sea/thai.htm for a direct link to Thailand-related material.

Several Web sites offer information on Northern Thailand. Most are commercial sites established by tour operators or hotels; the ratio of commercial to non-commercial sites is liable to increase over time if current Internet trends continue. Remember that all URL's (uniform resource locators) mentioned are subject to change without notice.

Many Web sites with information on Thailand travel earn revenue from hotel bookings and advertising paid for by travel suppliers, hence you should take any recommendations they make with a huge grain of salt.

Useful Web sites include:

Asia Travel Perhaps the best of the many commercial sites with travel-booking capabilities.
  W asiatravel.com/chiangmai.html
Bangkok Post Contains the entire newspaper (except for ads), and archives of stories for several years.
  W www.bangkokpost.com
The Nation Another good source of local news with a comprehensive searchable archive.
  W www.nationmultimedia.com
Tourism Authority of Thailand Good general selection of information about Northern Thailand.
  W www.tat.or.th/province/north/chi-mai/
Welcome to Chiang Mai & Chiang Rai This free tourist magazine posts many of its useful Northern Thailand listings on the Web.
  W welcome-to.chiangmai-chiangrai.com/
Chiang Mai News Very comprehensive but mostly limited to Chiang Mai itself.
  W www.chiangmainews.com

Aside from the Web, another Internet resource, soc.culture.thai, is a usenet newsgroup. It's very uneven, as it's basically a chat outlet for anyone who thinks they have something to say about Thailand. Still, it's not a bad place to start if you have a burning question that you haven't found an answer to elsewhere.

BOOKS
Lonely Planet
For those planning to travel beyond Northern Thailand, Lonely Planet's *Thailand* guidebook is full of indispensable information. The compact *World Food: Thailand*, by Joe Cummings, enables food-conscious visitors to Thailand, as well as residents, to appreciate the full range of Thai cuisine by providing explanations of the cooking methods, extensive menu glossaries and lots of cultural and historical background. A section on Northern Thai cuisine is included.

The hardcover pictorial *Buddhist Stupas of Asia: The Shape of Perfection* contains coverage of a number of Northern Thai *chedi* (stupas).

Other Lonely Planet publications of interest to anyone visiting Thailand include *Bangkok, Thailand's Islands & Beaches,* the *Thai phrasebook*, the *Hill Tribes phrasebook* and the *Thailand, Vietnam, Laos & Cambodia Road Atlas*.

Guidebooks
England's Christian Gooden publishes a trio of volumes that are part travelogue, part guidebook to some of the North's most out-of-the-way places: *Hinterlands: Sixteen Do-It-Yourself Jungle Treks in Nan & Mae Hong Son Provinces; Around Lanna: A Guide to Thailand's Northern Border Region from Chiang Mai to Nan;* and *Thee Pagodas: A Journey down the Thai-Burmese Border*. Maps provide graphic directions for duplicating many of the walks Gooden has done.

English expat Oliver Hargreave has written a colourful and authoritative guidebook to Chiang Mai entitled *Exploring Chiang Mai, City, Valley & Mountains* (Within Design, Chiang Mai), in which maps of driving circuits are particularly noteworthy.

David Unkovich's *A Motorcycle Guide to the Golden Triangle* (Silkworm Books, Chiang Mai) is indispensable for anyone wanting to make a motorcycling trip off the beaten track in the mountainous borderlands of Northern Thailand.

Travel
Carl Bock's illustrated *Temples and Elephants: The Narrative of a Journey through Upper Siam and Laos*, first published in 1884 and most recently republished by Bangkok's White Lotus, provides glimpses of Northern Thailand from a vanished era.

American missionary Daniel McGilvary's 1912-vintage *A Half Century among the Siamese and the Laos* goes much deeper than Bock and contains some of the most oft-quoted passages on life in late-19th-century Northern Thailand.

WAR Wood's *Consul in Paradise* takes a nostalgic look at a former British consul's sojourn in Chiang Mai in the early 20th century. Reginald Campbell's *Teak Wallah* carries on in a similar mode about the Chiang Mai teak trade in the same era.

Charles Nicholls' semi-fictional *Borderlines* (1992) takes the reader on a voyage to the Thai-Myanmar border in the company of a colourful group of travellers.

Asia Books' *A Golden Souvenir of Chiang Mai & Northern Thailand* contains sumptuous photos of the region by Jerry Alexander and is relatively inexpensive for a pictorial book.

Lanna: Thailand's Northern Kingdom, with text and photography by Michael Freeman, makes the upper North look like a virtual paradise.

Although it's marketed as a stylish coffee-table tome, and bears some similarities from the aforementioned Freeman book, *Lanna Style: Art & Design of Northern Thailand*, by William Warren, contains much solid historical information.

Natural History
Complete with sketches, photos and maps, *The Mammals of Thailand*, by Boonsong Lekagul & Jeffrey McNeely (Association for the Conservation of Wildlife, 1988), remains

the classic on Thai wildlife in spite of a few out-of-date references (it was first published in 1977). Bird lovers should seek out the *Bird Guide of Thailand*, by Boonsong Lekagul & EW Cronin (Association for the Conservation of Wildlife, 1972), for the comprehensive descriptions of Thailand's numerous avian species.

Detailed summaries of Thailand's national parks, along with an objective assessment of current park conditions, are available in *National Parks of Thailand* by Gray, Piprell & Graham (Communication Resources, Bangkok).

History & Politics

ML Manich Jumsai's *History of Laos, including the History of Lan Na Thai, Chiengmai* is one of the standard English histories for the region. *A Brief History of Lan Na* by Hans Penth (Silkworm Books) contains a detailed chronicle of the history of upper Northern Thailand.

Originally composed in Thai in 1827, the *Chiang Mai Chronicles* were translated into English by David Wyatt & Aroonrut Wichienkeo in the late 1990s, and comprise the most complete local historical record of the Lanna era. Much more than the title suggests, it begins with the founding of the Mon kingdom of Hariphunchai and continues as far afield as Laos and Yunnan before finishing with a Chiang Mai palace construction in the 1820s. Some of the narrative obviously relies heavily on oral legend, while in other parts exact dates and inscriptions are quoted.

Thailand's role in the international narcotics trade is covered thoroughly in Alfred McCoy's *The Politics of Heroin in Southeast Asia* and Francis Belanger's *Drugs, the US, and Khun Sa*. *Chasing the Dragon: Into the Heart of the Golden Triangle*, by Christopher R Cox, contains some decent writing and interesting news titbits as it traces a journalist's path to Khun Sa's former Ho Mong headquarters near the Thai-Myanmar border.

Culture & Society

Teak House, a Thai publishing company, produces a series of book-length monographs devoted to individual ethnic groups in Southeast Asia, including *The Haw: Traders of the Golden Triangle* (Andrew Forbes & David Henley) and *Khon Muang: People & Principalities of North Thailand* (Andrew Forbes & David Henley).

Culture Shock! Thailand & How to Survive It, by Robert & Nanthapa Cooper, is an interesting outline on getting along with the Thai way of life, although it's heavily oriented towards Bangkok. *Letters from Thailand* by Botan (translated by Susan Fulop Kepner) and Carol Hollinger's *Mai Pen Rai Means Never Mind* can also be recommended for their insights into traditional Thai culture, much of which applies equally to the North.

For information on books about Buddhism and how it is practised in Thailand, see the Religion section in the Facts about Northern Thailand chapter.

Hill Tribes

If you're interested in detailed information on hill tribes, seek out the hard-to-find *The Hill Tribes of Northern Thailand* by Gordon Young (Monograph No 1, The Siam Society). Young was born of third-generation Christian missionaries among the Lahu people, spoke several tribal dialects and was even an honorary Lahu chieftain with the highest Lahu title, the Supreme Hunter. The monograph covers 16 tribes, including descriptions, photographs, tables and maps.

Another Teak House hardcover, *The Akha: Guardians of the Forest* by Jim Goodman, is the definitive nonacademic introduction to perhaps Northern Thailand's most intriguing hill tribe.

From the Hands of the Hills, by Margaret Campbell, has lots of beautiful pictures. *Peoples of the Golden Triangle*, by Elaine & Paul Lewis, is also very good, very photo-oriented and expensive. Lonely Planet's *Thai Hill Tribes phrasebook* has descriptions of Thailand's major hill tribes, maps, and phrases in several hill-tribe languages.

Trekking through Northern Thailand, by Ada Guntamala & Kornvika Puapratum (Silkworm Books, Chiang Mai), contains good suggestions for trekking, whether you are going out on your own or with a guide. The small book includes route maps and lists of taboos for individual tribes. *The Hill Tribes of Thailand*, published by the Tribal Research Institute at Chiang Mai University, also contains sound advice for trekkers but the hill tribe information is rather skimpy.

See the special section 'People of Northern Thailand' for further information on these groups.

FILMS

A number of classic international films have used Northern Thailand as either a subject or as a location – more often the latter. In fact, nowadays location shooting in Thailand has become something of a boom industry as Thailand's jungles, rice fields and islands find themselves backdrops for all manner of scripts set in 'exotic' tropical countries. Thailand now maintains a substantial contingent of trained production assistants and casting advisers who work continuously with foreign companies – many of them from Japan, Hong Kong and Singapore – on location shoots.

The first film to come out of Thailand for foreign audiences was *Chang*, a 1927 silent picture shot entirely in Nan Province (then still a semi-independent principality with Siamese protection). Produced by American film impresarios Copper and Schoedsack (who later produced several major Hollywood hits, including the original *King Kong*), *Chang* contains some of the best jungle and wildlife sequences filmed in Asia to date. *Chang* is available on film or video from speciality houses.

Jean-Claude Van Damme's *The Kickboxer* brought Thai boxing to the big screen with a bit more class than the average martial arts flick; more than a few foreign pugilists have packed their bags for Bangkok after viewing the movie's exotic mix of ring violence and Thai Buddhist atmosphere. Some of the scenes were shot in the North, including some that used the old city of Sukhothai as a backdrop.

Two very forgettable 1980s comedy flicks were filmed in Mae Hong Son: *Volunteers*, a Tom Hanks and John Candy movie about a couple of Peace Corps workers falling afoul of dope peddlers and communists; and *Air America*, with a dashing Mel Gibson falling afoul of more Reds and dope peddlers. The dope-smuggling bridge that's a focus of *Volunteers* is based on a real bridge in Northern Thailand, the one that now links Mae Sai, Thailand's northernmost point, with Tachileik Myanmar.

NEWSPAPERS

Thailand's 1997 constitution guarantees freedom of the press, although the Royal Police Department reserves the power to suspend publishing licences for national security reasons. Editors nevertheless exercise self-censorship in certain realms, particularly with regard to the monarchy.

Monarchical issues aside, Thailand is widely considered to have the freest print media in Southeast Asia. In a survey conducted by the Singapore-based Political and Economic Risk Consultancy, 180 expatriate managers in 10 Asian countries ranked Thailand's English-language press the best in Asia. Surprisingly, these expats more frequently cited the *Bangkok Post* and the *Nation* as their source of regional and global news than either the *Asian Wall Street Journal* or the *Far Eastern Economic Review*.

These two English-language newspapers are published daily – the *Bangkok Post* in the morning and the *Nation* in the afternoon – and are available in many shops in Chiang Mai, and just about anywhere in the North where foreigners frequently travel. The *Bangkok Post*, Thailand's first English daily (established 1946), has a mixed Thai and international staff and tends to feature more objective reporting than the *Nation*. The latter often runs opinion pieces as news and has a habit of scapegoating the West for internal Thai problems. For international news, the *Bangkok Post* is the better of the two papers and is regarded by many journalists as the best English daily in the region. The *Nation*, on the other hand, is well regarded for its regional coverage.

The Singapore edition of the *International Herald Tribune* is widely available in Chiang Mai but rarely seen elsewhere in Northern Thailand.

The most popular Thai-language newspapers are *Thai Rath* and *Daily News*, but they're mostly full of blood-and-guts stories. The best Thai journalism is found in the somewhat less popular *Matichon* and *Siam Rath* dailies. All four newspapers are easily found in almost any town. Many Thais read the English-language dailies as they consider them better news sources. The *Bangkok Post* also publishes a Thai-language version.

MAGAZINES

English-language magazine publishing has faltered with the economic slowdown in Thailand and several mags failed after 1996. Now Thailand's biggest-selling English-language magazine, *Bangkok Metro* injects urban sophistication into the publishing scene with listings on art, culture, cuisine, film and music that include Chiang Mai and Northern Thailand.

In Chiang Mai, many popular magazines from the UK, USA, Australia and Europe – particularly those concerned with computer technology, autos, fashion, music and business – are available in bookshops that specialise in English-language publications (see Bookshops in the Chiang Mai chapter).

RADIO

Thailand boasts more than 400 radio stations, and each of the North's provincial capitals can claim a few. All in all, the radio offerings in Northern Thailand aren't nearly as interesting as in Bangkok, and there is virtually no English-language programming.

Each capital has a station affiliated with Radio Thailand and Channel 9 on Thai public television, and thus broadcasts CNN news coverage of the Asia region almost every hour between 5pm and 2am daily. In Chiang Mai, FM100.7, operated by the Mass Communications Organisation of Thailand, plays a variety of Thai and international pop and is the best all-around music station. Chiang Mai University has a student-run station at FM100.0. The Thai army, navy and police all lease time on their

stations, and the programming changes frequently. For a province-by-province guide to Northern Thai radio, check Ⓦ www.asiaradio.crosswinds.net/thalocs1.htm on the Internet.

The BBC World Service, Radio Canada, Radio Japan, Radio New Zealand, Singapore Broadcasting Company and Voice of America (VOA) all have English- and Thai-language broadcasts over short-wave radio. The frequencies and schedules, which change hourly, appear in the *Bangkok Post* and the *Nation*. BBC and VOA are the most easily received by the average short-wave radio.

Radio France Internationale and Deutsche Welle carry short-wave programs in French and German, respectively. Deutsche Welle also broadcasts 50 minutes of English programming three times daily.

TV

Thailand has five VHF TV networks. With a normal antenna, only Channels 3 and 9 can be received in Northern Thailand, but with cable or satellite hookups (see Satellite & Cable TV later in this section) all are available.

Channel 3 is privately owned and offers a wide variety of Thai comedy, dramas, news and movies, mostly in Thai language only; broadcast hours are 5.30am to midnight.

Channel 5 is a military network and broadcasts from 5am to 3.05am. Between 5am and 7am this network presents a mix of ABC, CNN International and English-subtitled Thai news programs; at noon it runs English-language news; then CNN headlines again at 12.07am.

Channel 7 (5.30am to 12.30am) is also military owned but the broadcast time is leased to private companies.

Channel 9, the national public television station, broadcasts from 5.30am until 2am the following morning. An English-language soundtrack is simulcast with Channel 9's evening news program at 7pm weekdays on radio station FM 107.

Channel 11 is run by the Ministry of Education and features educational programs from 4.40am to 11pm, including TV correspondence classes from Ramkhamhaeng and Sukhothai Thammathirat Open Universities. An English-language news simulcast comes over FM 88 at 8pm.

Satellite & Cable TV

As elsewhere in Asia, satellite and cable television services are swiftly multiplying in Thailand, and competition for the largely untapped market is keen. The main cable company in Thailand is UBC, available via CaTV, MMDS and DTH systems. Among the many satellite transmissions carried by UBC are six English-language movie channels (including HBO and Cinemax, both censored in Asia for language, nudity and violence), two to four international sports channels, imported TV series, MTV Asia, Channel V (a Hong Kong–based music video telecast), CNN International, CNBC, NHK, BBC World Service Television, the Discovery Channel and all the standard Thai networks. You can access further information on UBC's Web site (Ⓦ www.ubctv.com) or obtain a copy of the free monthly *UBC Magazine* by contacting the company.

Thailand has its own ThaiCom 1 and 2 as uplinks for AsiaSat and as carriers for the standard Thai networks and Thai Sky (TST). The latter includes five channels offering news and documentaries, Thai music videos and Thai variety programs. Other satellites tracked by dishes in Thailand include China's Apstar 1 and Apstar 2. Additional transmissions from these and from Vietnam, Myanmar and Malaysia are available with a satellite dish.

VIDEO SYSTEMS

The predominant VHS video format in Thailand is PAL, a system compatible with that used in most of Europe (France's SECAM format is a notable exception) as well as in Australia. This means if you're bringing video tapes from the USA or Japan (which use the NTSC format) you'll have to bring your own VCR to play them, or else acquire a 'multisystem' VCR with the capacity to play both NTSC and PAL (but not SECAM, except as black-and-white images). Some video shops (especially those that carry pirated or unlicensed tapes) sell NTSC as well as PAL and SECAM tapes.

Video CD (VCD) is beginning to replace VHS in Thailand. VCDs can be played on a VCD player or on any computer with a CD-ROM drive. For the latter you'll need to install VCD software, which can be downloaded free from the Internet. Many video shops and street vendors in larger cities sell VCDs of both Thai and international movies.

Digital video discs (DVDs) are still relatively rare in Thailand, although they are available at high-end audio shops and some video stores. Many Thai department stores and audio shops sell multiplayers that can play audio CDs, VCDs and DVDs.

PHOTOGRAPHY & VIDEO

Film & Equipment

Print film is fairly inexpensive and widely available throughout Thailand. Japanese print film costs around 100B per 36 exposures, US print film a bit more. Fujichrome Velvia and Provia slide films cost around 265B per roll, Kodak Ektachrome Elite is 230B and Ektachrome 200 about 270B. Slide film, especially Kodachrome, can be hard to find outside Chiang Mai, so be sure to stock up before heading upcountry. VHS video cassettes of all sizes are readily available in the major cities.

Processing

Film processing is generally quite good and inexpensive in the larger cities in Northern Thailand.

Dependable E6 processing is available at several labs in Bangkok but is untrustworthy elsewhere. Kodachrome must be sent out of the country for processing, so it can take up to two weeks to get it back. Pros will find that there are a number of labs in Bangkok that offer same-day pick-up and delivery within the city at no extra cost. IQ Lab (☎ 022 384 001), at 160 Thanon Silom, opposite the Silom Complex in Bangkok, offers the widest range of services, with all types of processing (except for Kodachrome), slide duping, scanning, digital prints, OutPut slides, photo CDs and custom printing.

Technical Tips

Pack some silica gel with your camera to prevent mould growing on the inside of your lenses. A polarising filter can be useful to cut down on tropical glare at certain times of day. Tripods are a must for shooting interiors in natural light.

For more tips, pick up a copy of *Travel Photography: A Guide to Taking Better Pictures*. Written by internationally renowned travel photographer Richard I'Anson, it's full colour throughout and designed to take on the road.

Photographing People

Hill-tribe people in some of the regularly visited areas expect money if you photograph them, while certain Karen and Akha will not allow you to point a camera in their direction. Use discretion when photographing villagers anywhere in Thailand, as a camera can be a very intimidating instrument. You may feel better leaving your camera behind when visiting certain areas.

Airport Security

In the wake of the terrorist attacks in the USA in September 2001, security checks at airports around the world have been upgraded. While in the past airport X-ray technology did not jeopardise film, new high-intensity machines now in use at some airports will fog all unprocessed film, whether exposed or not. At the time of writing it was unclear whether the right to request a hand-check for carry-on luggage would continue. The only way to guarantee undamaged images is to have film processed before boarding an airplane.

TIME

Thailand's time zone is seven hours ahead of GMT/UTC (London). Thus, noon in Chiang Mai is 9pm the previous day in Los Angeles – except during daylight saving time (DST), when it's 10pm; midnight in New York (DST 1am); 5am (the same day) in London; 6am in Paris; 1pm in Perth; and 3pm in Sydney (DST 4pm).

The current Thai government is discussing a proposal to revise Thailand's time zone to bring it into line with Singapore and Hong Kong, mainly to align with stock market opening and closing times in the latter cities.

Thai Calendar

The official year in Thailand is reckoned from 543 BC, the beginning of the Buddhist Era (BE), so that AD 2002 is BE 2545.

ELECTRICITY

Electric current in Thailand is 220V, 50 cycles. Electrical wall outlets are usually of the round, two-pole type; some outlets also accept flat, two-bladed terminals, and some will accept either flat or round terminals. Any electrical supply shop will carry adaptors for any international plug shape, as well as voltage converters.

WEIGHTS & MEASURES

Dimensions and weight are usually expressed using the metric system in Thailand. The exception is land measure, which is often quoted using the traditional Thai system of *waa, ngaan* and *râi*. Old-timers in the provinces will occasionally use the traditional Thai system of weights and measures in speech, as will boat-builders, carpenters and other craftspeople when talking about their work. Here are some conversions to use for such occasions:

Thai unit		metric unit
1 taaraang waa	=	4 sq m
1 ngaan	=	400 sq m
1 râi	=	1600 sq m
1 bàat	=	15g
1 tàleung or		
tamleung (4 bàat)	=	60g
1 châng (20 tàleung)	=	1.2kg
1 hàap (50 châng)	=	60kg
1 níu	=	about 2cm
		(or 1 inch)
1 khêup (12 níu)	=	25cm
1 sàwk (2 khêup)	=	50cm
1 waa (4 sàwk)	=	2m
1 sên (20 waa)	=	40m
1 yôht (400 sên)	=	16km

LAUNDRY

Virtually every hotel in Northern Thailand offers a laundry service. The charges are usually geared to room rates. Cheapest of all are public laundries, where you pay by the kilogram.

Many hotels and guesthouses also have laundry areas where you can wash your clothes at no charge; sometimes there's even a hanging area for drying. In accommodation where there is no laundry, do-it-yourselfers can wash their clothes in the sink and hang clothes out to dry in their rooms – see What to Bring earlier in this chapter for useful laundry tools. Laundry detergent is readily available in general mercantile shops and supermarkets.

Laundries that advertise dry-cleaning often don't really dry-clean (they just boil everything!), or they do it badly. Even luxury hotels in Northern Thailand rarely have dependable dry-cleaning services. It's probably better not to bring clothing that requires dry cleaning.

TOILETS

In Thailand, as in many other Asian countries, the 'squat toilet' is the norm, except in hotels and guesthouses geared towards tourists and international business travellers. Instead of trying to approximate a chair or stool like a modern sit-down toilet, a traditional Asian toilet sits more-or-less flush with the surface of the floor, with two footpads on either side of the porcelain abyss. For travellers who have never used a squat toilet it takes a bit of getting used to. If you find yourself feeling awkward the first couple of times you use one, you can console yourself with the knowledge that, according to those who study such matters, people who use squat toilets are much less likely to develop haemorrhoids than people who use sit-down toilets.

Next to the typical squat toilet is a bucket or cement reservoir filled with water. A plastic bowl usually floats on the water's surface or sits nearby. This water supply has a two-fold function: Toilet-goers scoop water from the reservoir with the plastic bowl and use it to clean their nether regions while still squatting over the toilet; and since there is usually no mechanical flushing device attached to a squat toilet, a few

extra scoops of water must be poured into the toilet basin to flush waste into the septic system. Even more rustic are the toilets in rural areas, which may simply consist of a few planks over a hole in the ground.

In larger towns, mechanical flushing systems are becoming more and more common, even with squat toilets. Even in places where sit-down toilets are installed, the plumbing may not be designed to take toilet paper. In such cases the usual washing bucket will be standing nearby or there will be a waste basket where you're supposed to place used toilet paper.

Public toilets are common in cinema houses, department stores, petrol stations, bus and train stations, larger hotel lobbies and airports. While on the road between towns and villages it is perfectly acceptable (for both men and women) to go behind a tree or bush, or even to use the roadside when nature calls.

BATHING

Some hotels and most guesthouses in Northern Thailand do not have hot water, although places in the larger cities will usually offer small electric shower heaters in their more expensive rooms. Very few boiler-style water heaters are available outside larger international-style hotels.

Many rural Thais bathe in rivers or streams. Those living in towns or cities may have washrooms where a large jar or cement trough is filled with water for bathing purposes. A plastic or metal bowl is used to sluice the water over the body. Even in homes where showers are installed, heated water is uncommon. Most Thais bathe at least twice a day (a good habit to get into in the tropics) and never use hot water.

If ever you find yourself having to bathe in a public place you should wear a phâakhamáa or phâasîn (a cotton wraparound); nude bathing is not the norm and most Thais will find it offensive.

HEALTH

Travel health depends on your predeparture preparations, your daily health care while travelling and how you handle any medical problem that does develop. While the potential dangers can seem quite frightening, in reality few travellers experience anything more than an upset stomach.

Predeparture planning

Immunisations Plan ahead for getting your vaccinations: Some of them require more than one injection, and certain vaccinations should not be given together. Note that some vaccinations should not be given during pregnancy or to people with allergies – discuss this with your doctor.

Although there is no risk of yellow fever in Thailand, you will need proof of vaccination if you're coming from a yellow fever–infected area (sub-Saharan Africa and parts of South America).

It is recommended you seek medical advice at least six weeks before travel. Be aware that there is often a greater risk of disease with children and during pregnancy.

It's a good idea to carry proof of your vaccinations. If you want immunisations while in Thailand, they are available from a number of sources, including both public hospitals and private clinics. Bangkok is your best bet in terms of finding less-common or more-expensive vaccines. Vaccinations you should consider having for Thailand include the following (for more

Everyday Health

Normal body temperature is up to 37°C (98.6°F); more than 2°C (4°F) higher indicates a high fever. The normal adult pulse rate is 60 to 100 per minute (children 80 to 100, babies 100 to 140). As a general rule the pulse increases about 20 beats per minute for each 1°C (2°F) rise in fever.

Respiration (breathing) rate is also an indicator of illness. Count the number of breaths per minute: Between 12 and 20 is normal for adults and older children (up to 30 for younger children, 40 for babies). People with a high fever or serious respiratory illness breathe more quickly than normal. More than 40 shallow breaths a minute may indicate pneumonia.

information about the diseases see the individual entries later in this section):

Cholera The current injectable vaccine against cholera gives poor protection and has many side effects, so it is not generally recommended for travellers.

Diphtheria & Tetanus Vaccinations for these two diseases are usually combined and are recommended for everyone. After an initial course of three injections (usually given in childhood), boosters are necessary every 10 years.

Hepatitis A The vaccine (eg, Avaxim, Havrix 1440 or VAQTA) provides long-term immunity (possibly more than 10 years) after an initial injection and a booster at six to 12 months. An injection of gamma globulin can provide short-term protection – two to six months, depending on the dose given. It is reasonably effective and, unlike the vaccine, is protective immediately, but because it is a blood product there are current concerns about its long-term safety. Hepatitis A vaccine is also available in a combined form, Twinrix, with hepatitis B vaccine. Three injections over six-months are required, the first two providing substantial protection against hepatitis A.

Hepatitis B Travellers who should consider vaccination against hepatitis B include those on a long trip, as well as those visiting countries where there are high levels of hepatitis B infection (of which Thailand is not one), where blood transfusions may not be adequately screened or where sexual contact or needle sharing is a possibility. Vaccination involves three injections, with a booster at 12 months. More rapid courses are available if necessary.

Japanese B Encephalitis Consider vaccination if you're spending a month or longer in rural Northern Thailand, making repeated trips to a risk area or visiting during an epidemic. It involves three injections over 30 days.

Polio Everyone should keep up to date with this vaccination, normally given in childhood. A booster every 10 years maintains immunity.

Rabies Vaccination should be considered if you're spending a month or longer in Thailand, especially if you're cycling, handling animals, caving or travelling to remote areas, and also for children (who may not report a bite). Pretravel rabies vaccination involves three injections over 21 to 28 days. Vaccinated persons who are bitten or scratched by a possibly rabid animal will require two booster injections of vaccine; those not vaccinated require more. Rabies vaccinations are available at nearly every public clinic or hospital in Thailand.

Tuberculosis The risk of TB to travellers in Thailand is usually very low.

Typhoid Vaccination against typhoid may be required if you are travelling for more than a couple of weeks in most parts of Asia. It is now available either as an injection or as capsules to be taken orally. A combined hepatitis A/typhoid vaccine was launched recently but its availability is still limited. Check with your doctor to find out its status in your country.

Malaria Medication

Antimalarial drugs do not prevent you from being infected, but kill the malaria parasites during a stage in their development and significantly reduce the risk of becoming very ill or dying. Expert advice on medication should be sought, as there are many factors to consider, including the area to be visited, the risk of exposure to malaria-carrying mosquitoes, the side-effects of medication, your medical history and whether you are a child or an adult or pregnant. Travellers to isolated areas in high-risk countries may like to carry a treatment dose of medication for use if symptoms occur. See Malaria under Insect-Borne diseases later in this section for information on the prevalence of malaria in Thailand.

Health Insurance

Make sure that you have adequate health insurance. See Travel Insurance under Visas & Documents earlier in this chapter for details.

Travel Health Guides

If you are planning to be away or travelling in remote areas for a long period of time, you may like to consider taking a more detailed health guide. Lonely Planet's *Healthy Travel Asia & India* is a handy pocket size and packed with useful advice, including pretrip planning, emergency first aid, immunisation and disease information and guidelines on what to do if you get sick on the road. *Travel with Children* from Lonely Planet also includes health tips for those who are travelling with children.

Guide to Healthy Living in Thailand, published by the Thai Red Cross Society, is available in Bangkok from the 'Snake Farm' (Queen Saovabha Memorial Institute; ☎ 022 520 161) and at most bookshops that carry English-language titles, such as Suriwong Book Centre in Chiang Mai. This book is rich in practical health advice on safe eating, child care, tropical heat, immunisations and local hospitals.

There are a number of excellent travel health sites on the Internet. From the Lonely Planet home page there are links at W www.lonelyplanet.com/weblinks/wlheal .htm to the World Health Organization (WHO) and the US Centers for Disease Control and Prevention (CDC).

Other Preparations

Make sure you're healthy before you start travelling. If you are going on a long trip make sure your teeth are OK. If you wear glasses take a spare pair and your prescription.

If you require a particular medication take an adequate supply, as it may not be available locally. Take part of the packaging showing the generic name rather than the brand, which will make getting replacements easier. To avoid any problems it's a good idea to have a legible prescription or letter from your doctor to show that you legally use the medication.

Basic Rules

Food Beware of ice cream that is sold in the street or anywhere it might have been melted and refrozen; if there's any doubt (eg, a power cut in the last day or two), steer well clear. Raw or undercooked shellfish such as mussels, oysters and clams should be avoided as well as undercooked meat, particularly in the form of mince.

If a place looks clean and well run and the vendor also looks clean and healthy, then the food is probably safe. In general, places that are packed with travellers or locals will be fine, while empty restaurants are questionable. The food in busy restaurants is cooked and eaten quite quickly with little standing around and is probably not reheated.

Water The number-one rule is be careful of water and especially ice. If you don't know for certain that the water is safe, assume the worst, although all water served in restaurants or to guests in an office or home will be purified. It's not necessary to ask for bottled water unless you prefer it. Reputable brands of Thai bottled water or soft drinks are generally fine, although in some places bottles may be refilled with tap water. Only use water from containers with a serrated seal – not tops or corks. Try to purchase glass water bottles, however, as these are recyclable (unlike the plastic disposable ones).

Fruit juices are made with purified water and are safe to drink. Milk in Thailand is always pasteurised. In rural areas villagers mostly drink collected rainwater.

Ice is generally produced from purified water under hygienic conditions and is therefore theoretically safe. During transit to the local restaurant, however, conditions are not so hygienic (you may see blocks of ice being dragged along the street), but it's very difficult to resist in the hot season. The rule of thumb is that if it's chipped ice it probably came from an ice block (which may not have been handled well) but if it's ice cubes or 'tubes' it was delivered from the ice factory in sealed plastic.

Water Purification Virtually no-one in Thailand bothers with filters, tablets or iodine since bottled water is so cheap and readily available. However, if you are stuck without bottled water, the simplest way of purifying water is to boil it thoroughly. Vigorous boiling should be satisfactory; however, at high altitude water boils at a lower temperature, so germs are less likely to be killed. Boil it for longer in these environments.

If you plan to do any long back-country camping trips, consider purchasing a water filter. There are two main kinds of filters. Total filters take out all parasites, bacteria and viruses and make water safe to drink. They are often expensive, but they can be more cost effective than buying bottled water. Simple filters (which can even be a nylon mesh bag) take out dirt and larger foreign bodies from the water so that chemical solutions work much more effectively; if water is dirty, chemical solutions may not work at all. It's very important when buying a filter to read the specifications so that you know exactly what it removes from the water and what it doesn't. Simple filtering will not remove all dangerous organisms, so

Medical Kit Check List

Following is a list of items you should consider including in your medical kit – consult your pharmacist for brands available in your country.

- ☐ **Aspirin or paracetamol (acetaminophen in the USA)** – for pain or fever
- ☐ **Antihistamine** – for allergies, eg, hay fever; to ease the itch from insect bites or stings; and to prevent motion sickness
- ☐ **Cold and flu tablets, throat lozenges and nasal decongestant**
- ☐ **Multivitamins** – consider for long trips, when dietary vitamin intake may be inadequate
- ☐ **Antibiotics** – consider including these if you're travelling well off the beaten track; see your doctor, as they must be prescribed, and carry the prescription with you
- ☐ **Loperamide or diphenoxylate** –'blockers' for diarrhoea
- ☐ **Prochlorperazine or metaclopramide** – for nausea and vomiting
- ☐ **Rehydration mixture** – to prevent dehydration, which may occur, for example, during bouts of diarrhoea; particularly important when travelling with children
- ☐ **Insect repellent, sunscreen, lip balm and eye drops**
- ☐ **Calamine lotion, sting relief spray or aloe vera** – to ease irritation from sunburn and insect bites or stings
- ☐ **Antifungal cream or powder** – for fungal skin infections and thrush
- ☐ **Antiseptic (such as povidone-iodine)** – for cuts and grazes
- ☐ **Bandages, Band-Aids (plasters) and other wound dressings**
- ☐ **Water purification tablets or iodine**
- ☐ **Scissors, tweezers and a thermometer** – note that mercury thermometers are prohibited by airlines
- ☐ **Sterile kit** – in case you need injections in a country with medical hygiene problems; discuss with your doctor

if you cannot boil water it should be treated chemically. Chlorine tablets will kill many pathogens, but not some parasites like giardia and amoebic cysts. Iodine is more effective in purifying water and is available in tablet form. Follow the directions carefully and remember that too much iodine can be harmful.

Medical Problems & Treatment

Self-diagnosis and treatment can be risky, so you should always seek medical help. Although there are drug dosages in this section, they are for emergency use only. Correct diagnosis is vital. An embassy, consulate or five-star hotel can usually recommend a local doctor or clinic.

In Thailand medicine is generally available over the counter is much cheaper than in the West. However, be careful when buying drugs, particularly where the expiry date may have passed or correct storage conditions may not have been followed. Bogus drugs are not uncommon and it's possible that drugs that are no longer recommended (or have even been banned) in the West are still being dispensed in Thailand.

Antibiotics should ideally be administered only under medical supervision. Take only the recommended dose at the prescribed intervals and use the whole course, even if the illness seems to be cured earlier. Stop immediately if there are any serious reactions and don't use the antibiotic at all if you are unsure that you have the correct one. Some people are allergic to commonly prescribed antibiotics such as penicillin; carry this information (eg, on a bracelet) when travelling.

Hospitals & Clinics

Thailand's most technically advanced hospitals are in Bangkok. In the North, Chiang Mai has the best medical care. Elsewhere in Northern Thailand, every provincial capital has at least one hospital (of varying quality) as well as several public and private clinics. The best emergency health care can usually be found at military hospitals (rohng pháyaabaan tháhǎan); they will usually treat foreigners in an emergency.

See the respective destination chapters for further information on specific hospitals, clinics and other health-care facilities.

Air Ambulance

Medical Wings (☎ 025 354 736, fax 025 354 355, ⓔ ew@bkk.a-net.net.th), in the domestic terminal at Bangkok International Airport, offers aeromedical transportation to or from any of 30 domestic airports in Thailand on a 24-hour basis.

Environmental Hazards

Air Pollution This type of pollution is something you'll become very aware of in Thailand, where heat, dust and motor fumes combine to form a powerful brew of potentially toxic air. Chiang Mai, during the hot season (March to May), is not a lot better. Air pollution can be a health hazard, especially if you suffer from lung conditions such as asthma. It can also aggravate coughs, colds and sinus problems and cause eye irritation or even infections. Consider avoiding badly polluted areas if you think they may jeopardise your health, especially if you have asthma, or invest in an air filter.

Heat Exhaustion Dehydration and salt deficiency can cause heat exhaustion. Take time to acclimatise to high temperatures, drink sufficient liquids and do not do anything too physically demanding.

Salt deficiency is characterised by fatigue, lethargy, headaches, giddiness and muscle cramps; salt tablets may help, but adding extra salt to your food is better.

Anhidrotic heat exhaustion is a rare form of heat exhaustion that is caused by an inability to sweat. It tends to affect people who have been in a hot climate for some time, rather than newcomers. It can progress to heatstroke. Treatment involves removal to a cooler climate.

Heatstroke This serious, occasionally fatal, condition can occur if the body's heat-regulating mechanism breaks down and the body temperature rises to dangerous levels. Long, continuous periods of exposure to high temperatures and insufficient fluids can leave you vulnerable to heatstroke.

The symptoms are feeling unwell, not sweating very much (or at all) and a high body temperature (39°C to 41°C, or 102°F to 106°F). Where sweating has ceased, the skin becomes flushed and red. Severe, throbbing headaches and lack of coordination will also occur, and the sufferer may be confused or aggressive. Eventually the victim will become delirious or convulse. Hospitalisation is essential, but in the interim get victims out of the sun, remove their clothing, cover them with a wet sheet or towel and then fan continually. Give fluids if they are conscious.

Motion Sickness Eating lightly before and during a trip will reduce the chances of motion sickness. If you are prone to motion sickness try to find a place that minimises movement – near the wing on aircrafts, close to midships on boats, near the centre on buses. Fresh air usually helps; reading and cigarette smoke don't. Commercial motion-sickness preparations, which can cause drowsiness, have to be taken before the trip commences. Ginger (available in capsule form) and peppermint (including mint-flavoured sweets) are natural preventatives.

Prickly Heat This is an itchy rash caused by excessive perspiration trapped under the skin. It usually strikes people who have just arrived in a hot climate. Keeping cool, bathing often, drying the skin and using a mild talcum or prickly heat powder or resorting to air-conditioning may help.

Sunburn In the tropics you can get sunburnt surprisingly quickly, even through cloud cover. Use a sunscreen, a hat, and a barrier cream for your nose and lips. Calamine lotion and aloe vera are good for mild sunburn. Protect your eyes with good-quality sunglasses, particularly if you will be near water or sand.

Infectious Diseases

Diarrhoea Simple things like a change of water, food or climate can all cause a mild bout of diarrhoea, but a few rushed toilet trips with no other symptoms is not indicative of a major problem.

Dehydration is the main danger with any diarrhoea, particularly in children or the elderly, in whom dehydration can occur quite quickly. Under all circumstances fluid replacement (at least equal to the volume being lost) is the most important thing to remember. Weak black tea with a little sugar, soda water, or soft drinks allowed to go flat and diluted 50% with clean water are all good.

With severe diarrhoea a rehydrating solution is preferable, as it will replace the minerals and salts that have been lost. Commercially available oral rehydration salts (ORS) are very useful; add these salts to boiled or bottled water. In an emergency you can make up a solution of six teaspoons of sugar and a half-teaspoon of salt to a litre of boiled or bottled water.

You need to drink at least the same volume of fluid that you are losing in bowel movements and vomiting. Urine is the best guide to the adequacy of replacement – if you have small amounts of concentrated urine, you need to drink more. Keep drinking small amounts often. Stick to a bland diet as you recover.

Gut-paralysing drugs such as loperamide diphenoxylate can be used to bring relief from the symptoms, although they do not actually cure the problem. Only use these drugs if you do not have access to toilets, eg, if you must travel. For children under 12 years old these drugs are not recommended. Do not use these drugs if the person has a high fever or is severely dehydrated.

In certain situations antibiotics may be required: diarrhoea with blood or mucus (dysentery), any diarrhoea with fever, profuse watery diarrhoea, persistent diarrhoea not improving after 48 hours and severe diarrhoea. These suggest a more serious cause of diarrhoea and in these situations gut-paralysing drugs should be avoided.

In these cases a stool test may be necessary to diagnose what bug is causing your diarrhoea, so you should seek medical help urgently. Where this is not possible the recommended drugs for bacterial diarrhoea (the most likely cause of severe diarrhoea in travellers) are norfloxacin 400mg twice daily for three days or ciprofloxacin 500mg twice daily for five days. These are not recommended for children or pregnant women. The drug of choice for children would be co-trimoxazole, with the dosage dependent on the child's weight. A five-day course should be given. Ampicillin or amoxycillin may be given in pregnancy, but medical care is necessary.

Two other causes of persistent diarrhoea in travellers are giardiasis and amoebic dysentery. Giardiasis is caused by a common parasite, *Giardia lamblia*. The symptoms include stomach cramps, nausea, a bloated stomach, watery, foul-smelling diarrhoea and frequent gas (farts). Giardiasis can appear several weeks after you have been exposed to the parasite. The symptoms may disappear for a few days and then return. Unfortunately this can continue for several weeks.

Amoebic dysentery, caused by the protozoan *Entamoeba histolytica*, is characterised by a gradual onset of low-grade diarrhoea, often with blood and mucus. Cramping, abdominal pain and vomiting are less likely than in other types of diarrhoea, and fever may not be present. Amoebic dysentery will persist until treated and can recur and cause other health problems.

You should seek medical advice if you think you have giardiasis or amoebic dysentery, but where this is not possible, tinidazole or metronidazole are the recommended drugs. Treatment is a 2g single dose of tinidazole or 250mg of metronidazole three times daily for five to 10 days.

Fungal Infections Fungal infections occur more commonly in hot weather and are usually found on the scalp, between the toes (athlete's foot) or fingers, in the groin and on the body (ringworm). You get ringworm (which is a fungal infection, not a worm) from infected animals or other people. Moisture encourages these infections.

To prevent fungal infections wear loose, comfortable clothes, avoid artificial fibres, wash frequently and dry yourself carefully. If you do get an infection, wash the infected area at least daily with a disinfectant or medicated soap and water, and rinse and dry well. Apply an antifungal cream or powder like tolnaftate. Try to expose the infected area to air or sunlight as much as possible and wash all towels and underwear in hot water, change them often and let them dry in the sun.

Hepatitis A general term for inflammation of the liver, hepatitis is a common disease worldwide. There are several different viruses that cause hepatitis, and they differ in the way that they are transmitted. The symptoms are similar in all forms of the illness, and include fever, chills, headache, fatigue, feelings of weakness and aches and pains, followed by loss of appetite, nausea, vomiting, abdominal pain, dark urine, light-coloured faeces, jaundiced (yellow) skin and yellowing of the whites of the eyes. People who have had hepatitis should avoid alcohol for some time after the illness, as the liver needs time to recover.

Hepatitis A is transmitted by contaminated food and drinking water. You should seek medical advice, but there is not much you can do apart from resting, drinking lots of fluids, eating lightly and avoiding fatty foods. Hepatitis E is transmitted in the same way as hepatitis A; it can be particularly serious in pregnant women.

There are almost 300 million chronic carriers of Hepatitis B in the world. It is spread through contact with infected blood, blood products or body fluids, eg, through sexual contact, unsterilised needles and blood transfusions, or contact with blood via small breaks in the skin. Other risk situations include having a shave, tattoo or body piercing with contaminated equipment. The symptoms of hepatitis B may be more severe than type A and the disease can lead to long-term problems such as chronic liver damage, liver cancer or a long-term carrier state.

Hepatitis C and D are spread in the same way as hepatitis B and can also lead to long-term complications.

There are vaccines against hepatitis A and B (see Immunisations earlier in this section) but there are currently no vaccines against the other types of hepatitis. Following the basic rules about food and water (hepatitis A and E) and avoiding risk situations (hepatitis B, C and D) are important preventative measures.

HIV & AIDS Infection with the human immunodeficiency virus (HIV) may lead to acquired immune deficiency syndrome (AIDS), which is a fatal disease. Any exposure to blood, blood products or body fluids may put the individual at risk.

According to the United Nations Human Development Program, Thailand – like the USA, Australia, and the UK – has belonged to the 'decrease or no growth' category since 1994. The World Health Organisation reports that the infection rate and projected future vulnerability to AIDS in Thailand is now lower than for any other country in Southeast Asia. As elsewhere around the globe, however, absolute numbers will only increase with time until or unless a cure is discovered.

In Thailand transmission is predominantly through heterosexual sexual activity (over 80%). The second most common source of HIV infection is intravenous injection by drug users who share needles (about 6%). Apart from abstinence, the most effective preventative is always to practise safe sex using condoms and never share syringes, even those that have been bleached.

The Thai phrase for 'condom' is *thŭng yaang ànaamai*. Since the 1970s, when health educator Mechai Viravaidya initiated a vigorous national program aimed at educating the public about contraception, the most common Thai nickname for 'condom' has been 'Mechai'. Good-quality latex condoms are distributed free by offices of the Ministry of Public Health (MPH) throughout the country – they come in numbered sizes, like shoes! Many Western men find that even the largest size issued by the MPH is too small; one of the better commercial brands available in Thailand is Durex.

HIV/AIDS can also be spread through infected blood transfusions, although this risk is virtually nil in Thailand due to vigorous blood-screening procedures. It can also be spread by dirty needles – tattooing, vaccinations, acupuncture and body piercing can potentially be as dangerous as intravenous drug use if the equipment is not clean.

If you do need an injection, ask to see the syringe unwrapped in front of you, or take a needle and syringe pack with you.

Intestinal Worms These parasites are most common in rural areas. Different worms have different ways of infecting people. Some may be ingested in food such as undercooked meat (eg, tapeworms) and some enter through your skin (eg, hookworms). Infestations may not show up for some time, and although they are generally not serious, if left untreated some can cause severe health problems later. Consider having a stool test when you return home to check for these and determine the appropriate treatment.

Liver Flukes These tiny worms (*pháyâat bai mái* in Thai) are occasionally present in freshwater fish. The main risk comes from eating raw or undercooked fish. Travellers should in particular avoid eating *plaa ráa* (called *háa* in Northern Thailand), an unpasteurised fermented fish used as an accompaniment for rice in the North. Plaa ráa is not commonly served in restaurants but is common in rural areas of the North, where it's considered a great delicacy. The Thai government is currently trying to discourage all Thais from eating plaa ráa and other uncooked fish products.

The intensity of symptoms depends very much on how many of the flukes get into your body. At low levels there are virtually no symptoms at all; at higher levels an overall fatigue, low-grade fever and swollen or tender liver (or general abdominal pain) are the usual symptoms, along with worms or worm eggs in the faeces. Persons suspected of having liver flukes should have a stool sample analysed by a doctor or clinic. The usual medication is 25mg per kilogram of body weight of praziquantel three times daily after meals for two days.

Schistosomiasis The overall risk of this disease is quite low, but it's highest in the southern reaches of the Mekong River and in the lakes of Northeastern Thailand – avoid swimming and bathing in these waterways. Heat bathing water to 50°C (122°F) for five minutes or treat the water with iodine or chlorine in a manner similar to that recommended for preparing drinking water.

Also known as bilharzia, this disease is transmitted by minute worms. They infect certain varieties of freshwater snails found in rivers, streams, lakes and particularly behind dams. The worms multiply and are eventually discharged into the water.

The worm enters through the skin and attaches itself to your intestines or bladder. The first symptom may be a general feeling of being unwell, or a tingling and sometimes a light rash around the area where it entered. Weeks later a high fever may develop. Once the disease is established abdominal pain and blood in the urine are other signs. The infection often causes no symptoms until the disease is well established (several months to years after exposure) and damage to internal organs irreversible.

A blood test is a reliable way to diagnose bilharzia, but the test will not show positive until a number of weeks after exposure.

Sexually Transmitted Infections Gonorrhoea, herpes and syphilis are among these diseases; sores, blisters or rashes around the genitals and discharges or pain when urinating are common symptoms. Symptoms of some sexually transmitted infections (STIs), such as wart virus and chlamydia, may be less marked or not observed at all, especially in women. Syphilis symptoms eventually disappear completely but the disease continues and can cause severe problems in later years. In Thailand gonorrhoea, nonspecific urethritis (NSU) and syphilis are the most common of these infections. The treatment of gonorrhoea and syphilis is with antibiotics. Different STIs each require specific antibiotics.

While abstinence from sexual contact is the only 100%-effective prevention, using condoms is also effective. A 2000 survey conducted by condom-maker Durex and a senior policy adviser to the WHO found that 82% of Thais between the ages of 16 and 45 always used condoms with casual partners, the highest rate among the 15 countries surveyed. Canada and Poland scored the lowest, with less than 25%. See HIV & AIDS earlier in this section for information on condom availability in Thailand.

Typhoid A dangerous gut infection caused by contaminated water and food, if typhoid is contracted medical help must be sought.

In its early stages sufferers may feel they have a bad cold or flu on the way, as early symptoms are a headache, body aches and a fever that rises a little each day until it is around 40°C (104°F) or higher. The victim's pulse is often slow relative to the degree of fever present – unlike a normal fever, where the pulse increases. There may be vomiting, abdominal pain, diarrhoea or constipation.

In the second week the high fever and slow pulse continue and a few pink spots may appear on the body; trembling, delirium, weakness, weight loss and dehydration may occur. Complications such as pneumonia, perforated bowel or meningitis may occur.

Insect-Borne Diseases

Filariasis, Lyme disease and typhus are all insect-borne diseases, but they do not pose a great risk to travellers in Northern Thailand. For more information on typhus see Less Common Diseases later in this section.

Malaria This serious and potentially fatal disease is spread by mosquito bites. Malaria risk exists throughout the year in rural Thailand, especially in forested and hilly areas. Thailand's high-risk areas are all outside of Northern Thailand.

According to the CDC and to Thailand's Ministry of Public Health, there is virtually no risk of malaria in urban areas of Northern Thailand.

If you are travelling in endemic areas it is extremely important to avoid mosquito bites and to take tablets to prevent the onset of this disease. The most recommended malarial preventive for Thailand travel is 100mg of doxycycline taken daily. Western doctors who know the situation in Thailand no longer recommend either chloroquine or mefloquine (Lariam) for travellers in the country, due to the malaria parasite's near-total resistance to these drugs. Side effects of doxycycline include photosensitivity, ie, your skin will be more easily affected by the sun.

On the other hand, the Malaria Division of Thailand's Ministry of Public Health, which is better acquainted with malaria in Thailand than any other health agency in the world, has issued an unequivocal announcement stating 'Malaria chemoprophylaxis is not recommended.' For more information contact the Hospital for Tropical Diseases (☎ 022 469 000), 420/6 Thanon Ratwithi, Bangkok.

Symptoms of malaria vary widely, ranging from fever, chills and sweating, headache, diarrhoea and abdominal pains to a vague feeling of ill-health, but one of the tell-tale long-term signs is the cyclic nature of the symptoms, coming on every 24 hours or every three days, for example. In general, if there is fever for two or three days you should seek medical advice for accurate diagnosis, perhaps by taking a blood test. Seek medical help immediately if malaria is suspected. Without treatment, malaria can rapidly become more serious and is sometimes fatal.

Every medical clinic or hospital in Thailand can easily test for malaria and treat the disease. If for some reason medical care is not available, certain malaria tablets can be used for treatment. These include Mefloquine, Fansidar and Malarone. If you took anti-malaria tablets before contracting malaria, you'll need to use a different malaria tablet for treatment as obviously the first one didn't work. It is strongly recommended that you seek medical advice for the medication and dosage that is right for you before you travel.

Travellers are advised to prevent mosquito bites at all times. The main messages are:

- Wear light-coloured clothing.
- Wear long trousers and long-sleeved shirts.
- Use mosquito repellents containing the compound DEET on exposed areas. (While prolonged overuse of DEET may be harmful, especially to children, its use is considered preferable to being bitten by disease-transmitting mosquitoes.)
- Avoid perfumes or aftershave.
- Use a mosquito net impregnated with mosquito repellent (permethrin) – it may be worth taking your own.
- Impregnate clothes with permethrin, which effectively deters mosquitoes and other insects.

Dengue Fever This viral disease is transmitted by mosquitoes and occurs mainly in tropical and subtropical areas of the world. Generally, there is only a small risk to travellers except during epidemics, which are usually seasonal (during and just after the rainy season). Chiang Mai does undergo a dengue fever epidemic every rainy season and we know several people who have contracted dengue in that city.

The *Aedes aegypti* mosquito, which transmits the dengue virus, is most active during the day, unlike the malaria mosquito, and is found mainly in urban areas in and around human dwellings.

Signs and symptoms of dengue fever include a sudden onset of high fever, headache, joint and muscle pains (hence its old name, 'breakbone fever') and nausea and vomiting. A rash of small red spots appears three to four days after the onset of fever. Dengue is commonly mistaken for other infectious diseases, including influenza.

You should seek medical attention if you think you may be infected. Infection can be diagnosed by a blood test. There is no specific treatment for dengue. You should avoid aspirin, as it increases the risk of haemorrhaging.

Recovery may be prolonged, with tiredness lasting for several weeks. Severe complications are rare in travellers but include dengue haemorrhagic fever (DHF), which can be fatal without prompt medical treatment. DHF is thought to be a result of a second infection due to a different strain (there are four major strains) and it usually affects residents of the country rather than travellers.

In 2000 Thailand's Mahidol University announced the development of a vaccine for all serotypes of dengue. The new vaccine began human trials late that year, and if successful should be available in 2003 or 2004. As with malaria, the best precaution is to avoid mosquito bites.

Japanese B Encephalitis Mosquitoes transmit this viral infection of the brain. Most cases occur in rural areas, as the virus exists in pigs and wading birds. Symptoms include fever, headache and alteration in consciousness. Hospitalisation is needed for correct diagnosis and treatment. There is a high mortality rate among those who have symptoms; of those who survive, many are intellectually disabled.

Cuts, Bites & Stings

Bedbugs & Lice Bedbugs live in various places, but particularly in dirty mattresses and bedding, evidenced by spots of blood on bedclothes or on the wall. Bedbugs leave itchy bites in neat rows. Calamine lotion or a sting-relief spray may help.

All lice cause itching and discomfort. They make themselves at home in your hair (head lice), your clothing (body lice) or in your pubic hair (crabs). You catch lice through direct contact with infected people or by sharing combs, clothing and the like. Powder or shampoo treatment will kill the lice and infected clothing should then be washed in very hot, soapy water and left in the sun to dry.

Bites & Stings Bee and wasp stings are usually painful rather than dangerous. Calamine lotion or sting-relief spray are good and ice packs will reduce the pain and swelling. However, in people who are allergic to these stings severe breathing difficulties may occur and require urgent medical care.

There are some spiders with dangerous bites but antivenins are usually available in local hospitals. Scorpions often shelter in shoes or clothing, and their stings are notoriously painful.

Cuts & Scratches Skin punctures can easily become infected in hot climates and may be difficult to heal. Wash well and treat any cut with an antiseptic, such as povidone-iodine. Where possible avoid bandages and Band-Aids, which can keep wounds wet. Coral cuts are notoriously slow to heal and if they are not adequately cleaned, small pieces of coral can become embedded in the wound. Avoid touching and walking on fragile coral in the first place, but if you are near coral reefs, then wear shoes and clean any cut thoroughly.

Leeches & Ticks Leeches may be present in damp rainforest conditions; they attach themselves to your skin to suck your blood. Trekkers often get them on their legs or in their boots. Salt or a lighted cigarette end will make them fall off and an insect repellent may keep them away. Do not pull them off, as the bite is then more likely to become infected. Clean and apply pressure if the point of attachment is bleeding.

You should always check all over your body if you have been walking through a potentially tick-infested area, as ticks can cause skin infections and other more serious diseases. If a tick is found attached, press down around the tick's head with tweezers, grab the head and gently pull upwards. Avoid pulling the rear of the body as this may squeeze the tick's gut contents through the attached mouth parts into the skin, increasing the risk of infection and disease. Smearing chemicals on the tick will not make it let go and is not recommended.

Snakes To minimise your chances of being bitten always wear boots, socks and long trousers when walking through undergrowth where snakes may be present. Don't put your hands into holes and crevices, and be careful when collecting firewood.

Snake bites do not cause instantaneous death and antivenins are usually available. Immediately wrap the bitten limb tightly, as you would for a sprained ankle, and then attach a splint to immobilise it. Keep the victim still and seek medical help, if possible with the dead snake for identification. Don't attempt to catch the snake if there is a possibility of being bitten again. Tourniquets and sucking out the poison are now comprehensively discredited.

Snakebite antivenin is available at hospitals throughout Thailand, as well as in pharmacies in larger towns and cities.

Women's Health

Gynaecological Problems Antibiotic use, synthetic underwear, sweating and contraceptive pills can lead to fungal vaginal infections, especially when travelling in hot climates. Thrush (yeast infection) or vaginal candidiasis is characterised by a rash, itch and discharge. Nystatin, miconazole or clotrimazole pessaries are the usual treatment, but some people use a more traditional remedy involving vinegar or lemon juice douches, or yoghurt. Maintaining good personal hygiene and wearing loose-fitting clothes and cotton underwear may help prevent these infections.

Sexually transmitted infections are a major cause of vaginal problems. Symptoms include a smelly discharge, painful intercourse and sometimes a burning sensation when urinating. Medical attention should be sought and sexual partners must also be treated. For more details see Sexu-ally Transmitted Infections earlier in this section. Apart from abstinence, the best thing is to practise safer sex using condoms.

Pregnancy It is not advisable to travel to some places while pregnant, as some vaccinations normally used to prevent serious diseases (eg, yellow fever) are not advisable during pregnancy. In addition, some diseases (eg, malaria) are much more serious for the woman in pregnancy and may increase the risk of a stillborn child.

Most miscarriages occur during the first three months of pregnancy. Miscarriage is not uncommon and can occasionally lead to severe bleeding. The last three months should be spent within reasonable distance of good medical care. A baby born as early as 24 weeks stands a chance of survival, but only in a good modern hospital. Pregnant women should avoid all unnecessary medication, although vaccinations and malarial prophylactics should still be taken where needed. Additional care should be taken to prevent illness and particular attention should be paid to diet and nutrition. Alcohol and nicotine, for example, should be avoided.

Less Common Diseases

The following diseases pose a small risk to travellers, and so are mentioned only in passing. Seek medical advice if you think you may have any of these diseases.

Nutrition

If your diet is poor or limited in variety, if you're travelling hard and fast and therefore missing meals or if you simply lose your appetite, you can soon start to lose weight and place your health at risk.

Make sure your diet is well balanced. Cooked eggs, tofu, beans, lentils (dhal in India) and nuts are all safe ways to get protein. Fruit you can peel (bananas, oranges or mandarins, for example) is usually safe and a good source of vitamins. Melons can harbour bacteria in their flesh and are best avoided. Try to eat plenty of grains (including rice) and bread. Remember that although food is generally safer if it is cooked well, overcooked food loses much of its nutritional value. If your diet isn't well balanced or if your food intake is insufficient, it's a good idea to take vitamin and iron pills.

In hot climates make sure you drink enough – don't rely on feeling thirsty to indicate when you should drink. Not needing to urinate or voiding small amounts of very dark yellow urine is a danger sign. Always carry a water bottle with you on long trips. Excessive sweating can lead to loss of salt and therefore muscle cramping. Salt tablets are not a good idea as a preventative, but in places where salt is not used much, adding salt to food can help.

Cholera Outbreaks of cholera are very rare in Thailand, and when they do occur they're generally widely reported, so you can avoid such problem areas. Fluid replacement is the most vital treatment – the risk of dehydration is severe as you may lose up to 20L a day. If there is a delay in getting to hospital, then begin taking tetracycline. The adult dose is 250mg four times daily. It is not recommended for children under nine years of age nor for pregnant women. Tetracycline may help shorten the illness, but adequate fluids are required to save lives.

Diphtheria Either a skin infection or a more dangerous throat infection, diptheria is spread by contaminated dust contacting the skin or by the inhalation of infected cough or sneeze droplets. Frequent washing and keeping the skin dry will help prevent skin infection. Treatment needs close medical supervision.

Rabies This fatal viral infection is found in many countries, including Thailand. Many animals (such as dogs, cats, bats and monkeys) can be infected and it is their saliva that is infectious. Any bite, scratch or even lick from an animal should be cleaned promptly and thoroughly. Scrub with soap and running water, and then apply alcohol or iodine solution. It is important that you seek medical help immediately to receive a course of injections.

Tetanus This disease is caused by a germ that lives in soil and in the faeces of horses and other animals. It enters the body via breaks in the skin. The first symptom may be discomfort in swallowing, or stiffening of the jaw and neck; this is followed by painful convulsions of the jaw and whole body. The disease can be fatal but can be prevented by vaccination.

Tuberculosis (TB) There is a world-wide resurgence of TB, and in Thailand it's the seventh leading cause of death. TB is a bacterial infection usually transmitted from person to person by coughing but which may be transmitted through consumption of unpasteurised milk. Milk that has been boiled is safe to drink, and the souring of milk to make yoghurt or cheese also kills the bacilli. Travellers are usually not at great risk, as close household contact with the infected person is usually required before the disease is passed on. You may need to have a TB test before you travel, as this can help diagnose the disease later if you become ill.

Typhus This disease is spread by ticks, mites and lice. It begins with fever, chills, headache and muscle pains followed a few days later by a body rash. There is often a large, painful sore at the site of the bite and nearby lymph nodes are swollen and painful. Typhus can be treated under medical supervision. Seek local advice on areas where ticks pose a danger and always check your skin carefully for ticks after walking in a danger area such as a tropical forest. An insect repellent can help, and walkers in tick-infested areas should consider having their boots and trousers impregnated with benzyl benzoate and dibutylphthalate (see Leeches & Ticks under Cuts, Bites & Stings earlier).

WOMEN TRAVELLERS
Attitudes towards Women
Chinese trader Ma Huan noted in 1433 that among the Thais 'All affairs are managed by their wives, all trading transactions large or small'. In rural areas female family members typically inherit the land and throughout the country they tend to control the family finances.

The most recent United Nations Development Program (UNDP) Human Development Report noted that on the Gender-related Development Index (GDI) Thailand ranks 40th among 130 countries included in the report, thus falling into the 'progressive' category. This ranking is 12 points higher than the overall UN human development index for Thailand, meaning gender-related development in Thailand is further along than the average of all other human development criteria for that country. The organisation also reports that the nation's GDI increase was greater than that of any country in the world between 1975 and 1995. According to the

UNDP, Thailand 'has succeeded in building the basic human capabilities of both women and men, without substantial gender imparity'. Noted Thai feminist and Thammasat University professor Dr Chatsumarn Kabilsingh has written that 'In economics, academia and health services, women hold a majority of the administrative positions and manifest a sense of self-confidence in dealing independently with the challenges presented by their careers'.

Thai women constitute 55% of all enrolments in secondary and tertiary schools and about 45% of Thailand's workforce, outranking both China and the USA in both categories.

So much for the good news. The bad news is that although women generally fare well in education, the labour force and in rural land inheritance, their cultural standing is a bit farther from parity. An oft-repeated Thai saying reminds us that men form the front legs of the elephant, women the hind legs (at least they're pulling equal weight).

On a purely legal level, men enjoy more privilege. Men may divorce their wives for committing adultery, but not vice versa, for example (although in actual practice, Thai men and women divorce at will for whatever reason they like). Men who take a foreign spouse continue to have the right to purchase and own land, while Thai women who marry foreign men lose this right. However, Article 30 of the 1997-ratified Thai constitution states 'Men and women hold equal rights' (few so-called developed countries in the Western world have charters containing such equal rights clauses); we can expect to see a reformation of such discriminatory laws as 'organic' legislation is put in place.

Safety Precautions

According to the latest TAT statistics, around 40% of all foreign visitors to Thailand are women, a ratio higher than the worldwide average and ahead of all other Asian countries (for which the proportion of female visitors runs lower than 35%) with the possible exception of Singapore and Hong Kong. This ratio is growing from year to year and the overall increase in women visitors has climbed faster than that of men for every year since 1993.

Everyday incidents of sexual harassment are much less common in Thailand than in India, Indonesia or Malaysia and this may lull women who have recently travelled in those countries into thinking that Thailand travel is safer than it is. Over the past decade several foreign women have been attacked while travelling alone in remote areas, and in August 2000 a British woman was murdered at a guesthouse in Chiang Mai. Such incidents, however, are extremely rare. If you're a woman travelling alone, try to pair up with other travellers when travelling at night or in remote areas. Make sure hotel and guesthouse rooms are secure at night – if they're not, demand another room or move to another hotel or guesthouse.

When in the company of single Thai males, keep an eye on food and drink. In 1999 and 2000 we received a couple of reports from women who alleged they had been drugged and raped by Thai trekking guides in Chiang Mai.

See Dangers & Annoyances for more information and advice.

Jík-Kôh Small upcountry restaurants are sometimes hangouts for drunken *jík-kôh*, an all-purpose Thai term that refers to the teenage playboy-hoodlum-cowboy who gets his kicks by violating Thai cultural norms. These oafs sometimes bother foreign women (and men) who are trying to have a quiet meal ('Are you married?' and 'I love you' are common conversation openers). It's best to ignore them rather than try to make snappy comebacks – they won't understand them and will most likely take these responses as encouragement. If the jík-kôh persist, leave and go to another restaurant. Unfortunately, restaurant proprietors will rarely involve themselves in such disturbances.

GAY & LESBIAN TRAVELLERS

Thai culture is very tolerant of homosexuality, both male and female. The nation has no laws that discriminate against homosexuals and there is a fairly prominent gay and lesbian scene. Hence there is no 'gay movement' in Thailand as such since there's no antigay establishment to move against. Whether speaking of dress or mannerism, lesbians and gays are generally accepted without comment.

Public displays of affection – both heterosexual and homosexual – are frowned upon. According to the gay-oriented guide *Thai Scene:*

For many gay travellers, Thailand is a nirvana with a long established gay bar scene, which, whilst often very Thai in culture, is particularly welcoming to tourists. There is little, if any, social approbation towards gay people, providing Thai cultural mores are respected. What people do in bed, whether straight or gay, is not expected to be a topic of general conversation nor bragged about.

The magazine *Pink Ink* writes:

Thai lesbians prefer to call themselves tom (for tomboy) or dee (for lady), as the term 'lesbian', in Thailand, suggests pornographic videos produced for straight men. Tom and dee, by contrast, are fairly accepted and integrated categories for Thai women, roughly corresponding to the Western terms 'butch' and 'femme'.

Organisations & Publications
Utopia (☎ 022 591 619, fax 022 583 250, e utopia@best.com), at 116/1 Soi 23, Thanon Sukhumvit, Bangkok, is a gay and lesbian multipurpose centre consisting of a guesthouse, bar, cafe, gallery and gift shop. It maintains a well-organised Web site called the Southeast Asia Gay and Lesbian Resources (Utopia Homo Page; W www .utopia-asia.com).

Thailand's premier (and only) lesbian society is Anjaree Group (☎/fax 024 771 776), PO Box 322, Ratchadamnoen, Bangkok 10200. Anjaree sponsors various group activities and produces a Thai-only newsletter.

Bilingual Thai-English Web sites of possible interest to visiting lesbians include W www.lesla.com.

The Web site W www.chiangmaigossip .com contains a great deal of information about the gay scene in Chiang Mai.

An in-depth resource for anyone interested in learning more about Thailand's gay and lesbian scene is *Lady Boys, Tom Boys, Rent Boys,* by Peter A Jackson.

DISABLED TRAVELLERS
Thailand presents one large, ongoing obstacle course for the mobility-impaired. With its high curbs, uneven sidewalks and nonstop traffic, Bangkok can be particularly difficult – many streets must be crossed via pedestrian bridges flanked with steep stairways, while buses and boats don't stop long enough for even the mildly disabled. Rarely are there any ramps or other access points for wheelchairs. Chiang Mai is a bit better: there's less traffic to worry about, and no pedestrian bridges with steep flights of steps. Some kerbs at intersections are ramped, but most are not.

Hyatt International Chiang Mai, Novotel Chiang Mai and Westin Chiang Mai are the only hotels in the region that make consistent design efforts to provide disabled access for each of their properties. Because of their high employee-to-guest ratios, homegrown luxury hotel chains such as those managed by Dusit, Amari and Royal Garden Resorts are usually very good about making sure that the mobility-impaired are well accommodated in terms of providing staff help where architecture fails. In other accommodation options you're pretty much left to your own resources.

For wheelchair travellers, any trip to Thailand will require a good deal of advance planning; fortunately, a growing network of information sources can put you in touch with those who have wheeled through Thailand before you. There is no better source of information than someone who's done it. A reader wrote with the following tips:

• The difficulties you mention in your book are all there. However, travel in the streets is still possible, and enjoyable, providing you have a strong, ambulatory companion. Some obstacles may require two carriers; Thais are by nature helpful and could generally be counted on for assistance.
• Don't feel you have to rely on organised tours to see the sights – these often leave early mornings

at times inconvenient to disabled people. It is far more convenient (and often cheaper) to take a taxi or hired car. It's also far more enjoyable as there is no feeling of holding others up.

- A túk-túk is far easier to get in and out of and to carry two people and a wheelchair than a taxi. Even the pedicabs can hang a wheelchair on the back of the carriage.
- Be ready to try anything – in spite of my worries, riding an elephant proved quite easy.

Organisations

International organisations with information on mobility-impaired travel include:

Access Foundation (☎ 516-887 5798) PO Box 356, Malverne, NY 11565, USA
Mobility International USA (☎ 541-343 1284, ⓔ info@miusa.org, ⓔ www.miusa.org) PO Box 10767, Eugene, OR 97440, USA
National Information Communication Awareness Network (Nican; ☎ 02-6285 3713, fax 6285 3714, Ⓦ www.nican.com.au) PO Box 407, Curtin, ACT 2605, Australia
Royal Association for Disability & Rehabilitation (Radar; ☎ 020-7250 3222, fax 250 0212, Ⓦ www.radar.org.uk) 12 City Forum, 250 City Rd, London EC1V 8AF, UK
Society for the Advancement of Travelers with Handicaps (SATH; ☎ 212-447 7284, ⓔ sathtravel@aol.com, Ⓦ www.sath.org) Suite 610, 347 Fifth Ave, New York, NY 11242, USA

The book *Exotic Destinations for Wheelchair Travelers,* by Ed Hansen & Bruce Gordon (Full Data, San Francisco), contains a useful chapter on seven locations in Thailand. Others books of value include *Holidays and Travel Abroad – A Guide for Disabled People* (RADAR, London).

Accessible Journeys (☎ 610-521 0339, Ⓦ www.disabilitytravel.com), at 35 West Sellers Ave, Ridley Park, Pennsylvania, USA, specialises in organising group travel for the mobility-impaired. Occasionally the agency offers Thailand trips.

SENIOR TRAVELLERS

Seniors' discounts aren't generally available in Thailand, but the Thais more than make up for this in the respect they show for the elderly. In Thai culture status comes with age; there isn't as heavy an emphasis on youth as in the Western world. Deference for age manifests itself in the way Thais will go out of their way to help older people in and out of taxis or with luggage, and – usually but not always – in waiting on them first in shops and post offices. Senior travellers are welcomed in Thailand with open arms. There is even a Retirement Visa for those 55 years of age and over, which is renewable year after year.

Nonetheless, some cultural spheres are for the young. In particular, cross-generational entertainment is less common than in Western countries. There is a strict stratification among discos and nightclubs, for example, according to age group. One place will cater to teenagers, another to people in their early 20s, one for late 20s and 30s, yet another for those in their 40s and 50s, and once you've reached 60 you're considered too old to go clubbing! Exceptions to this rule include the more traditional entertainment venues, such as rural temple fairs and other wát-centred events, where young and old will dance and eat together. For men, massage parlours are another place where old and young mix.

TRAVEL WITH CHILDREN

Like many places in Southeast Asia, travelling with children in Thailand can be a lot of fun as long as you come well prepared with the right attitudes, equipment and the usual parental patience. Lonely Planet's *Travel with Children,* by Cathy Lanigan, contains useful advice on how to cope with kids on the road and what to bring along to make things go more smoothly, with special attention paid to travel in developing countries.

Thais love children and in many instances will shower attention on your offspring, who will find ready playmates among their Thai counterparts and a temporary nanny service at practically every stop.

For the most part parents needn't worry too much about health concerns, although it pays to lay down a few ground rules – such as regular hand-washing – to head off potential medical problems. All the usual health precautions apply (see the Health section earlier for details); children should especially be warned not to play with animals, since rabies is relatively common in Thailand.

DANGERS & ANNOYANCES

Although Thailand is in no way a dangerous country to visit, it's wise to be a little cautious, particularly if you're travelling alone. There are no pirate taxis in Chiang Mai but solo women travellers should take special care on arrival at Bangkok International Airport, particularly at night. Don't take one of Bangkok's often very unofficial taxis (black-and-white licence plates) by yourself – it's better to take a licensed taxi (yellow-and-black plates) or even the public bus.

Both men and women should ensure their rooms are securely locked and bolted at night. Inspect cheap rooms with thin walls for strategic peepholes.

Take caution when leaving valuables in hotel safes. A few travellers have reported unpleasant experiences leaving valuables in Chiang Mai guesthouses while trekking. Make sure you obtain an itemised receipt for property left with hotels or guesthouses – note the exact quantity of travellers cheques and all other valuables.

When you're on the road, keep zippered luggage secured with small locks, especially while travelling on buses and trains. Several readers' letters have recounted tales of thefts from their bags or backpacks during long overnight bus trips, particularly between Bangkok and Chiang Mai. Such theft appears to be far more common on the private buses arranged via Thanon Khao San (a backpackers centre in Bangkok) than on buses boarded at the official government bus station. See the Getting Around chapter for more details.

Credit Cards

On return to their home countries, some visitors have received huge credit-card bills for purchases (usually jewellery) charged to their cards while the cards had, supposedly, been secure in the hotel or guesthouse safe. You might consider taking your credit cards with you if you go trekking – if the cards are stolen on the trail at least the bandits aren't likely to be able to use them. There are organised gangs in Bangkok specialising in arranging stolen credit-card purchases – and in some cases these gangs pay down-and-out foreigners to fake the signatures on the credit cards.

When making credit-card purchases, don't let vendors take your credit card out of your sight to run it through the machine. Unscrupulous merchants have been known to rub off three or four or more receipts with one credit-card purchase; after the customer leaves the shop, they use the one legitimate receipt as a model to forge your signature on the blanks, then fill in astronomical 'purchases'. Sometimes they wait several weeks – even months – between submitting each charge receipt to the bank, so that you can't remember whether you'd been billed at the same vendor more than once.

Drugging

In bars and on trains and buses beware of friendly strangers offering gifts such as cigarettes, drinks, cookies or sweets (candy). Several travellers have reported waking up with a headache sometime later to find that their valuables had disappeared.

Male travellers have also encountered drugged food or drink from friendly Thai women in bars and from prostitutes in their own hotel rooms. Female visitors have encountered the same with young Thai men, albeit less frequently. Conclusion: Don't accept gifts from strangers.

Assault

Robbery of travellers by force is very rare in Thailand, but it does happen. Isolated incidences of armed robbery have tended to occur along the Thai-Myanmar border. In February 2000 armed bandits robbed an Australian couple camping illegally in Doi Ang Khang National Park, near the Myanmar border. The couple tried to resist and, during the ensuing scuffle, one of the campers was shot and killed.

The safest practice in remote areas is not to go out alone at night and, if trekking in Northern Thailand, always walk in groups.

Touts

Touting – grabbing newcomers in the street or in train stations, bus terminals or airports to sell them a service – is a long-time tradition in Asia, and while Thailand doesn't have as many touts as, say, India, it does have its share. In the popular tourist spots it seems like everyone – young boys waving fliers, túk-túk drivers, sǎamláw (three-wheeled vehicle) drivers, schoolgirls – is touting something, usually hotels or guesthouses. For the most part they're completely harmless and sometimes they can be very informative. But take anything a tout says with two large grains of salt. Since touts work on commission and get paid just for delivering you to a guesthouse or hotel (whether you check in or not), they'll say anything to get you to the door.

Often the best (most honest and reliable) hotels and guesthouses refuse to pay tout commissions – so the average tout will try to steer you away from such places. Hence don't believe them if they tell you the hotel or guesthouse you're looking for is closed, full, dirty or 'bad'. Sometimes (rarely) they're right but most times it's just a ruse to get you to a place that pays more commission. Always have a careful look yourself before checking into a place recommended by a tout. Túk-túk and sǎamláw drivers often offer free or low-cost rides to the place they're touting; if you have another place you're interested in, you might agree to go with a driver only if he or she promises to deliver you to your first choice after you've had a look at the place being touted. If drivers refuse, chances are it's because they know your first choice is a better one.

This type of commission work isn't limited to low-budget guesthouses. Taxi drivers and even airline employees at Thailand's major airports – including Chiang Mai – reap commissions from the big hotels as well. At either end of the budget spectrum, the customer ends up paying the commission indirectly through raised room rates.

Bus Touts Watch out for touts wearing (presumably fake) TAT or tourist information badges at Bangkok's Hualamphong train station. They have been known to coerce travellers into buying tickets for private bus rides, saying the train is 'full' or 'takes too long'. Often the promised bus service turns out to be substandard and may take longer than the equivalent train ride, due to the frequent changing of vehicles. You may be offered a 24-seat VIP 'sleeper' bus to Chiang Mai, for example, and end up stuffed into a minivan all the way. Such touts are 'bounty hunters' who receive a set fee for every tourist they deliver to the bus companies. Avoid the travel agencies (many of which bear 'TAT' or even 'Lonely Planet' signs) just outside the train station for the same reason.

Border Areas

A little extra caution should be exercised along Northern Thailand's borders with Myanmar. The Myanmar border between Um Phang and Mae Sariang occasionally receives shelling from Burmese troops in pursuit of Karen or Mon rebels. Karen rebels are trying to maintain an independent nation called Kawthoolei along the border with Thailand. The situation is complicated by an ongoing split between the Christian and Buddhist Karen insurgents. Between Mae Sot and Tha Song Yang, south of Mae Sariang on the Thai side, are several Karen refugee camps (at last report 12 camps with a total of about 100,000 refugees) populated by civilians who have fled Burmese-Karen armed conflicts, as well as political dissidents from Yangon. The risk of catching a piece of shrapnel is substantially lower if you keep several kilometres between yourself and the Thai-Myanmar border in this area – fighting can break out at any time. Mae Sot itself is quite safe these days, although you can still occasionally hear mortar fire in the distance.

The presence of Shan and Wa armies along the Myanmar-Thai border in northern Mae Hong Son Province makes this area dangerous if you attempt to travel near opium- and amphetamine-trade border crossings; obviously these are not signposted, so take care anywhere along the border in this area.

Drug Penalties

drug	quantity	penalty
marijuana or hallucinogens		
consumption	any amount	1 year imprisonment & up to 10,000B fine
possession	any amount	up to 5 years imprisonment & up to 50,000B fine
cocaine or morphine		
consumption	any amount	6 months to 10 years imprisonment & up to 5000B fine
possession	less than 100g	5 years imprisonment & 5000B fine
possession	100g+	5 years to life imprisonment & 50,000B to 500,000B fine
heroin or amphetamines		
consumption	any amount	6 months to 10 years imprisonment & 5000B to 10,000B fine
possession	less than 20g	1 to 10 years imprisonment & 10,000B to 100,000B fine
possession	20g + to less than 100g	5 years to life imprisonment & 50,000B to 500,000B fine
possession	100g +	life imprisonment or execution

In early 1996 Khun Sa and 10,000 of his troops surrendered to Yangon, taking most of the punch out of the Mong Tai Army (MTA). However, as many as 8000 MTA fighters, split among four armies, are still active in the area bordering Mae Sai south to Mae Hong Son, so the area is not much safer than when Khun Sa was around. In March 1998 there was a three-way armed clash between Thai border police, Myanmar forces and the Shan States Army along the Mae Hong Son/Shan State border.

There is also potential for hostilities to break out between Myanmar government troops and the Thai army over a disputed Thai-Myanmar border section near Doi Lang, southwest of Mae Sai in Mae Ai district. The territory under dispute amounts to 32 sq km; at the moment the two sides are trying to work things out peaceably according to the 1894 Siam-Britain Treaty, which both countries recognise. The problem is that British mapping of the time made geographical naming errors that seem to favour the Burmese side. It is likely that Burmese and Thai troops will remain poised for action on either side of the border until the matter is resolved.

Drugs

Opium, heroin, amphetamines, hallucinogens and marijuana are widely used in Thailand, but it is illegal to buy, sell or possess these drugs in any quantity. (The possession of opium for consumption, but not sale, among hill tribes is legal.) A lesser-known narcotic, *kràthâwm* (a leaf of the *Mitragyna speciosa* tree), is used by workers and students as a stimulant. Kràthâwm leaves sell for around 200B for 100, or 5B to 15B each; the leaf is illegal and said to be addictive.

Crude amphetamine tablets called *yaa bâa* (crazy medicine) are imported in large quantities from Wa-controlled areas of northeastern Myanmar and sold inexpensively in Northern Thailand. The quality is low and dosages erratic. This is another illegal drug to be extremely careful of. In Chiang Mai we've heard of cases of yaa bâa being sold to tourists as the rave drug Ecstasy (MMDA).

Although in certain areas of the country drugs seem to be used with some impunity, enforcement is arbitrary – the only way not to risk getting caught is to avoid the drug scene entirely. Every year perhaps dozens of visiting foreigners are arrested in Thailand for drug use or trafficking and end up doing

Scams

Thais are generally so friendly and laid-back that some visitors are lulled into a false sense of security that makes them particularly vulnerable to scams and con schemes of all kinds.

In Northern Thailand – even in Chiang Mai, the North's tourism capital – the scams herein described appear to be far less common than in Bangkok. Nonetheless, we have had reports of some of the same scams occurring in Chiang Mai, and we provide this information as a preventive measure.

Scammers tend to haunt the areas where first-time tourists go, such as the area around Pratu Tha Phae or Wat Phra Sing in Chiang Mai.

Most scams begin the same way: A friendly Thai male (or, on rare occasions, a female) approaches a lone visitor – usually newly arrived – and strikes up a seemingly innocuous conversation. Sometimes the con man says he's a university student, other times he may claim to work for the World Bank or a similarly distinguished organisation (some even carry cellular phones). If you're on the way to Wat Phra Sing, for example, he may tell you it's closed for a holiday. Eventually the conversation works its way around to the subject of the scam – the better con men can actually make it seem like you initiated the topic. That's one of the most bewildering aspects of the con – afterwards victims remember that the whole thing seemed like their idea, not the con artist's.

The scam itself almost always involves either gems or card playing. With gems, the victims find themselves invited to a gem and jewellery shop – your new-found friend is picking up some merchandise for himself and you're just along for the ride. Somewhere along the way he usually claims to have a connection, often a relative, in your home country (what a coincidence!) with whom he has a regular gem export-import business. One way or another, victims are convinced (usually they convince themselves) that they can turn a profit by arranging a gem purchase and reselling the merchandise at home. After all, the jewellery shop just happens to be offering a generous discount today – it's a government or religious holiday, or perhaps it's the shop's 10th anniversary, or maybe they've just taken a liking to you! The latest wrinkle is to say it's a special 'Amazing Thailand' promotion. As one freshly scammed reader recently wrote in: 'Everybody we spoke to mentioned 'Amazing Thailand' before they ripped us off!'

There is a seemingly infinite number of variations on the gem scam, almost all of which end up with the victim making a purchase of small, low-quality sapphires and posting them to their home countries. (If they let you walk out with them, you might return for a refund after realising you've been taken.) Once you return home, of course, the cheap sapphires turn out to be worth much less than you paid for them (perhaps one-tenth to one-half).

Many have invested and lost virtually all their savings; some admit they had been scammed even after reading warnings in this guidebook or those posted by the Tourism Authority of Thailand (TAT) around Bangkok.

Even if you were somehow able to return your purchase to the gem shop in question (one fellow we knew actually intercepted his parcel at the airport before it left Thailand), chances are slim-to-none

time in Thai prisons. A smaller, but significant, number die of heroin overdoses. Guesthouses where foreigners hang out are targets of infrequent drug enforcement sweeps.

The legal penalties for drug offences are stiff: If you're caught using marijuana, mushrooms or LSD, you face a fine of 10,000B plus one year in prison; for heroin or amphetamines, the penalty for use can be anywhere from six months' to 10 years'

imprisonment, plus a fine of 5000B to 10,000B. The going rate for bribing one's way out of a small pot bust is 50,000B.

Drug smuggling – defined as attempting to cross a border with drugs in your possession – carries considerably higher penalties, including execution. Recent arrest records show that citizens of Myanmar, Laos, Malaysia, Cambodia and the UK top the list of those arrested in Thailand for drug traf-

Scams

they'd give a full refund. The con artist who brings the mark into the shop gets a commission of 10% to 50% per sale – the shop takes the rest.

The Thai police are usually no help whatsoever, believing that merchants are entitled to whatever price they can get. The main victimisers are a handful of shops that get protection from certain high-ranking government officials. These officials put pressure on police not to prosecute, or to take as little action as possible. Even TAT's tourist police have never been able to prosecute a Thai jeweller, even in cases of blatant, recurring gem fraud. A Thai police commissioner was recently convicted of fraud in an investigation into a jewellery theft by Thais in Saudi Arabia: He replaced the Saudi gems with fakes! (See the Jewellery entry in the Shopping section of this chapter for information on recent initiatives to protect consumers.)

The card-playing scam starts out much the same way: A friendly stranger approaches the lone traveller on the street, strikes up a conversation and then invites them to the house or apartment of his sister (or brother-in-law etc) for a drink or meal. After a bit of socialising a friend or relative of the con arrives on the scene; it just so happens a little high-stakes card game is planned for later that day. Like the gem scam, the card-game scam has many variations, but eventually the victim is shown some cheating tactics to use with help from the 'dealer', some practice sessions take place and finally the game gets under way with several high rollers at the table. The mark is allowed to win a few hands first, then somehow loses a few, gets bankrolled by one of the friendly Thais, and then loses the Thai's money. Suddenly your new-found buddies aren't so friendly any more – they want the money you lost. Sometimes the con pretends to be dismayed by it all. Sooner or later you end up cashing in most or all of your travellers cheques or making a costly visit to an ATM. Again the police won't take any action – in this case because gambling is illegal in Thailand so you've broken the law by playing cards for money.

Other minor scams involve túk-túk drivers, hotel employees and bar girls who take new arrivals on city tours; these almost always end in high-pressure sales situations at silk, jewellery or handicraft shops.

Follow TAT's number-one suggestion to tourists: Disregard all offers of free shopping or sightseeing help from strangers – they invariably take a commission from your purchases. I would add to this: Beware of deals that seem too good to be true – they're usually neither good nor true. You might also try lying whenever a stranger asks how long you've been in Thailand – if it's only been three days, say three weeks! Or save your Bangkok sightseeing until after you've been upcountry. The con artists rarely prey on anyone except new arrivals.

Contact the Tourist Police if you have any problems with consumer fraud. The Tourist Police headquarters (☎ 053 248 130, 053 248 974) for the North is located in Chiang Mai, about 100m north of the TAT office on Thanon Chiang Mai-Lamphun. In Bangkok a special police unit (☎ 022 541 067, 022 235 4017) deals specifically with gem swindles. A telephone hotline (☎ 1155) connects with the tourist police from any phone in Thailand.

ficking, followed by Australians, Germans, Americans and Italians.

LEGAL MATTERS

In general, Thai police don't hassle foreigners, especially tourists. If anything they usually go out of their way not to arrest a foreigner breaking minor traffic laws, rather taking the approach that a friendly warning will suffice.

One major exception is drugs (see Dangers & Annoyances earlier for a general discussion of this topic), which most Thai police view as either a social scourge with regard to which it's their duty to enforce the letter of the law, or as an opportunity to make untaxed income via bribes. The direction they'll go often depends on dope quantities; small-time offenders are sometimes offered the chance to pay their way out of an arrest, while traffickers usually go to jail.

If you are arrested for any offence, the police will allow you the opportunity to make a phone call to your embassy or consulate in Thailand if you have one, or to a friend or relative if not. There's a whole set of legal codes governing the length of time and manner in which you can be detained before being charged or put on trial, but a lot of discretion is left to the police. With foreigners the police are more likely to bend these codes in your favour. However, as with police worldwide, if you don't show respect you will make matters worse.

Thai law does not presume an indicted detainee to be either 'guilty' or 'innocent' but rather a 'suspect' whose guilt or innocence will be decided in court. Trials are usually speedy.

Thailand has its share of attorneys, and if you think you're a high arrest risk for whatever reason, it might be a good idea to get out the Bangkok *Yellow Pages,* copy down a few phone numbers and carry them with you.

Tourist Police Hotline

The best way to deal with most serious hassles regarding ripoffs or thefts is to contact the tourist police, who are used to dealing with foreigners, rather than the regular Thai police. The tourist police maintain a hotline – dial ☎ 1155 from any phone in Thailand. Call this number to lodge complaints or to request assistance with regards to personal safety 24 hours a day. You can also call this number between 8.30am and 4.30pm daily to request travel information.

The tourist police can also be very helpful in cases of arrest. Although they typically have no jurisdiction over the kinds of cases handled by regular cops, they may be able to help with translation or with contacting your embassy.

BUSINESS HOURS

Most government offices are open from 8.30am to 4.30pm weekdays, but close from noon to 1pm for lunch. Regular bank hours are 8.30am to 3.30pm weekdays.

Several banks in Chiang Mai have special foreign-exchange offices in tourist-oriented areas that are open longer (8.30am to 8pm) and every day of the week. Note that all government offices and banks are closed on public holidays.

Businesses usually operate between 8.30am and 5pm weekdays and sometimes on Saturday morning. Larger shops usually open from 10am to 6.30pm or 7pm but smaller shops may open earlier and close later. Department stores are usually open between 10am and 10pm.

PUBLIC HOLIDAYS & SPECIAL EVENTS

The number and frequency of festivals and fairs in Northern Thailand is incredible – there always seems to be something going on, especially during the cool season between November and February.

The exact dates for festivals may vary from year to year, either because of the lunar calendar, which isn't quite in sync with the solar calendar – or because local authorities have decided to change festival dates. The TAT (see Tourist Offices earlier for contact information) publishes an up-to-date *Major Events & Festivals* calendar each year that is useful for anyone planning to attend a particular event.

See the destination chapters for details on local festivals.

January

New Year's Day Public holiday, 1 January. A rather recent public holiday in deference to the Western calendar.

February

Chiang Mai Flower Festival Colourful floats and parades exhibit Chiang Mai's cultivated flora.

Magha Puja *(maakhá buuchaa)* Held on the full moon of the 3rd lunar month to commemorate Buddha preaching to 1250 enlightened monks who came to hear him 'without prior summons'. A public holiday throughout the country, it culminates with a candle-lit walk around the main chapel *(wian tian)* at every wát. This festival is especially well celebrated at Wat Chedi Luang in Chiang Mai.

Late February–Early March

Chinese New Year Called *trùt jiin* in Thai, Chinese all over Thailand celebrate their lunar New Year (the date shifts from year to year) with a week of house-cleaning, lion dances and fireworks.

April

Chakri Day This is a public holiday commemorating the founder of the Chakri dynasty, Rama I. It's held on 6 April.

Songkran This is the celebration of the lunar New Year in Thailand. Buddha images are 'bathed', monks and elders receive the respect of younger Thais by the sprinkling of water over their hands, and a lot of water is generously tossed about for fun. Songkran generally gives everyone a chance to release their frustrations and literally cool-off during the peak of the hot season. Hide out in your room or expect to be soaked; the latter is a lot more fun. It's held from 13 to 15 April.

May

Coronation Day Public holiday, 5 May.

Visakha Puja *(wísǎakhà buuchaa)* A public holiday that falls on the 15th day of the waxing moon in the 6th lunar month, this day commemorates the date of the Buddha's birth, enlightenment and *parinibbana,* passing away. Activities are centred on the wát, including candle-lit processions, much chanting and sermonising.

Mid-May–Mid-June

Bun Phra Wet This festival, more popular in the villages of Northern Thailand than in the larger towns and cities, commemorates a Buddhist legend in which a host of spirits *(phǐi)* appeared to greet the Buddha-to-be upon his return to his home town, during his penultimate birth as Prince Vessantara.

Mid- to Late July

Asalha Puja *(àsǎanhà buuchaa)* This festival commemorates the Buddha's first sermon.

Khao Phansa *(khǎo phansǎa)* A public holiday and the beginning of Buddhist 'lent', this is the traditional time of year for young men to enter the monkhood for the rainy season and for all monks to station themselves in a monastery for the three months. It's a good time to observe a Buddhist ordination.

August

Queen's Birthday This public holiday is celebrated on 12 August.

Mid-October–Mid-November

Kathin *(thâwt kàthǐn)* The kathin ceremony takes place during the last month of the rainy season, at the end of the Buddhist lent. New monastic robes and requisites are offered to the Sangha (monastic community). In Nan Province longboat races are held on Mae Nam Nan (Nan River).

October

Chulalongkorn Day Public holiday, 23 October. This holiday is in commemoration of King Chulalongkorn (Rama V).

November

Loi Krathong On the proper full-moon night, small lotus-shaped baskets or boats made of banana leaves containing flowers, incense, candles and a coin are floated on Thai rivers, lakes and canals. This is a peculiarly Thai festival that probably originated in Sukhothai and is best celebrated in the North. In Chiang Mai the festival is called Yi Peng, and residents also launch paper hot-air balloons into the sky. At the Sukhothai Historical Park there is an impressive sound-and-light show held at this time.

December

King's Birthday Public holiday, 5 December.

Constitution Day This is a public holiday held on 10 December commemorating the establishment of the constitutional monarchy in 1932.

ACTIVITIES
Cycling

Details on pedalling your way around Northern Thailand and bicycle hire can be found in the Getting Around chapter.

Trekking

Wilderness walking or trekking is one of Northern Thailand's biggest draws. Typical trekking programs run for four or five days (although it is possible to arrange from one- to 10-day treks) and feature daily walks through forested mountain areas coupled with overnight stays in hill-tribe villages to satisfy both ethno- and eco-tourism urges. See the 'Trekking' special section for more detail.

Other trekking opportunities are available in Northern Thailand's larger national parks, where park rangers may be hired as guides and cooks for a few days at a time.

Rates are reasonable. For more information, see the respective park entries later in this book.

River Rafting

Several local travel outfits in Chiang Mai, Pai, Mae Hong Son, Chiang Rai, Tha Ton and Um Phang can arrange rafting trips on Northern Thailand's abundant waterways. These range from relatively calm journeys on bamboo rafts drifting down Mae Nam Kok from Tha Ton to Chiang Rai, to whitewater excursions aboard rigid inflatable rafts down Mae Nam Pai.

In some cases river rafting can be combined with other wilderness activities, such as hiking and elephant trekking. An up-and-coming spot for this sort of combo is Um Phang in southern Tak Province.

COURSES
Language

Several language schools in Chiang Mai offer courses in Thai language. See the Chiang Mai chapter for details. AUA, the most popular Thai language school in Chiang Mai, also offers classes in Northern Thai dialect for those interested.

Thai Studies

Chiang Mai University (☎ 053 221 699, W www.chiangmai.ac.th), at 239 Thanon Huay Kaew, offers special summer programs in Thai studies – history, culture, politics and Thai language – for international students.

Meditation

Thailand has long been a popular place for Western students of Buddhism, particularly those interested in Buddhist meditation. Two basic systems of meditation are taught: *samatha* (calm) and *vipassana* (*wípàtsanaa;* insight). Samatha aims towards the calming of the mind and development of refined states of concentration, and as such is similar to other traditions of meditation and contemplation found in most of the world's religions.

Unique to Buddhism, particularly Theravada and to a lesser extent Tibetan Buddhism, is the system of meditation known as vipassana.

Foreigners who come to Northern Thailand to study vipassana can choose several temples and meditation centres (*sămnák wípàtsanaa*) specialising in these teachings. Teaching methods vary but the general emphasis is on observing mind-body processes from moment to moment. Thai language is usually the medium of instruction but several places also provide instruction in English. Some centres and monasteries teach both vipassana and samatha methods, others specialise in one or the other.

Details on some of the more popular meditation-oriented temples and centres are given in destination chapters. Instruction and accommodation are free of charge at temples, although donations are expected.

Short-term students will find that the two-month Tourist Visa is ample for most courses of study. Long-term students may want to consider getting a three- or six-month Non-Immigrant Visa (see Visas & Documents earlier in this chapter). A few Westerners are ordained as monks or nuns in order to take full advantage of the monastic environment. Monks and nuns are generally (but not always) allowed to stay in Thailand as long as they remain in robes.

Places where English-language instruction is usually available include:

Sivali Meditation Centre (☎ 053 464 592, @ malinee@sivalicentre.com) Hang Dong, Chiang Mai
Wat Phra That Chom Thong (☎ 053 362 067) 157 Ban Luang, Chom Thong, Chiang Mai
Wat Tapotaram (Wat Ram Poeng; ☎ 053 278 620) Chiang Mai

Before visiting one of these centres, it's a good idea to call or write to make sure space and instruction are available. Some places require that lay persons staying overnight wear white clothes. For even a brief visit, wear clean and neat clothing (ie, long trousers or skirt, and sleeves that cover the shoulder).

For a detailed look at vipassana study in Thailand, including visa and ordination procedures, read *The Meditation Temples of Thailand: A Guide* published by Silkworm Books (☎ 053 271 889), 104/5 Thanon

Chiang Mai-Hot, Mu 7, Tambon Suthep, Chiang Mai, or *A Guide to Buddhist Monasteries & Meditation Centres in Thailand* (available from the World Fellowship of Buddhists in Bangkok or online at Ⓦ www.dharmanet.org/thai_94.html).

Useful reading material includes Jack Kornfield's *Living Dharma*, which contains short biographies and descriptions of the teaching methods of 12 well-known Theravada teachers, including six Thais. Serious meditators will want to study *The Path of Purification (Visuddhi Maggha)*, a classic commentary that reveals every detail of canonical Buddhist practice and includes a Pali-English glossary defining all the tricky terms.

Muay Thai (Thai Boxing)

Many Westerners have trained in Thailand, but few last more than a week or two in a Thai camp – and fewer still have gone on to compete on Thailand's pro circuit.

Training in muay thai takes place at dozens of boxing camps (perhaps as many as a hundred) around the country. Most of them are relatively reluctant to take on foreign trainees, except in special cases where the applicant can prove a willingness to conform totally to the training system, the diet and the rustic accommodation, and most of all show an ability to learn the Thai language. Rates vary from US$50 to US$200 per week, including food and accommodation.

Lanna Boxing Camp (☎/fax 053 273 133, ⓔ muaythai@asiaplus.com) at 64/1 Soi 1 (Soi Chang Khian), Thanon Huay Kaew, Chiang Mai 50300, and Chiang Mai Olympia (☎ 01 671 4969, ⓔ chiangmaiolympia@loxinfo.co.th) both specialise in training for foreigners. Be forewarned, however: Muay thai training is gruelling and features full-contact sparring, unlike tae kwon do, kenpo, kung fu and other East Asian martial arts.

In Thailand look for copies of *Muay Thai World*, a biannual periodical published by Bangkok's World Muay Thai Council. Although it's basically a cheap martial arts flick, Jean-Claude Van Damme's *The Kickboxer*, filmed on location in Thailand, gives a more comprehensive, if rather exaggerated, notion of muay thai than most films on the subject.

The Web site Ⓦ www.muaythai.com contains loads of information on muay thai in Thailand, including the addresses of training camps.

Thai Massage

Described by some as a 'brutally pleasant experience', this ancient form of healing was first documented in the West by the French liaison to the Thai Royal Court in Ayuthaya in 1690, who wrote:

When any person is sick in Siam he causes his whole body to be moulded by one who is skilful herein, who gets upon the body of the sick person and tramples him under his feet.

Unlike most Western massage methodologies, such as Swedish and Californian techniques, Thai massage does not directly seek to relax through a kneading of the body with palms and fingers. Instead, a multipronged approach uses the hands, thumbs, fingers, elbows, forearms, knees and feet, and is applied to the traditional pressure points along the various *sên* (meridians; the human body is thought to have 72,000 of these, of which 10 are crucial).

The client's body is also pulled, twisted and manipulated in ways that have been compared to a 'passive yoga'. The objective is to distribute energies evenly throughout the nervous system so as to create a harmony of physical energy flows. The muscular-skeletal system is also manipulated in ways that can be compared to modern physiotherapy and chiropractic.

Northern Thailand offers ample opportunities to study its unique tradition of massage therapy. In fact, the Northern provinces boast a 'softer' version than the style emanating from Wat Pho in Bangkok, often considered the master source for all Thai massage pedagogy. Although Chiang Mai, as you might expect, is the most popular place to study massage, instruction is available in Pai as well. See the Massage sections in the relevant destination chapters.

Cooking

More and more travellers are coming to Thailand just to learn how to cook. Many foreign chefs seeking out recipe inspirations for East-West fusion cuisine make culinary pilgrimages to Thailand.

As for Thai language, massage and muay thai, Chiang Mai is the main centre for cooking lessons in the North. However, you may find smaller enterprises operating out of guesthouses in Pai, Mae Hong Son and Chiang Rai. Three particularly popular schools in Chiang Mai area are:

Chiang Mai Thai Cookery School (☎ 053 206 388, fax 053 399 036, ℮ nabnian@loxinfo .co.th) 1–3 Thanon Moon Muang. This place receives raves for its well-organised courses, which include market and garden visits.

Siam Chiang Mai Cookery School (☎ 053 271 169, fax 053 208 950) 5/2 Soi 1, Thanon Loi Khroh. This school offers three different courses and a free cookbook.

Sompet Thai Cookery School (☎/fax 053 280 901, ℮ sompet41@chmai.loxinfo.co.th) 100/1 Thanon Chang Khlan. Sompet teaches Thai and vegetarian cooking. Two courses per day are available, and the *Thai and Vegetarian Cookery* book is included in the course fee.

WORK

Thailand's steady economic growth has provided a variety of work opportunities for foreigners, although in general it's not as easy to find a job as in the more developed countries. The one exception is English teaching; as in the rest of East and Southeast Asia, there is a high demand for English speakers to provide instruction.

Teaching English

Those with academic credentials, such as teaching certificates or degrees in English as a second language (ESL) or English as a foreign language (EFL), get first crack at the better-paying jobs at universities and international schools. But there are dozens of private language-teaching establishments that hire noncredentialed teachers, by the hour, throughout the region. Private tutoring is also a possibility in the larger and more prosperous provincial capitals such as Chiang Mai, Lampang, Chiang Rai and Phitsanulok.

If you're interested in looking for teaching work, start with the English-language *Yellow Pages* of the *Greater Bangkok Metropolitan Telephone Directory*, which contains many upcountry listings. Check all the usual headings – Schools, Universities, Language Schools and so on. Some organisations, such as Teachers of English to Speakers of Other Languages (TESOL), Suite 300, 1600 Cameron St, Alexandria, VA 22314, USA; and International Association of Teachers of English as a Foreign Language, 3 Kingsdown Chamber, Kingsdown Park, Whitstable, Kent CT5 2DJ, UK, publish newsletters with lists of employment in foreign countries, including Thailand.

Web sites containing tips on where to find teaching jobs and how to deal with Thai classrooms, as well as current job listings include:

🅦 experiencethailand.netfirms.com/
   teachingenglish.htm
🅦 www.ajarn.com
🅦 www.asiatradingonline.com/teaching.htm
🅦 www.eslcafe.com/thailand

Other Jobs & Volunteer Positions

Voluntary and paid positions with organisations that provide charitable services in education, development or public health are available for those with the right educational and/or experiential backgrounds. However, you typically cannot ask for a certain region of Thailand, and thus can't be assured of an assignment in the North. Contact the usual prospects, such as: Voluntary Service Overseas (VSO; ☎ 020-8780 7200) in London; VSO Canada (☎ 613-234 1364) in Ottawa; Overseas Service Bureau (OSB; ☎ 03-9279 1788) in Melbourne; Volunteer Service Abroad (☎ 04-472 5759) in Wellington, New Zealand; or US Peace Corps (☎ 800-424 8580) in Washington, DC.

The UN supports a number of ongoing projects in the country. In Bangkok interested people can try contacting: United Nations Development Program (☎ 022 829 619); UN World Food Program (☎ 022 800 427); World Health Organization (☎ 022

829 700); Food & Agriculture Organization (☎ 022 817 844); Unicef (☎ 022 805 931); or Unesco (☎ 023 910 577). These organisations often list the locations of positions, so you may be able to specify Northern Thailand.

Mon, Karen and Burmese refugee camps along the Thailand-Myanmar border can use volunteer help. Since none of the camps is officially sanctioned by the Thai government, few of the big nongovernmental organisations (NGOs) and multilateral organisations are involved here. This means the level of overall support is low but the need for volunteers is definitely there. If this interests you, travel to the relevant areas (primarily Mae Sot) and ask around for the 'unofficial' camp locations.

Work Permits

All employment in Thailand requires a Thai work permit. Thai law defines work as 'exerting one's physical energy or employing one's knowledge, whether or not for wages or other benefits', and therefore, theoretically, even volunteer work requires a work permit.

A 1979 royal decree closed 39 occupations to foreigners, including architecture, civil engineering and clerical or secretarial services. In 1998 several jobs were reopened to foreigners; you may wish to contact your local Thai embassy or consulate (see Embassies & Consulates earlier) for the latest information on employment in Thailand.

Work permits should be obtained through an employer, who may file for the permit before you enter Thailand. The permit itself is not issued until you enter Thailand on a valid Non-Immigrant Visa.

The Thai government maintains the One-Stop Visa Centre (☎ 026 939 333, fax 026 939 340), 207 Thanon Ratchadaphisek, Krisda Plaza, Bangkok, which handles work permits and Non-Immigrant Visas for investors, businesspeople and foreign correspondents only. For information about work permits, contact any Thai embassy abroad or check out its Web site (W www.thaiembdc.org).

ACCOMMODATION

Places to stay in Northern Thailand are abundant, varied and very reasonably priced – in fact, the North, generally speaking, has the least expensive guesthouses and hotels of any region in Thailand.

A word of warning about touts: Don't believe them if they say a place is closed, full, dirty or crooked. Sometimes they're right but most times it's just a ruse to get you to a place that pays them more commission. (See Dangers & Annoyances earlier for more information about touts.)

Fire

If you're concerned about hotel fire safety, always check the fire exits at your hotel to make sure they're open and functioning. In 1997 the 17-storey Royal Jomtien Resort Hotel in Pattaya burned down, taking with it the lives of 80 people. The hotel had no sprinkler system and the fire exits were chained shut. In the wake of the fire, regulations were supposedly tightened around the country, but we've seen hotels in various locations that also chain or otherwise block off fire exits – to keep guests from skipping the room bill and to block potential thieves.

National Park Camping & Accommodation Facilities

All but two of the national parks in Northern Thailand have bungalows for rent that sleep as many as 10 people for rates of 500B to 1500B, depending on the park and the size of the bungalow. During the low seasons you can often get a room in one of these park bungalows for 100B per person (some parks will rent rooms in the larger bungalows for 100B any time of year).

Camping is allowed in all but two of the Northern Thai national parks (Doi Suthep/Doi Pui National Park and Khun Chae National Park, although Khun Chae is in the process of developing a campground) for only 5B to 20B per person per night. Some parks have tents for rent at 50B to 100B a night, but always check the condition of the tents before agreeing to rent one. It's a good idea to take your own sleeping bag or mat, and other basic camping gear. You should also take a torch (flashlight), rain gear, insect repellent, a water container and a small medical kit. A few parks also have *reuan thǎew* (longhouses) where rooms are around 150B to 200B for two people.

Advance bookings for accommodation are advisable at the more popular parks, especially on holidays and weekends. Most parks charge an entry fee to visit (Thais/foreigners 20/200B, children 14 and under half-price). Be sure to save your receipt for the duration of your stay. You may be asked by a ranger to show proof of having paid.

Temple Lodgings

If you are a Buddhist, or can behave like one, you may be able to stay overnight in some temples for a small donation. Facilities are very basic, however, and early rising is expected. Temple lodgings are usually for men only, unless the wát has a place for lay women to stay. Neat, clean dress and a basic knowledge of Thai etiquette are mandatory. See Meditation under Courses earlier for information on wát in Northern Thailand that will accommodate long-term lay students.

Hostels

There is a Thai branch of Hostelling International (☎ 022 820 950, fax 022 628 7416), formerly International Youth Hostel Federation, at 25/2 Thanon Phitsanulok, Sisao Thewet, Dusit, Bangkok 10300, with member hostels in Chiang Mai, Chiang Rai and Phitsanulok. Thai youth hostels range in price from 70B for a dorm bed to 280/350B per air-con single/double room. Only HI card holders are accepted as guests in Thai hostels; membership costs 300B per year (50B for a one-night membership).

University & School Accommodation

College and university campuses may have inexpensive accommodation during the summer vacation (March to June). There are universities in Chiang Mai, Lampang and Phitsanulok. There are also teachers colleges (*sa-thǎaban râatchaphát*) in every provincial capital that may offer summer vacation accommodation. The typical teachers' college dorm room lets for 50B to 100B per night.

Guesthouses

Guesthouses are generally the cheapest accommodation in Northern Thailand. Guesthouses vary quite a bit in terms of the facilities on offer, and are particularly numerous in Chiang Mai, Mae Hong Son and Pai, where stiff competition keeps the rates low. Some are especially good value, while others are mere flophouses. Many serve food, although there tends to be a bland sameness to meals in guesthouses wherever you are in Thailand.

YMCAs

Only the YMCAs in Chiang Mai and Chiang Rai offer guest facilities. Both YMCAs charge quite a bit more than guesthouses or hostels, and more than some local hotels, but they are well maintained and generally good value.

Resorts

In most countries 'resort' refers to hotels that offer substantial recreational facilities (eg, tennis, golf, swimming, sailing etc) in addition to accommodation and dining. In Thai hotel lingo, however, the term simply refers to any hotel that isn't located in an urban area. Hence a few thatched beach huts or a cluster of bungalows in a forest may be called a 'resort'. Several places in Northern Thailand fully deserve the resort title under any definition – but it pays to look into the facilities before making a reservation.

Chinese-Thai Hotels

The standard Thai hotels, often run by Chinese-Thai families, are usually found in busy central districts of provincial capitals. They generally have reasonable rates (average 180B for rooms without bathroom or air-con, 200B to 300B with fan and bathroom, 350B to 500B with air-con). These may be located on the main street of the town or near bus and train stations.

Typical rooms are clean and include a double bed and a ceiling fan. Some have attached Thai-style bathrooms (this will cost a little more). Rates may or may not be posted; if not, they may be increased for *faràng* (Westerners), so it is worthwhile bargaining.

Some of the cheapest Chinese-Thai hotels may double as quasi-brothels, where *phûu yǐng hǎa kin* (literally, women looking to eat; ie, prostitutes) maintain a few rooms for their work; the perpetual traffic in and out may be a bit noisy at times. Unaccompanied males are often asked if they want female companionship when checking into inexpensive hotels. Even certain middle-class (by Thai standards) hotels are reserved for the 'salesman' crowd, meaning travelling Thai businessmen, who frequently expect extra night-time services. Foreign women are usually left alone, but if you think you might feel uncomfortable being around such activity, by all means look for another hotel.

The cheapest hotels may have names posted in Thai and Chinese only, but with experience you will be able to identify them. Many of these hotels have restaurants downstairs; if they don't, there are usually restaurants and noodle shops nearby.

Getting a Good Room

For most hotels or guesthouses, it's best to have a look around before agreeing to check in, to make sure the room is clean, that the fan and lights work and so on. If there's a problem, request another room or a discount. If possible, always choose a room off the street and away from the front lounge to cut down on noise.

For a room without air-con, ask for a *hâwng thammádaa* (ordinary room) or *hâwng phát lom* (room with fan). A room with air-con is *hâwng ae*. Sometimes faràng asking for air-con are automatically offered a 'VIP' room, which usually comes with air-con, hot water, fridge and TV and is about twice the price of a regular air-con room.

Tourist-Class, Business & Luxury Hotels

These are found only in the main tourist and business destinations, eg, Chiang Mai, Chiang Rai, Lampang, Mae Hong Son, Mae Sot and Phitsanulok. Prices start at around 600B outside Chiang Mai and proceed to 2000B or more. These hotels will typically offer air-con, TV, Western-style showers and baths, toilets, IDD phones and restaurants. Added to room charges will be a 7% government tax (VAT), and most of these hotels will include an additional service charge of 8% to 10%.

Discounts Discounts of 30% to 50% for hotels charging 1000B or more per night can easily be obtained through many Thai travel agencies. Several top-end hotels offer discounts of up to 60% for reservations made via the Internet. In the arrival halls of both the international and domestic terminals at Bangkok Airport, the Thai Hotels Association (THA) desk can arrange discounts. If you are holding Thai Airways International (THAI) tickets, or flew in with THAI, the airline can arrange substantial discounts.

There is no reservation service at Chiang Mai airport, so if you're transiting through Bangkok it's best to use the ones there.

FOOD

Standing at the crossroads of India, China and Asian Oceania, Thailand has adapted cooking techniques and ingredients from all three of these major spheres of influence, as well as from the culinary kits carried by passing traders and empire-builders from the Middle East and southern Europe. Over the centuries, indigenous rudiments fused with imported elements to produce a distinctive native cuisine that is instantly recognisable to any discerning palate. Thai cuisine has become so globally appreciated that in a survey polling travel agencies in over 25 countries, Thailand ranked fourth after France, Italy and Hong Kong in the perceived excellence of cuisine.

As with other well-developed world cuisines, Thailand's can be categorically divided into several regional variations.

Northern Thailand of course has its own cuisine, even if it is difficult to find outside of municipal markets and a sprinkling of *ráan aahǎan phéun meuang* (local-style restaurants). However, the overall spirit of the cuisine – and a majority of the ingredients – are shared across Northern Thailand's regional boundaries.

Northern Style

In the traditional Northern home, the family takes meals sitting on the floor around a *tòhk,* a round, footed table made of lacquered wood or woven bamboo. The rim of the table is usually raised a few centimetres to prevent items from sliding off. Such tables are very practical in simple houses with few rooms, as they can easily be moved to any space in the household, or even outdoors, for a meal.

Food is served in *khǎn* (small lidded bowls), while slightly larger *kawng khâo* (cylindrical woven baskets) hold the sticky rice. Named for the bowls and table thus used, meals served in this fashion are known as *khǎn tòhk.* Nowadays only rural Northerners and a few culture revivalists in Chiang Mai eat khǎn tòhk style. However, tour companies and tourist hotels in Chiang Mai and Chiang Rai often arrange 'khǎn tòhk dinners' for their clients and guests, in which everyone eats in the Northern Thai style while watching performances of Northern Thai music and dance.

Because the North's relatively cooler climate is conducive to vegetable cultivation, Northern Thai cuisine *(aahǎan nĕua)* tends to feature a larger variety of vegetables than other regional cuisines. *Khâo nǐaw* (sticky rice) is preferred over the Central and Southern Thai–style white rice and, as in Northeastern Thailand and Laos, it is eaten with the hands. *Sôm-tam,* a tart and spicy salad usually made with green papaya, is very popular in the North but, unlike Northeastern Thais, Northerners tend to eat it as a between-meal snack rather than as part of a main meal.

Northern Thais make use of roots and herbs not found or seldom used elsewhere in the country. Culinary herbs with a somewhat bitter flavour are particularly favoured. The famous Northern soup *kaeng khae* – spicy, but not quite a curry – for example, contains a bitter acacia leaf called *cha-om* along with *phàk chii faràng* (a strong parsley-like leaf known in English as 'sawtooth coriander'), plus two types of eggplant known for their bitterness.

Sour tones are enjoyed in other Northern soups, so that *kaeng phàk hèuat* contains tamarind juice while *kaeng hó* features plenty of *nàw mái prîaw* (pickled bamboo shoots).

Neither bitter nor sour are two popular curries made from the heart of the banana palm *(kaeng yùak)* and jackfruit *(kaeng kha-nǔn).* Rich and fragrant *kaeng hangleh* (rich Burmese-style curry), a Burmese import, is popular at rural weddings and funerals.

Sausages of various kinds are famous in the North, especially *sâi ùa,* one of the most popular food items requested by Thais visiting from other regions. To make sâi ùa, Northerners make a typical Thai curry paste of dried chillies, garlic, shallots, lemongrass and kaffir-lime peel, blend it with ground pork, stuff it into pork intestines and then fry it to produce a spicy red sausage.

Another sausage, *nǎem mâw* (pot sausage) requires no cooking. Instead, ground pork, pork rind and cooked sticky rice are mixed with salt, garlic and chilli, then pressed into a clay pot and left to stand for exactly three days. After three days the nǎem mâw is wrapped in banana leaves and served or sold. The fermenting effects of the garlic and chilli 'cook' the mixture into a sour-tasting sausage, which must be eaten on the third day or disposed of before it spoils. Another sausage, *mǔu yâw,* is a more homogenised pork product with a look and texture resembling that of a large German frankfurter.

Three chilli pastes are considered quintessentially Northern. *Náam phrík nùm* (young chilli paste) is young fresh green chillies pounded together with roast eggplant into a thick green paste, into which are dipped steamed vegetables and fried pork rinds. To make *náam phrík àwng* the cook pounds together dried red chillies, ground pork, tomatoes, lemongrass and various other herbs and together then cooks them till the pork is done. Raw rather than steamed vegetables go best with this chilli dip.

Some people take to the food in Thailand immediately while others don't; Thai dishes can be pungent and spicy – lots of garlic and chillies are used, especially *phrík khîi*

nǔu (literally, mouse-shit peppers; these are the small torpedo-shaped devils that can be pushed aside if you are timid about red-hot curries).

Northern Style

The third, *náam phrík náam puu*, makes liberal use of *náam puu* (*nâam pǔu* in Northern Thai) a Northern Thai condiment made by pounding small field crabs into a paste and then cooking the paste with water till it becomes a slightly sticky black liquid. Many faràng visitors mistakenly believe that náam puu is uncooked and therefore unsafe to eat; whether they'll find it appetising even knowing it's cooked is another story. Mixed with shallots, garlic and dried chillies, it makes a good chilli dip best enjoyed with hot sticky rice and bamboo shoots.

A less well known Northern chilli dip, *náam phrík khàa*, is a bright red concoction redolent with galangal. It's often served with steamed or roasted fresh mushrooms. Fresh mushrooms – which are abundant just after the rainy season in October and November – also crop up on khon meuang menus as tasty *yam hèt hǎwm* (shitake mushroom yam) and *khài phàt hǔu nǔu* (eggs stirfried with mouse-ear mushrooms).

Although noodle dishes are popular all over Thailand, the North could be called the Noodle Crossroads of Thailand, since the region's mix of Yunnanese, Shan and Burmese heritages has produced a variety of *kǔaytǐaw* (rice noodles) and *khanǒm jiin* (literally, Chinese pastry; thin rice noodles) unparalleled elsewhere in the kingdom. In Chiang Mai the best-known local speciality of any kind is probably *khâo sawy*, a delicious bowl of wheat noodles with chicken or beef curry and flat, squiggly, egg noodles. It's served with small saucers of shallot wedges, sweet-spicy pickled cabbage, lime and a thick red chilli sauce. Noodle historians argue about whether this dish's origin is Shan or Yunnanese. Although the name may have come from a similar Shan noodle dish known in Myanmar as *hkauk swe*, the *jiin haw* (Chinese Muslims from Yunnan) seem to have been the original khâo sawy vendors in Chiang Mai. The jiin haw still command two of the best khâo sawy shops in town (near the Ban Haw Mosque), close to the very spot where the jiin haw mule caravans of yore used to tie up.

Those in the mood for more historical food debate can contemplate the origins of *khanǒm jiin náam ngíaw*. The name suggests Shan origins (*ngíaw* – alternately 'endearing' or 'pejorative', depending on the context – is a Northern Thai word referring to people of Shan descent); but once again it seems to be the local Yunnanese who most pride themselves on this dish, particularly in Mae Salong, a mountain village in Chiang Rai Province well known for its resident Yunnanese population. Recipes vary, but it commonly consists of pork rib meat, tomatoes and black bean sauce fried with a curry paste of chillies, coriander root, lemongrass, galangal, turmeric, shallots, garlic and shrimp paste. The resulting melange is served over fresh khanǒm jiin.

For a noodle that many people consider primarily Chinese, *wún sên* finds its way into a surprising number of dishes in the North, including *kaeng phàk wǎan* (a Northern soup with 'sweet greens'), kaeng yùak (curry made from banana-palm hearts), kaeng hó (soup with pickled bamboo shoots) and *phàt wún sên* (cellophane noodles stirfried with nǎem and eggs).

In the small Utaradit district of Laplae, restaurants specialise in *mìi pan*, a spicy mix of thin rice noodles, bean sprouts and coriander leaf wrapped into a rice-paper roll. It's very reminiscent of Vietnamese spring rolls, and since a majority of Laplae residents have Lao ancestry, it's likely there's some kind of connection. Slightly more common throughout the middle North is *kǔaytǐaw hâeng sùkhǒthai* (Sukhothai dry rice noodles), thin rice noodles served in a bowl with peanuts, barbecued pork, ground dried chilli, green beans and bean sprouts.

Almost all Thai food is cooked with fresh ingredients, particularly herbs. Plenty of lime juice, lemon grass and fresh coriander leaf are added to give the food its characteristic tang, and fish sauce (*náam plaa*, generally made from anchovies) or shrimp paste *(kà-pì)* to make it salty. Northern Thai cooking, however, tends to use less shrimp paste than Central or Southern Thai cuisine.

Other common seasonings include galanga root *(khàa)*, black pepper, three kinds of basil, ground peanuts (more often a condiment), tamarind juice *(náam mákhǎam)*, ginger *(khǐng)* and coconut milk *(kà-thí)*. The Thais eat a lot of what could be called Chinese food (there has always been a large Chinese migrant population), which is generally, but not always, less spicy.

Rice *(khâo)* is eaten with most meals; *kin khâo* (to eat) literally means 'eat rice'. Thais can be very picky about their rice, insisting on the right temperature and cooking times. Ordinary white rice is called *khâo jâo* and there are many varieties and grades. The finest quality Thai rice is known as *khâo hǎwm málí* (jasmine-scented rice) for its sweet, inviting smell when cooked.

Native Northern Thais prefer 'sticky' or glutinous rice (called *khâo nǐaw* in general, but *khâo nêung* in the North).

Where to Eat

Many small restaurants and food stalls do not have menus, so it is worthwhile memorising a standard repertoire of dishes. Most provinces have their own local specialities in addition to the standards and you might try asking for 'whatever is good', allowing the proprietors to choose for you. Of course, you might get stuck with a large bill this way, but with a little practice in Thai social relations you may also get some very pleasing results.

The most economical places to eat – and the most dependable – are noodle shops *(ráan kǔaytǐaw)*, curry-and-rice shops *(ráan khâo kaeng)* and night markets *(talàat tôh rûng)*. Most towns and villages have at least one night market and several noodle and/or curry shops. The night markets in Chiang Mai have a reputation for overcharging (especially for large parties), and it helps to

speak Thai as much as possible. Curry shops are generally open for breakfast and lunch only, and are a very cheap source of nutritious food. Another common food venue in larger cities is the *ráan khâo tôm* (literally, boiled-rice shop), a type of Chinese-Thai restaurant that offers not just boiled rice soups *(khâo tôm)* but an assortment of *aahǎan taam sàng* (food made to order). In the better places, cooks pride themselves in being able to fix any Thai or Chinese dish you name. One attraction of ráan khâo tôm is that they tend to stay open late – some are even open 24 hours.

Sponsored by the Shell oil company, Thai food critic Thanad Sri bestows upon his favourite dishes at restaurants around Thailand a sign (called Shell Chuan Chim) bearing the outline of a green bowl next to the familiar Shell symbol, which is displayed outside the restaurant. It's not a foolproof guarantee; some restaurants hang onto their signs long after the kitchen has lowered its standards.

What to Eat

Thai food is served with a variety of condiments and sauces, especially fish sauce with sliced chillies, and any number of dipping sauces for particular dishes.

Except for 'rice plates' and noodle dishes, Thai meals are usually ordered family-style, ie, two or more people order together, sharing different dishes. Traditionally, the party orders one of each kind of dish, eg, one of chicken, one of fish, one of soup etc. One dish is generally large enough for two people. One or two extras may be ordered for a large party. If you come to eat alone at a Thai restaurant and order one of these 'entrees', you had better be hungry or know enough Thai to order a small portion. This latter alternative is not really very acceptable socially: Thais generally consider eating alone in a restaurant unusual – but then, as a foreigner you're an exception anyway.

A cheaper alternative is to order dishes 'over rice' *(râat khâo)*. Curry (kaeng) over rice is called *khâo kaeng*; in a standard curry shop khâo kaeng is only 15B to 20B a plate.

Another category of Thai food is called *kàp klâem* – dishes meant to be eaten while drinking alcoholic beverages. On some menus these are translated as 'snacks' or 'appetisers'. Typical kàp klâem include *thùa thâwt* (fried peanuts), *kài săam yàang* (literally, three kinds of chicken; a plate of chopped ginger, peanuts, mouse-shit peppers and bits of lime – to be mixed and eaten by hand) and various kinds of *yam* (Thai-style salads made with lots of chillies and lime juice).

See the Language chapter for more food vocabulary.

Vegetarian Food Those visitors who wish to avoid eating meat and seafood can be accommodated with some effort. Vegetarian restaurants are increasing in number throughout the country, thanks largely to Bangkok's ex-Governor Chamlong Srimuang, whose strict vegetarianism inspired a nonprofit chain of vegetarian restaurants *(ráan aahăan mangsawírát)* in Bangkok and several provincial capitals. Many of these are sponsored by the Asoke Foundation, an ascetic (some would say heretic) Theravada Buddhist sect that finds justification for vegetarianism in the Buddhist sutras. The food is usually served buffet-style and is very inexpensive – typically 7B to 15B per dish. Most of these restaurants are open only from 7am or 8am until noon daily.

Other easy, though less widespread, venues for vegetarian meals include Indian restaurants, which usually feature a vegetarian section on the menu. Currently Chiang Mai is the only city we've found with Indian restaurants. Chinese restaurants are also a good bet, since many Chinese Buddhists eat vegetarian food during Buddhist festivals.

More often than not, however, visiting vegetarians are left to their own devices at the average Thai restaurant. In Thai the magic words are *phŏm kin jeh* (for men) or *dì-chăn kin jeh* (women). Like other Thai phrases, it's important to get the tones right – the key word, jeh, should rhyme with the English 'jay' without the 'y'. Loosely translated this phrase means 'I eat only vegetarian food'. It might also be necessary to

follow with the explanation *phŏm/dì-chăn kin tàe phàk* (I eat only vegetables). Don't worry – this won't be interpreted to mean no rice, herbs or fruit.

In Thai culture, brown or unpolished rice *(khâo klâwng)* was traditionally reserved for prisoners, but nowadays it's occasionally available in vegetarian restaurants.

Chiang Mai has more vegetarian restaurants per capita than any city in Thailand, and in 1999 it hosted the World Vegetarian Congress.

DRINKS
Non-alcoholic Drinks
Fruit Juices & Shakes The incredible variety of fruits to be found in Thailand means a corresponding availability of nutritious juices and shakes. The all-purpose term for fruit juice is *náam phŏn-lá-mái*. Put *náam* (water or juice) together with the name of any fruit and you can get anything from *náam mánao* (lime juice) to *náam taeng moh* (watermelon juice). When a blender or extractor is used, fruit juices may be called *náam khán*, or squeezed juice (eg, *náam sàpparót khán* – pineapple juice; *náam sôm khán* – orange juice). When mixed in a blender with ice the result is *náam pon* (literally, mixed juice) as in *náam málákaw pon*, a papaya smoothie or shake. Night markets will often have vendors specialising in juices and shakes.

Thais prefer to drink most fruit juices with a little salt mixed in. Unless a vendor is used to serving faràng, your fruit juice or shake will come slightly salted. If you prefer unsalted fruit juices, specify *mâi sài kleua* (without salt).

Sugar cane juice *(náam âwy)* is a Thai favourite and a very refreshing accompaniment to curry-and-rice plates. Many small restaurants or food stalls that don't offer any other juices will have a supply of freshly squeezed náam âwy on hand.

Coffee Over the last 15 years or so, Nescafé and other instant coffees have made deep inroads into the Thai coffee culture at the expense of freshly ground coffee. Typical Thai restaurants, especially those in hotels, guesthouses and other tourist-oriented establishments, will usually serve instant coffee with packets of artificial, non-dairy creamer on the side. Upmarket hotels and coffee shops sometimes also offer filtered and espresso coffees at premium prices.

Traditionally, coffee in Thailand is locally grown, roasted by wholesalers, ground by vendors and filtered just before serving. Thai-grown coffee may not be as full and rich-tasting as gourmet Sumatran, Jamaican or Kona beans but it's still considerably tastier than Nescafé or other instant products. Northern Thailand grows the best coffees in Thailand, mostly arabica bean.

Sometimes restaurants or vendors with the proper accoutrements for making traditional filtered coffee will keep a supply of Nescafé just for foreigners (or moneyed Thais, since instant always costs a few baht more per cup than filtered). To get real Thai coffee ask for *kaafae thŭng* (literally, bag coffee) or *kaafae tôm* (boiled coffee), which refers to the traditional method of preparing coffee by filtering hot water through a bag-shaped cloth filter. Outdoor morning markets are the best places to find kaafae thŭng.

The usual kaafae thŭng is served mixed with sugar and sweetened condensed milk – if you want black coffee, say *kaafae dam*; if you don't want sugar, be sure to specify *mâi sài náam-taan* (without sugar).

Tea Both Indian-style (black) and Chinese-style (green or semi-cured) teas are commonly served in restaurants in Northern Thailand. The latter predominates in Chinese restaurants and is also the usual ingredient in *náam chaa*, the weak, often lukewarm tea-water traditionally served in Thai restaurants for free. The aluminium teapots you find on every table in the average restaurant are filled with náam chaa; ask for a plain glass *(kâew plào)* and you can drink as much of this stuff as you like at no charge. For iced náam chaa ask for a glass of ice (usually 1B) and pour your own; for fresh, undiluted Chinese tea, ask for *chaa jiin*.

Black tea, both the imported and Thai-grown kind, is usually available in the same restaurants or food stalls that serve real coffee. An order of *chaa ráwn* (hot tea) almost always results in a cup (or glass) of black tea with sugar and condensed milk. As with coffee you must specify when you order whether you want the tea with or without milk and sugar. (See the relevant phrases in the Coffee entry earlier.)

Some fine oolong-style teas are cultivated and cured in Northern Thailand, and are widely available in towns and cities throughout the region.

Water Water that has been purified for drinking purposes is simply called *náam dèum* (drinking water), whether boiled or filtered. *All* water offered to customers in restaurants or to guests in an office or home will be purified, so you needn't fret about the safety of taking a sip (see the Health section earlier in this chapter). In restaurants you can ask for *náam plào* (plain water), which is always either boiled or taken from a purified source; it's served by the glass at no charge or you can order by the bottle. A bottle of carbonated water (soda) costs about the same as a bottle of plain purified water, but the bottles are smaller.

Alcoholic Drinks

Drinking in Thailand can be quite expensive compared to other consumer activities. The Thai government has placed increasingly heavy taxes on liquor and beer, so that now nearly half the price you pay for a large beer is tax. Whether this is an effort to raise more tax revenue (the result has been a sharp decrease in the consumption of alcoholic beverages and a corresponding decrease in revenue) or to discourage consumption, drinking can wreak havoc with your budget. One large bottle (630mL) of Singha beer costs about 70% of the minimum daily wage of a Chiang Mai worker.

According to the UN's Food & Agriculture Organization (FAO), Thailand ranks fifth worldwide in consumption of alcohol, behind South Korea, the Bahamas, Taiwan and Bermuda, and well ahead of Portugal, Ireland and France.

Beer Only a few brands of beer are readily available all over Thailand. Advertised with such slogans as *pràthêht rao, bia rao* (Our Land, Our Beer), the Singha label is considered the quintessential 'Thai' beer by foreigners and locals alike. Pronounced *sǐng*, it claims about half the domestic market. Singha is a strong, hoppy-tasting brew thought by many to be the best beer brewed in Asia. The alcohol content is a heady 6%.

Kloster, similarly inspired by German brewing recipes, is a notch smoother and lighter with an alcohol content of 4.7% and generally costs about 5B or 10B more per bottle.

Boon Rawd Breweries, makers of Singha, also produce a lighter beer called Singha Gold that only comes in small bottles or cans; most people seem to prefer either Kloster or regular Singha to Singha Gold, which is a little on the bland side. Better is Singha's new canned 'draught beer' – if you like cans.

Carlsberg, jointly owned by Danish and Thai interests, waded into the market in the early 1990s and proved to be a strong contender. In its first two years of business Carlsberg managed to grab around 25% of the Thai market. Like Kloster, it has a smoother flavour than Singha.

As the beer wars heated up, Singha retaliated with advertisements suggesting that drinking a Danish beer was unpatriotic. Carlsberg responded by creating Beer Chang (Elephant Beer), which matches the hoppy taste of Singha but ratchets the alcohol content up to 7%. Beer Chang has managed to gain an impressive market share mainly because it retails at a significantly lower price than Singha and thus easily offers more bang per baht. Predictably, the next offensive in the war was launched with the marketing of Boon Rawd's new cheaper brand, Leo. Sporting a black-and-red leopard label, Leo costs only slightly more than Chang but is similarly high in alcohol. To differentiate the new product from the flavour of the competition, Boon Rawd gave Leo a maltier taste.

Other Thailand-produced, European-branded beers you'll find in larger cities include a dark beer called Black Tiger, malty-sweet Mittweida, Heineken and Amstel lager.

The Thai word for beer is *bia*; draught beer is *bia sòt*.

Spirits Rice whisky is a big favourite in Thailand and somewhat more affordable than beer for the average Thai. It has a sharp, sweet taste not unlike rum, with an alcohol content of 35%. The most famous brand is Mekong (pronounced *mâe khǒng*). In rural areas you'll find several other labels, including Kwangthong, Hong Thong, Hong Ngoen, Hong Yok and Hong Tho. Mekong costs around 120B for a large bottle *(klom)* or 60B for the flask-sized bottle *(baen)*. An even smaller bottle, the *kòk,* is occasionally available for 30B to 35B. The Hong brands are less expensive.

More expensive Thai whiskies appealing to the can't-yet-afford-Johnnie-Walker set include Blue Eagle whisky and Spey Royal whisky, each with 40% alcohol content. These come dressed up in shiny boxes, much like the expensive imported whiskies they're imitating.

One company in Thailand produces a true rum, ie, a distilled liquor made from sugar cane, called Sang Som. Alcohol content is 40% and the stock is supposedly aged. Sang Som costs several baht more than the rice whiskies, but for those who find Mekong and the like unpalatable, it is an alternative worth trying. Thais usually mix it with soda and lime, or with Coke and lime or with soda, Coke and lime together.

Other Liquor A cheaper alternative to whisky is *lâo khǎo* (white liquor), of which there are two broad categories: legal and bootleg. The legal kind is generally made from sticky rice and is produced for regional consumption. Like Mekong and its competitors, it is 35% alcohol, but sells for 50B to 60B per klom, or roughly half the price. The taste is sweet and raw and much more aromatic than the amber stuff – no amount of mixer will disguise the distinctive taste.

The illegal kinds are made from various agricultural products, including sugar-palm sap, coconut milk, sugar cane, taro and sticky rice. In Northern Thailand almost all lâo khǎo is made from sticky rice. Alcohol content may vary from as little as 10% or 12% to as much as 95%. Also known as *lâo thèuan* (jungle liquor), this is the drink of choice for many Thais who can't afford the heavy government liquor taxes; prices vary but 10B to 15B worth of the stronger concoctions will intoxicate three or four people. These types of home-brew or moonshine are generally taken straight with pure water as a chaser. In smaller towns almost all garage-type restaurants (except, of course, Muslim restaurants) keep some under the counter for sale. Sometimes roots and herbs are added to jungle liquor to enhance flavour and colour.

Herbal liquors are somewhat fashionable throughout the North and can be found at roadside vendors, small pubs and in a few guesthouses. These liquors are made by soaking various herbs, roots, seeds, fruit and bark in lâo khǎo to produce a range of concoctions called *lâo yaa dawng*. Many of the yaa dawng preparations are purported to have specific health-enhancing qualities. Some of them taste fabulous, while others are rank.

Wine Thais are becoming increasingly interested in wine-drinking, but still manage only a minuscule average consumption of one glass per capita per year. Wines imported from France, Italy, the USA, Australia, Chile and other countries are available in restaurants and wine shops, but a 340% government tax makes them out of reach for most of us – or, at the very least, a poor bargain. If the government drops the tax, wine could become very fashionable in Thailand.

Various enterprises have attempted to produce wine in Thailand, most often with disastrous results. However, a successful wine was recently produced from a winery called Chateau de Loei, near Phu Reua in Loei Province. Dr Chaiyut, the owner, spent considerable time and money studying Western wine-making methods; his first vintage, a Chenin Blanc, is quite a drinkable wine. It's available at many of the finer restaurants in Chiang Mai.

ENTERTAINMENT

Bars

Northern Thailand has far fewer bars per capita than Bangkok, or even Central or Southern Thailand. Chiang Mai has more bars than anywhere else in the North, followed by Chiang Rai and Lampang. Outside cities, for the most part the closest you'll come to a bar is the rustic Thai interpretation of a karaoke lounge.

In mid-2001 the Thai government, prompted by Prime Minister Thaksin Shinawatra, mandated that all bars had to close by midnight. This was amended to 2am after it became apparent that tens of thousands of Thai workers were losing their jobs because people preferred to party later at private venues, and thus stopped going to clubs. Some bars get around the 2am closing but in most cases the law is strictly upheld.

Live Music

A handful of clubs in Chiang Mai have live music, often very good – see the Chiang Mai chapter for details.

In other towns in the North, live music is much less common, unless you count the occasional 'sing-song' cafe (the Thais simply call them *khaa-feh* – cafes) where a succession of untrained female singers take turns fronting a two- or three-piece band. Small groups of men sit at tables ogling the girls while putting away prodigious amounts of whisky. For the price of a few drinks, the men can invite one of the singers to sit at their table for a while.

The small town of Pai, about halfway between Chiang Mai and Mae Hong Son, is know for jam sessions at various places around town, as it's one of the few towns where no-one seems to care what time the bars close.

Discos

Discos can be found in Chiang Mai and a few other spots in the North, mostly attached to tourist or luxury hotels. The main clientele is Thai, although foreigners are welcome. Some provincial discos retain female staff as professional dance partners for male entertainment, but discos are generally considered fairly respectable nightspots for couples.

Thai law permits discos to stay open till 2am.

Cinemas

Chiang Mai boasts several cinema houses where the offerings tend towards US and European shoot-em-ups mixed with Thai comedies and romances, along with the occasional more serious film. In other provincial capitals violent action pictures are always a big draw. English-language films are only shown with their original soundtracks in Chiang Mai; elsewhere, all foreign films are dubbed in Thai. Ticket prices range from 70B to 100B.

Every film in Thailand begins with a playback of the royal anthem, accompanied by pictures of the royal family projected onto the big screen. All viewers are expected to stand during the royal anthem.

SPECTATOR SPORTS
Muay Thai (Thai Boxing)

Almost anything goes in this martial sport, both in the ring and in the stands. If you don't mind the violence (in the ring), a Thai boxing match is worth attending for the pure spectacle – the wild musical accompaniment, the ceremonial beginning of each match and the frenzied betting throughout the stadium.

Thai boxing is also telecast on Channel 7 from noon to 2pm every Saturday afternoon, which explains the quiet streets at these times.

History Most of what is known about the early history of Thai boxing comes from Burmese accounts of warfare between Myanmar and Thailand during the 15th and 16th centuries. The earliest reference (AD 1411) mentions a ferocious style of unarmed combat that decided the fate of Thai kings. A later description tells how Nai Khanom Tom, Thailand's first famous boxer and a prisoner of war in Burma, gained his freedom by roundly defeating a dozen Burmese warriors before the Burmese court. To this day, many Thais attribute their standing as the sole unconquered Asian nation to muay thai.

King Naresuan the Great (reigned 1590–1605) was apparently a top-notch boxer himself, and he made muay thai a required part of military training. Later, another Thai king, Phra Chao Seua (the Tiger King) further promoted Thai boxing as a national sport by encouraging prize fights and the development of training camps in the early 18th century. There are accounts of massive wagers and bouts to the death during this time. Phra Chao Seua himself is said to have been an incognito participant in many of the matches. Combatants' fists were wrapped in thick horsehide for maximum impact with minimum knuckle damage. They also used cotton soaked in glue and ground glass and, later, hemp. Tree bark and seashells were used to protect the groin from lethal kicks.

No-one trained in any other martial art has been able to defeat a ranking Thai *nák muay* (fighter trained in muay thai) and many martial-art aficionados consider the Thai style the ultimate in hand-to-hand fighting. On one famous occasion, Hong Kong's top five kung fu masters were all dispatched by knock-out in less than 6½ minutes. Hong Kong, China, Singapore, Taiwan, Korea, Japan, the USA, Netherlands, Germany and France have all sent their best and none of the challengers has yet beaten a top-ranked Ratchadamnoen/Lumphini Stadium Thai boxer (except in non-stadium-sponsored bouts). American Dale Kvalheim trained in muay thai and won a Northeastern championship around 25 years ago, becoming the first non-Thai to seize a regional title – but Isan stadiums are a far cry from Bangkok's two muay thai crucibles, Ratchadamnoen and Lumphini.

Modern Muay Thai The high incidence of death and physical injury led the Thai government to institute a ban on muay thai in the 1920s, but in the 1930s it was revived under a set of regulations based on the international Queensberry rules. Bouts were limited to five three-minute rounds separated with two-minute breaks. Contestants had to wear international-style gloves and trunks (always either red or blue) and their feet were taped – to this day no shoes are worn.

There are 16 weight divisions in Thai boxing, ranging from miniflyweight to heavyweight, with the best fighters said to be in the welterweight division. As in international-style boxing, matches take place on a 7.3-sq-metre canvas-covered floor with rope retainers supported by four padded posts, rather than in the traditional dirt circle.

In spite of these concessions to safety, today all surfaces of the body are still considered fair targets and any part of the body, except the head, may be used to strike an opponent. Common blows include high kicks to the neck, elbow thrusts to the face and head, knee hooks to the ribs and low crescent kicks to the calf. A contestant may even grasp an opponent's head between his hands and pull it down to meet an upward knee thrust. Punching is considered the weakest of all blows and kicking merely a way to 'soften up' one's opponent; knee and elbow strikes are decisive in most matches.

A Thai boxer's training and his relationship with his trainer are highly ritualised. When a boxer is considered ready for the ring, he is given a new name, usually with the name of the training camp as his surname. The relationship is perhaps best expressed in the *ram muay* (boxing dance) that precedes every match. The ram muay ceremony usually lasts about five minutes and expresses obeisance to the fighter's guru *(khruu)*, as well as to the guardian spirit of Thai boxing. This is done through a series of gestures and movements performed in rhythm to the ringside musical accompaniment of Thai oboe *(pìi)*, and percussion. Each boxer works out his own dance, in conjunction with his trainer and in accordance with the style of his particular camp.

The woven headbands and armbands fighters wear into the ring are sacred ornaments that bestow blessings and divine protection; the headband is removed after the ram muay ceremony, but the armband, which contains a small Buddha image, is worn throughout the match. After the bout begins the fighters continue to bob and weave in rhythm until the action begins to heat up. The musicians continue to play throughout the match and the volume and tempo of the music rise and fall along with the events in the ring.

Coloured belts denoting training ranks, such as those issued by karate schools, do not exist in muay thai.

Most provincial capitals in the North have at least one muay thai training camp, and some hold public matches at local sports stadiums.

Each year around the lunar New Year (Songkran) in April, near the town of Mae Sot on the Thai-Myanmar border, a top Thai fighter challenges a Burmese fighter of similar class from the other side of Mae Nam Moei; it's a no-holds barred, hemp-fisted battle that ends only after one of the opponents surrenders or is knocked out.

Tàkrâw

Tàkrâw, sometimes called Siamese football in old English texts, refers to games in which a woven rattan ball about 12cm in diameter is kicked around. The rattan (or sometimes plastic) ball itself is called a *lûuk tàkrâw.* Popular in several neighbouring countries, tàkrâw was introduced to the Southeast Asian Games by Thailand, and international championships tend to alternate between the Thais and Malaysians. The traditional way to play tàkrâw in Thailand is for players to stand in a circle (the size depends on the number of players) and simply try to keep the ball airborne by kicking it soccer-style. Points are scored for style, difficulty and variety of kicking manoeuvres.

A popular variation on tàkrâw – and the one used in international competitions – is played like volleyball, with a net, but with only the feet and head permitted to touch the ball. It's amazing to see the players perform aerial pirouettes, spiking the ball over the net with their feet. Another variation has players kicking the ball into a hoop

4.5m above the ground – basketball with feet, and no backboard!

SHOPPING

Because it's the centre of the nation's handicraft industry, Northern Thailand is the best region in the country to shop for Thai-made goods.

Always haggle to get the best price, except in department stores (see Tipping & Bargaining in the Money section, earlier in this chapter, for some pointers). And don't go shopping in the company of touts, tour guides or friendly strangers, as they will inevitably – no matter what they say – take a commission on anything you buy, thus driving prices up.

Textiles

Fabric may be the best all-round buy in Thailand. Thai silk is considered the best in the world – the coarse weave and soft texture of the silk means it is more easily dyed than harder, smoother silks, resulting in brighter colours and a unique lustre. Silk can be purchased cheaply in the North, and excellent and reasonably priced tailor shops can make your choice of fabric into almost any pattern. A Thai-silk suit should cost around 4500B to 6500B. Chinese silk is available at about half the cost – 'washed' Chinese silk makes inexpensive, comfortable shirts or blouses.

Cottons are also a good deal – common items like the phâakhamáa and the phâasîn make great tablecloths and curtains. Good ready-made cotton shirts are available, such as the *mâw hâwm* (Thai work shirt) and the *kúay hâeng* (Shan-style shirt). See the sections on Pasang in the Around Chiang Mai chapter for places to see cotton-weaving.

In the North you can find Lanna-style textiles based on intricate Thai Daeng, Thai Dam and Thai Lii patterns from Nan, Laos and China's Xishuangbanna. Chiang Mai has become a centre for antique textiles from all over the region.

The *mǎwn khwǎan*, a hard, triangle-shaped pillow, makes a good souvenir and comes in many sizes. Some are made in the North, some in the Northeast, but all are available in Chiang Mai's Night Bazaar or Talat Worarot, as well in as other markets. Likewise fairly nice batik *(paa-té)* made in Southern Thailand – similar to the batik found in Malaysia – can also be found in the North.

Clothing

Tailor-made and ready-made clothes are relatively inexpensive. If you're not particular about style you could pick up an entire wardrobe of travelling clothes in Pai or at Chiang Mai's Night Bazaar for what you'd pay for one designer shirt in New York, Paris or Milan.

You're more likely to get a good fit if you use a tailor, but be wary of the quickie 24-hour tailor shops; the clothing is often made of inferior fabric or the poor tailoring means the arms start falling off after three weeks' wear. It's best to ask Thais or long-time foreign residents for a tailor recommendation and then go for two or three fittings.

Shoulder Bags

Thai shoulder bags *(yâam)* come in many varieties, some woven by hill tribes, others by the Northern Thai cottage industry. The best are made by the Lahu hill tribes, whom the Thais call Musoe. The weaving is more skilful and the bags tend to last longer than those made by other tribes. For an extra-large yâam, the Karen-made bag is a good choice and is easy to find in the Mae Sot and Mae Hong Son areas. These days many hill tribes are copying patterns from tribes other than their own.

Overall, Chiang Mai has the best prices and selection of standard shoulder bags. Prices range from 70B for a cheaply made bag to 200B for something special.

Antiques

Northern Thailand has become a good source of Thai antiques – prices are about half what you'd typically pay in Bangkok. Real antiques cannot be taken out of Thailand without a permit from the Fine Arts Department. No Buddha image, new or old, may be exported without permission –

again, refer to the Fine Arts Department or, in some cases, the Department of Religious Affairs, under the Ministry of Education. Too many private collectors smuggling and hoarding Siamese art (Buddhas in particular) around the world have led to strict controls. See Customs earlier in this chapter for more information on the export of art objects and antiques.

Chiang Mai is the centre for antique dealers in Northern Thailand. However, you will also find the occasional antique shop in smaller towns, and along roadsides between towns – in fact, some of the latter shops sometimes sell to the Chiang Mai shops.

Jewellery

Thailand is the world's largest exporter of gems and ornaments, rivalled only by India and Sri Lanka. The International Colorstones Association (ICA) relocated from Los Angeles to Bangkok's Charn Issara Tower several years ago, and the World Federation of Diamond Bourses (WFDB) has established a Bourse in Bangkok – two events that recognise Thailand as the world trade-and-production centre for precious stones.

Rough stone sources in Thailand have decreased dramatically and stones are now imported from Australia, Sri Lanka and other countries to be cut, polished and traded. Native stones, such as sapphires, make up only about 25% of the business. At least 40% of all gem-related exports consist of diamond products, all of which are imported rough and then finished in Thailand by expert Thai gem-cutters. One of the results of this remarkable growth – in Thailand the gem trade has increased 10% every year for the last two decades – is that the prices are rising rapidly.

If you know what you are doing you can make some really good buys in both unset gems and finished jewellery. Gold ornaments are sold at a good rate, as labour costs are low. The best bargains in gems are jade, rubies and sapphires.

You'll face the least risk if you buy from reputable dealers only, preferably members of the Jewel Fest Club, a guarantee program

established by the TAT and the Thai Gem and Jewellery Traders Association (TGJTA). When you purchase an item of jewellery from a shop that is identified as a member of the Jewel Fest Club, a certificate detailing your purchase will be issued. This guarantees a refund less 10% if you return the merchandise to the point of sale within 30 days. A refund less 20% is guaranteed if the items are returned after 30 days but within 45 days of purchase. You can obtain a list of members direct from Jewel Fest Club (☎ 022 353 039, 022 675 233/7) or from the TAT. However, few shops in the North are Jewel Fest Club members, so you'd best visit the TAT in advance to see if they have list of places to avoid – they often do.

The biggest centres in Northern Thailand for gem stones native to Thailand, neighbouring Myanmar and Cambodia, include Mae Sot and Mae Sai, both Thai towns on the Myanmar border.

Warning Be wary of special 'deals' that are offered for one day only or that set you up as a 'courier' in which you're promised big money. Many travellers end up losing big. Shop around and don't be hasty. Remember: There's no such thing as a 'government sale' or 'factory price' at a gem or jewellery shop; the Thai government does not own or manage any gem or jewellery shops.

See the boxed text 'Scams' in this chapter for detailed warnings on gem fraud.

Hill-Tribe Crafts

Interesting embroidery, clothing, bags (see Shoulder Bags earlier in this section) and jewellery from the Northern provinces can be bought in Chiang Mai at the Night Bazaar, and at smaller venues in other Northern towns, as well as at various tourist shops around the North.

In Chiang Mai there are shops selling handicrafts all along Thanon Tha Phae and Thanon Loi Khroh, and there is a shop sponsored by missionaries near Prince Royal College. There is a branch of the Queen's Hillcrafts Foundation in Chiang

Rai. It's worth bargaining and shopping around for the best prices.

Lacquerware

Northern Thailand produces some good lacquerware, and also sells a lot that is made in Myanmar and sold along the northern Myanmar border. Try Mae Sot, Mae Sariang and Mae Sai for the best buys.

Today's styles originated in 11th-century Chiang Mai. In 1558 Myanmar's King Bayinnaung captured a number of Chiang Mai lacquer artisans and brought them to Bago in central Myanmar to establish the tradition of incised lacquerware. Lacquer (not to be confused with lac, which comes from an insect), comes from the *Melanorrhea usitata* tree and in its most basic form is mixed with paddy-husk ash to form a light, flexible, waterproof coating over bamboo frames.

To make a lacquerware object, a bamboo frame is first woven. If the item is top quality, only the frame is bamboo; horse or donkey hairs will be wound round the frame. In lower-quality lacquerware the whole object is made from bamboo. The lacquer is then coated over the framework and allowed to dry. After several days it is sanded down with ash from rice husks, and another coating of lacquer is applied. A high-quality item may have seven layers of lacquer.

The lacquerware is engraved and painted, then polished to remove the paint from everywhere except in the engravings. Multi-coloured lacquerware is produced by repeated applications. From start to finish it can take five or six months to produce a high-quality piece of lacquerware, which may have as many as five colours. Flexibility is one characteristic of good lacquerware: A top-quality bowl can have its rim squeezed together until the sides meet without suffering damage. The quality and precision of the engraving is another thing to look for.

Lacquerware is made into bowls, trays, plates, boxes, containers, cups, vases and many other everyday items. Octagonal folding tables are also popular lacquerware items.

Nielloware

This art came from Europe via Nakhon Si Thammarat and has been cultivated in Thailand for over 700 years. Engraved silver is inlaid with niello – an alloy of lead, silver, copper and sulphur – to form striking black-and-silver jewellery designs. Nielloware is one of Thailand's best buys, and even though it's a Southern Thai craft, you'll find it for sale in shops in the North.

Ceramics

Many kinds of hand-thrown pottery, old and new, are available throughout the kingdom. The best-known ceramics are the greenish Thai celadon products from the Sukhothai-Si Satchanalai area, and Central Thailand's *benjarong* (five-colour) style. The latter is based on Chinese patterns while the former is a Thai original that has been imitated throughout China and Southeast Asia. Rough, unglazed pottery from the North and Northeast can also be very appealing.

Other Crafts

Under the queen's Supplementary Occupations & Related Techniques (SUPPORT) foundation, a number of regional crafts from around Thailand have been successfully revived. *Málaeng tháp* collages and sculptures are made by artfully cutting and assembling the metallic, multicoloured wings and carapaces of female wood-boring beetles *(Sternocera aequisignata)*, harvested after they die at the end of their reproductive cycle. They can be found in craft shops all over the north.

For 'Damascene ware' *(khraam)*, gold and silver wire is hammered into a cross-hatched steel surface to create exquisitely patterned bowls and boxes. Look for them in Chiang Mai's Central Department Store and in more-upmarket craft shops.

Yaan líphao is a type of intricately woven basket made from a hardy grass in Southern Thailand. Ever since the queen and other female members of the royal family began carrying delicate yaan líphao purses, they've been a Thai fashion staple. It is found in many of the same places that sell khraam.

Furniture

Rattan and hardwood furniture items are often good buys and can be made to order. Not surprisingly, Chiang Mai has the best selection in the North. With the ongoing success of teak farming and teak recycling, teak furniture has once again become a bargain in Thailand if you find the right places. Asian rosewood is also a good buy.

Fake or Pirated Goods

In Chiang Mai there is black-market street trade in fake designer goods, particularly Benetton pants and sweaters; Lacoste and Ralph Lauren polo shirts; NBA-franchise T-shirts; Levi's jeans; Reebok sneakers; and Rolex, Dunhill and Cartier watches. Knockoff logo T-shirts of almost any brand are also big. No-one pretends they're the real thing, at least not the vendors.

In some cases foreign name brands are produced under licence in Thailand and represent good value. A pair of legally produced Levi's 501s, for example, typically costs US$10 from a Thai street vendor, and US$35 to US$45 in the company's home town of San Francisco! Careful examination of the product usually reveals tell-tale characteristics that confirm or deny its authenticity.

Unlicensed video compact discs (VCDs) are another illegal bargain in Northern Thailand, mainly Chiang Mai. The movies are 'pirated', ie, no royalties are paid to the copyright owners. Average prices are from 100B to 200B per VCD. We've also seen music CDs that may be pirated for sale in Chiang Mai's Night Bazaar.

At Computer Plaza in Chiang Mai, several shops sell MP3 discs on which as many as 11 or 12 CDs' worth of music is compressed onto one CD. To play these CDs you'll need an MP3 player (or you can play them on a computer CD drive with the proper software).

Other Goods

Chiang Mai is famous for its markets – Worarot, Ton Lam Yai, Ton Phayom, Thanin and, of course, the Night Bazaar. Even if you don't want to spend any money, they're great places to wander around.

For interesting shops with all of the aforementioned goods, the two main areas in Chiang Mai are Thanon Tha Phae and Thanon Loi Khroh. Two big shopping centres, Kat Suan Kaew and Airport Plaza, contain higher-end shops with clothing, electronics and houseware.

Getting There & Away

AIR

Although several international airlines fly direct to Chiang Mai (see Chiang Mai International Airport later), the majority of visitors to Thailand who arrive by air do so via Bangkok.

The per-air-kilometre expense of getting to Bangkok varies, depending on your point of departure, but in general Bangkok is one of the cheapest cities in the world to fly out of, due to the Thai government's loose restrictions on air fares and the high level of competition between airlines and travel agencies. The result is that with a little shopping around you can come up with some real bargains. If you can find a cheap one-way ticket to Bangkok, take it, because you are virtually guaranteed to find a ticket of equal or lesser cost for the return trip once you get there.

From most places around the world your best bet will be budget, excursion or promotional fares – when speaking to airlines ask for the various fares in that order. Each carries its own set of restrictions and it's up to you to decide which set works best in your case. Fares fluctuate, but in general they are cheaper from September to April (northern hemisphere) and from March to November (southern hemisphere).

Fares listed in this chapter should serve as a guideline only – don't count on them staying this way for long.

Airports & Airlines

In Northern Thailand only Chiang Mai fields international flights. Chiang Rai International Airport, though designated 'international', fields planes only to and from Bangkok so far, but Thai Airways International (THAI) hopes to establish international routes to and from other Asian capitals over the next few years. In 2001 Bangkok Airways announced a Sukhothai–Siem Reap flight but so far it has yet to materialise.

Bangkok International Airport A district directly north of Bangkok known as

Don Muang has been the main hub for international air traffic in and out of Thailand since 1931. Today it's home to Bangkok International Airport, the busiest airport in Southeast Asia.

A second airport, New Bangkok International Airport (NBIA), is intended to replace Don Muang at Nong Ngu Hao, 20km east of Bangkok, in 2004.

The national carrier, THAI, dominates inbound and outbound air traffic, but 80 other international airlines also fly in and out of Bangkok. Bangkok Airways flies between Bangkok and Phnom Penh and Siem Reap in Cambodia.

During the last decade the facilities at Bangkok International Airport have undergone a US$200 million redevelopment, including the construction of two new international terminals that are among the most modern and convenient in Asia. Immigration procedures have also been sped up, although it can still be slow-going during peak arrival times (11pm to midnight). Baggage claim is usually pretty efficient.

The foreign currency booths on the ground floor of the arrival hall and in the departure lounge of both terminals give a good rate of exchange, so there's no need to wait till you're in the city centre to change money. Each of these banks also operates automated teller machines (ATMs) in the arrival and departure halls.

Left-luggage facilities (70B per piece for under 24 hours, after which the charge is 35B for every 12 hours) are available in the departure hall in both terminals. Both are open 24 hours. In the transit lounge of Terminal 1, clean day rooms with washing and toilet facilities can be rented for US$86 a double per eight hours. Less expensive rooms without bathrooms are available for US$31 per four-hour block.

Hotel Reservations The hotel reservation desks operated by the Thai Hotels Association (THA) at the back of the arrival hall in both terminals offer a selection of accommodation options not only for Bangkok but for Chiang Mai and other Northern Thai locations. However, the listings comprise only places above the guesthouse price bracket (roughly 900B and above). THA staff can often arrange room rates well below normal walk-in rates.

There have been reports that reservations desks occasionally claim a hotel is full when it isn't, just to move you into a hotel that pays higher commissions. If you protest, the staff may ask you to speak to the 'reservations desk' on the phone – usually an accomplice who confirms the hotel is full. Dial the hotel yourself if you want to be sure.

There are usually one or two other desks in the arrival hall offering similar services, but THA seems to be the most reliable.

If you're continuing on to Chiang Mai or other destinations in the North, you'll have to proceed to the domestic terminal, either on foot via a connecting enclosed, air-con bridge, or via one of the free airport shuttle buses.

Terminal Shuttle THAI operates free air-con shuttle buses over two routes between the international and domestic terminals. Both routes go between Terminal 1 and the domestic terminal, so if you're just going between these buildings you can jump on any bus that comes along. In addition, Route A-1 continues to Cargo Agent 1 building and the VIP rooms building. This shuttle runs every 20 minutes from 5.20pm to 11pm daily.

Route A-2 adds stops at the customs bureau building, the four-storey car park, Cargo Agent 4 building and the office of AAT storage division. This shuttle starts at 6am and runs hourly between 6am and 5pm on weekdays.

Airlines Offices in Bangkok Following is a list of major airline offices in Bangkok.

Aeroflot (☎ 022 511 223) Regent House, Thanon Ratchadamri

Air India (☎ 022 350 557/8) 12th floor, One Pacific Place, 140 Thanon Sukhumvit

Air New Zealand (☎ 022 548 440) 14th floor, Sindhorn Bldg, 130–132 Thanon Withayu

All Nippon Airways (ANA; ☎ 022 385 121) 2nd & 4th floors, CP Tower, 313 Thanon Silom

American Airlines (☎ 022 541 270) 518/5 Thanon Ploenchit

Asiana Airlines (☎ 026 568 610–7) 18th floor, Ploenchit Center Bldg, Soi 2 Sukhumvit

Bangkok Airways (☎ 022 293 434, 022 534 014) 60 Queen Sirikit National Convention Centre, Thanon Ratchadaphisek Tat Mai, Khlong Toey

Biman Bangladesh Airlines (☎ 022 357 643/4) Chongkolnee Bldg, 56 Thanon Surawong

British Airways (☎ 026 361 700) 990 Thanon Phra Ram IV (Rama IV)

Canadian Airlines International (☎ 022 514 521, 022 548 376) Maneeya Center Bldg, 518/5 Thanon Ploenchit

Cathay Pacific Airways (☎ 022 630 606) 11th floor, Ploenchit Tower, 898 Thanon Ploenchit

China Airlines (☎ 022 535 733; reservations ☎ 022 534 242) 4th floor, Peninsula Plaza, 153 Thanon Ratchadamri

China Southwest Airlines (☎ 026 347 848–52) Ground floor, Bangkok Union Insurance Bldg, 175–177 Thanon Surawong

Emirates (022 607 402) 54 Sukhumvit 21

EVA Airways (☎ 023 673 388; reservations ☎ 022 400 890) 2nd floor, Green Tower, 3656/4–5 Thanon Phra Ram IV

Garuda Indonesia (☎ 022 856 470–3) 27th floor, Lumphini Tower, 1168/77 Thanon Phra Ram IV

Gulf Air (☎ 022 547 931–4) 12th floor, Maneeya Center Bldg, 518/5 Thanon Ploenchit

Japan Airlines (JAL; ☎ 026 925 185/6; reservations ☎ 026 925 151–60) JAL Bldg, 254/1 Thanon Ratchadaphisek

KLM-Royal Dutch Airlines (☎ 026 791 100, ext 2) 19th floor, Thai Wah Tower II, 21/133–4 Thanon Sathon Tai

Korean Air (☎ 022 670 985/6; reservations ☎ 026 350 465–72) 9th floor, Kongboonma Bldg, 699 Thanon Silom

Kuwait Airways (☎ 026 412 864–7) 12th floor, RS Tower, 121/50–51 Thanon Ratchadaphisek

Lao Aviation (☎ 022 369 822/3) Ground floor, Silom Plaza, 491/17 Thanon Silom

Lufthansa Airlines (☎ 022 642 484; reservations ☎ 022 642 400) 18th floor, Q House, Asoke Bldg, 66 Soi 21, Thanon Sukhumvit

Malaysia Airlines (☎ 022 630 520–32; reservations ☎ 022 630 565–71) 20th floor, Ploenchit Tower, 898 Thanon Ploenchit

Myanmar Airways International (☎ 026 300 334–8) 23rd floor, Jewelry Trade Center Bldg, 919/298 Thanon Silom

Northwest Airlines (☎ 022 540 789) 4th floor, Peninsula Plaza, 153 Thanon Ratchadamri

Qantas Airways (☎ 026 361 770; reservations ☎ 026 361 747) 14th floor, Abdulrahim Place, 990 Thanon Phra Ram IV

Royal Air Cambodge (☎ 026 532 261; reservations ☎ 026 532 261–6) 17th floor, Pacific Place Bldg, 142 Thanon Sukhumvit

Royal Nepal Airlines (☎ 022 165 691–5) 9th floor, Phayathai Plaza Bldg, 128 Thanon Phayathai

Scandinavian Airlines (SAS; ☎ 022 600 444) 8th floor, Glas Haus Bldg, 1 Soi 25, Thanon Sukhumvit

Singapore Airlines (SIA; ☎ 022 365 301; reservations ☎ 022 360 440) 12th floor, Silom Center Bldg, 2 Thanon Silom

Thai Airways International (THAI; head office ☎ 025 130 121; reservations ☎ 022 800 060) 89 Thanon Viphavadi Rangsit; (☎ 022 343 100–19) 485 Thanon Silom; (☎ 022 880 060, 022 800 110) 6 Thanon Lan Luang; (☎ 022 152 020/1) Asia Hotel, 296 Thanon Phayathai; (domestic ☎ 025 352 081/2; international ☎ 025 236 121) Bangkok International Airport, Don Muang; (☎ 022 239 746–8) 3rd floor, Room 310–311, Grand China Bldg, 215 Thanon Yaowarat

United Airlines (☎ 022 530 559; reservations ☎ 022 530 558) 14th floor, Sindhorn Bldg, 130–132 Thanon Withayu

Vietnam Airlines (☎ 026 569 056–8) 7th floor, Ploenchit Center Bldg, Soi 2 Thanon Sukhumvit

Chiang Mai International Airport Although rather small, Chiang Mai International Airport (☎ 053 270 222–34) is well equipped with facilities for the traveller. Upstairs on the departure level is a branch of Suriwong Book Centre and a large restaurant operated by THAI, serving Thai, Chinese and international food. On the ground floor there are fast-food places, a post office and an international (IDD and Home Country Direct) phone office (open from 8.30am to 8pm).

Airline Offices in Chiang Mai THAI has regular flights to Chiang Mai from Singapore, Kuala Lumpur, Hong Kong, Beijing, Kunming, Yangon, Mandalay and Vientiane; and several other airlines operate regularly scheduled international flights to and from Chiang Mai. Airlines with offices in Chiang Mai include:

Air Mandalay (☎ 053 818 049, fax 053 818 051) 107 Doi Ping Mansion, 148 Thanon Charoen Prathet (for flights to Yangon and Mandalay)

Bangkok Airways (☎ 053 281 519, fax 053 281 520) 2nd floor, Chiang Mai International Airport (Siem Reap)

Lao Aviation (☎ 053 404 033, 053 223 401) Nakorn Ping Condo 1st floor, 2/115 Thanon Ratchapreuk (Vientiane, Luang Prabang)

Mandarin Airlines (☎ 053 201 268/9, fax 053 922 237) 2nd floor, Chiang Mai International Airport (Taipei)

Silk Air (☎ 053 276 459, 053 276 595, fax 053 276 549) Imperial Mae Ping Hotel, 153 Thanon Si Donchai (Singapore)

Thai Airways International (☎ 053 211 044–6) 240 Thanon Phra Pokklao

Buying Tickets

Although other Asian centres are now competitive with Bangkok and Chiang Mai as places to buy discounted airline tickets, Thailand is still a good place for shopping around, especially with the baht trading low against most hard currencies.

Travellers should note, however, that a few Thai travel agencies have shocking reputations. Taking money and then delaying or not coming through with the tickets, as well as providing tickets with limited validity periods or severe use-restrictions, are all part of the racket. There are a large number of perfectly honest agents (see the following recommendations for some suggestions), but beware of the rogues.

Charal Business Chiang Mai (☎ 053 252 050, 🇪 charaltr@loxinfo.co.th) 123 Thanon Chang Moi

Chiang Mai PM (☎ 053 275 067, 🇪 pmtravel@loxinfo.co.th) 55/1 Thanon Moon Muang

Mau Travel Service (☎ 053 821 022, 🇪 mautour@loxinfo.co.th) 82/1 Thanon Charoen Prathet

Air Passes THAI occasionally has on offer special four-coupon passes – available only outside Thailand for foreign currency purchases – with which you can book any four domestic flights for one fare of around US$199 (50% less for children under 12) as long as you don't repeat the same leg. Additional coupons cost US$49 each, but you may not exceed a total of eight coupons. Unless you plan carefully this isn't much of a saving, since it's hard to avoid repeating the same leg in and out of Bangkok. Also, the baht is so low these days that it's often cheaper to make domestic flying arrangements in Thailand rather than from abroad.

For more information on the four-coupon deal, known as the 'Amazing Thailand fare', inquire at any THAI office outside Thailand.

Booking Problems Booking flights in and out of Bangkok during the high season (December to March) can be difficult. For air travel during these months you should make your bookings as far in advance as possible.

Also, be sure to reconfirm return or ongoing tickets when you arrive in Thailand (THAI claims this isn't necessary with its tickets). Failure to reconfirm can mean losing your reservation.

Departure Tax

All passengers leaving Thailand on international flights are charged an international departure tax (officially called 'airport service charge') of 500B. The tax is not included in the price of air tickets, but is paid at the checkout counter. Only baht is accepted. Be sure to have enough baht left over at the end of your trip to pay this tax – otherwise you'll have to revisit one of the currency exchange booths.

The USA

Discount travel agents in the USA are known as consolidators (although you won't see a sign on the door saying Consolidator). San Francisco is the ticket consolidator capital of America, although some good deals can also be found in Los Angeles, New York and several other big cities.

Council Travel (☎ 800-226 8624, ⓦ www.counciltravel.com), America's largest student travel organisation, has around 60 offices in the USA. Visit the Web site or call for the office nearest you. STA Travel (☎ 800-777 0112, ⓦ www.statravel .com) has offices in Boston, Chicago, Miami, New York, Philadelphia, San Francisco and other major cities. Call the toll-free 800 number or visit its Web site for office locations.

One of the most reliable discounters is Avia Travel (☎ 800-950 AVIA, 510-558 2150, fax 558 2158, ⓔ sales@aviatravel .com, ⓦ www.aviatravel.com) at Suite E, 1029 Solano Ave, Albany CA 94706. Avia specialises in custom-designed round-the-world fares; check its Web site for the latest on offer. The agency sets aside a portion of its profits for Volunteers in Asia, a non-profit organisation that sends grassroots volunteers to work in Southeast Asia.

It is cheaper to fly to Bangkok and Chiang Mai via West Coast cities rather than from the East Coast. Return fares to Bangkok from the West Coast start from around US$750 or US$870 for a connecting flight to Chiang Mai. The airlines that generally offer the lowest fares include China Airlines, EVA Airways, Korean Air and THAI. Several of these airlines also fly out of New York, Dallas, Chicago and Atlanta – add another US$150 to US$250 to their lowest fares.

Canada

Canadian discount air ticket sellers are also known as consolidators and their air fares tend to be about 10% higher than those sold in the USA.

Travel CUTS (☎ 800-667 2887, ⓦ www .travelcuts.com) is Canada's national student travel agency and has offices in all major cities.

Return low-season fares from Vancouver to Bangkok start from around C$1450 on Eva Airways or China Airlines, via Taipei. Travellers living in eastern Canada will usually find the best deals out of New York or San Francisco, adding fares from Toronto or Montreal (see The USA entry earlier).

Air Travel Glossary

Alliances Many of the world's leading airlines are now intimately involved with each other, sharing everything from reservations systems and check-in to aircraft and frequent-flyer schemes. Opponents say that alliances restrict competition. Whatever the arguments, there is no doubt that big alliances are the way of the future.

Courier Fares Businesses often need to send urgent documents or freight securely and quickly. Courier companies hire people to accompany the package through customs and, in return, offer a discount ticket which is sometimes a bargain. However, you may have to surrender all your baggage allowance and take only carry-on luggage.

Fares Airlines traditionally offer 1st class (coded F), business class (coded J) and economy class (coded Y) tickets. These days there are so many promotional and discounted fares available that few passengers pay full fare.

Lost Tickets If you lose your airline ticket, an airline will usually treat it like a travellers cheque and, after inquiries, issue you with another one. Legally, however, an airline is entitled to treat it like cash and if you lose it then it's gone forever. Take very good care of your tickets.

Onward Tickets An entry requirement for many countries is that you have a ticket out of the country. If you're unsure of your next move, the easiest solution is to buy the cheapest onward ticket to a neighbouring country or a ticket from a reliable airline which can later be refunded if you do not use it.

Open-Jaw Tickets These are return tickets where you fly out to one place but return from another. If available, this can save you backtracking to your arrival point.

Overbooking Since every flight has some passengers who fail to show up, airlines often book more passengers than they have seats. Usually excess passengers make up for the no-shows, but occasionally somebody gets 'bumped' onto the next available flight. Guess who it is most likely to be? The passengers who check in late. If you do get 'bumped', you are normally offered some form of compensation.

Reconfirmation Some airlines require you to reconfirm your flight at least 72 hours prior to departure. Check your travel documents to see if this is the case.

Restrictions Discounted tickets often have various restrictions on them – such as needing to be paid for in advance and incurring a penalty to be altered or cancelled. Others are restrictions on the minimum and maximum period you must be away.

Round-the-World Tickets RTW tickets give you a limited period (usually a year) in which to circumnavigate the globe. You can go anywhere the carrying airlines go, as long as you don't backtrack. The number of stopovers or total number of separate flights is decided before you set off and they usually cost a bit more than a basic return flight.

Ticketless Travel Airlines are gradually waking up to the realisation that paper tickets are unnecessary encumbrances. On simple one-way or return trips, reservations details can be held on computer and the passenger merely shows ID to claim their seat.

Transferred Tickets Airline tickets cannot be transferred from one person to another. Travellers sometimes try to sell the return half of their ticket, but officials can ask you to prove that you are the person named on the ticket. On an international flight, tickets are compared with passports.

Australia

Two well-known agents for cheap fares are STA Travel and Flight Centre. STA Travel (☎ 1300 360 960, W www.statravel .com.au) has offices in all major cities and on many university campuses. Call for the location of the nearest branch or visit the Web site. Flight Centre (☎ 131 600, W www.flightcentre.com.au) also has dozens of offices throughout Australia.

From the east coast of Australia, THAI and Qantas have direct flights to Bangkok starting from around A$1150 in the low season and A$1420 in the high season. Garuda Indonesia, Philippine Airlines and Malaysia Airlines also have frequent flights and some good deals, with stopovers, to Bangkok.

Flights to Chiang Mai via Singapore, flying Singapore/Silk Air, start from A$1300 in the low season and A$1600 in the high season.

New Zealand

Flight Centre (☎ 0800 243 544, W www .flightcentre.co.nz) has many branches throughout the country. Check its Web site for details. STA Travel (☎ 0800 874 773, W www.statravel.com) has offices in Auckland, Newmarket, Hamilton, Palmerston North, Wellington, Christchurch and Dunedin.

From Auckland, THAI has direct flights to Bangkok starting from NZ$1299 in the low season and NZ$1550 in the high season. Qantas, Malaysian Airlines and Garuda International also have flights to Bangkok, with stopovers.

The UK

Discount air travel is big business in London and London-to-Bangkok is arguably the most competitive air route in the world. Advertisements for many travel agencies appear in the travel pages of the weekend broadsheet newspapers, in *Time Out,* the *Evening Standard* and in the free magazine *TNT*.

For students or travellers under 26 years, popular travel agencies in the UK include STA Travel (☎ 0870-160 0599, W www

.statravel.co.uk), which has offices throughout the country; and USIT Campus Travel (☎ 0870-240 1010, W www.usitcampus .co.uk), with over 50 branches. Both of these agencies sell tickets to all travellers but cater especially to young people and students.

Other recommended travel agencies for all age groups include:

Bridge the World (☎ 020-7734 7447, W www .b-t-w.co.uk) 4 Regent Place, London W1
Flightbookers (☎ 020-7757 2000, W www.ebookers.com) 177–178 Tottenham Court Rd, London W1
North-South Travel (☎ 012-45 608 291, W www.nstravel.demon.co.uk) Moulsham Mill, Parkway, Chelmsford, Essex CM2 7PX. North-South Travel donates part of its profit to projects in the developing world.
Quest Travel (☎ 020-8547 3123, W www.questtravel.co.uk) 10 Richmond Rd, Kingston-upon-Thames, Surrey KT2 5HL
Trailfinders (☎ 020-7938 3939, W www .trailfinders.co.uk) 194 Kensington High St, London W8
Travel Bag (☎ 020-7287 5158, W www .travelbag.co.uk) 52 Regent St, London W1B 5DX

Typical low-season discounted air fares from London to Bangkok start from UK£340 to UK£430 return. Gulf Air, Qatar Airways, Air France and Eva Air all offer good deals between the two capitals. Eva Air and Singapore Airlines also have connecting flights from London to Chiang Mai starting from £620.

Qantas Airways and THAI both have non-stop flights starting from around UK£600 in the low season.

The Netherlands

Recommended agencies include NBBS Reizen (☎ 020-620 5071, W www.nbbs.nl), 66 Rokin, Amsterdam, which has branches in most cities; and Budget Air (☎ 020-627 1251), 34 Rokin, Amsterdam. Another agency, Holland International (☎ 070-307 6307), has offices in most cities.

KLM has direct flights from Amsterdam to Bangkok for around €800; China Airlines direct flights start at €710.

Germany

Recommended agencies in Germany include STA Travel (☎ 01805 456 422, Ⓦ www.statravel.de), which has branches in major cities across the country. Usit Campus (☎ 01805 788 336, Ⓦ www.usit-campus.de) also has several offices in Germany. Check the Web sites for details.

Kuwait Airways has flights from Frankfurt to Bangkok starting from €594 and Malaysian Airlines has flights starting at €779.

France

France has a network of student travel agencies that can supply discount tickets to travellers of all ages. OTU Voyages (☎ 0820 817 817, Ⓦ www.otu.fr), Voyageurs du Monde (☎ 01 42 86 16 40, Ⓦ www.vdm.com) and Nouvelles Frontières (☎ 08 25 00 08 25, Ⓦ www.nouvelles-frontieres.fr) have branches throughout the country and offer some of the best services and deals.

Return fares from Paris start from €690 with Emirates and Lufthansa. Thai has direct flights starting from €800.

Asia

There are regular flights to Bangkok International Airport from every major city in Asia and most airlines offer similar fares for intra-Asia flights. Following is a list of common one-way intra-Asia fares from Bangkok. Return tickets are usually double the one-way fare, although occasionally airlines run special discounts of up to 25% for such tickets. For fares in the reverse direction, convert to local currency.

destination	one-way fare
Calcutta	5900B
Colombo	7200B
Delhi	13,500B
Denpasar	8600B
Ho Chi Minh City	4500B
Hong Kong	8000B
Kathmandu	8600B
Kuala Lumpur	4300B
Kunming	5050B
Manila	7600B
Osaka	12,300B
Penang	3800B
Phnom Penh	3775B
Seoul	12,300B
Singapore	5600B
Taipei	7600B
Tokyo	12,300B
Yangon	3700B

Other Places in Thailand

Air fares between Bangkok and Northern Thai cities include:

destination	one-way fare
Chiang Mai	2170B
Chiang Rai	2200B
Lampang	1650B
Mae Sot	1595B
Nan	1735B
Phitsanulok	1080B
Phrae	1500B

There is also a flight between Chiang Mai and Phuket for 3920B.

LAND & RIVER

This section contains information on reaching Thailand from other countries, and general information on overland travel to the North from other parts of Thailand. You'll find more-detailed information on travelling to the North from elsewhere in Thailand in the respective Getting There & Away sections in the destination chapters.

Laos

Road The Thai-Lao Friendship Bridge (Saphan Mittaphap Thai-Lao) spans a section of the Mekong River between Ban Jommani (near Nong Khai, Thailand) and Tha Na Leng (near Vientiane, Laos) and is the main transportation gateway between the two countries. A parallel rail bridge is planned to extend the Bangkok-Nong Khai railway into Vientiane, although a construction schedule has yet to be announced.

In early 1996 construction began on a second Mekong bridge to span the river between Thailand's Chiang Khong and Laos' Huay Xai. Although this bridge was supposed to be operational by 1998, the project was abandoned in 1997 after the drastic

Northern Thailand to Yunnan, China

It's possible to travel from Thailand to China's Yunnan Province by road via Laos, a land route that ties together the Golden Triangle and Yunnan's Xishuangbanna district (called Sipsongpanna in Thailand) in Southwest China. The Thais, Shan and Lao all consider Xishuangbanna to be a cultural homeland.

One can easily cross into Laos from Northern Thailand via the border crossings at Chiang Khong/Huay Xai. Once in Laos, head to Luang Nam Tha or Udomxai, then proceed north to the Lao village of Boten on the Chinese border, close to the Xishuangbanna town of Mengla (Mong La). A road from Mengla leads to Jinghong. To reach Luang Nam Tha from Northern Thailand you may cross by ferry from Chiang Khong on the Thai side to Huay Xai on the Lao side. This crossing is fully operational; foreigners may enter Laos here with the proper visa. The Boten crossing is legal for all nationalities.

Another way to reach Boten is via Pakbeng in Laos' Udomxai Province. Pakbeng is midway along the Mekong River route between Huay Xai and Luang Prabang; from Pakbeng a Chinese-built road system continues all the way to Boten. To facilitate trade and travel between China and Thailand, the Chinese have offered to build a new road leading directly south to the Thai border (Nan Province) from the river bank opposite Pakbeng. For now, Thai authorities are not too happy about this proposed road extension, which is seen as a push towards an 'invasion' of Thailand. During the years of Thai communist insurgency, Communist Party of Thailand (CPT) cadres used the Pakbeng road to reach Kunming, China, for training in revolutionary tactics.

---

drop in the value of the baht. If construction ever resumes, the bridge will link Thailand and China with a road through Bokeo and Luang Nam Tha Provinces in Laos – it is part of an ambitious transport project known as the Chiang Rai to Kunming Road.

Boat The Mekong River ferry crossing from Huay Xai to Chiang Khong puts you right at Northern Thailand's doorstep, and is a popular way of travelling between Northern Thailand and northern Laos.

Myanmar
Several border crossings between Thailand and Myanmar are open to day-trippers or for short excursions in the vicinity.

Mae Sai to Tachileik The infamous bridge, Lo Hsing-han's former 'Golden Triangle' passageway for opium and heroin, spans the Mae Sai (Sai River) between Thailand's northernmost town and the border boom-town of Tachileik (called Thakhilek by the Thai, Shan and Khün peoples). Border permits for up to two weeks may be obtained from the Burmese immi-

gration facility at the border for excursions to Tachileik and as far north as Kengtung and Mengla. You can also use this border as a way of renewing your Thai visa if you happen to be in Northern Thailand.

This border crossing closed for a few months in 1994 and 1995, due to fighting between Shan insurgent armies and the Burmese, and it closed again in 1999 during and after the God's Army hostage-taking crisis in Ratchaburi. In 2001 further skirmishes led to another temporary closing, but at the time of publication everything had returned to normal and the border crossing was open in both directions as usual.

Rumour has it that an overland route going all the way to China via Kengtung will soon open here, but so far Mengla is the end of the line. The road continuing west from Kengtung to Taunggyi is in usable condition, although it runs through the opium-poppy harvesting area of the Golden Triangle, a common site of clashes between the Shan army and the Burmese military, and is definitely off-limits to non-Burmese. It's 163km on from Tachileik to Kengtung, and another 450km from Kengtung to Taunggyi. You are, however, permitted to

Northern Thailand to Yunnan, China

Another land route to China begins at the Burmese border town of Tachileik (opposite Mae Sai on the Thai side) and proceeds 164km northwards to Myanmar's Kengtung (known as Chiang Tung to the Thais) Shan State. At present the road from Kengtung to Tachileik is a rough track that takes all day to cover when road conditions are good; permission to cross here can be arranged in Mae Sai on the Thai side. From Kengtung the road continues another 100km north to Myanmar's Mengla (opposite Daluo on the Chinese border); this latter section is now approved for tourist travel upon registration in Kengtung. The Chinese have improved the Daluo to Kengtung section of the road in return for limited mineral and logging rights in Myanmar, so this section is much better than the longer stretch between Kengtung and Tachileik.

From Daluo it's 300km to Jinghong, capital of Xishuangbanna. If you have a valid Chinese visa, you may be able to cross the Chinese border by land from Myanmar at Mengla/Daluo, but this must be approved in advance by Myanmar and Chinese authorities.

In the long term, the river route is also promising. Chinese barges weighing up to 100 tonnes now ply the Mekong River eight months a year; from the Chinese border to Chiang Khong, Thailand, the trip takes about five days. During the drier months, however, river transport north of Luang Prabang is hampered by rocks and shallows. Blasting and dredging could make way for boats of up to 500 tonnes to travel year-round, but could have devastating effects on the watercourse and lands downstream.

travel by air from Tachileik or Kengtung to Mandalay and vice versa.

Chiang Dao A dirt track turns left 10km north of Chiang Dao in Chiang Mai Province and leads through the small town of Meuang Ngai to Na Ok at the border. This was the most popular opium route from Myanmar 25 or 30 years ago, but the main trade now is in water buffalo and lacquer. It'd be wise to be very careful in this area.

Mae Sot to Myawadi This crossing begins a route from Myawadi to Mawlamyaing (Moulmein) via Kawkareik along a rough road that has long been off limits to foreigners due to Mon and Karen insurgent activity. There are regular buses from Tak to Mae Sot in Tak Province. In 1994 the Myanmar government signed an agreement with Thailand to build a bridge across Mae Moei between Myawadi and Mae Sot (actually 6km from Mae Sot proper). The span was finally completed and opened in 1997, then quickly closed due to international bickering over reclamation of the river banks. In 1998 it was

open again for a short time, then closed again, but at the time of writing it was open again.

Foreigners are now permitted to cross from Mae Sot to Myawadi for the day. See the Mae Sot section in the Western Provinces chapter for details. For now, travel is allowed only between Myawadi and Mae Sot – beyond Myawadi is off limits. Myanmar's Yangon junta claims it has plans to open the road from Myawadi all the way to Pa-an in the Kayin State, and Thai groups have managed to receive permission to travel by chartered bus all the way to Yangon.

Just north of Myawadi is Wangkha, and to the south is Phalu (Waley on the Thai side), former Karen and Mon smuggling posts now controlled by Yangon. Foreigners are not permitted to cross here, although some do, via local connections.

China
Road The governments of Thailand, Laos, China and Myanmar have agreed to the construction of a four-nation ring road through all four countries. The western half of the loop will proceed from Mae Sai in

The Northern Loop

While the normal way of getting to Northern Thailand is to head directly from Bangkok to Chiang Mai, there are many interesting alternatives.

Starting north from Bangkok, visit the ancient capitals of Ayuthaya, Lopburi and Sukhothai, or take a less-travelled and longer route by going west to Nakhon Pathom and Kanchanaburi and then northeast by bus to Lopburi (backtracking to Ayuthaya if desired).

From Lopburi, either head north to Chiang Mai, or stop at Phitsanulok for side trips to Sukhothai, Tak and Mae Sot. It is possible to travel by road from Mae Sot to Mae Sariang, then on to Mae Hong Son or Chiang Mai.

Once you're in Chiang Mai, the usual route is to continue on to Fang for the Mae Nam Kok (Kok River) boat ride to Chiang Rai, then on into the Golden Triangle towns of Mae Sai and Chiang Saen. Travellers with more time might add to this the Chiang Mai-Mae Hong Son-Chiang Mai circle. Once you get to the Fang area a very rough but traversable road between Tha Ton and Doi Mae Salong (Mae Salong Mountain) is an alternative to the Mae Nam Kok trip.

From Chiang Mai, proceed to Northeastern Thailand via Phitsanulok and Lom Sak, entering the Northeast proper at either Loei or Khon Kaen. From there, Nong Khai, Udon Thani and Khon Kaen are all on the railway route back to Bangkok, but there are several other places in the area worth exploring before heading back to the capital.

A Northern Thailand–Laos loop, starting with the crossing of the Mekong River at Chiang Khong (Thailand) to Huay Xai (Laos) and then continuing by river to Luang Prabang and Vientiane, has become very popular over the last couple of years. From Vientiane you can loop back into Northeastern Thailand or continue on to Vietnam or China by road or air. This loop can be done in reverse, of course, from Bangkok to Vientiane, Luang Prabang and Huay Xai, then back into Thailand via Chiang Khong to Chiang Rai and eventually Chiang Mai.

Thailand to Jinghong in China, via Myanmar's Tachileik, Kengtung and Mengla (near Dalau on the China-Myanmar border); while the eastern half will extend from Chiang Khong in Thailand to Jinghong via Huay Xai (opposite Chiang Khong) and Boten (on the Yunnanese border south of Jinghong) in Laos.

The stretch between Tachileik and Dalau is still under construction (some sections towards the Chinese border are complete) but it's possible to arrange one- to three-day trips as far as Kengtung in Myanmar's Shan State (see the Mae Sai section in the Eastern Provinces chapter for details). There's already a road between Huay Xai and Boten (built by the Chinese in the 1960s and 1970s) but it needs upgrading. Once the roads are built and the visa formalities have been worked out, this loop will provide alternative travel connections between China and Southeast Asia, in much the same way as the Karakoram

Highway has forged new links between China and South Asia. It's difficult to predict when all the logistical variables will be settled, but progress so far points to a cleared path by 2006.

The eastern half of this loop, from Boten to Huay Xai, Laos, and across to Chiang Khong, Thailand, can be done relatively easily now, although roadways between Boten and Huay Xai are a little rough.

Boat You can reach China's Yunnan Province from Thailand by boat along the Mekong River. Several surveys of the waterway have been completed and a specially constructed express boat made its inaugural run between Sop Ruak in Chiang Rai Province, and China's Yunnan Province in early 1994. For the moment, permission for such travel is restricted to very infrequent private tour groups, but it's reasonable to assume that in the future a scheduled public service may become

Warning

The information in this chapter is particularly vulnerable to change: Prices for international travel are volatile, routes are introduced and cancelled, schedules change, special deals come and go, and rules and visa requirements are amended. Airlines and governments seem to take a perverse pleasure in making price structures and regulations as complicated as possible. You should check directly with the airline or a travel agent to make sure you understand how a fare (and ticket you may buy) works. In addition, the travel industry is highly competitive and there are many lurks and perks.

The upshot of this is that you should get opinions, quotes and advice from as many airlines and travel agents as possible before you part with your hard-earned cash. The details given in this chapter should be regarded as pointers and are not a substitute for your own careful, up-to-date research.

available. The boat trip takes six hours – it's considerably quicker than any currently possible road route. However, it's only navigable all the way to China during the rainy season and in the period immediately thereafter.

Other Places in Thailand

Bus The government-regulated public bus system – *bòrísàt khŏn sòng* (Baw Khaw Saw for short) – connects Northern Thailand with cities and towns in other regions of Thailand.

Buses leave from Bangkok's Northern and Northeastern Bus Terminal (☎ 029 363 660 for Northern routes) on Thanon Kamphaeng Phet, just north of Chatuchak Park. It's also called the Moh Chit station (*sathăanii măw chít*), or 'New' Moh Chit (*măw chít mài*). Air-con city bus Nos 4, 10 and 29, along with a dozen or more ordinary city buses, all pass this terminal. The Mo Chit Skytrain station is also within walking distance of the bus terminal.

Allow an hour to reach the Northern bus terminal from Banglamphu or anywhere

along the river, much less if you're on the Skytrain route.

Legally, all buses operating out of Bangkok, whether government-operated or privately licensed, must leave from the official Baw Khaw Saw terminals.

Buses to and from other parts of Thailand may operate from the local Baw Khaw Saw terminal or, in the case of private bus services, from private bus offices.

For a description of the various kinds of buses available, see the Getting Around chapter.

Fares For details on bus fares to/from towns and cities in Northern Thailand, see the Getting There & Away sections in the relevant destination chapters. Some sample bus fares include:

to/from Chiang Mai	fare
Bangkok	
ordinary	215B
1st class	403B
VIP	625B
Khon Kaen (via Tak)	
ordinary	243B
air-con	340B
1st class	437B
Khorat	
ordinary	243B
1st class air-con	437B
VIP	510B
Udon Thani	
ordinary	228B
air-con	319B
1st class	410B

to/from Chiang Rai	fare
Bangkok	
air-con	370B
1st class	452B
VIP	700B
Khon Kaen	
ordinary	239B
air-con	335B
1st class	430B
Khorat	
ordinary	262B
air-con	472B
VIP	550B

Train Northern Thailand is linked to Central Thailand via the State Railway of Thailand's northern trunk line between Bangkok and Chiang Mai. All trains that run north along this line originate from Bangkok's Hualamphong station.

For information on the different classes of trains, on general fare structuring and on making advance reservations, see the Getting Around chapter.

Fares For individual train fares to/from towns and cities in Northern Thailand, see the Getting There & Away sections in the relevant destination chapters. Generally speaking, train travel costs a bit more than bus travel, although it is considerably cheaper than domestic air travel.

Some sample train fares include:

to/from Chiang Mai*	fare
Bangkok	
3rd class	153B
2nd class	281B
1st class	593B
Lopburi	
3rd class	133B
2nd class	277B

to/from Phitsanulok*	fare
Bangkok	
3rd class	69B
2nd class	159B
1st class	324B
Ayuthaya	
3rd class	54B
2nd class	124B
1st class	258B

*These are basic fares that do not include surcharges for express trains, sleeping berths or air-conditioning, all of which cost extra. See the Getting Around chapter for a full explanation.

ORGANISED TOURS
Thai Companies

Many operators around the world can arrange guided tours of Thailand. Most of them simply serve as brokers for tour companies based in Thailand; they buy their trips from a wholesaler and resell them under various names in travel markets overseas. One is much like another and you might as well arrange a tour in Thailand at a lower cost – there are so many available. Two of the largest tour wholesalers in Bangkok are: World Travel Service (☎ 022 335 900, fax 022 367 169) at 1053 Thanon Charoen Krung; and Diethelm Travel (☎ 022 559 150, fax 022 560 248) at Kian Gwan Building II, 140/1 Thanon Withayu.

Motorcycle tours of Northern Thailand (with extensions into Laos and Southwest China) can be organised by Siam Bike Tour (ⓔ davidfl@chmai.loxinfo.co.th).

Bangkok-based Khiri Travel (☎ 026 290 491, fax 026 290 493, ⓔ info@khiri.com) specialises in ecologically oriented tours. It's located opposite the Viengtai Hotel on Soi Rambutri off Thanon Chakrapong.

Overseas Companies

The better overseas tour companies build their own Northern Thailand itineraries from scratch and choose their local suppliers based on which ones best serve these itineraries. Of these, several specialise in adventure and/or ecological tours, including:

Asia Transpacific Journeys (☎ 800-642 2742, 303-443 6789, fax 443 7078, Ⓦ www .southeastasia.com) 3055 Center Green Dr, Boulder, CO 80301, USA

Club Aventure (☎ 514-527 0999, fax 527 3999, ⓔ info@clubaventure.qc.ca) 759 ave du Mont-Royal Est, Montreal, QUE H2J 1W8, Canada

Exodus (☎ 020-8673 5550, fax 8673 0779, Ⓦ www.exodustravels.co.uk) 9 Weir Rd, London SW12 OLT, UK

Geographic Expeditions (☎ 800-777 8183, 415-922 0448, Ⓦ www.geoex.com) 2627 Lombard St, San Francisco, CA 94123, USA

Intrepid Travel (☎ 03-9473 2626, fax 9419 4426, Ⓦ www.intrepidtravel.com) 11–13 Spring St, Fitzroy, VIC 3065, Australia

Mountain Travel Sobek (☎ 800-227 2384, 510-527 8100, fax 525 7710, Ⓦ www.mtsobek .com) 6420 Fairmount Ave, Berkeley, CA 94530, USA

Getting Around

AIR
Regional Air Services
Two domestic carriers, Thai Airways International (commonly known as THAI) and Bangkok Airways, operate out of the domestic airports in 28 cities around the country, including cities in Northern Thailand.

Most domestic air services are operated by THAI, which flies Boeing 737s, ATR-72s and Airbus 300s on its main domestic routes.

Domestic Airlines
Bangkok Airways has flights along four main routes: Bangkok-Sukhothai-Chiang Mai; Bangkok-Ko Samui-Phuket; Bangkok-Ranong-Phuket; and U Taphao (Pattaya)–Ko Samui. Bangkok Airways' fares are competitive with THAI's but the company is small and it remains to be seen whether or not it will continue as a serious contender.

Bangkok Airways' Chiang Mai office (☎ 053 281 519, fax 053 281 520) is on the 2nd floor of Chiang Mai International Airport. The head office (☎ 022 293 434; reservations ☎ 022 293 456) is in Bangkok at 60 Queen Sirikit National Convention Centre, Thanon Ratchadaphisek Mai, Khlong Toey, Bangkok 10110. There is also an office in Sukhothai.

THAI Offices Offices for THAI's domestic services can be found throughout Thailand:

Bangkok (head office; ☎ 025 130 121) 89 Thanon Viphavadi Rangsit;
  (☎ 022 343 100) 3rd–5th floors, Silom Plaza Bldg, 485 Thanon Silom;
  (☎ 022 800 110) 6 Thanon Lan Luang;
  (☎ 022 152 020–4) Asia Hotel, 296 Thanon Phayathai;
  (☎ 022 239 746–48) 310–311, 3rd floor, Grand China Tower, 215 Thanon Yaowarat;
  (☎ 025 352 081/2, 025 236 121) Bangkok International Airport, Don Muang
Buriram (☎ 044 625 066) Phusiam Tours, 24/23 Thanon Romburi
Chiang Mai (☎ 053 210 210; reservations ☎ 053 211 044, 053 210 210) 240 Thanon Phra Pokklao;
  (☎ 053 277 782, 053 277 640) Chiang Mai International Airport
Chiang Rai (☎ 053 711 179, 053 222 279) 870 Thanon Phahonyothin;
  (☎ 053 793 048–57, ext 162, 163) Chiang Rai International Airport
Hat Yai (☎ 074 230 445/6, 074 244 282; reservations ☎ 074 233 433) 190/6 Thanon Niphat Uthit;
  (☎ 074 251 034) Hat Yai International Airport
Khon Kaen (☎ 043 227 701–5) 9/9 Thanon Prachasamoson;
  (☎ 043 246 305, 043 246 345) Khon Kaen airport
Lampang (☎ 054 217 078, 054 218 199) 314 Thanon Sanambin;
  (☎ 054 225 383) Lampang airport
Loei (☎ 042 812 344, 042 812 355) 22/15 Thanon Chumsai
Mae Hong Son (☎ 053 611 297, 053 611 194) 71 Thanon Singhanat Bamrung;
  (☎ 053 611 367) Mae Hong Son airport
Mae Sot (☎ 055 531 730, 055 531 440) 76/1 Thanon Prasat Withi
Nakhon Phanom (☎ 042 512 940) Bovon Travel Co Ltd, 13 Thanon Ruamjit Thawai;
  (☎ 042 513 357) Nakhon Phanom airport
Nakhon Ratchasima (Khorat; ☎ 044 252 114, 044 257 211–3) 40–44 Thanon Suranari
Nakhon Si Thammarat (☎ 075 342 491, 075 343 874) 1612 Thanon Ratchadamnoen
Nan (☎ 054 710 377, 054 710 498) 34 Thanon Mahaphrom;
  (☎ 054 771 729) Nan airport
Narathiwat (☎ 073 511 161, 073 513 090–2) 322–324 Thanon Phuphaphakdi;
  (☎ 073 511 595, 073 514 570) Narathiwat airport
Nong Khai (☎ 042 411 530) 102/2 Thanon Chonpratan
Pattani (☎ 073 335 939) 9 Thanon Prida
Pattaya (☎ 038 420 995–7) Dusit Resort Hotel, Thanon Hat Pattaya Neua
Phitsanulok (☎ 055 258 020, 055 251 671) 209/26-28 Thanon Borom Trailokanat
Phrae (☎ 054 511 123) 42–44 Thanon Ratsadamnoen
Phuket (☎ 076 258 236; reservations ☎ 076 258 237) 78/1 Thanon Ranong;
  (☎ 076 327 194) Phuket International Airport
Sakon Nakhon (☎ 042 712 259/60) 1446/73 Thanon Yuwaphattana

Songkhla (☎ 074 311 012, 074 314 007) 2 Soi 4, Thanon Saiburi

Surat Thani (☎ 077 273 710, 077 273 355, 077 272 610) 3/27–28 Thanon Karunarat; (☎ 077 200 605, 077 200 611/2) Surat Thani airport

Tak (☎ 055 512 164) 485 Thanon Taksin

Trang (☎ 075 218 066, 075 219 923) 199/2 Thanon Visetkul; (☎ 075 210 804, 075 215379) Trang airport

Ubon Ratchathani (☎ 045 313 340–2, 045 313 344) 364 Thanon Chayangkun; (☎ 045 243 037–9, 045 245 612, ext 127) Ubon Ratchathani airport

Udon Thani (☎ 042 246 697, 042 243 222) 60 Thanon Mak Khaeng; (☎ 042 246 567, 042 246 644) Udon Thani airport

THAI's 24-hour reservation number is ☎ 022 800 060.

Air Fares

The Air Fares map shows some of the fares on more popular routes. Note that through-fares are generally less than the combination fares; Chiang Rai–Bangkok, for example, is less than the sum of Chiang Rai–Chiang Mai and Chiang Mai–Bangkok fares.

All fares listed in this guide and appearing on the Air Fares map are economy fares. Business class fares cost around 35% more than economy fares.

BUS
Government Buses

The cheapest and slowest of the Thai buses are the ordinary government-run buses (*rót thammádaa*, or in Thai slang *rót daeng*, 'red bus') that stop in every little town and for every waving hand along the highway. For some destinations – such as smaller towns – these orange- or red-painted buses are your only choice, but at least they leave frequently.

The government also runs faster, more comfortable but less frequent air-con buses called *rót ae, rót pràp aakàat* or *rót thua*;

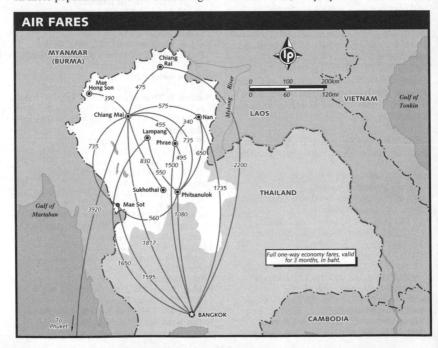

AIR FARES

Full one-way economy fares, valid for 3 months, in baht.

these are painted with blue markings. If these are available for your destination they are your very best choice, since they don't cost that much more than the ordinary stop-in-every-town buses. The government bus company is called Baw Khaw Saw, an abbreviation of *bòrísàt khŏn sòng* (literally, transportation company). Every city and town in Thailand linked by bus has a Baw Khaw Saw terminal, even if it's just a patch of dirt by the roadside.

The service on the government air-con buses is usually quite good and includes beverage service and video. On longer routes (eg, Bangkok–Chiang Mai) the air-con buses even distribute claim checks (receipt dockets) for your baggage. Longer routes may also offer two classes of air-con bus, 2nd class and 1st class; the latter have toilets. 'VIP' buses have fewer seats (30 to 34 instead of 44; some routes have Super VIP, with only 24 seats) so that each seat reclines more. Sometimes these are called *rót nawn* (sleepers). For small to medium-sized people they are more comfortable, but if you're big in girth you may find yourself squashed on the 34-seaters when the person in front of you leans back.

Occasionally you'll get a government air-con bus in which the air-con is broken or the seats are not up to standard, but in general they are more reliable than private tour buses.

Private Buses

Private buses are available between major tourist and business destinations all over the country. They can be booked through most hotels or any travel agency, although it's best to book directly through a bus office to be assured that you get what you pay for.

Fares may vary from company to company, but usually not by more than a few baht. However, fare differences between the government and private bus companies can be substantial. Private buses from Bangkok to Chiang Mai often cost less than government buses, although those that charge less offer inferior service. Some private companies' departures are more frequent than for the equivalent Baw Khaw Saw services.

There are also private buses running be-

tween major destinations within the various regions, eg, Chiang Mai to Sukhothai in the North. New companies are cropping up all the time. Minibuses are used consistently on hilly or winding routes (eg, Tak to Mae Sot, Chiang Mai to Pai).

Private air-con buses are usually no more comfortable than government air-con buses and feature similarly narrow seats and hair-raising rides. On either type of air-con bus the crew usually turns up the air-con until your knees knock, handing out pillows and blankets and serving free soft drinks. On overnight journeys the buses usually stop somewhere en route and passengers are awakened to get off the bus for a free meal of fried rice or rice soup. A few companies even treat you to a meal before a long overnight trip.

Like the state-run bus companies, private companies offer VIP (sleeper) buses on long hauls. In general, the private bus companies that deal mostly with Thais are good, while tourist-oriented ones – especially those connected with Thanon Khao San (Khao San Rd) in Bangkok – are awful.

The safest, most reliable private bus services from Bangkok to the North are the ones that operate from the official Baw Khaw Saw terminal rather than from hotels or guesthouses. Picking up passengers from any point that is not an official terminal is actually illegal, and services promised are often not delivered. Although it can be a hassle getting out to the Baw Khaw Saw terminal, you're generally rewarded with safer, more reliable and punctual service.

Service

Although on average the private companies charge more than the government does on the same routes, the service does not always match the higher relative cost. In recent years the service on many private lines has in fact declined, especially on the Bangkok–Chiang Mai route.

Sometimes the cheaper lines – especially the ones that are booked on Thanon Khao San in Bangkok – will pull a swifty and switch vehicles at the last moment so that you're stuck with a cramped van with broken air-con instead of the roomy air-con bus advertised. One traveller recounted how his Thanon Khao San bus stopped for lunch halfway to Chiang Mai and then zoomed off while the passengers were eating – leaving them to finish the journey on their own! To avoid situations like this it's always better to book bus tickets directly at a bus office – or at the government Baw Khaw Saw station – rather than through a travel agency.

Another problem with private companies is that they generally spend time cruising the city for passengers before getting under way, meaning that they rarely leave at the advertised departure time.

Our advice is to take a train or public bus and if this fails then sit at the back of the bus. The public bus journeys we took were far superior; two free meals, plenty of leg room and drivers who had at least a modicum of respect for human life.

Safety

Statistically, private buses meet with more accidents than government air-con buses. Turnovers on tight corners and head-on collisions with trucks are probably due to the inexperience of the drivers on a particular route.

Keep an eye on your bags when riding buses – pilfering by stealth is still the most popular form of robbery in Thailand; the risks are not that great – just be aware. Most pilfering seems to take place on the private bus runs between Bangkok and Chiang Mai, especially on buses booked on Thanon Khao San. Keep zippered bags locked and well secured.

When travelling on night buses take care of your belongings. Some of the long-distance buses leaving from Bangkok now issue claim checks for luggage stored under the bus, but valuables are still best kept on your person or within reach.

TRAIN

The railway network in Thailand, run by the Thai government through the State Railway of Thailand (SRT), is very well run, on the whole. It isn't possible to take the train everywhere in Thailand, but often it is the most preferable type of public transport. Third-class train travel is often the cheapest way to cover a long distance; 2nd-class travel costs about the same as a private tour bus but is much safer and more comfortable. Trains take a bit longer than chartered buses on the same journey but are worth the extra travel time, on overnight trips especially.

Trains offer many advantages: There is more space and more room to move and stretch out (even in 3rd class) than there is on even the best buses. The large windows are good for watching the passing sights. The scenery itself is always better along the train routes than along Thai highways – the trains regularly pass small villages, farmland, old temples etc. On non-air-con trains – our preference – the windows are usually open, so there is no glass between you and the scenery (good for taking photos). The pitch-and-roll of the railway cars is much easier on the bones, muscles and nervous system than the quick stops and starts, the harrowing turns and the pothole jolts endured on buses. The train is safer in terms of both accidents and robberies. Last, but certainly not least, you meet a lot more interesting people on trains, or so it seems to us.

Rail Routes

Four main rail lines stretch 4500km along the northern, southern, northeastern and eastern routes. The northern line runs through Lopburi, Phitsanulok, Den Chai (in Phrae Province) and Lampang before ending at Chiang Mai.

A spur from Den Chai to Chiang Rai in the North has also been under discussion, though nothing concrete has happened yet.

Classes

The SRT operates passenger trains in three classes – 1st, 2nd and 3rd – but each class varies considerably, depending on whether you're on an ordinary, rapid or express train.

3rd Class A typical 3rd-class car consists of two rows of bench seats divided into facing pairs. Each bench seat is designed to seat two or three passengers, but on a

CHRIS MELLOR

Traditional village set high in the mountains of Northern Thailand

HERMANN MOLL

Thailand is home to a colourful array of orchids

JOHN HAY

Farm worker, Chiang Mai Province

JOHN HAY

Heating things up: green chillies

Lisu (Lisaw) tribespeople, dressed in their most colourful garb, gather for a New Year celebration in Chiang Mai Province.

crowded upcountry line nobody seems to care about design considerations. On rapid trains 3rd-class seats are padded and reasonably comfortable for shorter trips. Rapid and Express trains do not carry 3rd-class cars at all. Commuter trains in the Bangkok area are all 3rd class and the cars resemble modern subway or rapid-transit trains, with plastic seats and ceiling hand-straps for standing passengers.

2nd Class Seating arrangements in 2nd-class cars are similar to those on a bus, with pairs of padded seats, usually recliners, all facing towards the front of the train.

In a 2nd-class sleeper, the seats convert into two fold-down berths, one over the other. Curtains provide a modicum of privacy and the berths are fairly comfortable, with fresh linen for every trip. A toilet stall and washbasins are located at one end of the car. Second-class cars are found only on rapid and express trains; some routes offer air-con 2nd class as well as ordinary 2nd class.

1st Class First-class cars provide private cabins. Each has individually controlled air-con (older trains also have an electric fan), a washbasin and mirror, a small table and long bench seats that convert into beds, one over the other. Drinking water and soap are provided free of charge. First-class cars are available only on rapid, express and special express trains.

Costs

There is a 60B surcharge for express trains (*rót dùan*) and 40B for rapid trains (*rót rehw*). These trains are somewhat faster than the ordinary trains, as they make fewer stops. Some 2nd- and 3rd-class services are air-con, in which case there is a 70B surcharge (note that there are no 3rd-class cars on either rapid or express trains). For the special express trains (*rót dùan phísèht*) that run between Bangkok and Chiang Mai there is an 80B surcharge (or 120B if a meal is included).

The charge for 2nd-class sleeping berths is 100B for an upper berth and 150B for a lower berth (or 130B and 200B, respec-

tively, on a special express). The difference between upper and lower is that there is a window next to the lower berth and a little more head room. The upper berth is still comfortable enough. For 2nd-class sleepers with air-con add 250/320B per upper/lower ticket. No sleepers are available in 3rd class.

Air-con really isn't necessary on night trains, since a steady breeze circulates through the train and cools things down quickly. In fact, air-con 2nd class can become uncomfortably cold at night and cannot be regulated by passengers; for this reason we recommend choosing non-air-con.

All 1st-class cabins come with individually controlled air-con. For a two-bed cabin the surcharge is 520B per person. Single 1st-class cabins are no longer available, so if you're travelling alone you may be paired with another rail passenger, although the SRT takes great care not to mix genders.

You can figure on 500km costing around 200B in 2nd class (not including the surcharges for the rapid and express services), roughly twice that in 1st class and less than half in 3rd. Surprisingly, basic fares have changed only slightly over the last decade, although supplementary charges have increased steadily. Currently the government continues to subsidise train travel, particularly 3rd class, to some extent. However, there has been some talk of privatising the railway – which would, of course, ring the death knell for the passenger rail system as it has in most other formerly rail-faring countries of the world.

Train Passes The SRT issues a couple of train passes that may save you on fares if you plan to ride Thai trains extensively within a relatively short interval. These passes are available only in Thailand, and may be purchased at Hualamphong train station.

The cost for 20 days of unlimited 2nd- or 3rd-class rail travel (blue pass) is 1100B (not including supplementary charges) or 2000B including all supplementary charges; children aged four to 12 pay half the adult fare. Supplementary charges include all extra charges for rapid, express, special express and aircon. Passes must be validated at a local station before boarding the first train. The price of the pass includes seat reservations that, if required, can be made at any SRT ticket office. The pass is valid until midnight on the last day. However, if the journey is commenced before midnight on the last day of validity, the passenger can use the pass until that train reaches its destination.

Do the passes represent a true saving over buying individual train tickets? The answer is yes only if you can average more than 110km by rail per day for 20 days. If you travel at this rate (or less), then you'll be paying the same amount (or more) as you would if you bought ordinary train tickets directly. On less crowded routes where there are plenty of available 2nd-class seats the passes save time that might otherwise be spent at ticket windows, but for high-demand routes (eg, Bangkok–Chiang Mai) you'll still need to make reservations.

Bookings

The disadvantage of travelling by rail, in addition to the time factor mentioned earlier, is that trains can be difficult to book. This is especially true around holiday time (eg, the middle of April approaching the Songkran Festival), since many Thais prefer the train. Trains out of Bangkok should be booked as far in advance as possible – a minimum of a week for popular routes such as the northern line to Chiang Mai, especially if you want a sleeper. Mid-week departures are always easier to book than weekends; during some months of the year you can easily book a sleeper even one day before departure, as long as it's on a Tuesday, Wednesday or Thursday.

Advance bookings can be made one to 60 days before your intended date of departure. If you want to book tickets in advance, go to Hualamphong station in Bangkok, walk through the front of the station house and go straight to the back right-hand corner where a sign says 'Advance Booking' (open from 8.30am to 4pm daily). The other ticket windows, lined up in front of the platforms, are for same-day purchases, mostly

3rd class. Advance bookings can also be made at window Nos 2 to 11 from 5am to 8.30am and from 4pm to 11pm.

Reservations are computerised in the Advance Booking office, and you simply take a queue number, wait until your number appears on one of the electronic marquees, report to the desk above which your number appears and make your ticket arrangements. Only cash baht is acceptable here.

Note that buying a return ticket does not necessarily guarantee you a seat on the way back, it only means you do not have to buy a ticket for the return. If you want a guaranteed seat reservation it's best to make it immediately upon arrival at your destination.

Booking trains back to Bangkok is generally not as difficult as booking trains out of Bangkok. Chiang Mai is an exception, and booking trains out of that city during or around holidays can be challenging. It's best to book as far in advance as possible.

Tickets between any station in Thailand can be purchased at Hualamphong station (☎ 022 233 762, 022 256 964, 022 247 788; 022 250 300, ext 5200 03). You can also make advance bookings at Don Muang station (across from Bangkok International Airport) and at the Advance Booking offices at train stations in larger cities.

Advance reservations can be made by phone from anywhere in Thailand. Throughout Thailand SRT ticket offices are generally open from 8.30am to 6pm on weekdays, 8.30am to noon on weekends and public holidays. Train tickets can also be purchased at certain travel agencies in Bangkok. It is much simpler to book trains through these agencies than to book them at the station; however, there is usually a surcharge of 50B to 100B added to the ticket price.

Dining Facilities

Meal service is available in dining cars and at your seat in 2nd- and 1st-class cars. Menus change as frequently as the SRT changes catering services. For a while there were two menus, a 'special food' menu with 'special' prices (generally given to tourists) and a cheaper, more extensive menu.

Nowadays all the meals seem a bit overpriced (75B to 200B on average) by Thai standards – if you're concerned with saving baht, bring your own food.

Several readers have written to complain about being overcharged by meal servers on the trains. If you do purchase food on board, be sure to check the prices on the menu rather than trusting server quotes. Also check the bill carefully to make sure you haven't been overcharged.

Station Services

Accurate, up-to-date information on train travel is available at the Rail Travel Aids counter in Hualamphong station. There you can pick up timetables and ask questions about fares and scheduling – one person behind the counter usually speaks a little English. There are two types of timetable available: four condensed English timetables with fares, schedules and routes for rapid, express and special express trains on the four trunk lines; and four Thai timetables for each trunk line, with side lines as well. These latter timetables give fares and schedules for all trains – ordinary, rapid and express. The English timetables only display a couple of the ordinary routes (eg, they don't show the wealth of ordinary trains that go to Ayuthaya and as far North as Phitsanulok).

For questions or problems other than booking, there is a special tourist service line at ☎ 022 828 773.

All train stations in Thailand have baggage storage services (sometimes called the 'cloak room'). The rates and hours of operation vary from station to station. At Hualamphong station the hours are 4am to 10.30pm daily and left luggage costs 10B per day per piece for up to five days, after which it goes up to 15B per day. Hualamphong station also has a 10B shower service in the rest rooms.

Hualamphong station has a couple of travel agencies where other kinds of transport can be booked, but beware of touts who try and drag you there saying the trains are fully booked when they aren't. Avoid the travel agencies outside the station, which

have very poor reputations. Near the front of the station, at one end of the foyer, a Mail Boxes Etc (MBE) provides mailing, courier and packing services from 7.30am to 7.30pm Monday to Friday, 9am to 4pm Saturday and 9am to 8pm Sunday.

CAR & MOTORCYCLE
Roadways

Thailand has over 170,000km of roadways, of which around 16,000km are classified 'national highways' (both two-lane and four-lane), which means they're generally well maintained. Route numberings are fairly consistent: Some of the major highways have two numbers, one under the national system and another under the optimistic 'Asia Highway' system that indicates highway links with neighbouring countries. Route 105 to Mae Sot on the Myanmar border, for example, is also called 'Asia 1'. For the time being, the only border regularly crossed by non-commercial vehicles is the Thai-Malaysian border.

Kilometre markers are placed at regular intervals along most larger roadways, but place names are usually printed on them in Thai script only. Highway signs in both Thai and Roman script that show destination and distance are becoming increasingly common.

Road Rules

Thais drive on the left-hand side of the road (most of the time). Other than that, just about anything goes, in spite of road signs and speed limits – the Thais are notorious scoff-laws when it comes to driving. Like many places in Asia, in Thailand every two-lane road has an invisible third lane in the middle that all drivers feel free to use at any time. Passing on hills and curves is common – as long as you've got the proper Buddhist altar on the dashboard, what could happen?

The main rule to be aware of is that right-of-way belongs to the bigger vehicle; this is not what it says in Thai traffic law, but it's the reality. Maximum speed limits are 50km/h on urban roads and 100km/h on most highways – but on any given stretch of highway you'll see vehicles travelling as slowly as 30km/h or as fast as 150km/h.

Indicators are often used to warn passing drivers about oncoming traffic. A flashing left indicator means it's OK to pass, while a right indicator means that someone's approaching from the other direction.

The principal hazard to driving in Thailand, besides the general disregard for traffic laws, is having to contend with so many different types of vehicles on the same road – bullock carts, 18-wheelers, bicycles, túk-túk (motorised pedicabs) and customised racing bikes. This danger is often compounded by the lack of running lights. In village areas the vehicular traffic is lighter but you have to contend with stray chickens, dogs, water buffaloes and goats. Once you get used to the challenge, driving in Thailand is very entertaining.

Checkpoints

Military checkpoints are common along highways throughout Northern Thailand, especially in border areas. Always slow down for a checkpoint – often the sentries will wave you through without an inspection, but occasionally you will be stopped and briefly questioned. Use common sense and don't act belligerently, or you're likely to be detained longer than you'd like.

Rental

Cars, four-wheel drives (4WD) and vans can be rented in Bangkok, Chiang Mai, Chiang Rai and Mae Hong Son. A Japanese sedan (eg, Toyota Corolla) typically costs around 1000B to 1500B per day; minivans (eg, Toyota Hi-Ace, Nissan Urvan) go for around 1800B to 2500B a day. International rental companies tend to charge a bit more; Avis, for example, rents Nissan 1.4 Sentras for 1500B a day (9000B weekly), slightly larger Mitsubishi 1.5 Lancers for 2000B a day (10,200B weekly) and Mitsubishi 4WD Pajeros for 2200B per day (13,200B weekly).

The best deals are usually on 4WD Suzuki Caribians or Daihatsu Miras, which can be rented for as low as 800B per day with no per-kilometre fees for long-term rentals and in low seasons. Unless you absolutely want the cheapest vehicle, you might be better off with a larger vehicle (eg, a Mitsubishi 4WD Strada, if you absolutely want a 4WD); Caribians are notoriously hard to handle at

ROAD DISTANCES (km)

	Ayuthaya	Bangkok	Chiang Mai	Chiang Rai	Kamphaeng Phet	Lampang	Lopburi	Mae Hong Son	Mae Sai	Nan	Phayao	Phetchabun	Phichit	Phitsanulok	Phrae	Sukhothai	Tak	Uttaradit
Ayuthaya	---																	
Bangkok	79	---																
Chiang Mai	607	686	---															
Chiang Rai	777	856	191	---														
Kamphaeng Phet	289	338	357	477	---													
Lampang	531	599	92	225	241	---												
Lopburi	98	153	579	672	247	489	---											
Mae Hong Son	767	846	225	406	569	412	814	---										
Mae Sai	845	924	259	68	545	293	740	474	---									
Nan	587	668	318	275	359	227	554	639	343	---								
Phayao	620	691	222	94	382	131	516	543	162	176	---							
Phetchabun	323	354	417	599	364	368	259	741	680	418	444	---						
Phichit	285	344	406	474	90	332	177	656	542	359	379	191	---					
Phitsanulok	298	377	309	479	103	244	259	637	547	295	319	158	73	---				
Phrae	479	551	201	235	241	109	371	432	528	118	141	331	359	176	---			
Sukhothai	358	427	298	400	77	207	316	578	468	282	337	214	125	59	176	---		
Tak	335	414	280	460	68	174	315	423	528	362	304	304	157	1657	244	79	---	
Uttaradit	419	491	231	400	177	140	377	552	468	191	214	251	189	118	74	100	179	---

speeds above 90km/h and tend to crumple dangerously in collisions. Cars with automatic shift are uncommon. Drivers can usually be hired with a rental vehicle for an additional 300B to 400B per day.

Check with travel agencies or large hotels for rental locations. It is advisable always to verify that a vehicle is insured for liability before signing a rental contract; you should also ask to see the dated insurance documents. If you have an accident while driving an uninsured vehicle you're in for some major hassles.

Motorcycles can be rented in major towns and many smaller tourist centres of Northern Thailand (eg Chiang Mai, Chiang Rai, Pai, Mae Hong Son and Mae Sai). Rental rates vary considerably from one agency to another and from city to city but average around 200B per day. Since there is a glut of motorcycles for rent in Chiang Mai these days, they can be rented there for as little as 150B per day (or as little as 100B per day off-season or long-term).

A substantial deposit is usually required to rent a car; motorcycle rental usually requires that you leave your passport.

Driving Permits

Foreigners who wish to drive motor vehicles (including motorcycles) in Thailand need an International Driving Permit. If you don't have one, you can apply for a Thai driver's licence at the Police Registration Division (PRD; ☎ 025 130 051–5) on Thanon Phahonyothin in Bangkok. Provincial capitals also have PRDs. If you present a valid foreign driver's licence at the PRD you'll probably only have to take a written test; other requirements include a medical certificate and two passport-size colour photos. The forms are in Thai only, so you may also need an interpreter. Some PRDs request an affidavit of residence, obtainable from your country's embassy in Thailand upon presentation of proof that you reside in Thailand (eg, a utility bill in your name).

Fuel & Oil

Modern petrol (gasoline) stations with electric pumps are in plentiful supply all over Thailand where there are paved roads. In more remote off-road areas petrol (ben-sin or náam-man rót yon) is usually available at small roadside or village stands – typically just a couple of ancient hand-operated pumps fastened to petrol barrels. The Thai phrase for 'motor oil' is náam-man khrêuang.

At the time of writing, regular (thammádaa, usually 91 octane) petrol costs about 15B per litre, while super (phísèht, which is 94 to 95 octane) costs a bit more. Diesel (dii-soen) fuel is available at most pumps for around 12B per litre. All fuel in Thailand is unleaded.

Motorcycle Touring

Motorcycle travel has become a popular way to get around Thailand, especially in the North. Dozens of places along the guesthouse circuit, including many guesthouses themselves, have set up shop with no more than a couple of motorbikes for rent. It is also possible to buy a new or used motorbike and sell it before you leave the country. A used 125cc bike can be purchased for as little as 20,000B to 25,000B; you'll pay up to 60,000B for a reconditioned Honda MTX or AX-1, and more for the newer and more reliable Honda Degree or Yamaha TTR 250.

Daily rentals range from 150B to 200B a day for a 100cc step-through (eg, Honda Dream, Suzuki Crystal) in low-season months to 500B for a good 250cc dirt bike. The motorcycle industry in Thailand has stopped assembling dirt bikes, so many of the rental bikes of this nature are getting on in years. When they're well maintained they're fine; when they're not so well maintained they can leave you stranded, or worse. The latest trend in Thailand is small, heavy racing bikes that couldn't be less suitable for the typical faràng (Western) body.

The legal maximum size for motorcycle manufacture in Thailand is 150cc, though in reality few bikes on the road exceed 125cc. Anything over 150cc must be imported, which means an addition of up to 600% in import duties. The odd rental shop specialises in bigger motorbikes (average 200cc to 500cc) – some were imported by foreign residents and later sold on the local market, but most came into the country as 'parts' and were discreetly assembled, and licensed under the table.

A number of used Japanese dirt bikes are available in Northern Thailand. The 250cc, four-stroke, water-cooled Honda AX-1 and Yamaha TTR combine the qualities of both touring and off-road machines, and feature economical fuel consumption. If you're looking for a more narrowly defined dirt bike, check out the Yamaha Serow.

While motorcycle touring is undoubtedly one of the best ways to see Northern Thailand, it is also undoubtedly one of the easiest ways to cut your travels short, permanently. You can also run up very large repair and/or hospital bills in the blink of an eye. However, with proper safety precautions and driving conduct adapted to local standards, you can see parts of Northern Thailand inaccessible by other modes of transport and still make it home in one piece. Some guidelines to keep in mind:

- If you've never driven a motorcycle before, stick to the smaller 100cc step-through bikes with automatic clutches. If you're an experienced rider but have never done off-road driving, take it slowly the first few days.
- Always check a machine over thoroughly before you take it out. Look at the tyres to see if they still have tread, look for oil leaks, test the brakes. You may be held liable for any problems that weren't duly noted before your departure. Newer bikes cost more than clunkers, but are generally safer and more reliable. Street bikes are more comfortable and ride more smoothly on paved roads than dirt bikes; it's silly to rent an expensive dirt bike if most of your riding is going to be along decent roads. A two-stroke bike suitable for off-roading generally uses twice the fuel of a four-stroke bike with the same engine size, thus lowering your cruising range in areas where roadside pumps are scarce.
- Wear protective clothing and a helmet (required by law in 17 provinces – most rental places can provide them). Without a helmet, a minor slide on gravel can leave you with concussion. Long pants, long-sleeved shirts and shoes are highly recommended as protection against sunburn and as a

second skin if you fall. If your helmet doesn't have a visor, wear goggles, glasses or sunglasses to keep bugs, dust and other debris out of your eyes. Gloves are also a good idea, to prevent blisters. It is practically suicidal to ride on Thailand's highways without taking these minimum precautions for protecting your body.

- For distances of over 100km or so, take along an extra supply of motor oil, and if riding a two-stroke machine carry two-stroke engine oil. On long trips, oil burns fast.
- You should never ride alone in remote areas, especially at night. There have been incidents where faràng bikers have been shot or harassed while riding alone, mostly in remote rural areas. When riding in pairs or groups, stay spread out so you'll have room to manoeuvre or brake suddenly if necessary.
- Distribute whatever weight you're carrying on the bike as evenly as possible across the frame. Too much weight at the back of the bike makes the front end harder to control and prone to rising up suddenly on bumps and inclines.
- Get insurance with the motorcycle if at all possible. The more reputable motorcycle rental places insure all their bikes; some will do it for an extra charge. Without insurance you're responsible for anything that happens to the bike. If an accident results in a total loss, or if the bike is somehow lost or stolen, you can be up for 25,000B plus. To be absolutely clear about your liability, ask for a written estimate of the replacement cost for a similar bike – take photos as a guarantee. Some agencies will only accept the replacement cost of a new bike. Health insurance is more than a good idea, it's an absolute neccessity; get it before you leave home and check the conditions in regard to motorcycle riding.

There's an excellent Web site (W www .geocities.com/goldentrianglerider) with detailed, up-to-date information on motorcycle touring in Northern Thailand.

BICYCLE

Just about anywhere outside Bangkok, bikes are the ideal form of local transport because they're cheap, nonpolluting and keep you moving slowly enough to see everything. Bicycles can be hired in many locations; guesthouses often have a few for rent at only 30B to 50B per day. Carefully note the condition of the bike before hiring; if it breaks down you are responsible and parts can be very expensive.

Many visitors are bringing their own touring bikes to Thailand these days. For the most part, drivers are courteous and move over for bicycles. Most roads are sealed, with roomy shoulders. Grades in most parts of the country are moderate; exceptions include the far North, especially Mae Hong Son and Nan Provinces, where you'll need iron thighs. There is plenty of opportunity for dirt-road and off-road pedalling, especially in the North, so a sturdy mountain bike makes a good alternative to a touring rig. Favoured touring routes include the two-lane roads along the Mekong River in the North – the terrain is mostly flat and the river scenery is inspiring.

One note of caution: Before you leave home, go over your bike with a fine-toothed comb and fill your repair kit with every imaginable spare part. As with cars and motorbikes, you won't necessarily be able to buy that crucial gismo for your machine when it breaks down somewhere in the back of beyond as the sun sets. In addition to bringing a small repair kit with plenty of spare parts, it is advisable to bring a helmet, reflective clothing and plenty of insurance.

No special permits are needed for bringing a bicycle into the country, although bikes may be registered by customs – which means if you don't leave the country with your bike you'll have to pay a huge customs duty. Most larger cities have bike shops (there are several in Bangkok and Chiang Mai) but they often stock only a few Japanese or locally made parts.

You can take bicycles on the train for a little less than the equivalent of one 3rd-class fare. Buses often don't charge (if they do, it will be something nominal); on ordinary buses they'll place your bike on the roof, and on air-con buses it will be put in the cargo hold.

The Thailand Cycling Club (☎ 022 435 139 or ☎ 022 412 023) in Bangkok serves as an information clearing house on biking tours and cycle clubs around the country. One of the best shops for cycling gear in Thailand is the centrally located Probike (☎ 022 533 384, fax 022 541 077), 237/1 Soi Sarasin, opposite Lumphini Park in Bangkok.

HITCHING

Hitching (bòhk rót in Thai) is never entirely safe in any country in the world, and we don't recommend it. Travellers who decide to hitch should understand that there's a small but serious risk. However, many people do choose to hitch, and the advice that follows should help to make the journey as fast and safe as possible.

People have mixed success with hitchhiking in Thailand; sometimes it's great and at other times no-one wants to pick you up. It seems easiest in the more touristy areas of the North, most difficult in the central and northeastern regions where faràng are a relatively rare sight. To stand on a road and try to flag every vehicle that passes by is, to the Thais, something only an uneducated village dweller would do.

If you're prepared to face this perception, the first step is to use the correct gesture used for flagging a ride – the thumb-out gesture isn't recognised by the average Thai. When Thais want a ride they stretch one arm out with the hand open, palm facing down, and move the hand up and down. This is the same gesture used to flag a taxi or bus, which is why some drivers will stop and point to a bus stop if one is nearby.

In general, hitching isn't worth the hassle, as ordinary (no air-con) buses are frequent and fares cheap. There's no need to stand at a bus terminal – all you do is stand on any road going in your direction and flag down a passing bus or sãwngthãew (pick-up truck).

The exception is in areas where there isn't any bus service, though in such places there's not liable to be very much private traffic either. If you do manage to get a ride it's customary to offer food or cigarettes to the driver if you have any.

LOCAL TRANSPORT
Bus

Only one town in Northern Thailand has a city bus service – Phitsanulok, where fares are between 4B to 13B (see the Phitsanulok section in the Lower North chapter for more information). For the rest, you must rely on sãwngthãew, túk-túk or sãamláw (three-wheeled pedicabs).

The Tuk-Tuk of Thailand.

Săamláw & Túk-Túk

Săamláw means 'three wheels', and that's just what they are – three-wheeled vehicles. There are two types of săamláw: motorised and nonmotorised. You'll find motorised săamláw (called túk-túk) throughout the country. They're small utility vehicles, powered by a horrendously noisy two-stroke engine (usually LPG-powered) – if the noise and vibration doesn't get you, the fumes will. The nonmotorised version, on the other hand, is the bicycle rickshaw, just like you find, in various forms, all over Asia. In either form of săamláw the fare must be established, by bargaining if necessary, before departure.

Săwngthăew

A săwngthăew (literally, two rows) is a small pick-up truck with two rows of bench seats down the sides, very similar to an Indonesian bemo and akin to a Filipino jeepney. Săwngthăew sometimes operate on fixed routes, just like buses, but they may also run a share-taxi type of service or even be booked individually just like a regular taxi. They are often colour-coded, so that red săwngthăew, for example, go to one destination or group of destinations while blue ones go to another.

Motorcycle Taxi

Many cities in Thailand offer *mawtoesai ráp jâang* – 100cc to 125cc motorcycles that can be hired, with driver, for short distances. They're not very suitable if you're carrying more than a backpack or small suitcase, but if you're empty-handed they can't be beat for quick transport over short distances. In addition to the lack of space for luggage, motorcycle taxis also suffer from lack of shelter from rain or sun.

In most cities you'll find motorcycle taxis clustered near street intersections, rather than cruising the streets looking for fares. Fares tend to run from 10B to 30B, depending on distance. Some motorcycle taxis specialise in regular, short routes, eg, from one end of a long *soi* (lane) to another. In such cases the fare is usually a fixed 10B, occasionally as low as 5B in small towns.

Chiang Mai

☎ 053 • postcode 50000 • pop 170,000

One of the many questions Thais may ask a foreigner visiting Thailand is 'Have you been to Chiang Mai yet?', underscoring the feeling that Chiang Mai is a keystone of any journey to the kingdom. Along with Sukhothai farther south, it was the first Southeast Asian state to make the historic transition from domination by Mon and Khmer cultures to a new era ruled by Thais.

Although Thais idealise their beloved northern capital as a quaint, moated and walled city surrounded by mountains with legendary, mystical attributes, the truth is Chiang Mai has all but left that image behind to become a modern, cosmopolitan city exhibiting many of the hallmarks of contemporary world culture and technology.

More than 700km northwest of Bangkok, Chiang Mai has over 300 temples (121 within the *thêtsabaan*, municipal limits) – almost as many as in Bangkok – a fact that makes it visually striking. Auspicious Doi Suthep rises 1676m above and behind the city, providing a picturesque backdrop for this fast-developing centre. Many visitors stay in Chiang Mai longer than planned because of the high quality and low price of accommodation, food and shopping, the cool nights (compared with Central Thailand), the international feel of the city and the friendliness of the people.

The city is small enough to navigate by bicycle. With the increasing number of cultural and spiritual learning experiences available in Chiang Mai these days – Thai massage, Thai cooking, Thai language, yoga and *vipassana* (insight) meditation – Chiang Mai has become much more than just a quick stop on the Northern Thailand tourist circuit.

Not all the foreigners you see in Chiang Mai are tourists – as many as 20,000 expatriates live in the Chiang Mai area part time or year-round. Chiang Mai residents often comment that living here has all the cultural advantages of being in Bangkok, but fewer of the disadvantages such as traffic gridlock and air pollution. In recent years, however, traffic has increased and the city's major thoroughfares have in fact become somewhat noisy and polluted. Still, the narrow winding *soi* (lanes) of the walled city and older neighbourhoods to the east maintain Chiang Mai's essential character.

The best time of year for a visit to Chiang Mai is between July and March, when the weather is relatively pleasant, the air is clearest, and the surrounding hills are green.

Preserving Chiang Mai

In efforts to preserve the city's character, the Chiang Mai government has legislated several conservation measures, most notably a 1991 ban on the building of any high-rise construction within 93m of a temple, thereby protecting about 87% of all land within municipal limits. Designed to halt any future condo developments along Mae Nam Ping (Ping River) in order to preserve the city's skyline, this law has been very effective.

Another positive development was the 1992 dredging of the formerly polluted city moat and installation of an automatic filtering system. Although not the most pristine of waterways, the moat now supports many fish and turtles.

A further boon was the establishment of a one-way traffic system that allowed the city to extinguish many traffic lights and improve overall traffic flow considerably. The city has also introduced the most comprehensive municipal recycling program in the country; there are recycling bins on roadsides around town to accept glass, plastic and paper.

The most drastic scheme thus far proposed would involve establishing a 'twin city' nearby to channel development away from the old city – possibly at San Kamphaeng to the east. Since the national economic crisis of 1997 however, this idea has been shelved.

From April to June it is hot and dry, and a thick haze tends to collect in the air over the surrounding valley. August is the rainiest month, although even then there usually are clear days.

HISTORY

One of the oldest and most popular literary accounts of how Chiang Mai came to be founded narrates how a Thai prince named Suwanna Kham Daeng tracked a deer a very long distance. He ended up in Northern Thailand, and delighted with the location he founded a city predecessor to Chiang Mai.

Chiang Mai's more verifiable history begins with a series of early settlements along the Mae Nam Ping (Ping River), which today runs through the eastern half of the city. Here Phaya Mang Rai, a prince from Ngoen Yang (today Chiang Saen) took over a Mon settlement to develop Nopburi Si Nakhon Ping Chiang Mai (shortened to Chiang Mai, 'New Walled City') in 1296. Historically, Chiang Mai Province succeeded Phaya Mang Rai's Chiang Rai kingdom after he conquered the post-Dvaravati kingdom of Hariphunchai (modern Lamphun) in 1281. Mang Rai built Chiang Mai's original city walls in 1296; traces of these earthen ramparts can still be seen today along Thanon Kamphaeng Din (Kamphaeng Din Rd).

Later, in the 14th and 15th centuries, Chiang Mai became a part of the larger kingdom of Lan Na Thai (Million Thai Rice Fields; often called Lanna), which extended as far south as Kamphaeng Phet and as far north as Luang Prabang in Laos. During this period Chiang Mai became an important religious and cultural centre – the eighth world synod of Theravada Buddhism was held there in 1477.

The Burmese capture of the city in 1556 was the second time the Burmese had control of Chiang Mai Province: Before Phaya Mang Rai's reign, King Anawrahta of Pagan (present-day Bagan) had ruled Chiang Mai Province in the 11th century. The second time around, the Burmese ruled Chiang Mai for over 200 years.

The Burmese allowed trade to continue and in 1587 the first known Westerner to visit Chiang Mai, London trader Ralph Fitch, spent several months in the city. Fitch regaled:

Tamakey [Chiang Mai] is a very fair and great town, with fair houses of stone, well peopled, the streets are very large, the men very well set and strong, with a cloth about them, bare headed and bare footed: for in all these countries they wear no shoes. The women be much fairer than those of Pegu. Hither to Tamakey come many merchants out of China, and bring great store of musk, gold, silver, and many other things of China work.

Another Englishman, Thomas Samuel of the East India Company, arrived in 1613, only to be captured by Burmese troops the following year. It is thought that he was taken back to Myanmar, where he later died.

In 1775 Chiang Mai was recaptured by the Thais under King Taksin, who appointed Chao Kawila, a *jâo meuang* (chieftain) from nearby Lampang principality, as viceroy of Northern Thailand. Chao Kawila paraded his troops into the city in 1797 and within three years had built the monumental brick walls around the inner city, expanded the city in southerly and easterly directions and established a river port at the end of what is today Thanon Tha Phae (*thâa phae* means 'raft pier').

Under Kawila, Chiang Mai became an important regional trade centre. Many of the later Shan and Burmese-style temples seen around the city were built by wealthy teak merchants who emigrated from Burma during the late 19th century. Not all the Shan residents were merchants, however. In 1902 several hundred labourers, most of them Shan, protested against the practice of corvee (involuntary service to the state) by refusing to construct roads or otherwise follow government orders. The ensuing skirmishes between corvee labourers and Chiang Mai troops – dubbed the Shan Rebellion by historians – didn't resolve the issue until the custom was discontinued in 1924.

The completion of the northern railway to Chiang Mai in 1921 finally linked the North with Bangkok, giving the region a new access to markets both in the Siamese capital and abroad. In 1927 King Rama VII and Queen Rambaibani rode into city at the head of an 84-elephant caravan, becoming the first Central Thai monarchs to visit the North, and in 1933 Chiang Mai officially became a province of Siam.

Long before tourists began visiting the region, Chiang Mai was an important centre for handcrafted pottery, weaving, umbrellas, silverwork and woodcarving. After the city was linked to the outside world, word soon spread among the Thais and foreign visitors that the quaint northern capital was a highly recommended destination for shopping and recreation. By the mid 1960s tourism had replaced commercial trade as Chiang Mai's number one source of outside revenue, a ranking that has been maintained since. Close seconds are the manufacture and sale of local handicrafts. In handicraft shops anywhere in Thailand, chances are at least someone working there will hail from the Chiang Mai area.

ORIENTATION

The old city of Chiang Mai is a neat square bounded by moats and partial walls. Thanon Moon Muang (Mun Meuang), along the eastern moat, is the centre for inexpensive accommodation and places to eat. Thanon Tha Phae runs straight from the middle of this side and crosses Mae Nam Ping, where it changes into Thanon Charoen Muang.

The train station and the main post office are farther down Thanon Charoen Muang, a fair distance from the centre. There are two inter-city bus terminals in Chiang Mai, one near Pratu Chang Pheuak (White Elephant Gate) and a larger one called Chiang Mai Arcade.

Several of Chiang Mai's important temples are within the moat area, but there are others to the north and west.

Maps

Finding your way around Chiang Mai is fairly simple, although a copy of Nancy Chandler's *Map of Chiang Mai*, sold in bookshops, is a very worthwhile investment

for 140B. It shows all the main points of interest, shopping venues (including detailed inset maps of the Night Bazaar and Talat Worarot) and oddities that you'd be most unlikely to stumble upon by yourself.

The Tourism Authority of Thailand (TAT) puts out a sketchy city map that is free and available from the TAT office on Thanon Chiang Mai–Lamphun. Several other giveaway maps are also available in tourist shops and restaurants.

INFORMATION
Tourist Offices

Chiang Mai has a friendly TAT office (Central Chiang Mai map; ☎ 053 248 604) on Thanon Chiang Mai–Lamphun opposite the Saphan Lek (Lek Bridge) just south of Saphan Nawarat. It's open 8am to 4.30pm daily.

Chiang Mai's Tourist Police (Central Chiang Mai map; ☎ 053 248 130, 053 248 974, 1155), who have a reputation for honesty and efficiency, have an office about 100m north of the TAT office on Thanon Chiang Mai–Lamphun. It's open 6am until midnight daily. Call ☎ 1155 in case of emergency (24 hours).

Foreign Consulates

Chiang Mai has several foreign consular posts where you may be able to arrange visas. The Indian consulate here is a familiar stopping-off point for travellers on their way to India; it takes about four days to process a visa.

Australia (Chiang Mai map; ☎ 053 221 083, fax 053 219 726) 165 Thanon Sirimankhalajan
Austria (Chiang Mai map; ☎ 053 400 231, fax 053 400 232) 15 Mu 1, Thanon Huay Kaew
Canada (Chiang Mai map; ☎ 053 224 851, 053 224 861, ☎/fax 053 850 147) 151 Thanon Chiang Mai–Lampang (Hwy 11)
China (Central Chiang Mai map; ☎ 053 276 125, 053 200 424, fax 053 274 614) 111 Thanon Chang Lor
Finland (Chiang Mai Night Bazaar map; ☎ 053 234 777, fax 053 251 512) 104–112 Thanon Tha Phae
France (Central Chiang Mai map; ☎ 053 281 466, 053 275 277, fax 053 821 039) 138 Thanon Charoen Prathet

Germany (☎/fax 053 838 735,
ⓔ dekonsul@loxinfo.co.th) 199/163 Mu 3,
Baan Nai Fan 2, Thanon Kan Khlong
Chonlaprathan

India (Chiang Mai map; ☎ 053 243 066, 053
242 491, fax 053 247 879) 344 Thanon Faham
(Charoen Rat)

Japan (Chiang Mai map; ☎ 053 203 367, fax
053 203 373) 104–107 Airport Business Park,
90 Thanon Mahidon

Sweden (Chiang Mai map; ☎ 053 220 844, 053
221 812, fax 053 210 877) YMCA
International Hotel, Santitham

UK & Northern Ireland (Central Chiang Mai
map; ☎ 053 263 015, fax 053 263 016) 198
Thanon Bamrungrat

USA (Eastern Chiang Mai map; ☎ 053 252
629–31, fax 053 252 633) 387 Thanon
Wichayanon

Immigration

The Thai immigration office (Chiang Mai
map; ☎ 053 201 755/6, 71 Thanon Sanam
Bin) is near the airport. Two-week visa extensions are available here for 500B. You
will need copies of your passport and two
passport photos for the extension application. The office is open 8.30am to 4.30pm,
Monday to Friday.

Money

All major Thai banks have several branches
throughout Chiang Mai, many of them
along Thanon Tha Phae; most are open
8.30am to 3.30pm on weekdays only.

In the well-touristed areas – for example,
the Night Bazaar, Thanon Tha Phae and
Thanon Moon Muang – there are automated
teller machines (ATMs) and the banks also
operate foreign-exchange booths that are
open as late as 8pm.

Chiang Mai International Business Center (☎ 053 252 801), diagonally opposite
Thai Farmers Bank on Thanon Tha Phae,
specialises in cash exchanges in several
currencies (although travellers cheques are
also accepted). It's open 8.30am to 3.30pm
Monday to Friday. There is a second
branch (☎ 053 216 283) located at 30/1
Thanon Chotana.

If you need to send or receive money by
wire, there's a Western Union (Chiang Mai
map; ☎ 053 224 979, Central Department

Store, 3rd floor, Kad Suan Kaew shopping
centre, Thanon Huay Kaew) in town.

Post & Communications

The main post office (Chiang Mai map;
☎ 053 241 070) is on Thanon Charoen
Muang near the train station. It's open
8.30am to 4.30pm weekdays and 9am to
noon on weekends.

More convenient to visitors staying west
of the river towards the old city, the Mae
Ping post office (Chiang Mai Night Bazaar
map), on Thanon Praisani near the flower
market, is open 8.30am to 4.30pm weekdays, 9am to noon Saturday. The old Mae
Ping post office, which is across the street
from the new post office, houses the Chiang
Mai Philatelic Museum (open 9am to 4pm
weekends and holidays).

Other useful branch post offices can be
found at Thanon Singarat/Samlan, Thanon
Mahidon, Thanon Phra Pokklao, Thanon
Chotana, Thanon Chang Khlan, and at
Chiang Mai University and Chiang Mai
International Airport.

Mail Boxes Etc (Chiang Mai Night
Bazaar map; ☎ 053 818 433), at 124
Thanon Chang Khlan near the Night Bazaar
offers the usual private mail services, including rental boxes, mailing supplies,
packing services, stationery and a courier
service. It also does passport photos and
photocopies.

DHL International (Central Chiang Mai
map; ☎ 053 418 501) has an office on
Thanon Mani Nopharat east of Pratu Chang
Pheuak (Chang Pheuak Gate).

Overseas telephone calls and faxes can
be arranged at the Overseas Call Office
around the side and upstairs from the main
post office on Thanon Charoen Muang; it's
open 24 hours. International calls can also
be made from larger hotels for a service
charge (up to 30%), at many Internet cafes
and at Mail Boxes Etc on Thanon Chang
Khlan. A few Internet cafes can arrange inexpensive Internet phone hook-ups.

Home Country Direct phones, with easy
one-button connection with foreign operators in a number of countries around the
world, are available at: Chiang Inn Plaza,

100/1 Thanon Chang Khlan, near the Night Bazaar; Chiang Mai International Airport; the main post office on Thanon Charoen Muang; the Thai Airways International (THAI) office at 240 Thanon Phra Pokklao; and the TAT office.

The list of places to log on in Chiang Mai is rapidly growing and you'll find plenty of Internet centres along the following streets: Tha Phae, Moon Muang, Ratchadamnoen, Ratchadamri, Huay Kaew, Suthep and Chang Khlan.

Chiang Mai Disabled Center (Central Chiang Mai map; ☎ 053 213 941, [e] assist@loxinfo.co.th), at 133/1 Thanon Ratchaphakhinai in the old city, offers several terminals with email and Internet access, along with fax and scanning services. Prices are the same as most other Internet centres in town, and all proceeds go to help local disabled people. The Foundation to Encourage the Potential of Disabled Persons, which runs the centre, has a Web site at [W] www.infothai.com/disabled.

Internet Resources

Chiang Mai Focus ([W] www.chiangmai-focus.com) is the best overall source of Web-based information on Chiang Mai so far. Pages include up-to-date data on attractions, activities, accommodations, transport and most importantly current events. Chiang Mai Online ([W] www.chiangmai-online.com) is a commercial site with an overall uneven information flow, although the accommodation listings are quite comprehensive and include room rates from guesthouses as well as hotels. Chiang Mai Newsletter ([W] www .chiangmainews.com) shows great potential as well and posts articles on culture and art.

Bookshops

Chiang Mai has several bookshops, the biggest being Suriwong Book Centre (Central Chiang Mai map) at its newly expanded location at 54 Thanon Si Donchai, and DK Book House (Eastern Chiang Mai map) on Thanon Kotchasan. A smaller place with a decent selection of books is The Book Zone (Eastern Chiang Mai map; ☎ 053 252 418)

on Thanon Tha Phae, directly opposite Wat Mahawan.

Bookazine (Chiang Mai Night Bazaar map; ☎ 053 281 370), in the basement of Chiang Inn Plaza, carries European and American newspapers and magazines, travel guides, maps and other English-language publications.

The American University Alumni (AUA; Eastern Chiang Mai map; ☎ 053 214 120) library on Thanon Ratchadamnoen has a large selection of English-language newspapers and magazines. The library is open 8.30am to 6pm weekdays, 9am to 1pm Saturday. Entry requires an annual 400B membership fee (100B for AUA students, 200B for other students) or a one-month temporary 150B membership fee for visitors. The British Council (Central Chiang Mai map; ☎ 053 242 103, fax 053 244 781) at 198 Thanon Bamrungrat also has a small English-language library. The Chiang Mai University library has a good collection of foreign-language titles.

Chiang Mai also has several shops specialising in used books. The Bookshop (Eastern Chiang Mai map) on Thanon Loi Kroh, in an alley next to L'Elephant Blanc restaurant, has especially good selections, going far beyond the usual airport pulp to include many books on arts and culture, including hardcovers. Most books for sale are in English, but books in French and German are also available.

Shaman Books (Eastern Chiang Mai map), on Soi 2, Thanon Tha Phae, is a branch of the well-known Bangkok used bookshop. Shaman specialises in travel, fiction and spirituality.

The Library Service (Eastern Chiang Mai map), next to New Saitum Guest House at 21/1 Soi 2, Thanon Ratchamankha, not far from Pratu Tha Phae, also offers used paperbacks for sale or trade, as does Gecko Books (Eastern Chiang Mai map) on Thanon Chang Moi Kao.

Media

Several free English-language publications are distributed at tourist spots throughout the city. The tourism-oriented *Guidelines*

CHIANG MAI

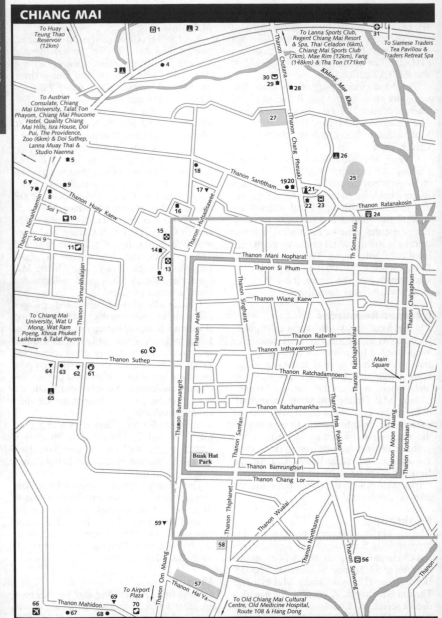

CHIANG MAI

To Huay Teung Thao Reservoir (12km)

To Lanna Sports Club, Regent Chiang Mai Resort & Spa, Thai Celadon (6km), Chiang Mai Sports Club (7km), Mae Rim (12km), Fang (148km) & Tha Ton (171km)

To Siamese Traders Tea Paviliou & Traders Retreat Spa

Thanon Chotana

Khlong Mae Kha

To Austrian Consulate, Chiang Mai University, Talat Ton Phayom, Chiang Mai Phucome Hotel, Quality Chiang Mai Hills, Isra House, Doi Pui, The Providence, Zoo (6km) & Doi Suthep, Lanna Muay Thai & Studio Naenna

Thanon Chang Pheuak

Thanon Santitham

Thanon Ratanakosin

Thanon Huay Kaew

Thanon Hutsadisawee

Thanon Mani Nopharat

Thanon Si Phum

Thanon Nimanhaemin

Soi 1

Soi 9

Thanon Sirimankhalajan

Thanon Wiang Kaew

Thanon Sughharat

Thanon Arak

Thanon Ratwithi

Thanon Inthawarorot

Thanon Ratchadamnoen

Main Square

Thanon Ratchaphakhinai

Th Soman Kila

Thanon Chaiyaphum

To Chiang Mai University, Wat U Mong, Wat Ram Poeng, Khrua Phuket Laikhram & Talat Payom

Thanon Suthep

Thanon Ratchamankha

Thanon Phra Pokklao

Thanon Moon Muang

Thanon Kotchasan

Thanon Bunreuangrit

Thanon Samfan

Buak Hat Park

Thanon Bamrungburi

Thanon Chang Lor

Thanon Thiphanet

Thanon Whalai

Thanon Nontharam

Thanon Sunwong

To Airport Plaza

Thanon Om Muang

Thanon Hai Ya

Thanon Mahidon

To Old Chiang Mai Cultural Centre, Old Medicine Hospital, Route 108 & Hang Dong

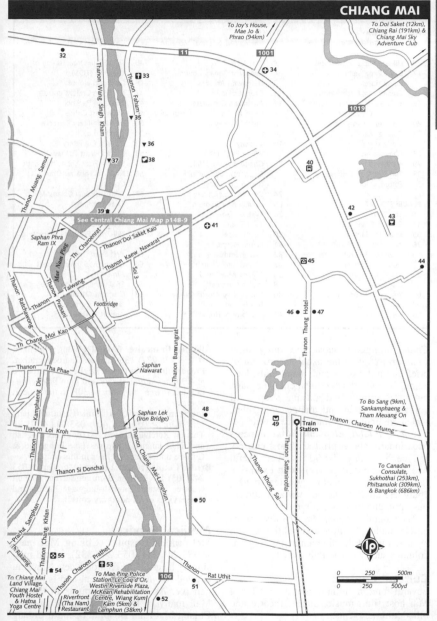

CHIANG MAI

To Joy's House,
Mae Jo &
Phrao (94km)

To Doi Saket (12km),
Chiang Rai (191km) &
Chiang Mai Sky
Adventure Club

● 32

11

1001

☩ 34

1019

🏨 33

Thanon Fa Ham

▼ 35

40
🏧

42 ●

43
🏧

▼ 36

🏧 38

▼ 37

Thanon Wiang Singh Kham

Thanon Muang Samut

39 🏛

See Central Chiang Mai Map p148-9

☩ 41

Saphan Phra
Ram IX

Th Charoenrat

Thanon Doi Saket Kao

📷 45

44

Mae Nam Ping

Thanon Kaew Nawarat

Soi 3

Thanon Praisani

Taiwang

46 ● ● 47

Thanon Thung Hotel

Thanon Ratchawong

Footbridge

Th Chang Moi Kao

Thanon Bamrungrat

Thanon Kamphaeng Din

Thanon
Tha Phae

Saphan
Nawarat

To Bo Sang (9km),
Sankamphaeng &
Tham Meuang On

Thiahon Loi Kroh

Saphan Lek
(Iron Bridge)

48
●

Thanon Charoen Muang

Thanon Si Donchai

🏧
49

🚉 Train
Station

Thanon Chiang Mai-Lamphun

Thanon Sattanrotfai

Thanon Khong Sai

To Canadian
Consulate,
Sukhothai (253km),
Phitsanulok (309km),
& Bangkok (686km)

● 50

L Pracha Samphan

Th Rakaeng

Thanon Chang Khlan

🏧 55

🏛 54

🏨 53

To Chiang Mai
Land Village,
Chiang Mai
Youth Hostel
& Hatna
Yoga Centre

Thanon Charoen Prathet

To Mae Ping Police
Station, Le Coq d'Or,
Westin Riverside Plaza,
McKean Rehabilitation
Centre, Wiang Kum
Kam (5km) &
Lamphun (38km)

To
Riverfront
(Tha Nam)
Restaurant

106

Thanon
Rat Uthit

● 51

● 52

0   250   500m
0   250   500yd

LP

CHIANG MAI

PLACES TO STAY		OTHER			
5	Amity Green Hills	1	Chiang Mai National Museum	42	Carrefour
8	Amari Rincome Hotel	2	Khuang Sing	43	Chiang Mai German Brewery
9	Hillside Plaza & Condotel	3	Wat Jet Yot	44	Payap University
12	Lotus Pang Suan	4	Anantasiri Tennis Courts	45	Telephone Organisation of
	Kaew Hotel	7	Nantawan Arcade		Thailand (TOT)
14	Chiang Mai Orchid Hotel	10	Drunken Flower	46	Duangjitt House
16	YMCA International Hotel;	11	Australian Consulate	47	Northern Crafts Centre
	Swedish Consulate	13	Kad Suan Kaew; Sri Sanpanmai	48	Talat San Pa Khoi
20	Novotel Chiang Mai	15	Vista 12 Huay Kaew	49	Main Post Office
22	Chiang Mai Phu	18	ITM	50	Kawila Military Barracks
	Viang Hotel	19	Velocity	51	Gymkhana Club
28	Chawala Hotel	21	White Elephant Monument	52	Foreign Cemetery
29	Iyara Hotel	23	Chang Pheuak (White	53	Sacred Heart Cathedral
39	Pun Pun Guest House		Elephant) Bus Terminal	55	Season Plaza Shopping Centre
54	Empress Hotel		(Provincial Buses)	56	National Theatre; Drama
		24	Devi Mandir Chiang Mai		College
PLACES TO EAT		25	Chiang Mai Stadium	57	Talat Dok Mai Chiang Mai
6	The Pub	26	Wat Ku Tao	58	Talat Thiphanet
17	Sa-Nga Choeng Doi	27	Talat Thanin	60	Maharaj Hospital
35	Khao Soi Samoe Jai	30	Post Office	61	Petrol Station
36	Khao Soi Lam Duan;	31	Lanna Hospital	63	Hill-Tribe Products Promotion
	Khao Soi Ban Faham	32	Talat Kamthiang		Centre
37	Heuan Soontaree	33	Chiang Mai Church	65	Wat Suan Dok
59	Vegetarian Centre of	34	Chiang Mai Ram 2	66	Chiang Mai International
	Chiang Mai	38	Indian Consulate		Airport
62	Yong Khao Tom Kui	40	Chiang Mai Arcade (New)	67	Thai Immigration Office
64	Suandok Vegetarian		Bus Terminal	68	Customs Office
69	Chez John	41	McCormick Hospital	70	Japanese Consulate;
					Airport Business Park

Chiang Mai and *Welcome to Chiangmai & Chiangrai* contain the usual assortment of brief cultural essays and maps embedded among stacks of advertisements for bars, pubs, restaurants and antique shops. All contain bus, train and airline timetables, which are updated perhaps once a year.

Chang Puak/L'Elephant Blanc appears occasionally and is printed almost entirely in French. *Chiang Mai Info* is a very useful booklet (published yearly), with extensive listings of government agencies, banks, churches, apartments, condos and current bus, train and plane schedules.

The monthly *Chiang Mai Newsletter* runs articles on local culture and politics as well as a listing of local events and regular columns such as 'The Pub Crawl'.

Cultural Centres

Several foreign cultural centres in Chiang Mai host film, music, dance, theatre and other cultural events.

Alliance Française (Central Chiang Mai map; ☎ 053 275 277) 138 Thanon Charoen Prathet. French films (subtitled in English) are screened at 4.30pm every Tuesday and 8pm Friday; admission is free to members, 30B to the general public.

American University Alumni (Eastern Chiang Mai map; ☎ 053 278 407, 053 211 377) 73 Thanon Ratchadamnoen. AUA offers English and Thai language courses (see Language & Culture under Courses later in this chapter).

British Council (Central Chiang Mai map; ☎ 053 242 103) 198 Thanon Bamrungrat. The council features a small English-language library and the services of an honorary consul.

Medical Services

McCormick Hospital (Chiang Mai map; ☎ 053 241 311, 053 240 832), an old missionary hospital on Thanon Kaew Nawarat, is good for minor treatment and is not expensive. As at most hospitals in Chiang Mai, many of the doctors speak English. Chiang Mai Ram Hospital (Central Chiang

Mai map; ☎ 053 224 861), on Thanon Bun-reuangrit near the Sri Tokyo Hotel, is the most modern hospital in town. It's full of gleaming new equipment and costs a bit more than the other Chiang Mai hospitals.

Other recommended medical facilities include Lanna Hospital (Chiang Mai map; ☎ 053 357 234) on Thanon Chang Khlan. The Malaria Centre (Central Chiang Mai map; ☎ 053 221 529) at 18 Thanon Bun-reuangrit can do blood checks for malaria.

Chip Aun Tong Dispensary (Central Chiang Mai map; ☎ 053 234 187), at 48–52 Thanon Chang Moi, offers traditional Chinese medicine and has a Chinese doctor. Mungkala (Eastern Chiang Mai map; ☎ 053 278 494, 053 208 431, fax 053 208 432, e mungkala@cm.ksc.co.th), at 21–25 Thanon Ratchamankha, is another good traditional Chinese clinic that offers acupuncture, massage and herbal therapy.

Alcoholics Anonymous (Chiang Mai map; ☎ 053 241 311, ext 235) holds open meetings at 6.30pm every evening at House No 11 behind McCormick Hospital. Closed meetings are held on Sunday at 9.30am.

Film & Processing
Outside of Bangkok, Chiang Mai has the best supply of quality photographic film in the country. Broadway Photo (Eastern Chiang Mai map; ☎ 053 251 253), on Thanon Tha Phae about 100m east of Pratu Tha Phae, has a good selection of slide film, including hard-to-find (in Chiang Mai) Fujichrome slide films. Souvenir print processing is fine, but professional photographers will do better to wait till they're in Bangkok or back home for processing, as Chiang Mai's photo labs are notoriously unreliable.

Dangers & Annoyances
All in all Chiang Mai is a very safe place to visit but as always it pays to be cautious, especially when you first arrive.

Watch out for travel agents who ask for cash up front to buy air tickets on your behalf. Either wait to pay till you have the correct ticket in hand, or better yet pay by credit card so that you can reverse the charges if scammed.

Don't accept drinks from strangers in guesthouses. There have been a few unconfirmed reports of druggings followed by attempted robbery and/or rape.

THINGS TO SEE
Wat Chiang Man
วัดเชียงมั่น

A stone slab inscription, engraved in 1581 and erected at Wat Chiang Man (Central Chiang Mai map; ☎ 053 375 368), bears the earliest known reference to the city's 1296 founding. It is thus thought to be the oldest wát (temple) in the city, supposedly founded by Phaya Mang Rai. The wát features typical Northern Thai temple architecture, with massive teak columns inside the bòt (central sanctuary), which in Northern Thai is called a sĭm.

Two important Buddha images are kept in a glass cabinet in the smaller wíhăan (Buddhist image sanctuary) to the right of the sĭm. The Phra Sila is a marble bas-relief Buddha standing 20cm to 30cm high. According to legend, it's supposed to have come from Sri Lanka or India 2500 years ago, but since no Buddha images were produced anywhere before around 2000 years ago it must have arrived later. The well-known Phra Satang Man, a crystal seated Buddha image, was shuttled back and forth between Thailand and Laos. It's thought to have come from Lavo (Lopburi) 1800 years ago and stands just 10cm high. A very interesting silver Buddha sits in front of the cabinet among a collection of other images.

The sĭm containing the venerated images is open 9am to 5pm daily. Wat Chiang Man is off Thanon Ratchaphakhinai in the northeastern corner of the old city.

Wat Phra Singh
วัดพระสิงห์

Started by King Pa Yo in 1345, the wíhăan that houses the Phra Singh image was completed between 1385 and 1400. The Phra Singh Buddha supposedly comes from Sri Lanka, but it is not particularly Singhalese in style. In fact it's a perfect example of the

Uncle Piang's River Triumph

The simple but striking Chedi Khao or 'White Stupa' on the corner of Thanon Faham and Thanon Wichayanon near the US consulate is of unverified date and provenance, but at least it has a story behind it. Legend says a hostile power from the south came to the edge of the river one day with a man who was an expert diver. The leaders of the invading force challenged Nakhon Ping (an old name for Chiang Mai) to find someone who could dive into the Mae Nam Ping and stay beneath the river's rippling surface longer than their champion. If the Chiang Mai resident won, Nakhon Ping would remain independent, and if not the invaders would seize the territory.

The Nakhon Ping Monarch sent out an appeal for someone in his kingdom who could respond to the challenge. As Chiang Mai was landlocked, finding someone skilled in timed diving was nigh impossible but after several days a man called Uncle Piang volunteered to defend his homeland. Wearing only sarongs, Uncle Piang and the diving expert dived into the Ping. An expectant crowd marvelled as the champion diver stayed underwater for four minutes, then came gasping to the river's surface. As the Chiang Mai citizenry cheered, Piang was declared the winner and Nakhon Ping, as the story goes, kept its sovereignty.

When Piang didn't surface for several more minutes, the king ordered several of his subjects into the river to search for him. They found his body at the bottom of the river, his sarong tied to a stake.

This isn't the only story attached to the White Stupa. A more modern and paranoid version claims the CIA maintains a powerful transmitter inside the *chedi* (stupa) that enables the adjacent US consulate to send and receive secret communiques. Of course the consulate denies all knowledge of such an instrument. 'Why would we use such a puny little chedi for our transmitter?', the consul allegedly retorted when asked about the story. 'We use Doi Suthep!'

classic Lanna style that was preferred from Chiang Mai to Luang Prabang during this period. As it is identical to two images in Nakhon Si Thammarat and Bangkok, and has quite a travel history (Sukhothai, Ayuthaya, Chiang Rai, Luang Prabang – the usual itinerary for a travelling Buddha image, involving much royal trickery), no-one really knows which image is the real one, nor can anyone document its place of origin. The image was finished in about 1600.

The wát's main *chedi* (stupa) displays classic Lanna style with its octagonal base. Wihan Lai Kham, near the chedi, contains impressive Lanna-style temple mural paintings and *laai kham* (gold stencil patterns on lacquer). See the special section 'Lanna-Style Temple Murals'.

Wat Phra Singh *(Central Chiang Mai map;* ☎ *053 814 164)* stands at the west end of Thanon Ratchadamnoen near Pratu Suan Dok.

Wat Chedi Luang

วัดเจดีย์หลวง

This temple complex *(Central Chiang Mai map;* ☎ *053 278 595)*, the name of which means 'Monastery of the Great Stupa', stands off Thanon Phra Pokklao. The centrepiece of the compound is a very large and venerable Lanna-style chedi dating from 1441. It's now in partial ruins, damaged either by a 16th-century earthquake or by the cannon fire of King Taksin in 1775 during the recapture of Chiang Mai from the Burmese.

The Phra Kaew ('Emerald' Buddha) – now in Bangkok's Wat Phra Kaew – sat in the eastern niche here in 1475. Now in the eastern niche sits a jade replica of the original Phra Kaew; its official name is Phra Phut Chaloem Sirirat, but it's more commonly known locally as the Phra Kaew Yok Chiang Mai (Chiang Mai Holy Jade Image). The image was financed by the Thai king and carved in 1995; the placement of the image celebrated the 600th anniversary of the chedi (according to some reckonings), and the 700th anniversary of the city.

A restoration of the great chedi, financed by Unesco and the Japanese government, has so far thankfully stopped short of creating a new spire, since no-one knows for sure how the original superstructure looked. New Buddha images have been placed in three of the four directional niches.

New porticoes and *naga* (serpent being) guardians for the chedi lack the finesse of the originals. On the southern side of the monument, six elephant sculptures in the pediment can be seen. Five are cement restorations; only the one on the far right – without ears and trunk – is original brick and stucco.

The *làk meuang* (guardian deity post) for the city is within the wát compound in the small building to the left of the main entrance. There are also some impressive dipterocarp trees (so named because of their 'twin winged' seed pods that come helicoptering down in the hot season) in the grounds.

Wat Phan Tao
วัดพันเถา

Diagonally adjacent to Wat Chedi Luang, this wát *(Central Chiang Mai map;* ☎ *053 814 689)* contains a large, old teak wíhǎan that is one of the unsung treasures of Chiang Mai. Constructed of moulded wooden teak panels fitted together and supported by 28 gargantuan teak pillars, the wíhǎan features naga bargeboards inset with coloured mirror mosaic. On display inside are old temple bells, some ceramics, a few old Northern-style gilded wooden Buddhas and antique cabinets stacked with old palm-leaf manuscripts. Also in the compound are some old monastic quarters.

There's a wall dividing Wat Phan Tao from Wat Chedi Luang, but you can walk through small gates from one to the other. Across Thanon Ratchadamnoen from here, at the Thanon Phra Pokklao intersection, is an uninteresting monument marking the spot where Phaya Mang Rai was struck by lightning!

Wat Jet Yot
วัดเจ็ดยอด

Out of town on the northern highway loop near the Chiang Mai National Museum, this wát *(Chiang Mai map;* ☎ *053 219 483)* was built to host the eighth World Buddhist Council in 1477. Based on the design of the Mahabodhi Temple in Bodhgaya, India, the proportions for the Chiang Mai version are quite different from the Indian original, so it was probably modelled from a small votive tablet depicting the Mahabodhi in distorted perspective. The seven spires *(jèt yâwt)* represent the seven weeks Buddha was supposed to have spent in Bodhgaya after his enlightenment. The main stupa, erected in 1487, contains the ashes of the Lanna king Phaya Tilok.

On the outer walls of the old wíhǎan is some of the original stucco relief. There's an adjacent stupa of undetermined age and a very glossy wíhǎan. The entire area is surrounded by well-kept lawns. It's a pleasant, relaxing temple to visit, although curiously it's not very active in terms of worship.

Wat Jet Yot is a bit too far from the city centre to reach on foot; by bicycle it's easy or you can take a red *sǎwngthǎew* (small passenger truck; also written songthaew).

Wat Suan Dok
วัดสวนดอก

Phaya Keu Na, the sixth Lanna king, built this temple *(Chiang Mai map;* ☎ *053 278 304)* in a forest grove in 1373 as a place where the visiting Phra Sumana Thera, a teaching monk from Sukhothai, could spend the rains retreat. The large, open wíhǎan was rebuilt in 1932. The bòt contains a 500-year-old bronze Buddha image and vivid *jataka* (Buddha's past-life stories) murals. Amulets and Buddhist literature printed in English and Thai can be purchased at quite low prices in the wíhǎan.

In the grounds is a group of whitewashed Lanna stupas, framed by Doi Suthep. The large central stupa contains a Buddha relic that supposedly self-multiplied. One relic was mounted on the back of a white elephant (commemorated by Chiang Mai's Pratu Chang Pheuak), which was allowed to wander until it 'chose' a site on which a wát could be built to enshrine it. The elephant stopped and died at a spot on Doi Suthep,

CHIANG MAI

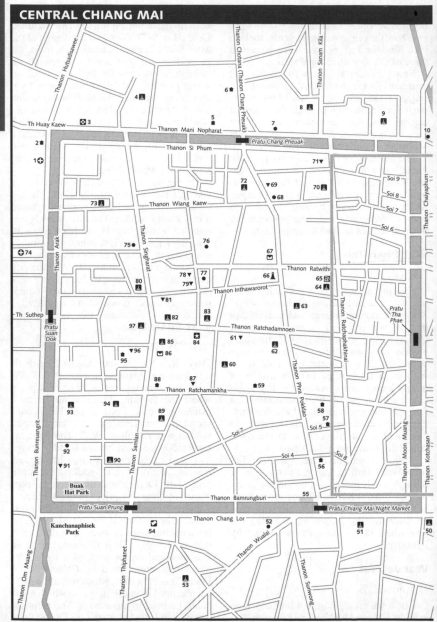

CENTRAL CHIANG MAI

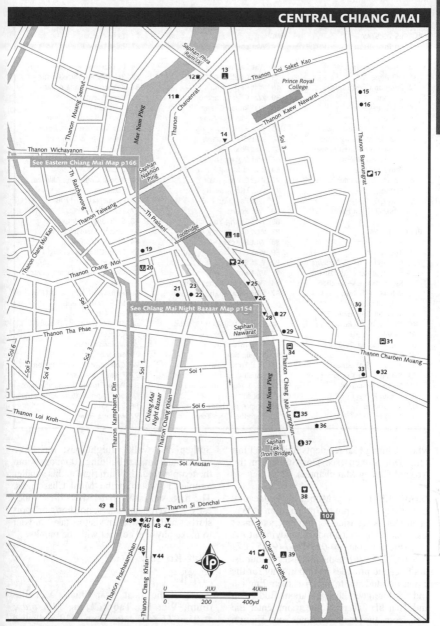

CENTRAL CHIANG MAI

PLACES TO STAY
- 2 Sri Tokyo Hotel
- 5 Northern Inn
- 6 Chang Peuk Hotel
- 11 Je t'Aime
- 12 Pun Pun Guest House
- 27 Le Pont
- 30 C&C Teak House
- 36 Ben Guest House
- 40 Baan Kaew Guest House
- 49 Imperial Mae Ping Hotel
- 56 Golden Fern Guest House
- 57 Julie Guest House
- 58 Anodard Hotel
- 59 Chiang Mai Garden Guest House
- 88 Felix City Inn
- 95 Wanasit Guest House

PLACES TO EAT
- 14 Khao Soi Prince
- 25 The Gallery
- 26 Good View Bar & Restaurant
- 28 Riverside Bar & Restaurant; Riverside Cookery School
- 42 Whole Earth Restaurant
- 44 Vihara Liangsan
- 45 Khao Soi Suthasinee 2
- 46 Giorgio Italian Restaurant
- 61 La Villa Pizzeria
- 69 The Amazing Sandwich
- 71 Jok Somphet
- 78 Khao Soi Suthasinee
- 79 Mangsawirat Kangreuanjam
- 81 Si Phen Restaurant
- 87 Heuan Phen
- 91 Rot Sawoei
- 96 Ta-Krite

WAT
- 4 Wat Lokmoli
- 8 Wat Chiang Yeun
- 9 Wat Pa Pao
- 13 Wat Chetuphon
- 18 Wat Ketkaram
- 39 Wat Chaimongkhon
- 50 Wat Phuak Chang
- 51 Wat Muang Mang
- 53 Wat Sisuphan
- 60 Wat Chedi Luang
- 62 Wat Phan Tao
- 63 Wat Duang Di
- 64 Wat U Mong Klang Wiang
- 70 Wat Chiang Man
- 72 Wat Hua Khwang
- 73 Wat Pa Phrao Nai
- 80 Wat Prasat
- 82 Wat Thung Yu
- 83 Wat Chai Phra Kiat
- 85 Wat Si Koet
- 89 Wat Phra Jao Mengrai
- 90 Wat Phuak Hong
- 93 Wat Meh Thang
- 94 Wat Meun Ngoen Kong
- 97 Wat Phra Singh

OTHER
- 1 Chiang Mai Ram Hospital
- 3 Computer Plaza; Icon
- 7 DHL International
- 10 Tui Big Bike
- 15 Thai Tribal Crafts
- 16 British Council
- 17 UK & Northern Ireland Consulate
- 19 Chip Aun Thong Dispensary
- 20 Namdhari Sikh Temple
- 21 Talat Warorot
- 22 Talat Lamyai
- 23 Flower Market
- 24 Le Brasserie
- 29 Raintree Resource Centre
- 31 Buses to Bo Sang & San Kamphaeng
- 32 Talat San Pa Khoi
- 33 Gawila Boxing Stadium
- 34 Buses to Lamphun, Pasang, Chiang Rai & Lampang
- 35 Tourist Police
- 37 Tourism Authority of Thailand
- 38 Zodiac
- 41 French Consulate; Alliance Française
- 43 Lanna Nakorn 1296
- 47 SEA Tours
- 48 Suriwong Book Centre
- 52 Chiang Mai Flying Club
- 54 Chinese Consulate
- 55 Pratu Chiang Mai Night Market
- 65 Chiang Mai Disabled Center (Internet)
- 66 Anusawari Sam Kasat (Three Kings Monument)
- 67 Post Office
- 68 Thai Airways International Office
- 74 Malaria Centre
- 75 School
- 76 Chiang Mai Central Prison
- 77 District Offices
- 84 Police (Inside the quadrangle on Thanon Ratchadamnoen)
- 86 Post Office
- 92 Mengrai Kilns

where Chiang Mai residents built Wat Phra That Doi Suthep (see Doi Suthep in the Around Chiang Mai chapter).

Monk Chat Every Monday, Wednesday and Friday from 5pm to 7pm, a room at Wat Suan Dok is set aside for foreigners to meet and chat with novice monks studying at the monastic university (☎ 053 273 149, 053 273 105, 053 273 120) on the monastery grounds. It's free, and provides an opportunity for the monastic students to practise their English and for foreigners to learn about Buddhism and Thai life. To reach the room, enter the wát from the main entrance on Thanon

Suthep and walk straight past the large wíhǎan to a smaller building 100m or so into the temple grounds. Turn right at this smaller temple, and watch for the 'Monk Chat' signs. The monastery asks that visitors dress modestly – covered shoulders, no shorts or short skirts – and that women visitors take care not to make physical contact with the monks.

Wat Ku Tao

วัดกู่เต้า

North of the moat, near Chiang Mai Stadium, Wat Ku Tao (Chiang Mai map; ☎ 053 211 842) dates from 1613 and has a unique chedi that looks like a pile of diminishing spheres, said to be of possible Yunnanese design. The chedi is said to contain the ashes of Tharawadi Min, a son of the Burmese king Bayinnaung, ruler of Lanna from 1578 to 1607.

Wat U Mong
วัดอุโมงค์

This forest wát was first used during Phaya Mang Rai's rule in the 14th century. Brick-lined tunnels in an unusual large, flat-topped hill were supposedly fashioned around 1380 for the clairvoyant monk Thera Jan. The monastery was later abandoned and wasn't reinstated until a local Thai prince sponsored a restoration in the late 1940s. The late Ajahn Buddhadasa, a well-known monk and teacher at Southern Thailand's Wat Suanmok, sent several monks to re-establish a monastic community at U Mong in the 1960s. One building contains modern artwork by various monks who have resided at U Mong, including several foreigners. A marvellously grisly image of the fasting Buddha – ribs, veins and all – can be seen in the grounds on top of the tunnel hill, along with a very large chedi. Also in the grounds is a small lake.

A small library/museum with English-language books on Buddhism is also on the premises. Resident foreign monks give talks in English on Sunday afternoons at 3pm by the lake.

To get to Wat U Mong (☎ 053 273 990), travel west on Thanon Suthep for about 2km and take the signed left turn past Talat Phayom (Phayom Market), then follow the signs for another 2km to Wat U Mong. Săwngthăew to Doi Suthep also pass the turn-off.

Wat Chetawan, Wat Mahawan & Wat Bupparam
วัดเชตวัน, วัดมหาวัน, วัดบุปผาราม

These three wát along Thanon Tha Phae feature highly ornate wíhăan and chedi designed by Shan or Burmese artisans. Most likely they were originally financed by Burmese teak merchants who immigrated to Chiang Mai a century or more ago. Burmese influence is evident in the abundant peacock motifs (a solar symbol common in Burmese and Shan temple architecture) and the Mandalay-style standing Buddhas found in wall niches. At Wat Mahawan (Eastern Chiang Mai map; ☎ 053 840 189) and Bupparam (Eastern Chiang Mai map; ☎ 053 276 771), no two guardian-deity sculptures are alike; the whimsical forms include monkeys or dogs playing with lions and mythical creatures. Wat Bupparam contains a precious little bòt constructed of teak and decorated in pure Lanna style. In one corner of the compound sit two spirit shrines, one for Jao Pho Dam, another for Jao Pho Daeng (Holy Father Black and Holy Father Red).

Wat Chai Phra Kiat
วัดชัยพระเกียรติ

On Thanon Ratchadamnoen a block-and-a-half east of Wat Phra Singh, this monastery (Central Chiang Mai map; ☎ 053 222 616) contains a huge bronze Buddha cast by order of a Burmese military commander in 1565.

Wat Sisuphan
วัดศรีสุพรรณ

This wát (Central Chiang Mai map; ☎ 053 200 332), off Thanon Wualai south of the moat, was founded in 1502 but little remains of the original structures except for some teak pillars and roof beams in the wíhăan. The murals inside show an interesting mix of Taoist, Zen and Theravada Buddhist elements. Wat Sisuphan is one of the few wát in Chiang Mai where you can see the Poy Luang (Poy Sang Long) Festival, a Shan-style group ordination of young boys as Buddhist novices, in late March.

Wat Phuak Hong
วัดพวกหงส์

Behind Suan Buak Hat off Thanon Samlan, this wát (Central Chiang Mai map; ☎ 053 278 864) contains the locally revered Chedi

CHIANG MAI

Si Pheuak. The stupa is over 100 years old and features the 'stacked spheres' style seen only here and at Wat Ku Tao, most likely influenced by the Dai stupas of China's Xishuangbanna district in Yunnan.

Wat Chiang Yeun

วัดเชียงยืน

Another unique local temple is the Burmese-built Wat Chiang Yeun *(Central Chiang Mai map; ☎ 053 211 654)* on the northern side of the moat, across Thanon Mani Nopharat, between Pratu Chang Pheuak and the northeastern corner of the old city. Besides the large Northern-style chedi here, the main attraction is an old Burmese colonial gate and pavilion on the eastern side of the school grounds attached to the wát.

Catering to Shan and Burmese temple-goers, a few shops and street vendors in the vicinity of Wat Chiang Yeun sell Burmese-style pickled tea *(mîang)* and Shan-style noodles.

Wat Sai Mun Mianma

วัดทรายมูลเมียนมา

While the other wát in Chiang Mai may have Burmese and/or Shan histories, this wát *(Eastern Chiang Mai map)* within the southeast corner of the old city has the strongest current connections with Myanmar. Several among the small monastic population are Burmese, and the walls of the wíhǎan are adorned with large pictures of sacred Buddhist sites in Myanmar. The main chedi is very Burmese in style, with an ornate umbrella topping a dome bearing garland reliefs.

Wiang Kum Kam

เวียงกุมกาม

These excavated ruins are near Mae Nam Ping, 5km south of the city via Hwy 106 (Thanon Chiang Mai–Lamphun). Apparently this was the earliest historical settlement in the Chiang Mai area, established by the Mon in the 11th century (before Phaya

Mang Rai's reign, although the settlement's founding is often mistakenly attributed to Mang Rai) as a satellite town for the Hariphunchai kingdom.

Burmese invaders under Bagan's King Anawrahta briefly occupied Mae Nam Ping settlements during the 11th century, leaving behind a damaged and possibly abandoned Wiang Kum Kam, thus leaving the area open to Phaya Mang Rai's expansion to Chiang Mai. The city was again abandoned in the early 18th century due to massive flooding, and visible architectural remains are few – only the four-sided Mon-style chedi of Wat Chedi Si Liam and the layered brick pediments of Wat Kan Thom (the Mon name; in Thai the temple was known as Wat Chang Kham) are left. Chedi Si Liam is said to have been inspired by the similar chedi at Wat Kukut in Lamphun.

Altogether, over 1300 inscribed stone slabs, bricks, bells and stupas have been excavated at the site – all are currently being translated at Chiang Mai University. So far, the most important archaeological discovery has been a four-piece inscribed stone slab now on display in the Chiang Mai National Museum. These early 11th-century inscriptions indicate that the Thai script actually predates King Ram Khamhaeng's famous Sukhothai inscription (introduced in 1292) by 100 or more years.

The stones display writing in three scripts of varying ages; the earliest is Mon, the latest is classical Sukhothai script, while the middle-period inscription is proto-Thai. Historical linguists studying the slabs now say that the Thai script was developed from Mon models, later to be modified by adding Khmer characteristics. This means Ram Khamhaeng was not the 'inventor' of the script as previously thought, but more of a would-be reformer. His reformations appear on only one slab and weren't accepted by contemporaries – his script, in fact, died with him.

An ideal way of getting to Wiang Kum Kam is to hire a bicycle; follow Thanon Chiang Mai–Lamphun southeast about 3km and look for a sign to the ruins on the right. From this junction it's another 2km to the ruins. You could also hire a *túk-túk* (motorised *săamláw*, a three-wheeled vehicle) or red săwngthăew to take you there for 50B or 60B (one way). Once you're finished looking around you can walk back to Thanon Chiang Mai–Lamphun and catch a săwngthăew or a blue Chiang Mai–Lamphun bus back into the city.

Muslim, Hindu & Sikh Temples Of the 12 mosques in Chiang Mai, the oldest and most interesting is **Matsayit Chiang Mai** *(Chiang Mai Mosque or Ban Haw Mosque; Chiang Mai Night Bazaar map)* on Soi 1, Charoen Prathet, between Thanon Chang Khlan and Thanon Charoen Prathet, not far from the Night Bazaar. Founded by *jiin haw* (Chinese Muslims) from China's Yunnan Province over a hundred years ago, it still primarily caters to this unique ethnic group; you'll hear Yunnanese spoken as often as Thai within the compound. Along this soi are several Yunnanese Muslim restaurants that serve *khâo sawy kài* (curried chicken and noodles) as a speciality.

The most colourful of Chiang Mai's two Hindu temples is the brightly painted, traditional *mandir*-and-*sikhara* **Devi Mandir Chiang Mai** *(Chiang Mai map)* on Thanon Ratanakosin, opposite Chiang Mai Stadium. At **Siri Guru Singh Sabha**, a Sikh temple off Thanon Charoenrat (behind Wat Ketkaram; see Central Chiang Mai map), free *prasada* (blessed vegetarian food) is distributed to temple-goers on Friday morning.

Namdhari Sikh Temple *(Central Chiang Mai map)*, on Thanon Ratchawong between Thanon Chang Moi and Thanon Tha Phae, is the place of worship for the Namdhari sect of Sikhism.

McKean Rehabilitation Centre
สถาบันแมคเคนเพื่อการ
ฟื้นฟูสภาพ

Southeast Asia's first leprosarium *(Chiang Mai map;* ☎ *053 277 049, Thanon Ko Klang, Km4; open 8am-4.30pm daily; tours by appointment only)*, now a rehabilitation centre for people with physical disabilities, owes its existence to the inspiration of American Presbyterian missionary Dr James McKean.

Dr McKean arrived in Chiang Mai in 1889 and asked the royal rulers of Chiang Mai if they would donate some land on which he might develop a treatment centre for Thais suffering from leprosy. In 1908 he was given an uninhabited 160-acre island in the Mae Nam Ping, Ko Klang, once used as a place of exile for elephants gone berserk. McKean's leprosy institute became world famous as a place where patients achieved self-sufficiency through training in various trades.

After modern pharmaceuticals virtually eliminated leprosy, the institute became a home for the disabled elderly, about 50 of whom still live in cottages in a village called Buraphaniwet at the northern end of the island. In 1993 a rehabilitation centre for the disabled was added to the facilities.

The older buildings on the island, including a meeting hall, former wards and a church, are constructed in an early 20th-century style reminiscent of colonial Asian architecture of the era.

Prospective visitors should call before coming to the centre. There is no charge for visiting the island, but donations to the centre are welcome.

Chiang Mai National Museum
พิพิธภัณฑสถานแห่งชาติเชียงใหม่

Established in 1954 with a single curator overseeing a small collection of Lanna Buddhas and potshards, Chiang Mai National Museum *(Chiang Mai map;* ☎ *053 221 308, 053 408 568; admission 30B; open 9am-4pm Wed-Sun)* has grown to employ a full-time staff of 20 cataloguing and caring for up to a million artefacts. These items are shared among four important national museums in Chiang Mai, Lamphun, Chiang Saen and Nan, all under the auspices of the Chiang Mai museum.

The museum displays a very good selection of Buddha images in all styles, including a very large bronze Buddha downstairs. Pottery is also displayed downstairs, while upstairs there are household and agricultural tools, along with historic weaponry. At present the museum is undergoing a major and much needed renovation, so many of the display rooms should have an entirely new look within the near future.

The museum is close to Wat Jet Yot on Hwy 11 (also called Superhighway Rd), which curves around the city.

Tribal Museum
พิพิธภัณฑ์ชาวเขา

Originally established in 1965 on the ground floor of the Tribal Research Institute on Chiang Mai University campus, this teaching museum (☎ 053 210 872; admission free; open 9am-4pm Mon-Fri; slide & video shows 10am to 2pm) moved to its new location overlooking a lake in Ratchamangkhala Park on the northern outskirts of the city in 1997. The new, octagonal facility houses a large collection of handicrafts, costumes, jewellery, ornaments, household utensils, agricultural tools, musical instruments and ceremonial paraphernalia, along with various informative displays concerning the cultural features and backgrounds of each of the major hill tribes in Thailand. There is also an exhibition on activities carried out by the Thai royal family on behalf of the hill

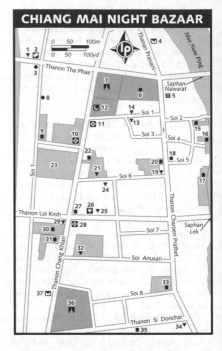

CHIANG MAI NIGHT BAZAAR

tribes, as well as various bits of research and development sponsored by governmental and nongovernmental agencies.

CHIANG MAI NIGHT BAZAAR

PLACES TO STAY
9 Chiang Inn
15 Galare Guest House
16 River View Lodge
17 Diamond Riverside Hotel
20 Porn Ping Tower Hotel
22 Night Bazaar Guest House
27 Royal Lanna
30 Suriwongse Hotel
31 Royal Princess
33 Chiangmai Souvenir Guest House (Viking Guest House)
35 Chiang Mai Plaza Hotel

PLACES TO EAT
1 Bacco
13 Sophia

14 Khao Soi Islam; Khao Soi Fuang Fah
19 Rot Neung
21 Galare Food Centre
24 Shere Shiraz
25 Red Lion English Pub & Restaurant
29 Starbucks
32 Anusan Night Market
34 Piccola Roma Palace

WAT
7 Wat Upakhut
36 Wat Si Don Chai

OTHER
2 Finnish Consulate
3 Eastern Arts
4 Mae Ping Post Office

5 Governor's House
6 Buddhist Association of Chiang Mai
8 The Peak Rock-Climbing Plaza
10 Chiang Inn Plaza; Sophet Thai Cookery School
11 CM Centre
12 Matsayit Chiang Mai (Ban Haw)
18 The Wild Planet – Contact Travel
23 Nakhon Ping Night Bazaar
26 German Hofbräuhaus
28 Chiang Mai Pavilion; OK Pizza
37 Mail Boxes Etc

Night Bazaar

The Night Bazaar, arguably Chiang Mai's biggest tourist attraction, is in fact the legacy of the original Yunnanese trading caravans that stopped over here along the ancient trade route between Simao (in China) and Mawlamyaing (on Myanmar's Gulf of Martaban coast).

Today the market sprawls along Thanon Chang Khlan between Thanon Tha Phae and Thanon Si Donchai every night of the year, rain or dry, holiday or no. Made up of several different roofed areas, ordinary glass-fronted shops and dozens of street vendors, the market offers a huge variety of Thai and Northern Thai goods, as well as designer goods (both fake and licensed, so look carefully) at very low prices – if you bargain well. Many importers buy here because the prices are so good, especially when buying in large quantities. You'll also find a smaller selection of goods from India, Nepal and China.

Chiang Mai University
มหาวิทยาลัยเชียงใหม่

The city's only public university (☎ 053 844 821) was established in 1964, when it became the first Thai university to be founded outside Bangkok. Today 3,360-acre CMU boasts over 15,000 students and close to 2000 lecturers divided among more than a hundred departments.

Although scholastically CMU doesn't compare overall to such notable Bangkok universities as Silpakorn, Thammasat or Chulalongkorn, it has earned special respect for its faculties of engineering and medical technology.

The main campus lies west of the city centre in a 239.4-hectare wedge of land between Thanon Suthep and Thanon Huay Kaew; entrances to the campus can be found along both roadways. Students live in over 20 dormitories on campus as well as in off-campus housing, found mostly to the south of the CMU off Thanon Suthep. The abundant green areas between the faculty buildings and student residences, along with the tree-shaded, tranquil **Ang Kaew** reservoir, are pleasant places for strolling. For more vigorous movement, the campus offers a **fitness park** and **sports track**, both open to the public at no charge, as well as a **swimming pool** with a small usage fee.

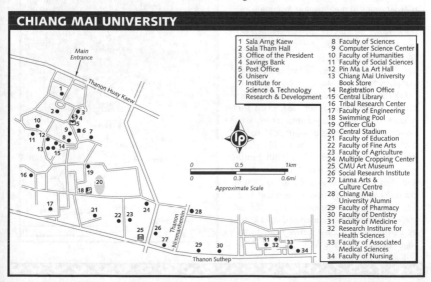

CHIANG MAI UNIVERSITY

Main Entrance

Thanon Huay Kaew

Thanon Nimmanhemin

Thanon Suthep

0   0.5   1km
0   0.3   0.6mi
Approximate Scale

1 Sala Arng Kaew
2 Sala Tham Hall
3 Office of the President
4 Savings Bank
5 Post Office
6 Uniserv
7 Institute for Science & Technology Research & Development
8 Faculty of Sciences
9 Computer Science Center
10 Faculty of Humanities
11 Faculty of Social Sciences
12 Pin Ma La Art Hall
13 Chiang Mai University Book Store
14 Registration Office
15 Central Library
16 Tribal Research Center
17 Faculty of Engineering
18 Swimming Pool
19 Officer Club
20 Central Stadium
21 Faculty of Education
22 Faculty of Fine Arts
23 Faculty of Agriculture
24 Multiple Cropping Center
25 CMU Art Museum
26 Social Research Institute
27 Lanna Arts & Culture Centre
28 Chiang Mai University Alumni
29 Faculty of Pharmacy
30 Faculty of Dentistry
31 Faculty of Medicine
32 Research Institure for Health Sciences
33 Faculty of Associated Medical Sciences
34 Faculty of Nursing

Other facilities on the main campus include restaurants, banks, a post office, an art gallery, bookshop and grocery store. Accommodation to the public is available at **Uniserv**, a large on-campus hostel (see Places to Stay later in this chapter).

Three Kings Monument
อนุสาวรีย์สามกษัตร

The Anusawari Sam Kasat (*Three Kings Monument; Central Chiang Mai map*) on Thanon Phra Pokklao near the THAI office

---

Caravans of Northern Thailand

Dating from at least the 15th century, Chinese-Muslim caravans from Yunnan Province (China) used Chiang Mai as a 'back-door' entry and exit for commodities transported between China and the Indian Ocean port of Mawlamyaing (Moulmein) in Myanmar (Burma) for international seagoing trade.

The main means of transport for the Yunnanese caravaneers were mules and ponies, beasts of burden that contrasted with the Southeast Asian preference of oxen, water buffalo and elephants. The Chinese Muslims who dominated the caravan traffic owed their preferred mode of conveyance, as well as their religious orientation, to mass conversions effected during the Mongol invasions of Yunnan in the 13th century. The equestrian nature of the caravans led the Thais to call the Yunnanese *jiin haw* (literally, galloping Chinese).

Three main routes emanated from the predominantly Thai Xishuangbanna (Sipsongpanna in Thai) region in southern Yunnan into Northern Thailand, and onward to the Gulf of Martaban via Mawlamyaing. The western route proceeded southwest from Simao to Chiang Rung (now known as Jinghong), then went on through Chiang Tung (Kengtung) to Fang or Chiang Rai.

The middle route went south to Mengla near the border of China and Laos, crossed Laos via Luang Nam Tha, and entered what is today Thailand at Chiang Khong (which was an independent principality at the time) on the Mekong River. At this point the middle route merged with the western route

at Chiang Rai Province, and formed a single route through Chiang Mai to Mae Sariang, a line that continued along the Salawin River to Mawlamyaing in present-day Myanmar.

The third route went from Simao to Phongsali in northern Laos then via Luang Prabang (Laos), crossing the Mekong River to Meuang Nan and Meuang Phrae (now Nan and Phrae Provinces) before curving northwestward via Lampang and Lamphun to Chiang Mai.

Principal southward exports along these routes included silk, opium, tea, dried fruit, lacquerware, musk, ponies and mules, while northward the caravans brought gold, copper, cotton, edible birds' nests, betel nut, tobacco and ivory. By the end of the 19th century many artisans from China, northern Burma and Laos had settled in the area to produce crafts for the steady flow of regional trade. The city's original transhipment point for such trade movements was a market district known as Ban Haw, a stone's throw from today's Night Bazaar in Chiang Mai.

is a set of three bronze sculptures depicting Phaya Ngam Meuang, Phaya Mang Rai and Phaya Khun Ram Khamhaeng (Phaya Ruang), the three Northern Thai–Lao kings most associated with early Chiang Mai history. Many Chiang Mai residents, considering the monument a sacred site, make offerings of candles and flowers at the kings' bronze feet.

The monument stands in front of the old *săalaa klaang* (provincial offices), which are being converted into a cultural centre now that a new săalaa klaang has been opened on the northern outskirts of town.

Suan Buak Hat
สวนบวกหาด

This well-maintained *suan* (park) in the southwestern corner of the moat *(Central Chiang Mai map)* is Chiang Mai's compact counterpart to Bangkok's Lumphini Park, with very pleasant grass expanses, fountains and palms; many people jog here.

Chiang Mai Zoo & Arboretum
สวนสัตว์และแหล่งเพาะพันธ์
ไม้ป่าเขตร้อนเชียงใหม่

At the foothills of Doi Suthep, 6km from the town centre, are the shady, nicely landscaped, hilly **Chiang Mai Zoo & Arboretum** (☎ 053 358 116, 053 222 479; *adult/child 30/5B; open 8am-5pm daily)*.

Reportedly over 5000 birds (150 species) fly about the zoo's Nakhon Ping Birdwatching Park. A few snack vendors scattered around the park offer simple rice and noodle dishes. The quiet, lush arboretum is a favourite local jogging spot. Except for the name of each species, most signs are in Thai only. Parking costs 30B per car or truck, 10B for a motorcycle or bicycle.

Foreign Cemetery
สุสานฝรั่ง

This slightly spooky cemetery *(Chiang Mai map)* off Thanon Chiang Mai–Lamphun near the Gymkhana Club contains century-old headstones marking the remains of American, English and European traders, missionaries and various other expats who have died in Chiang Mai. A bronze statue of Queen Victoria, imported from Calcutta, India, during the Raj era, stands sentinel.

ACTIVITIES
Aeronautics

Located at an airstrip in Lamphun, the **Chiang Mai Flying Club** *(Central Chiang Mai map;* ☎/fax 053 200 515, 01 952 0144, ✉ *alpharom@samart.co.th, 185/12 Thanon Wualai)* offers sightseeing flights that run for a half to 1½ hours, depending on the route (most are in the Lampang and Lamphun areas).

These flights cost from 1500B to 5500B per person, depending on the length of the flight and number of people. The cost includes transfers from Chiang Mai to Lamphun, the services of the pilot (also the guide) and membership in the club.

Overnight trips to Chiang Rai and Mae Hong Son are also offered at rates that depend on the number of passengers and include transfers from Chiang Mai, a day tour of the region by road, and accommodation.

The planes appear to be in fine condition. Sightseeing flights can also be booked through **Chiang Mai Newsletter** *(*☎ *053 225 201)*.

An ultralight-aircraft operation calling itself **Chiang Mai Sky Adventure Club** *(*☎ *053 868 460, 01 993 6861, fax 053 867 646,* ✉ *flying@cmnet.co.th, 143 Mu 6, Tambon Choeng Doi, Amphoe Doi Saket; flights 1200B per person)* offers 15-minute flights over the Doi Saket area. The rate includes transport from hotel to airfield.

Cycling

Chiang Mai Bicycle Club *(*☎ *053 943 018)* organises a trip almost every Sunday, starting between 7am and 7.30am from the square in front of Pratu Tha Phae. These trips typically take routes outside of town.

Rock Climbing

The largest rock-climbing wall in Southeast Asia was recently erected in Chiang Mai at

Gates & Walls Walking Tour

CC

The sleepy moats, timeworn bastions and carefully restored gates that encompass old Chiang Mai are a dominant feature of this ancient city. Evocative of a troubled past, symbolic of cultural continuity and Northern Thai pride, the inner city fortifications have come to epitomise historical Chiang Mai. What's more, they also make a good walking tour, though the full 6km circuit is really only for the dedicated walker. Although much of the walk is shaded by moat-side trees, except in the cool season it is probably better to go some of the way by bicycle or túk-túk.

A good place to start your tour is **Pratu Tha Phae**, the city's eastern entrance, which once linked the city with the main river crossing on the banks of the Mae Nam Ping. About 5m across (said to be 'the width of an elephant with one person on either side'), and protected by heavy, steel-bound wooden doors, the reconstructed gate sits on a flagstone square, dominating an area that has become the focal point for Chiang Mai's festivals and celebrations. A popular meeting place for locals and visitors alike, on ordinary evenings crowds of young men gather there to play *tà-krâw,* or simply to chat with other locals in *kham meuang,* the lilting Northern Thai dialect.

Turning southwards and proceeding clockwise, the first bastion you'll reach is **Jaeng Katam**, 'Fish Trap Corner', where local residents used to catch fish in a large pond which has long since disappeared. Today this bastion looks spectacular when Chiang Mai municipality turns on the fountains and – on festival nights – the illuminating floodlights.

Continuing clockwise around the old city, next comes **Pratu Chiang Mai** or Chiang Mai Gate. Erected by Phaya Mang Rai in 1296, restored by Chao Kawila in about 1800 and rebuilt entirely in 1966–69, this gateway used to lead to the old road to Lamphun. In its present incarnation Pratu Chiang Mai has been widened to accommodate more traffic, and an extensive market selling a wide variety of fresh and cooked foods, general household items and hardware has grown up just inside the moat. On a still day you may catch the fragrance of joss sticks burning at the shrine of **Chao Pu Pratu Chiang Mai**, the guardian spirit of the gateway.

Further to the west **Pratu Suan Prung**, perhaps the quietest and most attractive of the city gates, is something of a curiosity since it adds a second gateway in the southern wall (the other three walls have only one gate each). For centuries the citizens of Chiang Mai reserved this gate for carrying their dead out of the city for cremation. Although it's still used for the occasional funeral procession, today the gate also provides vehicular access to the old city like any other gate. Formerly surrounded by towering trees that were recently cut down to widen the rather narrow road, the gateway boasts a 'cemetery' for old spirit houses and a relatively low flow of traffic.

The next bastion reached, at the old city's southwest corner, is **Jaeng Ku Ruang**. The origins of this name are obscure, though Chiang Mai city council has erected a sign that helpfully explains that

The Peak Rock-Climbing Plaza *(Chiang Mai Night Bazaar map;* ☎ *053 820 777, 28/2 Thanon Chang Khlan,* e *josh@thepeakthailand .com; 1 trial 150B, 1 hour 200B, 2 hours 250B)* Built to international competition climbing standards, this new attraction stands 15m high and 16m wide, and is designed to accommodate beginners as well as seasoned veterans. Non-climbers can watch from several adjacent bars and restaurants.

All rates include equipment rental. The Peak offers a 500B membership that includes five two-hour climbing passes, a 20% discount on all goods in the retail store and on future climbing tickets, a T-shirt, sticker, key chain and a top-rope belay lesson.

The Peak also sponsors **rock climbing treks** *(1500B per person, minimum 2 persons)* of limestone cliffs, called Crazy Horse Buttress by local *faràng* (Western) climbers,

Gates & Walls Walking Tour

'the name means a stupa-like structure containing the ashes of a person called Ruang'. The bastion is in excellent condition, with well-preserved battlements offering clear views of Doi Suthep. The surrounding area, too, is pleasant, with children often seen swimming in the moats, and, at certain times of the year, a series of garden vendors offering potted plants for sale.

Continuing north beyond Jaeng Ku Ruang, the ancient walls extend for some distance towards Chiang Mai's western entrance, **Pratu Suan Dok** or 'Flower Garden Gate'. In former times the gardens of 14th-century Chiang Mai king Keu Na lay outside this gateway. This king later founded a monastery amid the gardens, and it came to be known as Wat Suan Dok, or 'Flower Garden Temple', today the most famous centre of Buddhist learning in the North. Jaeng Ku Ruang can be a fine place to watch the sun set over Doi Suthep to the west in the early evening.

Head north another 750m and you'll reach **Jaeng Hua Rin**, the city's northwestern corner. This bastion, which faces Thanon Huai Kaew and once again offers fine views of Doi Suthep, is also well preserved. The battlements on top are high enough to protect a small, circular redoubt, and the whole area is made more attractive by stands of red irises and tall palm trees lining the moat banks.

To the east, set square in the centre of the Old City's northern wall, stands venerable **Pratu Chang Pheuak**. Originally established by Phaya Mang Rai in 1296, this gate was once known as Pratu Hua Wiang, or 'Head of the City Gate', for it was the way by which Lanna rulers entered the capital en route to their coronations. During the reign of King Saen Muang Ma (1385–1401), however, the neighbouring Chang Pheuak (Albino, or 'White' Elephant) monument was erected, and the name of the northern gate was subsequently changed to Pratu Chang Pheuak.

The charming Chang Pheuak monument itself consists of two albino elephants – greatly revered in Thailand and customarily considered royal property – formed in brick and stucco, one looking north and the other westwards. Each has its own stone 'stable', and both are at all times bedecked with offerings from reverent local residents. Sweet-smelling jasmine and frangipani blossoms hang from their tusks, candles burn before their stylised front feet and incense wafts on the wind.

The fourth and last of the old city bastions, **Jaeng Si Phum** (Holy Land Bastion), is situated at the quadrangle's northeastern corner, about 750m due north of Pratu Tha Phae. According to legend this bastion marks the first point in the original city walls founded by Phaya Mang Rai more than 700 years ago. Not far from here, there once stood a giant banyan tree, held to be highly auspicious and regarded as a source of Chiang Mai's power, prosperity and security. Today, sadly, the banyan tree is no more, although a spirit shrine honouring the tree's spirit stands close by the bastion, and regularly receives offerings and reverence from the townspeople.

Andrew Forbes

Andrew Forbes, a long-time resident of Chiang Mai, writes frequently about Chiang Mai for CPA-Media. His writing can be found at ⊠ *www.cpamedia.com.*

behind Tham Meuang On about 20km east of Chiang Mai. The price includes two guides, transportation, food, fruit, drinking water, equipment rental, entry fee to the cave or hot springs and insurance. For more information about the cave, see the Tham Meuang On entry in the Around Chiang Mai chapter.

The Peak sells a very informative rock-climbing guide to Crazy Horse Buttress, complete with route maps, for 100B.

Jogging

Several public areas offer decent space for exercise walks, jogs or runs. Among the best are **Suan Buak Hat** at the southeastern corner of the city moat, the **arboretum** behind Chiang Mai Zoo, the **Chiang Mai University sports track**, the **Maharaj Hospital fitness park** off Thanon Suthep and the **700th Anniversary Stadium** north of town on the Chiang Mai–Mae Rim Hwy.

Hash House Harriers The **Chiang Mai Harriers** (☎ 053 206 822) meet each Saturday at the H3 Pub on the corner of Thanon Moon Muang and Soi 2, Thanon Moon Muang, and organise a 'hash' (foot race) at various locations in the area. Call for times.

Swimming

Landlocked Chiang Mai can get very hot, particularly from March to July. Fortunately, local opportunities for a refreshing swim – providing an alternative to the usual tourist solution (vegetating in refrigerated rooms most of the day) – are many.

City Pools Chiang Mai has several swimming pools for public use; you can pay on a per-day basis, or buy an annual membership. Typical per-use fees range from 30B to 90B (public pools are cheaper than hotel or private pools), while annual memberships cost around 200B to 300B.

Chiang Mai University (☎ 053 221 699)
Faculty of Education, Thanon Huay Kaew
Maharaj (Suandok) Hospital (☎ 053 221 310)
Faculty of Medicine, Thanon Suthep
Physical Education College (☎ 053 210 825)
Chiang Mai Stadium, Thanon Sanam Kila
Pongpat Swimming Pool (☎ 053 212 812) 73/2
Thanon Chotana

A few hotels and guesthouses with pools also allow nonguests to swim for a daily fee, including:

Amari Rincome Hotel (Chiang Mai map;
☎ 053 894 884) Thanon Huay Kaew at
Thanon Nimmanhemin.
Top North Guest House (Eastern Chiang Mai
map; ☎ 053 278 900) 15 Soi 2, Thanon Moon
Muang.

Huay Teung Thao Reservoir This sizable lake about 12km northwest of the city is a great place for an all-day swim and picnic, especially during the hotter months. Windsurfing equipment can be rented for around 150B an hour. By car or motorcycle you can get to Huay Teung Thao by driving 10km north on Rte 107 (follow signs towards Mae Rim), then west 2km past an army camp to the reservoir.

Cyclists would do best to pedal to the reservoir via Thanon Khan Khlong Chonlaprathan. Head west on Thanon Huay Kaew, then turn right just before the canal. Follow Thanon Khan Khlong Chonlaprathan north until it ends at a smaller road between the reservoir and the highway; turn left here and you'll reach the lake after another 1km or so of pedalling. From the northwestern corner of the moat, the 12km bike ride takes about an hour.

If you don't bring your own, food is available from vendors at the lake, who maintain small bamboo-thatch huts over the water's edge for people to sit in. The local speciality is *kûng tên*, 'dancing shrimp', freshwater shrimp served live in a piquant sauce of lime juice and Northern Thai spices. Fishing is permitted if you'd like to try your luck at hooking lunch.

Tennis

Anantasiri Tennis Courts (*Chiang Mai map;* ☎ *053 222 210*), off Hwy 11 and opposite the Chiang Mai National Museum, is the best public tennis facility in Chiang Mai. The eight courts are illuminated at night, and you can hire a 'knocker' (tennis opponent) for a reasonable hourly fee in addition to the regular court fee.

Other places with public tennis courts include:

Chiang Mai Land Village (Chiang Mai map;
☎ 053 272 821) Thanon Chiang Mai Land
Gymkhana Club (Chiang Mai map; ☎ 053 241
035) Thanon Rat Uthit
Lanna Sports Club (Chiang Mai map; ☎ 053
221 911) Thanon Chotana

There are also public tennis courts at the Amari Rincome Hotel on Thanon Huay Kaew.

COURSES
Language & Culture

The basic Thai course at *American University Alumni* (*AUA; Eastern Chiang Mai map;* ☎ *053 278 407, 053 211 377, fax 053 211 973,* ⓔ *aualanna@loxinfo.co.th, 73 Thanon Ratchadamnoen*) consists of three levels with 60 hours of instruction; there are

Discarded signs and numberplates, Chiang Mai Province

Brightly clad weaver

Adding a touch of colour to a rice-paper umbrella

Hmong woman, Chiang Mai

Searching for the perfect something in Chiang Mai.

Karen woman, Chiang Mai Province

Chiang Mai's Night Bazaar: the business of browsing

also 30-hour courses in 'small talk', reading and writing, and Northern Thai. Costs range from 2700B for the reading and writing and Northern Thai courses to 3500B per level for the 60-hour courses. Private tutoring is also available at 250B to 290B per hour.

The **Australia Centre** *(Eastern Chiang Mai map;* ☎ *053 810 552, fax 053 810 554, Soi 5, Thanon Suthep),* at the back of Chiang Mai University in an old traditional Thai house, offers a 30-hour course in 'survival Thai' over a two-week period.

Payap University *(Chiang Mai map;* ☎ *053 304 805, ext 250/251, fax 053 245 353)* offers intensive 30- and 60-hour Thai language courses at beginning, intermediate and advanced levels; these focus on conversational skills, as well as on elementary reading and writing, and Thai culture. Costs for each course are 6000B (60 hours) and 12,000B (120 hours). Payap University also offers a Thai Studies Certificate Program, which involves two semesters of classroom lectures and field trips. These consist of 12 hours of Thai language study and an additional 18 hours of electives such as Foundations of Thai Music, Thai Drama and Dance, Survey of Thai History, Buddhist Traditions and Contemporary Thai Politics. Costs include a US$40 application fee, plus US$1500 per semester for tuition. Single courses can be audited for 3500B each.

Chiang Mai Thai Language Center *(*☎*/fax 053 277 810,* e *cmat@loxinfo.co.th, 131 Thanon Ratchadamnoen),* not far from AUA, is run by a Thai couple and offers Thai language courses for beginners through advanced learners. Group classes (30-hour course) of reading/writing or speaking/conversation consist of no more than six students while private lessons are also available. Tuition for private lessons start at 200B while the 30-hour group courses range from 2000B to 2200B.

Cooking

A number of programs around the city offer one- to five-day courses in Thai cooking. Most classes include an introduction to Thai herbs and spices, an occasional local market tour, cooking instructions and recipe booklets. Of course, you get to eat the delicious Thai food as well – everything from Chiang Mai–style chicken curry to steamed banana cake.

Rates are around 700B to 900B a day. Virtually every guesthouse in Chiang Mai offers to arrange cooking classes as well.

We've also received good reports about the following:

Baan Thai (Eastern Chiang Mai map; ☎ 053 357 339, e baan_thai@yahoo.com) 11 Soi 5, Thanon Ratchadamnoen
Chiang Mai Thai Cookery School (Eastern Chiang Mai map; ☎ 053 206 388, fax 053 399 036, w www.thaicookeryschool.com) 1-3 Thanon Moon Muang
Gap's Thai Culinary Art School (Eastern Chiang Mai map; ☎/fax 053 278 140, e gap_house@hotmail.com) 3 Soi 4, Thanon Ratchadamnoen
Riverside Cookery School (Central Chiang Mai map; ☎ 053 243 239) Riverside Bar & Restaurant, 9–11 Thanon Charoenrat
Siam Thai Cookery School (☎ 053 271 169, 053 213 415, fax 053 208 950) 5/2 Soi 1, Thanon Loi Kroh
Sompet Thai Cookery School (Chiang Mai Night Bazaar map; ☎/fax 053 280 901, e sompet41@chmai.loxinfo.co.th) Chiang Inn Plaza, 100/1 Thanon Chang Khlan

Jewellery Making

Nova *(Eastern Chiang Mai map;* ☎ *053 273 058,* e *nova@thaiway.com, 201 Thanon Tha Phae)* This place teaches the fundamentals of jewellery craft for 850B per day, or 4000B for a five-day course. Workshops are kept to two to eight people per session.

Buddhist Meditation

Not far from Wat U Mong, Wat Ram Poeng is a large monastery that supports the well-known **Northern Insight Meditation Centre** *(*☎ *053 278 620, 1 Thanon Khan Khlong Chonlaprathan),* where many foreigners have studied vipassana. Twenty-six-day individual courses are taught by a Thai monk, with Western students or bilingual Thais acting as interpreters. If you can't make the whole 26 days you must commit to a minimum two weeks.

A reasonably large *Tripitaka* (Buddhist scriptures) library houses versions of the Theravada Buddhist canon in Pali, Thai, Chinese, English and other languages.

The formal name for this wát is Wat Tapotaram. To get there by public transport, take a săwngthăew west on Thanon Suthep to Talat Phayom. From Talat Phayom, take a săwngthăew south along Thanon Khan Khlong Chonlaprathan about 1km and get off when you see the wát entrance on the right. Or charter a săwngthăew or túk-túk all the way.

Meditation can also be learned from the monks at Wat U Mong. The best way to arrange something is to attend one of the Sunday talks (see the Wat U Mong entry earlier in this chapter).

Traditional Massage

Over the years Chiang Mai has become a centre for Thai massage studies. Not all of the places purporting to teach massage are equally good however.

Old Medicine Hospital *(OMH;* ☎ *053 275 085, 78/1 Thanon Chiang Mai Hot)* The oldest and most popular place to study, OMH is on Soi Siwaka Komarat off Thanon Wualai, opposite the Old Chiang Mai Cultural Centre. The 10-day course runs daily from 9am to 4pm and the 3500B fee includes all teaching materials. There are two courses a month year-round except for the first two weeks of April.

The OMH curriculum is very traditional, with a Northern Thai slant (the Thai name for the institute actually means Northern Traditional Healing Hospital). Classes tend to be large during the months of December to February.

International Training Massage *(*☎ *053 218 632, fax 053 224 197,* e *itm60@hotmail .com, 17/7 Thanon Morakot, Santitham)* This place features an OMH-inspired curriculum with a five-day, 2250B course.

Lek Chaiya *(Eastern Chiang Mai map;* ☎ *053 278 325,* W *www.nervetouch.com, 25 Thanon Ratchadamnoen)* Khun Lek is a Thai woman who has been massaging and teaching for 40 years, specialising in *jàp sên* (nerve-touch) healing massage and the use of medicinal herbs. Courses take three to five days, depending on the student's zeal or availability, and cost 4000B (including books).

Ban Nit *(Eastern Chiang Mai map; Soi 2, Thanon Chaiyaphum; 100B per hour)* The teacher is Mama Nit, an older woman who is a specialist in deep-tissue, nerve and herbal massages and offers a unique, one-on-one course. Her methods were handed down from a long line of ancestral Chinese healers. Some students live in and eat meals with Mama Nit and her family while studying.

Muay Thai

There are several boxing camps that offers authentic *muay thai* (Thai kickboxing) instruction to foreigners as well as Thais.

Lanna Muay Thai *(Kiatbusaba; Chiang Mai map;* ☎*/fax 053 221 621,* W *www .asiaplus.com/lannamuaythai/, 64/1 Soi Chiang Khian)* This boxing school is located off Thanon Huay Kaew. Several Lanna students have won stadium bouts, including the famous *kàthoey* (male transvestite) boxer Parinya Kiatbusaba (Thai fighters traditionally take the camp name as their ring surname), who wore lipstick and pink nail polish to his national weigh-in, then triumphed at Lumphini stadium in Bangkok. For nonresident boxers, training is held from 4pm to 8pm daily, while resident trainees also have morning sessions. Rates are 250B a day or 7000B a month; simple camp accommodation is available for 3000B a month. Thai food is available at low cost, Western food more expensively.

Muay Thai (Thai boxing)

According to the camp's management: 'Foreign boxers are much sought after and we offer match-ups with local boxers for all levels of competition'.

Yoga

Hatha Yoga Centre (☎/fax 053 271 555, e marcelandyoga@hotmail.com, 129/79 Chiang Mai Villa 1) Located at the Pa Daet intersection, this school conducts hatha yoga classes from 5.30am to 7.30am and 5pm to 7pm weekdays only.

Informal Northern Thai Group

The 16-year-old Informal Northern Thai Group (Central Chiang Mai map; 138 Thanon Charoen Prathet; admission 20B; 7.30pm every second Tues) meets monthly at the Alliance Française. The usual evening format involves a lecture from a resident or visiting academic on some aspect of Thailand or Southeast Asia, followed by questions and answers and an informal drink afterwards at a local bar or restaurant. Some of the more recent topics have included 'Community Forestry in Northern Thailand' and 'Is Thailand One of the Few Non-Homophobic Countries in the World?'.

RIVER CRUISES

Mae Ping River Cruises (Central Chiang Mai map; ☎ 053 274 822, Thanon Charoen Prathet) From a small pier on Mae Nam Ping behind Wat Chaimongkhon, this place offers two-hour tours between 8.30am to 5pm daily for 300B per person, and a Thai dinner cruise between 7.15pm to 9.30pm daily for 400B per person. Day cruises are in roofed boats that stop at a small fruit farm about 40 minutes away where free samples and a beverage are provided. The Thai dinner cruise offers a set menu. Alcoholic drinks cost extra.

The Riverside Bar & Restaurant also offers dinner cruises; see that entry under Places to Eat.

SPECIAL EVENTS

The week-long **Winter Fair** (thêtsakaan ngaan reuduu năo) in late December and early January is a great occasion. In late January the **Bo Sang Umbrella Festival** (thêtsakaan rôm) features a colourful umbrella procession during the day and a night-time lantern procession. Although it sounds touristy, this festival is actually a very Thai affair; one of the highlights is the many Northern Thai music ensembles that give performances in shopfronts along Bo Sang's main street.

Perhaps Chiang Mai's most colourful festival is the **Flower Festival** (thêtsakaan mái dàwk mái prà-dàp), also called the Flower Carnival, which is held annually in February (actual dates vary from year to year). Events occur over a three-day period and include displays of flower arrangements, a long parade of floats decorated with hundreds of thousands of flowers, folk music, cultural performances and the Queen of the Flower Festival contest. Most activities are centred at Suan Buak Hat near the southwestern corner of the city moats. People from all over the province and the rest of the country turn out for this occasion, so book early if you want a room in town.

In mid-April **Songkran Festival** (thêtsakaan sŏngkraan), the traditional Thai New Year, is celebrated here with an enthusiasm bordering on pure pandemonium.

In May the **Intakin Festival** (ngaan tham bun săo inthákin), held at Wat Chedi Luang and centred around the city's làk meuang (city pillar), propitiates the city's guardian deity to ensure that the annual monsoon will arrive on time. Also in May – when the mango crop is ripe – a **Mango Fair** (thêtsakaan má-mûang) is celebrated in Suan Buak Hat with lots of mango eating and the coronation of the Mango Queen.

During the festival of **Loi Krathong** (lawy krà-thong), usually celebrated in late October or early November, Chiang Mai's river banks are crowded with people floating the small lotus-shaped boats (krà-thong) that mark this occasion. In Chiang Mai this festival is also known as Yi Peng, and some khon meuang (Northern Thai people) celebrate by launching cylindrical-shaped hot-air balloons, lighting up the night skies with hundreds of pinpoints of light.

PLACES TO STAY – BUDGET

At any one time there are at least 300 hotels and guesthouses operating in Chiang Mai. Generally speaking Chiang Mai has the lowest-priced lodging of any larger city in Thailand, although prices range from a low 60B for a single room at Rose Guest House to US$425 for a garden-view room at the Regent Chiang Mai Resort & Spa.

As elsewhere in Thailand, at the cheaper hotels 'single' means a room with one large bed (big enough for two) while 'double' means a room with two beds; the number of people staying in the room is usually irrelevant.

Guesthouses

Guesthouse accommodation is spread all over the city, but areas where they're most concentrated include the following: along Thanon Moon Muang (the inside of the eastern moat) and on streets off Thanon

---

Songkran in Chiang Mai

In the middle of April the three-day Songkran or 'water festival' celebrates the start of the Thai lunar new year. Songkran, from the Sanskrit *samkranta* (fully passed over), signifies the passage of the sun from the sign of Pisces into the sign of Aries in the zodiac. All of Thailand observes this festival, but it is celebrated with particular fervour in Chiang Mai, where people turn out into the streets by the thousands to douse one another with water.

On a spiritual level, the Thai traditionally believe that during this period the old Songkran spirit departs and the new one arrives. On the first day of the festival, when the old spirit departs, believers give their homes a thorough cleaning. At various wát throughout the city people gather in the morning to build and decorate miniature sand stupas for good luck.

Shop owners will erect *pràtuu sa-wǎn* or 'heaven gates' – mock doorways made from coconut stems, banana leaves and banana tree trunks – in front of their shops to welcome the Songkran spirit. This is also where shop staff, friends and family will gather with barrels of water in which they dip buckets, bowls or water guns for dousing all passers-by. By 9am the water mayhem in the streets has begun in earnest. The streets bordering the city moats are the largest focus, with throngs of people using water-guns, buckets and even plastic cups to make sure every moving object in sight is thoroughly soaked.

On the second day civic groups mount a colourful parade down Thanon Ratchadamnoen and Thanon Tha Phae, as the sacred Buddha image from Wat Phra Sing is carried on a flower-bedecked float from the temple to the river. Thais gather along both sides of these streets to participate in a ritual cleansing of the image by tossing bowls of water – often scented with jasmine flowers – over the float.

The third day is considered especially crucial and cleansing rituals extend to the bathing of Buddha images at local wát by pouring water onto them. In the older Northern Thai temples such as Wat Chiang Man, the water is delivered through naga-ornamented wooden sluice pipes on raised stands. Senior monks receive a similar treatment, and younger Thai will also pour water over the hands (palms held together) of their elderly relatives in a gesture of respect. Unless you were to enter a wát, you might not have a clue that any religious activity was taking place, since out in the streets the water-fighting action remains constant.

Although the true meaning of the festival is kept alive by ceremonies held inside wát grounds, Songkran nowadays is mainly a festival of fun and a way for locals to literally cool off during the hottest month of the year. Foreigners are not exempt from the soaking, and it's pretty much useless trying to stay dry in Chiang Mai during Songkran unless you never leave your room. The best way to enjoy a Chiang Mai Songkran is to grab a bucket, get out in the streets and join the fun.

Moon Muang; along several sois running south off Thanon Tha Phae; and along Thanon Charoen Prathet, parallel to and west of Mae Nam Ping. Several others are scattered elsewhere around the western side of Chiang Mai and along Thanon Charoen-rat east of Mae Nam Ping.

The best Chiang Mai guesthouses seem to be those owned and managed by local families, rather than by Bangkok Thais out for a quick buck. There are basically two kinds of budget guesthouse accommodation – old family homes converted into guest rooms (these usually have the best atmosphere although the least privacy) and hotel- or apartment-style places with rows of cell-like rooms. Nowadays the latter predominate although there are still a few of the older-style places around. In both, the furnishings are basic – a bed and a few sticks of furniture. Usually you must supply your own towel and soap; the rooms are cleaned only after guests leave. You can assume that rooms under 100B will not have a private bathroom but will probably have a fan.

The cheaper guesthouses make most of their money from food service and hill-tribe trekking rather than from room charges, hence you may be pressured to eat and to sign up for a trek. Places that charge 200B or more don't usually hassle guests in this way.

Many of the guesthouses can arrange bicycle and motorcycle rental. If you phone a guesthouse, most will collect you from the train or bus terminal for free if they have a room (this saves them having to pay a commission to a driver).

The following list is not exhaustive but covers most of the more reliable, long-running places. Guesthouses that belong to the Chiangmai Northern Guest House Club (☎ 053 217 513) are probably more secure in terms of theft than those that are not. As members pay government taxes, they are generally more interested in long-term operation. Members also meet regularly to discuss tourism issues, accommodation standards and room rates. The TAT office on Thanon Chiang Mai–Lamphun can provide an up-to-date list of members.

Inner Moat Area Unless otherwise indicated, the following accommodation options can be found on the Eastern Chiang Mai map.

Banana Guest House (☎ 053 206 285, fax 053 275 077, e onanong32@hotmail.com, 4/9 Thanon Ratchaphakhinai) Dorm beds 70B, singles/doubles with hot-water bathroom 100/120B. Near Pratu Chiang Mai, this is a small but friendly place that is almost always full in the high season.

Rose Guest House (☎ 053 273 869, 053 276 574, 87 Thanon Ratchamankha-Ratchaphakhinai) Singles/doubles/triples with fan and shared bathroom 60/80/120B. This friendly spot has a large sitting area downstairs as well as room to sit or do laundry on the roof. Like the Banana Guest House, it's often full in the high season.

Julie Guest House (Central Chiang Mai map; ☎ 053 274 355, e julie_chiangmai@yahoo.com, 7/1 Soi 5, Thanon Phra Pokklao) Dorm beds 50B, rooms with shared bathroom 80B, singles/doubles/triples with private hot water bathroom 120/130/180B. In the same general area as the Rose and the Banana, this one's a little nicer. Rooms are on the small side but the public areas are cosy. Bicycle rental is available and videos are shown nightly in the restaurant. Call for free transport.

Pha Thai (☎ 053 278 013, fax 053 274 075, 48/1 Thanon Ratchaphakhinai) Rooms with private solar-heated bathroom 200-250B. This place in the same quiet southeastern corner of the inner moat area has clean rooms with fans in a modest three-storey building.

Golden Fern Guest House (Central Chiang Mai map; ☎ 053 278 423, fax 053 278 665, e thegoldenfern_chiangmai@hotmail.com, 20 Soi 8, Thanon Phra Pokklao) Rooms with hot-water bathroom, fridge & fan 250B, with TV & air-con 350B, deluxe rooms with better bedding & bathtub 450B. Down a fairly quiet soi, the faràng-managed Golden Fern has recently been converted from a small apartment complex into a clean 30-room guesthouse.

New Saitum Guest House (☎ 053 278 575, Soi 2, Thanon Moon Muang) Rooms

CHIANG MAI

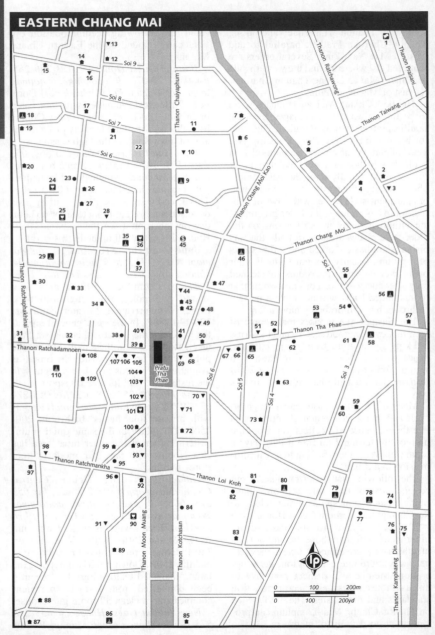

EASTERN CHIANG MAI

EASTERN CHIANG MAI

PLACES TO STAY
2 New Mitrapap Hotel
4 New Asia Hotel
5 Prince Hotel
6 Eagle House 1
7 Orchid House
12 SK House;
Libra Guest House
14 Supreme House;
SUP Court
15 Paneeda House
17 Northlands House;
Lamchang House
19 RCN Court
20 Sumit Hotel
21 CM Apartments;
Chiang Mai SP Hotel
26 Your House Guest House
27 Eagle House 2
30 Safe House Court
31 Rendezvous Guest House
33 Amphawan House; Kavil
Guest House & Restaurant;
Chiang Mai White House;
Chiangmai Kristi House
34 Nice Apartment
39 Moon Meuang Golden
Court; Montri Hotel
42 Daret's House
43 New City; Happy House
47 VK Guest House
50 Roong Ruang Hotel
55 Veerachai Court
57 Tapae Inn
59 Fang Guest House
60 Ratchada Guest House
61 Tapae Place Hotel
63 Midtown House; Thana
Guest House;
Baan Jongcome
64 Thapae
72 Little Home
Guest House
73 Sarah Guest House
76 Imperial Mae Ping Hotel
83 Center Place Guest House

85 Lai Thai Guest House
87 Pha Thai Guest House
88 Banana Guest House
89 Top North Guest House
92 Muang Thong Hotel;
Queen Bee
94 Somwang Guest House
97 Rose Guest House
99 Smile House
100 New Saitum Guest House;
Library Service
109 Gap's House; Gap's Thai
Culinary Academy

PLACES TO EAT
3 Han Yang Hong Kong
10 Somphet Night Market
13 Biaporn
16 Indian Restaurant Vegetarian
Food
28 Irish Pub
40 JJ Bakery & Restaurant
44 Thanam Restaurant
49 Da Stefano
51 Ratana's Kitchen
67 Dara Steakhouse
69 Art Cafe
70 El Toro Mexican Restaurant &
Cantina; Bake & Bite
71 Aroon (Rai) Restaurant
75 Kuaytiaw Kai Tun Coke
91 Pum Pui Italian Restaurant
93 Kuaytiaw Reua Koliang
Restaurant
98 Mitmai Restaurant
102 Jerusalem Falafel
103 AUM Vegetarian Food
105 Salom Joy
107 Easy Diner

WAT
9 Wat Chomphu
18 Wat Lam Chang
29 Wat Pan Ping
35 Wat Dok Euang
46 Wat U Sai Kham

53 Wat Chetawan
56 Wat Saen Fang
58 Wat Bupparam
65 Wat Mahawan
78 Wat Chang Khong
79 Wat Loi Khron
80 Wat Phan Tong
86 Wat Sai Mun Mianma
110 Wat Phan An

OTHER
1 US Consulate
8 Nice Illusion
11 Ban Nit
22 Talat Somphet
23 Baan Thai
24 Rasta Cafe
25 Yoy Pocket
32 American University Alumni
(AUA) Library
36 Kafé
37 North Wheels
38 VIP
41 Elephant Lightfoot
45 Money Exchange
48 Gecko Books
52 The Book Zone
54 Shaman Books
62 Nova
66 Broadway Photo
68 Journey Car Rent
74 Hangdong Rattan
77 Success Silk Shop
81 The Bookshop
82 Woven Dreams
84 DK Book House
90 H3 Pub
95 Lost Book Shop
96 Mungkala
101 Bierstube; Pinte Blues Pub;
Sax Music Pub
104 Chiang Mai Thai Cookery
School
106 Lek Chaiya
108 American University Alunmi
(AUA)

90-150B. New Saitum offers well-worn, basic but relatively livable wooden bungalows with private bathroom and balconies in a quiet setting.

Somwang Guest House (☎ *053 278 505, Soi 2, Thanon Moon Muang)* Rooms with bath 150B. Though a little cramped, Somwang can be recommended for its convenient location near Pratu Tha Phae.

Smile House (☎ *053 208 661, fax 053 208 663, 5 Soi 2, Thanon Ratchamankha)* Singles & doubles with fan 250B, with aircon & TV 400B. Smile House offers rooms in an old Thai house surrounded by a row of newer rooms. The charming outdoor eating area attached to the renovated house is a plus. Historical footnote: This house once served as the 'safe house' of infamous

CHIANG MAI

Shan-Chinese opium warlord Khun Sa whenever he came to Chiang Mai. The guesthouse rents motorcycles and bicycles and offers other travel services as well.

Chiang Mai Garden Guest House (Central Chiang Mai map; ☎/fax 053 278 881, 82-86 Thanon Ratchamankha) Rooms with bathroom & fan 120B, with air-con 350B, triples/quads with fan 150/200B. This friendly and centrally located guesthouse has clean rooms in an ageing two-storey building close to Heuan Phen, Mit Mai and several other restaurants. Wat Chedi Luang is in the next block. The Thai woman owner speaks French, German and English. Chiang Mai Garden will not pay commissions to túk-túk or săwngthăew drivers; call the guesthouse for free transport.

Eagle House 2 (☎ 053 210 620, fax 053 216 368, 26 Soi 2, Thanon Ratwithi) Dorm beds 70B, singles/doubles/triples with fan & cold-water bathroom 170/200/270B, doubles/triples with hot-water bathroom 240/320B, with air-con 290/360B. A newer, nicer branch of the original Eagle House (see under Pratu Tha Phae to the River later in this section), this three-storey, modern building has a pleasant garden sitting area and is fairly quiet. It is around the corner from Irish Pub and convenient to several Thai bars along Thanon Ratwithi.

Your House Guest House (☎ 053 217 492, fax 053 419 093, e yourhous@ cm.ksc.co.th, Soi 2, Thanon Ratwithi) Singles/doubles in a teak house with shared hot-water bathroom 140/160B, in a cement building with private bathroom 150/190B. This friendly guesthouse is a little farther north along the same soi as Eagle House 2.

Along the little, red-bricked soi off Thanon Moon Muang is a plethora of other cheap places in several tacky, newer buildings. Soi 9, off Moon Muang near the northeastern corner of the moat, is a particularly good area to look if you're having trouble finding a vacant room during festivals such as Songkran and the Flower Festival.

SK House (☎ 053 210 690, 30 Soi 9, Thanon Moon Muang) Singles/doubles 150/250B. This place is OK, but if you don't sign up for a trek first, good luck getting a room.

Libra Guest House (☎/fax 053 210 687, 26 Soi 9, Thanon Moon Muang) Singles & doubles with fan & cold-water bathroom 100B, with hot-water bathroom 150B. Next door to SK House, the clean rooms are decent, although they're often full, even in the low season, and one reader reported that there was too much pressure to buy treks.

Paneeda House (☎ 053 213 156, 45 Soi 9, Thanon Moon Muang) Rooms with bathroom 150B per person. This is a newer three-storey guesthouse run by an elderly Thai couple. The rooms may be a bit overpriced for the area, but the couple are very friendly and they don't push treks, food or anything else.

Supreme House (☎ 053 222 480, fax 053 218 545, 44/1 Soi 9, Thanon Moon Muang) Rooms with inside bathroom 100-250B.

SUP Court (☎ 053 210 625, 053 224 652, Soi 9, Thanon Moon Muang) Rooms from 2000B, offered on a monthly basis only. SUP Court is near the Supreme House.

Northlands House (☎/fax 053 218 860, 2 Soi 7, Thanon Moon Muang) Rooms 250-350B. Northlands House is west of Chiang Mai SP Hotel and CM Apartments (see Hotels later).

Lamchang House (☎ 053 210 586, 053 211 435, 24 Soi 7, Thanon Moon Muang) Rooms with shared hot-water bathroom & fan 80-150B. Lamchang House is a little farther west of Northlands House. The simple rooms are located in an atmospheric wooden Thai-style house run by a Thai family. There is a small garden restaurant and information service.

Wanasit Guest House (Central Chiang Mai map; ☎ 053 814 042, 6 Soi 8, Thanon Ratchamankha) Rooms with fan 150B. All rooms in this two-storey, modern Thai house come with bathroom. Air-con rooms are available for a bit more. Wanasit is down a quiet soi next to Ta-Krite restaurant, near Wat Phra Singh.

Bridging the gap between budget and mid-range places are a couple of comfortable guesthouses in the 200B to 400B range.

Gap's House (☎/fax 053 278 140, e gap_house@hotmail.com, 3 Soi 4, Thanon Ratchadamnoen) Singles/doubles 250/390B. Behind the AUA Thai Language Centre, this guesthouse has Northern Thai–style houses built around a quiet garden filled with antiques. All rooms have carpet, air-con and hot-water bathrooms; rates include a filling breakfast. Gap's offers a Thai cooking course, and there's a tasty 80B vegetarian buffet from 7pm to 9pm nightly.

Rendezvous Guest House (☎ 053 213 763, fax 053 419 009, 3/1 Soi 5, Thanon Ratchadamnoen) Singles/doubles with fan 180/250B, rooms with air-con 300B. This three-storey inn is on the other side of Thanon Ratchadamnoen down Soi 5. All rooms have hot water, TV, phone and fridge.

Farther north along the same soi is a short string of three- and four-storey apartment-style places: *Kavil Guest House & Restaurant* (☎/fax 053 224 740, e kavilgh@ chmai.loxinfo.co.th, 10/1 Soi 5, Thanon Ratchadamnoen), with rooms for 180B to 360B; *Amphawan House* (☎ 053 210 584, 10 Soi 5, Thanon Ratchadamnoen), with rooms for 200B to 250B, less for long-term stays; *Chiang Mai White House* (☎ 053 357 130, 12 Soi 5, Thanon Ratchadamnoen), which has rooms with fan for 250B, and rooms with air-con and cable TV for 350B, both with attached hot water bathrooms; and *Chiangmai Kristi House* (☎ 053 418 165, 14/2 Soi 5, Thanon Ratchadamnoen), with rooms for 150B to 180B. We especially liked Chiang Mai White House, with its spotless rooms and public areas, nice garden and security; the checkout time is an early 10am. An advantage of these last four is their quiet location.

Top North Guest House (☎ 053 278 900, 053 278 684, fax 053 278 485, 15 Soi 2, Thanon Moon Muang) Rooms with fan & hot-water bathroom 300B, with air-con 500B, with TV & bathtub 600B. This popular, efficiently run spot tucked down a winding soi features a swimming pool and a travel agency.

Safe House Court (☎ 053 418 955, 178 Thanon Ratchaphakhinai) Rooms with air-con, phone, fridge & hot-water bathroom 350-400B; monthly 3000B. The semi-classical architecture at centrally located Safe House Court is of a more pleasing design than most apartment courts in Chiang Mai.

RCN Court (☎ 053 418 280/2, 053 224 619, fax 053 211 969, e rcncourt@ chm.cscoms.com, 35 Soi 7, Thanon Moon Muang) Rooms with fan & hot-water bathroom 300-350B, with air-con 400-480B; monthly with fan/air-con 4000/5500B. Although the building exterior isn't as pleasing as that of Safe House Court, it's very clean and offers fax and laundering services, an attached minimart and a small restaurant. The security seems very good. Daily rates change depending on the season, although most residents are staying long term and it can be difficult to find a vacancy. Monthly rates don't include electricity and phone charges. All rooms come with a medium-sized fridge. A terrace with exercise equipment is available for guest use. Head north along Thanon Ratchaphakhinai past Sumit Hotel, then right on Soi 7.

Pratu Tha Phae to the River Unless otherwise indicated, the following accommodation can be found on the Eastern Chiang Mai map.

Daret's House (☎ 053 235 440, 4/5 Thanon Chaiyaphum) Singles/doubles with cold-water bathroom 70/100B, with hot-water bathroom 80/120B. Across the moat, quite close to Pratu Tha Phae, is this guesthouse with stacks of basic, well-worn rooms. The large sidewalk cafe in front is popular.

Happy House (☎ 053 252 619, fax 053 251 871, 11/1 Thanon Chang Moi Kao) Singles/doubles with fan & hot-water bathroom 100/180B, rooms with air-con 280B. The rooms in this multi-storey guesthouse are large and well tended. It is next door to Daret's House.

VK Guest House (☎ 053 252 559, 22/2 Soi 3, Thanon Chang Moi Kao) Singles & doubles 80B; one triple room with bathroom 40B per person. VK is a three-storey building down an alley off Thanon Chang Moi Kao, with fairly basic but adequate rooms.

CHIANG MAI

Eagle House 1 *(☎ 053 235 387, fax 053 216 368)* Singles with bathroom 90B, doubles with bathroom 120-150B. Eagle House, farther north on Thanon Chang Moi Kao across busy Thanon Chang Moi, has staff boasting French, German, English and Spanish language skills. The simple rooms could use some additional maintenance, but at these prices it's hard to complain. Trekking is big here.

Orchid House *(☎ 053 874 127)* Rooms with bathroom 100-150B. Farther north yet at Soi 2, Thanon Chaiyaphum, the friendly Orchid House offers simple accommodation with balcony in a modern four-storey building.

Soi 4, farther east (towards the river) along Thanon Tha Phae, has several newer, two-storey brick guesthouses with downstairs sitting areas and rooms in the 100B to 200B range: ***Midtown House*** *(☎ 053 273 191, 7 Soi 4, Thanon Tha Phae)*, ***Thapae*** *(☎ 053 271 591, 2/2 Soi 4, Thanon Tha Phae)* and ***Sarah Guest House*** *(☎ 053 208 271, 20 Soi 4, Thanon Tha Phae)*. All are fine – a step up from the Pratu Tha Phae places – but we'd choose Midtown House for its friendly service and sense of privacy. Sarah Guest House is in a nice garden setting.

Thana Guest House *(☎ 053 279 794, fax 053 272 285, 27/8 Soi 4, Thanon Tha Phae)* Singles/doubles with fan & hot-water 160/180B, with air-con 250/300B. Also on Soi 4, this guesthouse caters to Israeli travellers (the management boasts 80% Israeli occupancy), with all signs in Thai and Hebrew. The rooms are good and there is a small restaurant on the premises serving kosher food.

Baan Jongcome *(☎ 053 274 823, 47 Soi 4, Thanon Tha Phae)* Rooms with fan/aircon 350/450B. Next down this soi is this three-storey building; it's a little more upmarket, with more comfortable rooms.

Fang Guest House *(☎ 053 282 940, 46-48 Soi 1, Thanon Kamphaeng Din)* Singles/doubles with fan & hot-water bathroom 200/250B, with air-con & carpet 300B. Located in a newer, four-storey building well away from traffic, Fang offers clean rooms

with solar-heated hot-water showers, but hot water is available in the afternoon only. The small restaurant serves faràng food.

Ratchada Guest House *(☎ 053 275 556, 55 Soi 3, Thanon Tha Phae)* Singles/doubles with fan & hot-water bathroom 100/150B. This guesthouse has a quiet location.

Little Home Guest House *(☎ 053 206 939, fax 053 273 662,* e *littleh@ loxinfo.co.th, 1/1 Soi 3, Thanon Kotchasan)* Singles/doubles with fan & hot-water bathroom 200/280B. Not far from the moat and DK Book House, the efficient Little Home offers large, clean, comfortable rooms in a modern Thai-style building. Upstairs rooms have private balconies.

Center Place Guest House *(☎ 053 271 169, fax 053 208 950,* e *centerplace99@ hotmail.com, 17/2 Soi 1, Thanon Loi Kroh)* Singles & doubles with fan & bathroom 150B. This is off a good street for textile shopping and within walking distance of both the inner moat area and the Night Bazaar. The proprietors also offer instruction in Thai cooking.

Chiangmai Souvenir Guest House *(Viking Guest House; Chiang Mai Night Bazaar map; ☎ 053 818 786, 116 Thanon Charoen Prathet)* Rooms with fan & hot-water shower 130-180B, with air-con 330B. One block east of the Night Bazaar and right around the corner from Anusan Night Market, this is a pleasant and inexpensive urban haven, with an attractive outdoor eating area.

East of the River The following accommodation can be found on the Central Chiang Mai map.

Ben Guest House *(☎ 053 244 103, 4/11 Soi 2, Thanon Chiang Mai-Lamphun)* Rooms with fan & hot-water bathroom 150B. South of Saphan Nawarat and down a very narrow soi near the TAT office, this quiet compound has very clean rooms. Food service is available in an adjacent garden, and the staff can arrange bicycle rentals. Although it's on the eastern side of the river, Ben Guest House is within walking distance of the Night Bazaar.

There is a spare string of guesthouses along Thanon Charoenrat, parallel to the river – a bit far from the centre of town but recommended for those who are seeking a quiet atmosphere or the scenic river setting.

Le Pont (☎ *053 241 661, 053 241 712, fax 053 243 673, 14 Thanon Charoenrat*) Rooms with air-con & hot-water bathroom 450-550B. Opposite the Riverside Bar & Restaurant near Saphan Nawarat, this place looks impressive, with its office, sitting area and restaurant housed in a 120-year-old teak residence; the guest rooms are in an adjacent modern wing. Discounts are available with stays of a week or more. The only drawback is that you can hear the live music from the Riverside until the bands shut down around 1am.

Je t'Aime (☎ *053 241 912, 247-249 Thanon Charoenrat*) Singles 80-120B, doubles 100-160B. This quiet guesthouse has a variety of rooms in separate several-storey buildings on secure, landscaped grounds. The owner, a Thai artist, has placed paintings or some kind of original artwork in every room.

Pun Pun Guest House (☎ *053 243 362, fax 053 246 140,* e *armms@iname.com, 321 Thanon Charoenrat*) Bungalows with shared hot-water bathroom 150-200B, rooms with private bathroom 200-275B. Pun Pun offers very tidy bungalows as well as rooms with private bathroom in a quaint two-storey wooden Thai-style house. Rates depend on the number of people and the time of year. Assets include a fully stocked bar, snooker table and riverfront promenade.

C&C Teak House (☎ *053 246 966, 39 Thanon Bamrungrat*) Singles/doubles with shared bathroom 80/150B. Closer to the train station than Mae Nam Ping (rather far from the old city), this century-old teak house in a secure, gated compound contains quiet, comfortable rooms.

Thanon Chang Khlan The following accommodation can be found on the Chiang Mai Night Bazaar map.

Night Bazaar Guest House (☎ *053 272 067, 89/2 Thanon Chang Khlan*) Rooms with fan or air-con & hot-water bathroom 200-450B. In the heart of the Night Bazaar neighbourhood, and adjacent to the Galare

Food Centre, this might be just the place to stay if you're buying wholesale in the area.

Chiang Mai Youth Hostel (☎ *053 276 737, fax 053 204 025,* e *chiangmai@ tyha.org, 21/8 Thanon Chang Khlan*) Rooms with fan & hot-water bathroom 150B; with air-con 350B. A Hostelling International membership is required to stay here; a temporary membership valid for one night costs 50B. Call for free pick-up.

Thanon Huay Kaew This area northwest of the old city generally contains Chiang Mai's more expensive hotels and restaurants, hence few guesthouses have so far opened up here.

Isra House (*Chiang Mai map;* ☎ *053 214 924, 109/24 Thanon Huay Kaew*) Singles/doubles with shared bathroom 60/80B. Despite its street address, Isra House is actually on a soi off Huay Kaew, north of The Pub. There are only nine rooms. Its main virtue is that it's the cheapest place to stay in the city. Because it's so cheap, some people stay long-term, and some elect to pay by the month. If you do much sightseeing or dining in the old city, however, any savings over a slightly more expensive but more centrally located place will quickly disappear in săwngthăew fares.

Uniserv (*Chiang Mai University map;* ☎ *053 224 672, fax 053 216 244, Chiang Mai University*) Beds in dorm with fan & shared bathroom 100B; 2-bed room with air-con and private bathroom 400B, with TV & fridge 750B (but discounts to 500B usually available). The Uniserv hostel on CMU campus, close to the Thanon Huay Kaew side, is a large hotel-like structure with clean rooms, good service and a Thai restaurant downstairs. You do not have to be a student to stay here.

Hotels

Unless otherwise indicated, the following accommodation can be found on the Eastern Chiang Mai map.

New Mitrapap Hotel (☎ *053 235 436, fax 053 251 260, 94-98 Thanon Ratcha-wong*) Singles/doubles with fan & hot-water bathroom 320B, with air-con 400B.

CHIANG MAI

In Chiang Mai's small Chinatown, between the east moat and Mae Nam Ping, this hotel features adequate rooms; the air-con rooms are a better deal. It's close to several good, inexpensive Chinese restaurants, as well as Talat Warorot (Warorot Market).

Prince Hotel (☎ 053 252 025, fax 053 251 144, 3 Thanon Taiwang) Singles/ doubles with hot-water bathroom from 440B. The Prince offers good, if time-worn, air-con rooms. There's a restaurant, coffee shop and swimming pool.

Chiang Mai Phu Viang Hotel (Chiang Mai map; ☎ 053 221 632, 5-9 Soi 4, Thanon Chotana) Small rooms with fan & hot-water bathroom from 200B, larger rooms with air-con & TV 280B. Near the Chang Pheuak bus terminal, this very Thai hotel features a restaurant and coffee shop.

Muang Thong Hotel (☎ 053 248 378, fax 053 274 349, 5 Thanon Ratchamankha) Singles/doubles with hot-water bathroom 120/180B. Inside the city moat at the corner of Thanon Ratchamankha and Thanon Moon Muang is this old Thai-style hotel. Street noise from busy Thanon Moon Muang could be a problem.

Roong Ruang Hotel (Roong Raeng; ☎ 053 236 746, fax 053 252 409, 398 Thanon Tha Phae) Upstairs/downstairs rooms with fan & hot-water bathroom 250/280B; with air-con & cable TV 350/400B. This hotel on the eastern side of the city moat boasts a prime location near Pratu Tha Phae. The service is good and the rooms, which face an inner courtyard and are therefore quiet, have pleasant sitting areas out the front. This is a good place to stay for the Flower Festival in February as the Saturday parade passes right by the entrance, but it's probably not the best choice for the raucous Songkran and Loi Krathong festivals. There's another entrance on Thanon Chang Moi Kao.

Tapae Inn (☎ 053 234 640) Rooms with fan & bathroom 150B, with air-con 220B. This decent budget choice is just west of the canal on the northern side of Thanon Tha Phae.

Sumit Hotel (☎ 053 211 033, ☎/fax 053 214 014, 198 Thanon Ratchaphakhinai)

Rooms with fan & bathroom 200B, with hot-water bathroom and air-con 300B. On a relatively quiet section of Thanon Ratchaphakhinai inside the old city, this hotel offers very clean, large rooms in the classic Thai/Chinese style. You can choose a room with one big bed or two twin beds for the same rate. This is very good value for anyone avoiding the guesthouse scene – it's probably the best hotel deal in the old city.

YMCA International Hotel (Chiang Mai map; ☎ 053 221 819, 053 222 366, fax 053 215 523, e ytour@loxinfo.co.th, 11 Thanon Soemsuk Mengrairasmi) Old wing: dorm beds 75B, singles/doubles with fan & shared bath 130/190B, with fan & bathroom 220B, with air-con 250/350B; new wing: singles/doubles with air-con, bathroom, telephone & TV 500/600B. Outside the northwestern corner of the moat, this place has a travel agency, handicraft centre and cafeteria.

Montri Hotel (☎ 053 211 069, fax 053 217 416, e am-intl@cm.ksc.co.th, 2-6 Thanon Ratchadamnoen) Singles with air-con & hot water bathroom 575B, with cable TV 695B. Since it's at the busy intersection of Thanon Moon Muang and Thanon Ratchadamnoen, the street-facing rooms in this place are bombarded with noise from Thanon Moon Muang, which reflects off Tha Phae wall. One advantage is that JJ Bakery & Restaurant is downstairs. Tax, service and breakfast are included in room rates.

Nice Apartment (☎ 053 210 552, 053 218 290, fax 053 419 150, 15 Soi 1, Thanon Ratchadamnoen) Rooms with fan, hot-water bathroom & cable TV 200-250B, with air-con 300-350B. Clean, simple and well-run, you'll find this building on a soi behind the Montri Hotel; monthly rates are also available.

VIP (☎ 053 418 970, fax 053 419 199, 1 Soi 1, Thanon Ratchadamnoen) Rooms with fan, hot-water bathroom & TV 200-250B, with air-con 300-350B. On the same soi almost directly behind JJ Bakery & Restaurant, the VIP is very similar to Nice Apartment in layout and quality.

CM Apartments (☎ 053 222 100, 7 Soi 7, Thanon Moon Muang) Rooms with hot-water bathroom 250-450B. On Soi 7 off Thanon Moon Muang there are a couple of good apartment-style places, including this basic but clean building. There are many Thai residents; monthly rates are 2500B to 3000B.

Chiang Mai SP Hotel (☎ 053 214 522, fax 053 223 042, 7/1 Soi 7, Thanon Moon Muang) Rooms with hot-water bathroom 2500-3000B a month. This place is similar to CM Apartments – basic but clean rooms, and many Thai residents.

Veerachai Court (☎ 053 251 047, fax 053 252 402, 19 Soi 2, Thanon Phae 2) Rooms with air-con & hot-water bathroom 400B. This place features a nine-storey building on the eastern side of the soi, and a four-storey one on the western side. Clean, quiet, if smallish, rooms come with TV. The monthly rate is 3500B.

Moon Meuang Golden Court (☎ 053 212 779, Thanon Moon Muang) Rooms with fan & hot-water bathroom 200B, with air-con 300B. North of Pratu Tha Phae, this apartment-style place is clean enough and there's a small coffee shop attached.

Anodard Hotel (Central Chiang Mai map; ☎ 053 270 755, fax 053 270 759, 57-59 Thanon Ratchamankha) Rooms with air-con & hot-water bathroom from 450B. Well-kept rooms with air-con are in a building that would have been called 'modern' 30 years ago. There are a restaurant and swimming pool on the premises.

Pratu Chang Pheuak Area There are very few hotels north of the city walls. Although far from the Tha Phae action, there are some near the Chang Pheuak bus terminal (for Chiang Dao, Fang and Tha Ton).

Chawala Hotel (Chiang Mai map; ☎ 053 214 939, 053 214 453, 129 Thanon Chotana) Rooms with fan & shower 150B, with air-con 250B. Rooms at this place are basic.

Chang Peuk Hotel (Central Chiang Mai map; ☎ 053 217 513, fax 053 223 668, 133 Thanon Chotana) Rooms with air-con & hot-water bathroom 250B, with TV 350B. Near the Chang Pheuak bus terminal, this place has clean rooms and there's a good coffee shop on the premises.

PLACES TO STAY – MID-RANGE

In this range you can expect daily room cleaning, the option of air-con (some places have rooms with fan also) and – in the hotels – TV and telephone. If anything marks a guesthouse, it's the absence of these latter appliances, though some of the places in this price category (500B to 1500B) really blur the line between 'hotel' and 'guesthouse', the difference often being in name only.

Rooms in all accommodation described below come with air-con and hot-water bathroom unless otherwise noted.

Galare Guest House (Chiang Mai Night Bazaar map; ☎ 053 821 011, fax 053 279 088, ✉ galare_gh@hotmail.com, 7/1 Soi 2, Thanon Charoen Prathet) Rooms 860B. A good example of a place that could just as well be a hotel is this well-managed guesthouse. Spacious rooms which have air-con, TV and a refrigerator. It's popular with repeat visitors for its Mae Nam Ping location and proximity to both the Night Bazaar and post office.

River View Lodge (Chiang Mai Night Bazaar map; ☎ 053 271 110, fax 053 279 019, 25 Soi 2, Thanon Charoen Prathet) Rooms 1450-2000B. Almost next door to the Galare Guest House, this establishment features 36 well-appointed rooms in a two-storey, L-shaped building on spacious, landscaped grounds with a swimming pool. Up to 40% discount is offered from May to August. The friendly owner has a small collection of classic cars on display in the parking lot.

Porn Ping Tower Hotel (Chiang Mai Night Bazaar map; ☎ 053 270 099, fax 053 270 119, 46 Thanon Charoen Prathet) Rooms 1766B. Almost opposite the decaying Diamond Riverside Hotel on Thanon Charoen Prathet, from the ambience of the reception area, one might expect to pay much more. The Porn Ping is most famous for Bubbles, still the most popular disco in town. Rooms are often discounted to 790/890B a single/double.

Royal Lanna (Chiang Mai Night Bazaar map; ☎ 053 818 773, fax 053 818 776, 119 Thanon Loi Kroh) Rooms with hot-water bathroom with bathtub, air-con, TV, phone & refrigerator 900B. The Royal Lanna towers over the Night Bazaar. Rates also include a breakfast buffet, and discounts are available for monthly rentals. There's a medium-sized swimming pool on the 4th floor.

Baan Kaew Guest House (*Central Chiang Mai map;* ☎ *053 271 606, fax 053 273 436, 142 Thanon Charoen Prathet*) Rooms with fan/air-con 350/450B. Farther down Thanon Charoen Prathet, opposite Wat Chaimongkhon and two doors south of the Alliance Française, Baan Kaew Guest House has well-maintained and simple but well-designed rooms featuring cross-ventilation and mosquito coil containers. This guesthouse is set far back off the road, so it's very quiet. Meals are available in a small outdoor dining area. Be prepared to pay for the room every morning.

Tapae Place Hotel (*Eastern Chiang Mai map;* ☎ *053 270 159, 053 281 842, fax 053 271 982, 2 Soi 3, Thanon Tha Phae*) Rooms 700-1600B. This is a large, modern, L-shaped building facing busy Thanon Tha Phae. Although it's a bit worn, the hotel's main drawcard is that it's only a few steps away from the banks, shops and restaurants of the city's main tourist thoroughfare.

Felix City Inn (*Central Chiang Mai map;* ☎ *053 270 710, fax 053 270 709,* e *felix@cm.ksc.co.th, 154 Thanon Ratchamankha*) Rooms in high/low season 1900/942B. Inside the old city on a relatively quiet street, the friendly and efficient Felix City Inn offers 134 comfortable rooms. Room rates include breakfast.

Lai Thai Guest House (*Eastern Chiang Mai map;* ☎ *053 271 725, 053 271 534, fax 053 272 724, 111/4 Thanon Kotchasan*) Rooms 590-790B. Facing the eastern side of the moat the business-like Lai Thai has well-kept rooms, plus a swimming pool and garden.

New Asia Hotel (*Eastern Chiang Mai map;* ☎ *053 252 426, fax 053 252 427, 55 Thanon Ratchawong*) Rooms 266-406B. This is the place if you want to stay in Chiang Mai's bustling Chinatown. The lobby decor is 1970s-era Hong Kong; it's a bit tacky but rooms are decent. There are many Chinese clients.

Sri Tokyo Hotel (*Central Chiang Mai map;* ☎ *053 213 899, fax 053 211 102, 6 Thanon Bunreuangrit*) Rooms 250B, suites 450-600B. Close to the Japanese embassy, and next door to Chiang Mai Ram Hospital, Sri Tokyo has OK rooms but street noise can be a problem in the front.

Chiang Mai Phucome Hotel (*Chiang Mai map;* ☎ *053 211 026, fax 053 216 412, 21 Thanon Huay Kaew*) Rooms in old building 700B, in new building 900B. Strung out along Thanon Huay Kaew to the immediate northwest of the old city are perhaps a dozen mid-range and top-end hotels. Typical of the kind of places here is the Phucome. Once the best hotel in the city, it is now very middle-of-the-road but a fair deal for a room with all amenities. On the premises are a restaurant, coffee shop and massage centre. This hotel remains a favourite with visiting Thais.

Quality Chiang Mai Hills (*Chiang Mai map;* ☎ *053 210 030, fax 053 210 035, 18 Thanon Huay Kaew*) Rooms 1200-1500B. Near the Phucome, this place has 249 well-appointed rooms; rates include breakfast.

The Providence (*Chiang Mai map;* ☎ *053 893 123, fax 053 221 750, 99/9 Thanon Huay Kaew*) Singles & doubles from 380B. Farther out on Huay Kaew, all rooms at The Providence have air-con, and there's a restaurant, coffee shop and lobby bar.

Northern Inn (*Central Chiang Mai map;* ☎ *053 210 002, fax 053 215 828, 234/18 Thanon Mani Nopharat*) Rooms 450B. Close to Pratu Chang Pheuak and the Chang Pheuak bus terminal, the Northern Inn has fair rooms; middle-budget package tourists use this hotel extensively.

Iyara Hotel (*Chiang Mai map;* ☎ *053 222 245, 053 214 227, fax 053 214 401, 126 Thanon Chotana*) Rooms 450-700B. Several long blocks farther north of Pratu Chang Pheuak, opposite the teacher's college, the Iyara has good accommodation, but this is a very busy street and the only reason to stay here is if you have business at the teacher's college or everything else is full.

Joy's House (*Chiang Mai map;* ☎ *053 854 213, fax 053 248 960,* ⓔ *joys_house@ hotmail.com, 114 Mu 9, San Phi Seua*) Rooms from 950B. Joy's represents a new concept in upper mid-range lodgings, sort of a cross between a home-stay and a boutique hotel with personalised services. Rooms are spread out among several large Thai houses in a quiet area not far from the new City Hall on the city's northern outskirts. All come with fan, hot-water bathroom and mini-fridge. The more expensive 'Professor's Studio' has air-con and TV. A separate wing contains telephone, fax, computer with Internet access, TV and a bar. Prices include a welcome massage and herbal sauna, Thai dance and transport by private car to/from and around Chiang Mai as necessary. For separate rates, the staff offer a range of activities from handicraft village visits to temple tours, all customised for the guest.

PLACES TO STAY – TOP END

In general, hotel rates for luxury hotels are lower in Chiang Mai than in Bangkok. You can expect to pay 1500B to 5000B for large, well-maintained rooms with air-con, TV, IDD telephone, restaurant (usually more than one), fitness centre and swimming pool. Booking through a travel agency or via the Internet almost always means lower rates, or try asking for a hotel's 'corporate' discount.

The biggest single area in town for top-end hotels runs along Thanon Huay Kaew, a broad, straight avenue running northwest-ward from the northwestern corner of the moat. There are also a number of deluxe hotels in the vicinity of the Night Bazaar.

Chiang Mai Plaza Hotel (*Chiang Mai Night Bazaar map;* ☎ *053 270 036, fax 053 272 230, 92 Thanon Si Donchai*) Singles/doubles 2500B. Not far from the Night Bazaar this friendly hotel has a spacious, serene lobby with live Northern Thai music in the evenings, a lobby bar, restaurant, wood-panelled sauna, fitness centre and a well-kept pool area with shade pavilions. Room rates are often discounted to 1600B for singles and 1800B for doubles, including breakfast. Nonsmoking rooms are

available, which is unusual for a place charging less than 3000B.

Imperial Mae Ping Hotel (*Central Chiang Mai map;* ☎ *053 270 160, fax 053 270 181,* ⓔ *maeping@loxinfo.co.th, 153 Thanon Si Donchai*) Standard rooms 3000-3500B, deluxe rooms 3750-4250B. Also near the Night Bazaar; well-equipped rooms and a coffee shop, three restaurants and pool.

Chiang Inn (*Chiang Mai Night Bazaar map;* ☎ *053 270 070, fax 053 274 299,* ⓔ *chianginn@chiangmai.a-net.net.th, 10 Thanon Chang Khlan*) Rooms 1000-1200B. Behind the centre of the Night Bazaar, off Thanon Chang Khlan, Chiang Inn has comfortable rooms and amenities include a restaurant, popular disco and swimming pool. The Chiang Inn Plaza shopping centre, with several restaurants and shops, is just opposite the front of the hotel. Room rates include breakfast.

Royal Princess (*Chiang Mai Night Bazaar map;* ☎ *053 281 033, fax 053 281 044,* ⓔ *rpc@dusit.com, 112 Thanon Chang Khlan*) Rooms from 3000B. On Thanon Chang Khlan itself, in the middle of where the Night Bazaar vendors set up nightly, the Royal Princess boasts three restaurants, a lobby bar and a swimming pool. This one is mainly used by package tourists.

Suriwongse Hotel (*Chiang Mai Night Bazaar map;* ☎ *053 270 051, fax 053 270 063,* ⓔ *suriwongse_htl_cnx@hotmail.com, 1110 Thanon Chang Khlan*) Singles/ doubles 1292/1420B including tax, service and breakfast. Around the corner from the Royal Princess, on Thanon Loi Kroh, the Suriwongse contains a coffee shop, restaurant, swimming pool and massage centre. The 120B lunch buffet is popular with nonguests.

Empress Hotel (*Chiang Mai map;* ☎ *053 270 240, fax 053 272 467,* ⓔ *reservations@ empresshotels.com, 199 Thanon Chang Khlan*) Singles/doubles 3146/3630B including tax and service charges. South of the Night Bazaar area, the Empress offers plush surroundings, including a restaurant, coffee shop, swimming pool, fitness centre and disco.

Westin Riverside Plaza (Chiang Mai map; ☎ 053 275 300, fax 053 275 299, W www.westin-chiangmai.com, 318/1 Thanon Chiang Mai-Lamphun) Rooms from 6200B. On the eastern bank of Mae Nam Ping, this is the city's top property at the moment. Capacious rooms are commensurate in quality with the international reputation enjoyed by this management group. Facilities include three restaurants, a coffee shop, fitness centre, swimming pool, sauna and beauty salon.

Amari Rincome Hotel (Chiang Mai map; ☎ 053 221 130, 053 221 044, fax 053 221 915, e rincome@amari.com, 1 Thanon Nimmanhemin) Standard singles/doubles from US$88/96. At the corner of Huay Kaew and Thanon Nimmanhemin, the city's most expensive option offers large, comfortable rooms, a well-received Italian restaurant, coffee shop, lobby bar, conference facilities, tennis court and pool.

Lotus Pang Suan Kaew Hotel (Chiang Mai map; PSK; ☎ 053 224 444, fax 053 224 493, 99/4 Thanon Huay Kaew) Rooms 1000-2783B. Located behind Kad Suan Kaew shopping centre, PSK has attractive rooms, a beer garden, restaurant, coffee shop, fitness centre, nightclub, tennis and squash courts, swimming pool and, of course, sheltered access to the shopping centre.

Chiang Mai Orchid Hotel (Chiang Mai map; ☎ 053 222 091, fax 053 221 625, e cmorchid@loxinfo.co.th, 100 Thanon Huay Kaew) Rooms from 2825B. This is another top-drawer spot on Thanon Huay Kaew, and only about a hundred metres from the entrance to Kad Suan Kaew shopping centre.

Amity Green Hills (Chiang Mai map; ☎ 053 220 100, fax 053 221 602, e amity@loxinfo.co.th, 24 Thanon Chiang Mai-Lampang) Rooms 1000-1600B. A short distance northeast off Thanon Huay Kaew, on Hwy 11, the Amity has well-appointed rooms at a relatively low price, no doubt because the location is less than ideal in terms of being able to walk to restaurants or attractions. Facilities include a restaurant, coffee shop, lobby bar, busi-ness centre, conference room, fitness room and swimming pool.

Novotel Chiang Mai (Chiang Mai map; ☎ 053 225 500, fax 053 225 505, W www.novotel.co.th, 183 Thanon Chang Pheuak) Singles/doubles 2600/2800B, deluxe rooms 3000-3200B. North of Pratu Chang Pheuak, the reliable Novotel offers spacious and well-decorated rooms. You may be able to negotiate the rates downward, as this isn't the most popular part of town to stay in.

Out of Town

North of the city in the Mae Rim/Mae Sa area is a string of plush countryside resorts. Most offer free shuttle vans back and forth from the city.

The Regent Chiang Mai Resort & Spa (Chiang Mai map; ☎ 053 298 181, fax 053 298 190, Thanon Mae Rim–Samoeng Kao) Rooms from US$365 plus tax & service. The creme de la creme of these type of re-sorts, designed by noted Thai architect Chu-lathat Kitibutr, The Regent features 64 vaulted pavilion suites (each around 75 sq metres), plus two- and three-bedroom resi-dences spread amid eight hectares of land-scaped gardens and rice terraces worked by water buffalo. On the premises are two full-service restaurants, a bar-restaurant, a health club, two swimming pools and two illuminated tennis courts. The resort's 900-sq-metre Lanna Spa has earned much ac-claim since its 1999 opening.

Chiang Mai Sports Club (Chiang Mai map; ☎ 053 298 330, fax 053 297 897, e shotel@loxinfo.co.th, 284 Mu 3, Tambon Don Kaew, Mae Rim) Singles & doubles 2400B, suites 6500B (plus 400B high-season surcharge on holidays). Seven kilometres from town on Thanon Mae Rim, with 45 rooms and three two-storey luxury suites on 71 *râi* (11.3 hectares) of land, the resort lives up to its name, boasting air-con squash courts, a badminton hall, grass- and hard-court tennis, fitness centre, sauna, gymna-sium and swimming pool; you have to pay extra for the badminton, squash and tennis fa-cilities, but everything else is free for guests. Discounts of up to 50% are often available.

PLACES TO EAT

Chiang Mai has the best variety of restaurants of any city in Thailand outside of Bangkok. Most travellers seem to have better luck here than in Bangkok, though, simply because it's so much easier to get around and experiment.

Chiang Mai's guesthouses serve a typical menu of Western food along with a few pseudo-Thai dishes. If you're interested in authentic Thai cuisine, you'll have to leave the guesthouse womb behind.

Other than the obvious Northern Thai fare, you'll find noodles in Chiang Mai are wonderful and the variety astounding. *Khâo sawy* – a Shan–jiin haw concoction of chicken (or, less commonly, beef or pork), spicy curried broth and flat, squiggly, wheat noodles – is one of the most characteristic Northern Thai noodle dishes. It's served with small saucers of shallot wedges, sweet-spicy pickled cabbage and a thick red chilli sauce. Khâo sawy places can be found around the city – just look for the distinctive noodle shape and orange-brown broth.

Chiang Mai is blessed with over 25 vegetarian restaurants, most of them very inexpensive. All of the Indian restaurants in this section feature short vegetarian sections on their menus; the Indian Restaurant Vegetarian Food is all vegie. The Vegetarian Chiang Mai Club (☎ 053 222 571) collects and disperses information on the international vegetarian movement; call for further information. Also look for the brown 'Vegetarian Restaurant Map', drawn by an expat American and available at many vegie spots around town.

There are also a number of food centres, on-the-river dining spots, as well as a handful of bustling night markets.

Chiang Mai Night Bazaar

Along Soi 1, Charoen Prathet, between Thanon Chang Khlan and Thanon Charoen Prathet and near the Chiang Mai (Ban Haw) Mosque, are a number of simple restaurants and alley vendors selling inexpensive but tasty Muslim curries and khâo sawy. Néua òp hǎwm ('fragrant' Yunnanese Muslim-style dried beef), a speciality of Chiang Mai, is also sold along the lane.

You'll find the main faràng food district in Chiang Mai runs along Thanon Chang Khlan. This strip features the usual Western fast-food outlets, most of which are clustered within the Chiang Inn Plaza and Pavilion shopping centres.

Noodles The oldest area for khâo sawy is Ban Haw, the jiin haw area around the Matsayit Chiang Mai on Soi 1, Thanon Charoen Prathet, around the corner from the Diamond Riverside Hotel and Galare Guest House and not far from the Night Bazaar (in fact this is where the jiin haw caravans of yore used to tie up). Most khâo sawy places are open from around 10am till 3pm or 4pm.

Khao Soi Islam (Soi 1, Thanon Charoen Prathet) Khâo sawy 25B. Open 5am to 5pm daily. This place is alongside the similar *Khao Soi Fuang Fah*. Both serve up Muslim curries, *khanǒm jiin* (choice of two sauces) and *khâo mòk kài* (the Thai-Muslim version of chicken biryani). Khao Soi Islam also serves *khâo mòk pháe* (goat biryani).

Rot Neung (Thanon Charoen Prathet) Dishes 30B. Open 9am-9pm daily. Opposite the Diamond Riverside Hotel, this place serves some of the best *kǔaytǐaw lûuk chín plaa* (rice noodle soup with fish balls) in Chiang Mai. If you thought you didn't like fish balls – ground fish rolled into balls – give them a second try here, as this place makes them fresh and sells them to many other stands in town. A bowl is filled with noodles, fish balls, plus strips of fishcake and even delicious fish wonton.

Indian, Muslim & Israeli *Sophia (Soi 1, Thanon Charoen Prathet)* Dishes 20-30B. Open 8am-7pm Sat-Thur. On the opposite side of the soi from Khao Sawy Islam and Khao Soi Fuang Fah, this simple rice shop serves good curries and khâo mòk kài.

Shere Shiraz (☎ 053 276 132, Soi 6, Thanon Charoen Prathet) Dishes 50-100B. Open 9.30am-11pm daily. This establishment serves mostly north-Indian food, with a few south-Indian dishes. The extensive menu includes many vegetarian dishes.

Arabia (☎ 053 818 850, Anusan Night Market) Dishes 30-80B. Open 10am-10pm daily. Arabia does north-Indian/Pakistani/Arab-style cuisine very well, especially in terms of the freshness of the flavours. Don't let the fact that it's often empty or nearly so throw you off the trail; Arabia has a steady and discerning, if small, clientele.

A *rotii vendor stall* along Soi 1 does delicious *rotii* (Indian flat bread) and chicken martabak (*mátàbà kài;* rotii stuffed with chicken).

Italian *Bacco* (☎ 053 251 389, *Thanon Tha Phae*) Dishes 40-100B. Open noon-10.30pm Mon-Sat. In a very old Thai building towards the eastern end of Thanon Tha Phae, this is the least expensive Italian restaurant in town and has quite an enjoyable menu.

Piccola Roma Palace (☎ 053 271 256, *144 Thanon Charoen Prathet*) Dishes 100-200B. Open 11am-2pm & 5pm-11pm. For more of a splurge, the place to go is this luxurious new restaurant featuring subdued lighting, sharp service and great attention to culinary detail. It also has very high prices by Chiang Mai standards, the best salads in town and an excellent wine list – overall a good spot to celebrate an anniversary or the firing of your evil boss back home. Piccola Roma Palace offers free transportation to and from the restaurant – just call.

OK Pizza (☎ 053 818 499, *Chiangmai Pavilion, Cnr Thanon Chang Khlan & Thanon Loi Kroh*) Dishes 60-100B. Open 11am-10pm daily. Although it's hardly Italian, this spot gets a thumbs up for its fresh, light pizzas, good mixed salad, extreme cleanliness and friendly service.

International *Haus München* (☎ 053 274 027, *115/3 Thanon Loi Kroh*) Dishes 40-100B. Open noon-midnight daily. This place has better German food than the Bierstube, and is convenient to the Night Bazaar.

Next to Haus München are three more European eateries, all in a row along Thanon Loi Kroh: *Red Lion English Pub & Restaurant*, *German Hofbräuhaus* and *Cafe Benelux*, each serving the type of cuisine their names imply and all open approximately noon to midnight.

Food Centres *Galare Food Centre* (*Thanon Chang Khlan*) This is a large indoor/outdoor cluster of permanent food vendor booths opposite the main Night Bazaar building on Thanon Chang Khlan; free Thai classical dancing is featured every evening.

Night Markets *Anusan Night Market* (between Thanon Chang Khlan and Thanon Charoen Prathet near the Night Bazaar) attracts both tourists and Thais. If you wander over here, look for the stalls that are crowded – they're usually the best. All of the places have English menus. The large khâo tôm (rice soup) place near the market entrance, *Uan Heh-Hah,* still packs in the customers; the most popular dish is the khâo tôm plaa (fish rice soup), but other specialities worth trying include curried fish balls and curry-fried crab.

Eastern Chiang Mai

Chiang Mai has a small Chinatown in an area centred around Thanon Ratchawong north of Thanon Chang Moi. Here you'll find a whole string of Chinese rice and noodle shops, most of them offering variations on Tae Jiu (Chao Zhou) and Yunnanese cooking.

A New Golden Triangle Export

Starbucks, the US-based coffeeshop chain that opened its first branch in Chiang Mai in 2001, recently announced it would soon be selling coffee grown in Northern Thailand alongside such familiar sources as Jamaica, Kenya, Costa Rica, Java and so on. According to a report in the *Bangkok Post,* Starbucks will start with the domestic marketing of two hill tribe–produced brands and then move into international distribution. If successful, this move may bring international recognition to Northern Thailand's arabica coffee plantations. As of 1998 Thailand ranked seventh in worldwide coffee production.

Northern & Northeastern Thai *Aroon (Rai) Restaurant* (☎ *053 276 947, 45 Thanon Kotchasan*) Dishes 40-80B. Open 8am-10pm daily. Across the moat near Pratu Tha Phae is one of Chiang Mai's oldest and best-known restaurants. The large, open-air Aroon specialises in both Northern and Central Thai dishes and has a huge menu; prices are inexpensive to moderate. Look for Chiang Mai specialities like *kaeng hang-leh, kaeng awm* and *kaeng khae*. Despite the Thai word *kaeng* (curry) in these dish names, only the first is a curry by the usual definition – that is, made from a thick, spicy paste; the latter two dishes are more like stews and rely on local roots and herbs for their distinctive, bitter-hot flavours. Aroon's standard, Indian-inspired chicken curry – *kaeng kàrìi kài* – is the best in town. Downstairs you'll find more exotic dishes in trays near the cashier, including bamboo grubs *(rót dùan)* and other forest goodies. The spacious open-air dining area upstairs is favoured by night-time clientele, and in hot weather it's cooler than downstairs. Aroon is a good choice for a Thai breakfast of curry and rice.

Thanam Restaurant (*Thanon Chaiyaphum*) Dishes 30-75B. Open 11am-8pm daily. A little north of Daret's House (see Places to Stay – Budget earlier), the small and super-clean Thanam leans towards Central Thai cuisine, with a few Northern Thai dishes as well. Hallmark dishes include *phàk náam phrík* (fresh vegetables in chilli sauce), *plaa dùk phàt phèt* (spicy fried catfish), *kaeng sôm* (hot and sour vegetable ragout), as well as khâo sawy and *khanŏm jiin náam ngíaw* (Chinese noodles with spiced sauce). Thanam has a small, Roman-script sign inside. The restaurant doesn't serve alcohol and won't serve people wearing beach clothes (such as tank tops and singlets).

Central & Southern Thai *Ratana's Kitchen* (☎ *053 874 173, 320-322 Thanon Tha Phae*) Dishes 40-80B. Open 9am-11pm daily. Next to Bookzone, this air-con spot owned by an English-Thai couple serves good Thai dishes from several regions, as well as a few faràng items. Although parking can be tight along Thanon Tha Phae, if you're driving you can usually park in the compound of adjacent Wat Chetawan.

Noodles *Kuaytiaw Kai Tun Coke* (*Thanon Kamphaeng Din*) Dishes 40B. Open 10am-5pm daily. This small food stall directly opposite the main entrance to the Imperial Mae Ping Hotel specialises in chicken marinated in Coca Cola and spiced overnight before being steamed then served with rice noodles. It's actually quite good and has become famous as far away as Bangkok.

Kuaytiaw Reua Koliang Restaurant (*Cnr Thanon Ratchamankha & Thanon Moon Muang*) Dishes 25-30B. Open 8am-5pm daily. This spot has been serving authentic *kŭaytĭaw reua* ('boat noodles' – rice noodles served in a dark broth seasoned with ganja leaves) for many years now.

Chinese *Han Yang Hong Kong* (*Hong Kong Roast Goose; Thanon Ratchawong*) Dishes 25-35B. Open 8am-8pm daily. Next to the New Mitrapap Hotel (see Places to Stay – Budget earlier), this place has succulent roast duck, pork and goose, as well as dim sum. There are several other inexpensive Chinese restaurants along this street.

Mitmai Restaurant (☎ *053 275 033, 42/2 Thanon Ratchamankha*) Dishes 35-65B. Open 9am-9pm daily. Mitmai is a Yunnanese place specialising in delicious vegetable soups made with pumpkin, taro, mushrooms, snow peas or other Chinese vegetables. Especially tasty is the *tôm sôm plaa yâwt máphráo* (hot and sour fish soup with coconut shoots). The bilingual menu also includes *yam* (tangy, Thai-style salad) made with Chinese vegetables, as well as Yunnanese steamed ham, Chinese medicine chicken and many vegetarian dishes. No MSG is used in the cooking.

Salom Joy (*Thanon Ratchadamnoen*) Dishes 20-40B. Open around 6am-6pm Mon-Sat. For a quick Chinese breakfast, try the food stall opposite JJ Bakery. It has held out against the development of Pratu Tha Phae for many years and still serves cheap *jók* (rice congee), *paa-thâwng-kŏh* (Chinese 'doughnuts') and *náam tâo hûu* (hot soy milk). This is one of the few places in the Pratu Tha Phae area that opens for breakfast. Later in the day noodle and rice plates are available.

Indian, Muslim & Israeli *Indian Restaurant Vegetarian Food* (☎ 053 223 396, 27/3 Soi 9, Thanon Moon Muang) Dishes 25-60B. Open 8am-9pm daily. This friendly, family-owned place makes cheap and adequate vegetarian thalis, as well as individual Indian dishes. There's a *branch* (☎ 053 278 324) at 85/2 Thanon Ratchaphakhinai.

Jerusalem Falafel (☎ 053 270 208, 35/3 Thanon Moon Muang) Dishes 40-80B. Open 9am-11pm Sat-Thur. This restaurant and bakery serves a selection of felafels, shashlik, humus, and other Israeli specialities, as well as Thai and vegetarian food, baguette sandwiches, pizza, soups, salads, gelato and delicious home-made cakes and pies.

Italian *Da Stefano* (☎ 053 874 189, 2/1-2 Thanon Chang Moi Kao) Dishes 60-120B. Open 11.30am-11pm Mon-Sat, 5.30pm-11pm Sun. This is an intimate, well-decorated, air-con place that focuses on fresh Italian cuisine, with one of the better wine lists in town. Prices are moderate, and the food and service are very good.

Pum Pui Italian Restaurant (☎ 053 278 209, 24 Soi 2, Thanon Moon Muang) Dishes 50-120B. Open 11am-11pm daily. Near Top North Guest House, casual Pum Pui features a low-key garden setting and moderate prices; the menu includes olive pate and other antipasto, along with salads, Italian wines, several vegetarian selections, ice cream, breakfast and espressos. The complimentary Italian breads served at the beginning of all meals are excellent.

International *El Toro Mexican Restaurant & Cantina* (mobile ☎ 01 882 0345, 6 Soi 1, Thanon Kotchasan) Dishes 40-100B. Open noon-midnight daily. The menu here boasts 19 Mexican dishes, six Thai, four Indian, five pastas, plus a list of sandwiches, salads, desserts, beers and cocktails including margaritas and piña coladas. If Elvis showed up here, he'd order the chimichanga and a chicken vindaloo. A pool table and a good collection of recorded Latin tunes make this a good spot to party with friends.

Bake & Bite (☎ 053 285 185, 6 Soi 1, Thanon Kotchasan) Dishes 30-100B. Open 7am-6pm Sun-Fri, 7am-3pm Sat. This tiny spot wedged into a corner of the parking lot in front of El Toro prepares delicious European and American-style pastries, pies and sandwiches on your choice of several breads. Good coffee, too. There are only a few tables here.

Art Cafe (☎/fax 053 206 365, Cnr Thanon Tha Phae & Thanon Kotchasan) Dishes 40-100B. Open 10am-10pm daily. Facing Pratu Tha Phae, this popular air-con place offers a combination of vegetarian and nonvegetarian Italian, as well as Thai, Mexican and American food, including pizza, sandwiches, pasta, enchiladas, tacos, salads, ice cream, tiramisu, pies, shakes, fruit juices and coffees. Art Cafe is the perfect place to go if you have a small group who can't decide what kind of food they want to eat. It occasionally hosts 190B Mexican buffets on Saturday. This restaurant is 100% smoke-free.

JJ Bakery & Restaurant (☎ 053 213 088, Cnr Thanon Moon Muang & Thanon Ratchadamnoen) Dishes 50-140B. Open 6.30am-11.30pm daily. Although it's not as good nor as cheap as it once was, JJ's near Pratu Tha Phae still offers a very diverse menu of Western, Thai and Chinese dishes. There's another branch of JJ with the same hours on the ground floor of Chiang Inn Plaza, off Thanon Chang Khlan near the Night Bazaar.

Irish Pub (☎ 053 214 554, 24-24/1 Thanon Ratwithi) Dishes 50-100B. Open 9am-1am daily. The menu offers baked goods, good coffee, yogurt, muesli, sandwiches, pasta, pizza, vegetarian dishes, baked potatoes, ice cream, some Thai food, beer on tap, and fruit and vegetable juices. The homey indoor section is decorated with Irish kitsch and there's pleasant garden seating out the back.

Easy Diner (☎ *053 208 989, 27/29 Thanon Ratchadamnoen)* Dishes 50-120B. Open 8am-10pm Mon-Sat. An air-con place west of Pratu Tha Phae, Easy Diner specialises in American diner-style fare such as burgers (vegetarian and chicken burgers included), hot dogs, ribs, chicken, salads, milk shakes and apple pie. Breakfast (including British style) is served all day, and there's a takeaway and delivery service.

Dara Steakhouse *(Thanon Tha Phae)* Dishes 40-120B. Open 8am-9pm Mon-Sat. Across from Roong Ruang Hotel, this very casual spot boasts an extensive Thai and Western menu and low prices.

Bierstube (☎ *053 278 869, 33/6 Thanon Moon Muang)* Dishes 40-100B. Open 7.30am-11pm daily. A simple place with wooden tables, the Bierstube has been popular among German expats and visitors for many years.

Vegetarian *AUM Vegetarian Food* (☎ *053 278 315, 65 Thanon Moon Muang)* Dishes 30-70B. Open 8am-9pm daily. Near Pratu Tha Phae and long popular with travellers because of its easy location, this place features an all-vegie menu with a varied list of traditional Thai and Chinese dishes, including Northern and Northeastern Thai dishes prepared without meat or eggs. There is an upstairs eating area with well-worn cushions on the floor and low tables.

Biaporn *(Soi 1, Thanon Si Phum)* Dishes 20-30B. Open 10am-3pm daily. This very inexpensive Thai vegetarian place within the old city quadrangle, just north of SK House, has a limited selection of dishes but it's good.

Thip Thai Vegetarian Restaurant *(Thanon Moon Muang)* Dishes 10-30B. Open 8am-7pm daily. Thip Thai is just south of Soi 9 and in the same general area as Biaporn.

Night Markets Chiang Mai is full of interesting day and night markets stocked with very inexpensive and very tasty foods. *Talat Somphet* *(Thanon Moon Muang),* north of the Thanon Ratwithi intersection, sells cheap takeaway curries, yam, *lâap* (spicy minced meat), *thâwt man* (fried fish cakes), sweets and seafood. On the opposite side of the moat, the small *Somphet night market* *(Thanon Chaiyaphum)* has everything from noodles and seafood to the specialities of Yunnan. A lot of travellers eat here, so prices are just a bit higher than average, but the food is usually good.

There is also a large *fruit and vegetable market* *(Thanon Chang Moi near the Charoen Prathet intersection);* several *rice and noodle vendors* coexist alongside fruit stalls.

Central Chiang Mai

Eateries in the old city and along the river include many more traditional spots serving Northern Thai cuisine. There is also a host of rice and noodle shops.

Northern & Northeastern Thai *Si Phen Restaurant* (☎ *053 315 328, 103 Thanon Inthawarorot)* Dishes 25-60B. Open 9am-5pm Mon-Sat. Near Wat Phra Singh, Si Phen specialises in inexpensive Northern and Northeastern style dishes and prepares some of the best *sôm-tam* (spicy papaya salad) in the city, including a variation made with pomelo fruit. The *kài yâang khâo nǐaw* combo (grilled chicken and sticky rice) – another Isan (Northeastern) favourite – is also very good, as is the khâo sawy and *khanǒm jiin* (Chinese noodles) with either *náam yaa* (fish sauce) or *náam ngíaw* (sweet, spicy sauce) – always good.

Heuan Phen (☎ *053 277 103, 112 Thanon Ratchamankha)* Dishes 40-100B. Open 8.30am-3pm & 5pm-10pm daily. Heuan Phen is a highly regarded place for Northern Thai food. Among the house specialities here are Chiang Mai and jiin haw dishes such as khanǒm jiin náam ngíaw, khâo sawy, *lâap khûa* (Northern-style minced-meat salad), *náam phrík nùm* (chilli sauce made with roasted eggplant), kaeng hang-leh, kaeng awm, kaeng khae and other *aahǎan phéun meuang* (local food). It's almost opposite a kindergarten, east of the Felix City Inn. Daytime meals are served in a large dining room out front, while evening meals are served in an atmospheric antique-decorated house at the back.

Central & Southern Thai *Ta-Krite (Ta-Khrai; Soi 1, Thanon Samlan)* Dishes 30-80B. Open 10am-11pm daily. This pleasant indoor-outdoor place with ironwork chairs has a garden setting inside the moat on the soi that runs along the southern side of Wat Phra Singh. The kitchen focuses on Central Thai food. *Náam phrík* (thick chilli sauce) is a house speciality, along with *khâo tang nâa tâng* (sticky rice with meat, shrimp and coconut).

Noodles *Khao Soi Suthasinee (Soi 1, Thanon Inthawarorot)* Dishes 25-40B. Open 9am-4pm daily. Inside the old city, this is the best choice for exemplary khâo sawy. There's another branch at 164/10 Thanon Chang Khlan, near Lanna Commercial College, and yet a third at 267–269 Thanon Chang Khlan.

Rot Sawoei (Thanon Arak) Dishes 25-35B. Open 11am-2.30am daily. Around the corner from Suan Buak Hat, this unassuming place is famous for very delectable *kǔaytǐaw kài tǔn yaa jiin,* rice noodles with Chinese herb-steamed chicken that practically melts off the bone. A normal bowl costs 25B, while a *phísèht* (special) order with extra chicken costs 35B. *Khâo nâa kài* (sliced chicken over rice) is also good. In addition, Rot Sawoei serves juices made from fresh toddy palm, coconut, orange and guava. It's the perfect late-night spot for a snack.

Chinese *Jok Somphet (Cnr Thanon Ratchaphakhinai & Thanon Si Phum)* Dishes 20-30B. Open 6am-11pm daily. Popular for its namesake jók, this place also serves decent khâo sawy kài and other noodles – *bà-mìi,* kǔaytǐaw – with chicken, beef or pork.

Italian *Giorgio Italian Restaurant (☎ 053 818 236, 2/6 Thanon Prachasamphan)* Dishes 100-200B. Open 11am-11pm daily. Chiang Mai's newest Italian eatery features a full range of pastas, all of it home-made, including *bigoli.* The salads are particularly good, while the slightly upmarket decor is classy and retro.

La Villa Pizzeria (☎ 053 277 403, 145 Thanon Ratchadamnoen) Dishes 40-120B. Open 11am-11pm daily. In a large, old Thai house, La Villa serves delicious pizzas baked in a wood-fired oven, and the rest of the Italian food on the menu is tops.

International *The Amazing Sandwich (☎ 053 218 846, 252/3 Thanon Phra Pokklao)* Dishes 60-90B. Open 9am-8.30pm Mon-Sat. Three doors north of the THAI office, this is a small, very clean air-con place specialising in fresh baguette sandwiches with your choice of a dozen fillings, as well as lasagne, vegetable pie and quiche, plus juices, beers, wine, spirits and cocktails.

Vegetarian *Mangsawirat Kangreuanjam (Soi 1, Thanon Inthawarorot)* Dishes 10-20B. Open 8am till early afternoon (or until everything's sold) daily. The difficult-to-see English sign reads 'Vegetarian Food'; look for a cluster of stainless-steel pots a few doors down from Khao Soi Suthasinee away from Chiang Mai Central Prison. The cooks put out 15 to 20 pots of fresh, 100%-Thai vegetarian dishes daily at around 8am and when they're sold out, the restaurant closes. The dishes feature lots of bean curd, squash, peas, pineapple, sprouts and potato, and the desserts are good. Very good and very cheap – three items over rice cost just 15B to 20B, or figure 40B to 50B for three large bowls of food, two plates of rice, and two bottles of water, more than enough to engorge two hungry stomachs.

Whole Earth Restaurant (☎ 053 282 463, 88 Thanon Si Donchai) Dishes 90-200B. Open 11am-11pm daily. Associated with a Transcendental Meditation centre, Whole Earth serves Thai and Indian (vegetarian and nonvegetarian) food and the atmosphere is suitably mellow, although the food may be a bit overpriced and underspiced.

Vihara Liangsan (☎ 053 818 094, 199/23 Thanon Chang Khlan) Lunch about 25B. Open 9am-2pm daily. On Thanon Chang Khlan, take a left into a small soi past the all-white Season (Si Suan) Plaza shopping centre, and on your right you'll come to this modest veg spot. Here you serve yourself from a long buffet table (the food is a mix of Chinese and Thai vegetarian, with lots of tofu and gluten), then place your plate – including rice – on a scale, and pay by weight. It's best to get here between 11am and 1pm as the food sometimes runs out.

Night Markets In the upstairs section of *Talat Warorot* (*Cnr Thanon Chang Moi & Thanon Praisani*) are a number of great stalls for khâo tôm, *khâo man kài* (chicken rice), *khâo mǔu daeng* ('red' pork with rice), jók and khâo sawy, with tables overlooking the market floor. It's not the best cooking in Chiang Mai by a long shot, but it's cheap. A set of vendors on the ground floor specialise in inexpensive noodles – this area is particularly popular. The market is open 6am to 5pm daily.

A good hunting ground for food is the very large and popular *Pratu Chiang Mai night market* (*Thanon Bamrungburi near Pratu Chiang Mai*). People tend to take their time here, making an evening of eating and drinking – there's no hustle to vacate tables for more customers.

On the River *Riverside Bar & Restaurant* (☎ *053 243 239, Thanon Charoenrat*) Dishes 60-120B. Open 5pm-1am daily. Two hundred metres north of Saphan Nawarat, this place always has good food, and it's as popular with Thais as with faràng. Another plus is that you can choose from indoor and outdoor dining areas. The atmosphere is convivial and there's good live music nightly. There's also an 8pm dinner cruise – you can board the boat any time after 7.30pm.

Good View (☎ *053 241 866, 13 Thanon Charoenrat*) Dishes 60-120B. Open 6pm-1am daily. Good View is newer, with more open-air areas, and it is more popular with Thais than faràng. The 122-item menu covers everything Thai. There's live music here, also, usually cover bands.

The Gallery (☎ *053 248 601, 25-29 Thanon Charoenrat*) Dishes 60-120B. Open noon-2am daily. The Gallery is a 100-year-old teak house that's half art gallery, half restaurant. The quality of the food goes

up and down here; sometimes it's great, other times so-so. Ditto for service.

Greater Chiang Mai

The following eateries can be found on the Chiang Mai map.

Northern & Northeastern Thai *Heuan Soontaree* (☎ *053 252 445, 46/2 Thanon Wan Singkham*) Dishes 40-90B. Open 10am-11pm daily. A little north of Saphan Phra Ram IX, this is an open-air restaurant built on several levels on the west bank of the river. The owner – the famous Northern Thai singer Soontaree Vechanont – performs at the restaurant nightly beginning around 9pm. The menu is a pleasant blend of Northern, Northeastern and Central Thai specialities.

Central & Southern Thai *Khrua Phuket Laikhram* (*Classical Phuket Kitchen;* ☎ *053 278 909, 1/10 Thanon Suthep*) Dishes 40-100B. Open noon-10pm daily. Near Chiang Mai University, this is a small family-run restaurant that has delicious, cheap yet large portions of authentic home-style Southern-Thai cooking. If there are no seats downstairs, try the upstairs dining room. Specialities include *yâwt máphráo phàt phèt kûng* (spicy stir-fried shrimp with coconut shoots), *hèt hǔu nǔu phàt khài* (eggs stir-fried with 'mouse-ear mushrooms', black fungus) and *yam phuukèt laikhraam* (a delicious salad of cashew nuts and squid). The restaurant has daily specials, too.

Noodles *Khao Soi Prince* (*Thanon Kaew Nawarat*) Dishes 20-35B. Open 9am-3pm daily. Near Prince Royal's College, this place is cited by many locals as their favourite spot for authentic khâo sawy.

Khao Soi Lam Duan (*Thanon Faham*) Dishes around 30B. Open 9am-3pm daily. Just north of Saphan Phra Ram IX (Rama IX Bridge), this is one of the more famous khâo sawy places in Chiang Mai. Thanon Faham is an extension of Thanon Charoenrat, and sometimes called by the latter name. This place serves large bowls of beef, pork or chicken khâo sawy. Also on the menu are *kao-lǎo* (soup without noodles), *mǔu sà-té* (grilled spiced pork on bamboo skewers), khâo sawy with beef or pork instead of chicken, *khanǒm rang phêung* (literally, beehive pastry, a coconut-flavoured waffle), Mekong rice whisky and beer.

Two more khâo sawy places of similar quality along this same stretch of Thanon Faham are **Khao Soi Samoe Jai** and **Khao Soi Ban Faham**.

Chinese *Yong Khao Tom Kui (Cnr Thanon Suthep & Thanon Nimmanhemin)* Dishes 25-70B. Open 6pm-2am daily. This unassuming sidewalk place near Chiang Mai University is a favourite late-night haunt for those who are discerning about *khâo tôm kǔi*, boiled rice gruel served with pungent Thai and Chinese side dishes.

China Palace (☎ 053 275 300, Westin Riverside Plaza, 318/1 Thanon Chiang Mai-Lamphun) Dishes 80-180B. Open 11am-10pm daily. Probably the best place to totally splurge on Chinese food is this plush spot at the Westin. It specialises in excellent, if slightly pricey, Cantonese cuisine.

Indian, Muslim & Israeli *Sa-Nga Choeng Doi (7/1 Thanon Charoensuk)* Dishes 25-35B. Open 8am-4pm daily. Only a five-minute walk from the YMCA in Amphoe Santitham (Santitham district), this place has probably the best khâo mòk kài and mátàbà in town. The home-made, unsweetened yogurt here is also highly recommended. The restaurant has no Roman-script sign – just look for the appropriate dishes on the tables.

Italian *La Gritta (☎ 053 221 130, 053 221 044, ℮ rincome@amari.com, Amari Rincome Hotel, Thanon Huay Kaew)* Dishes 120-200B, buffet 240B. Open 11.30am-2pm and 5pm-11pm daily. The menu offers good, authentic Italian food at international prices. You can sample a wide variety of international and Thai dishes at La Gritta's daily buffet (11.30am-2pm).

International *The Pub (☎ 053 211 550, 189 Thanon Huay Kaew)* Dishes 70-150B. Open for dinner 6pm-midnight Tues-Sun.

Close to some of the large hotels on Thanon Huay Kaew, The Pub nowadays serves both international and Thai cuisines and draws Thais as well as Westerners. Newsweek magazine named it 'one of the world's best bars' in 1986 and although its glory days may have passed, it's still got a homey kind of class. European wines and draught beer are available, and there's also a dart board. One of the best things going at The Pub is the annual traditional Christmas dinner offered on the evenings of 24 and 25 December.

Chez John (☎ 053 201 551, 18/1 Thanon Mahidon) Dishes 80-160B. Open noon-2pm & 6.30pm-10pm daily. Near the airport and opposite the customs office, this restaurant offers moderately priced French cuisine and a large selection of wines.

Le Coq d'Or (☎ 053 282 024, ℮ lecoqd'or@d-d-web.com, 68/1 Thanon Ko Klang) Dishes 100-200B. Open 11am-2pm & 6pm-11pm daily. The most expensive and formal French eatery in town serves French haute cuisine in a lavishly decorated mansion off Thanon Chiang Mai–Lamphun east of the river.

Western franchise-style places can be found in the Kad Suan Kaew shopping centre on Thanon Huay Kaew and at Airport Plaza near the airport.

Vegetarian *Suandok Vegetarian (Thanon Suthep)* Dishes 10-20B. Open 7am-2pm daily. Just west of the entrance to Wat Suan Dok, Suandok offers an array of inexpensive, wholesome Thai vegetarian dishes and brown rice.

Vegetarian Centre of Chiang Mai (☎ 053 271 262, 14 Thanon Mahidon) Dishes 10-15B. Open 6am-2pm Sun-Thur. The Asoke Foundation operates an extremely cheap Thai vegetarian restaurant not far from the southwest corner of the city walls. The food is served cafeteria style – you push a tray down a rack and point to what you want. Warning: brown rice only. A small health food section to one side of the restaurant offers dried gluten, nuts, beans, herbs, vegetarian chilli sauces, natural beauty products, herbal medicines and Dhamma books (mostly in Thai). From

Thursday afternoon to Saturday it's closed so that the staff can visit a Santi Asoke retreat centre in the *amphoe* (district) of Mae Taeng.

Markets & Food Centres *Talat San Pa Khoi*, midway between the river and the train station on Charoen Muang, has a better selection and lower prices than Anusan. It is also where you'll find the *curry stand* that is probably the only place in Chiang Mai where you can find fresh Thai curries past 11pm. It stays open till around 5am and is very popular with late-night partiers.

A food centre on the 3rd floor of the *Kad Suan Kaew shopping centre* on Thanon Huay Kaew gathers together vendors selling all kinds of Thai and Chinese dishes at reasonable prices.

Airport Plaza also has a good food centre.

On the River *The Riverfront Restaurant* (*Tha Nam;* ☎ *053 275 125, 43/3 Thanon Chang Khlan*) Dishes 50-100B. Open 8am-11pm daily. On the west bank of Mae Nam Ping and housed in an old, Northern Thai–style building, The Riverfront is pretty reliable for Northern, Northeastern and Central Thai cuisine. A Northern Thai folk music ensemble performs in the evenings.

ENTERTAINMENT
Bars & Pubs

All bars mentioned in this section should be open from around 6pm until 2am, the legal closing time in Thailand. Unless otherwise indicated, the following bars and pubs are marked on the Eastern Chiang Mai map.

A section of Thanon Ratwithi extending a couple of blocks west of Thanon Moon Muang has become a good area for pubs where Thais and foreigners, women as well as men, meet for drinks and conversation. Mixed in among the pubs are a large art supplies store, a couple of homespun print shops, and other vaguely 'media-industrial' endeavours, some of them rather old.

Walking from Thanon Moon Muang, first is the long-running *Irish Pub* (*24/1 Thanon Ratwithi*) on the right, which has nothing particularly Irish about it other than some kitsch on the walls. The beers are all Thai-brewed, but it's quiet and the comfortable upstairs is even suitable for solo reading or writing. Next, at the corner of Ratwithi and the soi that leads around the corner to Eagle House 2, sits the diminutive *Yoy Pocket* (*Thanon Ratwithi*), a funky spot reminiscent of some of the homier cafes/pubs on Thanon Phra Athit in Bangkok.

Behind the building that holds Yoy Pocket, the outdoor *Rasta Cafe* plays recorded reggae, dub, African and Latin music and is quite popular in the peak tourist season. Look for other abandoned shopfronts along this street to give birth to more Thai pubs with creative decor – if the sagging economy permits.

The happy hour at *Kafé* (*Thanon Moon Muang, between Soi 5 & Soi 6*), near Talat Somphet, is popular among expats and Thais. Farther south along Thanon Moon Muang, between Thanon Ratchadamnoen and Soi 3, is a string of small *bars,* some strongly male-oriented in their overabundance of female staff, others good all-round places for a drink.

The long-running *Pinte Blues Pub* (*Thanon Moon Muang*) serves espresso and beer, and plays tapes from a huge blues collection. *Bierstube* (see Places to Eat for address) features German grub and beer, while *John's Place* (*Thanon Moon Muang*) and *Spotlight* (*Thanon Kotchasan*) are go-go bars frequented almost exclusively by men, both Thai and foreign. *Sax Music Pub* (*Thanon Moon Muang*) in this same area plays a wide variety of prerecorded tapes, DJ style. The Pinte Blues Pub is the only bar in the Pratu Tha Phae vicinity where you generally see couples or faràng women, although during the high season the crowd at the Sax Music Pub can be relatively mixed.

Farther south along Thanon Moon Muang is the *II3 Pub,* a rustic open-air bar that serves as the local Hash House Harriers headquarters.

The *Drunken Flower* (*Mao Dokmai; Chiang Mai map;* ☎ *053 212 081, Soi 1, Thanon Nimanhemin*) is a cosy indoor/

outdoor bar and restaurant with a mixed Thai and expat crowd, especially local non-governmental organisation staffers.

Discos

All the flashy hotels have discos with hi-tech recorded music and cover charges of 100B to 200B. The cover charge includes one drink, with the usual 'ladies free' nights sprinkled throughout the week. The most active hotel discos in town remain *Fantasy Discotheque (Chiang Inn)*, *Stardust (Westin Riverside Plaza)*, *Crystal Cave (Empress Hotel)* and the ever popular *Bubbles (Porn Ping Tower Hotel)*. Bubbles (the name has been 'updated' to Space Bubble, but everyone in town still calls it by the old name, which in Thai is pronounced 'Bubben') has the most regular local clientele.

One of the most popular non-hotel discos is *Zodiac (formerly Gi Gi's; Central Chiang Mai map; ☎ 053 302 340/1, Thanon Chiang Mai-Lamphun)* east of the river, along with *Discovery (Chiang Mai map; ground floor, Kad Suan Kaew shopping centre)*. In Thai parlance, these are 'kitchen discos' *(khrua thek)* – customers stand next to small, round, waist-high tables on the dance floor so that they dance close to their drinks and pocketbooks. Another popular spot is *Nice Illusion (Eastern Chiang Mai map; Thanon Chaiyaphum)* near the moat, where it gets so crowded some nights there's barely room to move. At all three, the crowd tends to be very young.

Gay Venues

Chiang Mai has several gay men's bars

Coffee Boy Bar (☎ 053 247 021, 248 Thanon Thung Hotel) Coffee Boy is located in a 70-year-old teak house not far from the Arcade bus terminal. On weekends there's a cabaret show.

Other popular gay meeting places include *Circle Pub (☎ 053 214 996, 161/7-8 Soi Erawan, Thanon Chotana)* and *Doi Boy (☎ 053 404 361, 27/1-2 Soi 4, Thanon Chang Pheuak)*, both not far from the Novotel, and both featuring weekend cabarets.

Adam's Apple (☎ 053 220 381, 132/46-47 Soi Wiang Bua, Thanon Chotana) The

three-storey Adam's Apple has a massage centre, go-go bar, gay pub and karaoke lounge.

House of Male (☎ 053 894 133, 269/2 Soi 3, Thanon Sirimangkhalajan) This place has a similar orientation to Adam's Apple but focuses on a pool, steam room and gym.

Live Music

Riverside Bar & Restaurant (Central Chiang Mai map; ☎ 053 243 239, Thanon Charoenrat) On Mae Nam Ping, the Riverside is one of the longest-running live music venues in Chiang Mai. It has good food, fruit shakes, cocktails and live music nightly – a variety of covers from The Beatles to reggae, as well as some Thai pop. It's usually packed with both foreigners and Thais on weekends, so arrive early to get a table on the veranda overlooking the river. There are two indoor bars, both full of regulars, with separate bands. Next door, *Good View Bar & Restaurant (Central Chiang Mai map; ☎ 053 241 866, Thanon Charoenrat)* features a good covers band and is also quite popular.

Le Brasserie (Central Chiang Mai map; ☎ 053 241 665, 37 Thanon Charoenrat). A block or so north of the Rim Ping, Le Brasserie has become a favourite late-night spot (11.15pm to 2am) to listen to a talented Thai guitarist named Took play energetic versions of Hendrix, Cream, Dylan, Marley, the Allman Brothers and other 1960s and 1970s gems. A couple of other local bands warm up the house before Took comes on, often to a packed house. Food service is available inside the bar or out the back by the river.

Massage & Spa Treatments

All of the places that teach massage (see under Courses earlier in this chapter) offer massage services as well, usually for around 200B per hour. There are also dozens of *nûat phǎen bohraan* (traditional massage) centres all around the city, often doing massage for as little as 100B per hour, but most people find that the massage schools give the best service.

Let's Relax (☎ *053 818 498, 145/27 Thanon Chang Khlan*) On the second floor of the Chiangmai Pavilion shopping centre (Night Bazaar map), massages given here are generally of superior quality, and are performed in a very clean and professional atmosphere. In addition to full-body massage, Let's Relax offers 30-minute back and shoulder massage, arm massage and foot massage.

Traders Retreat Spa (☎ *053 409 705,* e *info@siametraders.com, 85 Soi 2, Thanon Suksasem*) Near Lanna Hospital, this is a new day spa specialising in Thai massage, Thai herbal sauna and teakwood-tub mineral soaks in a tropical garden ambience. Prices are very reasonable.

Some of the top hotels have good massage staff. Perhaps the best massage you can find associated with a hotel property is at the new *Lanna Spa* (☎ *053 298 181, Thanon Mae Rim–Samoeng Kao)*, at the Regent Chiang Mai Resort & Spa, about 20 minutes drive north of Chiang Mai in Mae Rim. In addition to traditional Thai massage, the Lanna Spa offers skin-scrub massage using Thai herbs and spices as well as aromatherapy oil massage. Facials and other kinds of spa treatments are also available. Expect premium prices and premium service.

Cinemas

Major Cineplex (☎ *053 283 939, 4th Floor, 2 Thanon Mahidol)*, Located at Airport Plaza, this new movie house boasting a state-of-the-art sound system and 'honeymoon seats' – pairs of seats without a middle armrest for the convenience of romantic couples – is the best cinema in town. Along with the latest Thai films, first-run foreign films with English soundtracks are frequently shown.

Two other cinemas showing first-run foreign as well as Thai films are the *Vista cinemas* at two shopping centres opposite one another on Thanon Huay Kaew: Kad Suan Kaew and Vista 12 Huay Kaew.

The best source of info on current movie programming at all three cinema houses in Chiang Mai is w www.movieseer.com.

Cultural Shows

Old Chiang Mai Cultural Centre (*OCMCC;* ☎ *053 202 993/5, 053 274 093, 053 275 097, fax 053 274 094, 185/3 Thanon Wualai; admission & dinner 270B; performances 7pm-10pm daily)* Northern-Thai and hill-tribe dances are performed nightly at this place 500m south of the town centre. Performances include a *khan tòk* dinner (see the 'Northern Style' boxed text in the Facts for the Visitor chapter). It's a touristy affair but done well. Several big hotels around town offer similar affairs, but the OCMCC was the first and is still the best.

Lanna Nakorn 1296 (☎ *053 818 249, 84 Thanon Chang Khlan; admission 250B; performances 8pm and 10pm daily)* For a grander show that includes live elephants, try this newer place, housed in a former cinema house near the Night Bazaar.

SPECTATOR SPORTS

Gawila Boxing Stadium (*Sanam Muay Thai Kawila;* ☎ *053 279 507, Talat San Pa Khoi; admission 300B)* The stadium holds muay thai matches most Friday nights between November and May. Most bills will offer up to a dozen nightly bouts, including matches between local Thais and faràng kickboxers who have been training at local camps. The matches usually begin at 7pm.

SHOPPING

Hundreds of shops all over Chiang Mai sell hill-tribe and Northern Thai craftwork, but a lot of it is commercial and touristy junk churned out for the undiscerning. So bargain hard and buy carefully! The nonprofit outlets often have the best quality, and although the prices are sometimes a bit higher than at the Night Bazaar, a higher percentage of your money goes directly to the hill-tribe artisans.

Thai Tribal Crafts (*Central Chiang Mai map;* ☎ *053 241 043, 208 Thanon Bamrungrat)* Near the McCormick Hospital, this store is run by two church groups on a non-profit basis and has a good selection of quality handicrafts.

Hill-Tribe Products Promotion Centre (*Chiang Mai map;* ☎ *053 277 743, 21/17*

Thanon Suthep) This royally sponsored project is near Wat Suan Dok; all profits go to hill-tribe welfare programs.

The *YMCA International Hotel (Chiang Mai map)* also operates a nonprofit handicrafts centre.

The two commercial markets with the widest selections of Northern Thai folk crafts are *Talat Warorot* at the eastern end of Thanon Chang Moi Kao and the *Chiang Mai Night Bazaar* off Thanon Chang Khlan. See the separate entry on each of these under Markets further on.

As Chiang Mai is Thailand's main handicraft centre, it's ringed by small cottage factories and workshops where you can watch craftspeople at work. In general, though, merchandise you see at factories outside the city will cost more than it would in Chiang Mai unless you're buying in bulk.

Markets

Talat Warorot (Central Chiang Mai map) Locally called *kàat lǔang*, Northern Thai for 'great market', this is the oldest and most famous market in Chiang Mai. A former royal cremation ground, it has served as a marketplace since the reign of Chao Inthawararot (1870–97). Although the huge enclosure is quite dilapidated (ignore the scary-looking escalators, which haven't functioned for years), it's an especially good market for fabrics and cooking implements. You'll also find cosmetics, clothing, handicrafts, prepared foods (especially Northern Thai foods), housewares, picture frames, rope and string – practically anything one needs to manage the average Thai household.

Across the street from Talat Warorot is the very similar *Talat Lamyai (Central Chiang Mai map)*. Both markets are open from around 5am to 6pm daily. Vendors outside the markets, however, operate 24 hours a day, as this is a major off-loading spot for trucks from around the North.

Talat Pratu Chiang Mai (Central Chiang Mai map) on Thanon Bamrungburi near Pratu Chiang Mai, is a fresh market that's particularly busy with locals shopping for takeaway Thai and Northern Thai

food. The indoor area is open from 4am till around noon, while outside vendors continue to sell till nightfall. A night food market then sets up across the street next to the moat and stays open till past midnight.

Talat San Pa Khoi (Chiang Mai map) off Thanon Charoen Muang and *Talat Thiphanet (Chiang Mai map)* off Thanon Wualai are large municipal markets that offer all manner of goods and see few tourists. San Pa Khoi opens around 4am and does a brisk trade till around 10am, then slows until an hour before nightfall. A few vendors open again past midnight, serving curries over rice and other dishes for late-night revellers.

Our favourite market for prepared foods is the clean and well-run *Talat Thanin (Chiang Mai map)* off Thanon Chotana, north of Pratu Chang Pheuak. It's open from around 5am till early evening.

Just south of Talat Thiphanet, the *Talat Dok Mai Chiang Mai (Chiang Mai map)* is the perfect place to pick up some greenery to feather your Chiang Mai nest if you're settling in long term. It opens around 9am and closes around sunset. A quick stop for flowers only, and especially fresh *phuang má-lai* (jasmine garlands), is the nameless *flower market (talàat dàwk mái; Central Chiang Mai map)* on Thanon Praisani near Talat Warorot. Vendors here stay open long hours and you can be assured of finding at least a few open whether day or night – nights are particularly busy. For many years this market has consisted of a string of carts and booths along the west side of the street, but reportedly all will soon move into a large market building, complete with parking lot, which is currently under construction nearby.

Talat Ton Phayom (Chiang Mai map), on Thanon Suthep across from Chiang Mai University, features all manner of fresh produce and cooked foods. Because CMU students make up a good portion of the clientele, prices tend to be low.

On the Superhighway opposite Lanna Hospital, local farmers sell fresh produce and a large variety of flowering plants at *Talat Kamthiang (Chiang Mai map)*. It's open from around 6am to 6pm daily.

Night Bazaars

The *Chiang Mai Night Bazaar*, the mother of all tourist markets, stretches along Thanon Chang Khlan from Thanon Tha Phae to Thanon Si Donchai. Good buys include Phrae-style *sêua mâw hâwm* (Thai farmer's shirts), Northern- and Northeastern-Thai hand-woven fabrics, *yâam* (shoulder bags), hill-tribe crafts (many tribespeople set up their own stalls here; the Akha wander around on foot), opium scales, hats, silver jewellery, lacquerware, woodcarvings, iron and bronze Buddhas and many other items.

In the main Chiang Mai Night Bazaar Building there are dozens of permanent shops selling antiques, handicrafts, rattan and hardwood furniture, textiles, jewellery, pottery, basketry, silverwork, woodcarving and other items of local manufacture. Prices can be very good if you bargain hard. One of our favourite shops in this building is *Chiang Mai (2nd floor, Chiang Mai Night Bazaar Bldg)*, which carries a selection of well-made cotton T-shirts silk-screened with more than 30 different old Chiang Mai designs, along with equally well-designed silver-and-bead jewellery and a changing selection of interesting accessories.

If you're in need of new travelling clothes, this is a good place to look. A light cotton dress, trousers or yâam can be bought for less than 200B, and sêua mâw hâwm cost between 100B and 150B, depending on size. Spices – everything from a *tôm yam* (soup made with lemongrass, chilli, lime and usually seafood) herbal mix to pure saffron – are available from several vendors. Cashew nuts, roasted or raw, are often less expensive here than in Southern Thailand where they're grown.

Except in the few shops with fixed prices (like the aforementioned Chiang Mai), you must bargain patiently but mercilessly. The fact that there are so many different stalls selling the same items means that competition effectively keeps prices low, if you haggle. Look over the whole bazaar before you begin buying. If you're not in the mood or don't have the money to buy, it's still worth a stroll, unless you don't like crowds – most nights it's elbow to elbow.

Several restaurants and many food trolleys feed the hungry masses. Down Soi Anusan at the southern end of Thanon Chang Khlan, the *Anusan Night Market* has lots of good Thai and Chinese food at night, and in the early morning (5am-9am) you'll find fresh produce and noodle vendors.

Shopping Centres & Department Stores

Chiang Mai had 17 shopping centres with department stores at last count. The *Kad Suan Kaew shopping centre (Chiang Mai map; Thanon Huay Kaew)*, centred around a branch of Bangkok's Central department store, is the best, with *Airport Plaza* a close second. There are several upmarket shops in both complexes. *Computer Plaza (Central Chiang Mai map; Thanon Mani Nopharat)* and the adjacent *Icon (Thanon Mani Nopharat)*, near the northwestern corner of the moat, are the places to go for computer supplies.

Antiques

You'll see lots of antiques in the city, although Chiang Mai's shops are not always cheap. Also remember that worldwide there are a lot more instant antiques than authentic ones. The Chiang Mai Night Bazaar area is probably the best place to look for fake antiques. Inside the Chiang Mai Night Bazaar Building, towards the back on the second floor, are a few small shops with real antiques.

The Lost Heavens (☎ 053 278 185, Stall 2, 2nd floor, Chiang Mai Night Bazaar Bldg) The 'antiques corner' towards the back left specialises in Mien tribal artefacts. There is another location (☎ 053 251 557, 234 Thanon Tha Phae) opposite Wat Bupparam.

Under the Bo (☎ 053 818 831, Stall 22-23, 2nd floor, Chiang Mai Night Bazaar Bldg) This place carries many unique pieces in the form of furniture, antique bronze and wood figures, old doors, woodcarvings and weaving from Africa, South Asia and Southeast Asia. Neither this or the Lost Heavens stall is cheap, but many items are one-of-a-kind. Under the Bo has another shop out on the road to Hang Dong, about 5km southwest of Thanon Mahidon.

Many more antique shops can be found along Thanon Tha Phae and especially along Thanon Loi Kroh. Burmese antiques are becoming more common than Thai, as most of the Thai stuff has been bought by collectors. You can get some great buys of antique Burmese furniture from the British colonial period.

Eastern Arts (☎ *053 276 075, 49 Thanon Tha Phae*) This is one Tha Phae shop that stocks a large, good-quality selection of antiques and pseudo-antiques.

Hang Dong, 25km south of Chiang Mai, is even better for antique furniture of all kinds, especially the string of shops just east of Hang Dong on Thanon Thakhilek (the road to Ban Thawai), an area usually called Ban Wan. A couple of shops in Ban Wan make reproductions of Thai and Burmese antique furniture using salvaged old teak – these can be very good buys.

Srithong Thoprasert (☎ *053 433 112, Thanon Thakhilek*) One of the better ones is this small shop, about 500m from the main Hang Dong intersection.

Nakee's Asia Treasures (☎ *053 441 357, Thanon Thakhilek*) A few hundred metres towards Ban Thawai from Srithong Thoprasert, Nakee's has contemporary Thai furniture and design accessories based on older themes updated for form and function (including some fusion with Santa Fe styles). It also sells good antiques – all very tasteful and of high quality, if a bit pricey. Ban Thawai itself is a woodcarving village offering mostly new pieces, very little of which is high quality.

Ceramics

Thai Celadon (☎ *053 213 541, 053 213 245, 112 Thanon Chotana*) About 6km north of Chiang Mai, Thai Celadon turn out ceramics modelled on the Sawankhalok pottery that used to be made hundreds of years ago at Sukhothai and exported all over the region. With their deep, crackle-glaze finish, some ceramic pieces are very beautiful and the prices are often lower than in Bangkok.

Mengrai Kilns (*Central Chiang Mai map;* ☎ *053 272 063, 79/2 Thanon Arak*) In the southwestern corner of the inner moat area near Suan Buak Hat is this reliable store. Other ceramic stores can be found close to the Old Chiang Mai Cultural Centre.

There are also several celadon operations in the nearby town of Hang Dong.

Clothes

All sorts of shirts, blouses and dresses, plain and embroidered, are available at very low prices, but make sure that you check the quality carefully. The Night Bazaar and shops along Thanon Tha Phae and Thanon Loi Kroh have good selections. Also see under Tailors and Textiles later in this section for other clothing options.

Sri Sanpanmai (*Chiang Mai map;* ☎ *053 894 372, G-59 Kad Suan Kaew, Thanon Huay Kaew*) This shop sells good ready-made clothing made from Northern Thai textiles.

Lacquerware

Decorated plates, containers, utensils and other items are made by building up layers of lacquer over a wooden or woven bamboo base. Burmese lacquerware, smuggled into the North, can often be seen, especially at Mae Sai. There are several lacquerware factories in San Kamphaeng.

Musical Instruments

Lanna Music (☎ *053 274 144, 148/1 Thanon Phra Pokklao*) Lanna Music sells and repairs various Northern Thai musical instruments.

Bamboo Saxophones Perhaps because Northern Thailand is one of Asia's major locales for both wild and cultivated bamboo, Chiang Mai has attracted interest in the crafting of 'saxophones' from bamboo (although the first such instruments seem to have taken shape some 40 years ago in Jamaica). Actually a sort of hybrid between the saxophone and the recorder, the instruments come in several keys. For each saxophone the bamboo must be carefully selected, cut into short rings before being roasted over a fire to temper them, and then fitted and glued into the familiar curved shape. The sonic characteristics of the bamboo perfectly compliment the traditional cane sax reed to produce a very mellow, slightly raspy sound.

Two Chiang Mai residents make these delightful little instruments, which produce amazing volume considering their relatively small size. *Joy of Sax* sells bamboo saxes through The Lost Heavens (see earlier for details of the Thanon Tha Phae branch). You can also contact the Joy of Sax workshop directly at ☎ 053 222 505. A sax in the key of G costs 4500B, the slightly larger F sax 4800B; an instruction sheet and colourful hemp bag are included. *Elephant Lightfoot* (Eastern Chiang Mai map; ☎ 053 879 191, 4/1 Thanon Chaiyaphum) near Pratu Tha Phae, makes F, G, Bflat and Eflat models, for about the same price as Joy of Sax.

Rattan

Two cheaper rattan shops can be found along the northern side of Thanon Chang Moi two blocks east of the moat. This is the place to buy chairs, small tables, chaises longues, planters, floor screens, settees, bookshelves and other everyday household items. Most of the cheaper pieces, eg, a bookshelf or low-quality chair, cost around 800B, while a rattan chair of better, longer-lasting workmanship will cost 2000B to 5000B.

Hangdong Rattan (Eastern Chiang Mai map; ☎ 053 208 167, 54-55 Thanon Loi Kroh) Hangdong Rattan is a maker of higher-quality furniture and accessories made from this jungle vine. In addition to the many items on display, it takes custom orders.

Silverwork

There are several silverwork shops on Thanon Wualai close to Pratu Chiang Mai. *Sipsong Panna* (☎ 053 216 096, 6/19 Thanon Nimmanhemin) in the Nantawan Arcade opposite the Amari Rincome Hotel is a more upmarket place for jewellery collected in Thailand, Laos, Myanmar and Southwest China. Hill-tribe jewellery, which is heavy and chunky, is very nice.

Tailors

City Silk (☎ 053 234 388, 336 Thanon Tha Phae) More or less opposite Wat Mahawan, City Silk specialises in silk tailoring for women. English is spoken, and service is friendly and professional.

There are several tailor shops off Thanon Kotchasan near Aroon (Rai) Restaurant, including *Florida, Chao Khun, Chaiyo* and *Progress*. Another strip of tailors, catering mostly to tourists, can be found along Thanon Chang Khlan in the Night Bazaar area. Prices are reasonable, and often cheaper than in Bangkok. Ask to see some finished work before choosing a shop.

Teas

Siamese Traders Tea Pavilion (☎ 053 409 705, 053 409 171, fax 053 409 113, ⓔ info@ siamesetraders.com, 85 Thanon Sukkasem) Near Lanna Hospital, this place sells all kinds of teas, but especially locally grown oolongs. Free tastings, in which you can observe the Yunnanese way of brewing tea, are offered to anyone who visits the pavilion. Siamese Traders also offers organic Thai coffee, herbal teas, spice blends for tôm yam and tôm khàa soups and organic rice.

Textiles

Very attractive lengths of material can be made into all sorts of things. Thai silk, with its lush colours and pleasantly rough texture, is a particularly good bargain and is usually cheaper here than in Bangkok. *Talat Warorot* is one of the best and least expensive places to look for fabrics, but take care as many items said to be silk are actually polyester.

Several individual shops in town focus on high-quality traditional (sometimes antique) Thai and Lao fabrics, sold by the metre or made up into original-design clothes. A list of the best places in town would have to include *Sbun-Nga* and *Nandakwang*, both in a strip of shops opposite the Amari Rincome Hotel.

Studio Naenna (Chiang Mai map; ☎/fax 053 226 042, 053 226 138, 8 Soi Chang Khian, Thanon Huay Kaew) Open 8.30am-5pm daily, Oct-March; 9am-4pm

Mon-Fri, April-September. Another recommended shop, this place is operated by Patricia Cheeseman, an expert on Thai-Lao textiles who has written extensively on the subject.

The Loom (*Eastern Chiang Mai map; Chiang Inn Plaza, 100/1 Thanon Chang Khlan*) The Loom carries very fine fabrics from Northern and Northeastern Thailand, Laos and Cambodia.

Duangjitt House (*Chiang Mai map;* ☎ *053 242 291, 053 243 546*) A good source of textiles, Duangjitt House is on a soi off Thanon Thung Hotel opposite the Northern Crafts Centre building – call for an appointment.

You'll also find several shops selling antique Thai and Lao textiles along Thanon Loi Kroh.

Woven Dreams (*Eastern Chiang Mai map;* ☎ *053 272 569, 30/1 Thanon Loi Kroh*) and **Success Silk Shop** (*Eastern Chiang Mai map;* ☎ *053 208 853, 56 Thanon Loi Kroh*) These two shops feature Thai silk readymade and made-to-order clothes using fabrics from Thailand, Laos and Cambodia. Many are patched together from old hand-woven textiles and made into dresses, skirts, shirts and jackets. Also on offer are silk scarves, woven hats and yâam – all more or less sized for faràng.

If you want to see where and how the cloth is made, go to the nearby town of San Kamphaeng for Thai silk, or to Pasang, south of Lamphun, for cotton.

Umbrellas

At Bo Sang, the 'umbrella village' east of Chiang Mai (see the Around Chiang Mai chapter), you'll find hand-painted paper umbrellas of all kinds, from simple traditional brown ones to giant rainbow-hued parasols. These are also sold in shops in Chiang Mai, but in Bo Sang the selection is better.

Woodcarving

Many types of carvings are available, including countless elephants. Teak salad bowls are good and very cheap. Many shops along Thanon Tha Phae and near the

Night Bazaar stock wood crafts, or go to the source – Hang Dong and Ban Thawai south of town.

GETTING THERE & AWAY
Air

The THAI office (☎ 053 211 044–7) is within the city moat area at 240 Thanon Phra Pokklao, close to Wat Chiang Man. THAI operates 11 one-hour flights between Bangkok and Chiang Mai daily (plus additional flights on certain days of the week). The fare is 2170B one way in economy class.

Air fares between Chiang Mai and other Thai cities are:

destination	fare
Chiang Rai	775B
Mae Hong Son	690B
Mae Sot	1035B
Nan	875B
Phitsanulok	1035B
Phrae	755B
Phuket	4520B

Bangkok Airways (☎ 053 210 043/4, fax 053 281 520), on the 2nd floor of Chiang Mai International Airport, also operates daily flights to and from Bangkok via Sukhothai for 2170B.

See the Getting There & Away chapter for details on reaching Chiang Mai via international flights.

Bus

From Bangkok's Northern and Northeastern bus terminal (also known as Moh Chit) there are five ordinary buses daily to Chiang Mai, departing from 5.25am to 10pm. The 12-hour trip costs 215B via Nakhon Sawan and 200B via Ayuthaya. There are 13 2nd-class air-con buses – on which the air-con doesn't always work – a day between 6.30am and 10pm for 314B; these take 10 to 11 hours to reach Chiang Mai.

First-class air-con buses with toilets and 34 seats leave every 30 minutes between 7am and 8.45pm and cost 403B one way. The government VIP buses, with 24 seats that recline a bit more than the seats in 1st class air, cost 625B; there are only a couple of departures each day, from either Bangkok or Chiang Mai, between 7pm and 9pm. The 1st-class and VIP buses take from nine to 10 hours to reach Chiang Mai, depending on the traffic.

The public buses from the Northern and Northeastern bus terminal are generally more reliable and on schedule than the private ones booked in Banglamphu and other tourist-oriented places.

Ten or more private tour companies run air-con buses between Bangkok and Chiang Mai, departing from various points throughout both cities as well as from the official government terminals. Return tickets are always somewhat cheaper than one-way tickets. The fares on private air-con buses range from 300B to 400B, depending on the company and state of competition.

Travel agencies in Bangkok are notorious for promising services they can't deliver, such as reclining seats or air-con that works. It's better to stick to buses from the Northern & Northeastern bus terminal. Several Thanon Khao San agencies offer bus tickets to Chiang Mai for as little as 200B, including a night's free stay at a guesthouse in Chiang Mai. The bus companies can afford to charge such low fares because the guesthouses pay commissions for each tourist delivered to Chiang Mai. Sometimes this works out OK, but often the buses can be substandard and the 'free' guesthouse may charge you 40B for electricity or hot water, or apply heavy pressure for you to sign up for one of its treks before you can get a room. Besides, riding in a bus or minivan stuffed full of foreigners and their bulky backpacks is not the most cultural experience.

A couple of years ago a bus driver on a Thanon Khao San bus bound for Chiang Mai attacked a passenger with a machete when he asked why the promised air-con wasn't working. Several readers have complained that they purchased tickets for large air-con or even VIP buses and at the last minute were shunted into cramped minivans. We recommend avoiding these buses altogether; use public buses from Bangkok's Moh Chit terminal instead.

Public buses between Chiang Mai and other northern towns have frequent departures throughout the day (at least hourly), except for the Mae Sai, Khon Kaen, Udon, Ubon and Khorat buses, which have morning and evening departures only. (See the table for public fares and destinations for public buses.)

For buses to destinations within Chiang Mai Province use the Chang Pheuak terminal (☎ 053 211 586), while for buses outside the province use the Chiang Mai Arcade terminal (☎ 053 242 664). From the town centre, a túk-túk or chartered sǎwngthǎew to the Chiang Mai Arcade terminal should cost 30B to 40B; to the Chang Pheuak terminal you should be able to get a sǎwngthǎew at the normal 10B per person rate.

Train

Chiang Mai–bound rapid trains leave Bangkok's Hualamphong station (☎ 022 204 334, 022 201 690) daily at 6.40am (non-aircon 2nd class and 3rd class) and 10pm (non-air-con 2nd-class sleeper and 3rd class), arriving at 8.30pm and 12.20pm respectively. One rapid train offering 1st- and 2nd-class air-con sleeper and 3rd-class service departs daily at 3.15pm, arriving in Chiang Mai at 5.35am. Express diesel railcars depart at 8.25am and 7.25pm (2nd-class air-con only) and arrive at 7.20pm and 7.10am. Special express trains depart at 6pm (1st- and 2nd-class air-con sleeper and 2nd-class non-air-con sleeper) and 7.40pm (1st- and 2nd-class air-con only), reaching Chiang Mai at 6.50am and 8.30am respectively.

The basic 2nd-class one-way fare is 281B, plus special express (80B), express (60B) or rapid (40B) surcharges. Add 100B for upper berth and 150B for lower berth in a non-air-con 2nd-class rapid train (130B and 200B respectively on the special express). For air-con 2nd-class rapid trains, add 220/270B for upper/lower sleepers (250/320B on special express). For example, if you take a non-air-con 2nd-class upper berth on a rapid train, your total fare will be 461B (321+100+40B). Tickets for the 'express diesel railcar' (Nos 9 and 11) cost the same as 2nd-class air-con seats on an express.

Bus Destinations from Chiang Mai

destination	fare	duration (hrs)
Chiang Dao*	25B	1½
Chiang Khong	121B	6½
(air-con)	169B	6
(1st class air-con)	218B	6
Chiang Rai	77B	4
(air-con)	98B	3
(1st class)	139B	3
Chiang Saen	95B	4
(1st class air-con)	171B	3½
Chom Thong*	23B	2
Fang*	61B	3
Hang Dong*	8B	30 min
Khon Kaen (via Tak)	243B	12
(air-con)	340B	12
(1st class air-con)	437B	12
Khon Kaen (via Utaradit)	219B	11
(air-con)	307B	11
(1st class air-con)	394B	11
Khorat	243B	12
(1st class air-con)	437B	12
(VIP)	510B	12
Lampang	25B	2
(air-con)	52B	2
(1st class air-con)	70B	2
Lamphun	12B	1
Mae Hong Son (via Mae Sariang)	143B	8
(air-con)	257B	8
Mae Hong Son (via Pai)	100B	7
(air-con)	130B	7

The basic 1st-class fare is 593B; berths are 520B per person and are available on the special express and rapid trains only.

Trains leave Lopburi for Chiang Mai at 9.12am (rapid), 10.36am (express diesel railcar), 5.51pm (rapid), 8.26pm (special express), 9.33pm (express diesel), and 12.40am (rapid) arriving at the times listed for the same trains from Bangkok. Fares are 257/277B for 2nd-class rapid/express seats and 133/153B for 3rd-class rapid, including rapid/express surcharges.

Berths on sleepers to Chiang Mai are increasingly hard to reserve without booking well in advance; tour groups sometimes book entire cars. The return trip from Chiang Mai to Bangkok doesn't seem to be as difficult, except during the Songkran (mid-April) and Chinese New Year (late January to mid-February) holiday periods.

Chiang Mai's neat and tidy train station (☎ 053 245 363/4) has an ATM and two advance booking offices, one at the regular ticket windows outdoors (open 5am to 9pm daily), the other in a more comfortable air-con office (open 6am to 8pm daily). The booking office has a computerised reservation system through which you can book train seats for anywhere in Thailand up to 60 days in advance. There is also a left-luggage facility that is open 4.50am to 8.45pm daily. The cost is 10B per piece for the first five days and 15B per piece thereafter, with a 20-day maximum.

Bus Destinations from Chiang Mai		
destination	fare	duration (hrs)
Mae Sai	95B	5
(air-con)	108B	5
(1st class air-con)	171B	5
Mae Sariang	78B	4-5
(1st class air-con)	140B	4-5
Mae Sot	134B	6½
(1st class air-con)	241B	6
Nan	128B	6
(air-con)	179B	6
(1st class air-con)	230B	6
Pai	55B	4
(air-con)	80B	4
Phayao	67B	3
(air-con)	94B	2½
Phrae	79B	4
(air-con)	111B	3½
(1st class air-con)	142B	3½
Phitsanulok	132–140B	5–6
(air-con)	184–196B	5
Sukhothai	122B	6
(air-con)	171B	5
Tha Ton*	70B	4
Udon Thani	228B	12
(air-con)	319B	12
(1st class air-con)	410B	12
Utaradit	180B	6
(air-con)	300B	6
Wiang Haeng	70B	4

*Leaves from Chang Pheuak bus terminal. All other buses leave from the Chiang Mai Arcade bus terminal (also called New Terminal) off Thanon Kaew Nawarat.

GETTING AROUND
To/From Chiang Mai International Airport
The airport is 2km to 3km from the city centre. There are two legal airport taxi services, both charging 100B for cars that can take up to five passengers and their luggage. Pick up a ticket at the taxi kiosks just outside the baggage claim area and present it to the taxi drivers by the main arrival area exit.

You can charter a túk-túk or red săwng-thǎew from the centre of Chiang Mai to the airport for 50B or 60B.

Bus
Chiang Mai cancelled all bus services in the city in 1997, a lamentable but understandable fact, given the general lack of passengers. Most Chiang Mai residents now take săwngthǎew and many also have their own bicycles or motorcycles.

Car & Motorcycle
Cars, 4WDs and minivans are readily available at several locations throughout the city. Be sure that the vehicle you rent has insurance (liability) coverage – ask to see the documents and carry a photocopy with you while driving.

Two of the best agencies in town for service and price are North Wheels (Eastern Chiang Mai map; ☎ 053 216 189, fax 053 221 709, e sales@northwheels.com), at 127/2 Thanon Moon Muang near Talat

Somphet, and Queen Bee (Eastern Chiang Mai map; ☎ 053 208 988), next to Muang Thong Hotel on Thanon Moon Muang. Both offer hotel pick-up and delivery as well as 24-hour emergency road service; North Wheel's rates include insurance, while Queen Bee charges extra for insurance. Sample rentals at North Wheels include Suzuki Caribians for 1000B per 24-hour day, and Toyota 4WD pick-ups for 1500B a day. Discounted weekly and monthly rates are available.

It's important to choose a car rental agency carefully, by reputation rather than what's on paper. Also realise that whatever happens you're still responsible for personal injury and medical payments of anyone injured in connection with a traffic accident.

Other prominent rental agencies include:

Avis (☎ 053 201 574) 14/14 Thanon Huay Kaew; (☎ 053 201 798/9) Chiang Mai International Airport

Budget (☎ 053 202 871) Chiang Mai International Airport

Journey Car Rent (☎ 053 208 787, fax 053 273 428, e journeycnx@thaimail.com) 283 Thanon Tha Phae

National Car Rental (☎ 053 210 118) Amari Rincome Hotel

If you're looking to hire a motorcycle, Honda Dream 100cc step-throughs can be rented for 100B to 200B a day, depending on the season, the condition of the motorcycle and length of rental. Prices are very competitive in Chiang Mai because there's a real glut of motorcycles. For two people, it's cheaper to rent a small motorcycle for the day to visit Doi Suthep than to go up and back in a săwngthăew. Occasionally you'll see slightly larger 125cc to 150cc Hondas or Yamahas for rent for 200B to 250B a day.

Availability of bikes bigger than 150cc varies from year to year, but you can usually find Honda XL600s or Yamaha XT600s (800B to 900B a day), Honda AX-1 250s (500/350B high/low season), Honda Baja 250s (500/350B high/low season) and Honda XR 250s (400B) at a few of the agencies.

Motorcycle hire places come and go with the seasons. Many of them are lined up along

the eastern side of the moat on Thanon Moon Muang, Thanon Chaiyaphum and Thanon Kotchasan. One place to hire big bikes is Tui Big Bike (Central Chiang Mai map; ☎ 053 876 227) on the corner of Thanon Wichayanon and Thanon Chaiyaphum.

Among the more established and reliable are:

C&P Service 51 Thanon Kotchasan. Honda Baja 250s and Honda Dreams.

CVA Suzuki Co Ltd (☎ 053 216 666) 47/4-6 Thanon Chotana

Dang Bike Hire (☎ 053 271 524) 23 Thanon Kotchasan

Jaguar (☎ 053 214 694) 131 Thanon Moon Muang. Honda MRX 125s and Honda Baja 250s.

Lek Big Bike (☎ 053 251 830) 74/2 Thanon Chaiyaphum. Large fleet from 250cc to 750cc.

Mr Mechanic 4 Soi 5 Thanon Moon Muang. Small motorcycles and Suzuki 4WD vehicles (insurance included).

Pop Rent-A-Car (☎ 053 276 014) Near Soi 2 Thanon Kotchasan. Motorcycles and cars (insurance included).

SP Bike Rental (☎ 053 357 559) 99/1 Thanon Moon Muang, near Pratu Tha Phae

These agencies offer motorcycle insurance for around 50B a day – not a bad investment considering you could face a 25,000B to 60,000B liability if your bike is stolen. Most policies have a high deductible (excess), so in cases of theft you're usually responsible for a third to half of the bike's value – even with insurance.

More casual rental places that specialise in quick, easy and cheap rentals of 100cc bikes can be found along Thanon Moon Muang, including Mr Beer at 2 Thanon Moon Muang near Talat Somphet. Several car-rental places also rent motorcycles. See the Getting Around chapter for information on motorcycle touring.

Bicycle
As long as you can handle riding in some traffic, all of Chiang Mai is easily accessible by bike, including Chiang Mai University, Wat U Mong, Wat Suan Dok and the Chiang Mai National Museum on the outskirts of town.

One company that not only rents out bikes but also operates cycling tours around the province is The Wild Planet-Contact Travel (Chiang Mai Night Bazaar map; ☎ 053 277 178, fax 053 279 505, e adventure@thailine.com) at 73/7 Thanon Charoen Prathet between Thanon Loi Kroh and Thanon Tha Phae. It rents rugged 21-speed mountain bikes for 200B a day.

Basic bicycles can be rented for around 30B to 50B a day from some guesthouses or from places along the east moat.

Bike & Bite (☎ 053 418 534) 23/1 Thanon Si Phum. This is a combination Thai restaurant and mountain bike rental/tour company.
SP Bike Rental (☎ 053 357 559) 99/1 Thanon Moon Muang, near Pratu Tha Phae
Velocity (Central Chiang Mai map; ☎ 053 410 665) 177 Thanon Chang Pheuak. Velocity rents mountain and racing bikes, offers guided tours and carries all kinds of cycling accessories.

Săwngthăew, Túk-túk & Săamláw

Hordes of red săwngthăew ply the streets of Chiang Mai looking for passengers. Flag one down, state your destination, and if it is going that way you can ride for 10B. Săwngthăew come in various sizes and conditions – all based on small pick-ups – and take anywhere from 12 to 20 passengers. It's best to board one that already has passengers if you're worried about getting overcharged. Some drivers try to charge lone passengers (both Thais and faràng) 20B instead of the usual 10B. If you're the only passenger and you're going to an out-of-the-way place, that may be reasonable, but if you're going, say, from Pratu Tha Phae to Talat Warorot – a relatively short and well-travelled distance – you shouldn't have to pay more than the normal 10B fare. You can charter (măo) a săwngthăew anywhere in the city for 60B or less.

Túk-túk work only on a charter or taxi basis, at 30B for short trips and 40B to 60B for longer ones. After midnight in entertainment areas such as along Thanon Charoenrat near the Riverside and Le Brasserie, or down towards Zodiac, most túk-túk charge a flat 50B for any trip back across the river.

Around Chiang Mai

Chiang Mai is ringed with interesting attractions within a half-day's travel. Among the highlights are two small but significant museums in Mae Rim, sacred Doi Suthep (Mt Suthep) and the surrounding Doi Suthep & Doi Pui National Park, the traditional Northern Thai villages and natural environment of Doi Inthanon, the historic Lanna-style temples of Lamphun and Lampang and trekking around Chiang Dao and Tha Ton.

Chiang Mai Province

DOI SUTHEP
ดอยสุเทพ

Sixteen kilometres northwest of Chiang Mai and looming over the city like a doting mother stands Doi Suthep. Often shrouded in clouds during the rainy season, and obscured by haze in the dry season, the 1676m peak is named after the hermit Sudeva, who lived on the mountain's slopes for many years. Suthep is Chiang Mai's most potent geographical symbol and it is seen by many residents as a guardian entity.

Part of Suthep's sanctity comes from Wat Phra That Doi Suthep, a magnificent Lanna-style temple near the summit. First established in 1383 under King Keu Na, it's considered the most important Buddhist pilgrimage spot in the North and has also become an extremely popular tourist attraction. A *naga* (mythical serpent) staircase of 300 steps leads to the *wát* (temple) at the end of the winding road up the mountain. You also have the option of riding a tram from the parking lot to the wát grounds for 20B.

At the top, weather permitting, there are some fine views of Chiang Mai. Inside the cloister is an exquisite, Lanna-style, copper-plated *chedi* (stupa) topped by a five-tiered gold umbrella – one of the holiest chedi in Thailand.

About 4km beyond Wat Phra That Doi Suthep is **Phra Tamnak Phu Phing**, a winter palace for the royal family; here you might want to check out the **palace gardens** (*admission free; open 8.30am-12.30pm & 1pm-4pm Sat, Sun & holidays*).

The road that passes the palace splits off to the left, stopping at the peak of Doi Pui. From there a dirt road proceeds for a couple of kilometres to a nearby **Hmong hill-tribe village**. You can buy Hmong handicrafts here and see traditional homes and costumes, although these are mostly posed situations. A less touristy **Hmong village** can be found by taking a right fork in the road instead of a left, and walking or motorbiking 5km. Three kilometres beyond this village is a **coffee plantation** where you can taste fresh coffee. You can charter a *săwngthăew* (pick-up truck) to this village for 75B or ride a shared one for 20B per person.

If you're cycling or driving to the summit, you can stop off along the way at **Nam Tok Monthathon** (*Monthathon Waterfall; foreigners 200B*). The falls are 2.5km off the paved road to Doi Suthep. The trail is well marked; if you're interested in checking out the falls, have the săwngthăew driver drop you off on the way up the mountain. Pools beneath the falls hold water year-round, although swimming is best during or just after the annual monsoon. The falls can be crowded on weekends. The 200B fee allows you to visit other waterfalls on the road to Suthep; apparently the fees will be used to build cement parking lots and other infrastructure for the park, which could be good or bad depending on your point of view.

Doi Suthep & Doi Pui National Park
อุทยานแห่งชาติดอยสุเทพ ดอยปุย

Most visitors do a quick tour of the temple, the Hmong village and perhaps the winter

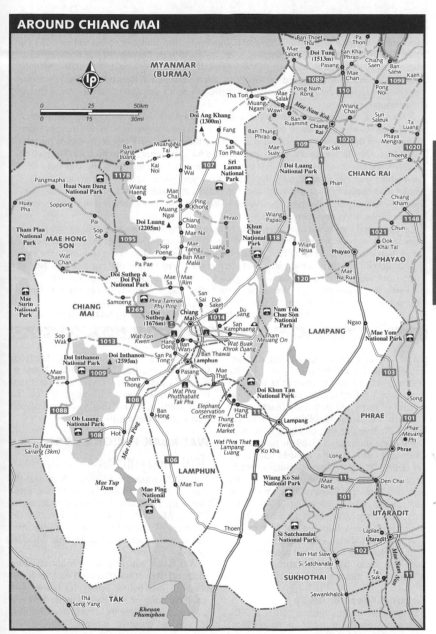

Reforesting Doi Suthep

Because of its proximity to urban Chiang Mai, the development and care of Doi Suthep & Doi Pui National Park has become a very sensitive issue. For many years the western side of the park has been severely disturbed by poachers and land encroachers, including around 500 resident hill-tribe families. In 1986 a Bangkok company tried to establish a cable-car system through the park to the temple, but protests, petitions and marches by the Group for Chiang Mai (Chomrom Pheua Chiang Mai) stopped the plan.

Meanwhile, Chiang Mai University's Forest Restoration Unit (FORRU) has developed a forest restoration strategy designed to conserve biodiversity and vital watersheds. FORRU, a joint initiative between the university's biology department and the national park service, models its program after the successful 'framework species method' used for forest restoration in Australia. The method involves planting 20 to 30 native forest tree species, selected for their ability to shade out weeds and attract seed-dispersing wildlife. The planted trees rapidly restore forest structure and function, whilst seed-dispersing birds and mammals, attracted into the planted plots by fruit and nectar, complete the recovery of biodiversity. The unit has tested various mulching, weeding and fertiliser treatments to ensure the trees' performance.

In three years the planted trees have created a closed canopy forest. An additional 30 non-planted tree species, sprouted from seeds brought in by wildlife, have established themselves in the planted plots. Leaf litter covers the forest floor, bird life has increased and wild pigs have returned to the area.

FORRU also runs an education program for schools and nongovernmental organisations (NGOs) and assists villagers to establish nurseries to grow framework tree species for planting.

For further information on reforestation, contact FORRU at e aquarius99@hotmail.com; for information on the INTG (Informal Northern Thai Group), contact e intg@thailand.com.

Adapted from a summary of an Informal Northern Thai Group talk

palace grounds, altogether missing the surrounding park *(adult/child under 14 200/100B)*. This 261 sq km reserve is home to more than 300 bird species and nearly 2000 species of ferns and flowering plants.

There are extensive **hiking trails** in the park, including one that climbs 1685m-high Doi Pui; the summit is a favourite picnic spot. Other trails pass **Hmong villages** that rarely get *faràng* (Western) visitors. Bungalow and dormitory *accommodation* is available near park headquarters (500m past the temple car park on the right). Depending on who's on duty, there are also maps available here. Mountain bikers will find lots of fat-tyre fun.

A 4km trail leads to the scenic and more isolated **Nam Tok Sai Yai**, and connects with a trail to **Nam Tok Monthathon** (see the previous Doi Suthep section).

Getting There & Away

Săwngthăew to Doi Suthep (30B to 50B, depending on the number of passengers) leave Chiang Mai throughout the day from the western end of Thanon Huay Kaew in front of Chiang Mai University, from Pratu Chang Pheuak and the Chiang Mai Zoo. To Phra Tamnak Phu Phing and Doi Pui add 20B in each direction.

WAT BUAK KHROK LUANG

วัดบวกครกหลวง

This little monastery, with its mid-19th-century *wíhǎan* (hall), is one of the most charming Northern Thai–style *wát* in the Chiang Mai area. The wíhǎan boasts a famous set of mural paintings – see the special section 'Lanna-Style Temple Murals' for a description.

Wat Buak Khrok Luang is about 300m south off Rte 1006 (the road to San Kamphaeng), just before Km4 and before you reach Bo Sang or San Kamphaeng. This is a good area to explore by bicycle or motorbike. If you're without wheels, take a Bo

Sang–bound săwngthăew and ask to be let off at *săam yâek wát bùak khrók lŭang,* the three-way junction for Wat Buak Khrok Luang.

BO SANG
ป่อสร้าง

Tourism brochures usually call Bo Sang (often spelt 'Baw Sang' or 'Bor Sang'), 9km east of Chiang Mai on Rte 1006, the 'Umbrella Village' because of its many umbrella manufacturers. Almost the entire village consists of craft shops selling painted umbrellas, fans, silverware, straw handiwork, bamboo and teak, statuary, china, celadon and lacquerware, along with tacky Chiang Mai and Northern Thai souvenirs and some quality items.

The larger shops can arrange overseas shipping at reasonable rates. As at Chiang Mai's Night Bazaar, discounts are offered for bulk purchases. Some of the places will also pack and post parasols, apparently quite reliably.

Less well known is the fact that Bo Sang is a centre for traditional Northern Thai music and makes Northern Thai instruments. Near soi 14 is a no-name *musical instrument shop* with beautiful hand-made *seung* (Northern Thai lutes) as well as other instruments. Look for a shopfront with drums and paintings of musicians in front.

One of the best times to visit Bo Sang is during the annual Umbrella Festival, which is quite local in flavour and features lots of Northern Thai music, food and colourful processions. It's usually held in late January.

Getting There & Away
To reach Bo Sang by public transport, board a white săwngthăew at the Chang Pheuak bus terminal or at Talat Worarot in Chiang Mai; the cost is 5B per person. You can also take the San Kamphaeng bus – see the following San Kamphaeng section.

SAN KAMPHAENG
สันกำแพง

Four or 5km farther down Rte 1006 is San Kamphaeng, which flourishes on cotton and silk weaving. Stores offering finished products line the main street, although the actual weaving is done in small factories down side streets. There are some good deals to be had here, especially in silk. For cotton, you'd probably do better in Pasang (see that section later), a lesser-known village near Lamphun, although you may see shirt styles here that are not available in Pasang.

Getting There & Away
Buses to San Kamphaeng (6B) leave Chiang Mai frequently during the day from the northern side of Thanon Charoen Muang, east of Mae Nam Ping (Ping River). The bus stop is towards the main post office and the train station and across from San Pa Khoi Market. White săwngthăew (6B) leave from Chang Pheuak bus terminal and from Talat Worarot.

THAM MEUANG ON
ถ้ำเมืองออน

This large limestone cave, long a sacred Buddhist site, can be found off Rte 1317, a pretty length of sealed road that runs parallel to Rte 1006 and then continues northeast beyond San Kamphaeng to Meuang On district.

The cave entrance is reached via a set of naga stairs. Several illuminated caverns are linked by passageways. Some of the cave formations are quite impressive. One very large stalagmite is considered a 'natural stupa' that arose, according to local legend, when the Buddha and a group of monks stopped here for shelter while on *thúdong* (wandering).

Snacks, including *kài yâang* (grilled chicken) and *sôm-tam* (green papaya salad), are available from *vendors* at the foot of the naga stairway.

On the other side of the mountain from Tham Meuang On is a set of high limestone cliffs that are a favourite destination for local rock climbers, who call the cliffs **'Crazy Horse Buttress'**. Over 50 routes have been bolted so far, with more on the way. For details on the climbing area, or to book a day trip with an experienced rock climber, contact The Peak Rock-Climbing Plaza (☎ 053 820 777, ✉ josh@thepeakthailand.com), at 28/2 Thanon Chang Khlan in Chiang Mai.

Getting There & Away

Biking and motorbiking along Rte 1317 is superb, so if you're up for it that's the best way to reach the cave or the rock-climbing area. There is no public transport along the stretch of road beyond San Kamphaeng, so the only other way to get here is to rent a car or charter a sǎwngthǎew from San Kamphaeng (around 150B one way, 300B for half a day, 500B all day). The signed turn-off for the cave comes at Km28 on Rte 1317. After turning, follow the road till it ends at the cave, about 1km along.

You can't easily reach Crazy Horse Buttress from the cave entrance. Instead you must take a dirt-road turn-off that comes a couple of kilometres before the turn-off for the cave. On Rte 1317 look for a small blue sign on the left that reads 'Muang On Cave 1km'. Beyond the sign you'll come to three dirt roads in a row; turn left onto the third road. About 500m up this road you'll be able to see the cliffs on the right.

MAE RIM

แม่ริม

Once a Northern Thai and Shan village a world apart from Chiang Mai, Mae Rim has a four-lane highway link to the capital and has grown into a major junction for local trade and tourism. At the northern end of Mae Rim, Rte 1096 heads southwest through the scenic Mae Sa valley to Samoeng (see Mae Sa & Samoeng later in this chapter).

The town of Mae Rim itself would seem to have little to offer the average visitor, but in fact there are two small museums here that make a visit worthwhile, especially if you're heading towards Samoeng anyway.

Dara Pirom Palace Museum

พิพิธภัณฑ์ดาราภิรมย์

This museum (☎ 053 299 175, Dara Rasmi Border Patrol Police Camp; adult/child 50/20B; open 9am-5pm Tues-Sun) was once the house of Chao Dara Rasmi, one of King Chulalongkorn's (the fifth King of the present Bangkok dynasty) favourite consorts.

The daughter of Phra Chao Inthara Wichayanon, the seventh king of Chiang Mai, Dara Rasmi was formally betrothed to King Chulalongkorn when she was 11 years old and became an official palace consort at age 13, in 1886. She was said to have been instrumental in strengthening relations between Siam and Lanna, and nine years after her instalment in Bangkok, Lanna became part of the Kingdom of Siam.

After Chulalongkorn's death in 1910, the Bangkok royal family granted permission for Chao Dara Rasmi to return to her Northern Thai homeland, where she built a splendid golden teak home of mixed European and Thai features. After she died in 1933, her home eventually became the property of Bangkok's Chulalongkorn University. The property decayed until 1998, when it was renovated for use as a museum chronicling its history and, more importantly, displaying Northern Thai cultural artefacts. With funding from the surviving members of the Lanna royal family along with Chulalongkorn University alumni, the palace opened as a museum in 1999.

The beautifully restored three-storey house contains 270 well-preserved and well-labelled pieces of furniture, decorative items and personal effects that once belonged to the princess. One room contains a very good display of Northern Thai loom-woven textiles, complete with technical notes and explanations.

To find the Dara Pirom Palace Museum you first have to get to the Mae Rim district office or main police station. Between these two public offices is a road that leads to a border police camp. The museum is about 200m beyond the camp entrance, past a short airstrip.

Kum-Une Art Museum

พิพิธภัณฑ์คำอูน

On the road to Samoeng (Rte 1096), 4km from Mae Rim and 1.5km past the turn-off for the Regent Chiang Mai Resort & Spa, this private museum (☎ 053 298 068, 259 Mu 1, Tambon Mae Raem, Mae Rim; open 9am-5pm, closed Tues) contains a quirky selection of Northern Thai antiques, textiles and easel art. It's best to call ahead, as hours are erratic.

The museum's best feature, however, is a 140-year-old raft house the owners brought up from Ayuthaya and lovingly restored. Possibly the most ornate and beautiful raft house ever constructed in Thailand, it's made entirely of teak and contains several rooms. Each room is filled with Thai antiques, including a number of old Buddhas and rare chinaware.

Inside the main house, one room is filled with one of the best collections of Thai – and especially Northern Thai – woven textiles in the North. Another room is dedicated to Chinese antiques and displays a Chinese wedding bed that equals the raft house in its rare and opulent design. Throughout the house are displayed paintings and other works of art from the hand of the owner, Ajahn Uap, a nationally famous artist and classical musician.

Baan Kwai Thai
บ้านควายไทย

If you have an interest in seeing how the Thais train and use water buffaloes for farm work, only one place in Northern Thailand is dedicated to satisfying that urge: Baan Kwai Thai (☎ 053 301 628, 300/2 Thanon Chiang Mai–Fang; 200B).

MH

Once the principal tool of trade for Thai farmers, water buffalo are being replaced by machines.

This rustic buffalo camp is 1.2km off Hwy 107 (the road from Chiang Mai to Fang), with the turn-off coming 1km north of the turn-off for Rte 1067 (the road to Samoeng). There are shows hourly from 8am to 11am, and at 3pm and 4pm.

MAE SA & SAMOENG
แม่สา/สะเมิง

This forested loop northwest of Chiang Mai via Mae Rim and/or Hang Dong makes a good day or overnight trip. Although dotted with tourist developments – resorts, orchid farms, butterfly parks, snake farms, elephant camps, botanic gardens, antique and handicraft shops – the Rte 1096/1269 loop through the Mae Sa Valley is very scenic in spots.

Nam Tok Mae Sa is only 6km from the Mae Rim turn-off from Rte 107, which in turn is 12km north of Chiang Mai. Many Thais come to these waterfalls to picnic on weekends; midweek there are far less visitors.

Farther along the loop are several Hmong villages, the most accessible being **Ban Nong Hoi** (turn off on the right near Km15) and **Ban Pha Nok Kok** (turn off on the left near Km16).

There are at least four places along the loop that call themselves elephant 'camp', 'farm', or 'village'. Best of the bunch is the **Maesa Elephant Camp** (☎ 053 297 060). Not far from Nam Tok Mae Sa, it has elephant shows (80B) at 8am and 9.40am daily, plus one at 1.30pm in the high season. The shows last one hour. You can feed the elephants sugar cane and bananas, and visit the baby elephants in their nursery and training school.

Samoeng, at the westernmost extension of the loop (35km from Mae Rim), is the most peaceful area for an overnight stay, since it's 5km north of the main loop junction between the highways to/from Mae Rim and Hang Dong via Rte 1269. About 1.5km outside Samoeng village itself is the **Samoeng Resort** (☎ 053 487 072), which has rooms from 700B in 15 quiet, well-designed fan or air-con bungalows.

Should you need money while in Samoeng, a Bangkok Bank near the market has an ATM.

Getting There & Away

Yellow săwngthăew to Samoeng from the Chang Pheuak bus terminal in Chiang Mai cost 35B per passenger. There are two daily departures, one at 9am and another at 11am. It takes two hours and 40 minutes to reach Samoeng from Chiang Mai. In Samoeng the vehicles stop near the market, across from Samoeng Hospital.

Since it's paved all the way, the winding loop road makes a good ride by bicycle or motorcycle. From Samoeng you can take a northwest detour along Rte 1265 to Rte 1095 for Pai and Mae Hong Son; the 148km road (136km unpaved, 12.2km paved) breaks north at the Karen village of Ban Wat Chan, where fuel is available. This is the longest stretch of unpaved road remaining in Northern Thailand and is recommended for experienced off-highway bikers only (and only in the dry season). The road passes a few Hmong and Karen villages.

The yellow săwngthăew from Chiang Mai continues from Samoeng on to Ban Wat Chan (100B, about four hours) twice a day, at 10.40am and 12.40pm.

HANG DONG TO SAN PA TONG
Wat Ton Kwen
วัดต้นเกว๋น

Ten kilometres south of Chiang Mai via Rte 108, Rte 1296 veers west-southwest and leads in the direction of this classic Lanna-style wát in the village of Ban Ton Kwen. If you're pedalling or driving, follow the signs and take the first road to your left after taking Rte 1296. Then take the second left and you'll see the wall of the temple compound on your right.

The wát's official name is Wat Intharawat, but the Northern Thai name comes from the very tall sugar palms (tôn kwĕn in Northern Thai) that stand just outside and inside the entrance. An entrance flanked with lion sculptures is very much in the old Lanna style, while the naga balustrade leading up to the portal of the wíhăan shows Thai Lü influence. The temple is thought to have been built in the middle of the 19th century and is remarkably well preserved given its age.

Take your time exploring the wíhăan, as there is much to peruse in the many carved wooden panels fitted together. Floral motifs abound in framing and cornices, and the ceiling is adorned with masterfully carved rosettes called dao phehdaan (ceiling stars).

If the wíhăan is locked, look around for a monk who can help find the key. The monastic quarters are in an adjacent compound with modern temple buildings.

Hang Dong, Ban Wan & Ban Thawai
หางดง,บ้านวันและบ้านถวาย

Fifteen kilometres south of Chiang Mai on Rte 108 is Hang Dong, well known for ceramics, woodcarving and antiques. Many of the shops here sell wholesale as well as retail, so prices are low. Catch a bus (6B) from Pratu Chiang Mai to Hang Dong. The shops are actually strung out along Rte 108, starting about 2km before Hang Dong.

Immediately east of Hang Dong there are more antique and furniture shops in Ban Wan, and beyond that, in Ban Thawai. Ban Wan generally has the best-quality furniture and antiques. Most of the goods churned out in Ban Thawai are for the tourist or overseas export market.

San Pa Tong & Mae Wang
สันป่าตอง/แม่วาง

Farther south down Rte 108, this village is known for its large **water buffalo and cattle market** (open 5.30am-10am Sat). In addition to livestock, the lively market purveys used motorcycles. If you want breakfast, there are also plenty of *food vendors*. You can catch a bus or săwngthăew to San Pa Tong from the bus queue near Pratu Chiang Mai.

West of San Pa Tong, in the foothills of the mountain range that eventually yields Thailand's highest peak, Doi Inthanon, Rte 1013 winds though the scenic valley district of Mae Wang. At the **Mae Wang Elephant Camp** (☎ 053 229 040, Km21, Rte 1013) elephant rides and river rafting along the Nam Khan can be arranged.

Places to Stay & Eat *Kao Mai Lanna Resort Hotel (☎ 053 834 470, fax 053 834 480, W www.kaomailanna.com, Km29, Thanon Chiang Mai–Hot)* Rooms without/ with bathtub 1200/1500B. As southern China supplanted Northern Thailand as a major source of tobacco for the world ciga- rette industry, many tobacco-curing sheds were either abandoned or destroyed. At Kao Mai Lanna, the sheds were converted into attractive tourist lodgings.

Built of brick and bamboo following de- signs imported by British tobacco brokers, each building has two floors divided into two units. All rooms are furnished with an- tiques or reproductions and feature air-con and medium-sized refrigerators.

Kao Mai Lanna offers free transport from the airport, train station or bus stations in Chiang Mai.

Even if you don't stay at the Kao Mai Lanna, the outdoor *restaurant* serves su- perb Thai food at very reasonable prices.

Mae Wang House (☎/fax 053 311 415, 5 Mu 8, Tambon Yuwa, San Pa Tong) Bun- galows 180B. On Mae Wang, not far from Mae Wang Elephant Camp, Mae Wang House offers six rustic bungalows with pri- vate hot-water bathrooms. Treks to nearby caves and Karen villages, along with bam- boo rafting and elephant tours, may be arranged here.

CHOM THONG & AROUND
จอมทอง

Chom Thong (pronounced 'jawm thawng') is a necessary stop between Chiang Mai and Doi Inthanon if you're travelling by public transport. The main temple is worth an hour's stop for its ancient *bòt* (ordination hall), or longer if you're interested in meditation.

Wat Phra That Si Chom Thong
วัดพระธาตุศรีจอมทอง

If you have time, walk down Chom Thong's main street to Wat Phra That Si Chom Thong. The gilded Burmese chedi in the compound was built in 1451 and the Burmese-style bòt, built in 1516, is one of the most beautiful in

Northern Thailand. Inside and out it is an in- tegrated work of art, and the whole is well looked after by the locals. Fine woodcarving can be seen along the eaves of the roof and inside on the ceiling, which is supported by massive teak columns. The impressive altar is designed like a small *praasàat* (enclosed shrine) in typical Lanna style, and is said to contain a relic from the right side of the Bud- dha's skull.

Nearby is a glass case containing ancient Thai weaponry. Behind the praasàat altar is a room containing religious antiques.

Vegetarian Restaurant (Watjanee) Dishes 25B. Open 8am-4pm daily. A few doors up from the wát compound, this restaurant offers simple one-plate rice and noodle dishes that substitute tofu and gluten for meat. Look for the yellow pennants out front.

Meditation Retreats Under the direction of Ajahn Thong, formerly of Wat Ram Poeng in Chiang Mai, meditation retreats in the style of the late Mahasi Sayadaw are held regularly. Meditation students are asked to stay a minimum of two weeks; the optimum course lasts 26 days. Students dress in white, and stay in a group of *kùtì* (meditation huts) at the back of the wát. The schedule is very rigorous.

Some students continue individual prac- tice at a forest monastery in the Chom Thong district known as Wat Tham Thong, 5km be- fore the town of Hot (west of Chom Thong) off Rte 108. The abbot at the latter monastery, Ajahn Chuchin Vimaro, teaches the same style of *vipassana* (insight meditation).

Doi Inthanon National Park
อุทยานแห่งชาติดอยอินทนนท์

Doi Inthanon (often called Doi In; 2595m), Thailand's highest peak, has four impres- sive waterfalls cascading down its slopes. Starting from the bottom, these are **Mae Ya** *(1.3km from Km1, Rte 1009)*, **Nam Tok Mae Klang** *(400m from Km7, Rte 1009; 200B)*, **Nam Tok Wachiratan** *(Km20, Rte 1009)* and **Nam Tok Siriphum** *(Km30, Rte 1009)*. The first three have picnic areas and *food ven- dors*. Nam Tok Mae Klang is the largest waterfall and the easiest to get to; you must stop here to get a bus to the top of Doi Inthanon. Nam Tok Mae Klang can be climbed nearly to the top, as there is a footbridge leading to rock formations over which the water cascades. Nam Tok Wachiratan is also very nice and less crowded.

The **Phra Mahathat Naphamethanidon** chedi, built by the Royal Thai Air Force to commemorate the king's 60th birthday in 1989, is off the highway between the Km41 and Km42 markers, about 4km before the summit of Doi Inthanon. In the base of the octagonal chedi is a hall containing a stone Buddha image.

At the summit of Doi Inthanon stands a large **shrine** built to commemorate the seventh king of Chiang Mai, Chao Inthanon (1870–97). Here you'll also find **Angka Nature Trail** near the visitors centre. The views from Inthanon are best in the cool dry season from November to February. You can expect the air to be quite chilly towards the top, so take a jacket or sweater. For most of the year a mist, formed by the condensation of warm humid air below, hangs around the highest peak. Along the 47km road to the top are many terraced rice fields, tremendous valleys and a few small hill-tribe villages. The mountain slopes are home to around 4000 Hmong and Karen tribespeople.

The entire mountain is a national park (482 sq km), despite agriculture and human habitation. One of the top destinations in Southeast Asia for naturalists and birdwatchers, the mist-shrouded upper slopes produce a bumper crop of orchids, lichens, mosses and epiphytes, while supporting nearly 400 bird varieties, more than any other habitat in Thailand. The mountain is also one of the last habitats of the Asiatic black bear, along with the Assamese macaque, Phayre's leaf-monkey and a selection of other rare and not-so-rare monkeys and gibbons, plus the more common Indian civet, barking deer and giant flying squirrel – around 75 mammalian species in all.

Most of the park's bird species are found between 1500m and 2000m; the best **birdwatching** season is from February to April,

and the best spots are the beung (bogs) near the top.

The 200B entry fee for foreigners collected for Nam Tok Mae Klang near the foot of the mountain is good for all stops on the Doi Inthanon circuit; be sure to keep your receipt.

Places to Stay *Little Home Guest House* (☎ *053 311 475, Km7, Rte 1192)* Rooms with bathroom 200B. Near the entrance to the National Park, just before the junction for Nam Tok Mae Klang and about 40km before the summit of Doi Inthanon, Little Home features simple motel-like rooms. There are a couple of other similar guesthouses in this vicinity.

Near the park headquarters (past the Chom Thong park entrance, 31km from Chom Thong) you'll find *forestry service bungalows,* with three-person/10-person bungalows for 800/2500B, and tents for 40B. For reservations, call National Park Division at the Royal Forest Department (☎ 025 797 223, 025 795 734). Reservations are advisable for weekends and long Thai holidays such as Songkran. Without reservations you can usually get a bed for 100B to 150B per person.

In Chom Thong, inquire at the *wát* for a place to sleep.

Mae Chaem (Mae Jaem)
แม่แจ่ม

Isolated until recently by long, semi-tortuous drives along dirt roads, Mae Chaem is now linked to the rest of Northern Thailand by sealed two-lane roads from Hot to the southeast and Doi Inthanon to the east. Although Mae Chaem receives only a small trickle of tourists so far – most of them Thai scholars or culture hounds interested in what may be one of the most well-preserved Lanna cultural 'islands' in the North – there's little doubt that this will change as Mae Chaem becomes better known.

Set in a narrow valley formed by Mae Chaem, the district is inhabited by a mixture of Northern Thai, Lawa and Sgaw Karen peoples. The Buddhists in the district

Black Swan Weaving

Mae Chaem weavers rely heavily on animal motifs when decorating *sîn tiin jòk*, particularly horses, elephants and the *hŏng* (Pali-Sanskrit: *hamsa*), a mythical swan sometimes identified with the Brahminy duck, the animals most associated with the Buddhist *jataka* (tales of the Buddha's past lives). The most difficult animal to weave is the *hŏng dam* (black swan). Once a weaver has learned to weave this motif, it is said, she has mastered the art of weaving and is an adult.

adhere to a unique set of Northern Thai customs no longer followed elsewhere in the North. During Songkran (Thai lunar New Year), for example, they launch sizable bamboo rafts, bedecked with flowers, tall reeds and star-like clusters of trimmed banana leaves, into Mae Chaem as a way of jettisoning the bad luck of the past year.

Mae Chaem also has a distinct weaving tradition, for which it is famous throughout Thailand. Of the several villages in the district where you can see weaving in action, the best choice is the Lawa and Northern Thai village of **Ban Thong Fai,** about 1km southeast of the *amphoe meuang* (district capital). A couple of shops in the district capital also sell local textiles, especially *sîn tiin jòk*, the highly decorative end-pieces for the traditional Northern Thai women's sarong.

Three wát in Mae Chaem are worth visiting for their Lanna-style features. **Wat Pa Daet** has a unique 1877 wíhăan built of timber posts alternating with plaster walls, an ancient building technique brought by the Thai Lü to Northern Thailand from Sipsongpanna in southern Yunnan, China. Note the narrow door, fitted between two posts, in a corner towards the back of the building, where the monks enter when there are many lay people present. The interior walls of the wíhăan are painted with Northern Thai–style folk murals along the upper half (for a discussion of the murals, see the special section 'Lanna-Style Temple Murals'). Outside, the barge-boards boast

naga motifs. A new bòt near the monastery entrance will contain Lanna-style murals by renowned Northern Thai artist Ajahn Dhamnu Haripitak. A small **weavers cooperative** on the wát grounds offers locally woven cotton and silk textiles for sale at very good prices.

The bòt at **Wat Yang Luang** boasts a large seated bronze Buddha in the Lanna style. Behind the Buddha stands a *khítchákùut* (a structure resembling a stupa, but with many more reliefs than the average stupa). Made of brick and stucco, it's covered in highly ornate stucco relief that combines Burmese and Lanna influences. There is a weavers cooperative across from the wát.

Wat Phuttha En features a rare wooden bòt on stilts in the middle of a pond.

Places to Stay & Eat So far there are only two places to stay in Mae Chaem.

Mae Chaem Hotel (Rte 1192) Rooms with shared/private bathroom 100/200B. In the district capital itself, this place is nothing to write home about, but if you're travelling by public transport it's the only place convenient to the bus stop.

Navasoung Resort (☎ 053 828 477, Rte 1192) Bungalows with fan & hot water 500B. The A-frame bungalows here are built on a slope with views of the valley. The resort is about 3km outside of town on the road to Doi Inthanon. If you have your own wheels, this is the better choice.

Navasoung Restaurant Dishes 25-75B. Open 8am-10pm daily. At the bungalows of the same name, this restaurant serves fairly good standard Thai and Chinese dishes.

There are a few *noodle stands* in the district capital of Mae Chaem.

Nong Sen Dishes 30-80B. Open 11am-11pm daily. This outdoor restaurant on a pond on the outskirts of town has individual thatched-roof shelters with wooden tables. The menu offers Northern, Northeastern and Central Thai food. It's a better choice than the noodle stands.

Getting There & Away

Buses to Chom Thong (23B, 58km) leave regularly from just inside Pratu Chiang Mai at the southern moat as well as from the Chang Pheuak bus terminal in Chiang Mai. Some buses go directly to Nam Tok Mae Klang and some go only as far as Hot, although the latter will let you off in Chom Thong.

From Chom Thong there are regular săwngthăew to Mae Klang (15B), about 8km north. Săwngthăew from Mae Klang to Doi Inthanon (30B) leave almost hourly until late afternoon. Most of the passengers are locals who get off at various points along the road, thus allowing a few stationary views of the valleys below.

For another 15B you can go from Chom Thong to Hot, where you can get buses on to Mae Sariang or Mae Hong Son. However, if you've gone to Doi Inthanon and the waterfalls, you probably won't have time to make it all the way to Mae Sariang or Mae Hong Son in one day, so you may want to stay overnight in the park or in Chom Thong.

Mae Chaem Before reaching the Inthanon summit, Rte 1192 splits west off Rte 1009 at Km38 and reaches the picturesque district of Mae Chaem after 22km. For the first few kilometres the road passes through beautiful primary and secondary forestlands.

Yellow săwngthăew go between Chom Thong and Mae Chaem, over Doi Inthanon.

NORTH TO THA TON
Mae Taeng & Chiang Dao
แม่แตง/เชียงดาว

The mountainous area around Mae Taeng in Chiang Mai Province – especially southwest of the junction of Rtes 107 and 1095 – has become a major trekking area because of the Lisu, Lahu, Karen and Hmong villages in the region.

Rafting along Mae Taeng is also popular. **Maetamann Rafting & Elephant Camp** (☎ 053 297 060, 053 297 283, fax 053 297 283, 535 Rim Tai, Mae Rim, off Rte 107; rafting/elephant rides 200/600B per hour) offers daytime bamboo rafting along the river as well as elephant rides, either separately or in combination. The elephant rides

operate from 8am until 3pm, rafting from 8am to 4pm. For the most part, the centre handles rafting groups on trips out of Chiang Mai.

The **Elephant Training Centre Taeng-Dao** (Km56, Rte 107, between Mae Taeng and Chiang Dao; adult/child 60/30B) is another centre in the area that puts on elephant shows for tourists. Shows are at 9am and 10am daily. If you haven't seen the one in Lampang Province (in Thung Kwian – see Around Lampang later in this chapter), this one's a reasonable alternative.

From the main four-way junction at Chiang Dao, those with their own wheels – preferably a mountain bike, motorcycle or truck – can head east to visit **Lahu**, **Lisu** and **Akha villages** within a 15km ride. Roughly 13.5km from Rte 107 is the Lisu village of **Lisu Huay Ko**, where rustic **accommodation** is available.

Fang Dao Forest Monastery, off the highway south of Chiang Dao near the 52km marker, is a meditation wát in the Northeastern forest tradition.

Tham Chiang Dao The main attraction along the way to Fang and Tha Ton is this **cave complex** (5B). It's located 5km west of Rte 107 and 72km north of Chiang Mai.

The complex is said to extend some 10km to 14km into 2285m-high Doi Chiang Dao; the interconnected caverns that are open to the public include **Tham Mah** (7365m long), **Tham Kaew** (477m), **Tham Phra Nawn** (360m), **Tham Seua Dao** (540m) and **Tham Nam** (660m).

Tham Phra Nawn and Tham Seua Dao contain religious statuary and are electrically illuminated (and thus easily explored on one's own), while Tham Mah, Tham Kaew and Tham Nam have no light fixtures. A guide with a pressurised gas lantern can be hired for 60B for up to eight people. The interior cave formations are quite spectacular in places – over 100 of them are named.

Local legend says this cave complex was the home of a reusĭi (hermit) for a thousand years. As the legend goes, the sage was on such intimate terms with the deity world that he convinced some thewádaa (the Buddhist equivalent of angels) to create seven magic wonders inside the caverns: a stream flowing from the pedestal of a solid-gold Buddha; a storehouse of divine textiles; a mystical lake; a city of naga; a sacred immortal elephant; and the hermit's tomb. No, you won't find any of the seven wonders; the locals say these are much deeper inside the mountain, beyond the last of the illuminated caverns.

The locals also say that anyone who attempts to remove a piece of rock from the cave will forever lose their way in the cave's eerie passages.

There is a wát complex outside the cavern and a collection of *vendors* selling roots, herbs and snacks (mostly noodles).

The surrounding area is quite scenic and largely unspoiled. From the summit of Doi Chiang Dao there are spectacular views. Beyond Tham Chiang Dao along the same rural road is a smaller sacred cave called **Tham Pha Plong**.

Places to Stay & Eat *Malee's Nature Lovers Bungalows (☎ 01-961 8387, 114/2 Mu 5)* Dorm beds/bungalows 80/300B. About 1.5km past Tham Chiang Dao on the right, under Thai and German management, is Malee's. The thatch-and-brick bungalows, most with a view of Doi Chiang Dao, have private cold-water showers; separate, shared hot-water showers are available. Malee's can arrange trekking, rafting and bird-watching trips in the area.

Pieng Dao Hotel (☎ 053 232 434, Ban Chiang Dao, Rte 107) Singles/doubles with shared cold-water bathroom 100/150B, rooms with private bathroom 200B. This is one of the last old wooden hotels operating in the North.

Chiang Dao Hill Resort (☎ 053 234 995, 053 232 434, Km100.5, Rte 107) Bungalows 900-1800B. This place has good tourist bungalows. A restaurant on the premises is open 7am to 10pm.

Getting There & Away Buses to Chiang Dao (25B, 1½ hours) from Chiang Mai's Chang Pheuak terminal depart every 30 minutes between 5.30am and 5.30pm.

WIANG HAENG TO DOI ANG KHANG

An interesting side excursion to make from the Chiang Dao area, especially if you're continuing on to Tha Ton, is the road to Wiang Haeng, Piang Luang and Doi Ang Khang off Hwy 107. This is a trip best done under your own steam, either by bicycle, motorcycle or car, but there is public transport as far as Wiang Haeng and Piang Luang.

Between the turn-off on Hwy 107 and Wiang Haeng you'll pass several Lisu, Lahu and Yunnanese Muslim villages.

Wiang Haeng & Piang Luang
เวียงแหง/เปียงหลวง

Approximately 54km from Hwy 107, via Rtes 1178 and 1322, Wiang Haeng is part of a mountain valley district that consists of a variety of peoples, including Shan, Yunnanese, Northern Thais, Lisu and Lahu. There is sufficient arable land to grow rice in the area, and the villages seem more prosperous than one might expect.

Wiang Haeng's claim to fame a decade or more ago was that the Shan States Army rebels printed their propaganda newspapers here and maintained a large military camp nearby.

Of more interest to the occasional visitor is the little Shan mountain town of Piang Luang farther along Rte 1322. Cool any time of year – cold in December and January – it's amusing to roam Piang Luang's winding streets, visit the market and local Shan-style Buddhist monasteries. At **Wat Piang Luang** the monks teach courses in Chinese, Shan, English and Thai.

A couple of kilometres beyond Piang Luang is the Myanmar border. The Thai side of the border is known as Ban Lak Taeng; the small town on the Myanmar side is Kam Ko.

Between Wiang Haeng and Piang Luang, in the village of Ban Nong Jong Kham, the very picturesque **Wat Nong Jong Kham** sits atop a forested hillock with views of rice fields below.

Places to Stay & Eat *Khum Wiang Haeng (☎ 053 477 177, Bang Kong Long,*

Wiang Haeng) Bungalows 500B. This place is about 3km past Wiang Haeng on the way to Piang Luang, in the village of Ban Kong Long. The large bungalows are fairly clean and serviceable but it would be considered rather expensive if it weren't the only place to stay anywhere near Wiang Haeng. A small attached restaurant serves standard Thai dishes.

Piang Luang Guesthouse *(Piang Luang, Wiang Haeng)* Rooms with fan & cold-water/hot-water bathroom 200/250B, with air-con 350B. In Piang Luang, this is a long row-house affair with decent all-cement rooms, each with two beds, a mirror and private facilities. There's no restaurant service. This is the only place to stay in Piang Luang to date.

You'll find a few *noodle shops* on the main street through town, but your best choice for most meals, as anyone in Piang Luang will tell you, is ***Bua Jin Phochana***, with dishes for 25B to 50B. It's open 7am to 9pm daily and serves surprisingly good Thai food. Half the shop is a *ráan cham* (sundries store), with all manner of tinned foods, toiletries and other necessities for maintaining a low-key household.

Getting There & Away A large săwngthăew travels between Chiang Mai and Piang Luang (70B, four hours) three times per day – early morning, late morning and mid-afternoon. It continues on to Piang Luang for an extra 10B.

If you're making your own way, note that Rte 1178 veers north-north-west off Hwy 107 at Km75. Then after exactly 19km, you should bear left onto Rte 1322, which leads to Wiang Haeng and Piang Luang. Fuel is scarce in the area, so be sure to fill up at the single petrol station in Wiang Haeng, whether you're coming or going.

Doi Ang Khang
ดอยอ่างขาง

About 20km before Fang is the turn-off for Rte 1249 to Doi Ang Khang, Thailand's 'Little Switzerland'. Twenty-five kilometres from the highway, this 1300m peak has a cool climate year-round and supports the cultivation of flowers, as well as fruits and vegetables that are usually found only in more temperate climates.

A few **hill-tribe villages** (Lahu, Lisu and Hmong) can be visited on the slopes. You can pick up a free map of the area at the main military checkpoint on Rte 1249.

Nineteen kilometres before the turn-off to Doi Ang Khang you can make a 12km detour west on a dirt road to visit **Ban Mai Nong Bua**, an ex-KMT village with an atmosphere like that of Doi Mae Salong (see the Eastern Provinces chapter).

Another way to reach Doi Ang Khang is from the direction of Wiang Haeng via Rtes 1178 and 1340. This brings you onto the mountain from the west, via Ban Arunothai. The scenery is particularly striking along this route, with lots of steep, forested limestone cliffs. You'll also pass more hill-tribe and Yunnanese Muslim villages.

Places to Stay & Eat Near the summit of Doi Ang Khang, near the Yunnanese village of Ban Khum, there are several places to stay. Most of them consist of relatively modest A-frame bungalows positioned along a hillside, such as ***Lung Kiat Chok Chai*** and ***Suwannaphum***, all charging from 100B for a very basic room with shared shower and toilet to 300B for a nicer one with private facilities.

Naha Guest House (☎ *053 450 008, Ban Khum, Tambon Mae Ngan, Fang)* 6/10-person bungalows 1500/2000B, or per person 100B. This place is also near the summit of Doi Ang Khang. Each of the bungalows here has shared hot-water shower and toilet.

Angkhang Nature Resort (☎ *053 450 110, fax 053 450 120, e angkhang@ amari.com, 1/1 Mu 5, Ban Khum, Tambon Mae Ngan, Fang)* Rooms 3300-3660B, from 20 Dec-10 Jan 4600-4240B. Part of the Amari Hotel Group, this unexpectedly plush hotel features large, tastefully designed bungalows spread out over a slope. There is a good restaurant on the premises.

[continued on page 216]

TREKKING IN NORTHERN THAILAND

Thousands of foreign travellers each year take part in treks into the hills of the North. Most come away with a sense of adventure, but there are a few who are disillusioned by the experience. The most important ingredient in a good trek is having a good leader/organiser, followed by a good group of trekkers – some travellers finish a tour complaining more about the other trekkers than about the itinerary, food or trek leader.

Before Trekking

Hill-tribe trekking isn't for everyone. Firstly, you must be physically fit to cope with the demands of sustained up-and-down walking, exposure to the elements and spotty food. Secondly, many people feel awkward walking through hill-tribe villages and playing the role of voyeur.

In cities and villages elsewhere in Thailand people are quite used to foreign faces and foreign ways (from TV if nothing else), but in the hills of Northern Thailand the tribes lead largely insular lives. Hence, hill-tribe tourism has pronounced effects, both positive and negative. On the positive side, travellers have a chance to see how traditional subsistence-oriented societies function. (See the 'People of Northern Thailand' special section.) Also, since the Thai government is sensitive about the image of their minority groups, tourism may actually have forced it to review, and sometimes improve, its policies on hill tribes. Hill tribespeople also have little opportunity to travel internationally, and visitation by foreigners thus offers hill-tribe villages a small window to the outside world. On the negative side, trekkers introduce many cultural items and ideas from the outside world that may erode tribal customs to varying degrees.

If you have any qualms about interrupting the traditional patterns of life in hill-tribe areas, you probably should not go trekking. It is undeniable that trekking in Northern Thailand is marketed like soap or any other commodity. Anyone who promises you an authentic experience is probably exaggerating at the very least, or at worst contributing to the decline of hill-tribe culture by leading travellers into untouristed areas.

Choosing a Company

Because of the inherent instability of the trekking business, it's difficult to make specific recommendations for particular trekking companies in Chiang Mai. Many of the trekking guides are freelance and go from one company to the next, so there's no way to predict which companies are going to give the best service at any one time. Many guesthouses that advertise their own trekking companies actually act as brokers for off-site operations; they collect a commission for every guest they book into a trek.

The Tourism Authority of Thailand (TAT) office in Chiang Mai (☎ 053 248 604) maintains and distributes a list of licensed agencies. It is also making efforts to regulate trekking companies operating out of Chiang Mai and recommends that you trek only with members of the Professional Guide Association of Chiang Mai or the Jungle Tour Club of Northern Thailand. Still, with more than 150 companies, it's very difficult to guarantee any kind of control. Ultimately the best way to shop for a trek is to talk to travellers who have just returned from one.

If you decide to do a trek keep these points in mind: Choose your trek operator carefully; try to meet the others in the group (suggest a meeting); and find out exactly what the tour includes and does not include, as usually there are additional expenses beyond the basic rate. In the cool season, make sure sleeping bags are provided, as the thin woollen blankets available in most villages are not sufficient for the average visitor. If everything works out, even an organised tour can be worthwhile. A useful check list of questions to ask includes:

- How many people will there be in the group? (Six to 10 is a good maximum range.)
- Can the organiser guarantee that no other tourists will visit the same village on the same day, especially overnight?
- Can the guide speak the language of each village to be visited? (This is not always necessary, as many villagers can speak Thai nowadays.)
- Exactly when does the tour begin and end? (Some three-day treks turn out to be less than 48 hours in length.)
- Does the organiser provide transport before and after the trek or is it just by public bus (which may mean long waits)?

In general, the trekking business has become more conscious of the need to tread carefully in hill-tribe villages than in previous decades. Most companies now tend to limit the number of visits to a particular area and are careful not to overlap areas used by other companies. Everyone benefits from this consciousness: There is less impact on hill tribes by trekkers, the trekkers have a better experience, and the trekking industry runs at a sustainable rate. Opium-smoking among guides continues to be a problem with some companies: A few companies are now advertising drug-free treks to avoid the pitfalls of opium-addicted guides and also to avoid the adverse influence the sight of constant opium-smoking has on young hill-tribe members.

cc

These days there are plenty of places apart from Chiang Mai where you can arrange treks, including Chiang Rai, Mae Hong Son, Pai, Mae Sai and Tha Ton. If you have a little time to seek out the right people, you can also go on organised treks from Mae Sariang, Khun Yuam,

Soppong (near Pai), Mae Sot, Um Phang and various out-of-the-way guesthouses that are springing up all over the North. You might find organisations in these places offer better and less-expensive tours from more remote and less-trekked areas. Also, they are generally smaller, friendlier operations and the trekkers are usually a more determined bunch since they're not looking for an easy and quick in-and-out trek. The treks are often informally arranged, usually involving discussions of duration, destination, cost etc.

The down side, of course, is that companies outside of Chiang Mai are generally subject to even less regulation than those in Chiang Mai, and there are fewer guarantees with regard to trekking terms and conditions.

Costs

Organised treks out of Chiang Mai average from 1800B to 2000B for a three-day, two-night trek, to 6000B to 7000B for a deluxe seven-day, six-night trek, both of which include transport, guide, accommodation, meals and rafting and/or elephant riding. Rates vary, so it pays to shop around – although so many companies are competing for your business that rates have remained pretty stable for the last few years. Elephant rides actually become quite boring and even uncomfortable after an hour or two. Some companies now offer quickie day treks or one-night, two-day programs.

Don't choose by price alone. It's better to talk to other travellers in town who have been on treks. Treks out of other towns in the North are usually less expensive than those from Chiang Mai.

The Professional Guide Association in Chiang Mai meets monthly to set trek prices and to discuss problems, and issues regular, required reports to the TAT about individual treks. All trekking guides and companies are supposed to be government-licensed and bonded. As a result, a standard for trekking operators has emerged whereby you can expect the price you pay to include: transport to and from the starting/ending points of a trek (if outside Chiang Mai); food (three meals a day) and accommodation in all villages visited; basic first aid; predeparture valuables storage; and sometimes the loan of specific equipment, such as sleeping bags in cool weather or water bottles.

Not included in the price are beverages other than drinking water or tea, lunch on the first and last days and personal porters.

Seasons

Probably the best time to do your trekking is November to February, when the weather is refreshing with little or no rain and poppies are in bloom everywhere. Between March and May the hills become dry and the weather is quite hot. The second-best time is early in the rainy season, between June and July, before the dirt roads become too saturated.

Safety

Every year or so there's a trekking robbery or two in Northern Thailand – the likelihood of this occurring to you is low. However, if it does happen keep in mind that often the bandits are armed with guns, which they will use if they meet resistance. Once they collect a load of money, cameras and jewellery, many bandit gangs hightail it across the border into Myanmar. In spite of this, police have had a good arrest record so far and have created hill-country patrols. One problem is that most people living in the rural North believe that all foreigners are very rich (a fair assumption in relation to hill-tribe living standards). Most of these people have never even

cc

been to Chiang Mai and, from what they have heard about the capital, consider Bangkok to be a virtual paradise of wealth. So don't take anything that you can't afford to lose, and don't resist robbery attempts.

If you leave your valuables with a guesthouse, make sure you obtain a fully itemised receipt before departing on a trek.

Conduct

There are several guidelines for minimising the negative impact your trekking may have on the local people:

- Always ask for permission before taking photos of tribespeople and/or their dwellings. You can ask through your guide or by using sign language. Because of traditional belief systems, many individuals and even whole tribes may object strongly to being photographed.

- Show respect for religious symbols and rituals. Don't touch totems at village entrances or any other object of obvious symbolic value without asking permission. Keep your distance from ceremonies being performed unless you're asked to participate.

- Exercise restraint in giving things to tribespeople or bartering with them. If you want to give something to the people you encounter on a trek, the best thing is to make a donation to the village school or other community fund. Your guide can help arrange this. While it's an easy way to get a smile, giving sweets to children contributes to tooth decay – remember they probably don't have toothbrushes and toothpaste like you do.

- Set a good example for hill-tribe youngsters by not smoking opium or using other drugs.

- Don't litter while trekking or staying in villages.

You might also want to check W www.lanna.com for 'Guidelines for Visitors to Northern Thailand's Mountain Peoples'.

Opium Smoking

Some guides are very strict now about forbidding the smoking of opium on treks. This seems to be a good idea, since one of the problems

trekking companies have had in the past is dealing with opium-addicted guides! Volunteers who work in tribal areas also say opium smoking sets a bad example for young people in the villages.

Opium is traditionally a condoned vice of the elderly, yet an increasing number of young people in the villages are now taking opium, heroin and amphetamines. This is possibly due in part to the influence of young trekkers who may smoke once and a few weeks later be hundreds of kilometres away, while villagers continue to face the temptation every day. Addiction has negative effects for the village as well as the individual's health, including a reduced male labour force (most addicts are men) and corresponding increase in women's workloads, and reduced overall agricultural production. Also, an increase in the number of villagers injecting heroin (needles are often shared) has led to sky-rocketing rates of HIV infection in hill-tribe villages. Given the already high incidence of HIV infection among Northern Thai prostitutes, some welfare groups say that entire tribal communities will be wiped out unless the rate of infection can be stopped.

Independent Trekking

You might consider striking out on your own in a small group of two to five people. Gather as much information as you can about the area you'd like to trek in from the Tribal Museum in Chiang Mai. Browsing the displays will help you identify different tribes, and the inscriptions offer cultural information. Don't bother staff with questions about trekking, as this is not their area of expertise. Maps, distributed mostly by guesthouses outside of Chiang Mai, pinpoint various hill-tribe areas in the North.

Be prepared for language difficulties. Few people will know any English. Usually someone in a village will know some Thai, so a Thai phrasebook can be helpful. Lonely Planet publishes the *Hill Tribes phrasebook*, with phrase sections for each of the six major hill-tribe languages.

As with Himalayan trekking in Nepal and India, many people in Northern Thailand do short treks on their own, staying in villages along the way. It is not necessary to bring a lot of food or equipment, just money for food that can be bought en route at small Thai towns and occasionally in hill-tribe settlements. Obviously, be sure to take plenty of water and some high-energy snacks. Note that the TAT strongly discourages trekking on your own because of the safety risk. Check with the police when you arrive in a new district so they can tell you if an area is considered safe or not. A lone trekker is an easy target for robbers.

{continued from page 210}

At the base of the slope studded with cheaper bungalows are a couple of *open-air restaurants* serving a variety of dishes with an emphasis on Thai and Yunnanese Muslim food.

In Ban Ma Luang, a Yunnanese village about 4km before the summit, is *Khao Soi Yunnan,* with khâo sawy (noodles) for 20B. It's open 9am to 6pm daily. This place serves real Yunnanese khâo sawy, ie, the broth contains no coconut milk. It also makes excellent *salabao* (steamed Chinese buns) filled with red bean paste.

FANG & THA TON
ฝาง/ท่าตอน

The present city of Fang was founded by Phaya Mang Rai in the 13th century, although as a settlement and trading centre for jiin haw caravans the locale dates back at least 1000 years.

Information
Two banks along the main street in Fang offer currency exchange. Near the bridge is a Tourist Police office open 8.30am to 4.30pm daily.

Things to See
From Rte 107, Fang doesn't look particularly inviting, but the town's quiet backstreets are lined with interesting little shops in wooden buildings. The Shan/Burmese-style **Wat Jong Paen** (near the Wiang Kaew Hotel) has a very impressive stacked-roof wíhǎan.

There are **Mien** and **Karen villages** nearby that you can visit on your own, but for most people Fang is just a road marker on the way to Tha Ton, the starting point for Mae Nam Kok trips to Chiang Rai, and for treks to the many hill-tribe settlements in the region. Most people prefer Tha Ton's more rural setting for spending the night. It's only half an hour or so by săwngthăew to the river from Fang or vice versa.

Through the Wiang Kaew Hotel in Fang you can arrange **tours to local villages** inhabited by Palaung (a Karennic tribe that

arrived from Myanmar around 18 years ago), Black Lahu, Akha and Yunnanese.

About 10km west of Fang at Ban Meuang Chom, near the agricultural station, is a system of **hot springs**, part of Doi Fang National Park. Just ask for the *bàw náam ráwn* (*baw nâam hâwn* in Northern Thai). On weekends there are frequent săwngthăew bringing Thai picnickers from Fang.

Tha Ton has a săwngthăew stand and a collection of river boats, restaurants, souvenir shops and tourist accommodation along a pretty bend in Mae Nam Kok. Climb the hill to **Wat Tha Ton** and the **Chinese shrine** for good views of the surrounding area. A large temple bell, which sounds every morning at 4am (wake-up call for monks) and again at 6am (alms-round call) can be heard throughout the valley surrounding Tha Ton.

Trekking & Rafting
There are some pleasant walks along Mae Nam Kok. Within 20km of Fang and Tha Thon you can visit Lahu and Palaung villages on foot, mountain bike or motorcycle.

Treks and raft trips can be arranged through **Thip's Travellers House** *(3-day raft trips 1800B per person, min 4 people)*. It uses bamboo house-rafts and the price includes all meals, lodging and rafting. Other places that can arrange trips are Mae Kok River Village Resort and the Thaton River View. All three are in Tha Ton.

On the first day you'll visit several villages near the river and spend the night in a Lisu village; on the second day rafters visit hot springs and more villages, and spend the second night on the raft; and on the third day you dock in Chiang Rai.

You could get a small group of travellers together and arrange your own house-raft with a guide and cook for a two- or three-day journey down river, stopping off in villages of your choice along the way. A house-raft generally costs 500B to 600B per person per day, including simple meals, and takes up to six people – so figure on 1500B to 1800B for a three-day trip. Police regulations require that an experienced boat navigator accompany each raft – the river has lots of tricky spots and there have been some mishaps.

Near the pier you can rent inflatable kayaks to do your own **paddling** in the area. Upstream a few kilometres the river crosses into Myanmar.

Places to Stay & Eat

Fang *Wiang Kaew Hotel (☎ 053 451 046, 22 Thanon Sai Rattabat)* Rooms with private bathroom 120-180B. In Fang there isn't much choice in the way of accommodation. On the budget end, Wiang Kaew Hotel is your best choice. The rooms are basic but clean; the higher priced ones have hot water.

Ueng Khum Hotel (UK Hotel; ☎ 053 451 268, 227 Thanon Tha Phae) Singles/doubles with fan 140/170B, rooms with air-con 350B. Around the corner from the Wiang Kaew, this place offers large bungalow-style accommodation around a courtyard. All rooms have hot-water showers.

Chok Thani (☎ 053 451 252, 425 Thanon Chotana) Rooms with air-con & private bathroom 290-450B. Near the market on the highway, slightly more upmarket digs are available here.

Fang Restaurant (Khun Pa, Thanon Sai Rattabat) Dishes 20-50B. Open 7am-9pm daily. Next to the defunct Fang Hotel entrance stands the Fang Restaurant, with a bilingual menu and quite decent food, including the speciality of the house, *khâo mǔu daeng* (barbecued pork over rice).

Parichat Restaurant (Thanon Rop Wiang Nok) Dishes 25-45B. Open 8am-8pm daily. Near the highway market, Parichat serves khâo sàwy with chicken or beef, plus *kǔaytǐaw* (rice noodles), *khâo phàt* (fried rice) and other standards.

Farther down this same road is a row of cheap *Isan restaurants* and *lâo dawng* (herbal liquor) bars.

A few *food vendors* – not quite enough to make a true 'night market' – set up near the bus terminal at night.

Tha Ton If you want to spend the night near the pier in Tha Ton, there are several options.

Thip's Travellers House (☎ 053 495 312, fax 053 495 312, 1/7 Thanon Tha Phae) Rooms without/with bathroom 80/100B. A short walk from the pier, quite near the bridge where the road from Fang meets the river, is this old standby. The walls are thin and the water is cold, but there's a nice little cafe out front.

AROUND CHIANG MAI

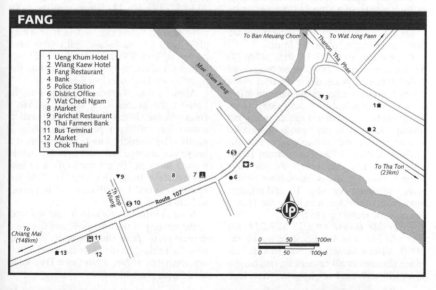

FANG

1 Ueng Khum Hotel
2 Wiang Kaew Hotel
3 Fang Restaurant
4 Bank
5 Police Station
6 District Office
7 Wat Chedi Ngam
8 Market
9 Parichat Restaurant
10 Thai Farmers Bank
11 Bus Terminal
12 Market
13 Chok Thani

To Ban Meuang Chom
To Wat Jong Paen
Thanon Tha Phae
Mae Nam Fang
To Tha Ton (23km)
'n Rop Wiang
Route 107
To Chiang Mai (148km)
0 50 100m
0 50 100yd

Chan Kasem (☎ *053 459 313, 209 Mu 3*) Rooms in older wooden section 80B, singles/ doubles with fan & bathroom 100B, rooms with hot water 150-250B, brick bungalow 300B. Chan Kasem is down near the pier. The rooms are none too clean but all have private bathrooms, except for those in the older wooden section. Chan Kasem has a restaurant on the river. Nearby is the friendly ***Naam Waan Guest House*** *(Thanon Tha Phae)*, with 10 tidy rooms, all with fan and cold-water shower, for 150B.

Apple Guest House *(Thanon Tha Phae)* Rooms with hot-water shower 300B, with small TV 400B. Opposite the boat landing in a new, two-storey building is this guest-house with an upmarket restaurant on the ground floor and spacious light-filled rooms above. Credit-card symbols on the front door seem to be merely decorative, as this place only accepts cash.

Maekok River Village Resort (☎ *053 459 355, fax 053 459 329,* [W] *www.track-of-the-tiger.com*) Pool-side suite 2250B, family villa 3250B. This newish place lies farther along the river. On the grounds are a pool and restaurant. A variety of activities, in-cluding massage, cooking classes, trekking, rafting, mountain biking and caving can be arranged through the resort.

On the opposite side of the river there are three other places to choose from.

Garden Home (☎ *053 373 015, 14 Mu 14*) Thatch bungalows 300B, stone bungalows 500-800B. This place, along the river about 150m from the bridge, is tranquil and offers very clean thatched-roof bungalows (with private hot-water shower) spaced well apart among lots of litchi trees and bougainvillea – most visitors will probably agree that this is the best deal in Tha Ton. Garden Home also offers a few stone bungalows and three larger, more luxurious bungalows on the river with small verandas, TV and refriger-ator. From the bridge, turn left at the Thaton River View Hotel sign to find it.

Riverside House (☎ *053 373 214, fax 053 373 215, 134 Mu 14*) Rooms with fan 300B, air-con bungalows 500-1000B. This place features small cement air-con bunga-lows with terraces back from the river, less-

expensive fan rooms in a cement building also back off the river and a couple of large air-con wooden bungalows with terraces right on the river. All rates include break-fast. The grounds are beautifully land-scaped, and an attached restaurant overlooks the river.

Thaton River View Hotel (☎ *053 373 173, fax 053 459 288, 302 Mu 14*) Rooms 1320B. This well-designed hotel is farther along the river, and has 33 immaculate, spa-cious rooms facing the water, joined by wooden walkways. Rates include breakfast (better value at this price than Maekok River Lodge). The hotel's restaurant is the best in the area, with Shell Chuan Chim honours (see the boxed text 'Northern Style' in the Facts for the Visitor chapter) for four differ-ent dishes on the menu. Facilities include a herbal sauna, massage, safe-deposit boxes, library, game room and jogging track.

Thaton Garden Riverside (☎ *053 459 286, 229 Mu 14*) Bungalows 300-400B. Also on the river, Thaton Garden offers good bungalows with fans and hot-water showers. The attached Rim Nam Restaurant is good.

Thaton Chalet (☎ *053 373 155, fax 053 373 158, 142 Mu 14*) Superior rooms 800-960B, deluxe rooms 1600B. Right on the river next to the bridge is this four-storey place with a stone facade. All rooms have carpet, air-con, TV and hot water. The hotel features a pleasant beer garden right on the river, as well as an indoor restaurant.

About 15km northeast of Tha Ton, in Lou-Ta, the nearest Lisu village, is ***Asa's Guest Home***. It has basic bamboo-walled rooms for 150B per person, including 2 meals. The friendly family who owns the house can arrange one- and two-day jungle trips in the area. To get here, take a yellow săwngthăew from Tha Ton for 15B (or motorcycle taxi for 30B) and ask to get off in Lou-Ta.

Several little ***noodle stands*** can be found in the vicinity of the bus queue and there are several rustic ***food stalls*** near the pier and near the bridge. At the latter the local culin-ary speciality is *lûu,* a Northern Thai salad made with pig's blood.

Getting There & Away

Bus & Săwngthăew Buses to Fang (61B, 3½ hours) leave from the Chang Pheuak bus terminal (☎ 053 211 586) in Chiang Mai every 30 minutes between 5.30am and 5.30pm. Air-con minivans (80B) make the trip to Fang every 30 minutes between 7.30am and 4.30pm, leaving from behind the Chang Pheuak bus terminal on the corner of Soi Sanam Kila.

From Fang it's 23km to Tha Ton. A săwngthăew does the 40-minute trip for 12B; the larger orange buses from Fang (12B) leave less frequently. Buses leave from near the market, or you can wait in front of the Fang Hotel for a bus or săwngthăew. Both operate from 5.30am to 5pm only.

Buses to Mae Sai (see the Eastern Provinces chapter) cost 36B from Tha Ton, 45B from Fang.

The river isn't the only way to get to points north from Tha Ton. Yellow săwngthăew leave for Mae Salong (50B, 2½ hours) in Chiang Rai Province every 30 minutes or so between 7am and 3pm from the northern side of the river in Tha Ton. You can charter an entire săwngthăew for 450/650B one way/return. Hold tight – the road is steep and winding.

If you're heading to or coming from Mae Hong Son Province, it's not necessary to dip all the way south to Chiang Mai before continuing westward or eastward. At Ban Mae Malai, the junction of Rte 107 (the Chiang Mai–Fang highway), you can pick up a bus to Pai for 45B; if you're coming from Pai, be sure to get off here to catch a bus north to Fang.

Motorcycle Motorcycle trekkers can travel between Tha Ton and Doi Mae Salong, 48km northeast along a fully paved but sometimes treacherous mountain road. There are a couple of Lisu and Akha villages along the way. The 27km or so between Doi Mae Salong and the village of Hua Meuang Ngam are very steep and winding – take care, especially in the rainy season. When conditions are good, the trip can be accomplished in 1½ hours.

For an extra charge, you can also take a motorcycle with you on most boats to Chiang Rai.

Lamphun Province

LAMPHUN
อ.เมืองลำพูน

postcode 51000 • pop 15,200

Most often visited as a day trip from Chiang Mai, Lamphun was, along with Pasang, the centre of the small Hariphunchai principality (AD 750–1281) originally ruled by the semi-legendary Mon queen Chama Thewi, said to be the daughter of the ruler of Lopburi (Lavo). Long after its progenitor, Dvaravati, was vanquished by the Khmer, Hariphunchai succeeded in remaining independent of both the Khmer and the Chiang Mai Thais.

Around AD 1050 a cholera epidemic prompted many Mon residents to emigrate to the Mon communities of Thaton and Bago in central Myanmar. Most returned six years later; today the city still boasts a small Mon-speaking community.

This oval-shaped provincial capital, on the western bank of Nam Mae Kuang, is fairly quiet but there are a few places to stay if you're looking to get away from the hustle and bustle of Chiang Mai or study Lamphun's temples in depth. The number of historic temples in the provincial capital is many times greater than the two described here.

Away from the modern facade of the town's main street you'll also find some interesting residential architecture tucked away in the back and side streets of Lamphun, including older wooden architecture and rare Shan-style mansions.

The village just north of Lamphun, Nong Chang Kheun, is known for producing the sweetest *lam yai* (*Nephelium longana*; longan) fruit in the country. During the second week of August Lamphun hosts the annual **Lam Yai Festival**, which features floats displaying the delicious fruit and, of course, a Miss Lam Yai contest.

Wat Phra That Hariphunchai
วัดพระธาตุหริภุญชัย

This wát, which was built on the site of Queen Chama Thewi's palace in AD 1044 (or 1108 or 1157, according to some datings), is on the western side of the main road into Lamphun from Chiang Mai. The temple lay derelict for many years until Khruba Siwichai, one of Northern Thailand's most famous monks, made renovations in the 1930s. It has some interesting post-Dvaravati architecture, a couple of fine Buddha images and two old chedi of the original Hariphunchai style. The nicely landscaped grounds boast some unusual plants, most of them labelled (in Thai only).

The very impressive main stupa, **Chedi Suwan**, dates from 1418 (or 1447, according to other sources); although not built during the Hariphunchai period, it was styled after Hariphunchai models. The chedi's 46m height is surmounted by a nine-tiered umbrella made with 6.5kg of pure gold. Thais consider this to be one of the eight holiest stupas in Thailand.

Eight bronze repousse panels of walking and standing Buddha figures in the Mon style, said to date to around 1330, were affixed to the *khaw rá-khang* ('bell neck'; the slender section of the stupa dome) when it was first erected. Although a 1980 restoration obscured the Buddhas with lacquer and gilt, the faint outlines of the figures can still be seen when the sun hits the stupa at the right angle.

Another stupa on the grounds, the **Pathumawadi Chedi**, has five brick terraces with niches for Buddha figures, similar to the more famous Chedi Kukut at Wat Chama Thewi (see that entry later in this section).

One of the world's largest bronze gongs hangs in a reddish pavilion on the grounds. Towards the back of the grounds is a very nice Lanna-style *hǎw trai* (Tripitaka library), high on its whitewashed pedestal, and a small stupa labelled 'Mount Meru'.

At a small open-air woodworking **museum** occupying a corner of the wát grounds there's a display of local wood carvings, some of them very nice.

Wat Chama Thewi (Wat Kukut)
วัดจามเทวี

A more unusual Hariphunchai chedi can be seen at Wat Chama Thewi (popularly called Wat Kukut), which is said to have been erected in the 8th or 9th century as a Dvaravati monument, then rebuilt by the Hariphunchai Mon in 1218. As it has been restored many times since then it is now a mixture of several schools. The stepped profile bears a remarkable resemblance to the 12th-century Satmahal Prasada at Polonnaruwa in Sri Lanka.

Each side of the chedi – known as **Chedi Suwan Chang Kot** – has five rows of three Buddha figures, diminishing in size on each higher level. The standing Buddhas are in Dvaravati style, although made recently.

A Lanna-style chedi nearby, **Ratana Chedi**, is supposed to have been built by order of Phaya Saphasit, a local prince of the 12th century. Although in basic form it's in the Lanna style, with its octagonal base, the stepped Buddha niches bring to mind Mon handiwork.

The Stupa Wars

Between AD 1130 and 1150, the kingdoms of Hariphunchai (Lamphun) and Lavo (Lopburi) found themselves on the brink of war. The respective rulers, both devout Buddhists, decided not to attack one another with weapons but to fight a *dhammayudha* (dharma war), a contest to see which kingdom could produce more Buddhist merit in a fixed interval of time.

It was decided that the best way to demonstrate Buddhist fervour was to see which kingdom could build the most stupas. Victory alternated between both sides on three different engagements, till during the fourth the Hariphunchai King Aditta captured the Lavo army. This time Aditta ordered both armies to work together to build the Great Army Stupa (Mahabalachetiya), which many people today believe to be Chedi Kukut at Lamphun's Wat Chama Thewi.

Wat Chama Thewi is on the opposite side of town from Wat Phra That Hariphunchai. To get there, walk west down Thanon Mukda, perpendicular to the Chiang Mai–Lamphun road (opposite Wat Hari), passing over the town moat, then past the district government offices until you come to the wát on the left.

Wat Phra Yeun
วัดพระยืน

This is another 11th-century temple centred on a chedi said to have been built by the Hariphunchai Mon. In this case the stupa has only four niches, each occupied by a large standing Buddha image, the temple's namesake *(phrá yeun* means 'standing Buddha').

Wat Phra Yeun is roughly 1km east of Wat Phra That Hariphunchai, across the river.

Lamphun National Museum
พิพิธภัณฑสถานแห่งชาติลำพูน

Across the street from Wat Phra That Hariphunchai is Lamphun's National Museum (☎ *053 511 186, 053 530 536; 30B; open*

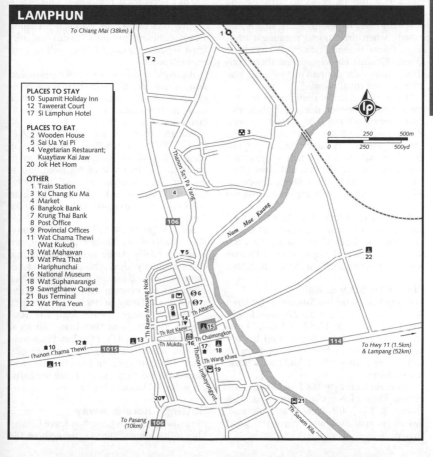

LAMPHUN

To Chiang Mai (38km)

Thanon Sar Pa Yang

Nam Mae Kuang

Thanon Rawp Meuang Nok

Th Rot Kaew

Th Mukda

Thanon Inthayongyot

Th Attarot

Th Chaimongkon

Th Wang Khwa

Th Sanam Kila

To Hwy 11 (1.5km) & Lampang (52km)

Thanon Chama Thewi

To Pasang (10km)

0   250   500m
0   250   500yd

PLACES TO STAY
10 Supamit Holiday Inn
12 Taweerat Court
17 Si Lamphun Hotel

PLACES TO EAT
2 Wooden House
5 Sai Ua Yai Pi
14 Vegetarian Restaurant; Kuaytiaw Kai Jaw
20 Jok Het Hom

OTHER
1 Train Station
3 Ku Chang Ku Ma
4 Market
6 Bangkok Bank
7 Krung Thai Bank
8 Post Office
9 Provincial Offices
11 Wat Chama Thewi (Wat Kukut)
13 Wat Mahawan
15 Wat Phra That Hariphunchai
16 National Museum
18 Wat Suphanarangsi
19 Sawngthaew Queue
21 Bus Terminal
22 Wat Phra Yeun

9am-4pm Wed-Sun). It has a small collection that includes artefacts from the Dvaravati, Hariphunchai and Lanna kingdoms.

Ku Chang Ku Ma
กู่ช้างกู่ม้า

About 1.5km north of the old city are two very old and large brick stupas that may have been constructed by the Mon. In their semi-ruined state (only the brick core, without stucco relief) they look very similar to stupa remains at Thayekhittaya in central Myanmar, which brings into question the claim that the latter were built by the Tibeto-Burman Pyu.

At any rate, who built these stupas and exactly when they did so remains a mystery. Local legend, however, says that Queen Chama Thewi ordered their construction to inter the remains of her royal elephant and royal horse.

Devotees of Chama Thewi, who has become a virtual deity to many Lamphun residents, make offerings of carved wooden elephants to the stupas (for some reason the horse is ignored). The larger chedi is wrapped in red and white cloth, which suggests it's more of an animist site than a Buddhist site, since red and white are colours associated with spirit worship throughout mainland Southeast Asia.

To reach Ku Chang Ku Ma under your own steam, follow the narrow road northeast along the banks of Mae Kuang for 1km, then take a lane to the right marked Thanon Ku Chang, which leads to the site in 500m.

Places to Stay & Eat
Si Lamphun Hotel (no Roman-script sign; ☎ 053 511 176, Soi 5, Thanon Inthayongyot) Singles/doubles 100/200B. This is the easiest accommodation to find but it's not the cleanest or best-kept hotel we've seen. It needs an overhaul, and traffic noise is a problem.

Taweerat Court (☎ 053 534 338, Thanon Chama Thewi) Rooms with fan 150B, with air-con & TV 300B. Near Wat Mahawan, this clean, apartment-style place is a good choice.

Supamit Holiday Inn (☎ 053 534 865, fax 053 534 355) Singles/doubles with fan 250/300B, with air-con 350/400B. Directly across from Wat Chama Thewi is this relatively new 50-room hotel. It's no relation to the international hotel chain, but the rooms, all with hot water and balconies, are clean and simple. An open-air restaurant on the 5th floor is quite good and offers a nice view of Lamphun. There's a karaoke lounge on the 5th floor, too.

Along Thanon Inthayongyot south of Wat Phra That is a string of OK *noodle and rice shops*.

Thai vegetarian restaurant Dishes 10-15B. Open 7am-7pm Mon-Sat. This place, on the road behind the National Museum, serves delicious meatless curries and stir-fried vegetables. Look for the yellow pennant out front.

A couple of doors down is *Kuaytiaw Kai Jaw*, which specialises in the unusual combination of rice noodles with a sausage made from chicken, carrots and seaweed. It tastes better than it sounds.

Jok Het Hom (Thanon Rop Wiang Nok) Dishes 20-25B. Open 7am-7pm daily. On Thanon Rop Wiang Nok, just as you turn to go up the western side of the moat, this is another place with an unusual interpretation of a common dish. The speciality here is *jók* (rice congee) made with fresh shitake mushrooms.

Sai Ua Yai Pi (☎ 053 561 381, Thanon Rop Wiang Nok) Dishes 20-40B. Open 11am-6pm daily. At the southwestern corner of the main city 'oval', this is mostly a take-away place but there are a couple of tables where you can sit down and eat. Here you can sample *sâi ùa* (spicy Northern Thai sausage).

Wooden House (Heuan Mai; Rte 106) Dishes 30-80B. Open 5pm-1am. This local pub is at the turn-off for the Lamphun train station, 1.7km north of the northern city gates. It's only open in the evenings, and has good Thai food. As the name suggests, it's in an old wooden house.

Getting There & Away
Blue săwngthăew to Lamphun leave Chiang Mai at 30-minute intervals throughout the

day from the Chiang Mai–Lamphun road near the southern side of Saphan Nawarat. Săwngthăew in the reverse direction leave Lamphun from the queue near the intersection of Thanon Inthayongyot and Thanon Wang Khwa. The 26km ride (10B) goes along a beautiful country road, parts of which are bordered by tall *yaang* (a kind of dipterocarp tree).

Ordinary buses to Chiang Mai (10B) leave from the bus terminal on Thanon Sanam Kila, and in the reverse direction, from the Chang Pheuak bus terminal or along the Chiang Mai–Lamphun road in Chiang Mai. Green buses on the Chiang Mai–Chiang Rai route also stop in Lamphun, but leave only from the Arcade terminal in Chiang Mai. From Lamphun, green buses depart for Lampang (29B) about 13 times a day between 6am and 5pm.

The turn-off for the quaint wooden Lamphun train station is 1.7km north of the old city gates, from where it's another 450m to the station itself.

Getting Around

Săamláw (three-wheeled pedicabs; also written *samlor*) around town cost 20B to most destinations.

PASANG

ป่าซาง

Do not confuse this village with Bo Sang, the umbrella village (see that section earlier in this chapter). In Pasang, found 11km south of Lamphun, cotton weaving is the cottage industry.

After Chiang Mai was invaded by the Burmese during the 18th century, Chao Kawila moved to Pasang. In 1782 he built a fortified city straddling Mae Tha, ordered the construction of Buddhist monasteries and established a system of farms to support the temporary capital.

Wat Chang Khao Noi Neua, off Rte 106 towards the southern end of town, features an impressive gilded Lanna-style chedi. **Wat Pasang Ngam** in the middle of town has an interesting Tripitaka library that dates to the 19th century.

Near the wát is a cotton products store called **Wimon** *(no Roman-script sign)*, where you can see people weaving. Wimon sells mostly floor coverings, cotton tablecloths and other utilitarian household items. **Nandakwang Laicum shop**, farther north along the main road, is recommended for its selection and tasteful designs, although it's mostly wholesale nowadays, with most of the output going to Chiang Mai and Bangkok. You'll also find a few shops near the main market in town, opposite Wat Pasang Ngam.

A few vendors in the market also blankets, tablecloths, *phâakhamáa* (cotton wraparounds), shirts and other woven cotton products.

Dhamma Park Gallery

อุทยานธรรมะแกลเลอรี่

Set amidst longan orchards and alongside a lily-filled canal, this relatively new Pasang attraction (☎/fax 053 521 609, ⓔ *dhamma parkgallery@yahoo.com, 109/2 Mu 1, Pasang Noi; adult/child 100/50B; open 9am-5pm Sat & Sun, by appointment Mon-Fri)* displays the Buddhist art of British artist Venetia Walkey.

Walkey's satirical sculptures are found in the gallery itself, built around a 8m spiral sculpture, the *Fountain of Wisdom*. Wood and metal sculptures by Thai Inson Wongsam adorn the rustic architecture dotting the grounds.

For those interested in overnighting, the Dhamma Park Gallery offers **dorm accommodation** in a converted rice barn. Visitors are also welcome to **camp**. There is no set fee for accommodation but donations are accepted.

The park bills itself as a contemporary, ecumenical centre for socially engaged Buddhism, and facilities are available for groups wanting to host seminars, performances or exhibitions.

Wat Phra Phutthabaht Tak Pha

วัดพระพุทธบาทตากผ้า

This regionally famous wát belonging to the popular Mahanikai sect, about 9km south of

Pasang or 20km south of Lamphun off Rte 106 in the subdistrict *(tambon)* of Ma-Kok (follow Rte 1133 1km east), is a shrine to one of the North's most renowned monks, Luang Pu Phromajakko (known in Northern Thai as Khruba Phromma), who died in 1984 at the age of 87. His former kùtì contains a lifelike resin figure of the deceased monk sitting in meditation.

One of his disciples, Ajahn Thirawattho, teaches meditation to a large contingent of monks who are housed in kùtì of laterite brick. Behind the spacious grounds is a park and a steep hill mounted by a chedi that honours Khruba Phromma's father and two brothers, who all became senior monks in the Mahanikai sect. If you want to take in the views without climbing the 469 steps up the hill, pedal, drive or hire a săwngthăew up the road at the back.

The wát is named after an unremarkable Buddha footprint *(phrá phúttábàat)* shrine in the middle of the lower temple grounds and another spot where Buddha supposedly dried his robes *(tàak phâa).*

A săwngthăew from Lamphun to the wát costs 20B.

Getting There & Away

A săwngthăew will take you from Lamphun to Pasang for 8B.

If you're heading south to Tak Province under your own power, traffic is generally much lighter along Rte 106 to Thoen than on Hwy 11 to Lampang; a winding 10km section of the road north of Thoen is particularly scenic. Both highways intersect Hwy 1 south, which leads directly to Tak's capital.

DOI KHUN TAN NATIONAL PARK

อุทยานแห่งชาติดอยขุนตาล

This park (☎ 053 519 216/7; adult/child under 14 200/100B) receives only around 10,000 visitors a year, one of Northern Thailand's lowest park-visitation rates. It's unique in that the main access is from the Khun Tan train station (five daily trains from Chiang Mai, 1½ hours). From the Khun Tan station, cross the tracks and follow a steep, marked path 1.5km to the park headquarters. By car take the Chiang Mai–Lampang highway to the Mae Tha turn-off, then follow signs along a steep unpaved road for 18km.

The park covers 255 sq km and ranges in elevation from 350m at the bamboo forest lowlands to 1363m at the pine-studded summit of Doi Khun Tan. Wildflowers, including orchids, ginger and lilies, are abundant. In addition to a well-marked trail covering the mountain's four peaks, there's also a trail to **Nam Tok Tat Moei** (7km round trip). Thailand's longest train tunnel (1352m), which opened in 1921 after six years of manual labour by a thousand Lao workers (several of whom are said to have been killed by tigers), intersects the mountain slope.

Bungalows that can accommodate six to nine people are available for around 600B to 1200B near the park headquarters and at Camp 1 on the first peak. At Camp 2 on the second peak it's 250B per person, or you can pitch your own *tent* for 10B; food is available at a small *shop* near the park headquarters. The park is very popular on cool season weekends.

Lampang Province

LAMPANG

อ.เมืองลำปาง

postcode 52000 • pop 44,700

One hundred kilometres from Chiang Mai, Lampang was inhabited as far back as the 7th century in the Dvaravati period and played an important part in the history of the Hariphunchai kingdom. Legend says the city was founded as Khelang by Chao Anantayot, the son of Hariphunchai's Queen Chama Thewi. More verifiably, it appears that Chao Kawila, who took Chiang Mai back from Burmese invaders in the late 18th century, was born here in 1742 to Chao Kaew, the ruler of Lampang.

Like Chiang Mai, Phrae and other older northern cities, Lampang was built as a walled rectangle alongside a river (in this case Mae Wang). At the end of the 19th and

Raw raft material, Mae Hong Song Province

PAUL DYMOND

Thailand's largest falls, Thilawsu, Tak Province

JOE CUMMINGS

A rock-climber takes on a cliff at Tham Meuang On, Chiang Mai Province

JOE CUMMINGS

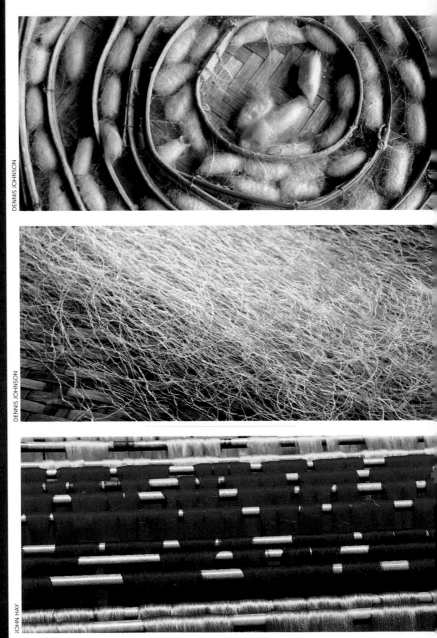

Only after they've eaten their fill of mulberry leaves do silk worms form their precious cocoons. The cocoons are boiled, washed and spun to produce the threads, which are then dyed.

beginning of the 20th centuries Lampang, along with nearby Phrae, became an important centre for the domestic and international teak trade. A large British-owned timber company brought in Burmese supervisors familiar with the teak industry in Burma to train Burmese and Thai loggers in the area. These well-paid supervisors, along with independent Burmese teak merchants who plied their trade in Lampang, sponsored the construction of more than a dozen impressive temples in the city. Burmese and Shan artisans designed and built the temples out of local materials, especially teak. Their legacy lives on in several of Lampang's best-maintained wát, now among the city's main visitor attractions.

Many Thais visit Lampang for a taste of urban Northern Thailand without the crass commercialism of Chiang Mai. Although the central area is quite busy, the shophouses provide a more traditional feel.

Information

At the northwestern corner of the clock tower circle there's a tourist information office staffed by members of the private Lampang Tourist Association Office. The city also maintains a tourist office in the new provincial complex a good distance outside of town, not very convenient for most visitors, even those who arrive by car.

Wat Phra Kaew Don Tao
วัดพระแก้วดอนเต้า

This wát, on the northern side of Mae Wang, was built during the reign of King Anantayot and was housed in the Emerald Buddha (now in Bangkok's Wat Phra Kaew) from 1436 to 1468. The main chedi shows Hariphunchai influence, while the adjacent *mondòp* (a square, spire-topped shrine room) was built in 1909. The mondòp, decorated with glass mosaic in typical Burmese style, contains a Mandalay-style Buddha image. A display of Lanna artefacts (mostly religious paraphernalia and woodwork) can be viewed in the wát's **Lanna Museum**. A small admission fee is charged.

Wat Chedi Sao
วัดเจดีย์เชา

About 6km north of town towards Jae Hom, this wát is named for the 20 whitewashed Lanna-style chedi on its grounds (*sao* is Northern Thai for '20'). It's a pretty, well-endowed wát, landscaped with bougainvillea and casuarina. At one edge of the wát stands a very colourful statue of Avalokiteshvara, while a pavilion in the centre features a gilded Buddha similar in style to the Phra Chinnarat in Phitsanulok (see the Lower North chapter). But the wát's real treasure is a 15th-century **solid-gold seated Buddha** on display in a glassed-in pavilion (*open 8am-5pm daily*) built over a pond. The image weighs 1507g, stands 38cm tall and is said to contain a piece of the Buddha's skull in its head and an ancient Pali-inscribed golden palm leaf in its chest; precious stones decorate the image's hairline and robe. A farmer reportedly found the figure next to the ruins of nearby Wat Khu Kao in 1983.

Monks stationed at Wat Chedi Sao make and sell herbal medicines; the popular **yaa màwng** is similar to tiger balm.

Other Temples

Two wát built in the late 19th century by Burmese artisans are **Wat Si Rong Meuang** and **Wat Si Chum**. Both have temple buildings constructed in the Burmese 'layered' style, with tin roofs gabled by intricate woodcarvings. The current abbots of these temples are Burmese.

Along with the wíhǎan at Wat Phra That Lampang Luang (see Around Lampang later in this chapter), the mondòp at **Wat Pongsanuk Tai** is one of the few remaining local examples of original Lanna-style temple architecture, which emphasised open-sided wooden buildings.

Baan Sao Nak
บ้านเสานัก

Baan Sao Nak (*Many Pillars House; ☎ 054 227 653, 30B; open 10am-5pm daily),* built in 1895 in the traditional Lanna style, is a huge teak house in the old Wiang Neua

AROUND CHIANG MAI

(North City) section of town. The local *khun yĭng* (a title equivalent to 'Lady') who owned the house died recently and left the house to the Thai government to be used as a museum. The entire house, supported by 116 teak pillars, is furnished with Burmese and Thai antiques; three rooms display antique silverwork, lacquerware, bronzeware, ceramics and other Northern Thai crafts. The area beneath the house is sometimes used for *khan tòk* ceremonial dinners (see the boxed text 'Northern Style' in the Facts for the Visitor chapter).

Opening hours can be erratic. The admission fee includes a soft drink.

Horse Carts

Lampang is known throughout Thailand as Meuang Rot Ma (Horse Cart City) because it's the only town in Thailand where horse carts are still used as public transport. These days, Lampang's horse carts are mainly for tourists. Trying to get a good price is difficult. A 20-minute horse-cart tour around town costs 150B; for 200B you can get a half-hour tour that goes along Mae Wang, and for 300B a one-hour tour that stops at Wat Phra Kaew Don Tao and Wat Si Rong Meuang. If there's little business you may be able to negotiate to bring the price down to 120B per half-hour or 200B per hour. The main horse-cart stands are in front of the provincial office and the Tipchang Lampang and Wieng Thong Hotels.

Traditional Massage

Next to Wat Hua Khuang in the Wiang Neua area, you can find traditional northern-Thai massage and herbal saunas at the **Northern Herbal Medicine Society** (*Samakhom Samunphrai Phak Neua; 149 Thanon Pratuma; massage 100/150B 30 mins/1 hour; sauna 100B; open 8am-8pm daily*). A 1½-hour massage is the recommended minimum for best effect. The outdoor sauna room is pumped with herbal steam created by heating a mixture of several medicinal herbs. Once you've paid you

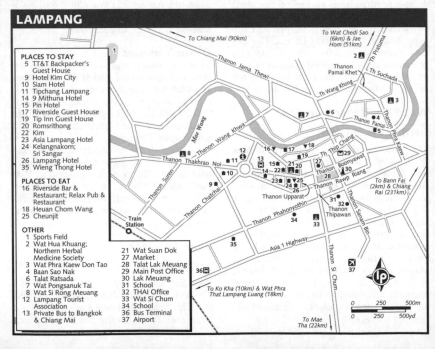

LAMPANG

To Chiang Mai (90km)

To Wat Chedi Sao (6km) & Jae Hom (51km)

PLACES TO STAY
5 TT&T Backpacker's Guest House
9 Hotel Kim City
10 Siam Hotel
11 Tipchang Lampang
14 9 Mithuna Hotel
15 Pin Hotel
17 Riverside Guest House
19 Tip Inn Guest House
20 Romsrithong
22 Kim
23 Asia Lampang Hotel
24 Kelangnakorn; Sri Sangar
26 Lampang Hotel
35 Wieng Thong Hotel

PLACES TO EAT
16 Riverside Bar & Restaurant; Relax Pub & Restaurant
18 Heuan Chom Wang
25 Cheunjit

OTHER
1 Sports Field
2 Wat Hua Khuang; Northern Herbal Medicine Society
3 Wat Phra Kaew Don Tao
4 Baan Sao Nak
6 Talat Ratsada
7 Wat Pongsanuk Tai
8 Wat Si Rong Meuang
12 Lampang Tourist Association
13 Private Bus to Bangkok & Chiang Mai
21 Wat Suan Dok
27 Market
28 Talat Lak Meuang
29 Main Post Office
30 Lak Meuang
31 School
32 THAI Office
33 Wat Si Chum
34 School
36 Bus Terminal
37 Airport

Thanon Jama Thewi
Thanon Pamai Khet
Th Pratuma
Th Suchada
Th Wang Khong
Thanon Pamai
Thanon Phra Kaew
Mae Wang
Thanon Wang Khwa
Thanon Thakhrao Noi
Th Thip Chang
Thanon Boonyawat
Thanon Rawp Riang
Thanon Suren
Thanon Chatchai
Thanon Upparat
Thanon Phahonyothin
Thanon Sanam Bin
Thanon Thipawan
Thanon Si Chum

Train Station

Asia 1 Highway

To Bann Fai (2km) & Chiang Rai (231km)

To Ko Kha (10km) & Wat Phra That Lampang Luang (18km)

To Mae Tha (22km)

0   250   500m
0   250   500yd

can go in and out of the sauna as many times as you want during one visit.

Places to Stay – Budget & Mid-Range

There are several economical choices in Lampang along Thanon Boonyawat, which runs through the centre of town.

Sri Sangar (Si Sa-Nga; ☎ 054 217 070, 213–215 Thanon Boonyawat) Singles/doubles 100/180B. This centrally located place has clean rooms, all with fan and bathroom.

9 Mithuna Hotel (☎ 054 217 438, 285 Thanon Boonyawat) Rooms with fan/air-con 204/286B. Off Thanon Boonyawat (with a second entrance off Thanon Rop Wiang Nok), this Thai-Chinese place is not the best deal.

Lampang Hotel (☎ 054 227 311, 696 Thanon Suan Dok) Rooms with fan/air-con 160/260B. This place is similar to 9 Mithuna. Rooms with a TV cost a bit more.

Kim (☎ 054 217 721, fax 054226929, 168 Thanon Boonyawat) Rooms 220B. The three-storey Kim is a more upmarket option, offering clean, comfortable accommodation with air-con, hot water and TV.

Kelangnakorn (☎ 054 216 137, 18 Thanon Suan Dok) Rooms with fan 280B, with air-con, TV & phone 420B. Diagonally across the street from Kim, Kelangnakorn is popular with travelling salesmen. It's farther off the road and has been refurbished.

Romsrithong (☎ 054 217 254, Cnr Thanon Boonyawat & Thanon Uparat) Rooms with fan & cold-water bathroom 200B, with air-con 300B, with TV & fridge 350B. This is a new three-storey place.

Riverside Guest House (☎ 054 227 005, fax 054 322 342, 286 Thanon Talat Kao) Rooms with fan 150B, with fan & bath from 250B, with river-view balcony 350B, with air-con & large living area 600B. Tucked away on narrow Thanon Talat Kao near the river, this place has comfortable rooms in old teak buildings surrounded by beautiful landscaping, with continental breakfast, fax service, international calls, motorcycle rental, laundry service and sightseeing tours. The owner speaks English, French and Italian.

Tip Inn Guest House (☎ 054 221 821, 143 Thanon Talat Kao) Singles without bathroom 100B, doubles with hot-water bathroom 160B. Near the Riverside Guest House, down a small alley marked by a small green sign 'Hotel', Tip Inn features nine basic, quiet rooms off the street. There is a small restaurant downstairs. The English-speaking Thai owners have a Thai silk shop on nearby Thanon Thip Chang.

Siam Hotel (☎ 054 217 472, 054 217 277, fax 054 217 277, Thanon Chatchai) Rooms with fan/air-con 250/380B. This friendly hotel is southwest of the clock circle. All rooms are clean and well kept; the air-con rooms have TV, phone and hot water.

TT&T Backpacker's Guest House (☎ 054 225 361, 01-951 5154, 55 Thanon Pamai) Beds in multibed rooms 100B, singles/doubles 180/200B. TT&T sits on the northern side of the river. The rooms are fairly clean; hot-water facilities are shared. A săwngthăew ride from the bus station to the guesthouse should cost about 20B per person.

Bann Fai (☎/fax 054 224 602, Mu 2, Tambon Lampang–Mae Ngao) Rooms 230-350B. About 2km outside town on Hwy 1, Bann Fai offers large rooms in a charming teak house decorated with Thai antiques and cotton hand woven on the premises. The landscaped grounds around the house encompass 300 plant species and river frontage, plus views of nearby rice fields and mountains. The four hot-water bathrooms are shared. Motorcycles are available for rent.

Places to Stay – Top End

Asia Lampang Hotel (☎ 054 227 844, fax 054 224 436, 229 Thanon Boonyawat) Rooms facing the street 350B, suite-style rooms 450-500B. All the rooms at the long-running Asia Lampang are good, but the larger suite-style rooms on the 5th floor are your best option. All rooms have air-con, TV and fridge. The pleasant street-level cafe is its best feature.

Pin Hotel (☎ 054 221 509, fax 054 322 286, 8 Thanon Suan Dok) Standard/deluxe rooms 450/650B, suites 900B. This four-storey place is right behind the Kim Hotel in the town centre. The less expensive rooms are in an older section, but are spacious and well maintained. The deluxe rooms and suites are in a relatively new wing. All 59 rooms come with air-con, satellite TV, phone and hot water. The Evergreen Restaurant is attached.

Tipchang Lampang Hotel (☎ 054 226 501, fax 054 225 362, 54/22 Thanon Thakhrao Noi) Rooms 600-800B. This is a slightly upmarket choice. Rates include American breakfast. The facilities include a coffee shop, cafe, supper club, cocktail lounge, tennis courts and pool.

Hotel Kim City (☎ 054 310 238, fax 054 226 635, 274/1 Thanon Chatchai) Rooms 500-900B. In the same category as the Tipchang, this place has good rooms and lots of on-site facilities.

Wieng Thong Hotel (☎ 054 225 801, fax 054 225 803, 138/109 Thanon Phahonyothin) Rooms with air-con from 850B. This is a modern multistorey hotel; rates include breakfast.

Places to Eat
Near the Kim and Asia Lampang Hotels are several good *rice and noodle shops*. Just east of the Kelangnakorn Hotel is a little row of *jók and noodle shops* open in the early morning.

Cheunjit (Thanon Boonyawat) Dishes 20-40B. Open late morning-early afternoon. Across from Wat Suan Dok, Cheunjit has good curries, especially *kaeng kà-rìi* (mild, Indian-style curry) and khâo sawy.

Riverside Bar & Restaurant (328 Thanon Thip Chang) Dishes 40-120B. Open 11am-midnight daily. This place is in an old teak structure on the river. It's a good choice for a drink or meal, with live folk music nightly and reasonable prices considering the high quality of the food and service. The proprietors also own the Riverside Guest House. A bit farther west, the more modern *Relax Pub & Restaurant* also has good food and live music.

Heuan Chom Wang Dishes 40-100B. Open 11am-11pm daily. If you walk east about 100m from the Riverside Guest House on Thanon Talat Kao, then north down an alley on the left, you'll come to this atmospheric open-air restaurant set in a beautiful old teak building overlooking the river. Ceramic pots filled with fragrant flower blossoms line the stairway leading into the restaurant. The local menu features Northern Thai food as well as more typical Central Thai fare.

Shopping
You can purchase beautiful Thai silk by the piece or by the metre at *Mudmee Silk (250/1–2 Thanon Thip Chang)*. Elegant royal silk designs are available (the Princess Mother was a customer here), but there are prices for every budget.

Getting There & Away
Air The THAI office (☎/fax 054 217 078) is at 314 Thanon Sanam Bin. THAI has two daily flights to Lampang from Bangkok for 1680B one way.

Bus There are air-con buses to Lampang from Phitsanulok's main bus terminal (140B, four hours via new route; 145B, five hours via old route). Buses for Lampang (25B ordinary, 50B to 65B air-con, two hours) leave from the Chiang Mai Arcade terminal about every half-hour during the day and also from next to Saphan Nawarat in the direction of Lamphun. Buses from Lamphun are 29B. Ordinary buses to/from Bangkok (four daily departures each way) cost 176B. There are also three 2nd-class air-con buses (246B), six 1st-class buses (317B) and one 24-seat VIP bus (490B). The bus terminal in Lampang is some way out of town – 10B by shared săwngthăew.

To book an air-con bus from Lampang to Bangkok or Chiang Mai there is no need to go out to the bus terminal, because the tour bus companies have offices in town along Thanon Boonyawat near the clock tower roundabout. Sombud, Thanjit Tour and Thaworn Farm each have 1st-class air-con buses to Bangkok (330B) leaving nightly around 8pm. In the same vicinity, New Wiriya has nine daily air-con departures to Bangkok (317B) between 9.30am and 10pm.

Train Two evening trains leave Lampang for Chiang Mai (37/15B 2nd/3rd class, two hours) at 5.27pm (2nd-class-only express diesel) and 6.03pm (2nd- and 3rd-class rapid) while one morning rapid train leaves at 10.27am.

AROUND LAMPANG
Wat Phra That Lampang Luang
วัดพระธาตุลำปางหลวง

Probably the most magnificent temple in Northern Thailand, Wat Phra That Lampang Luang is also the best compendium of Lanna-style temple architecture.

The centrepiece of the complex is the open-sided **Wihan Luang**. Thought to have been built in 1476, the impressive wíhǎan features a triple-tiered wooden roof supported by teak pillars. It's considered to be the oldest existing wooden building in Thailand. A huge gilded mondòp at the back of the wíhǎan contains a Buddha image cast in 1563; the faithful leave small gold-coloured Buddha figures close to the mondòp and hang Thai Lü weavings behind it.

Early 19th-century *jataka* (stories of the Buddha's past lives) murals are painted on wooden panels around the inside upper perimeter of the wíhǎan (for a discussion of this wát's murals, see the special section 'Lanna-Style Temple Murals'). The tall Lanna-style chedi behind the wíhǎan, raised in 1449 and restored in 1496, measures 24m at its base and is 45m high. The small, simple **Wihan Ton Kaew** to the right of the main wíhǎan (standing with your back to the main gate) was built in 1476. The oldest structure in the compound is the smaller 13th-century **Wihan Phra Phut** to the left of the main chedi; the wíhǎan to the right of the chedi (**Wihan Nam Taem**) was built in the early 16th century and, amazingly, still contains traces of the original murals.

Haw Phra Phutthabaht, a small white building behind the chedi, has been turned into a camera obscura. When you enter and shut the door an image of the chedi is projected, via a small hole in the door, onto a white sheet hanging on the wall. This seems to be part of a new camera obscura mania in the province, as two other temples, Wat Phra That Jom Ping (also in Ko Kha district) and Wat Ak Kho Chai Khiri (in Jae Hom) now boast such buildings.

The bòt or *sǐm* to the left of the Haw Phra dates from 1476 but was reconstructed in 1924.

The lintel over the entrance to the compound features an impressive dragon relief – once common in Northern temples but rarely seen these days. This gate supposedly dates back to the 15th century.

In the arboretum outside the southern gate, there are now three **museums** and they are all worthwhile. One displays mostly festival paraphernalia, plus some Buddha figures. Another, called 'House of the Emerald Buddha', contains a miscellany of coins, banknotes, Buddha figures, silver betelnut cases, lacquerware and other ethnographic artefacts, along with three small, heavily gold-leafed Buddhas placed on an altar behind an enormous repousse silver bowl. The third, a fine small museum, features shelves of Buddha figures, lacquered boxes, manuscripts and ceramics, all well labelled in Thai and English.

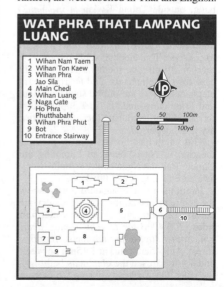

WAT PHRA THAT LAMPANG LUANG

1 Wihan Nam Taem
2 Wihan Ton Kaew
3 Wihan Phra Jao Sila
4 Main Chedi
5 Wihan Luang
6 Naga Gate
7 Ho Phra Phutthabaht
8 Wihan Phra Phut
9 Bot
10 Entrance Stairway

Wat Phra That Lampang Luang is located 18km southwest of Lampang in Ko Kha. To get there by public transport from Lampang, catch a blue săwngthăew south on Thanon Praisani to the market in Ko Kha (10B), then a Hang Chat–bound săwngthăew (5B) 3km north to the entrance of Wat Phra That Lampang Luang. A chartered motorcycle taxi from the Ko Kha săwngthăew station to the temple costs around 20B to 30B.

If you're driving or cycling from Lampang, head south on the Asia 1 highway and take the Ko Kha exit, then follow the road over a bridge and bear right. Note the police station on your left and continue for 2km over another bridge until you see the temple on the left. If you're coming from Chiang Mai via Hwy 11, turn south onto Rte 1034 18km northwest of Lampang at the Km13 marker – this route is a 50km short cut to Ko Kha that avoids much of Lampang.

Thai Elephant Conservation Centre
ศูนย์อนุรักษ์ช้างไทย

In Hang Chat district northwest of Lampang, outside Thung Kwian at the Km27 marker, is the Thai Elephant Conservation Centre (☎ 054 228 035, 054 228 108; adult/child 50/20B). Its main objectives are to conserve Thai elephants, to promote ecotourism, to provide medical treatment and care for sick elephants, and to train young elephants. There are public shows at 10am and 11am daily, and also at 1.30pm on Friday and Saturday during the June to February holiday period.

This camp has moved from its previous location in Ngao, between Lampang and Chiang Rai; the Ngao centre remains in use as a care facility for old tuskers.

In addition to the standard tourist show, the centre offers exhibits on the history and culture of elephants as well as **elephant rides** (200/400B for 15 min/30 min; available 8am-3.30pm) through the surrounding forest. At 9.45am (plus at 1.15pm on weekends) you can see the elephants bathing in the river. On weekends during the December to February high season, an ensemble of elephants plays oversized musical instruments, including drums, to create a sort of chaotic trance music.

The animals appreciate pieces of fruit – 'feels like feeding a vacuum cleaner with a wet nozzle', said one visitor. The centre now offers two- to three-day mahout workshops (3000B to 4000B), during which visitors can learn from elephant training experts how to ride and control elephants. These can be combined with an on-site homestay so that visitors may more closely observe elephant life.

To reach the camp, you can take a Chiang Mai–bound bus or săwngthăew from Lampang's main bus terminal and get off at the Km37 marker. Be forewarned: the showgrounds are about 2km off the highway and no túk-túk or motorcycle taxis are available.

Thung Kwian Market
ตลาดป่าทุ่งเกวียน

The famous Thung Kwian Market (ta-làat pàa thûng kwian; open 5am-noon Wed) at Thung Kwian in Hang Chat district (off Hwy 11 between Lampang and Chiang Mai) sells all manner of wild flora and fauna from the jungle, including medicinal and culinary herbs, wild mushrooms, bamboo shoots, field rats, beetles, snakes, plus a few rare and endangered species like pangolin. Officials are said to be cracking down on the sale of endangered species. If you're coming from Lampang, the market is before the Thai Elephant Conservation Centre.

The nearby Thung Kwian Reforestation Centre protects a 353-râi (56.5-hectare) forest under the Forest Industry Organisation.

Chae Son National Park
อุทยานแห่งชาติแจ้ช้อน

In Meuang Pan district, about 68km northeast of Lampang, begins 593-sq-km Chae Son National Park. Elevations in the park reach above 2000m, and rich floral zones consist mainly of lower montane evergreen forest, moist evergreen forest, pine forest, dry dipterocarp forest and tropical mixed

Elephants in Thailand

The elephant is one of the most powerful symbols in Thai culture, and until 1917 a white elephant appeared on the Thai national flag. Historically, Thais have worked side-by-side with elephants on farms and in the jungle, and elephants were the superweapons of Southeast Asian armies before the advent of tanks and big guns. Elephants are still revered in Thai society and are a strong drawcard for Western tourists.

JULIET COOMBE

Current estimates put the number of wild elephants in Thailand at 1300 to 2000, more than India but less than Myanmar. The number of domesticated elephants hovers at around 3800. However, numbers of both wild and domestic animals are steadily dwindling. Around the year 1900 it was estimated that there were at least 100,000 elephants working in Thailand; by 1952 the number had dropped to 13,397. Today Tak Province has the highest number of elephants and is one of only three provinces (the other two are Mae Hong Son and Surin) where the elephant population has actually increased over the last 20 years.

Elephant mothers carry their calves for 22 months. Once they are born, working elephants enjoy a brief childhood before they begin training at around three to five years of age. The training, which is under the guidance of their mahouts (elephant caretakers) takes five years. Tasks they learn include pushing, carrying and piling logs, as well as bathing and walking in procession.

Working elephants have a career of about 50 years; hence when young they are trained by two mahouts, one older and one younger – sometimes a father-and-son team – who can see the animal through its lifetime. Thai law requires that elephants be retired and released into the wild at age 61. They often live for 80 years or more.

Today the elephant is still an important mode of jungle transport, as it beats any other animal or machine for moving through a forest with minimum damage – its large, soft feet distribute the animal's weight without crushing the ground. Interestingly, an adult can run at speeds of up to 23km/h but put less weight on the ground per square centimetre than a deer!

Logging was recently banned in Thailand, resulting in much less demand for trained elephants. The plight of these unemployed creatures is becoming an issue of national concern. Many domesticated elephants are increasingly neglected, mistreated or abandoned by owners who often cannot afford to care for them. Meanwhile, destruction of forests and ivory-trade poaching are placing the wild elephant population in increasing jeopardy.

Of course, some owners continue to work their elephants in the illegal logging industry along the Thai-Myanmar border. Sadly, some animals are pumped full of amphetamines so they can work day and night.

The rising number of unemployed elephants also means unemployed mahouts; many elephant owners have begun migrating with their elephants to large cities, even Bangkok, in search of money, which can be earned simply by walking the animal through the streets and selling bananas and vegetables to people to feed it. The elephants often suffer in these urban environments; in 1998 an elephant died in Bangkok after getting one of its legs caught in a sewer culvert.

For more information about the state of elephants in Thailand check the Friends of the Asian Elephant Web site (W www.elephant.tnet.co.th).

deciduous forest (depending on climate, elevation and soil types). Inhabitants of the park include barking deer, mousedeer, wild pigs, Asian golden cats, serows, flying lemurs, monkeys and bears.

For most tourists, the park's biggest attractions are its waterfalls and hot springs. **Nam Tok Chae Son**, about 1km from the park headquarters, has six drops, each with its own pool. Close to the falls are nine hot springs, where small huts contain bathtubs (recessed into the floor and lined with clay tiles) that are continuously filled with water direct from the springs. For 20B you can take a 20-minute soak, followed by an invigorating cold-water shower.

Another waterfall, **Nam Tok Mae Mon**, is a 5km walk from the headquarters via a dirt track.

The park has a visitor centre, 12 *bungalows* for hire and a *restaurant*, but food must be ordered in advance of your visit. Several privately run *food/snack stalls* can provide sustenance as well. For further information, contact Chae Son National Park (☎ 054 229 000), at Tambon Chae Son, Amphoe Muang Ban, Lampang; or the Natural Resources Conservation Office, Royal Forest Department (☎ 025 797 223, 025 795 734), at Thanon Phahonyothin, Chatuchak, Bangkok.

Doi Luang National Park
อุทยานแห่งชาติดอยหลวง

Three more waterfalls can be found within Wang Neua district, roughly 120km north of the provincial capital via Rte 1053: **Wang Kaew**, **Wang Thong** and **Than Thong (Jampa Thong)**. Wang Kaew is the largest, with 110 tiers. Near the summit of Doi Luang is a Mien hill-tribe village. This area became part of the 1172-sq-km Doi Luang National Park in 1990; animals protected by the park include serow, barking deer, pangolin and the pig-tailed macaque.

For further information contact the Natural Resources Conservation Office at the Royal Forest Department (☎ 025 797 223, 025 795 734).

Other Attractions

North and east of Lampang are the cotton-weaving villages of **Jae Hom** and **Mae Tha**. You can wander around and find looms in action; there are also plenty of shops along the main roads.

Tham Pha Thai is 66km north of Lampang, between Lampang and Chiang Rai about 500m off Hwy 1. Besides the usual formations (stalagmites and stalactites), the cave has a large Buddha image.

Eastern Provinces

The four northeasternmost provinces of the North – Chiang Rai, Phrae, Nan and Phayao – together boast the lengthiest Thai cultural histories of any region in Thailand. Despite the venerable age of their origins, they were among the last to become provinces of the kingdom of Siam. Their relative isolation from the kingdom's main road and rail arteries has meant that Northern Thai art and culture have been particularly well-preserved here.

Chiang Rai Province

CHIANG RAI

อ.เมืองเชียงราย

postcode 57000 • pop 40,000

About 180km from Chiang Mai, Chiang Rai (called 'Siang Hai' in Northern Thai dialect) is known in tourist literature as 'the gateway to the Golden Triangle'. Most visitors to the town are interested in trekking or have just arrived after taking the boat trip down Mae Nam Kok (Kok River) from Tha Ton. Few people stay more than a night or two.

Phaya Mang Rai, the Lao–Thai Lü ruler of Ngoen Yang near present-day Chiang Saen, founded Chiang Rai in AD 1262 as his first stepping stone in the establishment of the Lanna kingdom. This was during a time when Kublai Khan's Mongols were moving southward, and Mang Rai may have chosen the location on the southern banks of Mae Nam Kok primarily because the river provided a natural line of defence against invasion from the north.

After periods of expansion alternating with Burmese invasions, Chiang Rai became a Siamese territory in 1786 and a province in 1910. The city's most historic monument, Wat Phra Kaew, once hosted the Emerald Buddha during its travels (the image eventually ended up at the *wát* of the same name in Bangkok). It now houses a replica of Chiang Mai's Wat Phra Singh Buddha image and a new 'Emerald Buddha' of its own.

Lots of wealthy Thais began moving to Chiang Rai in the 1980s and in the early 1990s the area saw a development boom as local entrepreneurs speculated on the city's future. Things have calmed down a bit and a few guesthouses have closed down, although having an airport has increased its potential as a major tourist destination. From a tourism marketing point of view, Chiang Rai is becoming a touted alternative to Chiang Mai, although it's not nearly as colourful and there's less to do in town. On the other hand it's a little more laid-back, and anyone interested in trekking will find they can reach village areas quicker than from Chiang Mai.

Information

Tourist Office The Tourism Authority of Thailand (TAT) office (☎ 053 744 674, 053 711 433) on Thanon Singkhlai, north of Wat Phra Singh, distributes maps of Chiang Rai as well as useful brochures on accommodation and transport. It's open daily from 8.30am to 4.30pm.

Money Chiang Rai is well supplied with banks, especially along Thanon Thanalai and along Thanon Utarakit. Bangkok Bank on Thanon Thanalai has an ATM, as do several other banks in town.

Post & Communications The main post office, on Thanon Utarakit south of Wat Phra Singh, is open from 8.30am to 4.30pm weekdays, and 9am to noon on Saturday, Sunday and public holidays.

A Communications Authority of Thailand (CAT) office on the corner of Thanon Ratchadat Damrong and Thanon Ngam Meuang offers international telephone, telegram, telex and fax services from 7am to 11pm weekdays.

There are several Internet cafes in the city centre, particularly in the vicinity of

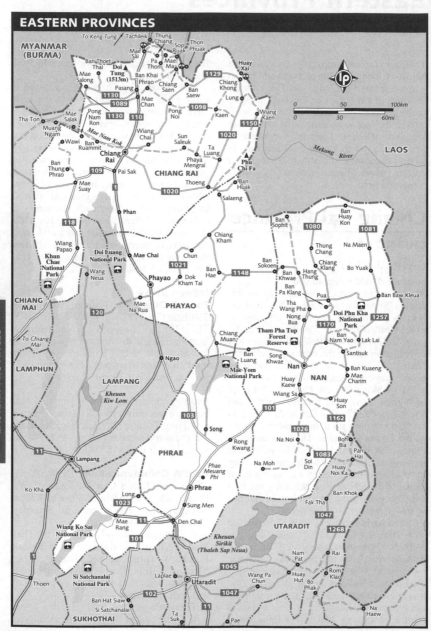

the Wang Come Hotel. The CAT and main post offices also offer Internet service.

Wat Phra Kaew
วัดพระแก้ว

Originally called Wat Pa Yia (Bamboo Forest Monastery) in local dialect, this is the city's most revered wát. Legend says that in 1434 lightning struck the temple's octagonal *chedi* (stupa), which fell apart to reveal the Phra Kaew Morakot (Emerald Buddha; actually made of jade).

Around 1990 Chiang Rai commissioned a Chinese artist to sculpt a new image from Canadian jade. Named the Phra Yok Chiang Rai (Chiang Rai Jade Buddha), it was intentionally a very close but not exact replica of the Phra Kaew Morakot in Bangkok, with dimensions of 48.3cm across the base and 65.9cm in height, just 0.1cm shorter than the original. The image is housed in the impressive Haw Phra Kaew, which sits towards the back of the wát compound.

The main *wíhǎan* (hall) is a medium-sized, nicely preserved wooden structure with unique carved doors. The chedi behind it dates to the late 14th century and is typical Lanna style.

Wat Jet Yot
วัดเจ็ดยอด

The namesake for this wát is a seven-spired *(jèt yâwt)* chedi similar to the chedi in Chiang Mai's Wat Jet Yot but without stucco ornamentation. Of more aesthetic interest is the wooden ceiling of the front veranda of the main *wíhǎan*. This wooden ceiling features a unique Thai astrological fresco.

Wat Phra Singh
วัดพระสิงห์

Housing yet another copy of a famous Buddha image, this temple was built in the late 14th century during the reign of Chiang Rai's Phaya Mahaphrom. A sister temple to Chiang Mai's Wat Phra Singh, its original buildings are typical Northern-style wooden structures with low, sweeping roofs. The impressive dragon-carved gate looks to be of Thai Lü design.

The main wíhǎan houses a copy of Chiang Mai's Phra Singh Buddha. Of more interest to art historians is the relatively new door for the bòt, which was designed by the famous contemporary artist Thawan Duchanee and carved to represent the four elements – earth, wind, water and fire.

Also on the grounds is a Buddha footprint shrine.

Other Temples

Wat Phra That Doi Chom Thong is a hilltop wát northwest of Wat Phra Kaew with views of the river and an occasional river breeze. The Lanna-style stupa here was supposedly built in 940. Nearby **Wat Ngam Meuang** was founded in 1670 next to a stupa containing the ashes of Phaya Mang Rai; the stupa was reportedly built by Mang Rai's son Phaya Khram. During the Burmese incursions into Lanna the wát was abandoned and fell to ruin, and the stupa was plundered. In 1952 the wát was rebuilt, and the brick pedestal of the Phaya Mang Rai stupa can still be seen.

Wat Pa Ko, near the entrance to the old Chiang Rai airport south of town, is a Shan-built temple with distinctive Burmese designs. Also near the old airport is **Wat Phra That Doi Phra Baht**, a Northern-style temple perched on a hillside.

Wat Rong Khun, around 12km south of the city near Km817 on Hwy 1, is notable for an ongoing contemporary Buddhist mural project by Thai artist Chalermchai Kositpipat. Chalermchai started the paintings in 1997 and expects to finish by 2004.

Hilltribe Museum & Education Center
ศูนย์การศึกษาชาวเขา

The nonprofit Population & Community Development Association (PDA) operates this combination museum/handicrafts centre (☎ *053 719 167, 053 711 475, fax 053 718 869,* ✉ *crpda@hotmail.com, 620/1 Thanon Thanalai; open 9am-7pm Mon-Fri,*

EASTERN PROVINCES

10am-7pm Sat & Sun). Crafts for sale are displayed on the ground floor. The 3rd floor of the facility serves as a museum with typical clothing for six major tribes, folk implements and other anthropological exhibits. The centre also offers a 25-minute slide show (50B) on Thailand's hill tribes with narration in English, French, German, Japanese and Thai.

If you've already been to the Tribal Museum in Chiang Mai, or the Tribal Research Institute at Chiang Mai University, you'll have seen it all before; otherwise, it's a good place to visit before undertaking any hill-tribe treks. A branch of Bangkok's Cabbages & Condoms restaurant is on the premises (see Places to Eat). See Trekking for information on the PDA's trekking agency.

Up Kham (Oup Kham) Museum
พิพิธพัณฑ์อูปคำ

This private museum (☎ 053 713 349, 81/1 Thanon Na Khai; adult/child 100/50B; open 10am-9pm daily) contains a small but impressive collection of silverwork, textiles, clothing and other memorabilia once owned or used by Northern Thai nobility. This includes rare Tai artefacts from parts of northeastern Myanmar (Burma), southwestern China and northwestern Vietnam. The museum is named for the collector's masterpiece, an ùup kham (golden bowl) used by Northern Thai royals for ritual purposes.

Labels are in Thai only but if owner/teacher/collector Ajahn Julak Suriyachai is around, he may be gracious enough to offer a few English explanations. The Lanna-style buildings stand on nicely landscaped grounds.

The museum is situated next to Talat Den Ha and near a military camp, about 1km west of the town centre. A túk-túk will take you there for 20B to 30B.

Tham Tu Pu
ถ้ำตุ๊ปู

If you follow the road across Saphan Mae Fah Luang (Mae Fah Luang Bridge) to the northern side of Mae Nam Kok, you'll come to a turn-off for Tham Tu Pu 800m from the bridge. Follow this dirt road 1.2km to arrive at this network of caves in the side of a limestone cliff. At the base of the cliff is Tham Tu Pu Meditation Centre (Samnak Vipassana Tham Tu Pu), where you'll find a steep set of stairs leading up to one of the main chambers.

Hat Chiang Rai
หาดเชียงราย

Chiang Rai Beach is a municipal recreation area along Mae Nam Kok about 3km west-northwest of town. On weekends it's crowded with local Thai picnickers but during the week there are few people around. The best time of all to visit is the hot season, when the river recedes to expose a pretty white-sand beach, and swimming is popular. During the rainy season the river is not suitable for swimming here.

Food vendors serve grilled chicken, sôm-tam (spicy green papaya salad), kûng tên (live freshwater shrimp served in a sauce of lime juice, chillies and herbs), sticky rice, beer, rice whisky and soft drinks.

Thai Language Study
YMCA (☎ 053 713 786, Thanon Ko Loi) 20-hour Thai language courses 3000B. Classes at the YMCA are one-on-one, two hours per day, four days per week. Don't confuse this YMCA with the YMCA International Hotel on the northern outskirts of town. This can be found by taking the road next to the TAT north onto the large river island of Ko Loi. The YMCA is on your left just past the bridge.

Trekking
More than 20 travel agencies, guesthouses and hotels offer trekking, typically in the Doi Tung, Doi Mae Salong and Chiang Khong areas. Chiang Rai's guesthouses were the first places to offer treks in the area and generally have the most experienced guides. Many of the local travel agencies merely act as brokers for guides associated with one of the guesthouses, so it may be cheaper to book directly through a guest-

house. As elsewhere in Northern Thailand, you're more assured of a quality experience if you use a TAT-licensed guide.

Trek pricing depends on the number of days and the number of participants, but averages 3000B per person for a four-day trek in a group of five to seven people (and as high as 3500B to 4500B per person in a smaller group of two to four people).

Three agencies in Chiang Rai operate treks and cultural tours where profits from the treks go directly to community development projects.

Dapa Tours (☎ 053 711 354, fax 053 750 172, ℮ info@dapatours.com) 115 Mu 2, Tambon Rim Kok. Run by Akha, this company specialises in tours to Akha areas.

Natural Focus (☎/fax 053 715 696, ℮ natfocus@loxinfo.co.th) 129/1 Mu 4, Thanon Pa-Ngiw, Soi 4, Rop Wiang. This company specialises in nature tours.

PDA Tours & Travel (☎ 053 740 088) Hilltribe Education Center

From Tha Mac Nam Kok (Kok River pier), boats can take you upriver as far as Tha Ton (see Fang & Tha Ton in the Around Chiang Mai chapter). An hour's boat ride from Chiang Rai is Ban Ruammit, which is a fair-sized Karen village. From here you can trek on your own to Lahu, Mien, Akha and Lisu villages – all of them within a day's walk. Inexpensive room and board (50B per person, meals 25B to 40B) are available in many villages in the river area. Another popular area for do-it-yourself trekkers is Wawi, south of the river town of Mae Salak near the end of the river route (see the Tha Ton to Chiang Rai & Chiang Mai section later in this chapter).

Places to Stay – Budget & Mid-Range

Guesthouses *Mae Kok Villa* (☎ 053 711 786, 445 Thanon Singkhlai) Dorm beds 80B, bungalows with fan & cold-water bathroom 120/150B, large singles/doubles with fan & hot-water bathroom 140/190B. This rambling place is next to the river, convenient if you're coming from Tha Ton by boat. The owner, who speaks good English, keeps over 10 dachshunds on the property.

Chat House (☎ 053 711 481, 3/2 Soi Saengkaew, Thanon Trairat) Dorm beds 60B, singles & doubles with shared bathroom 80B, with private hot-water shower 100-150B. The rooms are in an old Thai house. There are bicycles and motorcycles for rent, and 4WD and car rentals as well as guided treks can be arranged.

A bit east of here in a network of soi off Thanon Singkhlai is a trio of small family-run guesthouses.

Bowling Guest House (☎ 053 712 704, 399 Soi Nang Ing, Thanon Singkhlai) Singles/doubles 80/100B. This clean and friendly place has five rooms with attached cold-water shower. A separate hot-water shower is available.

Mae Hong Son Guest House of Chiang Rai (☎ 053 715 367, 126 Thanon Singkhlai) Singles/doubles with shared hot-water bathroom from 100/120B, with private bathroom 150/180B. This guesthouse is so named because it was once run by the same family as the original guesthouse in Mae Hong Son. Now under Dutch-Thai management, the guesthouse has a nice garden cafe although the rooms are in need of refurbishing; the owners also rent motorcycles, hold cooking courses and organise treks.

Lotus Guest House (Soi Nang Ing, Thanon Singkhlai) Singles/doubles without bathroom 80/100B, with cold-water bathroom 120/150B, singles with hot-water bathroom 150B. On the same soi as Bowling, the guesthouse has 16 well-kept rooms in row houses surrounding a grassy courtyard. Although only one room is available with an attached hot-water bathroom, there are hot showers outside that anyone can use.

Chian House (☎ 053 713 388, 172 Thanon Si Bunruang) Accommodation 100-200B. North of Lotus Guest House on a large island separated from the city by a Mae Nam Kok tributary is Chian House. The rooms here are simple but nicely done and bungalows all come with private hot-water showers. There's a pool on the premises, unusual for a place this inexpensive.

Lek House (☎ 053 713 337, 95 Thanon Ratchayotha) Rooms with shared bathroom

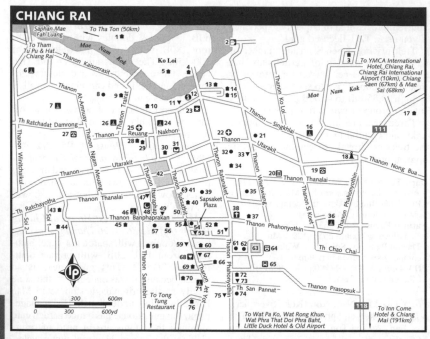

CHIANG RAI

in old house 70B, small bungalows with private bathroom 120B, row-house rooms with private bathroom 130B. Near the city centre, Lek rents motorcycles and a 4WD.

Ben Guest House (*☎ 053 716 775, 351/10 Soi 4, Thanon Sankhong Noi*) Singles/doubles without bathroom 80/100B, upstairs/downstairs rooms in teak house with bathroom 120/160B, rooms in newer brick building with bathroom 200B. If you follow Soi 1 Ratchayotha south till it ends, then turn left, you'll come to this ambitious place. All the rooms are clean and come with fans, and all bathrooms have hot water. The Northern-style building is made of salvaged teak. The few rooms without facilities are above the reception area. The owners speak English very well and can arrange treks with licensed guides. They also offer motorcycle and 4WD rentals.

Pintamorn Guest House (*☎ 053 714 161, 053 715 427, fax 053 713 317, 509/1 Thanon Ratanaket*) Rooms with fan & shared facilities 100B, singles/doubles/triples with private bathroom 200/250/300B, doubles with air-con 350B, adjoining air-con rooms (sleep up to 6) 600B. This spot in the city centre is convenient to restaurants and sightseeing, and the staff is very helpful with tourist information.

Boonbundan Guest House (*☎ 053 717 040, fax 053 712 914, 1005/13 Thanon Jet Yot*) Small rooms with fan & hot-water shower 140B, larger singles/doubles with fan 200/250B, with air-con 300/350B. The choice of accommodation at this walled compound in the southern part of town includes small rooms off the garden, in huts or in the air-con building overlooking the garden – something to suit all budgets. The 140B rooms are small and dingy and are not such good value compared with other budget places in town. Better value are the larger rooms in the new building.

Boonbundan Inn (*☎ 053 752 413*) Rooms with fan/air-con & TV 250/350B. If

CHIANG RAI

PLACES TO STAY
1 Rimkok Resort
3 Chian House
4 YMCA
5 Dusit Island Resort
9 Chat House
10 Mae Kok Villa
13 Bowling Guest House
14 Lotus Guest House
15 Mae Hong Son Guest House of Chiang Rai
17 Wang Din Place
28 Ruang Nakhon Hotel
29 Kijnakorn Guest House
30 Siriwattana Hotel
34 Pintamorn Guest House
37 Golden Triangle Inn
40 Chiengrai Hotel
43 Lek House
44 Ben Guest House
45 Saenphu Hotel
52 Siam Hotel
56 Suknirand Hotel
58 Krung Thong Hotel
60 Wang Come Hotel; Mayura Bakery & Cafe
66 Baan Bua
69 Boonbundan Guest House
70 Boonbundan Inn

72 Wiang Inn
76 Tourist Inn

PLACES TO EAT
11 Cham Cha
33 Thai Vegetarian Restaurant
47 Thai-Muslim Restaurant
49 Phetburi Restaurant; Ratburi Restaurant
50 Rice and Noodle Restaurants
51 Nakhon Pathom
53 La Cantina
59 Khao Soi Po Sai
63 Night Market
67 Mongkhon
73 Muang Thong Restaurant
75 Bierstube

OTHER
2 Tha Mae Nam Kok
6 Wat Phrat That Doi Chom Thong
7 Wat Ngam Meuang
8 Government Office; Town Hall
12 TAT Office
16 Wat Bunreuang
18 King Mang Rai Monument
19 TOT Office

20 Hilltribe Museum & Education Center; Cabbages & Condoms Restaurant
21 Chiang Rai Business School
22 Provincial Health Centre
23 Police Station
24 Wat Phra Singh
25 Hospital
26 Wat Phra Kaew
27 CAT Office
31 Main Post Office
32 School
35 Old Jail
36 Wat Si Koet
38 Chiang Rai First Church
39 District Office
41 Bangkok Bank
42 Market
46 Wat Ming Meuang
48 Daru Aman Mosque
54 ST Motorcycle
55 Clock Tower
57 DK Books
61 THAI Office
62 Night Bazaar
64 Rama II Theatre
65 Bus Terminal
68 Marquee Bar
71 Wat Jet Yot
74 KM Car Rent

you take a left at the end of the soi from Boonbundan Guest House and go down about 50m, you'll find the related Boonbundan Inn. Rooms are in a two-storey L-shaped building.

Tourist Inn (☎ 053 714 682, 1004/5-6 Thanon Jet Yot) Rooms with fan & bathroom in old house 150B, with fan/air-con in new building 200/400B. The friendly and efficient Tourist Inn offers large, clean rooms. The proprietors speak English, Thai and Japanese, and there is a good bakery on the premises. Car and motorcycle rentals can be arranged.

Kijnakorn Guest House (☎ 053 744 150/1, 24 Thanon Reuang Nakhon) Rooms with fan 300B, with air-con 400 500B. All rooms in this centrally located, four-storey building are clean and new and come with TV, fridge and phone as well as hot-water showers. It's a bit short on atmosphere, but basically OK.

Baan Bua (☎ 053 718 880, 879/2 Thanon Jet Yot) Singles/doubles with fan 180/200B, rooms with air-con 300B. In a quiet spot off Thanon Jet Yot, the friendly Baan Bua offers 10 large, very clean rooms in a cement row house, each with screen doors on either side to allow for insect-free cross-ventilation.

Hotels *Chiengrai Hotel* (☎ 053 711 266, 519 Thanon Suksathit) Singles/doubles/triples with fan & bathroom 160/220/350B. On Thanon Suksathit near the clock tower and district government building, the well-run, clean Chiengrai Hotel is a favourite with Thai truck drivers and travelling salespeople.

Suknirand Hotel (☎ 053 711 055, fax 053 713 701, 424/1 Thanon Banphaprakan) Rooms with fan from 300B, with air-con from 500B. Near the Chiengrai Hotel, the Suknirand is recently renovated.

Siam Hotel (☎ 053 711 077, 531/6-8 Thanon Banphaprakan) Rooms with fan & bathroom 250/300B. Funkier and cheaper than the Chiengrai or Suknirand hotels, this is a decent choice for someone who doesn't like guesthouses.

Ruang Nakhon Hotel (☎ 053 745 000, fax 053 745 003, 25 Thanon Reuang Nakhon) Rooms with fan & bathroom 200B, with air-con 300-400B. This place is in the same category as the Chiengrai Hotel and, though not quite as nice, allows four people to share a two-bed room.

Siriwattana Hotel (☎ 053 711 466, 485 Thanon Utarakit) This old-fashioned Thai-Chinese hotel next to the main post office was still closed for renovations when we last visited, but it's worth keeping an eye on.

Krung Thong Hotel (☎ 053 711 033, fax 053 717 848, 412 Thanon Sanambin) Singles/doubles with fan & bathroom 250/290B, rooms with air-con 340B. Rooms here are large and clean, and the staff is efficient.

YMCA International Hotel Chiangrai (☎ 053 713 785, fax 053 714 336, 70 Thanon Phahonyothin) Dorm beds 90B, singles/doubles with fan & private bathroom 300/400B, with air-con 400/500B. Out of town on the highway to Mae Sai, this is a very modern establishment. All rooms come with hot water and a telephone. Facilities include a restaurant, convention room, daycare centre and a small swimming pool. Thai massage and herbal sauna are recent additions.

Golden Triangle Inn (☎ 053 711 339, 053 716 996, fax 053 713 963, 590/2 Thanon Phahonyothin) Singles/doubles 650/950B Nov-Feb, 500/600B Apr-Oct. The 39 tasteful, but well-worn, rooms all have tile floors, air-con and hot water (even bathtubs); rates include American breakfast. Also on the landscaped grounds are a cafe, a Japanese-Thai garden, a Budget car rental office and an efficient travel agency. It's a popular place, so book in advance to ensure you get in.

Saenphu Hotel (☎ 053 717 300, fax 053 717 309, 389 Thanon Banphaprakan) Singles & doubles from 500B. This centrally located place is a pretty good value – all rooms come with air-con, TV, phone and fridge. The hotel's basement nightclub has live music and is a very popular local rendezvous spot.

Inn Come Hotel (☎ 053 717 850, fax 053 717 855, 176/2 Thanon Ratbamrung) Rooms from 650B. South of the city centre, this place has a restaurant, coffee shop, karaoke and a popular disco.

Places to Stay – Top End

Wiang Inn (☎ 053 711 533, fax 053 711 877, ℮ wianginn@samart.co.th, 893 Thanon Phahonyothin) Standard singles/doubles 1400/1600B, deluxe rooms 2100/2300B. Facilities here include a swimming pool, massage parlour, bar, restaurant, coffee shop and karaoke.

Wang Come Hotel (☎ 053 711 800, fax 053 712 973, 869/90 Thanon Premawiphat; in Bangkok ☎ 022 527 750) Rooms 1060-1600B, suites 2000-5500B. This hotel has comfortable rooms with air-con, carpet, TV, fridge and phone. Amenities consist of a pool, banquet room, disco, coffee shop, two restaurants and a nightclub. The hotel also rents golf clubs and provides transport to a golf course for 100B.

Dusit Island Resort (☎ 053 715 777-9, fax 053 715 801, ℮ chiangrai@dusit.com; in Bangkok ☎ 026 363 333) Rooms from 2800B. Perched on its own island in Mae Nam Kok (you can't miss seeing its stacked white facade if you arrive in Chiang Rai by boat), this hotel is an island unto itself, insulating its guests from the rigours of laidback Chiang Rai. Facilities include Chinese and European restaurants, a coffee shop, pub, swimming pool and fitness centre. Discounts are often available.

Rimkok Resort (☎ 053 716 445, fax 053 715 859, 6 Mu 4, Thanon Chiang Rai-Tha Ton; in Bangkok ☎ 022 790 102) Rooms 1806-2477B. Chiang Rai's most beautiful hotel, the Rimkok is set in lush grounds opposite the Dusit Island Resort on the other side of the river. The Thai-style architecture contains 256 spacious rooms with all the amenities. One drawback is the lack of a nearby bridge, so it's a 15-minute trip back and forth from Chiang Rai via the highway bridge at the eastern end of town.

Wang Din Place *(☎ 053 713 363, fax 053 716 790, 341 Thanon Khae Wai)* Rooms 800B. Situated in the northeastern corner of town near the river, this hotel offers sturdy, Thai-style bungalows with fridge, TV, aircon and private hot-water shower.

Little Duck Hotel *(☎ 053 715 620, fax 053 715 639,* 📧 *chitpong@loxinfo.co.th, 199 Thanon Phahonyothin; in Bangkok ☎ 026 915 941-6)* Rooms 900-1200B. South of the city past the old airport, the Little Duck Hotel has picked up a regular clientele of Thai politicos and entrepreneurs in spite of its distance from the new airport and town. Amenities include a pool and a restaurant.

Places to Eat
Thai The food scene in Chiang Rai continues to improve, and you'll find plenty of restaurants, especially along Thanon Banphaprakan and Thanon Thanalai. ***Phetburi*** and ***Ratburi*** on Thanon Banphaprakan are cheap and good. The Phetburi has a particularly good selection of curries and other Thai dishes.

Nakhon Pathom *(no English sign; Thanon Phahonyothin near the Banphaprakan intersection)* Dishes 30-80B. Open 8am-3pm daily. Yet another local restaurant named after a Central Thailand city, this place is very popular for inexpensive *khâo man kài* (Hainanese chicken rice) and *kǔaytǐaw pèt yâang* (roast duck with rice noodles).

Mongkhon *(Thanon Premawiphat)* Dishes 25-35B. Open 7am-9pm daily. We found the best duck noodles in town at this place, across from the Wang Come Hotel.

Muang Thong Restaurant *(☎ 053 711 162, Thanon Phahonyothin)* Dishes 30-80B. Open 11am-10pm daily. Just south of the Wiang Inn, the Muang Thong has an extensive Thai and Chinese menu that includes a frog section.

Thai-Muslim restaurant *(Thanon Itsaraphap)* Dishes 20-30B. Next to the mosque, this place has delicious *khâo mòk kài,* a Thai version of chicken biryani.

Cham Cha *(Thanon Singkhlai)* Dishes 35-90B. Open 7am-4pm daily. Beside the

TAT office, this is a very good place for breakfast or lunch if you arrive at TAT tired and hungry. It has all the usual Thai and Chinese standards, along with a few Isan dishes such as *lâap* (meat salad) and *sôm-tam* (spicy green papaya salad) not on the English menu – ice cream, too.

Tong Tung Restaurant *(no English sign; ☎ 053 756 403, 1/1 Thanon Sanambin)* Dishes 40-100B. Open 5pm-11pm daily. For Northern Thai food, try this semi-outdoor place on the western side of the road about 1km south of Thanon Banphaprakan. Most evenings the restaurant presents a program of Northern Thai dancing. So far the clientele is mostly Thai; as there's no sign in English, look for a small fountain in front of the bar pavilion.

Cabbages & Condoms *(C&C; ☎ 053 740 784, 620/1 Thanon Thanalai)* Dishes 35-90B. Open 11am-10pm daily. On the grounds of the Hilltribe Museum & Education Center, C&C serves Northern Thai food in a casual indoor and outdoor eating area. Profits from the restaurant are used by the PDA for HIV/AIDS education with the intention to make condoms as easy to find as cabbages (we would say that objective has been achieved, as any corner store in Thailand now has condoms and you have to visit a vegetable market to find cabbage!).

There's a small, pleasant family-run ***Thai vegetarian restaurant*** *(Thanon Wisetwiang),* opposite the Chiang Rai Condotel, serving dishes for 10B to 30B. It's open 7am to 2pm daily.

Near the bus terminal are the usual ***food stalls***; the ***night market*** next to the station and Rama I cinema is also good. There's a string of inexpensive ***rice and noodle restaurants*** along Thanon Jet Yot between Thanon Thanalai and Wat Jet Yot, near the Chiengrai Hotel. A *khâo sawy* (noodle) vendor called ***Khao Soi Po Sai,*** not far from the Wang Come Hotel in this stretch, is particularly recommended. ***Mayura Bakery & Cafe,*** attached to the Wang Come, sells baked goods and a selection of Thai and Western dishes.

International *Bierstube (☎ 053 714 195, Thanon Phahonyothin south of the Wiang*

Inn) Dishes 40-80B. Open 9am-11pm daily. Bierstube has been recommended for German food; there are several other *Western-style pubs* along here and on Thanon Suksathit/Jet Yot near the Wang Come Hotel.

La Cantina (Thanon Jet Yot) Dishes 45-100B. Open 8am-10pm daily. This long-established restaurant serves decent Italian for breakfast, lunch and dinner.

Entertainment

Chiang Rai is pretty quiet at night. A string of bars along Thanon Jet Yot capture most of the expat business. Among these the *Marquee Bar (☎ 053 714 653; open 6pm-1am),* run by an ex-professional musician from London, has the best recorded music and occasional jam sessions. Sapkaset Plaza, an L-shaped soi between Thanon Banphaprakan and Thanon Suksathit, has become a *go-go bar* centre.

Free *Northern Thai music and dance performances* are given nightly on a stage set in the night market area. There is another cluster of bars catering to both tourists and residents next to the night market.

Shopping

Prices for antiques and silverwork are sometimes lower in Chiang Rai than in Chiang Mai. Several shops worth checking for handicrafts, silver and antiques can be found along Thanon Phahonyothin, including *Gong Ngoen* at No 873/5, *Silver Birch* at No 891 and *Chiangrai Handicrafts Center* at No 237. *Ego (869/81 Thanon Premawiphak)* carries upmarket items like antique textiles.

It's cheaper to buy direct from the *craft vendors* who set up on the sidewalk in front of the northern entrance to the bus station nightly. Adjacent to the bus station is a tourist-oriented *night market* that resembles Chiang Mai's but on a much smaller scale.

Getting There & Away

Air Chiang Rai International Airport is 10km north of the city. The terminal has several snack vendors, souvenir shops, a Chinese tea shop, a money exchange, a post office (open 7am to 7pm daily) and rental

car booths. THAI has a restaurant on the upper floor. THAI flies twice daily between Chiang Rai and Chiang Mai (775B, 35 minutes). Daily flights are also available to/from Bangkok (2500B, 1¼ hours). There has been talk of flights from Hong Kong, Kunming, Vientiane and Mandalay, but as long as Chiang Mai's airport fields flights from these cities they're not likely to be added to the schedule. Chiang Rai must also compete with Bangkok Airways' Northern hub, Sukhothai.

Chiang Rai's THAI office (☎ 053 711 179, 053 222 279) is at 870 Thanon Phahonyothin, not far from the Wang Come Hotel.

Taxis into town from the airport cost 150B. Out to the airport you can get a túk-túk for 80B to 100B.

Bus There are two routes to Chiang Rai from Chiang Mai: an old and a new. The old route *(săi kào)* heads south from Chiang Mai to Lampang before heading north through Ngao and Phayao to Chiang Rai. If you want to stop at these cities, this is the bus to catch, but the trip will take up to seven hours. In Chiang Mai the bus leaves from Thanon Chiang Mai–Lamphun, near Saphan Nawarat; the fare is 83B (ordinary only).

The new route *(săi mài)* heads northeast along Hwy 118, stopping in Doi Saket and Wiang Papao (77B ordinary, 98B 2nd-class air-con, 139B 1st-class air-con, four hours). New-route 'green buses' *(rót meh khĭaw)* leave from Chiang Mai's Arcade bus terminal. Chiang Mai to Chiang Rai buses are sometimes stopped for drug searches by police.

The bus terminal is located on Thanon Prasopsuk, several blocks south of Thanon Phahonyothin.

The following table shows other bus services from Chiang Rai:

destination	fare	duration (hrs)
Bangkok		
air-con	370B	10
1st class	452B	10
VIP	700B	10

Ban Huay Khrai (for Doi Tung)
ordinary	15B	1

Chiang Khong
ordinary	42B	2½

Chiang Saen
ordinary	25B	1½

Fang
ordinary	45B	2½

Khon Kaen
ordinary	239B	13
air-con	335B	13
1st class	430B	13

Khorat
ordinary	262B	14
air-con	472B	13
VIP	550B	13

Lampang
ordinary	35B	2½
air-con	55B	2
1st class	80B	2

Mae Chan
ordinary	15B	¾

Mae Sai
ordinary	20B	1½
air-con	37B	1½

Mae Sot
ordinary	200B	7½
air-con	350B	7½

Mae Suay
ordinary	18B	1¼
air-con	34B	1
1st class	40B	1

Nan
ordinary	110B	6

Pasang
ordinary	15B	¾

Phayao
ordinary	25B	1¾
air-con	45B	1¾
1st class	55B	1¾

Phitsanulok
ordinary	153B	7
air-con	214B	6
1st class	290B	6

Phrae
ordinary	80B	4
air-con	124B	4
1st class	155B	4

Tak
ordinary	150B	6½
air-con	200B	6½

Boat One of the most popular ways of getting to Chiang Rai is the river trip from Tha

Ton (see the Tha Ton to Chiang Rai & Chiang Mai section later in this chapter).

For boats heading upriver on Mae Nam Kok, go to the pier in the northwestern corner of town. The boats leave daily at 10.30am. Regular long boats from Chiang Rai stop at the following villages along the Kok (times are approximate for ideal river conditions):

destination	fare	duration (hrs)
Ban Ruammit	50B	1
Pong Nam Ron	60B	1½
Hat Yao	100B	2¼
Pha Khwang	130B	2½
Kok Noi	150B	3
Mae Salak	170B	4
Tha Ton	250B	5

You can charter a boat to Ban Ruammit for 650B or all the way to Tha Ton for 1600B. Call Chiang Rai Boat Tour (☎ 053 750 009) for further information.

Getting Around

A sǎamláw ride anywhere in central Chiang Rai should cost 20B to 30B. Túk-túk cost twice as much. A city sǎwngthǎew (passenger pick-up truck) system (10B fare) circulates along the main city streets; there are also route túk-túk that charge 15B to 20B.

Several small agencies near the Wang Come Hotel rent cars (around 1200B a day), vans (1300B to 1500B) and Suzuki Caribian 4WDs (800B). The following charge a little more than the local offices:

Avis Rent-A-Car (☎ 053 793 827) Chiang Rai International Airport
Budget Rent-A-Car (☎ 053 740 442/3) 590 Thanon Phahonyothin, Golden Triangle Inn complex
National Car Rental (☎ 053 793 683) Chiang Rai International Airport; Dusit Island Resort

Bicycles and motorcycles can be hired at ST Motorcycle (☎ 053 713 652), who appear to take good care of their motorcycles. They are near the clock tower on Thanon Banphaprakan, but get there early as they often run out in the morning. Daily bike rental costs 60B to 100B a day. Motorcycle rentals start at 150B per day for older Honda Dreams (200B for newer ones) and up to 660B per day for a 250cc Yamaha TTR. ST has a second location (☎ 053 752 526) on Thanon Wat Jet Yot. Motorcycles can also be rented at many of the guesthouses.

THA TON TO CHIANG RAI & CHIANG MAI

From Tha Ton (see the Around Chiang Mai chapter) you can make a half-day longtail boat trip to Chiang Rai down Mae Nam Kok. The regular passenger boat takes up to 12 passengers, leaves at 12.30pm and costs 200B per person. You can also charter a boat all the way for 1600B, which between eight people works out to the same per person but gives you more room to move. The trip is a bit of a tourist trap these days as the passengers are all tourists (what local will pay 200B to take the boat when they can catch a bus to Chiang Rai for less than 40B?), and the villages along the way sell cola and souvenirs – but it's still fun. The best time to go is at the end of the rainy season in November when the river level is high.

To catch one of these boats on the same day from Chiang Mai you'd have to leave by 7am or 7.30am and make no stops on the way. The 6am bus is the best bet. The travel time down river depends on river conditions and the skill of the pilot, taking anywhere from three to five hours. You could actually make the boat trip in a day from Chiang Mai, catching a bus back from Chiang Rai as soon as you arrive, but it's better to stay in Fang or Tha Ton, take the boat trip, then stay in Chiang Rai or Chiang Saen before travelling on. You may sometimes have to get off and walk or push the boat if it gets stuck on sand bars.

Mae Salak, Wawi & Ban Ruammit

แม่สะลัก, วาวีและบ้านรวมมิตร

Some travellers take the boat to Chiang Rai in two or three stages, stopping first in Mae Salak, a large Lahu village that is about a third of the distance, or Ban Ruammit, a Karen village about two-thirds of the way down. Both villages are well touristed these days (charter boat tours stop for photos and elephant rides), but from here you can trek to other Shan, Thai and hill-tribe villages, or do longer treks south of Mae Salak to Wawi, a large multiethnic community of jiin haw (Yunnanese Chinese), Lahu, Lisu, Akha, Shan, Karen, Mien and Thai peoples.

The Wawi area has dozens of hill-tribe villages of various ethnicities, including the largest Akha community in Thailand (Saen Charoen) and the oldest Lisu settlement (Doi Chang). The little town of Wawi itself is very Yunnanese. Tea cultivation is a relatively new cash crop in the Wawi area, replacing the opium poppy that once blanketed nearby mountain slopes.

Near the Karen village of **Ban Thung Phrao**, about 15km from Mae Suay off Hwy 109, there are several Karen, Lahu, Akha, Lisu and Mien villages. Ban Thung Phrao has reliable accommodation, so is a good choice to do day treks from.

Near Ban Ruammit on the opposite river bank (50B, 1½ hours by boat from Chiang Rai) are some very pretty **hot springs**. Don't even think about entering the water – it's scalding hot.

Another alternative is to trek south from Mae Salak all the way to the town of **Mae Suay**, where you can catch a bus on to Chiang Rai or back to Chiang Mai. You might also try getting off the boat at one of the smaller villages (see the boat fares table in the Getting There & Away section later). Another alternative is to make the trip (much more slowly) upriver from Chiang Rai – this is possible despite the rapids.

Several of the guesthouses in Tha Ton now organise raft trips down the river – see Fang & Tha Ton in the Around Chiang Mai chapter.

CHIANG MAI TO CHIANG RAI

Highway 118 is the most direct road link between Chiang Mai and Chiang Rai. This is the 'new route' used by buses between the cities, but it's also a fairly easy car, motorcycle or bicycle ride. The road to

Wawi, Hwy 109, links with Hwy 118 near the town of Mae Suay.

With your own transport, you could make an interesting circuit by moving from Chiang Mai to Mae Suay, then over Doi Wawi to Fang and back to Chiang Mai. By public transport an alternative would be to bus from Chiang Mai to Tha Ton, then take the boat to Chiang Rai, returning to Chiang Mai via Hwy 118.

If you have time, consider stopping at Trekker Lodge, off Hwy 118 between Km63 and Km64, to go hiking in the surrounding hills. A **hot springs** just off the highway at Km64 has bathing pools where you can warm chilled bones in the cool season, or enjoy a meal at one of several open-air restaurants near the road's edge.

Khun Chae National Park

Established in 1995, this new, 270-sq-km park named for Nam Tok Khun Chae is easily visited via the main entrance on Hwy 118. Among the attractions are several waterfalls, mountain peaks and nature trails. At a reservoir called **Ang Nam Mae Chang Chao**, which serves as the chief water supply for the town of Wiang Papao and surrounding villages, you can hire bamboo rafts for 100B to 150B per hour for picnicking, fishing or swimming; it's at the northern end of the park.

The forests of Khun Chae are said to be home to barking deer, wild pig, pangolin, porcupine, flying lemur, hog badger, gibbons, several species of civets and squirrels, over a hundred species of birds, mountain turtles, a variety of snakes and 60 species of butterfly.

Because the park is so new, the staff is not yet charging admission unless you plan to climb **Doi Pha Ngom**, in which case there is a 20B fee. The peak of most interest is **Doi Langka Luang**, which at over 2000m is the fifth-highest peak in Thailand. It's near the extreme southern end of the park. A trail ascending the peak usually takes four days and three nights to climb. There are camping areas along the way but you'll need your own gear. You can arrange to take one of the park staff with you at no charge (except you must

pay for their food), or the staff can arrange for a local villager to guide you to the summit for 300B per day (and also provide food).

A two-hour trail walk will take you to the top of seven-level **Nam Tok Mae Tho**. Two self-guided nature trails, each around 2km long, offer insight into the different habitats and resources of the park. Bird-watchers will see a good variety of species along both trails. **Chom Wana Trail** features 15 different interpretive stations, while **Jurjling Trail** – which traverses steep terrain and can be very wet during the rainy season – has 11 interpretive stations. Each trail takes about two hours at a slow pace.

Two spacious *guesthouses* with capacities of up to 15 persons, two bathrooms with Western toilets and large observation decks with beautiful views of the area can be found near the park headquarters, not far off Hwy 118. At this point the staff claim there are no set fees for staying in the guesthouses, but that donations will be gratefully accepted. A *campground* is currently under development.

Khun Chae National Park is 56km northeast of Chiang Mai and 129km southwest of Chiang Rai via Hwy 118. You can reach here from Chiang Mai by taking a Wiang Papao–bound săwngthăew and getting off in front of the well-signed park headquarters on Hwy 118.

Places to Stay

Akha Hill House (☎ 01 460 7450, fax 053 715 451, Ⓔ apuehouse@hotmail.com) Dorm beds 40B, singles 50-60B, doubles 80-90B (all with shared bathroom); singles with private bathroom 70B, doubles 100-120B. This rustic guesthouse, owned and managed by Akha tribespeople, is in a beautiful setting overlooking a mountain valley about an hour's hike from the hot springs near Ban Ruammit. A waterfall and several villages (Akha, Mien, Lisu, Karen and Lahu) are within walking distance. The staff can organise overnight trips into the forest with guides who build banana-palm huts and cook meals using sections of bamboo. Akha Hill House can also be reached by road from Chiang Rai, 26km away. Call for free pick-up (once daily between 3.30pm and 4pm). It maintains an office opposite Wat Phra Sing in Chiang Rai (☎ 053 718 957) at 18/10 Thanon Phakdiwarong. Bring your own sleeping bag or an extra blanket during the colder months, December and January, when the provided blankets may not quite do the job.

Karen Hilltribe Guesthouse (☎ 01 224 6998, ⓔ karenguesthouse@hotmail.com, Ban Thung Phrao, Doi Wawi) Bungalows with shared hot-water bathroom 90-100B, with private hot-water bathroom 200-250B. Located in a peaceful mountainous area in the village of Ban Thung Phrao, this Swiss-Thai guesthouse offers rustic but comfortable bungalows, plus plenty of information on local hiking and sightseeing.

My Dream Guest House (Kaeng Wua Dam) Bungalows with fan & hot-water bathroom 300B. In the Karen village of Kaeng Wua Dam, on Mae Nam Kok across from Mae Salak, My Dream offers four new clean, comfortable and quiet bungalows. There are some good walks nearby.

The town of Wawi has a couple of very basic *hotels* costing 100B to 200B a night.

Charin Garden Resort (Suan Charin; ☎ 01 224 6984, fax 01 224 6983, 83 Mu 1) Bungalows with air-con & hot-water bathroom 600B. This place is a little north of Mae Suay on Hwy 118 and a good choice if you're travelling between Chiang Rai and Chiang Mai, or have just come from Wawi. Even if you don't need a place to stay, this is the best coffee stop along Hwy 118, as the restaurant has the best coffee for a 100km radius and the best pies outside of Bangkok.

Trekker Lodge (10km off Hwy 118 between Km63 & Km64) Bungalows with private hot-water bathroom 300B. The widely separated bungalows, each named for a different hill tribe, sit on a slope overlooking a pretty valley inhabited mostly by Lahu (Musoe). Each bungalow has a small fireplace, making this a particularly cosy spot during December and January when many rural guesthouses in Northern Thailand can be uncomfortably cold. The friendly staff can arrange one-day or multi-day trekking in the area. Trekker Lodge's restaurant serves good food, and there are outdoor tables with

good views. Since Trekker Lodge is nearly 10km off Hwy 118, you must either have your own transport or be prepared to hitch a ride with villagers who use the road.

Getting There & Away

Bus & Săwngthăew You can catch infrequent buses or săwngthăew along Hwy 109 between Mae Suay and Wawi. It's 40B all the way to Wawi, 25B as far as Ban Thung Phrao.

From Wawi north to Mae Salak on the banks of Mae Nam Kok there is no regular transport, though you may be able to hitch a ride with the intermittent truck traffic. If you have your own wheels, be aware that the road is sealed uphill from Wawi but once you start downhill towards Mae Salak it is a steep, winding dirt road. It can be dicey in the wet season, in fact impassable by ordinary passenger car, though a motorbike or pick-up truck can usually make it down. This stretch will probably be sealed in the next year or two. Highway 109 between Mae Suay and Wawi is a beautiful and easy drive.

Boat A boat leaves once daily for Chiang Rai from Tha Ton at 12.30pm. The following table shows boat fares from Tha Ton:

destination	fare
Ban Mai	70B
Mae Salak	80B
Pha Tai	90B
Jakheu	100B
Kok Noi	110B
Pha Khwang	120B
Hat Wua Dam	180B
Ban Nong Ram	200B
Ban Ruammit	200B
Chiang Rai	250B

For further information, call the Tha Ton boat office at ☎ 053 459 427.

MAE SALONG (SANTIKHIRI)
แม่สลอง(สันติคีรี)

postcode 57240 • pop 10,000
Aside from Bangkok's Yaowarat district, there is no place in Thailand that more re-

sembles China than Mae Salong, but here, rather than calling to mind brash Hong Kong or Taipei, the atmosphere is more reminiscent of a small Chinese mountain village. The combination of pack horses, hill tribes (Akha, Lisu, Mien, Hmong) and southern Chinese–style houses conjures up images of a small town or village in China's Yunnan Province.

The weather is always a bit cooler on Doi Mae Salong than on the plains below. During the cool and dry months, November to February, nights can actually get cold – be sure to bring sweaters and socks for visits at this time of year.

History

Yunnan is indeed the ancestral home of many of the residents of Doi Mae Salong, which was originally settled by the 93rd Regiment of the 5th Kuomintang (KMT) Army. Following the 1949 communist victory in China, this mostly Yunnanese regiment had no way of joining the main KMT exodus from Shanghai and Fujian to Taiwan, so they fled to northern Myanmar. After futile intermittent rear-guard action against the Chinese communists, the renegades were forced to leave Myanmar in 1961 when the Yangon government decided they didn't want the KMT presence to anger their powerful neighbour to the north. Crossing into Northern Thailand with their pony caravans (the Yunnanese immigrants' equestrian history, alien to the Thais, has led the latter to refer to them as jiin haw or 'galloping Chinese'), the ex-soldiers and their families settled into mountain villages and re-created a society much like the one they left behind in Yunnan.

After the Thai government granted the KMT refugee status in the 1960s, efforts were made to incorporate the Yunnanese and their families into the Thai nation. Until the late 1980s they didn't have much success, as many ex-KMT were deeply involved in the Golden Triangle opium trade in a three-way partnership with opium warlord Khun Sa and the Shan United Army (SUA). Because of the rough, mountainous terrain and lack of sealed roads, the outside world was rather cut off from the goings-on in Mae Salong.

The KMT never denied its role in drug trafficking, but justified it by claiming that the money was used to buy weapons to fight the communists. The KMT were merely a link in a chain that included high-level Thai military officers and politicians, but the Thais, as a sovereign state, were less forthcoming about their role, and pointed the finger at the KMT as the perpetrators of this illicit trade.

However, when the Thais needed battle-seasoned troops to fight indigenous communist insurgents in the 1970s they wasted no time in requesting troops and officers from the KMT forces in Northern Thailand. The bloodiest operation against the communists lasted from 1970 until 1974, during which nearly 1000 KMT soldiers died. As a reward for their contributions to Thailand's national defence, the Thai government bestowed Thai nationality upon many of the KMT soldiers and their families.

Infamous Khun Sa made his home in nearby Ban Hin Taek (now Ban Thoet Thai) until the early 1980s when he was finally routed by the Thai military. Khun Sa's retreat to Myanmar seemed to signal a change in local attitudes and the Thai government finally began making progress in its pacification of Mae Salong and the surrounding area. His 1996 surrender/retirement to Yangon also had a palpable effect on the region, cutting down on the Shan opium trade while increasing traffic in illicit amphetamines produced and traded by the Wa, another ethnic army in northeastern Myanmar.

Along with Thai language courses and crop substitution, in a further effort to separate the area from its old image as an opium fiefdom, the Thai government officially changed the name of the village from Mae Salong to Santikhiri (Hill of Peace).

Today the town feels very Chinese, helped along by the hand-painted Chinese character scrolls around doorways, the sight of old men with wispy beards smoking tobacco in immense bamboo water pipes and the crisp climate. It's not unusual for hotels and restaurants in Mae Salong to boast

EASTERN PROVINCES

satellite reception of three TV channels from China and three from Hong Kong. Although the Yunnanese dialect of Chinese remains the lingua franca, the new generation of young people look more to Bangkok than Taipei for their social and cultural inspirations. Many have left for greater educational and career opportunities.

Things to See & Do

One of the most important government programs is the crop-substitution plan to encourage hill tribes to cultivate tea, coffee, corn and fruit trees. This seems to be quite successful, as there are plenty of these products for sale in the town markets, and tea and corn are abundant in the surrounding fields.

At several **tea factories** in town you can taste the fragrant Mae Salong teas, cultivated from cuttings that originally hailed from Taiwan. The highest quality local tea is *kâan àwn* (soft-stem oolong). Another local favourite is *chaa náam phêung* (honey tea), prized for its natural sweetness.

Oolong teas are prized for their fragrance as well as taste, hence the two-cup serving method; the tall and narrow cup is emptied into the round cup, and the fragrance inhaled. Let the vendor instruct you. The tea shops also sell a variety of Chinese tea pots, and other tea wares, imported from Taiwan.

Chinese herbs, particularly the kind that are mixed with liquor *(yaa dawng)*, are also popular. Thai and Chinese tourists who come to Mae Salong frequently take back a bag or two of assorted Chinese herbs or tea. The local illicit corn whisky is much in demand – perhaps an all-too-obvious substitution for the poppy.

An interesting **morning market** convenes from around 5am to 7am (5am to 6am is the peak time) at the T-junction near Shin Sane Guest House and is attended by hill tribespeople from the surrounding districts. A more tourist-oriented **day market** lining the road in front of the Khumnaiphol Resort (see Places to Stay later) sells dried fruits, several varieties of fresh mushrooms, Chinese herbs and tea.

Behind the Khumnaiphol Resort is a **viewpoint** where you can look out over the town of Mae Salong. Near the viewpoint is a grand **memorial to the KMT**. Stairs lead to the **tomb of General Tuan Shi Wen**, commander of the 5th Division of the Anti-Communist Liberation Army of Yunnan of the Republic of China. Tuan, who also profited handsomely from the opium trade, died in 1980; his son runs the resort.

At Mae Salong Resort, which was a training camp for KMT soldiers until as late as 1987, there is a small **museum** containing photos and other artefacts chronicling the KMT history in the area.

On the road leading uphill to Mae Salong Resort, **Wat Santikhiri** encompasses a recently constructed Thai wíhǎan adjacent to an older Chinese temple dedicated to Kuan Yin, the goddess of compassion. Behind the wíhǎan a steep path continues on to **Phra Boromathat Chedi**, a stupa dedicated to the late Princess Mother.

Minivans full of Thai day-trippers begin arriving in Mae Salong around 10am and leave by 4pm. If you can stay overnight you'll pretty much have the place to yourself in the mornings and evenings.

Ban Hin Taek (Ban Thoet Thai)
บ้านหินแตก(บ้านเทิดไทย)

Khun Sa, Southeast Asia's most famous insurgent rebel and opium warlord, made his headquarters in the village of Ban Hin Taek – officially known today as Ban Thoet Thai – from 1976 until 1982, operating from Northern Thailand with virtual impunity.

The one-storey wooden house he once lived in is being turned into a museum that will display some of his personal effects and chronicle the history of his life and struggle for Shan independence.

Today many of Ban Hin Taek's 3000 residents – a mix of Shan, Yunnanese, Akha, Lisu and Hmong – claim to have fond memories of the man once hunted, but never captured, by heroin-consuming countries.

A busy morning market – part of which was once used to store the SUA arsenal – trades in goods from Thailand, Myanmar and China. Khun Sa was also responsible for the construction of Wat Phra That Ka Kham, a Shan-style monastery.

Rim Than Guest House (☎/fax 01 961 6961, 15 Mu 1) Rooms 300-500B. Comfortable bungalows are available at this place near the banks of the Nam Than. Next door to the guesthouse, *Ting Ting Restaurant* serves simple meals.

Trekking

Shin Sane Guest House has a wall map showing approximate routes to Akha, Mien, Hmong, Lisu, Lahu and Shan villages in the area. Nearby Mien, Akha and Lisu villages are less than half a day's walk away.

The best hikes are north of Mae Salong between Ban Hin Taek and the Myanmar border. Ask about political conditions before heading off in this direction (towards Myanmar), however. Shan and Wa armies competing for control over this section of the Thailand-Myanmar border occasionally clash in the area. A steady trade in amphetamines and, to a lesser extent, heroin, flows across the border via several conduit villages.

It's possible to walk south from Mae Salong to Chiang Rai in three or four days, following trails that pass through fairly remote hill-tribe villages. There are also several easily reached hill-tribe villages along the highway between Pasang and Mae Salong, but these days they're full of day tourists from Chiang Rai.

Shin Sane Guest House (see Places to Stay following) arranges treks to nearby villages for about 600B per day. It's possible to hire ponies as pack animals, or horses for riding. You could also trek the 12km to the Lahu village of Ja-Ju on your own. A basic guesthouse there offers rooms and two meals a day for 50B per person.

Places to Stay

Since the road from Mae Salong to Tha Ton opened, fewer visitors are opting to overnight in Mae Salong. The resulting surplus of accommodations often make prices negotiable, except during holidays, when they tend to increase.

Shin Sane Guest House (Sin Sae; ☎ 053 765 026, 32/3 Thanon Mae Salong) Rooms with shared hot-water bathroom 50B, cabins with private hot-water bathroom 200B. This guesthouse, Mae Salong's first hotel, is a wooden affair with a bit of atmosphere. The rooms with shared facilities are pretty basic, while the cabins at the back are newer and have good beds. Information on trekking is available, including a good trekking map; there is also a nice little eating area and a place for doing laundry. Calls to prayer from a mosque behind Shin Sane will bring you closer to Allah bright and early in the morning.

Golden Dragon Inn (☎ 053 765 009, 13/1 Thanon Mae Salong) Bungalows with hot-water bathroom 300B, hotel-type rooms with hot-water bathroom 500B. The clean bungalows in this place, directly opposite the mosque, have balconies. Hotel-type rooms each come with two double beds. During low season prices may be negotiable.

Mae Salong Villa (☎ 053 765 114-9, fax 053 765 039, 5 Mu 1) Rooms 600-1200B. The clean bungalow-style accommodation in this place just below the town centre is in a garden setting – it's better value than the Mae Salong Resort. The restaurant offers a nice view of the mountains, and the food is quite good. High-quality tea, grown on the proprietor's tea estate, can be purchased here.

Mae Salong Resort (☎ 053 765 014, fax 053 765 135, 8/8 Mu 1) Rooms & bungalows 500-2000B. At the top of the price range is this 59-room resort. The variety of rooms and bungalows look good from a distance but are none too clean. An exhibit hall on the grounds displays interesting old photographs, captioned in English, from the KMT era. The Yunnanese restaurant here, originally a cantina for KMT troops, is very good – especially tasty are the fresh mushroom dishes.

Khumnaiphol Resort (☎ 053 765 001-3, fax 053 765 004, 58 Mu 1) Singles & doubles 500B. On the opposite side of town near the afternoon market, on the road to Tha Ton, this once-upmarket resort is under new management and the modern hotel-style rooms are not as well kept as they once were.

Places to Eat

Paa-thâwng-kŏh (Chinese doughnuts) and hot soybean milk at the morning market are a good way to start the day. Don't miss the many *street noodle vendors* who sell *khanŏm jiin náam ngíaw,* a delicious Yunnanese rice-noodle concoction topped with a spicy pork sauce – Mae Salong's most famous local dish and a gourmet bargain at 15B per bowl.

Around town you'll find a variety of places serving simple Chinese snacks like fluffy *mantou* (plain steamed Chinese buns) and *saalaapao* (pork-stuffed Chinese buns) with delicious pickled vegetables. Many of the Chinese in Mae Salong are Muslims, so you'll find several *Muslim Chinese restaurants* serving khâo sawy.

Salema Restaurant, located halfway between the Shin Sane Guest House and the day market, serves tasty Yunnanese dishes using locally grown shitake mushrooms at moderate prices.

Of the hotel restaurants, the *Mae Salong Villa's* is best. Try the local speciality of black chicken steamed in Chinese medicinal herbs

Several *tea houses* in town selling locally grown teas offer complimentary tastings in very traditional, elaborate procedures involving the pouring of tea from a tall, narrow cup into a round cup to enhance the experience of the tea's fragrance.

Getting There & Away

Until the 1980s pack horses were used to move goods up the mountain to Mae Salong, but today the 36km road from Pasang is

Warning

In February 2001, Burmese forces, apparently in pursuit of Shan State Army rebels, shelled and fired on parts of Mae Sai, invoking retaliatory shelling from the Thai army. During the fighting the whole of Mae Sai was evacuated and the border area was subsequently closed for a time. At the time of publication it was open again, but check the current situation before travelling to Mae Sai.

paved and well travelled, and there is now a second route available as well. The original road, Rte 1130, winds west from Pasang, about 2km north of Mae Chan. Newer Rte 1234 approaches from the south, allowing easier access from Chiang Mai. The older route is definitely more spectacular.

To get to Mae Salong by public transport, take a bus from Mae Sai or Chiang Rai to Pasang. From Pasang, there are săwngthăew up the mountain to Mae Salong for 50B per person (down again costs 40B); the trip takes about an hour. This service stops at around 5pm; you can charter a săwngthăew in either direction for 300B.

The bus fare from Chiang Rai to Pasang is 15B. You can also reach Mae Salong by road from Tha Ton. See the Fang & Tha Ton section in the Around Chiang Mai chapter for details.

MAE SAI

แม่สาย

postcode 57130 • pop 60,000

The northernmost point in Thailand, Mae Sai is a good place from which to explore the Golden Triangle, Doi Tung and Mae Salong. It's also a good spot to observe border life, as Mae Sai is one of only two official land crossings open between Myanmar and Thailand. Don't come expecting bags of atmosphere; the town is little more than a modern trading post.

Foreigners are permitted to cross the border to Tachileik (the town opposite Mae Sai, spelt Thakhilek by the Thais) and continue as far as Kengtung, 163km from Thailand and 100km short of China. Within a few years, the road should be open all the way to the Chinese border – already the town is gearing up for Thailand-China traffic. (See the Around Mae Sai section for current details on this trip.) In spite of the opening, Thai tourists are much more commonly seen in Mae Sai than *faràng* (Westerners).

Burmese lacquerware, gems, jade and other goods from Laos and Myanmar are sold in shops along the main street. Many Burmese come over during the day from Tachileik to work or do business, hurrying back by sunset. Gem dealers from as far away as Chanthaburi frequent the gem market opposite the police station.

Take the steps up the hill near the border to **Wat Phra That Doi Wao**, west of the main street, for superb views over Myanmar and Mae Sai. This wát was reportedly constructed in memory of a couple of thousand Burmese soldiers who died fighting KMT here in 1965 (you'll hear differing stories around town, including a version wherein the KMT are the heroes). There are also some interesting trails in the cliffs and hills overlooking the Mae Sai Guest House

and the river. A persistent rumour says there's a gated cave tunnel that crosses to Myanmar beneath the Nam Ruak; the entrance is supposedly within the grounds of **Wat Tham Pha Jum**.

Mae Sai is a base for exploring the nearby caves of Tham Luang, Tham Pum and Tham Pla, as well as the trip to Doi Tung (see Around Mae Sai).

Places to Stay

Guesthouses *Chad House (☎ 053 732 054, fax 053 642 496, 32/1 Thanon Phahonyothin)* Dorm beds 50B per person, singles/

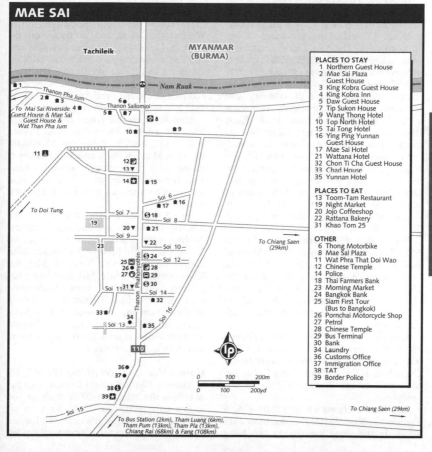

MAE SAI

Tachileik

MYANMAR (BURMA)

Nam Ruak

Thanon Pha Jum
Thanon Sailomjoi

To Mai Sai Riverside
Guest House & Mae Sai
Guest House &
Wat Than Pha Jum

To Doi Tung

Soi 6
Soi 7
Soi 8
Soi 9
Soi 10
Soi 12

Thanon Phahonyothin

Soi 11
Soi 14
Soi 13
Soi 16

To Chiang Saen
(29km)

110

To Bus Station (2km), Tham Luang (6km),
Tham Pum (13km), Tham Pla (13km),
Chiang Rai (68km) & Fang (108km)

To Chiang Saen (29km)

0   100   200m
0   100   200yd

PLACES TO STAY
1 Northern Guest House
2 Mae Sai Plaza
   Guest House
3 King Kobra Guest House
4 King Kobra Inn
5 Daw Guest House
7 Tip Sukon House
9 Wang Thong Hotel
10 Top North Hotel
15 Tai Tong Hotel
16 Ying Ping Yunnan
   Guest House
17 Mae Sai Hotel
21 Wattana Hotel
32 Chon Ti Cha Guest House
33 Chad House
35 Yunnan Hotel

PLACES TO EAT
13 Toom-Tam Restaurant
19 Night Market
20 Jojo Coffeeshop
22 Rattana Bakery
31 Khao Tom 25

OTHER
6 Thong Motorbike
8 Mae Sai Plaza
11 Wat Phra That Doi Wao
12 Chinese Temple
14 Police
18 Thai Farmers Bank
23 Morning Market
24 Bangkok Bank
25 Siam First Tour
   (Bus to Bangkok)
26 Pornchai Motorcycle Shop
27 Petrol
28 Chinese Temple
29 Bus Terminal
30 Bank
34 Laundry
36 Customs Office
37 Immigration Office
38 TAT
39 Border Police

EASTERN PROVINCES

doubles with shared hot-water bathroom 100/150B, bungalows with private bathroom 200B. Chad House is off the main street in a residential neighbourhood near the town entrance and the bus terminal. The English-speaking Thai-Shan family that runs it is friendly and helpful, and the food is good.

Chon Ti Cha Guest House (☎ 053 732 068, Soi 14, Thanon Phahonyothin) Rooms with fan 180B, with air-con & TV 300B. This guesthouse offers 12 clean, well-worn motel-style rooms, all with Thai-style toilet and cold-water shower. A Thai restaurant is attached, but little English is spoken.

Ying Ping Yunnan Guest House (☎ 053 640 507, Soi 6, Thanon Phahonyothin) Rooms 200-250B. The 12 very clean rooms with fan, TV, phone and hot-water shower are good value. There's a Chinese restaurant on the premises. Not much English is spoken.

Northern Guest House (☎ 053 731 537, 402 Thanon Tham Pha Jum) Rooms with shared bathroom from 60B, doubles with hot-water bathroom, air-con & river view up to 350B. Right on Nam Ruak (Ruak River) west of the international bridge, the friendly Northern Guest House has a variety of rooms and huts; the new air-con building has fancier rooms. The guesthouse maintains a nicely landscaped sitting area along the river; a restaurant on the premises offers room service, and is open from 7am to midnight. Add 50B to100B to prices in the high season.

King Kobra Guest House (☎ 053 733 055, Thanon Tham Pha Jum) Singles/doubles with shared facilities 100/120B, apartment-style rooms with fan & hot water 150/250B. East of the Northern Guest House on the southern side of the road (no river frontage), this place has simple but adequate rooms.

King Kobra Inn (☎ 053 733 055, Thanon Tham Pha Jum) Rooms with air-con 350B, VIP rooms 450B. Next door to King Kobra Guest House, the affiliated King Cobra Inn has email service. The room rates include breakfast.

Daw Guest House (☎ 053 640 476, 9 Thanon Sailomjoi) Singles/doubles 160/200B. In the same vicinity as the King Cobra Inn, the Yunnanese-owned Daw Guest House has five very large rooms with fan and hot-water shower. The proprietor speaks excellent English.

Tip Sukon House (☎ 053 642 816, 01-883 7318, 734 Thanon Sailomjoi) Rooms on 1st/2nd/3rd floor 200/400/300B. A bit east of Daw Guest House is this new three-storey place; all rooms are spotless and have private hot-water bathrooms. On the 1st floor there are one-bed rooms. On the second floor are the air-con VIP rooms, each with TV and a balcony overlooking the street. The 3rd floor houses doubles with fan and TV.

Mae Sai Plaza Guest House (☎ 053 732 230, Thanon Sailomjoi) Rooms 80-120B. West of Tip Sukon, and just back from the river, this rambling, 71-room hillside bamboo and wood complex has a laid-back atmosphere and a cafe overlooking the road. We've received complaints about the general lack of cleaning and maintenance here. Add 50B to prices in the high season.

Mae Sai Riverside Guest House (☎ 053 732 554, Thanon Tham Pha Jum) Rooms with cold/hot-water bathroom 150/200B. Between Mae Sai Plaza and Mae Sai Guest House, next to the river landing for local Thai-Burmese trade, this place has clean and secure rooms, all with fan and private bathroom.

Mae Sai Guest House (☎ 053 732 021, Thanon Sailomjoi) Bungalow singles/doubles with shared hot-water bathroom 100/200B, with private bathroom 200-500B. Another 150m west of Mai Sai Riverside Guest House, this guesthouse has a nicely landscaped and scenic location on the river across from Myanmar. It's a walk of about 1km from the end of Mae Sai's main road and thus very quiet. The bungalows are well designed. There's a restaurant and treks can be arranged.

Hotels *Mae Sai Hotel* (☎ 053 731 462, Soi 6, Thanon Phahonyothin) Rooms with fan & cold-water bathroom 200B, with air-con & hot-water bathroom 350B. This isn't a bad budget choice, as it's centrally located yet off the main road so it's relatively quiet.

Wattana Hotel (☎ *053 731 002, 24 Thanon Phahonyothin)* Rooms with fan/aircon 200/300B. Across from Mae Sai's market area, the Wattana is fairly well kept; all rooms come with private shower and toilet.

Yunnan Hotel (☎ *053 642 169, 688 Thanon Phahonyothin)* Rooms with fan, hot water & TV 350B, VIP rooms with air-con 500B. About 100m before the turn-off for Chad Guest House, done up in Chinese kitsch but friendly, the Yunnan has comfortable rooms that sleep up to three people. VIP rooms are the same, with the addition of a sofa and fridge. There's a beer garden in front.

Top North Hotel (☎ *053 731 955, fax 053 732 331, 306 Thanon Phahonyothin)* Singles/doubles with fan 300/400B, rooms with hot water 500B, with air-con 550B, with air-con, fridge & TV 600B. This popular hotel is only about five minutes walk from the bridge crossing to Myanmar.

Tai Tong Hotel (*Thai Thong;* ☎ *053 731 975, fax 053 640 988, 6 Thanon Phahonyothin)* Standard rooms 300B, larger rooms 500B, suites 900B. The rates for the larger rooms and suites include breakfast for two. All come with air-con and hot water.

Wang Thong Hotel (☎ *053 733 389, fax 053 733 399, 224 Thanon Phahonyothin)* Rooms 900B, suites up to 1500B. In the northern part of town off Thanon Phahonyothin, the nine-storey Wang Thong entertains brisk traffic among business travellers. Spacious, international-class rooms have all the amenities. Facilities include a swimming pool, pub, disco and restaurant. Off-street parking is available in a guarded lot behind the hotel.

Places to Eat

Many *food stalls* offering everything from khâo sawy to custard set up at night on the sidewalks along Thanon Phahonyothin. The night market is rather small but the *Chinese vendors* do excellent *kŭaytĭaw phàt sii-íu* (rice noodles stir-fried in soy sauce) and other noodle dishes. You can also get fresh paa-thâwng-kŏh and hot soy milk.

Jojo Coffeeshop (☎ *053 731 662, 233/1 Thanon Phahonyothin)* Dishes 25-50B.

Open 6.30am-4.30pm. Popular Jojo serves good Thai curries and Thai vegetarian dishes, plus ice cream and Western snacks. You'll eat well while contemplating the collection of Lanna-style wooden Buddhas along the walls.

Rattana Bakery, (☎ *053 731 230, 18 Thanon Phahonyothin)* Dishes 10-35B. Open 8am-5pm. Rattana has Thai- and Western-style pastries and cakes.

Khao Tom 25 (*near Chad House, Thanon Phahonyothin)* Dishes 20-45B. Open around noon-4am daily. This is your best bet for late-night eats.

Toom-Tam Restaurant (*Thanon Phahonyothin)* Dishes 20-35B. South of the Chinese temple and north of the police station, this Muslim place has good curries and khâo mòk.

Getting There & Away

Buses to Mae Sai leave frequently from Chiang Rai (20/37B ordinary/air-con, 1½ hours). The bus trip to/from Chiang Saen costs 20B via Mae Chan. See Getting Around in the Chiang Saen section later for details on different routes between Mae Sai and Chiang Saen.

There are buses to/from Chiang Mai (95B ordinary, three times daily, 108/171B 2nd/1st-class air-con, seven times daily, four to five hours). VIP buses to Bangkok leave Mae Sai at 6.30pm, 7pm and 7.10pm.

There are also direct buses to Mae Sai from Fang (45B) and Tha Ton (36B) via the paved Tha Ton–Mae Chan road. Other destinations include Doi Tung (40B), Mae Chan (14B), Mae Salong (60B) and Sop Ruak (34B). Mae Sai's main bus terminal (☎ 053 646 403) is 2km south of the immigration office, a 5B shared săwngthăew ride.

Bangkok Siam First Tour operates VIP 'sleeper' buses from Mae Sai to Bangkok (450B to 640B depending on the number of seats, 5.30pm or 6pm daily; 13 hours).

Government buses to Bangkok range from around 250B for ordinary buses to around 700B VIP. These depart from Thanon Phahonyothin around 5.30am to 6am and again between 4pm and 5.30pm.

Getting Around

Săwngthăew around town are 5B shared. Túk-túk cost 20B to 30B and motorcycle taxis 10B to 20B. Guesthouses in Mae Sai have stopped renting motorcycles, but Honda Dreams can be rented at Pornchai Motorcycle Shop, on Thanon Phahonyothin between Siam First Tour and the petrol station, for 150B per day. Thong Motorbike, across from Tip Sukon House, rents motorcycles at similar rates.

AROUND MAE SAI
Tham Luang
ถ้ำหลวง

About 6km south of Mae Sai off Rte 110 is Tham Luang, a large cave that extends into the hills for at least a couple of kilometres. The first cavern is huge, and a narrow passage at the back leads to a series of other chambers and side tunnels of varying sizes. The first 1km is quite easy going but after that you have to do some climbing over piles of rocks to get farther in. At this point the roof formations become more fantastic and tiny crystals make them change colour according to the angle of the light. For 30B you can borrow a gas lantern from the caretakers in front of the cave or you can take someone along as a guide (for which there's no fixed fee; just give them whatever you want). Guides aren't always available during the week.

Tham Pum & Tham Pla
ถ้ำปุ่ม/ถ้ำปลา

Only 13km south of Mae Sai, just off Rte 110 at Ban Tham, are a couple of caves with freshwater lakes inside. Bring a torch to explore the caves as there are no lights. Another attraction here is the unique chedi in front of the cave entrance. Its wide, multi-tiered, 'cake-like' structure is stylistically different from any other we've seen in Thailand.

Doi Tung
ดอยตุง

About halfway between Mae Chan and Mae Sai on Rte 110 is the turn-off west for Doi Tung. The name means 'Flag Peak', from the Northern Thai word for flag (tung). Legend says Phaya Achutarat of Chiang Saen ordered a giant flag to be flown from the peak to mark the spot where two chedi were constructed in AD 911; the chedi are still there, a pilgrimage site for Thai, Shan and Chinese Buddhists.

But the main attraction of Doi Tung is getting there. The 'easy' way is via Rte 1149, which is mostly paved to the peak of Doi Tung. But it's winding, steep and narrow, so if you're driving or riding a motorcycle, take it slowly.

Along the way are Shan, Akha and Musoe (Lahu) villages. Opium cultivation, once common all over Doi Tung, has been virtually eliminated following royal crop substitution projects. However amphetamine trafficking from nearby Myanmar means Doi Tung can still be a slightly dicey area to explore alone if you go far off the main roads. Travelling after 4pm – when traffic thins out – is not advised except along the main routes. It is not safe to trek in this area without a Thai or hill-tribe guide. You may hear gunfire from time to time, which might indicate that the Thai border patrol are in pursuit of Shan or Wa army units or others who have been caught between two hostile governments.

On the theory that local hill tribes would be so honoured by a royal presence that they would stop cultivating opium, the late Princess Mother (the king's mother) built the **Doi Tung Royal Villa** (admission 100B), a summer palace, on the slopes of Doi Tung near Pa Kluay Reservoir. The beautifully landscaped **Mae Fah Luang Garden** is open to the public, and the royal villa itself has been converted into a museum that preserves everything in the house almost exactly as it was before the Princess Mother's 1995 death.

Another royal project nearby, **Doi Tung Zoo** (admission 30B; open 9am-5pm daily) covers an open space of over 32 hectares. The zoo was first established as a wildlife breeding and animal conservation station, to help reintroduce many species to a reforested Doi Tung. These include Siamese fireback pheasants, peacocks, bears, sambar deer, barking deer and hog deer.

At the peak, 1800m above sea level, **Wat Phra That Doi Tung** is built around the twin Lanna-style chedi. The chedi were renovated by famous Northern Thai monk Khruba Siwichai early in the 20th century. Pilgrims bang on the usual row of temple bells to gain merit. Although the wát isn't that impressive, the high forested setting will make the trip worthwhile. From the walled edge of the temple you can get an aerial view of the snaky road you've just climbed.

A walking path next to the wát leads to a spring, and there are other short walking trails in the vicinity. A bit below the peak is the smaller **Wat Noi Doi Tung**, where food and beverages are available from vendors.

Places to Stay & Eat *Baan Ton Nam* (☎ *053 767 003, fax 053 767 077)* Rooms 1500B Jan-Sep, 2500B Oct-Dec. Opened in 2000 as part of the Doi Tung Development Project, this well-designed facility offers 45 deluxe twin rooms with attached hot-water shower, air-con, refrigerators and satellite TV. A semi-outdoor *restaurant*, open 7am-9pm, offers excellent meals made with local produce, including lots of fresh mushrooms.

Getting There & Away Buses to the turn-off for Doi Tung are 15B from either Mae Chan or Mae Sai. From Ban Huay Khrai, at the Doi Tung turn-off, a săwngthăew to Ban Pakha is 30B, or 60B all the way to Doi Tung, 18km away.

Road conditions to Doi Tung vary from year to year depending on the state of repair; during bad spells, the section above Pakha can be quite a challenge to climb, whether you're in a truck, 4WD or motorcycle.

You can also travel by motorcycle between Doi Tung and Mae Sai along an even more challenging 16km unevenly sealed road that starts in the Akha village of Ban Phame, 8km south of Mae Sai (4km south along Rte 110, then 4km west), and joins the main road about two-thirds of the way up Doi Tung – about 11km from the latter. You can also pick up this road by following the dirt road that starts in front of Mae Sai's

Wat Doi Wao. West of Ban Phame the road has lots of tight curves, mud, rocks, precipitous drops, passing lorries and occasional road repair equipment – figure on at least an hour by motorcycle or 4WD from Mae Sai. Although now sealed this is a route for experienced bikers only. The road also runs high in the mountains along the Myanmar border and should not be travelled alone or after 4pm. Ask first in Mae Sai about border conditions.

If you want to do a full loop from Mae Sai, ride/drive to Doi Tung via Rte 110 south of Mae Sai, then Rte 1149 up to Doi Tung. Once you've had a look around the summit, return to Mae Sai via the Ban Phame aforementioned roads; this means you'll be running downhill much of the way.

Cross-Border Trips to Tachileik & Beyond

Foreigners are ordinarily permitted to cross the bridge over the Nam Ruak into Tachileik in Myanmar. On occasion – such as in May 1994 when the MTA bombed the Tachileik dyke (draining the reservoir that supplied the town with water) and in early 2001 when Yangon forces engaged with local insurgents – the border closes for a while for security reasons, so be prepared for possible disappointment if the situation deteriorates again.

For now you can enter Myanmar at Tachileik and travel to Kengtung or Mengla for two weeks upon payment of a US$10 fee and the exchange of US$100 for 100 FEC (foreign exchange certificates), the parallel currency Myanmar's government uses to dampen black-market money exchange. You can use the FEC to pay for hotel rooms and plane tickets, but that's about all. Or change them for Myanmar kyat at the going black-market rate. Your two-week tourist visa can be extended for another two weeks at the immigration office in Kengtung.

If you only want to cross the border into Tachileik for the day, the cost is US$5 or 250B. There is no FEC exchange requirement for day trips.

Whether you're crossing for a day or for two weeks, you must check out with the Thai immigration near the entrance to Mae Sai, a couple of kilometres before the border itself. Once you cross the bridge, stop at the Burmese immigration checkpoint and pay the Myanmar immigration fees as appropriate. Upon returning to Thailand, you will be given a 30-day tourist visa automatically if you don't already have a Thailand visa.

Three-night, four-day excursions to the town of Kengtung (called Chiang Tung by the Thais and usually spelt Kyaingtong by the Burmese), 163km north, may be arranged through King Kobra Guest House in Mae Sai.

Tachileik About 3000 to 4000 people cross the bridge to Tachileik daily, most of them Thais shopping for dried mushrooms, herbal medicines, cigarettes and other cheap imports from China. At the **Myanmar Travels & Tours office**, on the left just after you cross the bridge, you can pick up an informative sketch map of the town for 5B.

The town boasts several Buddhist monasteries, including one with a **meditation centre** staffed by monks from Yangon and attended by Thais from Mae Sai as well as local Shan and Burmese. The **Mahamyatmuni Paya** contains a replica of the giant Rakhaing-style Buddha from the temple of the same name in Mandalay.

Be wary of cheap cartons of Marlboros and other Western-brand cigarettes, as many are filled with Burmese cigarettes instead of the real thing. Two of the better buys for foreigners are Shan handicrafts and untaxed imported wines.

If you're seriously interested in seeing Tachileik, your best option is to seek out one of the pedicab drivers parked near the MTT office. Several of them can speak decent English and can take you on a two-hour pedicab tour of the city for 100B.

Kengtung A bit more than halfway between the Thai and Chinese borders, Kengtung is a sleepy but historic capital for the Shan State's Khün culture. The Khün speak a Northern Thai language related to Shan and Thai Lü

and use a writing script similar to the ancient Lanna script. The original Khün are in fact said to have been 13th-century migrants from Chiang Mai, and their rulers claim to be descendants of the Lanna dynasty.

Although Kengtung lies about midway between the Salween River and Mekong River valleys, it is more or less cut off from the former by a series of north-south mountain ranges. Hence, culturally, the area has more of an affinity for the nearby cultures of the Mekong – Laos, Xishuangbanna (southeastern Yunnan) and Thailand – than for the Shan and Burmese cultures west of the Salween.

Before the Khün began paying tribute to the Burmans under King Anawrahta, they had their own independent kingdom variously called Meuang Tamilap, Meuang Ong Pu, Meuang Sanlawachilakam, Meuang Khemmaratungkburi and Tungkalasi before settling on Kengtung, which means 'Walled City of Tung'. 'Tung' is a reference to the kingdom's mythical founder, a hermit named Tungkalasi who used his magic staff to drain a lake of near-sea proportions, leaving behind the current town lake. Remains of the original city walls and gates can still be seen.

At various times in Thai history, Kengtung paid tribute to Thai kingdoms, most recently during WWII when Thai troops occupied the town. Nowadays it's a strategic Burmese government stronghold in the middle of the shifting seas of Shan and Wa insurgency. Its position is doubly strategic since the area is a crossroads with outlets in four different countries – Myanmar, China, Thailand and Laos – and is thus a critical linchpin in the country's defence.

Built around a small lake, and dotted with over 30 historic Buddhist temples and crumbling British colonial architecture, it's a much more scenic town than Tachileik, and one of the most interesting towns in Myanmar's entire Shan State. About 70% of all foreign visitors to Kengtung are Thais seeking a glimpse of ancient Lanna. Few Westerners are seen around town save for contract employees working for the UNDCP (United Nations Drug Control Project).

{continued on page 262}

EASTERN PROVINCES

Lanna-Style Temple Murals

Title page: Northern Thai stories: A mural depicts Katthana Kuman and his mother entering the forest (Photograph by Panupong Laohasom).

Top: Daily life and traditional Lanna architecture: Wihan Lai Kham, Wat Phra Singh, Chiang Mai

Middle: Detail from Khatthana Kuman mural, Wat Phumin, Nan

Bottom: Stories of Northern Thailand life: detail of courtship scene, Wat Phumin, Nan

PANUPONG LAOHASOM

Full of colourful, vibrant scenes depicting local people and everyday life, Northern Thai temple murals provide a wealth of information about the beliefs, customs and traditional culture of the Northern Thai people. Although there is evidence to suggest that a temple mural tradition in Northern Thailand dates to the 15th-century Lanna kingdom, no examples of this early vintage remain and most existing temple murals date back no more than 150 years. However, because stylistically the paintings are linked with the Lanna period, Thai art historians refer to them as 'Lanna-style' murals, regardless of age.

Originally all Thai temple murals fulfilled the twofold function of decorating the temple and educating those who came to worship by depicting Buddhist stories with moral messages. However, unlike the elegant, structured murals of Bangkok, whose painters followed carefully prescribed formulas approved by the court, Lanna murals are characterised by their spontaneity, down-to-earth descriptiveness and strong local flavour. An intriguing mix of Burmese, Shan, Lao, Thai Lü and Siamese influences reflects the multiethnic makeup of Northern Thailand now as in the past. This blending of outside influences with local traditions and sensibilities enhances the distinctive charm of Northern Thai temple murals. The use of natural mineral and plant pigments, including malachite, cinnabar, ochre and indigo, make for soft, pleasing colour schemes.

Lanna murals are almost always found in the wát's *wíhǎan*, a building at the heart of the temple complex where monks chant their daily Buddhist verses and proselytise to the community. The murals themselves draw their inspiration from events in the *jataka* (tales of the Buddha's past lives) as well as from a number of popular local stories taken from Northern Thai religious texts. Buddhist monks related these same stories time and again to their congregation, and the paintings, which can be viewed from the floor where worshippers sat, provided visual accompaniment to their *Dhamma* (Buddhist teachings) discourses.

In addition to the colourful narrative stories painted along the main walls of the wíhǎan, Lanna artists often used a mural technique called *laai kham* to further embellish the building's interior. Literally 'gold patterns', laai kham involves the stencilling of gold leaf onto a red or black lacquered surface. This technique has been used mainly to decorate the wooden architectural elements of the building's interior – pillars, beams and panels – as well as the wall immediately behind the main Buddha image.

Because of the difficulties inherent in stencil-cutting, laai kham is better suited to floral and geometric patterns or icons than it is to rendering detailed stories. Most popular among iconic depictions are stupas *thewádaa* (celestial beings), lotus flowers, Bodhi trees, Buddhas and mythical creatures such as the half-human, half-bird *kinnari*. The effect of light filtering in through the wíhǎan doorway and reflecting off the gold-and-red patterned surfaces is stunning and gives the visitor the feeling of having entered into a sacred, otherworldly space.

Murals deteriorate quickly in Thailand's hot, moist climate, a process sped along by poor temple maintenance due to lack of funds and/or expertise, along with a lack of appreciation for the historical and cultural value of the murals. Many of those that could be viewed just 20 years ago are now gone, and along with them, a part of Northern Thailand's precious cultural heritage. Thankfully, growing awareness and interest has meant that major efforts to restore and preserve important mural sites have been underway in recent years. Hopefully this trend will continue far into the future and guarantee the safekeeping of these windows onto Lanna's past.

Wat Buak Khrok Luang
วัดบวกครกหลวง

The wíhǎan at Wat Buak Khrok Luang, down a small *soi* (alley) off the main Chiang Mai–San Kamphaeng highway 4km from San Kamphaeng, offers a fine example of traditional Lanna architecture. A Shan artist painted the outstanding interior Lanna murals around 1870. Despite the damage inflicted on the paintings when windows were cut into the walls in a later renovation, and despite one badly deteriorated section, the paintings have retained their unique character and lively immediacy.

One can clearly see a Shan/Burmese influence in the palace architecture and costuming in the murals. A depiction of the *Mahasadha Jataka* on the northern wall shows a large group of Chinese undertaking the construction of a Lanna-style building, testimony to the presence of Chinese traders and residents from Bangkok and from neighbouring Yunnan Province. As one enters the wíhǎan, the scene immediately on the left depicts a procession of beautifully dressed merit-makers on their way to the temple loaded with offerings for the monks. On the right, exactly opposite, gruesome scenes of torture and mayhem evoke the Buddhist equivalent of hell. This clever layout reminds visitors of their options – do good deeds and offer generously to the temple in this life or reap the karmic consequence of being reborn into one of the frightening cosmic realms of hell in the next.

Wat Pa Daet
วัดป่าแดด

Nestled amid the lush, terraced rice fields of Mae Chaem Valley, west of Thailand's tallest peak, Doi Inthanon, Wat Pa Daet was constructed in 1887 and its mural paintings were completed in the following year. The soft blues and reds of the colour scheme, accented by bold, black outlines, lend a poetic quality to the paintings, which in their rusticity could almost be classified folk art. Here, lively depictions of rural Northern Thai life serve as a backdrop for classic jataka stories. Worth noting are the ploughing and rice planting scenes on the northern wall, the traditional horizontally striped *phâa sîn* worn by the women and the fantastic blue tattoos of the Northern Thai men, patterns which extend from their waists to their knees and look very much like short pants. The now faded inscriptions that run below each mural just beyond the painted frame records the names of the donors who sponsored the paintings and their intentions to earn merit through their donations.

Wat Prasat
วัดปราสาท

Close to historic Wat Phra Sing stands the wíhăan Wat Prasat, one of the oldest unreconstructed temple structures in Chiang Mai. Its multi-tiered roofs and wood-and-plaster walls are characteristic of traditional Lanna-style architecture. Inside, at the far end of the wíhăan before the walled chamber containing the main Buddha image, striking laai kham designs decorate the walls. Unlike most Northern Thai laai kham, which tend to be purely decorative or iconic, the gold-stencilled patterns at Wat Prasat narrate episodes from the Buddha's life.

On the southern wall a painting depicts a smiling Buddha passing into *parinibbana* (nirvana after death), his disciples grieving around him. On the opposite wall, Prince Siddhartha renounces the world by cutting off his long tresses, while in an adjacent scene he achieves enlightenment under the Bodhi tree. These murals are thought to have been executed circa 1900.

Wihan Lai Kham
วิหารลายคำ

The small Wihan Lai Kham, located next to the main chedi in the Wat Phra Sing temple complex in Chiang Mai, takes its name from the laai kham designs on its interior back wall. The wíhăan is also well known for the narrative murals that run along its main walls and date to circa 1870. The mural on the southern wall, depicting the popular Northern Thai story of a divine golden swan, Phra Suwannahong, is thought to have been painted by a local Chiang Mai artist.

Paintings on the northern wall, executed by an ethnic Chinese thought to have trained in Bangkok, display a much higher level of skill. A small figure above one of the windows is thought to be a self portrait of the artist. The mural here narrates Sang Thong (Golden Conch), a tale about a princess who refuses all of the princes of neighbouring kingdoms who come seeking her hand in marriage. Much to her father's regret, she falls madly in love with a terribly ugly common fellow from a nearby village. In the end, of course, he turns out to be a prince in disguise.

Wat Chiang Man
วัดเชียงมั่น

The murals in the wíhăan of Wat Chiang Man, Chiang Mai's oldest temple, were completed in 1996 to celebrate the 700th anniversary of the founding of Chiang Mai. Although the murals were recently painted, Ajahn Vithi Phanichapan of Chiang Mai University's Fine Arts Department and several other local artists drew their inspiration from traditional Lanna laai kham by covering the walls with red lacquer and gold-stencilled pictures depicting scenes from the life of Chiang Mai's founding father, Phaya Mang Rai. The result is surprisingly authentic and a welcome alternative to the jarring colours of the modern, acrylic-painted 'poster style' murals that are in vogue today in temples throughout Thailand.

Wat Phra That Lampang Luang
วัดพระธาตุลำปางหลวง

Several interesting examples of Lanna-style mural painting can be found in this large and highly venerated temple complex in Ko Kha, Lampang Province. To the north of the main chedi, open-sided Wihan Nam Taem contains the oldest surviving Northern Thai murals, painted around 1750. Although in an advanced state of deterioration, these murals, which were painted onto wooden panels positioned below the roofline, reveal a bold and skilful use of line and colour as well as careful observation of the natural world. The subject of the murals is Indra, the Hindu king of the gods and the first Hindu god, in Buddhist myth, to pay homage to the Buddha. On the back wall behind the main altar, a particularly fine laai kham Bodhi tree provides a dramatic backdrop to the sculpted Buddha images.

In the Wihan Luang (Main Wihan) the series of murals painted along the wooden panels on both the northern and southern sides of the building date back to circa 1900. These jataka paintings feature the yellow-and-blue colour scheme characteristic of Lampang painting in general, and show both Burmese and Chinese influence, especially in the costumes of the various figures depicted.

The small Wihan Phra Phut to the south of the chedi contains laai kham depicting the 'Buddhas of the Past', seated in rows on a lotus pedestal base. The designs etched in gold leaf on the lower portion of the wíhǎan's columns, depicting dancing figures, soldiers on horseback and mythical creatures such as the kinnari, are especially noteworthy.

Wat Phumin
วัดภูมินทร์

Far off the beaten path in the sleepy provincial capital of Nan Province one finds perhaps Thailand's finest and best-preserved example of Lanna-style murals at Wat Phumin. This temple is unusual in that its perfectly cruciform layout is said to encompass all three of the major elements of Buddhist temple architecture – the wíhǎan, the bòt and the chedi – within its interior space. Mural paintings cover all four walls of the expansive wíhǎan, adding to the structure's overall sense of symmetry.

Above each of the four entryways the visitor can view scenes from the Buddha's life story. On three of the walls we see the Buddha seated in the *bhumisparsa* (earth-touching) posture with disciples to either side. On the western wall, the Buddha passes into parinibbana as his disciples mourn.

Below these large iconic figures, the local Northern Thai story *Katthana Kuman* is depicted on a much smaller scale. This running narrative, about a hero who does battle with a number of formidable adversaries while on a quest to find his father, is full of local colour and considerable humour as well. The distinctive Lanna script written above and below the painted scenes helps to narrate the story and identify the various characters.

Also of note are some of the life-sized portraits painted either side of several of the entryways and at the top of the pilasters. Most likely these represent well-known Nan residents of the time. The figure in the red cape on the eastern wall is thought to portray the Nan governor who ordered the restoration of the temple, and on the western wall, next to the door, the tattooed male figure shown whispering to his female companion is believed to be a portrait of the artist himself. This latter scene is one of the most popularly copied in art produced for the tourist market.

Wat Nong Bua
วัดหนองบัว

The obvious similarities in the style and character of the murals at Wat Phumin with those of Wat Nong Bua, in Nong Bua, Nan Province, have caused many to speculate as to whether or not they are the work of the same artist or school of artists working together in the area at that time. The sense of liveliness and fun, use of gesture and facial expression to show emotion and the attention to detail are very similar in both temples. Here too, it is a Northern Thai text, the *Candagadha Jataka,* which is depicted. The eight Buddhas painted on the wíhǎan's western wall behind the main altar show the Enlightened One in seated and standing postures, and are particularly beautiful. The soft reds, pinks and blues of the colour scheme are much admired by the Thai art history community.

Claudine Triolo
A graduate in art history, Claudine resides in Chiang Mai and leads tours of Thailand and neighbouring countries.

{continued from page 256}

Wát worth visiting include **Wat Jom Kham**, which features a tall gilded chedi topped by a gold umbrella inlaid with silver, rubies, diamonds, sapphires and jade, and hung with tiny gold bells. The interior walls bear older gold-leaf-on-lacquer jataka (stories of the Buddha's past lives) as well as modern painted ones, sparkling mirrored pillars and a dozen or so Buddha images on an altar draped with gilded cloth. Much intricate tinwork outlines the gables and plinths of the temple. Legend says the stupa contains six strands of the Buddha's hair. Most likely the site dates to the 13th century Chiang Mai migration. The temple was substantially renovated in 1906 and 1936, when the height of the stupa rose to 38 metres.

Harry's Guest House & Trekking (☎ 101-21418, 132 Mai Yang Lan) Rooms US$5 per person. Harry is an English-speaking Kengtung native who spent many years as a trekking guide in Chiang Mai. He rents basic rooms in his large house and can arrange local treks.

The *Noi Yee Hotel* near the centre of town costs US$8 to US$15 per person per night in large multibed rooms.

For a complete description of Kengtung and the surrounding area, see Lonely Planet's *Myanmar* guidebook.

Beyond Kengtung Eighty-five kilometres north of Kengtung lies the Sino-Burmese border district of Mengla (or Mong La as it's sometimes spelt). Although Mengla is mainly a Thai Lü district, in a deal worked out with the Myanmar military it's currently controlled by ethnic Wa, who once fought against Yangon troops but who now enjoy peaceful relations with Yangon (in return for a sizable share in the Wa's thriving amphetamine and opium trade, it is suspected). A Drug Free Museum contains an exhibit on how to refine heroin from opium. The district receives lots of Chinese tourists, who come to peruse Mengla's well-known wildlife market and to gamble in the district's several casinos. The largest and

plushest, the Myanmar Royal Casino, is an Australian-Chinese joint venture. There are also plenty of karaokes, discos and other staples of modern Chinese entertainment life. The main currency used in town is the Chinese yuan.

In order to proceed to Mengla from Kengtung, you must first register at the Kengtung immigration office. The staff at Harry's Guest House can help you accomplish this, or if you take a tour via King Kobra Guest House, these details will be taken care of for you.

The obvious question is, can you cross the border from Mengla into Daluo, China? A few foreigners have done so successfully, after arranging tourist visas in advance for both Myanmar and China, and obtaining letters that allow them to cross the Myanmar-China border at Daluo.

Getting There & Away The cheapest form of transport to Kengtung is the săwngthăew that leave each morning from Tachileik, but reports say Myanmar authorities aren't allowing foreigners to board these. Give it a try anyway, as this sort of situation tends to change. You can rent 4WDs on either side of the border, but Thai vehicles with a capacity of five or fewer passengers are charged a flat US$50 entry fee, US$100 for vehicles with a capacity of over five. Burmese vehicle hire is more expensive and requires the use of a driver. Whatever the form of transport, count on six gruelling hours (depending on road conditions) to cover the 163km stretch between the border and Kengtung. The road trip allows glimpses of Shan, Akha, Wa and Lahu villages along the way.

CHIANG SAEN
เชียงแสน

postcode 57150 • pop 55,000
Once the site of an important Northern Thai kingdom, Chiang Saen today is a small crossroads town on the banks of the Mekong River. Scattered throughout the town are ruins of the 14th-century Chiang Saen kingdom. Surviving architecture in-

cludes many chedi, Buddha images, wíhǎan pillars and earthen city ramparts.

Unlike at Sukhothai or Kamphaeng Phet, where new cities grew up apart from historic ruins, the modern town of Chiang Saen developed in and around the old temple sites. This has made it difficult if not impossible for Thailand's Department of Fine Arts to establish a protected historical park. On the other hand this means that you can explore the old sites any time of day or night, and, with one exception, pay no admission.

The sleepy town hasn't changed much over the last decade in spite of Golden Triangle commercialisation, which is concentrated in nearby Sop Ruak. Practically everything in Chiang Saen closes by 9pm.

Chiang Saen is an official border crossing for Thai and Lao citizens travelling by ferry to and from the Lao PDR town on the opposite side of the river, Thon Phuak. Despite persistent rumours that the Chiang Saen crossing is open for foreigners (even the Australian embassy in Vientiane made such an announcement), this crossing has never been open to other than Lao or Thai citizens.

History
Phaya Mang Rai, the Thai Lü–Lao prince who founded the original Lanna kingdom, was born into a *meuang* (city-state) known as Ngoen Yang, said to be at or near Chiang Saen. He reportedly inherited the rule of Ngoen Yang from his father Phaya Lao Mang in 1259 and expanded his kingdom to include all meuang in the Kok River Basin, calling the conglomeration 'Yonok'. A few of the old monuments still standing in Chiang Saen today predate the Chiang Saen kingdom by a couple of hundred years, though whether these belonged to Yonok or another state has not been confirmed. Phaya Mang Rai is said to have moved his capital from Ngoen Yang to Chiang Rai in 1262.

Local written history as found in dated epigraphs begins in 1328 when Phaya Mang Rai's nephew Phaya Saen Phu established a new principality, Chiang Saen, in his own name. Saen Phu moved the Lanna capital from Chiang Mai to Chiang Saen. He ordered his followers to dig moats and build earthen walls for the city on the three sides, leaving the Mekong River to protect the city's eastern flank. During its heyday, the Chiang Saen kingdom maintained six major piers along the river (today's residents make do with only two).

Phaya Saen Phu invited many artisans to reside in the new capital, and Chiang Saen became especially renowned for its bronze-casting. Buddha castings that today are known as 'Lanna period' usually hail from 14th-century Chiang Saen. Phaya Pa Yu, Phaya Saen Phu's grandson, moved the capital back to Chiang Mai around 1346.

After suffering the 17th- and 18th-century Burmese invasions, Chiang Saen's glory quickly faded, although it remained independent of Siam longer than most other Lanna states, including Chiang Mai: Chiang Saen didn't become a Siamese possession until the 1880s.

Yunnanese trade routes extended from Simao, Yunnan, through Laos to Chiang Saen and then on to Mawlamyaing in Burma, via Chiang Rai, Chiang Mai and Mae Sariang. A lesser-used route proceeded through Utaradit, Phayao and Phrae.

Today huge river barges from China moor at Chiang Saen, carrying fruit, engine parts and all manner of other imports, keeping the old China-Siam trade route open.

Information
Tourist Offices The visitors centre, on the left-hand side as you come into town from the west, has a good relief display showing the major ruin sites as well as photos of various stupas before, during and after restoration. The centre is open 8.30am to 4.30pm Monday to Saturday.

Immigration Chiang Saen's immigration office is on the southwestern corner of the main intersection in town.

Money Siam Commercial Bank on Thanon Phahonyothin, the main street leading from the highway to the Mekong River, has an ATM and currency exchange.

Chiang Saen National Museum

พิพิธภัณฑสถานแห่งชาติ
เชียงแสน

Near the town entrance is a small museum (☎ 053 777 102, 702 Thanon Phahon-yothin; admission 30B; open 9am-4pm Wed-Sun) that displays artefacts from the Lanna period and prehistoric stone tools from the area, as well as hill-tribe crafts, dress and musical instruments.

Wat Chedi Luang

วัดเจดีย์หลวง

Behind the museum to the east are the ruins of Wat Chedi Luang, which features an 18m octagonal chedi in the classic Chiang Saen or Lanna style. Archaeologists argue about its exact construction date but agree it dates to some time between the 12th and 14th centuries.

Wat Pa Sak

วัดป่าสัก

About 200m from Pratu Chiang Saen (Chiang Saen Gate) are the remains of Wat Pa Sak (admission 20B), where the ruins of seven monuments are visible. The main mid-14th century stupa combines elements of the Hariphunchai and Sukhothai styles with a possible Burmese Bagan influence. Since these ruins form part of a historical park, there is an admission fee.

Wat Phra That Chom Kitti

วัดพระธาตุจอมกิตติ

About 2.5km north of Wat Pa Sak on a hill top are the remains of Wat Phra That Chom Kitti and Wat Chom Chang. The round chedi of Wat Phra That is thought to have been constructed before the founding of the kingdom. The smaller chedi below it belonged to Wat Chom Chang. There's noth-

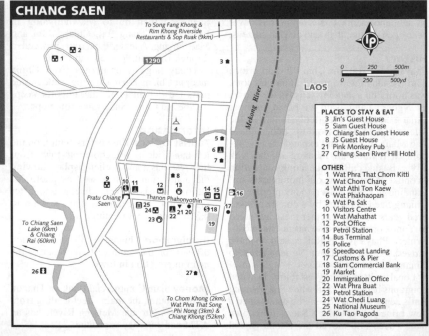

CHIANG SAEN

To Song Fang Khong & Rim Khong Riverside Restaurants & Sop Ruak (9km)

1290

LAOS

Mekong River

Pratu Chiang Saen

Thanon Phahonyothin

To Chiang Saen Lake (6km) & Chiang Rai (60km)

To Chiang Saen Lake (6km) & Chiang Rai (60km)

To Chom Khong (2km), Wat Phra That Song Phi Nong (3km) & Chiang Khong (52km)

0   250   500m
0   250   500yd

PLACES TO STAY & EAT
3   Jin's Guest House
5   Siam Guest House
7   Chiang Saen Guest House
8   JS Guest House
21 Pink Monkey Pub
27 Chiang Saen River Hill Hotel

OTHER
1   Wat Phra That Chom Kitti
2   Wat Chom Chang
4   Wat Athi Ton Kaew
6   Wat Phakhaopan
9   Wat Pa Sak
10 Visitors Centre
11 Wat Mahathat
12 Post Office
13 Petrol Station
14 Bus Terminal
15 Police
16 Speedboat Landing
17 Customs & Pier
18 Siam Commercial Bank
19 Market
20 Immigration Office
22 Wat Phra Buat
23 Petrol Station
24 Wat Chedi Luang
25 National Museum
26 Ku Tao Pagoda

EASTERN PROVINCES

ing much to see at these chedi, but there's a good view of Chiang Saen and the river from the top of the hill.

Wat Phakhaopan
วัดผ้าขาวป้าน

Inside the grounds of this living wát near the river stands a magnificent Lanna-period chedi. Legend says it was built by Phaya Lao Klao Kaew to inter the remains of a *taa phâa khăo*, a devout Buddhist layperson wearing white cloth, who drowned while bathing in the nearby river. The king reportedly placed 1050 small stupas in the base of the 22m chedi. The large square base contains walking Lanna-style Buddhas in niches on all four sides. The Buddha facing east is sculpted in the so-called 'calling for rain' mudra, with both hands held straight at the image's sides – a pose common in Laos and not so common in Thailand.

Wat Athi Ton Kaew
วัดอาทิต้นแก้ว

This moderately sized brick stupa has broken open to reveal an older stupa inside. One often reads that many important stupas – such as Phra Pathom Chedi in Central Thailand or Shwedagon Paya in Yangon – have been built over earlier ones. Chedi Athi Ton Kaew is one of the very few instances where non-archaeologists can see for themselves that some stupas really are built on top of earlier stupas. In this case the inner stupa, with much of its ornamented stucco covering intact, is in better condition than the outer stupa. The stupa encasement was undertaken in 1515, but the age of the earlier stupa is unknown.

Mekong River Trips

A relatively new boat landing and customs station stand alongside the Chiang Saen waterfront. Boats from China, Laos and Myanmar can be seen unloading their cargoes in the mornings.

Six-passenger speedboats *(reua rehw)* will go to Sop Ruak (half an hour) for 400B per boat one way or 700B return, or all the

way to Chiang Khong (1½ to two hours) for 1300B one way or 1700B return, depending on your bargaining skills.

See Mekong River Cruises in the Sop Ruak section later in this chapter for information on services from that town.

Places to Stay

Chiang Saen does not have any accommodation standouts. With a few exceptions, guesthouse rooms are in need of repair and bathrooms need better maintenance.

JS Guest House (☎ 053 770 60, 129 *Thanon Sai 1)* Dorm beds 60B, singles & doubles with shared bathroom 100B. The guesthouse is about 100m off the main road near the post office. Tidy, simple rooms are located in a long concrete building, and the shared bathroom is clean. A solar hot-water shower is available in the proprietor's house, and vegetarian Thai meals can be arranged. The guesthouse also rents bicycles for 40B per day.

Chiang Saen Guest House (Thanon Chiang Saen-Sop Ruak) Singles/doubles with shared bathroom 70/90B, bungalows with private bathroom 200B. On the road to Sop Ruak, opposite the river, this faded guesthouse offers rooms with shared bathroom in a house, and A-frame bungalows in need of repair – not good value and useful only if everything else is full.

Siam Guest House (Thanon Chiang Saen-Sop Ruak) Singles/doubles with shared bathroom in huts with mosquito nets 70/120B, with private bathroom 130/160B. This guesthouse is near the Chiang Saen Guesthouse and is similarly uninviting overall, although there is a nice looking cafe attached.

Jin's Guest House (☎ 053 650 847, 71 *Mu 8, Thanon Rim Khong)* Rooms 200-300B. Farther north on the edge of town (about 1.5km from the bus terminal), Jin's offers a variety of accommodation possibilities and prices. All rooms come with private bathroom. An upstairs veranda is a good place to watch the Mekong flow by. Jin also puts together custom tours with car, driver and guide.

Chiang Saen River Hill Hotel (☎ 053 650 826, fax 053 650 830, 714 Mu 3 Tambon

Wiang; in Bangkok ☎ 027 489 046-8, fax 027 489 048) Rooms 1000B. Quite a bit more upmarket is this clean, four-storey hotel featuring good service and some nice Northern Thai touches to the furnishings. All the rooms contain a fridge, TV and phone, along with a floor sitting area furnished with Thai axe pillows, a Thai umbrella and a small rattan table.

Places to Eat

Cheap noodle and rice dishes are available at *food stalls* in and near the market on the river road and along the main road through town from the highway, near the bus stop. A small *night market* sets up each evening at the latter location and stays open till around midnight.

During the dry months, *riverside vendors* sell sticky rice, sôm-tam, grilled chicken, dried squid and other fun foods for people to eat while sitting on grass mats along the river bank in front of Chiang Saen Guest House – a very pleasant way to spend an evening. Local specialities include fish or chicken barbecued inside thick joints of bamboo, eaten with sticky rice and sôm-tam.

Pink Monkey Pub Dishes 40-80B. Open noon-midnight daily. This is a friendly little wooden pub in the centre of town with cold beer and Thai *kàp klâem* (drinking snacks) as well as regular Thai meals.

Two *sŭan aahăan* (food garden)–style riverside restaurants off the river road out of Chiang Saen towards Sop Ruak, *Song Fang Khong* and *Rim Khong,* offer extensive menus of Thai, Chinese and Isan food. Bring your Thai-language skills. Dishes cost 35B to 100B, and opening hours are 11am to 11pm daily.

Chom Khong (2km south of town via Rte 1129) Dishes 35-100B. Open 11am-11pm daily. This is a very nice spot set back from the river with fruit gardens.

Getting There & Away

There are frequent buses from Chiang Rai to Chiang Saen (20B, 40 minutes to 1½ hours).

From Chiang Mai, ordinary/air-con buses (5 hours) cost 95/171B. In either direction,

be sure to ask for the new route (sǎi mài) via Chiang Rai. The old route (sǎi kào) passes through Lamphun, Lampang, Ngao, Phayao and Phan (seven to nine hours). You can also take a bus first to Chiang Rai then change to a Chiang Saen bus (4½ hours).

Laos A 30B ferry service between Thon Phuak, in Laos, and Chiang Saen is open only to Thai and Lao citizens. The crossing is open 8am to 6pm.

Getting Around

A good way to see the Chiang Saen–Mae Sai area is on two wheels. Mountain bikes (50B a day) and motorcycles (15B to 200B) can be rented at Jin's Guest House, while JS rents regular bicycles for 40B.

From Mae Sai to Chiang Saen there's a choice of two scenic paved roads (one from the centre of Mae Sai and one near the town entrance), or a wider, busier paved road via Rte 110 to Mae Chan and then Rte 1016 to Chiang Saen.

The roads out of Mae Sai are considerably more direct but there are several forks where you have to make educated guesses on which way to go (there are occasional signs). The two roads join near the village of Mae Ma, where you have a choice of going east through Sop Ruak or south through Pa Thon. The eastern route is more scenic.

If you're heading south to Chiang Khong, Rte 1129 along the river is the road to take.

AROUND CHIANG SAEN
Phra That Song Phi Nong
พระธาตุสองพี่น้อง

About 3km south of Chiang Saen on the road to Chiang Khong, near the riverside in the village called Ban Chiang Saen Noi, stand a pair of highly revered Northern Thai chedi. Now part of Wat Phra That Song Phi Nong, together they're known as the Two Siblings Stupas.

Reportedly this area was once a temporary campsite for Phaya Saen Phu when he was scouting for a capital to replace Chiang

Mai. Although architecturally the two chedi differ they're assumed to have been constructed in the 14th and 15th centuries. Much of the sculpted stucco ornamentation on the stupa nearest the centre of the wát grounds remains intact, and the niches on three out of four sides contain standing Buddhas. The niche facing east is empty and appears to have been used as a portal for treasure-seeking looters. The second chedi farther towards the river is less impressive. A wíhăan stands in front of each chedi.

The wát grounds themselves are nicely landscaped and this is a spot well worth visiting. You could easily bicycle here from Chiang Saen or hop a Chiang Khong–bound săwngthăew, asking to get off at Phra That Song Phi Nong.

Sop Ruak

สบรวก

Nine kilometres north of Chiang Saen is Sop Ruak, the official 'centre' of the Golden Triangle where the borders of Myanmar, Thailand and Laos meet, at the confluence of Nam Ruak and the Mekong River. In historical terms, 'Golden Triangle' actually refers to a much larger geographic area, stretching thousands of square kilometres into Myanmar, Laos and Thailand, within which the opium trade is prevalent. Nevertheless hoteliers and tour operators have been quick to cash in on the name by referring to the tiny village of Sop Ruak as 'the Golden Triangle', conjuring up images of illicit adventure even though the adventure quotient here is close to zero. In Northern Thai this village is pronounced 'sop huak'; many out-of-town Thais don't know either Thai name and simply call it 'Sam Liam Thong Kham' (săam lìam thawng kham; Thai for 'golden triangle').

Tourists have replaced opium as the local source of gold. Sop Ruak has in fact become something of a tourist trap, with souvenir stalls, restaurants, a massage place and bus loads of package-tour visitors during the day. In the evenings things are quieter.

One place worth a visit is the **House of Opium** (admission 20B; open 7am-6pm daily). This is a small museum with historical displays pertaining to opium culture. Exhibits include all the various implements used in the planting, harvest, use and trade of *Papaver somniferum* resin, including pipes, weights, scales and so on, plus photos and maps. Most labels are in Thai only. The museum is at the Km30 marker, at the southeastern end of Sop Ruak. A little shop at the front of the museum sells souvenir opium pipes for 80B, more authentic ones from China for 1500B to 1800B, and antique ones for 10,000B or more.

On the southern edge of town a huge pier and attached Thai-Lao-Chinese-Myanma Department Store shopping centre complex are under construction. The pier is meant to serve passenger-boat traffic between Sop Ruak and China – once the red tape has cleared and such a service can become established.

On the Burmese side of the river junction stands the **Golden Triangle Paradise Resort**, a huge hotel and casino financed by Thai and Japanese business partners who have leased nearly 3000 *râi* (480 hectares) from the Myanmar government. Only two currencies – baht and dollars – are accepted at the hotel.

Ten kilometres north of Chiang Saen on a plot of about 40 hectares opposite Le Meridien Baan Boran (see Places to Stay & Eat later in this section), the Mae Fah Luang Foundation is building a 5600-sq-metre **Opium Exhibition Hall**. This educational centre intends to become the world's leading exhibit and research facility for the study of the history of opiate use around the world; it should be completed by the time you read this.

Mekong River Cruises Local longtail boat or speedboat trips can be arranged through several local agents. The typical trip involves a 40-minute circuit around a large island and upriver for a view of the Burmese casino hotel for 400B per person. Longer trips head down river as far as Chiang Khong for 1800B per person return.

On longer trips you can stop off at a Lao village on the large river island of Don Sao, roughly halfway between Sop Ruak and

Chiang Saen. The Lao immigration booth here is happy to allow day visitors onto the island without a Lao visa. A 20B arrival tax is collected from each visitor. There's not a lot to see, but there's an official post office where you can mail letters or postcards with a Lao PDR postmark, a few shops selling T-shirts and Lao handicrafts, and the Sala Beer Lao, where you can drink Lao beer and munch on Lao snacks.

Places to Stay & Eat Virtually all the former budget places in Sop Ruak have given way to souvenir stalls and larger tourist hotels, so most budget travellers stay in Chiang Saen these days.

Akha Guest House (Thanon Chiang Saen-Sop Ruak) Huts 200B. A kilometre south of Sop Ruak on the road to Chiang Saen, Akha Guest House offers very simple but adequate huts with shared facilities.

Bamboo Hut (☎ 053 650 077, 053 769 084, Thanon Chiang Saen-Sop Ruak) Huts 190B. Just south of Akha Guest House is this similar cluster of bamboo huts with Mekong views.

Imperial Golden Triangle Resort (☎ 053 784 001-5, fax 053 784 006, 222 Ban Sop Ruak; in Bangkok ☎ 026 532 201) Rooms 2500B. This hotel offers 1st-class accommodation on a hillside overlooking the river; rates include buffet breakfast.

Le Meridien Baan Boran Hotel (☎ 053 784 084, fax 053 784 096, 229 Mu 1; in Bangkok ☎ 026 532 201) Rooms 4180-10,260B (plus tax & service). This 110-room hotel sits on a secluded hillside spot off the road between Sop Ruak and Mae Sai. It melds classic Northern Thai design motifs with modern resort hotel tricks like cathedral ceilings and skylights. To fit the naughty Golden Triangle image, one of the restaurants is called Suan Fin (Opium Field) and is decorated with poppy motifs; windows off the dining area serve up a view of Myanmar and Laos in the distance. The hotel bar is called Trafficker Rendezvous. A swimming pool, Jacuzzi, tennis and squash courts, gym, sauna, medical clinic, karaoke and two restaurants round out the amenities.

Of the several tourist-oriented restaurants overlooking the Mekong in Sop Ruak, the best is *Sriwan,* opposite the Imperial Golden Triangle Resort.

Getting There & Away Sǎwngthǎew run every 20 minutes or so throughout the day from Chiang Saen to Sop Ruak (10B). It's an easy bike ride from Chiang Saen to Sop Ruak.

Chiang Khong
เชียงของ

postcode 57140 • pop 9000
At one time Chiang Khong was part of a small river-bank meuang called Juon, founded in AD 701 by Phaya Mahathai. Over the centuries Juon paid tribute to Chiang Rai, then Chiang Saen and finally Nan before being occupied by the Siamese in the 1880s. Chiang Khong's territory extended all the way to Yunnan Province in China until the French turned much of the Mekong River's northern bank into French Indochina in 1893.

More remote yet more lively than Chiang Saen, Chiang Khong is an important market town for local hill tribes and for trade with northern Laos. Nearby are several villages inhabited by Mien and White Hmong. Among the latter are contingents who fled Laos during the 1975 communist takeover and who are rumoured to be involved in an organised resistance movement against the current Lao government.

Trade between Thailand and China via Chiang Khong is steady. Thai goods going north include dried and processed food and beverages, cosmetics, machinery, spare parts and agro-industrial supplies.

Huay Xai, opposite Chiang Khong on the Lao side of the river, is a legal point of entry for Laos. Anyone with a valid Laos visa may cross by ferry. From Huay Xai it's 250km to Luang Nam Tha, a short distance from Boten, a legal border crossing to and from China – see Border Crossing (Laos) later in this section for more information.

Money The Si Ayuthaya, Thai Farmers and Siam Commercial Banks have branches in town with ATMs and foreign exchange services.

Things to See & Do Several Northern Thai–style wát of minor interest can be seen in town. **Wat Luang**, on the main road, was once one of the most important temples in Chiang Rai Province and features a chedi dating to the 13th century (restored in 1881).

On a hill overlooking the town of Chiang Khong and the river is a **Nationalist Chinese Soldiers (KMT) Cemetery** where over 200 KMT soldiers have been buried. The grave mounds are angled on the hill so that they face China. A shrine containing old photos of KMT soldiers-in-arms stands at the top of the hill.

The village of **Ban Hat Khrai**, about 1km south of Chiang Khong, is famous as being one of the few places where *plaa bèuk* (giant Mekong catfish) are still caught (see the 'Plaa Bèuk' boxed text). During the plaa bèuk season, April and May, you can watch the small fishing boats coming and going from Tha Pla Beuk, about 2km south of Chiang Khong on the Mekong; the turn-off is near the Km137 marker.

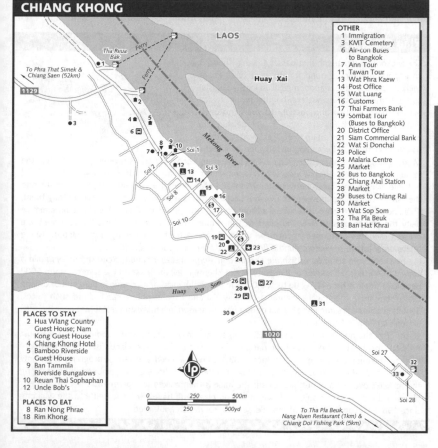

CHIANG KHONG

LAOS

Huay Xai

Mekong River

To Phra That Simek & Chiang Saen (52km)

1129

Tha Reua Bak

Ferry

OTHER
1 Immigration
3 KMT Cemetery
6 Air-con Buses to Bangkok
7 Ann Tour
11 Tawan Tour
13 Wat Phra Kaew
14 Post Office
15 Wat Luang
16 Customs
17 Thai Farmers Bank
19 Sombat Tour (Buses to Bangkok)
20 District Office
21 Siam Commercial Bank
22 Wat Si Donchai
23 Police
24 Malaria Centre
25 Market
26 Bus to Bangkok
27 Chiang Mai Station
28 Market
29 Buses to Chiang Rai
30 Market
31 Wat Sop Som
32 Tha Pla Beuk
33 Ban Hat Khrai

Soi 1
Soi 2
Soi 3
Soi 8
Soi 10
Huay Sop Som
1020
Soi 27
Soi 28

PLACES TO STAY
2 Hua Wlang Country Guest House; Nam Kong Guest House
4 Chiang Khong Hotel
5 Bamboo Riverside Guest House
9 Ban Tammila Riverside Bungalows
10 Reuan Thai Sophaphan
12 Uncle Bob's

PLACES TO EAT
8 Ran Nong Phrae
18 Rim Khong

0   250   500m
0   250   500yd

To Tha Pla Beuk, Nang Nuen Restaurant (1km) & Chiang Doi Fishing Park (5km)

EASTERN PROVINCES

About 3km northwest of town on the road to Chiang Saen, a gravel and dirt road (Rte 1129) climbs a hill 300m to **Phra That Simek**, a new stupa under construction. While digging the foundation for the stupa, workers uncovered a buried Lanna–Lan Xang style Buddha that will eventually be housed in an adjacent wíhǎan that is yet to be constructed. A board under a rustic pavilion bears photos of the discovery. From the hill there are views of the Mekong and Laos.

About 11km from Chiang Khong along the same road, more sweeping views of the river as well as surrounding farmlands are available at a well-marked **viewpoint** with tables and shelters for picnickers.

River Cruising You can hire longtail boats from a floating restaurant that's near the pier for 300B per hour.

Places to Stay There are several guesthouses at the northern end of town in a neighbourhood called Ban Wiang Kaew. There are two places near the old ferry pier.

Nam Khong Guest House (☎ *053 655 102, fax 053 655 277,* ⓔ *phayao98@ hotmail.com, Thanon Rim Khong)* Rooms with shared bathroom 60-150B. This place offers a variety of simple hut accommodations overlooking the Mekong.

Hua Wiang Country Guest House (Thanon Rim Khong) Rooms with shared bathroom 50-150B. As with the Nam

---

Plaa Bèuk

The Mekong River stretch that passes Chiang Khong is an important fishing ground for the plaa bèuk (giant Mekong catfish, *Pangasianodon gigas* to ichthyologists) probably the largest freshwater fish in the world. A plaa bèuk takes at least six and possibly 12 years (no-one's really sure) to reach full size, when it will measure 2m to 3m in length and weigh up to 300kg. Locals say these fish swim all the way from Qinghai Province (where the Mekong originates) in northern China. In Thailand and Laos its flesh is revered as a delicacy; the texture is very meaty but has a delicate flavour, similar to tuna or swordfish, only whiter.

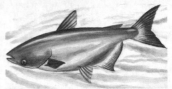

MH

These fish are only taken between mid-April and May when the river depth is just 3m to 4m and the fish are swimming upriver to spawn in Erhai Lake, Yunnan Province, China. Before netting them, Thai and Lao fishermen hold a special annual ceremony to propitiate Chao Mae Pla Beuk, a female deity thought to preside over the giant catfish. Among the rituals comprising the ceremony are chicken sacrifices performed aboard the fishing boats. After the ceremony is completed, fishing teams draw lots to see who casts the first net, and then take turns casting.

Anywhere from 15 to 60 catfish are captured in a typical season, and the catfish hunters guild is limited to 40 men, all natives of Ban Hat Khrai. Fishermen sell the meat on the spot for up to 500B per kilo (a single fish can bring up to 100,000B in Bangkok); most of it ends up in Bangkok or Chiang Mai restaurants, since local restaurants in Huay Xai and Chiang Khong can't afford such prices. Sometimes you can sample the catfish during harvest season in a makeshift restaurant near the fishermen's landing in Ban Hat Khrai.

Although the plaa bèuk is on the CITES list of endangered species, there is some debate as to just how endangered it is. Because of the danger of extinction, Thailand's Inland Fisheries Department has been taking protective measures since 1983, including a breed-and-release program. Every time a female is caught, it's kept alive until a male is netted, then the eggs are removed (by massaging the female's ovaries) and put into a pan; the male is then milked for sperm and the eggs are fertilised in the pan. As a result, well over a million plaa bèuk have been released into the Mekong since 1983. Of course, not all of the released fish survive to adulthood.

Khong, accommodation here overlooks the Mekong.

Bamboo Riverside Guest House *(☎ 053 791 621, 053 791 629, Thanon Rim Khong)* Dorm beds in thatched hut 70B, private thatched huts with fan & attached hot shower 150-250B. A little farther southeast of the Nam Khong, this place has a restaurant perched on a deck overlooking the river.

Chiang Khong Hotel *(☎ 053 791 182, 68/1 Thanon Sai Klang)* Singles/doubles with fan & hot-water bathroom 150/200B. Opposite the Bamboo Riverside, the Chiang Khong has plain but nicely kept rooms.

Ban Tammila Riverside Bungalows *(☎ 053 791 234, e baantammila@hotmail .com, 113 Thanon Rim Khong)* Huts without/with bathroom 200/300B. An old standby, Ban Tammila offers simple huts overlooking the river; there's also a very pleasant sitting/dining area by the river. This place receives a lot of repeat business.

Reuan Thai Sophaphan *(☎ 053 791 023, Thanon Sai Klang)* Rooms 350-600B. Next door to Ban Tammila Riverside Bungalows, this more upmarket place has rooms in nicely designed multi-floor wooden buildings.

Uncle Bob's *(☎ 053 791 929, Thanon Sai Klang)* Dorm beds 50B, singles/doubles with shared hot-water bathroom 80/120B. A little northwest of Wat Phra Kaew, Uncle Bob's is housed in a comfortable-looking, older wooden building.

Places to Eat There are a number of *rice and noodle shops* along the main street, none of them particularly good.

Ran Nong Phrae Dishes 20-40B. Open 8am-8pm daily. Just northwest of the entrance to Ban Tammila Riverside Bungalows, Nong Phrae serves good khâo sawy, Western breakfasts, *kǔaytǐaw* (rice noodles) and *aahǎan taam sàng* (food made to order).

Rim Khong Dishes 30-80B. Open 11am-9pm daily. On a narrow road down by the river, this is a simple indoor/outdoor restaurant overlooking the river. The bilingual menu is much shorter than the Thai menu; yam are the house speciality, but the kitchen can make just about anything.

Nang Nuan Dishes 40-120B. Open 9am-midnight daily. Next to Tha Pla Beuk, this pleasant open-air place overlooking the Mekong specialises in fresh river fish, including plaa bèuk.

Chiang Doi Fishing Park *(☎ 053 701 701, Km5, Rte 1020, Tambon Tha Sai)* Dishes 40-90B. Open 10am-11pm daily. If you're travelling by road along Rte 1020 from Chiang Rai, this unassuming roadside place is a food stop worth mentioning. The fare is excellent. You don't have to fish your own meal from the adjacent lake, though some people try.

Getting There & Away From Chiang Saen, graded and paved 52km-long Rte 1129 is the quickest way to come from the west. A second 65km road curving along the river has also been paved and provides a slower but less trafficked alternative. With mountains in the distance and the Mekong to one side, this road passes through picturesque villages and tobacco and rice fields before joining Rte 1129 just outside Chiang Khong.

Buses leave hourly between Chiang Rai and Chiang Khong from around 4am to 5pm; ditto to/from Chiang Saen. Buses from Chiang Rai (37B, 2½ hours) and beyond use roads from the south (primarily Rte 1020) to reach Chiang Khong; there are hourly departures approximately from 6am to 5pm daily. These stop more or less opposite the Bamboo Riverside Guest House.

Boats taking up to 10 passengers can be chartered up the Mekong River from Chiang Khong to Chiang Saen for 1800B. Boat crews can be contacted near the customs pier behind Wat Luang, or farther north at the pier for ferries to Laos.

Border Crossing (Laos) Ferries to Huay Xai, Laos, leave frequently between 8am and 5.30pm from Tha Reua Bak, a pier at the northern end of Chiang Khong, for 20B each way. A new pier was recently built about 100m southeast of Tha Reua Bak, but is used for cargo only.

As long as you hold a visa valid for Laos, there should be no problem crossing. If you don't already have a visa, Ann Tour (☎ 053 655 198, fax 053 791 218), on the main road in town near Ban Tammila Guest House, can arrange a 15-day visa in one day (except on weekends and holidays) for US$50 or the baht equivalent; if you submit your passport to the office at 8am, they'll have it back to you, complete with visa, by 3pm – in time to get across the river and start your Laos journey. If you can wait three working days, your visa will only cost 1300B. A 30-day visa takes three to five days to process; the fee ranges from 1450B to 2050B depending on your nationality. Ann Tour can also arrange vehicle permits to take cars (7000B) or motorcycles (4000B to 5000B) into Laos.

Plans to build a bridge across the Mekong here were aborted in 1997 following the baht crash. If the bridge ever gets built, it will, of course, replace the ferry service. Completion of a bridge might also affect the visa situation. Either way there is talk of allowing visas on arrival in Huay Xai. Ask at the local guesthouses for the latest information.

Once on the Lao side you can continue on by road to Luang Nam Tha and Udomxai or by boat down the Mekong to Luang Prabang and Vientiane. Lao Aviation flies from Huay Xai to Vientiane a couple of times a week.

Phrae Province

Phrae Province is probably most famous for the distinctive *sêua mâw hâwm*, the indigo-dyed cotton farmers shirts seen all over Thailand. 'Made in Phrae' has always been a sign of distinction for these staples of rural Thai life, and since the student-worker-farmer political solidarity of the 1970s, even Thai university professors like to wear them. The cloth is made in Ban Thung Hong outside the town of Phrae. A good place to buy mâw hâwm clothes in Phrae is Mo Hom Anian, a shop about 60m from the south-eastern gate (Pratu Chai) into the old city.

The annual **Rocket Festival** kicks off the rice-growing season in May. In Phrae the biggest celebrations take place in Long and Sung Men districts. Look for launching towers in the middle of rice fields for the exact location.

Sung Men district is also known for **Talat Hua Dong**, a market specialising in carved teak wood. Phrae has long been an important teak centre. Along Rte 101 between Phrae and Nan you'll see a steady blur of teak forests (they are the thickest around the 25km marker). Since the 1989 national ban on logging, these forests are all protected by law. Most of the provincial teak business now involves recycled timber from old houses. Specially licensed cuts taken from fallen teak wood may also be used for decorative carvings or furniture (but not in house construction).

The province of Phrae and its neighbouring province of Nan have been neglected by tourists and travellers alike because of their remoteness from Chiang Mai, but from Den Chai – on the northern train route – they're easily reached by bus along Rte 101.

PHRAE

อ.เมืองแพร่

postcode 54000 • pop 21,200

Like Chiang Mai and Lampang, Phrae has an old city partially surrounded by a moat alongside a river (here, Mae Nam Yom). Unlike Chiang Mai, Phrae's old city still has lots of quiet lanes and old teak houses – if you're a fan of traditional Thai teak architecture, you'll find more of it here than in any other city of similar size anywhere in Thailand. The local temple architecture has successfully resisted Central Thai influence over the centuries as well. It's a bit unusual since you'll find a mix of Burmese, Northern Thai (Nan and Lanna) and Lao styles.

Southeast of the old city, the newer, more modern Phrae looks like any other medium-sized town in Thailand.

History

Written records chronicling the history of Phrae are scarce and even the early names for the state are much debated. The meuang appears to have been annexed by Lanna's Phaya Tilokarat around AD 1500, and while under Lanna rule it was known as Pholarat or Phon Nakhon, meaning 'City of Strength'. Before that era, legend says it was an Angkor satellite called Kosaya Nakhon and inhabited by Thai Khün and Thai Lü. It is said that *kosaya* once meant 'silk' and that early on the settlement was known for its fine silk weaving. However it's more probable that 'Kosaya' is derived from the Pali-Sanskrit *kosiya*, an epithet for Indra, the Hindu-Buddhist king of the gods, and thus it would have meant 'City of Indra'.

Locals insist that Phrae existed as a Thai kingdom as far back as the 12th or 13th centuries, which is quite possible although confirming evidence is virtually nonexistent.

Eventually the Thais came to call the city Wiang Phrae or Wiang Phae, depending on which sources you believe. 'Phae' is a Northern Thai/Lao word for 'victory' in which case the name would mean City of Victory. However some Northern Thais pronounce the city name, even today, as Wiang Hae, and it may be that the city was named for Phra That Cho Hac (Silk Flag Stupa), the most significant religious monument in the city and province of Phrae.

During the late 19th and throughout much of the 20th century, the area surrounding Phrae was the most important centre in Thailand for the felling of teak timber. During this time many Shan immigrated to Phrae to work in the teak business. They apparently enjoyed Phrae's independence from Siam, since during the early years of Siamese rule a number of migrant Shans, with the backing of the local Northern Thai rulers, successfully seized the city and killed over twenty officials from the central region.

Phrae has suffered economically since the 1989 logging ban, although the city's skilled woodworkers continue to thrive on the processing of recycled teak and the rare specially licensed tree into furniture and art objects.

Information

Phrae's main post office stands near the centre of the old city near the traffic circle; hours are 8.30am to 4.30pm weekdays and 9am to noon on Saturday. Long-distance calls can be made at the CAT office (attached to the main post office) daily from 8am to 8pm.

Bangkok Bank and Krung Thai Bank, both on Thanon Charoen Meuang, have ATMs and offer foreign exchange services during normal banking hours (8.30am to 3.30pm weekdays).

Wat Luang

วัดหลวง

This is the oldest *wát* in the city, purportedly dating to the 12th or 13th century. Phra That Luang Chang Kham, a large octagonal Lanna-style chedi, sits on a square base with elephants supporting it *(cháang khám)* on all four sides, surrounded by *kùtì* (monastic residences) and coconut palms. As is sometimes seen in Phrae and Nan, the chedi is usually swathed in Thai Lü satin-like fabric.

The veranda of the main wíhǎan is in the classic Luang Prabang–Lan Xang style but has unfortunately been bricked in with laterite. Opposite the front of the wíhǎan is Pratu Khong, part of the city's original entrance gate. No longer used as a gate, it now contains a statue of Chao Pu, an early Lanna ruler. The image is sacred to local residents, who leave offerings of fruit, flowers, candles and incense.

Also on the temple grounds is a museum displaying temple antiques, ceramics and religious art dating from the Lanna, Nan, Bago and Mon periods. A 16th-century, Phrae-made sitting Buddha on the 2nd floor is particularly exquisite. There are also some 19th-century photos with English labels on display, including some gruesome shots of a beheading. The museum is usually open weekends only, but the monks will sometimes open it on weekdays upon request.

Wat Phra Non

วัดพระนอน

Southwest a few hundred metres from Wat Luang is a 300-year-old *wát* named after its

highly revered reclining Buddha image
(*phrá nawn*). The bòt was built around 200
years ago and has an impressive roof with a
separate two-tiered portico and gilded
carved wooden facade with Ramayana
scenes. The wíhǎan behind the bòt contains
the Buddha image, swathed in Thai Lü
cloth with bead and foil decoration.

Wat Jom Sawan
วัดจอมสวรรค์

Outside the old city on Thanon Ban Mai, this
temple was built by local Shan in the late
19th and early 20th centuries, and shows
Shan and Burmese influence throughout.
The well-preserved wooden wíhǎan and bòt
have high, tiered, tower-like roofs like those
found in Mandalay. A large copper-crowned
chedi has lost most of its stucco to reveal the
artful brickwork beneath. A prized temple
possession in the main wíhǎan is a Tripitaka
section consisting of 16 ivory 'pages' engraved in Burmese.

Other Temples

Across from the post office in the old city,
Wat Phra Baht Ming Meuang houses a Buddhist school, an old chedi, an unusual octagonal drum tower made entirely of teak
and the highly revered Phra Phut Kosai Buddha image, which closely resembles the
Phra Chinnarat in Phitsanulok. Just outside
the northeastern corner of the moat, **Wat Sa
Bo Kaew** is a Shan-Burmese-style temple
similar to Wat Jom Sawan. **Wat Phra Ruang**,
inside the old city, is typical of Phrae's
many old city wát, with a Nan-style,
cruciform-plan bòt, a Lao-style wíhǎan and
a Lanna chedi. Or is this unique mix a co-
herent design of local (Nan-Phrae) provenance that has yet to be identified?

Vongburi House
บ้านวงศ์บุรี

In 1997, this two-storey teak house was
opened as a private museum (☎ 054 620
153, Thanon Kham Leu; admission 30B;
open 8am-5pm daily). It was constructed between 1897 and 1907 for Luang Phongphi-

bun (the last prince of Phrae) and his wife
Chao Sunantha, who once held a profitable
teak concession in the city. Elaborate carvings on gables, eaves, balconies and above
doors and windows are in very good condition. Inside, many of the house's 20 rooms
display late 19th-century teak antiques,
documents (including early 20th-century
slave concessions), photos and other artefacts from the bygone teak dynasty era.
Most are labelled in English as well as Thai.

Ban Prathup Jai
บ้านประทับใจ

On the outskirts of town is Ban Prathup Jai,
also called Ban Sao Roi Ton (*Hundred-
Pillar House;* ☎ 054 511 008, Rte 1020,
Tambon Pa Maet, 10km west of town; admission 20B; open 8am-5pm daily). It's a
large Northern-style teak house that was
built using more than 130 teak logs, each
over 300 years old. Opened in 1985, the
house took four years to build, using timber
taken from nine old rural houses. The interior pillars are ornately carved. It's also
filled with souvenir vendors and is rather
tackily decorated, reinforcing the fact that
'impressive' is a relative term.

Special Events

During the fourth month of the Thai lunar
calendar (usually late April) the **Phra Baht
Chamlong** festival honours Phrae's most
sacred Buddha image, the Phra Phut Kosai,
with a procession from Wat Phra Baht Ming
Meuang through the centre of town.

Places to Stay – Budget

Several inexpensive hotels can be found
along Thanon Charoen Meuang, including
the basic *Ho Fa Hotel (no Roman-script
sign;* ☎ 054 511 140, 94 Thanon Charoen
Meuang), with rooms with bathroom for
100B to 150B, and the *Thepwiman Hotel
(☎ 054 511 103, 228 Thanon Charoen
Meuang),* with rooms with private bathroom for 110B to 160B; Thepwiman is still
the better of the two.
*Toongsri Phaibool Hotel (Thung Si
Phaibun;* ☎ 054 511 011, 84 Thanon Yan-

tarakitkoson) Rooms with fan 130-180B, with air-con 300B. This friendly place is a good choice. All the rooms are clean and have private bathrooms.

Sawatdikarn Hotel *(76-78 Thanon Yantarakitkoson)* is similar to the Toongsri Phaibool but not as well kept; rooms start at 100B.

Busarakham Hotel *(☎ 054 511 437, Thanon Ratsadamnoen)* Rooms with fan/air-con 180/300B per person. Southeast of the Nakhon Phrae Hotel (see Places to Stay – Mid-Range & Top End following), this rambling, one-storey place is fairly quiet since most rooms are well off the road.

Places to Stay – Mid-Range & Top End

Nakhon Phrae Hotel *(☎ 054 511 122, fax 054 521 937, 29 Thanon Ratsadamnoen)* Singles & doubles with fan & hot water in the old wing 200B, with TV 250B, rooms with fan & TV in new wing 350B, with air-con & TV 500B, with air-con, TV & fridge 560B. A mere two-minute walk from the old city, Nakhon Phrae's two wings are on opposite sides of the street; rooms are large. Local tourist information is available in the lobbies of both wings.

Paradorn Hotel *(Pharadon; ☎ 054 511 177, 177 Thanon Yantarakitkoson)* Singles/doubles with fan & bathroom 200/250B, rooms with air-con 350B. Formerly the best hotel in town, the Paradorn is starting to look a bit run-down these days, but at least the room rates have dropped commensurately.

Maeyom Palace Hotel *(☎ 054 521 028-38, fax 054 522 904, 181/6 Thanon Yantarakitkoson)* Rooms 1000-2000B. One hundred metres northeast of the Paradorn, this hotel offers rooms with air-con, carpet, TV, phone and fridge. Hotel facilities include a pool and two restaurants; the hotel also provides free transport to and from the Phrae bus terminal and airport. Room rates are usually discounted to 650-800B.

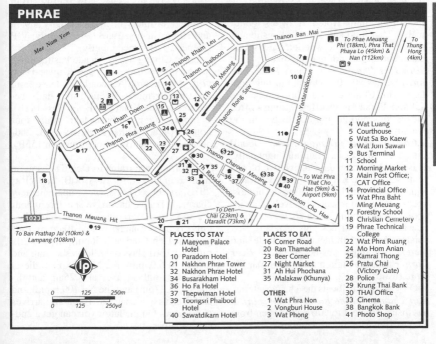

PHRAE

EASTERN PROVINCES

4	Wat Luang
5	Courthouse
6	Wat Sa Bo Kaew
8	Wat Jom Sawan
9	Bus Terminal
11	School
12	Morning Market
13	Main Post Office; CAT Office
14	Provincial Office
15	Wat Phra Baht Ming Meuang
17	Forestry School
18	Christian Cemetery
19	Phrae Technical College
22	Wat Phra Ruang
24	Mo Hom Anian
25	Kamrai Thong
26	Pratu Chai (Victory Gate)
28	Police
29	Krung Thai Bank
30	THAI Office
33	Cinema
38	Bangkok Bank
41	Photo Shop

PLACES TO STAY
7 Maeyom Palace Hotel
10 Paradorn Hotel
21 Nakhon Phrae Tower
32 Nakhon Phrae Hotel
34 Busarakham Hotel
36 Ho Fa Hotel
37 Thepwiman Hotel
39 Toongsri Phaibool Hotel
40 Sawatdikarn Hotel

PLACES TO EAT
16 Corner Road
20 Ran Thamachat
23 Beer Corner
27 Night Market
31 Ah Hui Phochana
35 Malakaw (Khunya)

OTHER
1 Wat Phra Non
2 Vongburi House
3 Wat Phong

Nakhon Phrae Tower (☎ *054 521 321, fax 054 521 937, 3 Thanon Meuang Hit)* Standard rooms from 1200B. Nakhon Phrae offers quality similar to that found at the Maeyom Palace. Room rates are readily discounted to 660B.

Den Chai If you are in Den Chai waiting for a train, basic lodging is available at *Yaowarat Hotel* (☎ *054 613 293, 11 Thanon Yantarakitkoson)*, with rooms with shared bathroom for 80B to 120B.

Places to Eat

A very good *night market* convenes just outside the Pratu Chai intersection every evening. Several *food vendors* also set up nightly in the soi opposite the Sawatdikarn Hotel. There's another *night market* a block or two behind the Paradorn Hotel on weekday evenings only.

Malakaw (*Khunya; Thanon Ratsadamnoen)* Dishes 40-80B. Open 3.30pm-midnight daily. For a slow evening repast, try this open-air place diagonally opposite the Busarakham Hotel. It offers good-quality Thai food and drink in a rustic ambience of rough-cut wooden tables and chairs beneath lots of hanging plants.

Ah Hui Phochana (*Thanon Ratsadamnoen)* Dishes 20-60B. Open 5pm-midnight daily. This Chinese coffee shop next to the Nakhon Phrae Hotel offers strong coffee and various noodle and rice dishes in the evening.

Corner Road (*Thanon Kham Doem)* Dishes 40-90B. Open 11am-midnight daily. This popular spot in the old city, two blocks southwest of the traffic circle, is decorated with lots of wood and old movie photos, and has an outdoor section as well as an indoor air-con dining room. It serves good rice and noodle dishes plus standard Thai cuisine. An English menu is available, and there's live music in the evenings. *Beer Corner* near the night market is similar but more rustic.

On Thanon Saisibut is the Thai vegetarian *Ran Thamachat* (*no Roman-script sign)*. It has dishes for 15B to 40B and is open from 7am to 7pm Monday to Saturday.

Shopping

If you're in the market for baskets or woven mats, a shop called *Kamrai Thong* (*no Roman-script sign)* near Pratu Chai carries a fine selection of hand-woven basketry. In this same vicinity, a few *clothing shops* specialise in mâw hâwm shirts and pants.

Getting There & Away

Air THAI flies to Phrae thrice weekly from Bangkok (1800B, 1½ hours). There are also flights to/from Chiang Mai (755B, four times weekly), Phitsanulok (765B, four times weekly) and Nan (640B, once daily). The THAI office (☎ 054 511 123) is at 42–44 Thanon Ratsadamnoen, near the Nakhon Phrae Hotel. The Phrae airport is 9km southeast of town via the same road that goes to Wat Phra That Cho Hae (see Around Phrae later); THAI operates a free shuttle service between the airport and the THAI office.

Bus There are buses to Phrae from Bangkok's Northern and Northeastern bus terminal (ordinary 172B, twice daily at 9am and 10pm; air-con 295B twice nightly; VIP sleeper 500B, twice nightly).

From Chiang Mai's Arcade bus terminal, ordinary buses leave daily at 6.30am and 9am (79B, four hours). Air-con buses leave from the same terminal several times daily between 8am and 10pm (111B, 1st class 142B).

From Chiang Rai buses take around four hours to reach Phrae (ordinary 80B, 2nd-class air-con 124B, 1st-class air-con 155B).

Train There are trains to Den Chai station from Bangkok (3rd class 90B, 2nd class 207B, 1st class 431B, plus supplementary charges). Trains that arrive at a decent hour are the No 101 rapid (2nd and 3rd class only, departs Bangkok at 6.40am and arrives in Den Chai at 3.56pm), the No 205 ordinary (3rd class only, leaves at 7am and arrives at 6.05pm), the No 9 express diesel (2nd class only, leaves at 8.25am and arrives at 3.27pm) and the No 109 rapid (2nd and 3rd class, departs at 10pm and arrives at 5.14am). On the latter you can get a 2nd-class sleeper.

Blue săwngthăew and red buses leave the Den Chai station frequently for the 23km jaunt to Phrae and cost 20B. You can catch them anywhere along the southern end of Thanon Yantarakitkoson.

Getting Around

A săamláw anywhere in the old town costs 20B to 30B; farther afield to somewhere like Ban Prathup Jai it can cost up to 40B. Motorcycle taxis are available at the bus terminal; a trip from here to, say, Pratu Chai should cost around 20B.

Shared săwngthăew ply a few of the roads – mainly Thanon Yantarakitkoson – and cost 5B to 10B depending on the distance.

AROUND PHRAE
Wat Phra That Cho Hae

วัดพระธาตุช่อแฮ

On a hill about 9km southeast of town off Rte 1022, this wát is famous for its 33m-high gilded chedi. Cho Hae is the name of the cloth that worshippers wrap around the chedi – it's a type of satin thought to have originated in Xishuangbanna (Sipsong-panna in Northern Thai) in China. Like Chiang Mai's Wat Doi Suthep, this is an important pilgrimage site for Thais living in the North. The Phra Jao Than Jai Buddha image here – similar in appearance to Phra Chinnarat in Phitsanulok – is reputed to impart fertility to women who make offerings to it.

The bòt has a gilded wooden ceiling, ro-coco pillars and walls with lotus-bud mosaics. Tiered *naga* (serpent-being) stairs lead to the temple compound; the hill top is surrounded by a protected forest of mature teak trees.

Săwngthăew between the city and Phra That Cho Hae (12B) are frequent.

Phra That Phaya Lo

พระธาตุพะยาเลาะ

This 400-year-old stupa is said to contain the ashes Phaya Lo, ruler of a Thai city-state called Nakhon Maen Suan. The im-pressive Lanna-style chedi stands near the village of **Ban Klang**, in Amphoe Song, 45km north of Phrae off Hwy 103.

Phae Meuang Phi

แพะเมืองผี

The name means 'Ghost-Land', a reference to this strange geological phenomenon about 18km northeast of Phrae off Rte 101. Erosion has created bizarre pillars of soil and rock that look like giant fungi. The area has recently been made a provincial park. There are shaded tables and food vendors near the entrance – you may need a drink after wandering around the baked surfaces between the eroded pillars.

Getting there by public transport entails a bus ride 9km towards Nan, getting off at the signposted turn-off for Phae Meuang Phi, and then catching a săwngthăew another 6km to a second right-hand turn-off to the park. From this point you must walk or hitch about 2.5km to reach the entrance.

Mabri Hill Tribe

ชนเผ่ามาบรี

Along the border of Phrae and Nan Provinces live the remaining members of the Mabri (sometimes spelt Mrabri or Mlabri) hill tribe, whom the Thais call *phĭi tawng lĕuang* (spirits of the yellow leaves). The most nomadic of all the tribes in Thailand, the Mabri customarily move on when the leaves of their temporary huts turn yellow, hence their Thai name. Now, however, their numbers have been greatly reduced (possibly to as few as 150) and experts suspect that few of the Mabri still migrate in the traditional way.

Traditionally, the Mabri are strict hunter-gatherers but many now work as field labourers for Thais, or other hill-tribe groups such as the Hmong, in exchange for pigs and cloth. Little is known about the tribe's belief system, but it is said that the Mabri believe they are not entitled to cultivate the land for themselves. A Mabri woman typically changes partners every five or six years, taking any children from the previous union with her. The Mabris' knowledge of medicinal plants is said to be enormous, encompassing the effective use of herbs for fertility and contraception, and for the treatment of snake or centipede poisoning. When a member of the tribe dies, the body is put in a tree top to be eaten by birds.

In Phrae Province there is a small settlement of around 40 Mabri living in Rong Khwang district (northeast of the provincial capital, near Phae Meuang Phi) under the protection (control) of American missionary Eugene Long. Long calls himself 'Boonyuen Suksaneh' and the Mabris' village 'Ban Boonyuen' – a classic scenario right out of Peter Mathiessen's *At Play in the Fields of the Lord*. Ban Boonyuen can only be reached on foot or by elephant; the nearest village, which is linked by road, is about 12km away.

Several Mabri families abandoned Ban Boonyuen in early 1992 and are now living in Hmong villages in Phrae and Nan. The remaining 100 or so Mabri live across the provincial border in Nan.

The Thai government operates a 'Pre-Agricultural Development of Mabri Society Project' in both provinces to ease the Mabri into modern rural society without an accompanying loss of culture.

According to project leaders, the effort is necessary to protect the Mabri from becoming a slave society within Northern Thailand's increasingly capitalist rural economy. Because of their anti-materialist beliefs, the Mabri perform menial labour for the Hmong and other hill tribes for little or no compensation.

Nan Province

Just over 668km from Bangkok, little-known Nan was one of Thailand's formerly government-designated 'remote provinces'. Before the early 1980s the area was so choked with bandits and PLAT (People's Liberation Army of Thailand) insurgents that travellers were discouraged from visiting. With the successes of the Thai army and a more stable political machine in Bangkok during the last two decades, Nan has opened up considerably, though a small area along Nan's 227km common border with Laos is still 'restricted' for 'security reasons'.

Nan remains a largely rural province with not a factory or condo in sight. The roads that link the provincial capital with the nearby provinces of Chiang Rai, Phrae and Utaradit pass through exquisite scenery of rich river valleys and rice fields.

Most of the inhabitants are agriculturally employed, growing sticky rice, beans, corn, tobacco and vegetables in the fertile river plains. Nan is also famous for two fruits: *fai jiin* (a Chinese version of Thailand's indigenous *máfai*) and *sôm sĭi thawng*, golden-skinned oranges. The latter are Nan's most famous export, commanding high prices in Bangkok and Malaysia. Apparently the cooler winter weather in Nan turns the skin orange (lowland Thai oranges are mostly green) and imparts a unique sweet-tart flavour. Thung Chang district supposedly grows the best sôm sĭi thawng in the province. Nan is also famous for its *phrík yài hâeng,* long hot chillies similar to those grown in China's Sichuan Province. During the hot season, you'll see lots of these chillies drying by the roadside.

Only 25% of the land is arable (and only half of that actively cultivated), as most of the province is covered by heavily forested mountains; Doi Phu Kha, at 2000m, is the highest peak. Half the forests in the province are virgin upland monsoon forest. Most of the province's population of 364,000 live in Mae Nam Nan valley, a bowl-shaped depression ringed by mountains on all sides.

The major river systems in the province include the Nan, Wa, Samun, Haeng, Lae and Pua. At 627km, Mae Nam Nan is Thailand's third-longest river after the Mekong and the Mun.

History

For centuries Nan was an isolated, independent kingdom with few ties to the outside world. Ample evidence of prehistoric habitation exists, but it wasn't until several small meuang consolidated to form Nanthaburi on Mae Nam Nan in the mid-14th century – concurrent with the founding of Luang Prabang and the Lan Xang (Million Elephants) kingdom in Laos – that the city became a power to contend with. Associated with the powerful Sukhothai kingdom, the meuang took the title Waranakhon and played a significant role in the development of early Thai nationalism.

Towards the end of the 14th century Nan became one of the nine Northern Thai–Lao principalities that comprised Lanna and the city-state flourished throughout the 15th century under the name Chiang Klang (Middle City), a reference to its position roughly midway between Chiang Mai (New City) and Chiang Thong (Golden City), today's Luang Prabang in Laos).

The Burmese took control of the kingdom in 1558 and transferred many inhabitants to Myanmar as slaves; the city was all but abandoned until western Thailand was wrested from the Burmese in 1786. The local dynasty then regained sovereignty and remained semi-autonomous until 1931, when Nan finally accepted full Bangkok sponsorship.

NAN
อ.เมืองน่าน

postcode 55000 • pop 23,000
In the capital, parts of the old city wall and several early wát dating from the Lanna period can be seen. Meuang Nan's wát are distinctive: Some temple structures show Lanna influence, while others belong to the Thai Lü legacy brought from Xishuangbanna, the Thai Lü's historical homeland.

Orientation & Information
Tourist Offices The provincial office on Thanon Suriyaphong has a friendly tourist centre, although not much English is spoken. Maps are sometimes available. It's open weekdays from 9am to 4.30pm and Saturday from 9am to noon.

Money Bangkok Bank and Thai Farmers Bank on Thanon Sumonthewarat, near the

Nan Fah and Dhevaraj Hotels (see Places to Stay later), operate foreign exchange services and ATMs.

Post & Communications The main post office on Thanon Mahawong, in the centre of the city, is open 8.30am to 4.30pm weekdays and 9am to noon on weekends and holidays. The attached CAT office offers a Home Country Direct phone and is open 7am to 10pm daily.

Internet services are available at Vichart Telecom on Thanon Anantaworarittidet and at R&T Computer on the corner almost opposite Fhu Travel Service.

Nan National Museum
พิพิธภัณฑสถานแห่งชาติน่าน

The 1903-vintage palace of Nan's last two feudal lords (Phra Jao Suriyapongpalidet and Jao Mahaphrom Surathada) houses the Nan National Museum (☎ 054 772 777, 054 710 561; admission 30B; open 9am- 4pm daily). This museum first opened its doors in 1973 under the auspices of Chiang Mai National Museum; recent renovations have made it one of the most up-to-date provincial museums in Thailand. Unlike most provincial museums in the country, this one has English labels for many items on display.

The ground floor is divided into six exhibition rooms with ethnological exhibits covering the various ethnic groups found in the province, including the Northern Thais, Thai Lü, Htin, Khamu, Mabri, Hmong and Mien. Among the items on display are silverwork, textiles, folk utensils and tribal costumes. On the 2nd floor of the museum are exhibits on Nan history, archaeology, local architecture, royal regalia, weapons, ceramics and religious art.

The museum's collection of Buddha images includes some rare Lanna styles as well as the floppy-eared local styles. Usually made from wood, these standing images are in the 'calling for rain' posture (with hands at the sides, pointing down) and they show a marked Luang Prabang influence. The astute museum curators posit a Nan style of art in Buddhist sculpture; some examples on

EASTERN PROVINCES

People of Nan

Nan is a sparsely populated province, and the ethnic groups found here differ significantly from those in other Northern provinces. Outside Mae Nam Nan valley, the predominant hill tribes are Mien (around 8000), with smaller numbers of Hmong. During the Vietnam War many Hmong and Mien from Nan (as well as from Chiang Rai and Phetchabun) were recruited to fight with the Communist Pathet Lao, which promised to create a Hmong-Mien king following a Pathet Lao victory in Laos. Some of these so-called 'Red Meo' even trained in North Vietnam.

Along the southwestern provincial border with Phrae are a few small Mabri settlements. What makes Nan unique, however, is the presence of three lesser-known groups seldom seen outside this province: the Thai Lü, Htin and Khamu.

Thai Lü

Originally from Xishuangbanna (Sipsongpanna) in China's Yunnan Province, the Thai Lü migrated to Nan in 1836 in the wake of a conflict with a local *jâo meuang* (lord). Phra Jao Atityawong, ruler of the Nan kingdom at the time, allowed the Thai Lü to stay and grow vegetables in what is now Tha Wang Pha district. Their influence on Nan (and, to a lesser extent, on Phrae) culture has been very important. Like most Siamese Thai, the Thai Lü are Theravada Buddhists, and the temple architecture at Wat Phra That Chae Haeng, Wat Phumin and Wat Nong Bua – typified by thick walls with small windows, two- or three-tiered roofs, curved pediments and *naga* (serpent-being) lintels – is a Thai Lü inheritance. Thai Lü fabrics are among the most prized in Northern Thailand and the weaving motifs show up in many Nan handicrafts.

The Thai Lü build traditional wooden or bamboo-thatched houses on thick wooden stilts, beneath which they place their kitchens and weaving looms. Many still make all their own clothes, typically sewn from indigo-dyed cotton fabrics. Many Thai Lü villages support themselves by growing rice and vegetables. In Nan they maintain a strong sense of tradition; most Thai Lü communities still recognise a jâo meuang and *măw meuang* (state astrologer), two older men in the community who serve as political and spiritual consultants.

---

display seem very imitative of other Thai styles, while others are quite distinctive, with the ears curved outwards. Also on display on the 2nd floor is a rare 'black' (actually reddish-brown) elephant tusk said to have been presented to a Nan lord over 300 years ago by the Khün ruler of Chiang Tung (Kengtung). Held aloft by a wooden Garuda sculpture, the tusk measures 97cm long and 47cm in circumference. A building adjacent to the museum has a few books on Thai art and archaeology for sale.

Wat Phumin
วัดภูมินทร์

Nan's most famous temple is celebrated for its cruciform bòt, constructed in 1596 and restored during the reign of Chao Ananta-vorapitthidet (1867–74). The bòt exterior

exemplifies the work of Thai Lü architects. Thai Lü artists painted the interior murals depicting the Khattana Kuman and Nimi jataka during the 19th-century restoration. These murals have historic as well as aesthetic value, since they incorporate scenes of local life from the era in which they were painted. (See the special section ' Lanna-Style Temple Murals'.)

The ornate altar sitting in the centre of the bòt has four sides with four Sukhothai-style sitting Buddhas in *maan wíchai* (victory over Mara; one hand touching the ground) posture, facing in each direction.

Wat Phra That Chae Haeng
วัดพระธาตุแช่แห้ง

Two kilometres past the bridge that spans Mae Nam Nan, heading southeast out of

People of Nan

Htin

Pronounced 'Tin', this Mon-Khmer group of about 3000 lives in villages of 50 or so families spread across remote mountain valleys of Chiang Klang, Pua and Thung Chang districts. A substantial number also live across the border in Sayaburi Province, Laos. They typically subsist by hunting for game, breeding domestic animals, farming small plots of land and, in Bo Kleua, extracting salt from salt wells.

Htin houses are usually made of thatched bamboo and raised on bamboo or wooden stilts. No metal (not even nails) – is used in the construction of houses because of a Htin taboo.

The Htin are particularly skilled at manipulating bamboo to make everything needed around the house; for floor mats and baskets they interweave pared bamboo with a black-coloured grass to create bold geometric patterns.

They also use bamboo to fashion a musical instrument of stepped pipes – similar to the *angklung* of Central Thailand and Indonesia – which is shaken to produce musical tones. The Htin don't weave their own fabrics, often buying clothes from neighbouring Miens.

Khamu

Like the Thai Lü, the Khamu people migrated to Nan around 150 years ago from the Xishuangbanna area in China and Laos. There are now over 5000 Khamu living in Nan (a greater number than anywhere else in Thailand), most of them in the Wiang Sa, Thung Chang, Chiang Klang and Pua districts. Their villages are established near streams; their houses have dirt floors like those of the Hmong but their roofs sport crossed beams similar to the Northern Thai *kàlae* (locally called kapkri-aak).

The Khamu are skilled at metalwork and they perform regular rituals to placate Salok, the spirit of the forge. Khamu villages are usually very self-sufficient; villagers hold fast to tradition and are known to value thrift and hard work. Ban Huay Sataeng in Thung Chang district is one of the largest and easiest Khamu villages to visit.

town, this temple dating from 1355 is the most sacred wát in Nan Province. It is set in a square, walled enclosure on top of a hill with a view of Nan and the valley. The Thai Lü–influenced bòt features a triple-tiered roof with carved wooden eaves, and dragon reliefs over the doors.

A gilded Lanna-style chedi sits on a large square base next to the bòt with sides 22.5m long; the entire chedi is 55.5m high. Phaya Phu Kha supposedly ordered the construction of this chedi in 1359 to hold a Buddha relic he acquired from the Sukhothai kingdom.

Wat Phra That Chang Kham

วัดพระธาตุช้างค้ำ

After Wat Phra That Chae Haeng, this is the second-most important temple in the city.

The main wíhǎan, reconstructed in 1458, has a huge seated Buddha image and faint murals in the process of being painstakingly uncovered. Sometime in the mid-20th century an abbot reportedly ordered the murals to be whitewashed because he thought they were distracting worshippers from concentrating on his sermons!

Also in the wíhǎan is a collection of Lanna-period scrolls inscribed (in Lanna script) not only with the usual Buddhist scriptures but with the history, law and astrology of the time. A *thammâat* (dharma seat; used by monks when teaching) sits to one side.

The magnificent chedi behind the wíhǎan dates to the 14th century, probably around the same time the temple was founded. It features elephant supports similar to those seen in Sukhothai and Si Satchanalai.

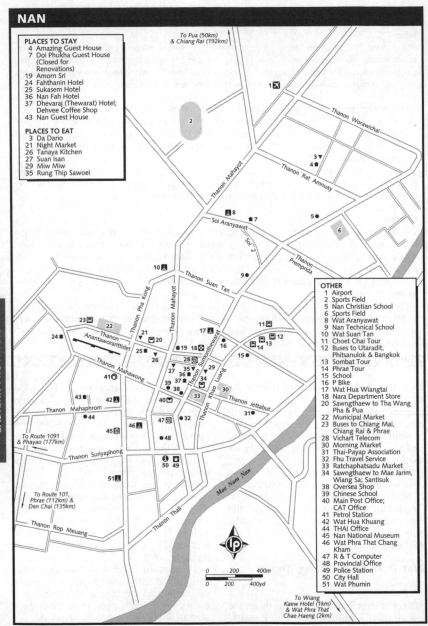

NAN

PLACES TO STAY
4 Amazing Guest House
7 Doi Phukha Guest House (Closed for Renovations)
19 Amorn Sri
24 Fahthanin Hotel
25 Sukasem Hotel
36 Nan Fah Hotel
37 Dhevaraj (Thewarat) Hotel; Dehvee Coffee Shop
43 Nan Guest House

PLACES TO EAT
3 Da Dario
21 Night Market
26 Tanaya Kitchen
27 Suan Isan
29 Miw Miw
35 Rung Thip Sawoei

OTHER
1 Airport
2 Sports Field
5 Nan Christian School
6 Sports Field
8 Wat Aranyawat
9 Nan Technical School
10 Wat Suan Tan
11 Choet Chai Tour
12 Buses to Utaradit, Phitsanulok & Bangkok
13 Sombat Tour
14 Phrae Tour
15 School
16 P Bike
17 Wat Hua Wiangtai
18 Nara Department Store
19 Sawngthaew to Tha Wang Pha & Pua
22 Municipal Market
23 Buses to Chiang Mai, Chiang Rai & Phrae
28 Vichart Telecom
30 Morning Market
31 Thai-Payap Association
32 Fhu Travel Service
33 Ratchaphatsadu Market
34 Sawngthaew to Mae Jarim, Wiang Sa; Santisuk
38 Oversea Shop
39 Chinese School
40 Main Post Office; CAT Office
41 Petrol Station
42 Wat Hua Khuang
44 THAI Office
45 Nan National Museum
46 Wat Phra That Chang Kham
47 R & T Computer
48 Provincial Office
49 Police Station
50 City Hall
51 Wat Phumin

To Pua (50km) & Chiang Rai (192km)

Thanon Worawichai

Thanon Rat Amnuay

Soi Aranyawat

Soi 2

Thanon Premprida

Thanon Suan Tan

Thanon Mahayot

Thanon Pha Kong

Thanon Anantaworarittidet

Thanon Mahawong

Thanon Sumonthewarat

Thanon Khao Luang

Thanon Jettabut

Thanon Mahaphrom

To Route 1091 & Phayao (177km)

Thanon Suriyaphong

To Route 101, Phrae (112km) & Den Chai (135km)

Thanon Rop Meuang

Thanon Thali

Mae Nam Nan

EASTERN PROVINCES

0   200   400m
0   200   400yd

To Wiang Kaew Hotel (1km) & Wat Phra That Chae Haeng (2km)

Next to the chedi is a small, undistinguished bòt from the same era. Wat Chang Kham's current abbot tells an interesting story involving the bòt and a Buddha image that was once kept inside. According to the venerable abbot, in 1955 art historian AB Griswold offered to purchase the 145cm-tall Buddha inside the small bòt. The image appeared to be a crude Sukhothai-style walking Buddha moulded of plaster. After agreeing to pay the abbot 25,000B for the image, Griswold began removing the image from the bòt – but as he did it fell and the plaster around the statue broke away to reveal an original Sukhothai Buddha of pure gold underneath. Needless to say, the abbot made Griswold give it back, much to the latter's chagrin. The image is now kept behind a glass partition, along with other valuable Buddhist images from the area, in the abbot's kùtì. Did Griswold suspect what lay beneath the plaster? The abbot refuses to say.

Wat Chang Kham is also distinguished by having the largest hăw trai (Tripitaka library) in Thailand. It's as big as or bigger than the average wíhăn, but now lies empty.

The wát is opposite the Nan National Museum on Thanon Pha Kong.

Wat Hua Khuang
วัดหัวข่วง

Largely ignored by art historians, this small wát diagonally opposite Wat Chang Kham features a distinctive Lanna/Lan Xang–style chedi with four Buddha niches, a wooden Tripitaka library now used as a kùtì and a noteworthy bòt with a Luang Prabang–style carved wooden veranda.

Inside are a carved wooden ceiling and a huge naga altar. The temple's founding date is unknown, but stylistic cues suggest this may be one of the city's oldest wát.

Wat Suan Tan
วัดสวนตาล

Reportedly established in 1456, Wat Suan Tan (Palm Grove Monastery) features an interesting 15th-century chedi (40m high) that combines prang (Khmer-style tower)

and lotus-bud motifs of obvious Sukhothai influence. The heavily restored wíhăn contains an early Sukhothai-style bronze sitting Buddha.

Wat Suan Tan is on Thanon Suan Tan, near the northeastern end of Thanon Pha Kong.

Trekking

Nan has nothing like the organised trekking industry found in Chiang Rai and Chiang Mai, but there is one company that leads two- or three-day excursions into the mountains. Fhu Travel Service (☎ 054 710 636, 054 710 940, mobile 01-472 8951, fax 054 775 345, ⓔ fhutravel@hotmail.com) at 453/4 Thanon Sumonthewarat offers treks to Mabri, Hmong, Mien, Thai Lü and Htin villages.

A one-day 'soft' trek costs 700B to 1200B per person, depending on the number of participants (two-person minimum); a two-day, one-night journey costs 1200B to 2000B per person; and three days and two nights costs 1500B to 2700B per person. The trekking fees include transport, meals, accommodation, sleeping bag and guide services.

Fhu also runs boat trips on Mae Nam Nan in December and January when the water level is high enough. White-water rubber-rafting trips on the Nam Wa in Mae Charim are offered year-round. The prices run from 1300B per person (for trips of seven to eight people) to 2500B per person (for trips of two people). This price includes transport, guide, lunch and safety equipment. Three-day rubber-rafting trips are 3000B to 6000B per person, depending on the number of people. Elephant tours are also available.

Tours of the city and surrounding area cost 500B for up to five people.

Places to Stay
Guesthouses *Nan Guest House (☎ 054 771 849, 57/16 Thanon Mahaphrom)* Singles/doubles/triples with shared bathroom 70/100/130B, rooms with private shower & toilet 200B. In a large house at the end of a soi off Thanon Mahaphrom, this guesthouse is close to the centre of town and

near the THAI office; it also offers tours and rents mountain bikes for 30B.

Amazing Guest House (☎ *054 710 893, 23/7 Thanon Rat Amnuay*) Singles/doubles/triples/quads 100/160/210/260B. In a tidy two-storey house on a quiet soi off Thanon Rat Amnuay, this place offers five fan rooms upstairs, all with wooden floors, clean beds and hot shared showers. Discounts are available for long-term stays.

Doi Phukha Guest House (☎ *054 751 517, 94/5 Soi 1 Thanon Sumonthewarat*) An old favourite, Doi Phukha has been closed for renovation for some time but is due to reopen soon.

Hotels *Sukasem Hotel* (☎ *054 710 141, fax 054 771 581, 29/31 Thanon Anantaworarittidet*) Rooms with fan & private bathroom 200-300B, with air-con 350B. The Sukasem is centrally located and offers fairly clean and adequate rooms.

Amorn Sri (*no Roman-script sign;* ☎ *054 710 510, 62/1 Thanon Anantaworarittidet*) Singles/doubles with fan 170/250B. The hotel is at a very busy intersection so it may not be the quietest choice. The rooms are also very basic and ought to be lower-priced for this market, but if the Sukasem is full and you don't want to stay in a guesthouse, this is your only budget choice.

Dhevaraj Hotel (*Thewarat;* ☎ *054 710 094, fax 054 771 365, 466 Thanon Sumonthewarat*) 2nd-floor singles/doubles with fan 300/400B, 3rd-floor singles/doubles with air-con 500/600B, 4th-floor VIP rooms 700B. One of the best hotels Nan has to offer, the four-storey Dhevaraj is built around a tiled courtyard with a fountain – very atypical for Thailand. It's not really fancy but it's a pleasant place. The large, clean fan rooms are a cut above the usual room with fan. Rooms towards the back of the hotel are quieter than those towards the front. The VIP rooms feature double-glazed windows, carpet, cable TV and minifridge.

Nan Fah Hotel (☎ *054 710 284, 438-440 Thanon Sumonthewarat*) Singles/doubles 440/540B. Next door to the Dhevaraj, the all-wood Nan Fah is well known for a sup-porting teak pillar that extends for three storeys. All rooms come with air-con and hot-water showers; rates include breakfast.

Wiang Kaew Hotel (☎ *054 750 573, fax 054 774 573, Km1, Rte 1168*) Rooms with fan/air-con 240/380B. On the road that leads to Wat Phra That Chae Haeng, the friendly Wiang Kaew offers rooms in row houses that almost have the appearance of separate bungalows. There's no lounge or karaoke, so it's quiet at night. All rooms come with hot water, TV, refrigerator and phone.

Fahthanin Hotel (☎ *054 757 321, fax 054 757 324, 303 Thanon Anantaworarittidet*) Rooms 700-800B. The seven-storey Fahthanin, the newest hotel in town, has rooms with TV, air-con, hot shower and minifridge. The more expensive rooms are slightly larger and have bathtubs. The restaurant/coffee shop has very good Thai food; room rates include breakfast.

Places to Eat
A *night market* assembles on the corner of Thanon Pha Kong and Thanon Anantaworarittidet every night; it's not that spectacular, but the vendors along the sidewalks nearby have fairly good food. Another group of *food vendors* sets up along the soi opposite the Dhevaraj Hotel.

Rung Thip Sawoei (*Thanon Sumonthewarat*) Dishes 25-60B. Open 7am-9pm daily. The most dependable Thai-Chinese restaurant in the vicinity of the Nan Fah and Dhevaraj hotels is this old brick-and-wood standby.

Miw Miw (*no Roman-script sign; Thanon Sumonthewarat, opposite Thai Farmers Bank*) Dishes 20-50B. Open 8am-10pm daily. This one's a bit cleaner than Rung Thip Sawoei and has good jók, noodles and real coffee.

Suan Isan (*Thanon Sumonthewarat*) Dishes 25-60B. Open 11am-11pm daily. If you turn left at the soi next to Rung Thip Sawoei and follow it about 200m, you'll come to this semi-outdoor spot with the best Northeastern Thai food in town.

{continued on page 290}

ANDREW LUBRAN

PEOPLE OF NORTHERN THAILAND

About 75% of all Thailand's residents are ethnic Thais or Tai, defined as those who speak a form of Thai/Tai as a first language (see the boxed text 'Austro-Thai Migration' in the Facts about Northern Thailand chapter). These can be divided into the Thai Phak Klang (Central Thai or Siamese) of the Chao Phraya Delta (the most densely populated region of the country); the Thai Lao or Thai Isan of Northeastern Thailand; the Thai Pak Tai of Southern Thailand; and the Khon Meuang (Northern Thais). Each group speaks its own Thai dialect and to a certain extent practises customs unique to its region. Politically and economically the Central Thais are the dominant group, although they barely outnumber the Thai Lao of the Northeast.

Khon Meuang

In the North, the Northern Thais are the most numerous group, accounting for an estimated 50% of the population, or around five million people. Historically some peoples in the region have called them Yuan (Thai Yuan) or Yün, or less frequently Phayap, but nowadays the Northern Thais consider these to be pejorative names and they prefer the term Khon Meuang (People of the Principalities).

Aside from language, there are many cultural differences that set Khon Meuang apart from Central and Southern Thais in particular. While the Central Thais cremate their dead in temple crematoriums, Northern Thais traditionally use cremation grounds purposely located outside the village perimeter, for example. This custom probably has its origins in pre-Buddhist Thai tribal societies, in which special areas were set aside for funeral rites. Virtually all ethnic Thais practise a combination of Buddhism and animism, but Northern Thais tend to add more animism to the mix than do the Central or Southern Thai.

On the other hand, Khon Meuang have many affinities with the Thai Lao of Northeastern Thailand. In fact, in the long history of Northern Thailand, the distinction between 'Thai' and 'Lao' was almost nonexistent until relatively recently, the two terms being used interchangeably throughout the Lan Na Thai (upper Northern Thailand) and Lan Chang (Laos) kingdoms. The aforementioned animistic beliefs of the Khon Meuang, for example, have much in common with those of the Thai Lao, and the two cultures share folk tales unknown to the Central and Southern Thais. Much vocabulary in Northern Thai – known locally as *kham meuang* (words of the principalities) – is identical to Lao, particularly the Northern Lao dialect as spoken in Luang Prabang, Luang Nam Tha and Bokeo. See the Language chapter for more detail.

Significant minority groups who speak Thai dialects in the North include the Thai Lü (or Lú, numbering 78,000), Shan (also known as

Thai Yai or Ngiaw, numbering approximately 56,000) and Black Thai (Thai Dam, around 20,000), all of whom share many customs with the Khon Meuang.

The Chinese

Chinese residents form a small but active minority in provincial capitals, particularly in Chiang Mai, Chiang Rai, Lampang, Lamphun and Phichit, where they tend to operate small businesses in downtown areas. Chinese – or those of mixed Chinese and Thai parentage – also run many of the factories of the North. Most trace their ancestry to Fujian and Guangzhou Provinces in China.

Perhaps more numerous are the Jin Haw or Hui, Chinese Muslims who emigrated from Yunnan to Thailand in the late 19th century to avoid religious and ethnic persecution during the Qing dynasty. In Northern Thailand they are joined by ex-Kuomintang (KMT) soldiers from southwestern China who fled into northern Myanmar and Thailand after the communist takeover of China in the late 1940s.

Hill Tribes

Ethnic minorities living in the mountainous regions of Northern Thailand are often called 'hill tribes' or, in the common Thai vernacular, chao khăo (mountain people). Each hill tribe has its own language, customs, mode of dress and spiritual beliefs.

Most are of semi-nomadic origin, having migrated to Thailand from Tibet, Myanmar, China or Laos during the past 200 years or so, although some groups may have been in Thailand much longer. They are 'fourth-world' people in that they belong neither to the main aligned powers nor to the developing nations. Rather, they have crossed and continue to cross national borders, usually fleeing oppression by other cultures, paying little attention to nationhood.

Language and culture constitute the borders of their world. Some groups are caught between the 12th and 21st centuries, while others are gradually being assimilated into modern life. Many tribespeople are also moving into lowland areas as montane lands become deforested by both traditional swidden (slash-and-burn) cultivation and illegal logging.

The Tribal Research Institute (☎ 053 210 872) in Chiang Mai recognises 10 different hill tribes in Thailand, but there may be up to 20. The institute estimates the total hill-tribe population to be around 550,000, although other sources give figures as great as one million.

The tribes most likely to be encountered in the region can be divided into three main linguistic groups: the Tibeto-Burman (Lisu, Lahu, Akha), the Karennic (Karen, Kayah) and the Austro-Thai (Hmong, Mien). Within each group there may also be several subgroups, eg, Blue Hmong, White Hmong; these names usually refer to predominant elements of clothing.

The hill tribes tend to have among the lowest standards of living in Thailand. Although it's tempting to correlate this with the traditional lifestyles they lead, their situation is compounded, in most cases, by lack of Thai citizenship. Without the latter, they don't have the right to own land or even to receive the national minimum wage, plus they may be denied access to health care and schooling. In the last couple of decades, efforts to integrate chao khảo into Thai society via free education and the issuing of Thai identity cards may have improved the lot of a minority of tribespeople. Of course the irony is that further Thai assimilation will threaten their cultural identities.

The Shan (Thai: Thai Yai, meaning 'large Thai') are not included in the descriptions below as they are not a hill-tribe group per se – they have permanent habitations and speak a language similar to Thai. Thai scholars consider them to have been the original inhabitants of the area. Nevertheless, Shan villages are often common stops on hill-tribe treks.

The following comments on dress refer mostly to the female members of each group, as hill-tribe men tend to dress like rural Thais. Population figures are taken from 1995 estimates. For more detailed descriptions on Thailand's hill tribes, see some of the recommendations in the Books section of the Facts for the Visitor chapter, or visit the Tribal Research Institute's informative Web site (**W** www.tribal.or.th).

Akha
Pop 48,500
Thai: I-kaw
Origin: Tibet
Present locations: Thailand, Laos, Myanmar, Yunnan
Economy: rice, corn, opium
Belief system: animism, with an emphasis on ancestor worship
Distinctive characteristics: Women wear a headdress of beads, coloured string and dangling silver ornaments.

The Akha are among the poorest of Thailand's ethnic minorities and tend to resist assimilation into the Thai mainstream. Like the Lahu, they often cultivate opium for their own use.

Akha houses are constructed of wood and bamboo, usually atop short wooden stilts and roofed with thick grass. Guests are often received on a raised, open verandah at the entrance of the house.

Villages are built along mountain ridges or on steep slopes from 1000m to 1400m in altitude. At the entrance of every traditional Akha village stands a simple wooden gateway consisting of two vertical struts joined by a lintel. Akha shamans affix various charms made from bamboo strips to the gateway to prevent malevolent spirits from entering the village. Standing next to the gateway are crude wooden figures of a man and a woman, each bearing exaggerated sexual organs, in the belief that human sexuality is abhorrent to the spirit world.

The well-known Akha Swing Ceremony takes place from mid-August to mid-September, between planting and harvest. As their annual rice crop ripens, the Akha erect a simple swing consisting of four tall saplings lashed into a pyramid configuration. Vines are hung from the top of the tree pyramid and tied to a wooden plank to form the swing. For four days, amid much feasting and merrymaking, the villagers – especially pubescent girls – will take turns riding the swing.

Lahu
Pop 73,200

Thai: Musoe
Origin: Tibet
Present locations: southern China, Thailand, Myanmar
Economy: rice, corn, opium
Belief system: theistic animism (supreme deity is Geusha); some groups are Christian
Distinctive characteristics: Women wear black-and-red jackets with narrow skirts; men wear bright green or blue-green baggy trousers.

There are five main groups (in descending number): Red Lahu, Black Lahu, White Lahu, Lahu Sheleh and Yellow Lahu. They tend to live at about 1000m altitude. The Lahu are known to be excellent hunters, and in fact the Thai term for this tribe, *musoe,* is derived from a Burmese word meaning 'hunter'.

Lahu houses are built of wood, bamboo and grass, and usually stand on short wooden posts. Intricately woven Lahu shoulder bags *(yâam)* are prized by collectors. Lahu food is probably the spiciest of all hill-tribe cuisines.

Lisu
Pop 28,000

Thai: Lisaw
Origin: Tibet
Present Locations: Thailand, Yunnan
Economy: rice, opium, corn, livestock
Belief system: animism with ancestor worship and spirit possession
Distinctive characteristics: Women wear long multicoloured tunics over trousers and sometimes black turbans with tassels. Men wear baggy green or blue pants pegged in at the ankles.

Patrilineal clans have pan-tribal jurisdiction, which makes the Lisu unique among hill-tribe groups (most of which have power centred either on a shaman or a village headman). Lisu villages are usually in the mountains at about 1000m. Homes are built on the ground, rather than on stilts, and consist mostly of bamboo and grass. Older homes – today quite rare – may be made from mud brick or mud and bamboo-thatch.

Having no written language, the Lisu rely on oral histories for the relay of culture from generation to generation.

Mien
Pop 40,300

Thai: Yao
Origin: central China
Present Locations: Thailand, southern China, Laos, Myanmar, Vietnam
Economy: rice, corn, opium
Belief system: animism with ancestor worship and Taoism

Distinctive characteristics: Women wear trousers and black jackets with intricately embroidered patches and red fur-like collars, along with large dark blue or black turbans.

The Mien have been heavily influenced by Chinese traditions and use Chinese characters to write their language. They tend to settle near mountain springs at between 1000m and 1200m. Mien houses, made from wood or bamboo walls with grass or wood shingle roofs, are built directly onto the ground. The Mien are highly skilled at embroidery and silversmithing. Kinship is patrilineal and marriage is polygamous.

Hmong
Pop 124,000

Thai: Mong or Meo/Maew
Origin: southern China
Present locations: southern China, Thailand, Laos, Vietnam
Economy: rice, corn, opium
Belief system: animism
Distinctive characteristics: Female tribespeople wear simple black jackets and indigo or black baggy trousers (White Hmong) with striped and/or embroidered borders, or indigo skirts (Blue Hmong), plus silver jewellery. Sashes may be worn around the waist, and embroidered aprons draped front and back. Most women wear their hair in a large bun. Hmong men wear black trousers and a short-waisted, long-sleeved jacket with an embroidered chestpiece.

The Hmong are Thailand's second-largest hill-tribe group and are especially numerous in Chiang Mai Province. They usually live on mountain peaks or plateaus above 1000m. Houses, made of wood or thatch, sit on the ground. Kinship is patrilineal and polygamy is permitted.

Karen
Pop 322,000

Thai: Yang or Kariang
Origin: Myanmar
Present Locations: Thailand, Myanmar
Economy: rice, vegetables, livestock
Belief system: animism, Buddhism, Christianity, depending on the group
Distinctive characteristics: Tribespeople wear thickly woven V-neck tunics of various colours (unmarried women wear white), towel-like turbans and yarn-strung earrings.

There are four distinct Karen groups – the Skaw (or White) Karen, Pwo Karen, Pa-O (or Black) Karen and Kayah (or Red) Karen. These groups combined form the largest hill tribe in Thailand, numbering about half of all hill-tribe people. The Karen tend to live in lowland valleys and practise crop rotation rather than swidden agriculture. Their homes are built on low stilts or posts, with the roofs swooping quite low. Kinship is matrilineal and marriage is monogamous.

[continued from page 284]

Tanaya Kitchen (75/23-24 Thanon Anantaworarittidet) Dishes 15-35B. The clean Tanaya Kitchen serves a range of reasonably priced vegetarian and non-vegetarian dishes.

Dhevee Coffee Shop (☎ 054 710 094, fax 054 771 365, Dhevaraj Hotel, 466 Thanon Sumonthewarat) Dishes 40-100B. Open 6am-2am. The Dhevaraj's modest restaurant is clean, reliable and open when many other places are closed.

Da Dario (☎ 054 750 258, 37/4 Thanon Rat Amnuay) Dishes 50-100B. Open 10am-2pm & 5pm-10pm Mon-Sat, 5pm-10pm Sun. Da Dario is a Swiss-run Italian/Thai restaurant; prices are reasonable and the food and service are very good.

Shopping

Good buys include local textiles, especially the Thai Lü weaving styles from Xishuangbanna. Typical Thai Lü fabrics feature red and black designs on white cotton in floral, geometric and animal designs; indigo and red on white is also common. A favourite is the *laai náam lǎi* (flowing-water design), with stepped patterns representing streams, rivers and waterfalls.

Local Mien embroidery and Hmong applique are of excellent quality. Htin grass-and-bamboo baskets and mats are worth a look, too.

Thai-Payap Association (☎ 054 710 230, 24 Thanon Jettabut) This nonprofit association, one of Thailand's most successful village self-help projects, has a shop near the morning market and Nan bus terminal. Supported by Britain's Ockenden Venture from 1979 to 1990, the association now involves over 20 villages and has become totally self-sufficient. The handiwork offered through Thai-Payap is among the highest quality available, often including intricate, time-consuming designs. All proceeds go directly to the participating villages – even the administrative staff are trained village representatives.

There are several small artisan-operated shops along Thanon Sumonthewarat and along Thanon Mahawong and Thanon Anantaworarittidet.

Getting There & Away

Air You can fly to Nan on THAI from Chiang Mai (875B, four weekly), Phitsanulok (950B, four weekly), Phrae (640B, daily) or Bangkok (2035B, three weekly). The THAI office (☎ 054 710 377) is at 34 Thanon Mahaphrom. THAI offers free transport from its office to the airport.

Bus Baw Khaw Saw (government) buses run from Chiang Mai, Chiang Rai and Phrae to Nan. The fare from Chiang Mai's Arcade bus terminal is 128B ordinary, 179B air-con or 230B 1st class air-con; the trip takes from six to seven hours. From Chiang Rai there's one daily bus at 9.30am (No 611, 110B, six to seven hours) that goes via treacherous mountain roads – get a window seat as there's usually lots of motion sickness. Buses from Phrae to Nan leave frequently (44/62B ordinary/air-con, two to 2½ hours).

From Nan, buses to Chiang Mai, Chiang Rai and Phrae leave from a terminal west of the large market along Thanon Anantaworarittidet. Most other buses arrive at and depart from the Baw Khaw Saw terminal off Thanon Khao Luang.

Regular government-run air-con buses run to and from Bangkok for 300B (8am, 8.30am and 7pm daily); 1st-class air-con is 420B (daily 8am and 7pm) and 24-seat VIP buses are 620B (daily 7pm). The journey takes 10 to 13 hours.

Private 1st-class and VIP Bangkok buses leave from offices located along the eastern end of Thanon Anantaworarittidet, not far from the Baw Khaw Saw terminal. Sombat Tour and Phrae Tour both run VIP buses to Bangkok for as low as 450B – check the number of seats before booking, though. Choet Chai Tour offers 1st-class air-con buses to Bangkok. Most of these private buses depart between 6.15pm and 6.45pm

Train The northern railway makes a stop in Den Chai, which is a 46B, three-hour bus ride from Nan.

A Bangkok-bound Sprinter leaves Den Chai at 12.25pm and arrives in Bangkok at 7.50pm. The rapid trains leave at 7pm and 8.25pm (arriving at Bangkok's Hualamphong station at 4.55am and 6.25am respectively); the special express trains leave at 8.48pm and 10.25pm, arriving in Bangkok at 5.30am and 6.50am respectively. To be sure of meeting any of these trains, take an early afternoon (1pm or 2pm) Den Chai–bound bus from Nan's Baw Khaw Saw bus terminal.

Trains bound for Chiang Mai (74/31B 2nd/3rd class) depart Den Chai at 7.58am (rapid), 3.27pm (express), and 3.56pm (rapid), arriving at Chiang Mai at 12.20pm, 7.20pm and 8.30pm respectively.

See Getting There & Away in the Phrae section for more Den Chai train information.

Săwngthăew Pick-ups to districts in the northern part of the province (Tha Wang Pha, Pua, Pha Tup) leave from the petrol station opposite Sukasem Hotel on Thanon Anantaworarittidet. Southbound săwngthăew (for Mae Charim, Wiang Sa and Na Noi) depart from the car park opposite the new Ratchaphatsadu Market on Thanon Jettabut.

Getting Around

P Bike (no Roman-script sign; ☎ 054 772 680), opposite Wat Hua Wiangtai at 331–333 Thanon Sumonthewarat, rents Honda Dreams for 150B a day including helmet and third-party insurance. Bicycles are also available, and P Bike does repair work.

Oversea Shop (☎ 054 710 258) at 488 Thanon Sumonthewarat (a few doors down from the Dhevaraj Hotel) rents bicycles and motorbikes and can also handle repairs.

Săamláw around town cost 20B to 30B. Green săwngthăew circulating around the city centre charge 5B to 10B per person depending on distance.

AROUND NAN
Doi Phu Kha National Park
อุทยานแห่งชาติดอยภูคา

This national park is centred around 2000m-high Doi Phu Kha in the Pua and Bo Kleua districts of northeastern Nan (about 75km from Nan). There are several Htin, Mien, Hmong and Thai Lü villages in the park and vicinity, as well as a couple of caves and waterfalls and endless opportunities for forest walks.

The park offers 14 *bungalows* that rent for 250B per double room. You must bring food and drinking water in from town, as the park office no longer offers food service.

Bamboo Hut (103 Mu 10, Tambon Phu Kha, Amphoe Pua, Nan 55120) Huts 100B. Located in Ban Toei, a Lawa-Thai village near the summit at the edge of the park, Bamboo Hut was opened in 2000 by an English- and Dutch-speaking Lawa and his Thai wife. They offer five clean, well-spaced bamboo-thatch huts with shared bathroom and stupendous mountain and valley views. The owner is happy to lead guests on one- to three-day treks for 500B per day, including all meals. Treks visit local waterfalls, limestone caves (Tham Long is the biggest cave – about a one-day walk from the guesthouse) and hill-tribe villages. This area gets quite cool in the winter months – evening temperatures of 5°C to 10°C are not uncommon – so dress accordingly.

The standard national park entry fees apply.

To reach the park by public transport you must first take a bus or săwngthăew north of Nan to Pua (25B), and then pick up one of the infrequent săwngthăew to the park headquarters or Bamboo Hut (30B). The one going from Nan to Pua leaves about 6am, the one from Pua to Ban Toei at about 7am.

Bo Kleua
บ่อเกลือ

This is a Htin village southeast of Doi Phu Kha National Park where the main occupation is the extraction of salt from local salt wells *(bàw kleua)*. Rte 1256 meets Rte 1081 near Bo Kleua; Rte 1081 can be followed south back to Nan (107km) via a network of unpaved roads.

EASTERN PROVINCES

Nong Bua
หนองบัว

This neat and tidy Thai Lü village near the town of Tha Wang Pha, approximately 30km north of Nan, is famous for Lü-style **Wat Nong Bua**. Featuring a typical two-tiered roof and carved wooden portico, the bòt design is simple yet striking – note the carved naga heads at the roof corners. Inside the bòt are some noteworthy but faded jataka murals, thought to have been painted by the same artist who painted the murals at Wat Phumin in the provincial capital. The building is often locked when religious services aren't in progress, but there's usually someone around to unlock it. Be sure to leave a donation at the altar for temple upkeep and restoration.

You can also see Thai Lü weaving in action in the village. The home of Khun Janthasom Phrompanya, near the wát, serves as a local weaving centre – check there for the locations of looms, or to look at fabrics for purchase. Large *yâam* (shoulder bags) are available for just 50B, while nicely woven neck scarves cost more. There are also several weaving houses just behind the wát.

Getting There & Away Săwngthăew to Tha Wang Pha (15B) leave from opposite Nan's Sukasem Hotel. Get off at Samyaek Longbom, a three-way intersection before Tha Wang Pha, and walk west to a bridge over Mae Nam Nan, then left at the dead end on the other side of the bridge to Wat Nong Bua. It's 3.1km from the highway to the wát.

If you're coming from Nan via your own transport on Rte 1080, you'll cross a stream called Lam Nam Yang just past the village of Ban Fai Mun but before Tha Wang Pha. Take the first left off Rte 1080 and follow it to a dead end; turn right and then left over a bridge across Mae Nam Nan and walk until you reach another dead end, then left 2km until you can see Wat Nong Bua on the right.

Tham Pha Tup Forest Reserve
ถ้ำผาตูบ

This limestone cave complex is about 10km north of Nan and is part of a relatively new wildlife reserve. Some 17 caves have been counted, of which nine are easily located by means of established (but unmarked) trails.

From Nan, you can catch a săwngthăew bound for Pua or Thung Chang; it will stop at the turn-off to the caves for 10B. The vehicles leave from the petrol station opposite the Sukasem Hotel.

Sao Din
เสาดิน

Sao Din (Earth Pillars) is an erosional phenomenon similar to that found at Phae Meuang Phi in Phrae Province – tall columns of earth protruding from a barren depression. The area covers nearly 20 râi (3.2 hectares) off Rte 1026 in Na Noi district about 60km south of Nan.

Sao Din is best visited by bicycle or motorcycle since it's time consuming to reach by public transport. If you don't have your own wheels, take a săwngthăew to Na Noi from the southbound săwngthăew station opposite the Ratchaphatsadu Market in Nan. From Na Noi you must get yet another săwngthăew bound for Fak Tha or Ban Khok, getting off at the entrance to Sao Din after 5km or so. From here you'll have to walk or hitch 4km to Sao Din itself. There are also occasional direct săwngthăew from Na Noi.

Northwest of Sao Din, off Rte 1216, is another set of earth pillars called Hom Chom.

Other Attractions

There are a couple of interesting destinations in and around the Thai Lü village of Pua, roughly 50km north of Nan. In Pua itself you can check out a famous Thai Lü temple, **Wat Ton Laeng**, which is admired for its classic three-tiered roof. **Nam Tok Silaphet** is southeast of Pua, just off the road between Pua and Ban Nam Yao. The water falls in a wide swath over a cliff and is best seen at the end of the monsoon season in November. On the way to the falls and west of the road is the Mien village of **Ban Pa Klang**, worth a visit to see silversmiths at work. This village supplies many silver shops in Chiang Mai and Bangkok. Other silverwork Mien villages can be found on Rte 101 between Nan and Phrae.

Off Rte 1148, north of the village of Ban Sakoen, is a huge, 200m-wide cave called **Tham Luang**. The path to the cave is not signposted, but if you ask at the police checkpoint in Ban Sakoen you should be able to get directions or you might even find a guide.

Thaleh Sap Neua (Northern Lake) formed by Kheuan Sirikit is an important freshwater fishery for Nan, as well as a recreational attraction for Nan residents. Ban Pak Nai on its northwestern shore is the main fishing village. Just before Mae Nam Nan feeds into the lake at its extreme northern end, there is a set of river rapids called Kaeng Luang.

Border Crossing (Laos)

Ban Huay Kon (140km north of Nan) in Thung Chang District is now a legal border crossing for Lao and Thais, and it may be promoted to an international crossing in the foreseeable future. From this crossing it's just 152km to Luang Prabang and about 300km to the Chinese border at Boten, Laos. From the Lao side of the border crossing, a dirt road leads north-northeast about 45km to the banks of the Mekong River in Laos' Udomxai Province. From here you can either take a boat down river to Luang Prabang or cross the river and pick up Rte 2 to Meuang Xai, the provincial capital. From Meuang Xai it's only a couple of hours to the international border with China's Yunnan Province.

Nan residents with an interest in history are excited by the prospect of linking again the five *chiang* (cities) of the Lanna–Lan Xang–Xishuangbanna Diaspora: Chiang Mai, Chiang Rai, Chiang Thong (the original name for Luang Prabang), Chiang Rung (Yunnan's Jinghong) and Chiang Klang (Nan).

There is an immigration office in the district capital of Thung Chang, 100km north of Nan; if you find out that the border crossing is open to foreigners, you should stop in to get a Thai exit stamp in your passport.

Every Saturday morning from around 5am to 11am there's a lively **Lao-Thai market** in Thung Chang.

Phayao Province

PHAYAO

อ.เมืองพะเยา

postcode 56000 • pop 21,500

Lying at the heart of the Chiang Rai–Phayao Valley, Phayao reigns over one of the North's major agricultural areas. The fertile Mae Nam Ing basin, coupled with a large wetlands network of ponds, swamps and natural canals, has always endowed the inhabitants of Phayao with a steady source of nourishment and cash crops.

Today the plains around Kwan Phayao, the lake adjacent to the provincial capital, are studded with rice fields and fish farms. The town itself thus serves mainly as a supply and trade relay point for surrounding farms. The large, placid Kwan Phayao also provides a scenic foreground for the calm city, yet few tourists seem to find their way to Phayao.

History

Archaeologists believe that an unbroken series of at least four old settlements existed in the area before the Lanna period. Sandstone found in nearby mountains was used for building, for tool-making and for the sculpture of Buddhist statuary. During these eras the meuang may have had many names, two of which were Dok Kham Tai (the name of a local flower), and Phukam Yao, later shortened to Phayao.

When Phaya Mang Rai was establishing Chiang Mai as a power centre along Mae Nam Ping towards the end of the 13th century, Phaya Ngam Meuang ruled over Phayao as an independent state. His power extended over Nan and Ngao as well. Mang Rai and Ngam Meuang joined the famous triple alliance with Phaya Ruang (Ram Khamhaeng), but after these kings passed on, Chiang Saen annexed Phayao in the early 14th century and Nan regained its independence.

Phayao never quite recovered from the Burmese invasion of 1558, when most of the population was carried off either to Hanthawady (later called Bago or Pegu) in Myanmar or to Vientiane in Laos. Although the area was gradually repopulated, Phayao remained dependent on other states in the region. The people of Phayao were drawn into several frontier wars, the most notable of which were the three Kengtung expeditions in 1849, 1852 and 1854. Many Phayao men were recruited for these forces.

After Siam abolished the *monthon* (cluster of satellite states) system in favour of the *jangwàt* (province) system, Phayao became part of Chiang Rai Province. Only in 1977 did the Thai government grant Phayao provincial status.

Information

A branch of Bangkok Bank on Thanon Don Sanam, near the Tharn Thong and Wattana Hotels, offers foreign exchange and ATM services. Several other major Thai banks can be found in the same general vicinity.

Wat Si Khom Kham (Wat Phra Jao Ton Luang)
วัดศรีโคมคำ

At the eastern edge of Kwan Phayao, Wat Si Khon Kham is the most important wát in Phayao, due to the presence of the Phra Jao Ton Luang, a very large and sacred Buddha image. The figure was originally built without a shelter at the edge of the lake between 1491 and 1524. Standing 18m tall and measuring 16m across its lap, it's the largest Lanna-style Buddha in existence. A wíhǎan was built around the image in 1922 under the direction of Khruba Siwichai (1877–1938). Khruba Siwichai, a native of Lamphun and the most famous monk Northern Thailand has yet produced, directed a number of important restoration projects around the North during his career. Phayao

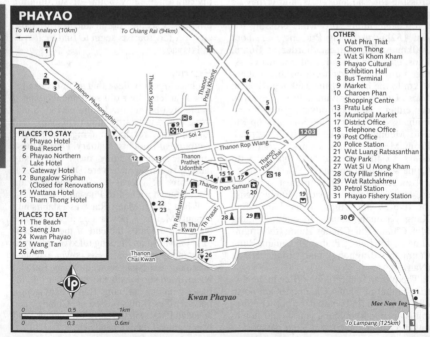

PHAYAO

To Wat Analayo (10km)
To Chiang Rai (94km)

Thanon Phahonyothin
Thanon Susan
Thanon Pratu Khlong

Thanon Rop Wiang
Thanon Prathet Udonthit
Thanon Don Saman
Th Ratchawong
Th Tha – Kwan
Th Prasat
Th Kwan
Thanon Chai Kwan

Kwan Phayao

Mae Nam Ing

To Lampang (125km)

PLACES TO STAY
4 Phayao Hotel
5 Bua Resort
6 Phayao Northern Lake Hotel
7 Gateway Hotel
12 Bungalow Siriphan (Closed for Renovations)
15 Wattana Hotel
16 Tharn Thong Hotel

PLACES TO EAT
11 The Beach
23 Saeng Jan
24 Kwan Phayao
25 Wang Tan
26 Aem

OTHER
1 Wat Phra That Chom Thong
2 Wat Si Khom Kham
3 Phayao Cultural Exhibition Hall
8 Bus Terminal
9 Market
10 Charoen Phan Shopping Centre
13 Pratu Lek
14 Municipal Market
17 District Office
18 Telephone Office
19 Post Office
20 Police Station
21 Wat Luang Ratsasanthan
22 City Park
27 Wat Si U Mong Kham
28 City Pillar Shrine
29 Wat Ratchakhreu
30 Petrol Station
31 Phayao Fishery Station

0   0.5   1km
0   0.3   0.6mi

residents are proud, however, that he served as Phayao's *jâo kháná* (ecclesiastical district chicf). In the temple grounds is a small **museum** dedicated to Khruba Siwichai.

The wát also contains a Buddhist University and maintains the adjacent Phayao Cultural Exhibition Hall (see separate entry).

A long pier belonging to the wát juts out over some wetlands at the edge of the lake.

Other Temples & Shrines

Several other temples in the city are worth visiting for those interested in Thai Buddhist art. **Wat Si U Mong Kham** contains a Lanna-period chedi in remarkably good condition, as well as a Lanna-period bronze sitting Buddha image called Phra Jao Lan Teu that many people believe is the most beautiful Lanna image outside of museums or private collections.

Opposite Wat Si Khom Kham a road climbs a hill to **Wat Phra That Chom Thong**, where you'll find a large white-washed Lanna-style chedi, a small forest grove and views of Kwan Phayao and the city. **Wat Lee** is famous for its Buddha carved from sandstone.

The **San Lak Meuang** (City Pillar Shrine) stands in the middle of a large green square with park benches and is one of the better-maintained city pillar shrines in the North. As the pillar is believed to harbour Phayao's guardian spirit, many local residents make offerings of flowers, candles and incense at the shrine.

Kwan Phayao
กว๊านพะเยา

'Kwan' *(kwáan)* is local dialect for 'lake' and Kwan Phayao is not only an important source of livelihood for farmers and fishers, but the main source of recreation for local townsfolk. Besides fishing for sport, swimming and boating, Phayao residents dine at lakeside restaurants and walk along the relatively new promenade.

Before Mae Nam Ing was dammed in 1941, the area now occupied by the lake was a large area of low-lying wetlands dotted with ponds and swamps, all linked by small waterways. One of the largest ponds was Nong Iang, a natural lagoon that now forms the part of the lake near Wat Si Khom Kham. The dam sits where Mae Nam Ing exits the lowlands at the current southeastern corncr of Kwan Phayao.

The damming expanded the natural lagoon so that now Kwan Phayao's waters occupy an area of 12,800 râi or around 18 sq km. The Phayao Fishery Office has become famous for breeding freshwater fishes, including the giant Mekong catfish (released into the Mekong, not into the lake). Among the fish commonly found in this lake is the sailfin shark (not an actual shark, so don't fear going in the water), which is also found in the Salween River, the Mekong and various other waterways in Southeast Asia.

Phayao Cultural Exhibition Hall
หอวัฒนธรรมนิทัศน์

Next to Wat Si Khom Kham on the Kwan Phayao, this well-designed and well-curated museum *(☎ 054 410 058; admission 10B; open 9am-4pm Wed-Sun)* is dedicated to local history and culture. The collection of historic sandstone sculptures alone is worth the small admission price. Included are lots of old *bai sêhmaa* (carved stone slabs used to mark areas where Buddhist monastic ordinations may be held), Buddha images, Buddha heads and inscribed pillars, including a pillar with a Lanna inscription dated 1493.

Other exhibits include an impressive selection of lacquerware, ceramics and textiles, plus an equally impressive set of candle rails that go in front of Buddhist altars. The ceramics collection covers the Phayao School, a sub-style of the general Lanna style dating to the 16th and 17th centuries, as distinguished by a blackish-grey clay.

Natural history and geology are well represented by educational displays as well. Most labels are in English and Thai, though a few are in Thai only.

Special Events

In May Phayao residents celebrate the Phra Jao Ton Luang Festival with processions to and from Wat Si Khom Kham through the city, with plenty of food and handicrafts vendors in evidence at the wát and along the roadways.

Loi Krathong, in late October or early November, is also a major Phayao event, with the Kwan Phayao providing a perfect setting for the launching of *krà-thong* (small banana-leaf rafts containing offerings to the water spirits).

Places to Stay
Phayao doesn't have a huge variety of accommodation, and what there is exists mainly to serve business travellers.

Two hotels in the semi-busy central district, along Thanon Don Sanam, offer the least expensive rooms.

Wattana Hotel (☎ 054 431 203, 69 Thanon Don Sanam) 1-bed/2-bed rooms with fan 140/180B. This is a typical modern Thai-Chinese hotel with rooms stacked around a central parking lot. All rooms have hot-water showers.

Tharn Thong Hotel (☎ 054 431 302, 56-59 Thanon Don Sanam) Rooms with fan & 2 beds 230B, with TV 280B, with TV & air-con 370B. This is very similar to the Wattana but with nicer rooms and lobby.

Bungalow Siriphan (☎ 054 431 319, Thanon Phahonyothin) Perched on a small peninsula at Kwan Phayao's southeastern edge, this set of bungalows appears to be the only lodging in Phayao that's on or near the lake. The location is also within convenient walking distance of the town centre and the lakefront promenade, and is less than 500m from the bus terminal. It was closed for renovations when we visited, but we would project rates of 300-500B when it reopens.

Gateway Hotel (☎ 054 411 330-9, fax 054 410 519, 7/36 Thanon Pratu Klong, Soi 2) Standard/deluxe rooms 1500/1800B, suites 3500-5000B. This nine-storey hotel has large, comfortable air-con rooms with TV. On the premises are a disco, karaoke, snooker club, coffeeshop and large parking lot. It's within easy walking distance of the main municipal market, and not far from the downtown area.

Phayao Northern Lake Hotel (☎ 054 481 538, 15/7 Thanon Rop Wiang) Rooms 1200-3000B. The city's newest hotel offers similar quality to the Gateway but is closer to the highway.

Most of Phayao's other places to stay are out on the Hwy 1, the Chiang Rai–Phayao highway.

Bua Resort (☎ 054 481 596, 262 Hwy 1, near Km738) Bungalows from 600B. The tiled-roof bungalows here look comfortable enough; a karaoke and snooker club are part of the complex.

Phayao Hotel (☎ 054 481 970, fax 054 481 973, 445 Hwy 1) Rooms with fan/air-con 300/400B. This is one of the older highway hotels.

Places to Eat
Several open-air restaurants can be found along Thanon Chai Kwan, opposite Kwan Phayao's lakefront promenade. The local specialty is *plaa phǎo*, fresh grilled fish (usually fish farmed in the lake), along with kûng tên (live freshwater shrimp served in a sauce of lime juice, chillies and herbs), *kài yâang* (grilled chicken), sôm-tam and *plaa mèuk yâang* (roast squid).

Wiang Tan (17/9 Thanon Chai Kwan) Dishes 40-100B. Open 10am-11pm daily. This is currently the most popular spot along the lakefront. The extensive menu includes standard Thai and Thai-Chinese dishes along with plenty of Isan dishes. Similar places along Thanon Chai Kwan worth trying include *Aem*, *Wang Thang* and *Saeng Jaan*.

There is also a sprinkling of restaurant along the lake northwest of Wat Si Khom Kham.

The Beach (Thanon Phahonyothin) Dishes 50-120B. This outdoor spot on a little cape in the lake is one of the best along this stretch. As the name suggests, it is decorated to look like it could be on a Southern Thai beach. It's well done, however, and the food and service are good.

Getting There & Away
The town bus terminal is off Soi 2, Thanon Pratu Klong, near the Gateway Hotel and

the Charoen Phan shopping centre. There are buses to Chiang Rai (25B ordinary, 41B to 55B air-con, 1¾ to two hours) and Chiang Mai (67B ordinary, 94B air-con, 2½ to three hours).

AROUND PHAYAO
Wat Analayo
วัดอนาลโย

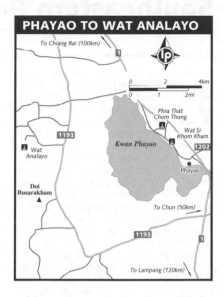

Spread out along a long ridge atop Doi Busarakham, 20km west of town to the north, this very well-endowed forest wát could almost be called a Buddhist resort. The rambling set of structures represents a hodgepodge of architectural styles, some old, some new. Wealthy Buddhists have contributed all manner of Buddhist art to the wát, including some very precious Buddha images from various periods in Thai art history. One hall in the compound contains a small Buddha in the style of Bangkok's Emerald Buddha – except that this one really is carved from emerald.

At the top of the first set of stairs is a highly stylised version of India's Mahabodhi Stupa. Bronze Sukhothai-style Buddhas sit at either side of the stupa. The monks' kùtì, among the most elaborate you're ever likely to see in Thailand, resemble Alpine cottages with tile roofs. Several ultra-large kùtì, modern in design and containing huge Buddha halls, appear to be reserved for wealthy donors.

Although much of the temple is surrounded by forest, you can glimpse views of Kwan Phayao and the town below in a few spots.

To reach Doi Busarakham, take the Phayao–Chiang Rai highway north about 7km and make a left onto Rte 1127. After 4km more, make another left onto Rte 1193. From here it's 9km to the last turnoff at Rte 1316, which leads up the mountain to a parking lot from where you can easily walk to Wat Analayo. Săwngthăew drivers

waiting at the parking lot charge 50B for the short hop to the main gate. There is no public transport to the temple but if you happen to be in Phayao on a Buddhist holiday, you could probably hitch a ride fairly easily.

Thai Lü Villages
หมู่บ้านไทยลื้อ

Many Thai Lü live in the districts of Chiang Kham (52km from Phayao) and Chiang Muan (84km), in the province's northeastern and southeastern corners respectively. If you're interested in Lü weaving, you'll find several shops selling textiles in Chiang Kham, and households in villages in both districts are good places to observe looms and techniques.

Around 25km northeast of Chiang Kham via Rtes 1210 and 1095, at Ban Huak on the Thai-Lao border, a Thai-Lao market is held on the 10th and 30th of each month.

Southeastern Provinces

Northern Thailand's largest river valley network, which covers much of the region's southeast quarter, cradled its grandest capitals – Sukhothai, Si Satchanalai, Kamphaeng Phet and Si Thep – between the 11th and 14th centuries. Following a string of interregional wars, as well as Burmese invasions, these cities were for the most part abandoned. After national power shifted to Bangkok in the 18th century, new towns and cities in what's sometimes called the 'Lower North' (*nĕua lâang*) developed to provide goods and services for a multitude of growing agricultural and forestry enterprises in the area.

Today the stone and brick ruins of the once-great Buddhist monasteries which sat at the centres of these former capitals have become attractions for scholars and tourists alike, and tourism supplements farming as an important source of local income. In addition to the incomparable wát-watching available at four different historical parks, the North's southeastern provinces offer a number of well-endowed national parks as well as traditional Northern Thai villages where one can observe original loom weaving techniques or simply soak up the rural ambience of what could be called 'the Old North.'

Phitsanulok Province

PHITSANULOK
อ.เมืองพิษณุโลก

postcode 65000 ● pop 85,500

Phitsanulok, often abbreviated as 'Phi-lok', straddles Mae Nam Nan (Nan River) near a junction with Mae Nam Khwae Noi. Because of its river junction location, it's sometimes referred to as Song Khwae (Two Tributaries), and it's the only city in Thailand where it's legal to reside on a houseboat within municipal boundaries. No new houseboats are permitted, however, so it's likely that they will gradually disappear.

Just as Chiang Mai dominates the upper North, this is the economic capital of the lower North. With its position at the geographical crossroads of three regions – Northern, Northeastern and Central Thailand – it is of major strategic importance to the kingdom in terms of national communications, transport, trade and defence.

This vibrant city makes an excellent base from which to explore the southeastern provinces of the North. Besides the temples of Wat Phra Si Ratana Mahathat and Wat Chulamani, you can explore the attractions of historical Sukhothai, Kamphaeng Phet and Si Satchanalai, as well as the national parks and wildlife sanctuaries of Thung Salaeng Luang and Phu Hin Rong Kla, the former strategic headquarters of the Communist Party of Thailand (CPT). All of these places are within 150km of Phitsanulok.

History

Khmer-style, Lopburi-period (10th- to 13th-century) monuments at Wat Chulamani, on the southern outskirts of the provincial capital, indicate that Phitsanulok was a small Khmer satellite at one time. Virtually no written records of that era exist, however, and it is not until the Sukhothai era that history stands on firmer ground.

Sukhothai Phaya (King) Li Thai built a Thai city here, using the river junction as a line of defence against Ayuthaya and naming the city Meuang Song Khwae. Despite the effort, Song Khwae was eventually absorbed by Ayuthaya, and during the reign of Ayuthaya King Borom Trailokanat (1448–88) it served as the capital of Siam for 18 years.

When Burmese King Bayinnaung (Burengnong in Thai) conquered Northern Thailand in the mid-16th century, a Thai prince by the name of Naresuan was installed as

Song Khwae's new ruler. Naresuan changed the name of the city to Phitsanulok (Pali-Sanskrit: Vishnuloka, or 'Realm of Vishnu', the Hindu preserver god).

The city was abandoned when Naresuan declared Thai independence in 1584 and moved all residents to Ayuthaya to fight the Burmese. After a short-lived victory against the Burmese, Thais began filtering back to Phitsanulok, which again served as a Northern Thai capital; at the same time Nakhon Si Thammarat rose to prominence in the South.

After the Burmese defeated Ayuthaya in 1767, Phitsanulok held onto its independent status until 1775, when the Burmese attacked the city and reduced it to ruins. When Siam finally regained the upper hand with the 1782 establishment of a capital in Bangkok, Phitsanulok began rebuilding the once great Northern Thai city. In 1894 Siamese King Chulalongkorn bestowed *monthon* (cluster of satellite states) status upon Phitsanulok, with dominion over the lower North (ie, Utaradit, Phichit, Sawankhalok, Sukhothai and Phetchabun). In 1917 Phitsanulok became a province of Siam.

Information

Tourist Offices The Tourism Authority of Thailand (TAT) office (☎/fax 055 252 742/3, ✉ tatphs@loxinfo.co.th) at 209/7–8 Thanon Borom Trailokanat has knowledgeable and helpful staff who give out free maps of the town and a sheet that describes a walking tour. The office also has information on Sukhothai and Phetchabun Provinces. It's open 8.30am to 4.30pm daily.

If you plan to travel by road from Phitsanulok to Lom Sak, ask for the sketch map that marks several waterfalls and resorts along Hwy 12.

Money Several banks in town offer foreign-exchange services and ATMs. Only the Bangkok Bank, at 35 Thanon Naresuan, has an after-hours exchange window (usually open till 8pm). There's also an ATM inside the Wat Phra Si Ratana Mahathat compound.

Post & Communications The main post office on Thanon Phuttha Bucha is open 8.30am to 4.30pm weekdays, 9am to noon weekends. The attached Communications Authority of Thailand (CAT) phone office offers Internet services and is open from 7am to 11pm daily.

Shops offering Internet access dot the central area of town near the train station. The highest concentration of Internet cafes is on the western bank of the river, near Saphan Ekathotsarot (Ekathotsarot Bridge). Internet House, opposite Naresuan University, is the closest spot to the Phitsanulok Youth Hostel, although it probably won't be long before the hostel itself offers email services to guests.

Wat Phra Si Ratana Mahathat (Wat Yai)
วัดพระศรีรัตนมหาธาตุ

The full name of this temple is Wat Phra Si Ratana Mahathat, but the locals call it Wat Phra Si or Wat Yai. The wát is next to the bridge over Mae Nam Nan (on the right as you're heading out of Phitsanulok towards Sukhothai). The main *wíhǎan* (hall) contains the **Chinarat Buddha (Phra Phuttha Chinarat)**, one of Thailand's most revered and copied images. This famous bronze image is probably second in importance only to the Emerald Buddha in Bangkok's Wat Phra Kaew. In terms of total annual donations collected (about 12 million baht a year), Wat Yai follows Wat Sothon in Chachoengsao.

The image was cast in the late Sukhothai style, but what makes it strikingly unique is the flame-like halo around the head and torso that turns up at the bottom to become dragon-serpent heads on either side of the image. The head of this Buddha is a little wider than standard Sukhothai, giving the statue a very solid feel.

According to Northern Thai chronicles, Phaya Li Thai commissioned construction of this wát in 1357. When it was completed, Li Thai wanted it to contain three high-quality bronze images, so he sent for well-known sculptors from Si Satchanalai, Chiang Saen

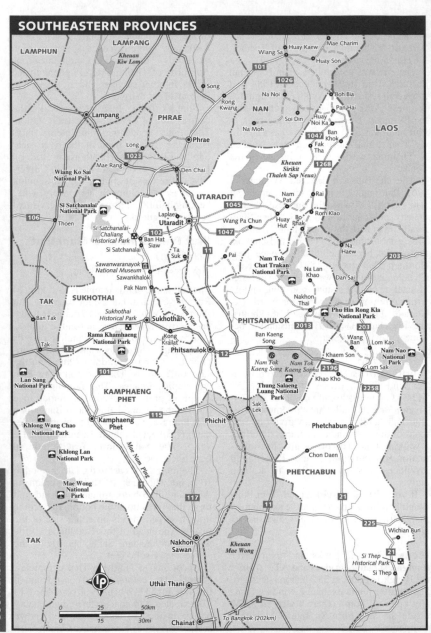

SOUTHEASTERN PROVINCES

and Hariphunchai (Lamphun), as well as five Brahman priests. The first two castings worked well, but the third required three attempts before it was decreed the best of all. Legend has it that a white-robed sage appeared from nowhere to assist in the final casting, then disappeared. This last image was named the Chinarat (Victorious King) Buddha and it became the centrepiece in the wíhǎan. All three Buddhas were kept at Wat Phra Si Ratana Mahathat for 400 years, after which the Phra Chinasi and Phra Satsada were moved to the royal temple of Wat Bowonniwet in Bangkok. Only the Chinnarat image has the flame-dragon halo.

The walls of the Lanna-style wíhǎan *(open 7am-6pm daily)* are low to accommodate the low-swept roof, typical of Northern temple architecture, so the image takes on larger proportions than it might in a Central or Northeastern wát. The brilliant interior architecture is such that when you sit on the Italian marble floor in front of the Buddha, the lacquered columns draw your vision towards the image and evoke a strong sense of serenity. The doors of the building are inlaid with mother-of-pearl in a design copied from Bangkok's Wat Phra Kaew.

Another sanctuary to one side has been converted into a **museum** *(admission free; open 9am-4pm Wed-Sun)* displaying antique Buddha images, ceramics and other historic artefacts.

Behind the Phra Chinarat wíhǎan stands a tall **prang** *(praang;* Khmer-influenced tower) with complex reticulated lines and 'corncob' shape typical of the Sukhothai period.

Dress appropriately when visiting this most sacred of temples – no shorts or sleeveless tops.

City buses Nos 1, 3 and 5 all pass this wát.

Wat Ratburana
วัดราชบูรณะ

Near Wat Yai, on the same side of the river, Wat Ratburana is of about the same age as Wat Yai, ie, it's a Sukhothai-era temple. When crossing Saphan Naresuan it's impossible not to spot the white-washed spire

of the monastery's main **chedi** (stupa). The latter sits on a multi-tiered octagonal base. Local legend says the remains of King Borom Trailokanat are encased in this stupa.

The brick-and-stucco **wíhǎan** next to the stupa has wooden doors impressively carved with floral designs. Inside on the wall over the main entry is a 10th-century mural of Mae Thorani (Dharani, the Hindu-Buddhist earth goddess) squeezing water out of her hair to wash away the temptations of Mara – the Buddhist equivalent of Satan – during the Buddha's final meditation before attaining nirvana.

In the *bòt* (central sanctuary), which stands next to the northern wall of the monastery compound, a more extensive set of murals relates scenes from the *Ramakian* (Thai version of the Indian epic *Ramayana*). In style these murals are very similar to those at Wat Phra Kaew in Bangkok and, like the paintings at the latter, date to the early Ratanakosin period.

City buses Nos 1, 3 and 5 pass this wát.

Wat Chulamani
วัดจุฬามณี

Five kilometres south of the city via Thanon Borom Trailokanat is Wat Chulamani, the ruins of which date from the Sukhothai period. The original buildings must have been impressive, judging from what remains of the ornate Khmer-style prang. The latter dates to the Lopburi period (10th to 13th centuries) and features a triple-tiered, 20-cornered base, along with Ayuthaya-style plasterwork added later. King Borom Trailokanat was ordained as a monk here and there is an old Thai inscription to that effect on the ruined wíhǎan, dating from the reign of King Narai.

The prang itself has little left of its original height, but Khmer-style door lintels remain, including one with a walking Buddha and a *dhammachakka* (Buddhist wheel of law) in the background.

Besides the prang and the wíhǎan, the only original structures left are the remains of the monastery walls. Still, there is a peaceful, neglected atmosphere about the place.

City bus No 5, originating at the train station, goes to Wat Chulamani.

Buddha-Casting Foundry
โรงหล่อพระ

On Thanon Wisut Kasat, not far from the Phitsanulok Youth Hostel, is a small factory *(open 8.30am-4.30pm Wed-Sun)* where bronze Buddha images of all sizes are cast. Most are copies of the famous Phra Chinarat Buddha at Wat Yai (see earlier in this section). Visitors are welcome to watch and there are even detailed photo exhibits describing step-by-step the lost-wax method of metal casting. Some of the larger images take a year or more to complete. The foundry is owned by Dr Thawi, an artisan and nationally renowned expert on Northern Thai folklore.

There is a small gift shop at the foundry where you can purchase bronze images of various sizes. To get here take city bus No 8.

Folk Museum
พิพิธภัณฑ์พื้นบ้าน

Across the street and a short distance north of the foundry is a folk museum *(admission by donation; open 8.30am-4.30pm Tues-Sun)*. Established by Dr Thawi, exhibits include items from his personal collection of traditional farm implements, hunting equipment, musical instruments, cooking utensils and other folkloric artefacts from throughout the northern region. It's the best collection of its kind in the country and many of the objects on display are virtually nonexistent in modern Thai life. If you're lucky, Dr Thawi may be around to offer you an impromptu demonstration of rustic devices used for calling birds and other animals, including elephants! City bus No 8 passes by the museum.

Places to Stay – Budget

Phitsanulok has good coverage in the budget accommodation category.

Phitsanulok Youth Hostel *(☎ 055 242 060, e phitsanulok@tyha.org, 38 Thanon Sanam Bin)* Rooms with shared shower &

toilet 120B, row house singles/doubles/triples/quads with private facilities 200/300/450/600B. Standing well above all other Thai hostels associated with Hostelling International, this one consists of a collection of historic wooden buildings collected by the owner and converted for residential use. Set amid a lush garden with aromatic jasmine vines and a spring, a 50-year-old house has been transformed into a restaurant featuring Thai and European food. A lofty teak-wood *săalaa* (sala; open-sided pavilion) behind the house is built of salvaged timber from seven old Tak Province teak houses to create a pleasant, open-air sitting-and-dining area – a good place to sit back and relax over a glass of wine or freshly brewed locally grown coffee while listening to the cadence of frogs and crickets.

Row-house rooms behind the săalaa are each furnished with Northern Thai antiques and feature unique semi-outdoor bathrooms. All rates include breakfast. From the train station you can get to the hostel by săamláw (20B to 30B) or No 4 city bus. From the airport take a túk-túk (30B) or a No 4 bus that passes by the hostel (on the right). From the bus terminal, take a săamláw (30B) or a No 1 city bus (get off at Thanon Ramesuan and walk the last 300m or so).

Lithai Guest House *(☎ 055 219 626, fax 055 219 627, Thanon Phayalithai)* Rooms with fan & shared bath 200B, with private bath & TV 220B, with air-con, TV, hot shower & breakfast 300B, with fridge 360B. Sixty clean, quiet rooms with plenty of light are strung out over three floors of the large Lithai Building, giving more the feel of an apartment complex than a guesthouse. This might be a good choice for a long-term stay and, in fact, the Lithai offers one night free for every 15 you pay for. There's a low-key coffee shop downstairs, and parking at the back.

Near the train station are several inexpensive hotels and places to eat.

Pisanuloke Hotel *(☎ 055 247 555, 055 247 999)* 1-bed & 2-bed rooms with fan/air-con 280/350B. This classic old two-storey building is conveniently located right next to the train station. There's a *khâo kaeng* (rice-and-curry) vendor downstairs in the lobby, and plenty of places to eat nearby.

Asia Hotel (☎ 055 258 378, fax 055 230 419, Thanon Ekathotsarot) Doubles with fan/air-con 200/300B. This four-storey hotel is not far from the train station. The rooms are quite decent, but street noise can be deafening, so ask for a room towards the back of the hotel.

Samai Niyom Hotel (☎ 055 258 575, 055 247 528, Thanon Ekathotsarot) Singles/doubles 280/380B. The rooms in this three-storey place are decent and all have air-con.

Pansombat Hotel (☎ 055 258 179, Thanon Saireuthai) Rooms 150B with private shower & shared toilet. If you turn left out of the station and then take the first right onto Thanon Saireuthai, you will come to this hotel. It's noisy and has a bit of night traffic.

Sukkit (☎ 055 258 876, 20/1-2 Thanon Saireuthai) Rooms 150B. Although it's strictly basic and a little dark, this is a better deal than Pansombat for a clean room with fan and private bathroom. It's centrally located a block from the river and is less noisy than hotels towards the station.

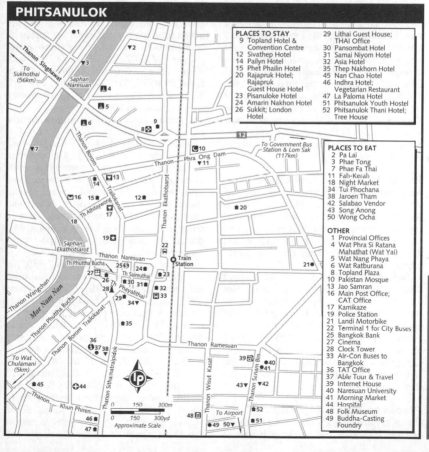

PHITSANULOK

PLACES TO STAY
9 Topland Hotel & Convention Centre
12 Sivathep Hotel
14 Pailyn Hotel
15 Phet Phailin Hotel
20 Rajapruk Hotel; Rajapruk Guest House Hotel
23 Pisanuloke Hotel
24 Amarin Nakhon Hotel
26 Sukkit; London Hotel
29 Lithai Guest House; THAI Office
30 Pansombat Hotel
31 Samai Niyom Hotel
32 Asia Hotel
35 Thep Nakhorn Hotel
45 Nan Chao Hotel
46 Indhra Hotel; Vegetarian Restaurant
47 La Paloma Hotel
51 Phitsanulok Youth Hostel
52 Phitsanulok Thani Hotel; Tree House

PLACES TO EAT
2 Pa Lai
3 Phae Tong
7 Phae Fa Thai
11 Fah-Kerah
18 Night Market
34 Tui Phochana
38 Jaroen Tham
42 Salabao Vendor
43 Song Anong
50 Wong Ocha

OTHER
1 Provincial Offices
4 Wat Phra Si Ratana Mahathat (Wat Yai)
5 Wat Nang Phaya
6 Wat Ratburana
8 Topland Plaza
10 Pakistan Mosque
13 Jao Samran
16 Main Post Office; CAT Office
17 Kamikaze
19 Police Station
21 Landi Motorbike
22 Terminal 1 for City Buses
25 Bangkok Bank
27 Cinema
28 Clock Tower
33 Air-Con Buses to Bangkok
36 TAT Office
37 Able Tour & Travel
39 Internet House
40 Naresuan University
41 Morning Market
44 Hospital
48 Folk Museum
49 Buddha-Casting Foundry

To Sukhothai (56km)
To Government Bus Station & Lom Sak (117km)
Train Station
To Wat Chulamani (5km)
To Airport

0 150 300m
0 150 300yd
Approximate Scale

London Hotel (☎ 055 225 145, 21-22 Soi 1, Thanon Phuttha Bucha) Rooms with fan 100-150B. If you keep walking towards the river, Thanon Saireuthai changes name to Soi 1, Thanon Phuttha Bucha, where you'll find the best cheapie in this area. The rooms and shared cold-water facilities are clean. It's an old wooden Thai-Chinese hotel that has been spruced up and painted in cheery colours.

Phet Phailin Hotel (☎ 055 258 844, 4/8 Thanon Athitayawong) Rooms with fan/air-con 300/450B. Formerly called the Siam Hotel, this is a friendly, old-fashioned four-storey place a half-block from the river and main post office. The rooms are large, and were recently refurbished; those towards the back are considerably quieter. You might want to have a look at the rooms before taking one – some are cleaner than others; if you get a clean, quiet one, this is good value.

Rajapruk Guest House Hotel (☎ 055 259 203) Rooms with fan/air-con 200/300B. You'll find this hotel behind the more upmarket Rajapruk Hotel on Thanon Phra Ong Dam. All the rooms have hot-water showers; both fan and air-con rooms are good value. Guests may use the Rajapruk Hotel swimming pool.

Places to Stay – Mid-Range

Rajapruk Hotel (☎ 055 258 477, fax 055 251 395, 99/9 Thanon Phra Ong Dam) Rooms 500-800B. This hotel offers good upper-mid-range value. All rooms come with air-con, hot-water showers, carpeting, TV and telephone; there are also more-expensive suites.

Indhra Hotel (☎ 055 217 934, 103/8 Thanon Sithamatraipidok) Singles & doubles with air-con 300B, with TV 350B. Next to the upmarket La Paloma Hotel, the 45-room Indhra offers clean, comfortable rooms.

Sivathep Hotel (☎ 055 244 933, 110/21 Thanon Prasongprasat) Rooms 290-400B. Once the top end place in Phitsanulok, the fading Sivathep offers clean rooms with fan or air-con and TV.

Places to Stay – Top End

Prices at Phitsanulok's upper-end hotels all start at 1000B or less, making it one of Thailand's bargain provincial capitals. This is also where the main hotel growth is, so a room glut will probably keep prices stable or even slightly depressed, especially at the older places.

Thep Nakhorn Hotel (☎ 055 244 070, fax 055 251 897, 43/1 Thanon Sithamatraipidok) Rooms/suites 450/1000B. The six-storey, centrally located Thep Nakhorn offers quiet air-con accommodation.

Pailyn Hotel (☎ 055 633 334-6, fax 055 258 185, 38 Thanon Borom Trailokanat) Rooms from 900B, including breakfast. This is another centrally located place, with somewhat nicer rooms.

Others in this category – places that were once Phitsanulok's flashiest digs but are now a little worn at the edges yet still quite comfortable – include *Nan Chao Hotel* (☎ 055 244 702-5, fax 055 244 794), with rooms from 600B; and *Amarin Nakhon Hotel* (☎ 055 219 069-75, fax 055 219 500, 3/1 Thanon Chao Phraya Phitsanulok), with rooms from 800B.

Topland Hotel & Convention Centre (☎ 055 247 800, fax 055 247 815, Cnr Thanon Singhawat & Thanon Ekathotsarot) Singles/doubles 1030/1250B. Connected to Topland Plaza shopping centre, this semi-luxurious place features a beauty salon, cafe, snooker club, fitness centre, several restaurants and other facilities. The room rates, which include breakfast, are a bargain compared with Bangkok or Chiang Mai prices for similar quality. Free airport transfer is available.

La Paloma Hotel (☎ 055 217 930, fax 055 217 937, 103/8 Thanon Sithamatraipidok) Rooms from 800B. This six-storey, 249-room luxury hotel has more of a family orientation than most places in town and can arrange day care for children with advance notice. The rooms are spacious and well maintained, and the parking lot is large.

Phitsanulok Thani Hotel (☎ 055 211 065, fax 055 211 071; in Bangkok ☎ 023 143 168) Standard rooms 1600B, singles/doubles often discounted to 880/980B. Right next door to the Phitsanulok Youth Hostel, this relatively new hotel is part of the Dusit chain. It features 110 air-con

Exquisite in pink: water lily, Sukhothai

Wat Mahathat, Old Sukhothai

Flowers in the hand of Buddha, Old Sukhothai

Water lilies afloat in a Sukhothai pond

Unfinished bronze Buddha figures, Phitsanulok

Buddha fingers, Sukhothai Historical Park

Wat Phra Si Ratana Mahathat, Phitsanulok

Monks deep in discussion, Sukhothai Historical Park

rooms, 21 of which are luxury rooms designed for business travellers.

Places to Eat

Phitsanulok is a great town for eating – there must be more restaurants per capita here than in just about any other town in Thailand.

There's a cluster of inexpensive market-style *food stalls* just west of the London Hotel near the cinema.

Tui Phochana (Thanon Phayalithai, east of the Lithai Bldg) Dishes 20-45B. Open 8am-7pm daily. Excellent, inexpensive Thai food can be had at this place. Tui makes fabulous *yam khanŭn* (curried jackfruit) at the beginning of the cool season, plus many other outstanding Thai curries year-round. There are plenty of other cheap Thai restaurants in this area too.

Close to the Phitsanulok Youth Hostel are several *small noodle and rice shops*.

Wong Ocha (no Roman-script sign) Dishes 15-30B. Open 10am-8pm daily. South around the corner from the Phitsanulok Youth Hostel, this permanent vendor stand sells delicious *kài yâang* (grilled chicken), *khâo nĭaw* (sticky rice) and *yam phàk kràchèt* (water mimosa salad).

Song Anong (Thanon Sanam Bin) Dishes 25B or less. Open 9am-3pm daily. Across from the Naresuan University campus, the very popular and very inexpensive Song Anong outdoor restaurant offers an excellent selection of curries, noodles and Thai desserts. Try the *săo náam,* a mixture of pineapple, coconut, dried shrimp, ginger and garlic served over *khanŏm jiin* (Chinese noodles) – it's delicious. Also good is the *kaeng yûak,* a curry made from the heart of a banana palm, and *kŭaytĭaw sùkhŏthai,* thin rice-noodles served dry in a bowl with peanuts, barbecued pork, spices, green beans and bean sprouts.

Early risers can try the small but lively *street vendor* selling *saalaapao* (Chinese steamed buns), *paa-thâwng-kŏh* and *jók* (2B to 10B). It's open from 6am to 10am daily.

Fah-Kerah (Thanon Phra Ong Dam) Dishes 7-20B. Open 7am-7pm daily. There are several Thai-Muslim cafes near the mosque on Thanon Phra Ong Dam; this one is very famous, and sells thick rotii served with *kaeng mátsàmàn* (Muslim curry), which is unusual this far north. Ask for *rotii kaeng* to get the set plate. This small cafe also has fresh milk and yoghurt.

A small *Thai vegetarian restaurant* next to the Indhra Hotel offers very inexpensive vegetable dishes. *Jaroen Tham*, around the corner from TAT, is similar. Both are open 8am to noon only.

Steak Cottage (Lithai Bldg) Dishes 40-120B. Open 11am-11pm daily. If you'd rather have a steak, try Steak Cottage. It also serves other European dishes, as well as Thai cuisine.

If you're out past midnight, your best bet is the very good *24-hour khâo tôm place* (dishes 15B to 40B), next to the train station. The *24-hour restaurant* (dishes 30B to 80B) attached to the Amarin Nakhon Hotel serves Chinese and Northeastern Thai cuisine.

On the River Floating restaurants light up Mae Nam Nan at night. Some good choices include the *Phae Fa Thai* (dishes 30B to 80B), and *Phae Tong* (dishes 40-80B). Both are open 11am to 11pm daily. South of the main string of floating restaurants is a pier where you can board a *restaurant-boat*, owned by Phae Fa Thai, that cruises Mae Nam Nan every night. You pay a small fee – 20B to 40B – to board the boat and then order from a menu as you please – there is no minimum charge.

Also along the river are a couple of *street vendors* preparing *phàk bûng lawy fáa* (literally, floating-in-the-sky morning glory vine), which is usually translated as 'flying vegetable'. This food fad originated in Chonburi but has somehow taken root in Phitsanulok. There are several of these places in town as well as along the river. The dish is nothing glorious – basically morning glory vine stir-fried in soya bean sauce and garlic – but there is a performance thrown in: The cook fires up a batch of phàk bûng in the wok and then flings it through the air to a waiting server who catches it on a plate. The eating places on the river are now so performance-oriented that the server climbs to the top of a van to catch the flying vegetable! Tour companies bring tour groups here and invite tourists to try the catch – it's just as amusing watching the tourists drop phàk bûng all over the place as it is to watch the cook. Dishes cost 40B to 80B, and the vendors are open 5pm to midnight daily. During the day this area is a sundries market.

In the same riverside night market, *Midnight Kai Ton* prepares excellent *khâo man kài* (Hainanese-style chicken rice). Most vendors here open between 5pm and 6pm and close around midnight, although a couple of *khâo tôm vendors* stay open till 2am.

Pa Lai Dishes 20-30B. Open 10am-4pm daily. Just back from the river and north of Wat Phra Si Ratana Mahathat, this old and established place is famous for *kǔaytǐaw hâwy khǎa* (literally, leg-dangling rice noodles). The name comes from the way customers sit on a bench facing the river, with their legs dangling below. At least two copycat places in this area also offer *kǔaytǐaw hâwy khǎa*.

Entertainment

Along Thanon Borom Trailokanat near the Pailyn Hotel is a string of really popular Thai pubs. Popular *Jao Samran (Thanon Borom Trailokanat)* features live Thai-folk and pop. The food service starts around 5pm or 6pm, while the music comes on around 8pm.

More or less across from the Phet Phailin Hotel, the *Kamikaze Pub* is a good spot for a quiet drink.

The Phitsanulok Thani Hotel's semi-outdoor *Tree House* features live bands playing Thai and faràng covers.

Getting There & Away

Air The THAI office (☎ 055 258 020, fax 055 251 671) is in the Lithai Building on Thanon Phayalithai. THAI has four 55-minute flights to Phitsanulok from Bangkok daily for 1380B one way. There are also flights between Phitsanulok and Chiang Mai (1035B, four weekly), Nan (950B, four weekly), Lampang (850B, two daily) and Phrae (765B, four weekly).

Phitsanulok's airport is just out of town. Sǎwngthǎew leave the airport for town every 20 minutes (10B); otherwise, you can catch the No 4 city bus (4B). The big hotels in town run free buses from the airport, and THAI has a door-to-door van service for 30B per person.

Bus Phitsanulok lies about 390km from Bangkok. Transport choices out of Phitsanulok are great, as it's a junction for bus lines running both north and northeast. Bangkok is six hours away by bus and Chiang Mai 5½ hours. Buses leave Bangkok's Northern and Northeastern bus station for Phitsanulok several times daily (125 ordinary, 185B 2nd-class air-con, 240B 1st-class air-con).

Be sure to get the new route *(sǎi mài)* bus via Nakhon Sawan (Rte 117), as the old route *(sǎi kào)* via Tak Fa (Hwy 11) takes six hours and costs more. Phitsanulok Yan Yon Tour and Win Tour (at the bus station) both run VIP buses between Bangkok and Phitsanulok for 250B.

Buses to destinations in other northern and northeastern provinces leave several times a day from the Baw Khaw Saw (government bus station) just outside town, except for the air-con buses that may depart only once or twice a day.

destination	fare	duration (hrs)
Chiang Mai (via Den Chai)		
ordinary	132B	5½
air-con	184B	5
Chiang Mai (via Tak)		
ordinary	140B	6
air-con	196B	6
Chiang RaiB		
ordinary	153B	6½
air-con	214B	6
1st class	290B	6
Khon Kaen		
ordinary	130B	6
air-con	173B	6
1st class	208B	6
Mae Sot		
air-con minivan	118B	5
Nakhon Ratchasima (Khorat)		
ordinary	154B	6
air-con	241B	6
VIP	290B	6

Nan
ordinary	112B	9
air-con	148B	8

Udon Thani
ordinary	125B	7
air-con	205B	7

Buses to the following points leave on the hour (*), every two hours (**) or every three hours (***) from early morning until 5pm or 6pm (except for Sukhothai buses, which leave every half-hour):

destination	fare	duration (hrs)
Kamphaeng Phet*		
ordinary	43B	3
air-con	58B	2
Lom Sak*		
ordinary	55B	2
Phetchabun***		
ordinary	67B	3
Sukhothai		
ordinary	24B	1
air-con	33B	1
Tak*		
ordinary	58B	3
air-con	74B	3
Utaradit*		
ordinary	48B	3
air-con	72B	2

Train Two ordinary trains (69B 3rd-class only, eight to nine hours) leave Bangkok for Phitsanulok at 7.05am (or Ayuthaya at 9.04am) and 8.35am (Ayuthaya 10.26am). For most people this is a more economical and convenient way to reach Phitsanulok from Bangkok than with the bus, since you don't have to go out to Bangkok's Northern and Northeastern bus station.

Rapid trains from Bangkok depart at 6.40am, 3.15pm, 6.10pm, 8pm and 10pm (about seven hours). The basic fare is 159B for 2nd class or 69B for 3rd class, plus a 40B surcharge for the rapid service. There are also three all air-con, 2nd-class express diesel trains ('Sprinter' Nos 3, 5 and 7), at 9.30am, 4pm and 11.10pm daily, that are about an hour quicker than the rapid service.

First class is available on the 3.15pm rapid train (2nd and 3rd class are also available) and the 6pm special express train (2nd

class also available). The basic 1st-class and 2nd-class fares are 324B and 159B, not including the rapid and special express surcharges of 40B and 80B, plus any berth arrangements. Other basic 3rd/2nd/1st-class train fares to and from Phitsanulok include: Chiang Mai 52/122/269B; Lopburi 41/95/201B; and Ayuthaya 54/124/258B.

If you're going straight on to Sukhothai from Phitsanulok, a túk-túk ride from the train station to the bus station 4km away costs 30B to 40B. From there you can get a bus to Sukhothai, or you can catch a Sukhothai-bound bus in front of the Topland Hotel on Thanon Singhawat; a túk-túk to Thanon Singhawat costs 20B from the train station.

Getting Around

Sǎamláw rides within the town centre should cost 20B to 30B per person. Ordinary city buses cost 4B, and there are 13 lines making the rounds, so you should be able to get just about anywhere by bus. A couple of the lines also feature air-con coaches costing 6B to 13B, depending on distance. The station for city buses is near the train station, off Thanon Ekathotsarot.

Motorcycles can be rented at Landi Motorbike (☎ 055 252 765) at 57/21-22 Thanon Phra Ong Dam. Rates are 150B a day for a 100cc and 200B for a 125cc or 150cc.

A reliable agency for car rental is Able Tour & Travel (☎ 055 242 206) on Thanon Borom Trailokanat near the TAT office.

PHU HIN RONG KLA NATIONAL PARK

อุทยานแห่งชาติภูหินร่องกล้า

From 1967 to 1982, the mountain known as Phu Hin Rong Kla served as the strategic headquarters for the CPT and its tactical arm, the People's Liberation Army of Thailand (PLAT). The remote, easily defended summit was perfect for an insurgent army. Another benefit was that the headquarters was only 50km from the Lao border, so lines of retreat were well guarded after 1975 when Laos fell to the Pathet Lao. China's Yunnan Province is only 300km away and it was there that CPT cadres received their training in revolutionary tactics (until the 1979 split between the Chinese and Vietnamese communists, when the CPT sided with Vietnam).

For nearly 20 years the area around Phu Hin Rong Kla and nearby Khao Kho – part of the so-called 'Guerrilla Triangle' – served as a battlefield for Thai troops and the communists. In 1972 the Thai government launched a major offensive against the PLAT in an unsuccessful attempt to rout them from the mountain. The CPT camp at Phu Hin Rong Kla became especially active after the Thai military killed hundreds of students in Bangkok during the October 1976 student-worker uprising. Many students subsequently fled here to join the CPT, setting up a hospital and a school of political and military tactics. By 1978 the PLAT ranks here had swelled to 4000. In 1980 and 1981 the Thai armed forces tried again and were able to recapture some parts of CPT territory. But the decisive blow to the CPT came in 1982, when the government declared an amnesty for all the students who had joined the communists after 1976. The departure of most of the students broke the spine of the movement, which had by this time become dependent on their membership. A final military push in late 1982 effected the surrender of the PLAT, and Phu Hin Rong Kla was declared a national park in 1984.

Orientation

The park (Thais/foreigners 20/200B, children half-price) covers about 307 sq km of rugged mountains and forest. The elevation at park headquarters is about 1000m, so it is refreshingly cool even in the hot season. The major attractions on the main road through the park are the remains of the CPT stronghold, including a rustic meeting hall, the school of political and military tactics and the CPT administration building. Across the road from the school is a water wheel designed by exiled engineering students.

Things to See & Do

A trail leads to **Pha Chu Thong** (Flag Raising Cliff, sometimes called Red Flag Cliff), where the communists would raise the red flag to announce a military victory. Also in this area are an **air-raid shelter**, a lookout and the remains of the main **CPT headquarters** – the most inaccessible point in the territory before a road was constructed by the Thai government. The buildings in the park are made out of wood and bamboo and have no plumbing or electricity – a testament to how primitive the living conditions were.

At the park headquarters is a small **museum** that displays relics from CPT days, including medical instruments and weapons. At the end of the road into the park is a small White Hmong village called **Phu Hin Rong Kla Patthana**, where visitors may catch a glimpse of traditional Hmong life. When the CPT was in this area, the Hmong were important allies.

One wonders what would have happened if the CPT had succeeded in its revolutionary goal. Perhaps the Thai army's headquarters in Phitsanulok would now be a museum instead.

If you're not interested in the history of Phu Hin Rong Kla, there are **hiking trails**,

PHU HIN RONG KLA NATIONAL PARK

To Nakhon Thai & Phitsanulok

Nam Tok Phatcharin Ton (800m from road)

Lan Hin Taek

Camp Ground & Bungalows

0   100   200m
0   100   200yd
Approximate Scale

Nam Tok Rom Klao (250m from road)

● Park Headquarters

2331

Water Wheel

School of Political & Military Tactics

Nam Tok Huay Khamin Noi (100m from road)

To Hmong Village, Lom Sak & Phetchabun

Pha Chu Thong (Flag Raising Cliff)

● CPT Administration
● Air-Raid Shelter

waterfalls and scenic views, plus some interesting rock formations – an area of jutting boulders called Lan Hin Pum, and an area of deep rocky crevices where PLAT troops would hide during air raids, called Lan Hin Taek. At Lan Hin Taek a natural weathering of sandstone uplift created rows of deep cavern-like fissures. Thick layers of lichens and mosses, ferns, wolf's claws, orchids and flowering shrubs cover these *râwng klâa* (hardened channels) for which the park is named.

Phu Hin Rong Kla can become quite crowded on weekends and holidays; schedule a more peaceful visit for mid-week.

Places to Stay & Eat
Royal Forest Department bungalows & tents 5/8/10/14-person bungalows 600/800/1000/1500B, large permanent 20-person tents 800B, tent sites 10B, park tents 40B per person (no bedding provided, except blankets for 20B a night). If you want to build a fire, you can buy chopped wood for 150B a night. Book accommodation through the Royal Forest Department (☎ 055 389 002; in Bangkok ☎ 025 614 292) or Golden House Tour Co (☎ 055 259 973, 055 389 002) in Phitsanulok.

Near the camp ground and bungalows are some vendors. The best are *Duang Jai Cafeteria* – try famous carrot *sôm-tam* (spicy salad) – and *Rang Thong*.

Getting There & Away
The park headquarters is about 125km from Phitsanulok. To get here, first take an early bus to Nakhon Thai (30B, two hours, hourly from 6am to 6pm). From there you can catch a săwngthăew to the park (25B, three daily from 7.30am to 4.30pm).

A small group can charter a pick-up and driver in Nakhon Thai for about 600B to 800B for the day. Golden House Tour Co operates a van service from Phitsanulok once a day for 40B per person or 650B to charter the van one way.

This is a delightful trip if you're on a motorbike as there's not much traffic along the way. A strong engine is necessary to make it up the hills to Phu Hin Rong Kla.

PHITSANULOK TO LOM SAK
Along Hwy 12 between Phitsanulok and Lom Sak (the scenic 'gateway' to Northeastern Thailand) there are several resorts and waterfalls. As in Phu Hin Rong Kla, the sites here tend to be more popular on weekends and holidays.

The Phitsanulok TAT office distributes a sketch map of attractions along this 130km stretch of road that marks the resorts and three waterfalls. You may want to bypass the first two waterfalls, Nam Tok Sakhunothayan *(Km33)* and Kaeng Song *(Km45)*, which are on the way to Phu Hin Rong Kla and hence get overwhelmed with visitors. The third, Nam Tok Kaeng Sopha *(Km72)*, is a larger area of small falls and rapids where you can walk from rock formation to rock formation – there are more or fewer rocks depending on the rains. Food vendors provide inexpensive *sôm-tam* and *kài yâang*.

Farther east along the road is 1262-sq-km Thung Salaeng Luang Wildlife Sanctuary *(entrance at Km80)*, one of Thailand's largest and most important protected areas. Thung Salaeng Luang encompasses vast meadows and dipterocarp forests, and like Phu Hin Rong Kla and Khao Kho was once home to the PLAT. Among bird-watchers it's known as a habitat for the colourful Siamese fireback pheasant.

If you have your own wheels, you can turn right at Km100 onto Rte 2196 and head for Khao Kho (Khao Khaw), another mountain lair used by the CPT during the 1970s. See Khao Kho in the Phetchabun section later in this chapter.

Places to Stay & Eat
There are several resorts just off Hwy 12 west of the Rte 2013 junction for Nakhon Thai.

Rainforest Resort (☎ *055 293 085, fax 055 293 086, Km44)* 4-person cottages 1000-1800B, 7-person cottage 2400B. This place is the best in the area. The spacious, tastefully designed cottages are spread over a hillside facing Mae Nam Khek. All come with air-con and hot water. An indoor-outdoor restaurant serves locally grown coffee and good Thai food.

Dipterocarps

The dipterocarp is a member of a family of trees commonly found in south Asia and Africa, named for its helicopter-like seed pods. It is generally a large tree, known for its leathery leaves and aromatic resins. The tree can be used as a source of timber and in the production of varnishes and herbal remedies.

Other resorts in the area, **Wang Nam Yen** and **Thanthong**, are similarly priced. **SP Huts** (☎ 055 293 402, fax 055 293 405), with rooms from 500B, is a bit cheaper.

Stop at **Blue Mountain Coffee** (Km42), **Rainforest Resort** (Km44) or **Thawee Fresh Coffee** (Km45), all on Hwy 12 near Ban Kaeng Song (close to Nam Tok Kaeng Song). These restaurants serve some of the best fresh coffee outside of Bangkok; the beans are locally grown kaafae jàak râi (literally, coffee from the fields) but have names like Blue Mountain and Brazil. Freshly brewed coffee costs 15B to 25B, but it's worth it for 100% arabica beans.

Getting There & Away

Buses between Phitsanulok and Lom Sak cost 55B each way, so any stop along the way will cost less. During daylight hours it's easy to flag down another bus to continue your journey, but after 4pm it gets a little chancy.

Sukhothai Province

SUKHOTHAI

อ.เมืองสุโขทัย

postcode 64000 • pop 25,800

As Thailand's first capital, Sukhothai (Rising of Happiness) flourished from the mid-13th century to the late 14th century. The Sukhothai kingdom is viewed as the 'golden age' of Thai civilisation – the religious art and architecture of the era are considered to be the most classic of Thai styles. For more on the history of Sukhothai, see History in the Facts about Northern Thailand chapter.

The new town of Sukhothai is undistinguished except for its good municipal market in the town centre. The meuang kào (old city) of Sukhothai features around 45 sq km of ruins (which have been made into a historical park – see the following Sukhothai Historical Park section), making an overnight stay in New Sukhothai worthwhile, although you can make a day trip to the old city ruins from Phitsanulok.

History

Formerly a Khmer client state, as the Angkor culture declined in the early 13th century, the kingdom of Sukhothai declared its independence in 1238 under Phaya Si Intharathit. Although often touted as Thailand's 'first kingdom', Sukhothai was of course preceded by Ngoen Yang (Chiang Saen) and possibly other Thai states. Furthermore, during the rule of Sukhothai's first two monarchs, these kingdoms to the north – particularly Phaya Mang Rai's Lanna – appear to have been larger and stronger.

Sukhothai's fortunes changed when its third king, originally called Phaya Ruang but eventually assuming the name Ram Khamhaeng (Rama the Brave; reigned 1279–1317), turned out to be a very clever ruler as well as a fearless warrior. Ram Khamhaeng's reputation in the region meant that oftentimes his would-be opponents surrendered without a battle. He also wisely courted favour with the Mongols in China, making two trips (in 1294 and 1300) to pay homage to Kublai Khan, who spared

Kings of Sukhothai

Si Intharathit	1238–?
Ban Meuang	?–1279
Ram Khamhaeng	1279–1317
Loet Thai	1317–?
Ngua Nam Thom	?–1347
Li Thai (Thammaracha I)	1347–1368/1374
Thammaracha II	1368/1374–1399
Thammaracha III	1399–1419
Thammaracha IV	1419–1438

Sukhothai during his raids on Southeast Asia.

After forging a peace alliance with Lanna, during his reign he was able to expand the kingdom's influence to include most of Thailand, western Cambodia, the entire Malay peninsula and Laos. Even the Mon of central Myanmar paid tribute to Ram Khamhaeng.

The learned king also appears to have been the royal sponsor for the codification of the Thai alphabet, although his exact role in its development remains a scholarly controversy. Whatever role he played, the oldest

known Thai writing at Sukhothai – a stone slab inscription dated to 1292 – appears to have been the work of Ram Khamhaeng.

The monarchs who followed Ram Khamhaeng were not as impressive and the kingdom's borders began receding once again. One former Thai vassal prince, Ramathibodi I, rebelled and declared a new kingdom called Ayuthaya on Mae Nam Chao Phraya farther south. Sukhothai's sixth monarch, the devoutly Buddhist Phaya Li Thai, recognised Ramathibodi I's power to lead and allowed Ayuthaya to annex Sukhothai in 1376.

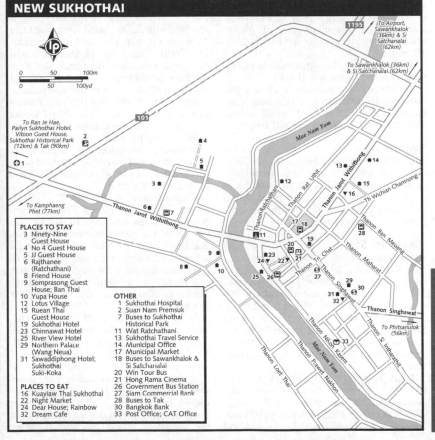

NEW SUKHOTHAI

PLACES TO STAY
3 Ninety-Nine Guest House
4 No 4 Guest House
5 JJ Guest House
6 Rajthanee (Ratchathani)
8 Friend House
9 Somprasong Guest House; Ban Thai
10 Yupa House
12 Lotus Village
15 Ruean Thai Guest House
19 Sukhothai Hotel
23 Chinnawat Hotel
25 River View Hotel
29 Northern Palace (Wang Neua)
31 Sawaddiphong Hotel; Sukhothai Suki-Koka

PLACES TO EAT
16 Kuayiaw Thai Sukhothai
22 Night Market
24 Dear House; Rainbow
32 Dream Cafe

OTHER
1 Sukhothai Hospital
2 Suan Nam Premsuk
7 Buses to Sukhothai Historical Park
11 Wat Ratchathani
13 Sukhothai Travel Service
14 Municipal Office
17 Municipal Market
18 Buses to Sawankhalok & Si Satchanalai
20 Win Tour Bus
26 Government Bus Station
27 Siam Commercial Bank
28 Buses to Tak
30 Bangkok Bank
33 Post Office; CAT Office

Because Sukhothai controlled a large chunk of mainland Southeast Asia, because the arts (particularly sculpture and architecture) flourished and because the Thai writing system was founded during that era, many Thais today consider Sukhothai to be the birthplace of their nation.

Information

A branch of the Siam Commercial Bank is located on the southwestern corner of Thanon Singhawat and Thanon Tri Chat. It has an ATM, as do several other banks found in the vicinity.

The post office on Thanon Nikon Kasem is open 8.30am to noon and 1pm to 4.30pm on weekdays and 9am to noon on weekends and holidays. The attached CAT office offers international phone services 7am to 10pm daily.

There are several Internet centres in the vicinity of the Chinnawat Hotel.

The tourist police maintain an office in the Sukhothai Historical Park (see the Sukhothai Historical Park section later) directly across from the Ramkhamhaeng National Museum.

Swimming

Suan Nam Premsuk *(Km4 on Route 101; admission 40B; open 7am-9pm)* is a modest sports complex with a clean swimming pool, tennis courts and ping pong table. Look for a couple of tall brick pillars supporting a blue-and-white sign.

Places to Stay

Guesthouses Most of the guesthouses in New Sukhothai offer reasonably priced accommodation in family homes (dorms and/or private rooms) and all rent out bicycles and motorcycles. Places continue to multiply, and competition keeps the prices low. The local taxi mafia has its hooks in the guesthouse proprietors, so expect lots of opinions from the săamláw drivers about where to go.

Lotus Village *(☎ 055 621 484, fax 055 621 463, ℮ lotusvil@yahoo.com, 170 Thanon Ratchathani)* Rooms with shared shower & toilet 120B per person (480B for whole house), singles/doubles in bungalows with private facilities 400B, deluxe rooms with fan/air-con 500/800B. Near the eastern bank of Mae Nam Yom, Lotus Village offers a wide range of rooms, all in teak buildings. All showers have hot water. Set in spacious grounds with a garden sitting area, the guesthouse is quite suitable for long-term stays. The multilingual staff are friendly and knowledgeable.

Yupa House *(☎ 055 612 578, Soi Mekhapatthana, 44/10 Thanon Prawet Nakhon)* Dorm beds 40B, private rooms 80-100B. Near the western bank of Mae Nam Yom you'll find this family-run place with a nice view of the city from the roof.

Somprasong Guest House *(☎ 055 611 709, 32 Thanon Prawet Nakhon)* Singles /doubles with fan & shared shower & toilet 120B, rooms with air-con & private facilities 300B. Near Yupa House, the rooms here are arranged hotel-like on the 2nd floor of a large family house. The family rents out bicycles and there's ample off-road parking.

Ban Thai *(☎ 055 610 163, 38 Thanon Prawet Nakhon)* Rooms with shared shower & toilet 120B, bungalows with private shower & toilet 200B. Next door to the Somprasong, this newer hotel is run by yet another friendly family and is a good place for reliable information on things to see and do in the Sukhothai area.

Friend House *(☎ 055 610 172, 52/7 Soi Nissan, Off Thanon Loet Thai)* Singles/ doubles with fan 100/120B, rooms with air-con 250B. The guesthouse has a small garden dining area, free bikes, and motorcycles for rent. All rooms come with private bathroom, and discounts for stays of more than two nights are available. The proprietor teaches English to Thais so it's a good place to meet students.

No 4 Guest House *(☎ 055 610 165, 140/4 Soi Khlong Mae Ramphan, Thanon Jarot Withithong)* Bungalows 150-180B. No 4 Guest House has moved a couple of times and is now in its third location. It offers rustic bamboo-thatch bungalows with private, open-air, cold-water bathrooms, fan and nicely furnished outdoor lounging areas. Prices depend on the size of the bungalow. There are several sitting areas on the property. The guesthouse offers information and a local area map as well as a two-day Thai cooking course and a five-day Thai massage course.

JJ Guest House Rooms 150B. Next door to No 4, this guesthouse has basic rooms in a wood-and-cement house with shared cold-water bathroom.

Ninety-Nine Guest House (☎ *055 611 315, mobile 01-972 9308, 234/6 Soi Panitsan*) Dorm beds/singles/doubles 80/120/150B. About 150m southwest on the southern side of the canal, this friendly guesthouse offers rooms in a clean two-storey teak house surrounded by gardens. You'll find shared cold-water facilities upstairs, hot water downstairs.

Dream Cafe (☎ *055 612 081, 055 622 157, fax 055 622 157, 86/1 Thanon Singhawat*) Rooms 250/350B. This restaurant offers a few charming guest rooms in a wooden building behind the restaurant; all have fan and attached hot-water shower. The owner has used recycled architectural features from old Thai houses throughout, and the rooms are nicely decorated with local crafts and antiques. More rooms will be added in the future.

Ruean Thai Guest House (☎ *055 612 444, 181/20 Soi Pracha Ruammit, Thanon Jarot Withithong*) Rooms with fan/air-con 250/600B. On a soi between Thanon Jarot Withithong and Thanon Wichian Chamnong, in a nice residential neighbourhood, Ruean Thai has traditional Thai style but with modern facilities. The house contains large and well-spaced guest rooms, with lots of inviting sitting areas in between. All the rooms have modern, private hot-water facilities. The guesthouse rents out bicycles for 15B.

Vitoon Guest House (*Opposite main entrance of Sukhothai Historical Park*) Rooms with fan, cold-water shower & toilet 250B, with air-con, TV & hot water 500B. The air-con rooms are large and comfortable. Vitoon also rents out bicycles.

Hotels *Sawaddiphong Hotel* (☎ *055 611 567, 56/2-5 Thanon Singhawat*) Singles with fan 150B, doubles with/without TV 220/180B, doubles with air-con 260-400B.

The comfortable rooms at friendly Sawaddiphong all have private bathrooms.

Sukhothai Hotel (☎ *055 611 133, 15/5 Thanon Singhawat*) Singles/doubles with fan 170/250B, rooms with air-con 280B. Once a travellers' favourite, but now very much an also-ran, this place is not particularly well kept. All rooms have an attached cold-water shower.

Chinnawat Hotel (☎ *055 611 385, 1-3 Thanon Nikon Kasem*) Rooms with fan 150-180B, with air-con 350B. This is another place that could really benefit from some renovation though most people seem to like it. The price of a fan room depends on whether it's in the old or new wing – the old wing is cheaper and a bit quieter. In the more expensive rooms, be sure to check that the air-con works before booking in. All rooms come with a private shower and toilet.

Rajthanee (*Ratchathani;* ☎ *055 611 031, fax 055 612 583, 229 Thanon Jarot Withithong*) Rooms with air-con & hot water 300B, with TV & refrigerator 600B. This was once the top hotel in town but is now rather faded.

River View Hotel (☎ *055 611 656, fax 055 613 373, 38 Thanon Nikon Kasem*) 1/2-bed rooms 350/450B, nicer rooms with TV 500B. Still a favourite among small traders, the all air-con River View has clean rooms and a large sing-song coffee shop downstairs.

Northern Palace (*Wang Neua;* ☎ *055 613 522, fax 055 612 038, 43 Thanon Singhawat*) Rooms 450B. All rooms here have air-con, small TVs and refrigerators. The hotel has a coffee shop and swimming pool.

Pailyn Sukhothai Hotel (☎ *055 633 336, fax 055 613 317; 10/2 Mu 1, Thanon Jarot Withithong; in Bangkok* ☎ *022 157 110, fax 022 155 640*) Rooms from 1200B. About 8km from the city centre on the road between the old and new cities of Sukhothai sits the huge Pailyn. It caters mostly to tour groups and has a pool, disco, health centre and several restaurants.

Places to Eat

Rainbow (*Thanon Nikon Kasem*) Dishes 20-60B. Open 7am-10pm daily. The menu features a variety of noodle dishes, Thai curries, sandwiches, Western breakfasts and ice cream at very reasonable prices.

Dear House (Thanon Nikon Kasem) Dishes 30-80B. Open 7.30am-11pm daily. Dear House serves sandwiches, burgers, Western breakfasts and Thai and Chinese food in wagon-wheel decor.

Sukhothai Suki-Koka (Thanon Singhawat) Dishes 30-90B. Open 11am-11pm daily. Thai-style sukiyaki is the speciality at this place in front of the Sawaddiphong Hotel.

Dream Cafe (☎ 055 612 081, 86/1 Thanon Singhawat) Dishes 40-100B. Open 11am-10pm daily. This air-con cafe is decorated with 19th-century Thai antiques. Despite catering primarily to tourists, the cafe serves good food and the staff is attentive. The extensive menu includes a long list of herbal liquors ('stamina drinks'), ice cream and very well-prepared Thai and Chinese food. Unlike many Thai restaurants, most of the Thai menu items are also on the bilingual menu. One dish that isn't listed in English is *thâwt man khâo phôht* (tasty corn fritters with a dipping sauce).

Ran Je Hae (Thanon Jarot Withithong, about 350m west of Rte 101) Dishes 25-30B. Open 10am-9pm daily. Ran Je Hae specialises in Sukhothai-style kǔaytǐaw – pork, coriander, green onions, pickled cabbage, pork skins, peanuts, chilli and green beans are added to the basic kǔaytǐaw recipe.

Kuaytiaw Thai Sukhothai (Thanon Jarot Withithong) Dishes 20-30B. Open 9am-8pm daily. This is another good spot to try Sukhothai-style kǔaytǐaw, about 20m south of the turn-off for Ruean Thai Guest House. The restaurant is in a nice wooden building with a fountain fashioned from ceramic pots out front.

Getting There & Away

Air The so-called 'Sukhothai' airport is 27km outside of town off Rte 1195 about 11km from Sawankhalok. It's privately owned by Bangkok Airways, and, like its Ko Samui counterpart, is a beautifully designed small airport that uses tropical architecture to best advantage. Bangkok Airways (☎ 055 633 266/7, fax 055 610 908; at the airport ☎ 055 612 448), with an office at the airport, operates a daily flight from Bangkok (1820B including 30B departure tax, one hour and 10 minutes). In the reverse direction, the flight costs 1890B (including the 100B domestic/international 'airport tax' charged at this airport). Bangkok Airways charges 80B to transport passengers between the airport and Sukhothai.

Bangkok Airways flies daily from Chiang Mai to Sukhothai (830B), or from Sukhothai to Chiang Mai (750B). Fares for children are half the adult price. Bangkok Airways at one time had plans to fly between Sukhothai and Siem Reap in Cambodia but the flight has yet to materialise. Bangkok Airways tickets can be purchased from any travel agency in town.

Bus Sukhothai can be reached by road from Phitsanulok, Tak or Kamphaeng Phet. If you arrive in Phitsanulok by rail or air, take a city bus No 1 to the air-con bus station in the centre, or to the Baw Khaw Saw (government bus station), for buses out of town. The bus to Sukhothai (24/33B ordinary/air-con, one hour) leaves regularly throughout the day.

From Tak, get a Sukhothai bus at the Baw Khaw Saw just outside town (48B, 1½ hours); at last count there were 10 departures daily. Buses from Kamphaeng Phet cost 46B (one to 1½ hours).

There are Baw Khaw Saw buses to/from Chiang Mai along the slower, older route (132/184B, five hours), and along the faster new route (140/196B, 4½ hours). Buses between Bangkok and Sukhothai cost 152B or 198B air-con (seven hours). Buses to Chiang Rai cost 153B or 214/290B air-con/1st-class air-con (six hours); there are two departures a day of both air-con and ordinary buses.

Phitsanulok Yan Yon Tour has six daily VIP buses (with reclining seats) to Bangkok for 260B. Win Tour has nine departures for the same price. Ordinary buses to destinations outside Sukhothai Province leave from the government bus station; tour buses leave from Win Tour or Phitsanulok Yan Yon Tour near the night market area. Buses to Tak leave from Thanon Ban Meuang, two streets east of Thanon Singhawat.

Buses to Sawankhalok (20B, 45 minutes) and Si Satchanalai (24/31B, one hour) leave hourly between about 6am and 6pm from the intersection of Thanon Singhawat and Thanon Jarot Withithong.

Getting Around

Around New Sukhothai, a săamláw ride should not cost more than 20B to 30B. Săwngthăew run frequently from 6.30am to 6pm between New Sukhothai and Sukhothai Historical Park, leaving from Thanon Jarot Withithong near Mae Nam Yom (10B, 20 to 30 minutes).

The best way to get around the historical park is by bicycle; these can be rented at shops outside the park entrance for 20B a day, or you can borrow or rent one at any guesthouse in New Sukhothai. Don't rent the first bikes you see at the bus stop at meuang kào (old city), as the better bikes tend to be found at shops around the corner, closer to the park entrance.

If you rent a bike in town, instead of taking Hwy 12 straight to the park consider a more scenic (if slower) route to the ruins: Turn right (north) off the highway about 2.5km west of the main junction of Hwy 12 and Rte 101. The best place to turn off is right into the compound of Wat Kamphaeng Ngam, in the village of Ban Kluay. Pedal through the wát compound and out the back entrance, where you'll see a canal. Follow the road along the canal – you must cross some canal bridges, as the road changes sides from time to time. You shouldn't get lost as long as you keep the canal in sight, and along the way you'll get a taste of village life. When you reach the ruins of Wat Chang Lom (the one with elephants along the base), continue another 200m or so and look for a bridge on the left that will take you back to Hwy 12 and the main entrance to the park.

The park operates a tram service through the old city for 20B per person.

SUKHOTHAI HISTORICAL PARK
อุทยานประวัติศาสตร์สุโขทัย

The original capital of this early Thai kingdom was surrounded by three concentric ramparts and two moats bridged by four gateways. Today the remains of 21 historical sites and four large ponds can be seen within the old walls, with an additional 70 sites within a 5km radius. The Sukhothai ruins are one of Thailand's World Heritage sites.

The ruins are divided into five zones – central, north, south, east and west – each of which has a 30B admission fee, except for the central section, which costs 40B. For 150B you can buy a single ticket that allows entry to all the Sukhothai sites, plus the Sawanwaranayok National Museum, Ramkhamhaeng National Museum and the Si Satchanalai and Chaliang ruins in nearby Sawankhalok. The ticket is good for repeated visits over 30 days. There are additional charges for bicycles (10B), motorcycles (20B), săamláw/túk-túk (30B) and cars or vans (50B). Tickets can be purchased at the front gate to the park. The park's official hours are from 6am to 6pm. At the Information Centre opposite Wat Phra Pai Luang you can browse historical displays.

Sukhothai temple architecture is most typified by the classic lotus-bud stupa, which features a conical spire topping a square-sided structure on a three-tiered base. Some sites also exhibit other rich architectural forms introduced and modified during the period – bell-shaped Singhalese and double-tiered Srivijaya stupas.

See the Sukhothai section earlier for details on getting to the park and getting around it.

Ramkhamhaeng National Museum
พิพิธภัณฑสถานแห่งชาติ
รามคำแหง

The museum *(admission 30B; open 9am-4pm daily except public holidays)* provides a good starting point for an exploration of the ruins. A replica of the famous Ram Khamhaeng inscription (see Wiang Kum Kam in the Chiang Mai chapter) is kept here among a good collection of Sukhothai artefacts.

Wat Mahathat

วัดมหาธาตุ

The largest wát in the city, circa 13th-century Wat Mahathat is surrounded by brick walls (surrounding an area 206m long and 200m wide) and a moat, said to represent the outer wall of the universe and the cosmic ocean. The stupa spires feature the famous lotus-bud motif, and some of the original stately Buddha figures still sit among the ruined columns of the old wíhǎan (main hall). The main image, a seated Buddha, measures 8m high.

There are 198 chedi within the monastery walls – a lot to explore in what many consider to have been the spiritual and administrative centre of the old capital. The surviving base of one of the larger chedi still has some of its original stucco ornamentation, including figures of elephants, lions, angels and demons.

Wat Si Sawai

วัดศรีสวาย

Just south of Wat Mahathat, this shrine dating from the 12th and 13th centuries features

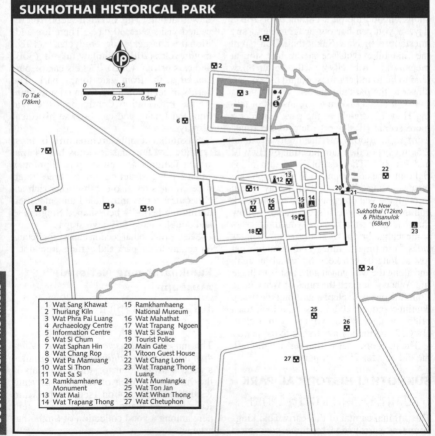

SUKHOTHAI HISTORICAL PARK

To Tak
(78km)

To New
Sukhothai (12km)
& Phitsanulok
(68km)

1 Wat Sang Khawat
2 Thuriang Kiln
3 Wat Phra Pai Luang
4 Archaeology Centre
5 Information Centre
6 Wat Si Chum
7 Wat Saphan Hin
8 Wat Chang Rop
9 Wat Pa Mamuang
10 Wat Si Thon
11 Wat Sa Si
12 Ramkhamhaeng
   Monument
13 Wat Mai
14 Wat Trapang Thong

15 Ramkhamhaeng
   National Museum
16 Wat Mahathat
17 Wat Trapang Ngoen
18 Wat Si Sawai
19 Tourist Police
20 Main Gate
21 Vitoon Guest House
22 Wat Chang Lom
23 Wat Trapang Thong
   Luang
24 Wat Mumlangka
25 Wat Ton Jan
26 Wat Wihan Thong
27 Wat Chetuphon

SOUTHEASTERN PROVINCES

three prang and a picturesque moat. It was originally built by the Khmers as a Hindu temple and thus predates Sukhothai. Later it was converted into a Buddhist wát.

Wat Sa Si
วัดสระศรี

Wat Sa Si (Sacred Pond Monastery), sits on an island west of the bronze monument of Ram Khamhaeng. It's a simple, classic Sukhothai-style wát with one large Buddha, one chedi and the columns of the ruined wíhǎan.

Wat Trapang Thong
วัดตระพังทอง

Next to the museum, this small, still functioning wát is reached by a footbridge across the large lotus-filled pond that surrounds it. This reservoir, the original site of Thailand's Loi Krathong Festival, supplies the Sukhothai community with most of its water. The wíhǎan here bears fine stucco reliefs. A ruined *mondòp* (square shrine hall) contains a Buddha footprint slab reportedly built by order of Phaya Li Thai in 1360.

Wat Phra Phai Luang
วัดพระพายหลวง

Outside the city walls in the northern zone, this somewhat isolated wát features three 12th-century Khmer-style prang, bigger than those at Wat Si Sawai. This may have been the centre of Sukhothai when it was ruled by the Khmers of Angkor prior to the 13th century. Two of the prang have crumbled into rubble, but the northernmost one has retained some of its original stucco ornamentation.

Four Buddha images in the classic four postures – sitting, standing, walking and reclining – occupy a ruined mondòp.

Wat Si Chum
วัดศรีชุม

This wát is northwest of the old city and contains an impressive, much-photographed mondòp with a 15m, brick-and-stucco

seated Buddha. Archaeologists theorise that this image is the 'Phra Atchana' mentioned in the famous Ram Khamhaeng inscription. A passage in the 3m-thick mondòp wall that leads to the top has been blocked so that it's no longer possible to view the *jataka* (stories of the Buddha's past lives) inscriptions that line the tunnel ceiling.

Wat Chang Lom
วัดช้างล้อม

Off Hwy 12 in the eastern zone, Wat Chang Lom (Elephant Circled Monastery) is about 1km east of the main park entrance. A large bell-shaped chedi is supported by 36 elephants sculpted into its base. Similar elephant-supported monuments can be seen in Si Satchanalai and Kamphaeng Phet (see those sections later in this chapter).

Wat Saphan Hin
วัดสะพานหิน

Wat Saphan Hin is a couple of kilometres to the west of the old city walls, on the crest of a hill that rises about 200m above the plain. The name of the wát, which means 'stone bridge', is a reference to the slate path and staircase leading to the temple, which are still in place. The site affords a good view of the Sukhothai ruins to the southeast and the mountains to the north and south.

All that remains of the original temple are a few chedi and the ruined wíhǎan, consisting of two rows of laterite columns flanking a 12.5m-high standing Buddha image on a brick terrace.

Wat Chang Rop
วัดช้างรอบ

On a hill west of the city, just south of Wat Saphan Hin, this wát features an elephant-base stupa, similar to that at Wat Chang Lom.

Thuriang Kilns
เตาเผาท่วยชามทุเรียง

Several kilns that once stood in this area of around 100m by 700m were used to create the famous celadon pottery for which the Sukhothai period became famous. Each consisted of a fire pit, a large dome-like oven and a flue – much like the Thai kilns of today.

AROUND SUKHOTHAI
Si Satchanalai-Chaliang Historical Park
อุทยานประวัติศาสตร์
ศรีสัชชนาลัย/ชะเลียง

The 13th- to 15th-century ruins in the old cities of Si Satchanalai and Chaliang, about 60km north of Sukhothai, are in the same basic style as those in the Sukhothai Historical Park. This historical park *(admission 40B, plus 10/30/40/50B per bicycle/motorcycle/săamláw/car; open 8am to 6pm)* has been classified as a World Heritage Site. It covers over 7 sq km and is surrounded by a 12m-wide moat. Chaliang, 1km to the

southeast, is an older city site (dating to the 11th century), though its two temples date to the 14th century.

The ruins at Si Satchanalai are set among hills and are very attractive in the sense that they're not as heavily visited as the Sukhothai ruins. Some people actually prefer the more unrestored atmosphere at Si Satchanalai over Sukhothai. Those listed in this section represent only the more distinctive of the numerous Si Satchanalai ruins.

There are bicycles for rent near the entrance to the park for 20B. For details on getting to the park, see Getting There & Away later in this section.

Wat Chang Lom This fine temple, marking the centre of the old city of Si Satchanalai, has 39 elephants surrounding a bell-shaped stupa, but is somewhat better preserved than its counterpart in Sukhothai. An inscription says the temple was built by Ram Khamhaeng between 1285 and 1291.

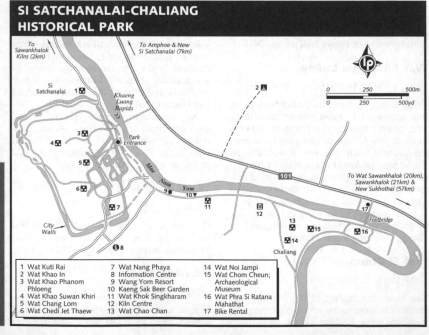

SI SATCHANALAI-CHALIANG HISTORICAL PARK

To Sawankhalok Kilns (2km)

To Amphoe & New Si Satchanalai (7km)

Si Satchanalai

Khaeng Luang Rapids

Park Entrance

Mae Nam Yom

To Wat Sawankhalok (20km), Sawankhalok (21km) & New Sukhothai (57km)

City Walls

Yom

Chaliang

Footbridge

1 Wat Kuti Rai
2 Wat Khao In
3 Wat Khao Phanom Phloeng
4 Wat Khao Suwan Khiri
5 Wat Chang Lom
6 Wat Chedi Jet Thaew
7 Wat Nang Phaya
8 Information Centre
9 Wang Yom Resort
10 Kaeng Sak Beer Garden
11 Wat Khok Singkharam
12 Kiln Centre
13 Wat Chao Chan
14 Wat Noi Jampi
15 Wat Chom Cheun; Archaeological Museum
16 Wat Phra Si Ratana Mahathat
17 Bike Rental

Wat Khao Phanom Phloeng On the hill overlooking Wat Chang Lom to the right are the remains of Wat Khao Phanom Phloeng, including a large seated Buddha, a chedi and stone columns that once supported the roof of the wíhǎan. From this hill you can make out the general design of the once great city. The slightly higher hill west of Phanom Phloeng is capped by a large Sukhothai-style chedi – all that remains of Wat Khao Suwan Khiri.

Wat Chedi Jet Thaew Next to Wat Chang Lom, these ruins contain seven rows of chedi, the largest of which is a copy of one at Wat Mahathat in Sukhothai. An interesting brick-and-plaster wíhǎan features barred windows designed to look like lathed wood (an ancient Indian technique used all over Southeast Asia). A *praasàat* (palace-like structure) and chedi are stacked on the roof.

Wat Nang Phaya South of Wat Chang Lom and Wat Chedi Jet Thaew, this stupa is Singhalese in style and was built in the 15th or 16th century, a bit later than other monuments at Si Satchanalai. Stucco reliefs on the large laterite wíhǎan in front of the stupa – now sheltered by a tin roof – date to the Ayuthaya period when Si Satchanalai was known as Sawankhalok. Goldsmiths in the district still craft a design known as *naang phayaa*, modelled after these reliefs.

Wat Phra Si Ratana Mahathat These ruins at Chaliang consist of a large laterite chedi (dating from 1448–88) between two wíhǎan. One wíhǎan contains a large seated Sukhothai Buddha image, a smaller standing image and a bas-relief of the famous walking Buddha, so exemplary of the flowing, boneless Sukhothai style. The other wíhǎan contains some less distinguished images.

There's a separate 10B admission for this wát.

Wat Chao Chan These wát ruins are about 500m west of Wat Phra Si Ratana Mahathat in Chaliang. The central attraction is a large Khmer-style prang similar to later prang in Lopburi and probably built during the reign of Khmer King Jayavarman VII (1181–1217). The prang has been restored and is in fairly good shape. The roofless wíhǎan on the right contains the laterite outlines of a large standing Buddha that has all but melted away from weathering.

Sawankhalok Kilns
เตาเผาสังคโลก

The Sukhothai–Si Satchanalai area has long been famous for its beautiful pottery, much of which was exported to countries throughout Asia. In China – the biggest importer of Thai pottery during the Sukhothai and Ayuthaya periods – the pieces came to be called 'Sangkhalok', a mispronunciation of Sawankhalok. Particularly fine specimens of this pottery can be seen in the national museums of Jakarta and Pontianak in Indonesia.

At one time more than 200 huge pottery kilns lined the banks of Mae Nam Yom in the area around Si Satchanalai. Several have been carefully excavated and can be viewed at the **Si Satchanalai Centre for Study & Preservation of Sangkhalok Kilns** (*admission 30B; open 9am-4pm Wed-Sun*). Opened in 1987, the centre has thus far exhibited two phases of its construction to the public: a small museum in Chaliang with excavated pottery samples and one kiln; and a larger outdoor kiln site 2km northwest of the Si Satchanalai ruins. The exhibits are very well presented, although there are no English labels. More phases are planned, including one featuring a working kiln.

Sawankhalok pottery rejects, buried in the fields, are still being found. Shops in Sukhothai and Sawankhalok sell misfired, broken, warped and fused pieces.

Sawanwaranayok Museum
พิพิธภัณฑ์สวรรค์วรนายก

In Sawankhalok town, near Wat Sawankhalam on the western bank of the river, the Sawanwaranayok Museum (☎ 055 641 571; *admission 30B; open 8.30am-4pm Wed-Sun*) displays original pottery and Buddha images unearthed by local villagers and donated to the wát. Thai Celadon near Chiang Mai is a ceramics centre producing a modern interpretation of the old craft.

Ban Hat Siaw
บ้านหาดเสี้ยว

Ban Hat Siaw is a colourful village southeast of Si Satchanalai. It is home to the Thai Phuan, a Thai tribal group that immigrated from Xieng Khuang Province in Laos about 100 years ago when the Annamese and Chinese were in Northeastern Laos.

The local Thai Phuan are famous for **hand-woven textiles** (*phâa hàat sîaw*), particularly the *phâa sîn tiin jòk*, a traditional long skirt featuring patterns of horizontal stripes bordered by weft brocade. These are made entirely of handspun cotton threads which are boiled in rice soup overnight to toughen the fibres. Once the threads are ready, it then takes at least two weeks to weave a skirt.

Traditionally every Thai Phuan woman is taught weaving skills, which are passed on from generation to generation. Practically every stilt house in the village has a loom beneath it; cloth can be purchased at the source, but if you can't make it to Ban Hat Siaw you can buy it from shops in Sawankhalok or from small shops and vendors along the main road through the town of Si Satchanalai. Vintage Hat Siaw textiles 80 to 200 years old can be seen in central Si Satchanalai at the **Village Old Clothes Museum** (*admission free; open 9am-4pm daily*).

Another Thai Phuan custom is the use of **elephant-back processions** in local monastic ordinations; these usually take place in early April.

Places to Stay & Eat

Wang Yom Resort (*Sunanthana;* ☎ *055 631 380, 78/2 Mu 5, Tambon Si Satchanalai*) Rooms with fan/air-con 1200/1500B. Just outside the Si Satchanalai Historical Park, 400m before the southeastern corner of the old city, it has spacious but overpriced bungalows and a 'handicraft village' set amid beautifully landscaped grounds along Mae Nam Yom. Bargaining is in order. Wang Yom's large restaurant is reportedly very

good. Food and drink are also available at a coffee shop in the historical park until 6pm.

Kaeng Sak Beer Garden Dishes 40-100B. Open 9am-3.30pm daily. Sharing a compound with several 'antique' shops by the river near the park entrance, this popular tour-bus stop features a moderately priced Thai and Chinese menu.

Sawankhalok This charming town on Mae Nam Yom, about 11km south of the historical park, has a couple of more economical possibilities for visitors wishing to explore the area.

Saengsin Hotel (☎ *055 641 818, fax 055 641 828, 2 Thanon Thetsaban Damri 3*) Singles/doubles with fan 150/210B, with air-con 280/320B. Centrally located on the main street that runs through Sawankhalok, the reliable Saengsin has clean and comfortable rooms and a decent coffee shop.

Muang Inn Hotel (☎ *055 641 622, 21 Thanon Kasemrat*) Rooms with fan/air-con 160/350B. There is a dark coffee shop and sing-song cafe downstairs from the hotel.

This isn't a big town for eating; most food places sell noodles and khâo man kài and not much else. There is a **night market**, bigger than the one in New Sukhothai, in Sawankhalok, which is held along the main streets.

Ko Heng is an old riverside Chinese restaurant that's well past its prime and is now primarily a place for old Chinese cronies to sit and drink tea.

Kung Nam Dishes 40-70B. Open 10am-11pm daily. This Thai and Chinese garden restaurant is probably the best spot for eating. It's on the outskirts of Sawankhalok towards Sukhothai, not far from the Muang Inn Hotel.

Getting There & Away

Bus Si Satchanalai–Chaliang Historical Park is off Rte 101 between Sawankhalok and New Si Satchanalai. From New Sukhothai, take a Si Satchanalai bus (24/31B ordinary/air-con) and ask to get off at meuang kào.

There are two places along the left-hand side of the highway where you can get off the bus and reach the ruins in the park; both involve crossing Mae Nam Yom. The first leads to a footbridge over Mae Nam Yom to Wat Phra Si Ratana Mahathat at Chaliang; the second crossing is about 2km farther northwest just past two hills and leads directly into the Si Satchanalai ruins.

Train King Rama VI had a 60km railway spur built from Ban Dara (a small town on the main northern trunk) to Sawankhalok just so that he could visit the ruins. The original train station in Sawankhalok is one of the main local sights. A vendor in the station sells real filtered coffee.

Amazingly, there is a daily special express from Bangkok to Sawankhalok, No 7, which leaves the capital at 11.10pm and arrives in Sawankhalok at 6.10am. Don't look for this train on your English train schedule, as it's only listed on the Thai timetable. It's a 'Sprinter', which means 2nd-class air-con, no sleepers, and the fare is 372B (this includes dinner and breakfast). You can also pick up this train in Phitsanulok at 5.30am; expect to pay about 33B for this shorter distance. In the reverse direction, No 4 leaves Sawankhalok at 7am.

There is also one local train a day, No 405, leaving Phitsanulok at noon and arriving in Sawankhalok at 2.45pm (21B 3rd class). The No 406 leaves Sawankhalok at 2.30pm and arrives at Phitsanulok at 4.45pm.

Getting Around
Bicycle is the best way to see the ruins. You can rent bikes (20B a day) from outside a barber shop at the gateway to Wat Phra Si Ratana Mahathat.

Kamphaeng Phet Province

KAMPHAENG PHET
อ.เมืองกำแพงเพชร

postcode 62000 • pop 25,500
Formerly an important front line of defence for the Sukhothai kingdom, Kamphaeng Phet is now mostly known for the monastery ruins – a World Heritage site – and for producing the tastiest *klûay khài* ('egg banana', a kind of small banana) in Thailand. It's a nice place to spend a day or two wandering around the ruins and experiencing a small northern provincial capital that receives few tourists.

History
Northern Thai chronicles refer to a 1004 founding date for Kamphaeng Phet (Diamond Wall), which would make it over two hundred years older than Sukhothai. Most likely it was an Angkor satellite much like Sukhothai was before Thai independence.

Also known as Chakangrao or Nakhon Chum, Kamphaeng Phet at various times paid tribute to Lanna, Sukhothai and Ayuthaya. The meeting of these three spheres of influence made for a unique Kamphaeng Phet style of Buddhist sculpture. The city was greatly amplified during the reign of Sukhothai's fourth king, Loet Thai.

As the fortunes of its sponsor kingdoms waxed and waned, so did those of Kamphaeng Phet. During the Burmese invasions the city was laid to ruin, and never really recovered from backwater status afterwards. Today it is an agricultural centre with a very small tourist industry.

Information
A privately sponsored tourist information centre (the sign reads 'Chamber of Commerce') on Thanon Thesa can answer general queries about accommodation and restaurants. It also has a good map of the town.

Thai Farmers Bank and Siam Commercial Bank have branches with ATMs on Thanon Charoensuk, the road coming into town from Phitsanulok. Most of the major banks also have branches with ATMs along the main streets along the river.

The main post office is just south of the old city on Thanon Thesa.

Old City
เมืองเก่า

Only 2km off Rte 1 are some ruins within the old city area of Kamphaeng Phet, as well as some very fine remains of the long city wall.

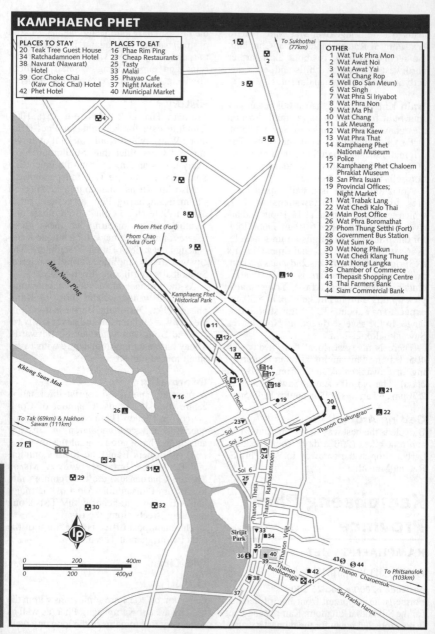

KAMPHAENG PHET

PLACES TO STAY
20 Teak Tree Guest House
34 Ratchadamnoen Hotel
38 Navarat (Nawarat) Hotel
39 Gor Choke Chai (Kaw Chok Chai) Hotel
42 Phet Hotel

PLACES TO EAT
16 Phae Rim Ping
23 Cheap Restaurants
25 Tasty
33 Malai
35 Phayao Cafe
37 Night Market
40 Municipal Market

OTHER
1 Wat Tuk Phra Mon
2 Wat Awat Noi
3 Wat Awat Yai
4 Wat Chang Rop
5 Well (Bo San Meun)
6 Wat Singh
7 Wat Phra Si Iriyabot
8 Wat Phra Non
9 Wat Ma Phi
10 Wat Chang
11 Lak Meuang
12 Wat Phra Kaew
13 Wat Phra That
14 Kamphaeng Phet National Museum
15 Police
17 Kamphaeng Phet Chaloem Phrakiat Museum
18 San Phra Isuan
19 Provincial Offices; Night Market
21 Wat Trabak Lang
22 Wat Chedi Kalo Thai
24 Main Post Office
26 Wat Phra Boromathat
27 Phom Thung Setthi (Fort)
28 Government Bus Station
29 Wat Sum Ko
30 Wat Nong Phikun
31 Wat Chedi Klang Thung
32 Wat Nong Langka
36 Chamber of Commerce
41 Thepasit Shopping Centre
43 Thai Farmers Bank
44 Siam Commercial Bank

To Sukhothai (77km)

Mae Nam Ping

Phom Phet (Fort)

Phom Chao Indra (Fort)

Kamphaeng Phet Historical Park

Khlong Suan Mak

To Tak (69km) & Nakhon Sawan (111km)

Thanon Thesa

Thanon Chakungrao

Soi 1
Soi 2
Soi 6

Thanon Thesa

Thanon Ratchadamnoen

Thanon Wijit

Sirijit Park

Thanon Banthoengjit

Thanon Charoensuk

Soi Pracha Hansa

To Phitsanulok (103km)

0   200   400m
0   200   400yd

Established at the old city site and now cared for by the Fine Arts Department is the **Kamphaeng Phet Historical Park** (*admission 40B for ruins within the city wall; 10/20 /30/50B per bicycle/motorcycle/túk-túk/car; open 6am-6pm daily*). The park was declared a Unesco World Heritage site in 1991. Here you'll find the all-sandstone **Wat Phra Kaew**, which used to be adjacent to the royal palace (now in ruins). The weather-corroded Buddha statues have assumed slender, porous forms that remind many visitors of Giacometti sculptures. About 100m southeast of Wat Phra Kaew is **Wat Phra That**, distinguished by a large round-based, laterite and brick chedi surrounded by columns.

Wat Phra Non once contained a large reclining Buddha but today consists of the ruins of a large wíhǎan, a laterite quadrangle and a pavilion supported by a 6m laterite column, said to the largest single piece of laterite in Thailand. A few sěhmaa (ordination-ground marker) stones and a lion sculpture are still intact.

This park is a popular spot for joggers and walkers.

San Phra Isuan

ศาลพระอิศวร

Near the Kamphaeng Phet National Museum (see its entry in this section), San Phra Isuan (Shiva Shrine) has a sandstone base upon which stands a Khmer-style bronze sculpture of Shiva (Isvara). This image is actually a replica: The original is on display in the Kamphaeng Phet National Museum.

In the 1880s a German tourist stole the Shiva figure's head and hands and took them to a museum in Berlin. Upon the personal request of Rama V, the museum eventually returned the art to Kamphaeng Phet in return for copies.

Wat Phra Boromathat

วัดพระบรมธาตุ

Across Mae Nam Ping are neglected ruins in an area that was settled long before Kamphaeng Phet's heyday, although visible remains are post-classical Sukhothai. Wat Phra Boromathat has a few small chedi and one large chedi of the late Sukhothai period that is now crowned with a Burmese-style umbrella added early in the 20th century.

Other Wát

Northeast of the old city walls, **Wat Phra Si Iriyabot** has the shattered remains of standing, sitting, walking and reclining Buddha images sculpted in the classic Sukhothai style. Northwest of here, **Wat Chang Rop** (Elephant-Encircled Temple) is just that – a temple with an elephant-buttressed wall.

Kamphaeng Phet National Museum

พิพิธภัณฑสถานแห่งชาติ กำแพงเพชร

Within the walls of the old city is a national museum (☎ 055 711 570; 30B; open 9am-4pm Wed-Sun). Downstairs is the usual survey of Thai art periods while upstairs is a collection of artefacts from the Kamphaeng Phet area, including terracotta ornamentation from ruined temples and Buddha images in the Sukhothai and Ayuthaya styles.

Kamphaeng Phet Chaloem Phrakiat Museum

พิพิธพัณฑ์เฉลิมพระเกียรติ กำแพงเพชร

Just south of the Kamphaeng Phet National Museum is this newer museum (☎ 055 722 341; admission free; open 9am-4pm daily), which consists of a series of Central Thai–style wooden structures on stilts set among nicely landscaped grounds. There are three main buildings: One focuses on history and prehistory, one features displays about geography and materials used in local architecture, and the third houses an ethnological museum featuring encased displays of miniature doll-like figures representing various tribes. Push-button recordings in

English and Thai explain the displays. A shrine hall in the grounds houses a Buddha figure.

Places to Stay

Teak Tree Guest House (☎ *016 756 471*, e *teakkpp@hotmail.com, Soi 1 Thanon Chakungrao*) Singles/doubles with fan 130/200B. Next to the old city wall, this was the only guesthouse in town when we visited. It offers three fan rooms in a tidy wooden house on stilts with shared modern hot-water bathroom. The guesthouse is only 10 minutes' walk from the historical park. Bicycles are available for 30B per day.

Gor Choke Chai Hotel (Kaw Chok Chai; ☎ *055 711 247, 19/3-4 Thanon Ratchadamnoen)* Rooms with private hot-water shower, toilet & fan/air-con 270/310B. In the centre of the new town, not far from the municipal market, the bustling but friendly Gor Choke Chai offers the best-value hotel in town.

Ratchadamnoen Hotel (☎ *055 711 029, 164 Thanon Ratchadamnoen)* Rooms 180-310B. On the eastern side of Thanon Ratchadamnoen, this four-storey hotel is rather tattered and the adjacent disco can be noisy.

Navarat Hotel (Nawarat; ☎ *055 711 211, Thanon Thesa)* Newer rooms with air-con from 550B, older rooms 400B. Near the river and set back from the road, the five-storey Navarat offers clean, comfortable rooms, and a coffee shop downstairs. The staff here speak some English.

Phet Hotel (☎ *055 712 810, fax 055 712 816, 99 Thanon Wijit)* Standard/deluxe rooms 550/650B, suites 2500B, including American breakfast for two. This hotel features well-maintained air-con rooms with TVs.

Places to Eat

A small *night market* sets up every evening in front of the provincial offices near the old city walls and there are also some *night markets* on Thanon Thesa with vendors selling Thai food.

In the centre of town is a larger *municipal market* at the intersection of Thanon Wijit and Thanon Banthoengjit. Several restaurants can be found along Thanon Thesa across from Sirijit Park by the river.

Malai (*77 Thanon Thesa)* Dishes 40-75B. Open 10am-10pm daily. Try this place for good Isan food in an outdoor setting.

Also on Thanon Thesa are a couple of similar air-con restaurants featuring Thai food and ice cream, *Phayao Cafe* and *Tasty*. Phayao also has a bakery next door to the restaurant.

There are also a few floating restaurants on the river, including *Phae Rim Ping*, where dishes cost 40B to 100B. It's open 11am to midnight daily.

Getting There & Away

The bus fare from Bangkok is 125B ordinary and 165B 2nd-class air-con. Most visitors arrive from Sukhothai (46B), Phitsanulok (41/58B ordinary/air-con) or Tak (28B). The government bus station is located across the river from town.

Getting Around

The least expensive way to get from the bus station into town is to take a shared săwngthăew (6B per person) to the roundabout across the river, and from there take a săamláw anywhere in town for 20B.

Phetchabun Province

Ringed by mountains providing a steady ration of water into the surrounding bowl-shaped valley, Phetchabun has always been one of the region's most important farming areas, especially for such thirsty crops as corn, tobacco and tamarind. Mulberry farms here also support a large proportion of the silkworms that produce the material for Thailand's famous loom-woven silk textiles. Over half the local population work in agriculture. The local dialect (Lao Lom, or Lao Neua), blends linguistic influences from Northern Thailand, the Khorat dialect and from Phuan, a Lao migrant group once hailing from Laos' Xieng Khuang Province.

The northern half of the province is home to the Phetchabun mountain range, which in its lengthy west-to-east extent incorporates one of Thailand's largest national parks, Nam Nao, along with the Khao Kho mountain resort area. From the 1960s into the early 1980s, this mountainous area was classified a 'pink zone', although since communist insurgents made their headquarters at Khao Kho (see later in this section) and at Phu Hin Rong Kla (see the Phitsanulok section earlier in this chapter), this was easily Thailand's 'reddest' province. Skirmishes between Thai government troops and the PLAT on the battlefields of Khao Kho took the lives of many soldiers on both sides.

Today the same mountains that were once off-limits to civilians have become a popular destination for Thais who seek out the exotically cold weather of the 'Thai Switzerland' from November to March. For more well-heeled Bangkok Thais who have built second homes in the Khao Kho area, Phetchabun provides an escape from the stifling heat of the Chao Phraya plains during the hot and dry season (March to May). Phetchabun in fact boasts Thailand's only provincial seal that incorporates mountains into its symbolic design.

There is little to see in the provincial capital itself. Most visitors to Phetchabun are interested in either cooling off in the northern mountains or in visiting the historic ruins of Si Thep Historical Park at the southern edge of the province.

PHETCHABUN
อ.เมืองเพชรบูรณ์

postcode 67000 • pop 55,000
Sitting at the cultural and historical crossroads of Northern and Northeastern Thailand, yet bypassed by the nation's major road arteries, Phetchabun is one of Thailand's least visited provincial capitals. Its apparent isolation today belies the important role it played as trade and supply station between the early Buddhist cultures of Central Thailand and Brahmanist cultures of Funan and later Angkor in northwestern Cambodia and southern Laos. Around

1940, Thai Prime Minister Phibul Songkhram devised a plan to move the capital to Phetchabun because of its perceived central location and because he felt that Bangkok was vulnerable to naval invasion via the Gulf of Thailand. Although Phibul even transferred some assets of the royal treasury to Phetchabun in preparation for the move, he fell from power before the transition was completed.

Wat Mahathat
วัดมหาธาตุ

This highly revered monastery on Thanon Nikon Bamrung is thought to stand on an earlier site that was sacred to the Dvaravati culture. The main chedi at Wat Mahathat, built during the Sukhothai period, is said to contain Buddha relics and the ashes of an enlightened monk. During a 1967 restoration, artisans dismantled part of the base and discovered Sukhothai-era jars, Ming ceramics, over 500 bronze Buddha amulets and an inscribed gold plaque stating that the chedi was constructed in 1383.

The bòt and wíhǎan each contain Buddha images dating to the U Thong period (13th to 15th centuries).

Wat Traiphum
วัดไตรภูมิ

A bronze Buddha image seated in meditation and dating to the Lopburi period (10th to 13th centuries) is the centre of attention at this wát on Thanon Phetcharat. Legend says that this image, called Phra Phut Thammaracha, was a gift from Angkor's Jayavarman VII to Phaya Pha Meuang, Phetchabun's Thai founder. Reportedly when a rival ruler attacked Phetchabun, and the image was being ferried across the nearby Mae Nam Pa Sak, the raft on which it was sitting broke apart and the image sank to the bottom of the river. After being recovered and installed at Wat Traiphum the image reportedly disappeared again and was found at the same spot in the river.

Hence during the annual Songkran festival (mid April), when Thais traditionally sprinkle

Buddha images with water in a ritual cleansing, the people of Phetchabun carry the Phra Phut Thammaracha in a procession to Mae Nam Pa Sak, and the provincial governor gives the image a ritual dunking in the river. Nowadays you will in fact see two identical images sitting on the altar in the bòt. The upper one is the original, the lower one a copy used in the annual ceremony.

Places to Stay

Siam Hotel (☎ 056 711 301, Thanon San Khu Meuang) Rooms with fan & cold-water shower 150B, with fan/air-con & hot-water shower 250/350B. Near the municipal market in the centre of town, this standard Thai-Chinese style hotel has the best location in Phetchabun if you want to be near a good selection of places to eat.

Phetchabun Hotel (☎ 056 711 348, Thanon San Khu Meuang) Rooms with shared/private cold-water shower & toilet 100/160B. This hotel is also centrally located, with more basic rooms.

Burapha Hotel (☎ 056 711 155, Thanon Saraburi-Lom Sak) Rooms with fan/air-con from 250/350B. At the northern edge of town, this place has parking available.

Kosit Hill Hotel (☎ 056 711 293, Thanon Charoen Phattana/Hwy 21) Rooms from 800B. This is the nicest hotel in town and although it's on the main north-south artery is still close to the centre. Parking is available.

Places to Eat

Talat Thetsaban 2 (Municipal Market No 2; Thanon Charoen Phattana) Dishes 10-30B. Beginning around 5.30am or 6am, permanent vendor stands in this market offer real coffee, coddled eggs *(khài lûak),* hot soya milk, *saalaapao* and *paa-thâwng kŏh* (Chinese 'doughnuts'). Of course Phetchabun Province grows good coffee, and the best coffee stand in Talat Thetsaban 2 is *Ko Se.* By around 10am or 11am the Talat Thetsaban 2 menu switches to *aahǎan taam sàng* (food according to order, ie, short-order fare) such as khâo kaeng (curry and rice), *yam* (tangy and spicy Thai salad), *náam phrík phàk tôm* (chilli dip with boiled veggies) and *plaa thuu thâwt* (fried mackerel).

Mae Lek (Thanon San Khu Meuang) Open 3pm-9pm daily. Good, old-fashioned Thai-style coconut ice cream is available at this place on the traffic circle around the City Pillar (Sao Nakhon Phetchabun).

Chang Meng Phochana (☎ 056 711 326, Thanon Kasemrat, behind district governor's residence) Dishes 50-100B. Open 10am-9pm daily. This place serves reliable Chinese food, including dim sum.

Khanom Jin Lan Sao Khun Ta (Thanon Charoen Meuang, near main post office) Dishes 10-20B. Open 10am-8pm daily. Phetchabun, along with Trang in Southern Thailand, is famous throughout the country for *khanǒm jiin* (thin white rice noodles doused with curried *plaa châwn,* serpent-fish). Khanom Jin Lan Sao Khun Ta is one of the best places in town for this dish. It's in the southwestern part of town.

Along Thanon San Khu Meuang near the Siam Hotel are several good eateries.

Khao Man Kai Sukhothai (Thanon San Khu Meuang) Dishes 20-30B. Open 4pm-10pm daily. This is the best spot for Hainanese chicken rice.

Phat Thai Boran (Thanon San Khu Meuang) Dishes 15-25B. Open 10am-8pm daily. Phat Thai Boran is good for *kǔay-tǐaw phàt thai* (rice noodles stir-fried with egg, tofu and dried shrimp).

Talat Toh Rung Phetchabun (Thanon San Khu Meuang) Dishes 15-40B. Open 7pm-5am daily. Midnight eats are available at Phetchabun's night market.

Pa Luan (☎ 056 799 199, 99/1 Mu 12) Dishes 20-35B. Open 9am-midnight. Near the entrance to Si Thep Historical Park, good Thai curries can be found at Pa Luan. It is especially known for *kaeng khǐaw-wǎan* (green curry with chicken) and *kaeng khûa* (dry-fried curry).

Nearby Wichianburi is famous for kài yâang, and the most famous roadside stand of several at the three-way intersection in Wichian is *Kai Yang Ta Pae.* Dishes cost 10B to 25B, and it's open 10am to 7pm daily.

In rural areas of the province mulberry worms *(tua dàk dâe),* either fried *(thâwt)* or dry-roasted *(khua hâeng),* are considered a delicacy and are especially popular as an accompaniment to beer or whisky drinking.

Shopping

Phetchabun's most famous agricultural product is *mákhăam wăan* (sweet tamarind), and plump tamarind pods are sold in shops all over town as well as along roadsides throughout much of the province. The best tamarind is said to come from Lom Kao and Lom Sak, so roadside stands are particularly plentiful along Hwy 12, the main road leading to those districts. Expect to pay 30B to 120B per kilo, depending on the type. Most expensive is *mákhăam sĭi thawng* (golden tamarind), meant to be eaten straight from the pod as a sweet-tart snack. The pods have dry, brittle shells that are easily cracked; once you've got the shell off, separate the stringy matter surrounding the individual fruit, then suck the tamarind flesh away from the large, hard seeds inside. The cheapest tamarind is *mákhăam náam plaa dùk* (catfish sauce tamarind), meant to be used as a cooking ingredient to add a sour taste and deep red colour to various Thai dishes.

Tamarind House Handicraft Centre (Sun Hattakam Ban Mai Makham; ☎ *056 568 065, 111 Mu 2, Tambon Wang Chomphu)* Open 8am-6pm daily. Phetchabun residents also use the tamarind tree to make furniture and handicrafts. One of the best places to shop for tamarind-wood items is this handicraft centre, which can be found on Hwy 21 near the southern entrance to the capital.

Getting There & Away

From Bangkok's Northern & Northeastern bus station, ordinary buses cost 165B and leave every hour from 7.30am to 11.30pm. The journey takes around five hours. Less frequent air-con buses cost 210B.

Ordinary buses to/from Phitsanulok cost 67B and take around three hours.

NAM NAO NATIONAL PARK
อุทยานแห่งชาติน้ำหนาว

One of Thailand's most beautiful and valuable parks, Nam Nao *(Thais/foreigners 20B/200B, half price for children 14 &*

under) covers nearly 1000 sq km, at an average elevation of 800m, at the intersection of Chaiyaphum, Phetchabun and Loei Provinces. Temperatures are fairly cool year-round, especially nights and mornings; the best time to go is from November to February, when morning frost occasionally occurs.

Although the park was first opened in 1972, it remained a PLAT stronghold until the early 1980s. Marked by the sandstone hills of the Phetchabun mountain range, the park features dense, mixed evergreen and deciduous forest on mountains and hills, open dipterocarp pine-oak forest on plateaus and hills, dense bamboo mountain forest with wild banana stands in river valleys, and savannah on the plains. A fair system of trails branches out from the park headquarters; the scenic and fairly level **Phu Khu Khao Trail** cuts through pine forest and grass meadow for 24km.

Although Nam Nao is adjacent to 1560-sq-km Phu Khiaw Wildlife Sanctuary, a highway bisecting the park has unfortunately made wildlife somewhat more accessible to poachers, so many native species are in decline. There are no villages within the park boundaries, however, so incidences of poaching and illegal logging remain fairly minor. Elephants and banteng (wild cattle) are occasionally spotted, as well as Malayan sun bears, tigers, leopards, Asian jackals, barking deer, gibbons, langurs and flying squirrels. Rumours of the bizarre fur-coated Sumatran rhinoceros (last seen in 1971, but tracks were observed in 1979) persist. **Phu Khiaw Wildlife Sanctuary** itself is a sandstone mountain in Khon San district covered with thick forest that harbours crocodiles, banteng, gaurs, tigers, elephants, serows, leopards and barking deer. Three rivers are sourced at Nam Nao: the Chi, Saphung and Phrom.

The park's highest peak, **Phu Pha Jit**, reaches 1271m. For a good sunrise view of the peak, follow the signs at Km45 off Hwy 12 along a 100m trail to the top of a nearby hill. Here you can perch yourself on mushroom-shaped rocks for a sweeping view of forests and peaks; the peak on your right is

Phu Pha Jit, while the one on your left is Phu Kradeung in Loei Province.

The park also boasts several waterfalls and caves. **Tham Pha Hong** (Swan Cliff Cave) can be found off Hwy 12 near Km39. Walk 300m through a bamboo forest to reach the cave. The front chamber is small and very dark (bring a torch), but the steps lead to a much larger and more open upper level where you can view large stalactites and stalagmites. About 100m before you reach the cave, a path to the left leads to a very good sunset view. Around the cave other trails lead to extensive bamboo groves and striking limestone cliffs.

Stop at Km67 and take a 100m walk to visit **Nam Tok Hehw Sai**. Near the base of the 20m falls is a pool suitable for swimming. A fork in the same trail follows the bamboo-shaded Huay Sanam Sai to **Nam Tok Sai Thong** after 1.5km. Hornbills are sometimes sighted in this area. These falls, approximately 4m tall and 30m wide, form a solid curtain of water over a cliff during the rainy season.

A small museum in the **visitors centre** near Km50 off Hwy 12 contains a collection of confiscated guns and traps used by poachers, an ecological map and a bird list.

The Royal Forest Department (☎ 025 614 292) operates *accommodation* including 500B units that sleep up to eight people, as well as 1000B units sleeping up to 24. Two-person tents are available for rent for 40B. *Vendors* next to the visitors centre offer noodles and Thai and Isan food.

Daily buses run through Nam Nao National Park from Lom Sak (or anywhere east of there on the Khon Kaen–Chiang Mai bus route) for around 40B. From Phetchabun ordinary buses run to Nam Nao (35B, every 45 minutes 9am to 11.30am) from Phet Tour on Thanon Samakhi Chai. Look for the park office sign on Hwy 12 at Km50; the office is 2km from here.

KHAO KHO
เขาค้อ

This mountainous district, a 'tourist recreation area' rather than a national park, lies 47km northwest of the provincial capital via Rte 2258. Aside from being dotted with Thai-style resorts and vacation homes, Khao Kho supports many farms growing cool-weather fruits and vegetables as well as very good arabica coffee. At Km17.5 on Rte 2258 is **Noen Mahatsajan** (Amazing Hill), where visitors have a merry time turning off their car engines and appearing to roll backwards uphill, an obvious optical illusion.

About 8.5km beyond Noen Mahatsajan is a **farmers market** that sells locally gown fruit and vegetables between November and April each year. Here you can sit beneath a large săalaa and drink fresh-roasted arabica coffee or mulberry-leaf tea brewed in clay pots, or a glass of fresh-squeezed passion-fruit juice *(náam săowárót)* while contemplating the view.

Off this roadway on a peak called Khao Ya stands **Khao Kho Palace** *(Phra Tamnak Khao Kho;* ☎ *056 722 011; admission 20B; open 6am-6pm daily).* Built in 1985 and one of the smaller royal palaces in Thailand, the 15-room, two-story semi-circular concrete structure is fairly uninteresting but has quite a nice rose garden. Be sure to dress appropriately. Near the palace are *vendors* selling snacks and fresh locally grown coffee. From the vendor stalls you can climb about 300m to the summit of Khao Ya, 1100m above sea level. It's possible to rent a room at the *guest lodge (*☎ *056 722 011)* behind the palace.

Rte 2258 joins Rte 2196 farther on, and off the latter stands the **Phiphithaphan Awut** *(Weapons Museum; admission 10B; open 7am-5pm daily).* Outside the museum are large 105mm and 155mm cannon emplacements once used during the suppression of communist insurgency. Inside the museum are yet more weapons, large and small.

Built with funds collected locally to make merit for people who died in PLAT-RTA struggle (1968–82), the **Phra Boromathat Chedi** *(open 7am-4pm daily)* stands near the town of Khao Kho itself. The 63m, white-and-gold monument features four niches facing the cardinal directions and containing Buddha images. Inside the hollow chedi, in a shrine hall lined with marble and teak, are more Buddha images.

Phetchabun's best coffee – arabica grown at Khao Kho – can be purchased at shops in town or from stands lining both sides of the road into Khao Kho (near the viewpoint and fruit market). Dried green beans cost around 30B per kilogram, and roasted coffee already ground for filtering costs about 500B per kilogram.

Getting There & Away

Regular săwngthăew run between Phetchabun (from behind the Phetchathani cinema on Thanon Charoen Phattana/Hwy 21) and amphoe Khao Kho every 40 minutes from 7am to 4pm for 50B. However to have a good look around Khao Kho it's best to bring your own wheels or charter a săwngthăew for 700B to 800B a day.

SI THEP HISTORICAL PARK
อุทยานประวัติศาสตร์ศรีเทพ

Tucked away in the southwestern corner of the province, 107km from the capital, is the least visited of Thailand's 10 historical parks. Si Thep (☎ 056 791 787; admission 30B, vehicles extra; open 8.30am-4.30pm daily) contains ruins that for the most part show Khmer cultural origins. A few ruins from an earlier era may indicate that Si Thep was once an important culture and trade relay point between the Dvaravati culture of Mae Nam Chao Phraya valley and the Funan and early Angkor empires. Another theory claims it represented the northernmost reach of the Srivijaya Empire, which was based in Southern Thailand, Sumatra or Java, depending on which sources you believe. Ancient skeletons with decorative jewellery unearthed in recent archaeological digs suggest this may have been an inhabited site for over 2000 years.

The foundation for one very large religious structure near the centre of the old city, **Khao Klang Nai**, still bears ornamental stucco thought to date to the Dvaravati period (6th to 11th centuries) and is considered to be one of the most important existing examples of Thailand's artistic heritage. Motifs bear a strong resemblance to similar monuments in Ratchaburi, Lopburi and

Nakhon Pathom, including renderings of the dhammachakka (Buddhist wheel of law) and deer (symbolic of the Buddha's presence at the deer park of Sarnath, India). As the Dvaravati culture declined, Si Thep was probably taken over by the Khmer, who built most of the structures visible today. The latter may have added the still-visible reservoirs that held water to be used in religious rituals. At one time there were over a hundred brick or laterite monuments standing in this city, but today only a few pediments and a couple of prang remain intact.

Prang Si Thep consists of a brick Khmer-style tower sitting on a laterite base. A sandstone superstructure that once sat atop the tower has toppled. Art historians say the style of Prang Si Thep is akin to the Baphuan style (11th to 12th centuries) at Angkor.

Prang Song Phi Nong is a typical mandapa-sikhara (shrine-tower complex) consisting of two towers of unequal height. A stone slab at the entrance may indicate that an older monument was used in the construction of a newer one – possibly a Khmer adaptation of an earlier Dvaravati shrine. A lintel of Parvati (Shiva's consort, also known as Uma Mahesvara) over the doorway exhibits the Baphuan style once again. This lintel was kept at the national museum in Lopburi for 15 years before it was returned to Si Thep in 1998.

Other sculptures found on site, including life-size (or larger) statues of Vishnu considered to be among the highest sculptural achievements in Southeast Asia, are now housed at the national museum in Bangkok.

A **visitors centre** contains informative displays chronicling Si Thep's history.

Getting There & Away

Ordinary buses going to Wichianburi (40B, 1½ to two hours), the closest town to Si Thep, leave frequently from Phetchabun's Baw Khaw Saw (government) bus terminal (at the intersection of Thanon Phra Phutthabaht and Thanon Kasemrat in the southeastern quarter of town) between 5.40am and 8.30pm. From Wichianburi you can hire a săwngthăew to Si Thep for 150B to 200B. On weekends there are regular săwngthăew running between Wichianburi and Si Thep for 20B per person.

Utaradit Province

Not a big tourist destination, Utaradit Province is noted for the cultivation of langsat fruit and for Kheuan Sirikit (Sirikit Dam), an impoundment of the Mae Nam Nan 55km from the city.

UTARADIT
อ.เมืองอุตรดิตถ์

postcode 53000 • pop 164,800
Utaradit, pronounced 'oo-ta-ra-dit' and often spelt Uttaradit, means 'northern landing', a reference to its former importance as a trade centre when the Mae Nam Nan was the most convenient way to transport people and goods through Northern Thailand. It's now a major stop on the Bangkok to Chiang Mai railway.

Some time in the past the capital developed a reputation as a city of widows and virgins – perhaps because it served as a battle front during Burmese invasions. A local hero, Phraya Phichai Dap Hak, repelled a Burmese invasion in 1772.

Things to See & Do
The **Utaradit Cultural Centre**, opposite the Governor's residence, displays various historical artefacts in a lovely traditional wooden structure built during the reign of Rama V (1868–1910).

Wat Tha Thanon, opposite the Utaradit train station, houses an important brass-and-tin alloy Chiang Saen–style Buddha image sitting in full lotus position. The striking image was found in 1893 when an abbot visiting Laplae noticed the Buddha *ùtsànít* (*usnisa*, or flame crown) sticking out of a termite mound. The image was uncovered and is now kept at Wat Tha Thanon.

Six kilometres west of Utaradit near the village of Laplae is **Wat Phra Taen Sila-at**, thought to have been constructed in the Sukhothai period. It is built around a rock that is believed to resemble a Buddha foot-print. When fire destroyed the original temple in 1908, Rama V ordered its restoration. The resident monks have established a small museum containing local artefacts upstairs in a wooden building in the compound. The temple holds a festival in March.

Wat Phra Non Phutthasaiyat, on a hill across the road from Wat Phra Taen Sila-at, is reached by a dramatic naga staircase. The view from the top of the hill is good. A wíhăan contains the wát's large namesake reclining Buddha.

Wat Phra Boromathat Thung Yang, located between Utaradit and Laplae (about 3km from the town centre via Hwy 102), contains jataka murals believed to have been painted during the Ayuthaya or early Ratanakosin period. A large and very old chedi on the grounds features a hemispherical Singhalese-style stupa on a triple-level square base.

In mid-January Utaradit residents celebrate the **Phraya Phichai Daphak Festival** in honour of the warrior prince who saved the town from a Burmese invasion during the reign of Siamese Phraya Taksin. Along with food, musical entertainment and processions, the festival features *muay thai* (Thai Boxing).

On the last weekend in September, when the local langsat crop is fully ripe, the province organises a **Langsat Festival** to promote Utaradit's favourite fruit. Activities include a beauty contest, agricultural exhibitions from each district, and lots of local products and foods on sale. Nightly entertainment ranges from singing contests to traditional dance.

Places to Stay – Budget & Mid-Range
P Vanich 2 Hotel (Phaw Wanit; ☎ *055 411 499, 1 Thanon Si Utara)* Rooms with fan 140-170B, with air-con 300B. This modest but comfortable hotel stands near the river in the old section of town, within walking distance of the train station.

P Vanich 3 Hotel (☎ *055 411 559, 51 Thanon Charoenrat)* Rooms with fan 120-150B, with air-con 300B. The town's least expensive hotel has adequate rooms but little charm.

Namchai Hotel (☎ 055 411 753, 213 *Thanon Boromat*) Rooms with fan/air-con 180/350B. This is a Thai-Chinese-style hotel near the bus terminal with decent rooms.

Vivat Hotel (☎ 055 411 778, 159 *Thanon Boromat*) Rooms with fan 240-285B, with air-con from 350B. Also close to the bus terminal, this was the top place in town before the Seeharaj and Friday Hotels were built. Facilities include a coffee shop, restaurant and night club.

Reuan Ton-Sak Hotel (☎ 055 440 394, 27 *Thanon Injaimi*) Rooms with air-con & TV from 380B. Rajabhat Institute Utaradit (the government teachers college) lets rooms to nonstudents whenever there's space. On weekends it's often full with adult students attending weekend classes.

Places to Stay – Top End

Seeharaj Hotel (☎ 055 411 106, 163 *Thanon Boromat*) Rooms with air-con from 750B, including breakfast. Not far from the bus terminal, Seeharaj boasts a coffee shop, restaurant, nightclub, swimming pool, fitness facility and massage service. It's close to the Friday department store and a night market.

Friday Hotel (☎ 055 440 292, 172 *Thanon Boromat*) Rooms with air-con from 750B, including breakfast. Located above the very modern Friday department store and Sunny's Supermarket, Friday Hotel offers a restaurant, coffee shop and meeting rooms.

Places to Eat

Several *rice shops* near the Seeharaj Hotel on Thanon Boromat specialise in *khâo man kài* (Hainanese-style chicken rice). *Chanchai* and *Laplae* on Thanon Sukkasem are two of many restaurants in town that serve standard Thai and Chinese dishes.

Vegetarians can take advantage of two *Thai vegetarian restaurants* run by the Santi Asoke Buddhist sect. There is a small one on Thanon Injaimi, opposite the exit gate for the Rajabhat Institute Utaradit, and a larger restaurant south of the town-centre area near the river. The latter grows organic vegetables in the surrounding lot for use in the restaurant's many dishes.

There is a good *night market* near the train station. Look for the local speciality *khanŏm thian sawŏei* (a mixture of corn flour and sweetened coconut milk coated with sesame seeds and wrapped in a banana leaf) here, in the *morning market* and elsewhere in town. Another local specialty is *mìi pan*, a spicy mix of noodles, bean sprouts and coriander wrapped in rice paper from Laplae.

Laplae district is known for delicious *khâo thâwt* (fried wonton sheets), *nàw mái thâwt* (fried bamboo shoots) and *khâo pan phàk* (steamed vegetables wrapped in a very thin rice flour crepe). You'll find these and more at *Laplae Restaurant* on Thanon Sukkasem in Utaradit.

The *Fern Restaurant*, just north of Laplae and set in a beautiful garden, offers an extensive menu and excellent service.

The restaurants in the *Friday* and *Seeharaj* Hotels serve a variety of Thai, Chinese and Western dishes in air-con comfort.

Shopping

Good buys include local textiles from nearby Laplae. A favourite is the flowing water design *(laai náam lăi)* showing stepped patterns representing streaming rivers and waterfalls. Good-quality textiles can be purchased at the *Sunarin Shop* (*Thanon Injaimi*) across from the exit gate of Rajabhat Institute Utaradit, and at several small shops in Laplae. The most traditional way to purchase such fabrics is in the form of *sîn tiin jòk*, a long women's sarong of a certain weft.

Rustic brooms made from *tawng kong*, a kind of grass, also hail from nearby Laplae and are a popular purchase for Thais visiting Utaradit.

The *morning market* is near the river within easy walking distance of the Utaradit train station.

Getting There & Away

Bus From the Utaradit bus terminal on Thanon Boromat, there are many government and private buses leaving for all destinations in the north, plus Bangkok. It takes about six hours to reach Chiang Mai (180/300B ordinary/air-con) and about eight hours to get to Bangkok (260B to 420B).

Train All Chiang Mai–bound trains stop in Utaradit. Few visitors board in Bangkok with Utaradit as their travel objective, but if you're one of those few, the Rapid No 109 has the best departure (10pm) and arrival (6.06am) times. Fares are 82/190/394B for 3rd/2nd/1st class, not including surcharges for rapid service, air-con or sleeping arrangements.

Faster is the Special Express No 9, which leaves Hualamphong station at 8.40am and arrives in Utaradit at 2.45pm. If you're heading back to Bangkok from Utaradit, all 11 daily departures are reasonably scheduled; again the fastest is the Special Express No 10, departing at 12.04am and arriving at 6.15am.

Utaradit may also be reached by train from either Phitsanulok (about two hours) or Chiang Mai (about six hours).

Getting Around

Car taxis – mostly old beaten-up Toyotas – park and wait at both the train station and bus terminal, as well as near the morning market near the Utaradit post office. You can sometimes flag down a taxi, but expect to share the car with other passengers. A taxi anywhere in town usually costs around 40B or 50B. There are a few sǎamláw in Utaradit and the cost will depend on your destination.

A white city bus goes by both the train and bus terminals. It's air-conditioned and costs 6B.

AROUND UTARADIT
Laplae
ลับแล

This district around 6km west of Utaradit is renowned for its natural beauty, lovely old wooden houses, hand-woven textiles and tawng kong brooms. You can see and purchase weaving at a women's cooperative on the main road through Laplae just south of the market area. Laplae and environs are also known for the cultivation of high-quality durian and langsat. Look for *khâo krìap* (thin discs of rice paper often embedded with chillies and black sesame seeds) drying on layers of thatch.

Nam Tok Mae Phun
น้ำตกแม่พูล

The multilevel waterfall, 12km north of Laplae off Rte 1043, is part of a pleasant park where local families picnic on weekends and holidays. There's a nice view from the small temple at the top of the falls.

Kheuan Sirikit
เขื่อนสิริกิติ์

Kheuan Sirikit (Sirikit Dam) is in Tha Pla district, 60km northeast of the capital via Rte 1045. The largest earth-filled dam in Thailand, it impounds the Mae Nam Nan to create a huge reservoir called Thaleh Sap Suriyanchantha. Boats are available for rent, and you can spend the night in a 50-room *row house* for 600/1200B for a double with fan/air-con. For reservations call the Electricity Generating Authority of Thailand (EGAT; ☎ 024 363 179) in Bangkok.

Ban Nam Phi
บ้านน้ำพี้

Iron ore from this district, 56km east of the capital via Rte 1245, is used to forge *dàap* and *krà-bìi*, traditional Thai swords. Several mines in the district produce exceptionally strong iron; the best of them, Bo Phra Khan, can only be used to make swords for the king. It is said that you can hear the ring of iron being hammered at nearly every house in the village of Ban Nam Phi.

Uthayan Ton Sak Yai
อุทยานต้นสักใหญ่

Teak was once a major local product in Utaradit. The largest teak tree in the world is found at Uthayan Ton Sak Yai (Big Teak Tree Park) in Ban Bang Kleua, 92km northeast of the provincial capital. Measuring 9.87m in circumference, the 1500-year-old tree is still alive despite damage from a storm that reduced its height from 48.5m to 37m. Park protection of the teak forest assures that all or at least most of the trees will live to a ripe old age.

Western Provinces

Tak and Mae Hong Son together make up one of Thailand's least populous regions. During much of early Thai history they were of course even less populated, and covered with vast teak forests that later became the currency upon which burgeoning Northern Thai cities such as Chiang Mai and Lampang built their economies.

Until around 30 years ago, all three were classified by the Thai government as 'remote' provinces, ie, provinces over which the central Bangkok government had little control. The 1968–82 communist insurgency movement thrived here and found willing recruits among disaffected Northern Thai villagers and hill tribes.

For Mae Hong Son and Tak the sense of separateness was compounded by their shared borders with Myanmar and even today there is much interchange, legal and illegal, between peoples on both sides of the border.

For visitors, these provinces offer many opportunities to get off the beaten tourist track and in touch with a multitude of minority cultures, as well as enjoy relatively pristine mountains, rivers and forests.

Tak Province

In the 1970s the mountains of western Tak were a hotbed of communist guerrilla activity. Since the 1980s the former leader of the local Communist Party of Thailand (CPT) movement has been involved in resort-hotel development and Tak is very much open to outsiders, but the area still has an untamed feeling about it. The entire province has a population of only around 471,600 people, but boasts Thailand's largest population of domesticated elephants, which are still commonly used by Karen villagers for transport and agricultural tasks.

Tak has always presented a distinct contrast with other parts of Thailand because of strong Karen and Burmese cultural influences. The Thailand-Myanmar border districts of Mae Ramat, Tha Song Yang and Mae Sot are dotted with refugee camps, an outcome of the firefights between the Karen National Union (KNU) and the Myanmar government, which have driven Karen civilians across the border. Most recent estimates indicate there are around 10,000 Burmese and Karen refugees along the border.

The main source of income for people living on both sides of the border is legal and illegal international trade. The main smuggling gateways on the Thailand side are Tha Song Yang, Mae Sarit, Mae Tan, Wangkha, Mae Sot and Waley. One important contraband product is teak, cut by the Karen or the Karenni (Kayah) and brought into Thailand from Myanmar on big tractor trailers at night. None of the trade is legal since the Thai government cut off all timber deals with the Burmese military in 1997.

Most of the province is forested and mountainous and is excellent for trekking. Organised trekking occurs, some farther north out of Chiang Mai, most of it locally organised. There are Hmong, Musoe (Lahu), Lisu and White and Red Karen settlements throughout the west and north.

TAK

อ.เมืองตาก

postcode 63000 • pop 49,200
Lying along the eastern bank of Mae Nam Ping (Ping River), Tak's provincial capital of the same name is not particularly interesting except as a point from which to visit the Lan Sang and Taksin Maharat National Parks to the west and Kheuan Phumiphon to the north. Travellers heading to the Thailand-Myanmar border town of Mae Sot occasionally find themselves here for a few hours or overnight.

Information

The Tourism Authority of Thailand (TAT; ☎ 055 514 341) has an office in a beautiful

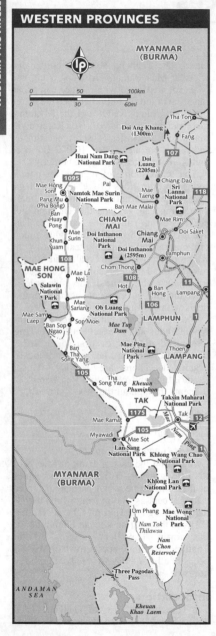

WESTERN PROVINCES

MYANMAR
(BURMA)

contemporary Thai building at 193 Thanon
Taksin, where you can ask questions or pick
up tourist pamphlets and brochures. The
hours are 8.30am to 4.30pm daily.

Several banks have branches along
Thanon Mahat Thai Bamrung and Thanon
Taksin, all with ATMs.

Things to See & Do

Although most of Tak exhibits nondescript,
cement-block architecture, the southern section of the city harbours a few **old teak
homes**. Residents are proud of the **suspension bridge** (for motorcycles, pedicabs, bicycles and pedestrians only) over Mae Nam
Ping, which flows quite broadly here even in
the dry season. There's also a larger highway
bridge (Saphan Kittikachon) over the river.

Places to Stay

Most of Tak's hotels are lined up along
Thanon Taksin and Thanon Mahat Thai
Bamrung in the town centre.

*Mae Ping Hotel (☎ 055 511 807, 619
Thanon Taksin)* Rooms with fan/air-con
110/250B. The slightly worn but atmospheric Mae Ping offers large clean rooms
with private shower and toilet in an old
wooden building. It's surprisingly quiet considering its location opposite the market.

*Sa-Nguan Thai Hotel (no Roman-script
sign; ☎ 055 511 155, Thanon Mahat Thai
Bamrung)* Singles/doubles with fan 170/
200B, with air-con 300/350B. This classic,
wooden two-storey place can be identified
by the red Chinese lanterns on the 2nd-floor
veranda. There's a decent Chinese-Thai
restaurant downstairs.

*Viang Tak 2 Hotel (☎ 055 511 910, 236
Thanon Chomphon)* Standard rooms 650B,
deluxe rooms 800-900B. Along Mae Nam
Tak, the eight-storey Viang Tak 2 features
comfortable air-con rooms along with a coffee shop, karaoke bar and swimming pool.

*Viang Tak Hotel (☎ 055 511 950, 25/3
Thanon Mahat Thai Bamrung)* Standard
rooms 650B, deluxe rooms 800-900B. The
Viang Tak 2's older sibling features 100 recently renovated rooms.

*Racha Villa (☎ 055 512 361, 307/1
Thanon Phahonyothin)* Rooms with fan/

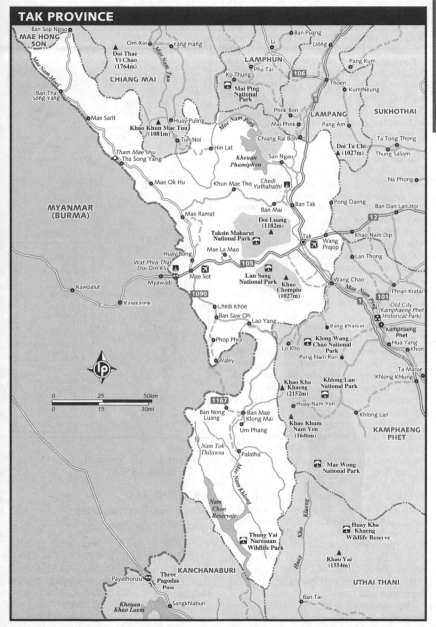

TAK PROVINCE

Ban Sop Ngao
MAE HONG
SON
Ban Puang
Om Koi
Yang Piang
Li
Dong
Pang Kum
Doi Thae
Yi Chao
(1764m)
LAMPHUN
Kum Neung
Ko Thung
Pha Tai
106
Thoen
CHIANG MAI
Mai Ping
National
Park
1
Huay Puling
Phrik Bon
LAMPANG
SUKHOTHAI
Khao Khun Mae Tun
(1081m)
Mai Phrik
Pang Am
Ta Tong Thong
Mae Sarit
Tun Noi
Mae Nam Ping
Chiang Rai Bon
Doi Ta Chi
(1027m)
Thung Saliam
Hin Lat
Tham Mae'Usu
Tha Song Yang
Kheuan
Phumiphon
Na Phong
Ban Tha
Song Yang
San Ngao
Mae Ok Hu
Chedi
Yuthahathi
Khun Mae Tho
Ban Tak
Pong Daeng
Ban Dan Lan Hoi
MYANMAR
(BURMA)
Mae Ramat
Ban Mai
12
Doi Luang
(1182m)
Tak
Khao Nam Dip
Taksin Maharat
National Park
Wang
Prajop
Huay Bong
Mae La Mao
Lan Thong
Wat Phra That
Doi Din Klu
105
Lan Sang
National Park
Wang Chao
Mae Nam Ping
Phran Kratai
Kawpalut
Myawadi
Mae Sot
Khao
Chomplu
(1027m)
101
Old City
(Kamphaeng Phet
Historical Park)
Kawkareik
1090
Chedi Khoe
Kamphaeng
Phet
Hua Yang
Khon
Ban Saw Oh
Lao Yang
Klong Wang
Chao National
Park
Phop Phra
Lo Kho
Pang Khanun
Ta Marue
Khlong Khlung
Pong Nam Ron
Waley
Khao Kha
Khaeng
(2152m)
Khlong Lan
National Park
1167
Huay Nam Yen
Khlong Lan
Ban Nong
Luang
Ban Mae
Klong Mai
Khao Khum
Nam Yen
(1646m)
KAMPHAENG
PHET
Um Phang
Nam Tok
Thilawsu
Palatha
Mae Wong
National Park
Nam
Chon
Reservoir
Kha
Khaeng
Huay Kha
Khaeng
Wildlife Reserve
Huay
Kha
Kha
Khaeng
Khao Yai
(1554m)
Thung Yai
Naresuan
Wildlife Park
KANCHANABURI
UTHAI THANI
Three
Pagodas
Pass
Payathonzu
Ban Tai
Kheuan
Khao Laem
Sangkhlaburi

0   25   50km
0   15   30mi

air-con 230/320B. Near the intersection of Rte 105 and Hwy 1, the rooms here are fairly well-appointed and come with carpet, TV, video and hot water.

Panasan Hotel (☎ *055 511 436, Off Thanon Phahonyothin*) Bungalows with private bathroom and fan 110-160B, with air-con 250B. Near the intersection of Hwys 1 and 12, the Panasan's bungalows are basic but clean; it's a good value, if a little removed from the town centre.

Places to Eat

Pond (*Thanon Taksin*) Dishes 15-30B. Open 8am-3pm daily. This simple place near the market specialises in Thai curries.

Cheap food can be bought in the *municipal market* (*Thanon Taksin*), across the street from the Mae Ping Hotel; dishes cost 10B to 30B, and it's open 6am to 6pm daily.

On the southeastern corner of Thanon Taksin and Thanon Charot Withi Thong you'll find a *vegetarian restaurant* (*no Roman-script sign*), open 8am to 4pm daily, with dishes for 10B to 30B.

Getting There & Away

Tak airport, 15km out of town towards Sukhothai on Hwy 12, isn't operating at the moment; the nearest functioning airports are in Phitsanulok and Mae Sot. THAI provides a free shuttle van a few times a day between Phitsanulok airport and Tak. In Tak the vans stop at the Viang Tak 2 Hotel.

There are frequent buses to Tak from Sukhothai (48B ordinary, 1½ hours). The Tak bus station is just outside town, but a túk-túk will take you to the town centre for around 20B.

Ordinary government buses depart for Bangkok three times daily (151B, 10 hours), while a 2nd-class air-con bus leaves once each day (184B, eight hours). There are four daily 1st-class air-con departures from Tak to Bangkok and one 10pm departure in the reverse direction (240B, six hours). Thanjit Tour and Choet Chai Tour offer 1st-class air-con buses with similar departures and fares.

Ordinary buses to Mae Sot (50B) leave at 2pm, 4pm and 5pm. Minivans to Mae Sot

TAK

0   50   100m
0   50   100yd
Approximate Scale

1   TAT Office
2   King Maha Taksin Shrine
3   Wat Botmani Sibunruang
4   Vegetarian Restaurant
5   Provincial Hall
6   Bus Station
7   Police Station
8   Thanjit Tour
9   Siam Commercial Bank
10 Viang Tak Hotel
11 Thai Military Bank
12 Sa-Nguan Thai Hotel
13 Bangkok Bank
14 Pond
15 Municipal Market
16 Mae Ping Hotel
17 Wat Mani Banphot
18 Taksin Hospital
19 Viang Tak 2 Hotel
20 Fire Station
21 Wat Sitalaram

leave much more frequently from the main station in Tak (35B).

AROUND TAK
Wat Phra Boromathat
วัดพระบรมธาตุ

In Ban Tak, 25km upstream along Mae Nam Tak from Tak, you can visit Wat Phra Boromathat, the original site of a Thai chedi that, according to legend, was constructed during the reign of Phaya Ram Khamhaeng (1275–1317) to celebrate his elephant-back victory over King Sam Chon, ruler of an

Across the Mekong from Chiang Rai Province

Hunter in Chiang Rai Province

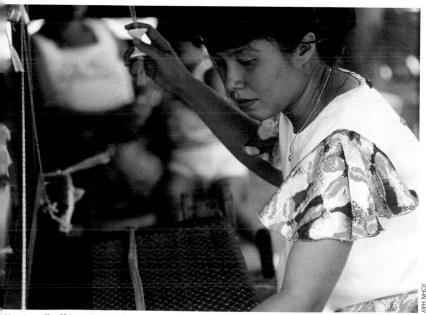
Weaving silk, Chiang Rai Province

Threshing the rice harvest, Chiang Rai Province

Chiang Rai man in ceremonial headgear

Akha woman, Chiang Rai Province

Novice monk admiring the view, Nan Province

independent kingdom once based at or near Mae Sot. The wát's main feature is a large, slender, gilded chedi in the Shan style surrounded by numerous smaller but similar chedi. Many Thais flock to the temple each week in the belief that the chedi can somehow reveal to them the winning lottery numbers for the week.

Taksin Maharat & Lan Sang National Parks

อุทยานแห่งชาติตากสิน มหาราชและลานสาง

These small national parks receive a steady trickle of visitors on weekends and holidays, but are almost empty during the week. Established in 1981, Taksin Maharat *(Thais/foreigners 20/200B, children half-price)* covers 149 sq km; the entrance is 2km from the Km26 marker on Rte 105/Asia Rte 1 (the so-called Pan-Asian Hwy, which would link Istanbul and Singapore if all the intervening countries allowed land crossings) to Mae Sot.

The park's most outstanding features are the 30m, nine-tiered **Nam Tok Mae Ya Pa** (Mae Ya Pa Falls) and a record-holding *tà-bàak*, a dipterocarp that is 50m tall and 16m in circumference. **Bird-watching** is said to be particularly good here; known resident and migratory species include the tiger shrike, forest wagtail and Chinese pond heron.

Nineteen kilometres from Tak, Lan Sang National Park *(Thais/foreigners 20/200B, children half-price)* preserves 104 sq km of rugged, 1000m-high granite peaks, part of the Tenasserim Range. A network of trails leads to several **waterfalls**, including the park's 40m-high namesake. To reach the park entrance, take Rte 1103 3km south off Rte 105.

Places to Stay Lan Sang National Park rents *bungalows* (150B to 600B), and also *tents* (30B). Taksin Maharat National Park offers rustic *rooms* (250B each), and has a *camp ground* (10B to pitch your own tent). *Food service* can be arranged in both parks.

Prospective overnighters can call the reservations number (☎ 025 614 292) in Bangkok, but you can usually arrange accommodation on the spot without any trouble.

Kheuan Phumiphon

เขื่อนภูมิพล

Approximately 45km north of Meuang Tak via Rte 1 and then 17km west (between the Km463 and Km464 markers) via the road to Sam Ngao, is Kheuan Phumiphon (Bhumibol Dam), which impounds Mae Nam Ping at a height of 154m, making it the tallest dam in Southeast Asia and the eighth-tallest in the world. The **shores** and **islands** of the reservoir are a favourite canoeing, swimming, fishing and picnicking destination for Tak residents.

Places to Stay For the use of visitors, the Electrical Generating Authority of Thailand (EGAT) maintains several *bungalows and longhouses (reservations & information: EGAT in Bangkok ☎ 024 363 179, Kheuan Phumiphon Visitors House ☎ 055 549 509).* Multibed units cost 400B to 1000B.

Ban Tak Youth Hostel (☎/fax 055 591 286, 9/1 Mu 10) Beds 120B. Between the provincial capital and the reservoir, in Ban Tak (on the western side of the village adjacent to Mae Nam Yom), is Thailand's smallest and most remote hostel. It offers a few rooms in a house with a large garden and a view of the mountains. The hostel can accept only eight visitors at a time. Bikes are available for hire.

MAE SOT

แม่สอด

postcode 63110 • pop 40,000

Eighty kilometres from Tak on Rte 105, this Burmese-Chinese-Karen-Thai trading outpost has become a small but simmering tourist destination. A decade or so ago, several public billboards in town carried the warning (in Thai): 'Have fun, but if you carry a gun, you go to jail' – underscoring Mae Sot's reputation as a free-swinging, profiteering wild-East town. The billboards are long gone but the outlaw image lingers. Black-market trade between Myanmar and Thailand is the primary source of local revenue, with most transactions taking place in the districts of Mae Ramat, Tha Song Yang, Phop Phra and Um Phang. Mae Sot has also become the most important jade and gem centre along the border, with most of the trade controlled by Chinese and Indian immigrants from Myanmar.

Border skirmishes between Myanmar's central government and the weakening Karen and Kayah ethnic insurgencies can break out at any time, sending thousands of refugees – and the occasional mortar rocket – across the Thai-Myanmar border, elements that add to the area's perceived instability.

Walking down the streets of Mae Sot, you'll see an interesting mixture of ethnicities – Burmese men in their *longyi* (sarongs), Hmong and Karen women in traditional hill-tribe dress, bearded Indo-Burmese men and Thai army rangers.

Shop signs along the streets are in Thai, Burmese and Chinese. Most of the temple architecture in Mae Sot is Burmese. The town's Burmese population is largely Muslim, and the Karen mostly Christian, while those living outside town are Buddhist.

The Thai-Myanmar Friendship Bridge was completed in 1996, linking Mae Sot with Myawadi and the highway west to Mawlamyaing (Moulmein) and Yangon, an exciting prospect for overland travel. At the moment foreigners can go no farther than Myawadi, although there are rumours that the route to Hpa-an and Mawlamyaing will soon open.

Information
Tourist Police The tourist police (☎ 055 533 523, 055 534 341) have an office 100m east-northeast of No 4 Guest House.

Money Thai Military Bank, Siam Commercial Bank and Krung Thai Bank offer ATM services in the centre of town.

Email & Internet Access You can check your email at Cyber Space on the southern side of Thanon Prasat Withi, near the THAI office. It's open 10am to 10pm.

Books & Maps DK Book House is attached to the DK Hotel on Thanon Intharakhiri. The only English-language books it stocks so far are Penguin classics, but there are a few maps of the area for sale, including a detailed Thai military-surveyed topographic map (1:250,000) of the border area, entitled *Moulmein*. This map covers as far north as Mae Ramat, to the south almost to Um Phang, west to Mawlamyaing and only about 50km east of Mae Sot.

Herbal Sauna
ห้องอบสมุนไพร

At Wat Mani men can take a herbal sauna *(20B; open 3pm-7pm)*. The sauna volunteers also sell herbal medicines made by the monks. The sauna is towards the back of the monastery grounds, past·the monks' *kùtì* (monastic residences).

Ban Mae Tao
บ้านแม่เฒ่า

Wat Wattanaram (Phattanaram) is a Burmese temple at Ban Mae Tao, 3km west of Mae Sot on the road to the Thailand-Myanmar border. A large alabaster Buddha sits in a shrine with glass-tile walls – it's very Burmese in style. In the main *wíhǎan* (hall) on the 2nd floor is a collection of Burmese musical instruments, including tuned drums and gongs.

Wat Phra That Doi Din Kiu (Ji)
วัดพระธาตุดอยดินกิว(จี)

Wat Phra That Doi Din Kiu (Ji) is a forest temple 11km northwest of Mae Sot on a 300m-high hill overlooking Mae Nam Moei and Myanmar. A small chedi mounted on what looks like a boulder that has been balanced on the edge of a cliff is one of the attractions, and is reminiscent of the Kyaiktiyo Paya in Myanmar.

The trail that winds up the hill provides fairly good views of the thick teak forests

MAE SOT

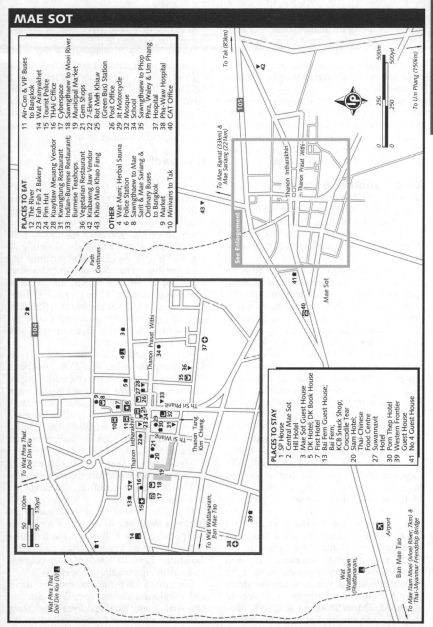

PLACES TO EAT
12 The River
23 Fah Fah 2 Bakery
24 Pim Hut
28 Kuaytiaw Meuang Vendor
31 Kwangtung Restaurant
33 Indian-Burmese Restaurant; Burmese Teashops
36 Vegetarian Restaurant
42 Krabawng Jaw Vendor
43 Khao Mao Khao Fang

OTHER
4 Wat Mani; Herbal Sauna
6 Police Station
8 Sawngthaew to Mae Sarit & Mae Sariang & Ordinary Buses to Bangkok
9 Market
10 Minivans to Tak
11 Air-Con & VIP Buses to Bangkok
14 Wat Aranyakhet
15 Tourist Police
16 THAI Office
17 Cyberspace
18 Sawngthaew to Moei River
19 Municipal Market
21 Gem Shops
22 7-Eleven
25 Rot Meh Khiaw (Green Bus) Station
26 Post Office
29 Jit Motorcycle
32 Mosque
34 School
35 Sawngthaew to Phop Phra, Waley & Um Phang
37 Hospital
38 Pha-Waw Hospital
40 CAT Office

PLACES TO STAY
1 SP House
2 Central Mae Sot Hill Hotel
3 Mae Sot Guest House
5 DK Hotel; DK Book House
7 First Hotel
13 Bai Fern Guest House; Bai Fern; KCB Snack Shop; Crocodile Tear
20 Siam Hotel; Thai-Chinese Food Centre
27 Suwannavit Hotel
30 Porn Thep Hotel
39 Western Frontier Guest House
41 No 4 Guest House

across the river in Myanmar. On the Thai side a scattering of smaller trees is visible. There are a couple of small limestone caves in the side of the hill on the way to the peak. The dirt road that leads to the wát from Ban Mae Tao passes through a couple of **Karen villages**.

During Myanmar's dry-season offensives against the KNU, this area is sometimes considered unsafe and the road to the temple is occasionally blocked by Thai rangers. Ask in town about the current situation before heading up the road.

Border Market & Border Crossings (Myanmar)

Săwngthăew (10B) frequently go to the border, 7km west of Mae Sot: Ask for Rim Moei (Edge of the Moei). The last săwngthăew back to Mae Sot leaves Rim Moei at 5pm.

A market about 100m from the river on the Thai side sells Burmese goods – dried fish and shrimp, dried bamboo shoots, mung beans, peanuts, woven-straw products, teak carvings, thick cotton blankets, lacquerware, tapestries, jade and gems. Dried and preserved foods are sold by the *pan* (pound), the Burmese/Karen unit of weight measurement, rather than by the kilogram (the usual measure in Thailand). You can also buy black-market kyat (Burmese currency) here at very favourable rates.

Since 1999 the border has been officially open to foreigners and you can cross the bridge to Myawadi for day visits. Travel isn't yet permitted beyond Myawadi. The prospect of the road all the way from Myawadi to Mawlamyaing on the Gulf of Mottama (Martaban) opening is probably still a couple of years away.

If your Thai visa is about to expire, you can cross the border here, turn around, and walk back into Thailand for an instant 30-day visa. Immigration procedures are taken care of at the Thai immigration booth at the bridge, although if you have any problems there's a larger immigration office in nearby Mae Moei Shopping Bazaar. It takes about 15 minutes to finish all the paper-

work to leave Thailand officially, and then you're free to walk across the arched bridge (open 6am to 6pm daily).

At the other end of the bridge is a rustic Myanmar immigration booth where you'll fill out permits for a one-day stay, pay a US$10 fee and leave your passports as a deposit. Then you're free to wander around Myawadi as long as you're back at the bridge by 5pm to pick up your passport and check out with immigration.

Myawadi

เมียวะดี

Myawadi is a fairly typical Burmese town with a number of monasteries, schools, shops and so on. The most important temple is **Shwe Muay Wan**, a traditional bell-shaped stupa gilded with many kilos of gold leaf and topped by over 1600 precious and semiprecious gems. Surrounding the main stupa are 28 smaller stupas, and these in turn are encircled by 12 larger ones. Colourful shrines to Mahamuni Buddha, Shin Upagot and other Buddhist deities follow the typical Mon and central-Burman style, with lots of mirrored mosaics.

Another noted Buddhist temple is **Myikyaungon**, called Wat Don Jarakhe in Thai and named for its crocodile-shaped sanctuary. A hollow stupa at Myikyaungon contains four marble Mandalay-style Buddhas around a central pillar, while niches in the surrounding wall are filled with Buddha figures in other styles, including several bronze Sukhothai-style Buddhas.

Myawadi's 1000-year-old earthen city walls, probably erected by the area's original Mon inhabitants, can be seen along the southern side of town.

If you're looking for a good traditional Burmese meal, one of the best places is the inexpensive *Daw Y Bon*, on the left-hand side of the main street leading away from the bridge. Look for a row of curry pots and an English sign reading 'Tea House'.

Because of long-time commercial, social and religious links between Mae Sot and Myawadi, many local residents speak some Thai. *The Riverside Club*, a casino on the river about 1km north of town, serves a mostly Thai clientele.

Special Events
Mae Sot hosts a large **Thai-Burmese gem fair** in April, when gem dealers from near and far gather to haggle over rubies, sapphires, jade and other stones.

Around this same time Thai and Burmese boxers meet for a **muay thai competition** held somewhere outside town in the traditional style. Although such Thai-Burmese match-ups occur in or around Mae Sot at other times of year, the much-advertised April bouts draw the best fighters from both sides of the border, and spectators pour in from as far away as Bangkok and Yangon. Up to 16 matches are fought in circular rings under temporary pavilions. Each match goes for five rounds. The first four rounds last three minutes; the fifth has no time limit. Hands bound in hemp, the boxers fight till surrender or knockout. You'll have to ask around to find the changing venue for the annual slug fest, as it's not exactly legal.

Organised Tours
SP House, Mae Sot Guest House and Western Frontier Guest House (see Places to Stay following) can arrange trekking and rafting trips north and south of Mae Sot.

Places to Stay – Budget
Guesthouses *Mae Sot Guest House* (☎ *055 532 745, Thanon Intharakhiri*) Singles/doubles with fan & shared bathroom 80/120B, with air-con & private bathroom 280B. The cheaper but not-so-great rooms here have shared facilities, the nicer air-con rooms (with cold-water showers) are in a row house. The guesthouse's best features are the pleasant open-air sitting area at the front and the fact that it's only a 10-minute walk to the bus station. Local maps and information are available and the owner speaks English well.

Bai Fern Guest House (☎ *055 533 343, 660/2 Thanon Intharakhiri*) Singles/doubles with shared hot-water bathroom 100/150B. Near Crocodile Tear (see Places

to Eat in this section), this guesthouse offers basic rooms in a rambling Thai house.

No 4 Guest House (☎/fax *055 544 976, 736 Thanon Intharakhiri*) Dorm beds/singles/doubles 50/80/100B. Farther west along Intharakhiri, the simple but well-run No 4 offers rooms in a large teak house well off the road. Hot-water facilities are shared.

Western Frontier Guest House (☎ *055 532 638, 18/2 Thanon Bua Khun*) Rooms 100B. In the southern part of town, near Pha-Waw Hospital, this guesthouse features six rooms in a two-storey brick-and-wood house. The staff boasts language skills in English, Japanese, Thai, Karen and Burmese and can arrange local trekking and rafting trips. Rental bikes are also available.

SP House (☎ *055 531 409, 14/21 Thanon Asia*) Rooms 50B per person. On the northwestern outskirts of town, this place has adequate wooden rooms. Although it's a bit far from the centre of town, good travel information is available. The staff can arrange various treks around the province.

Hotels *Suwannavit Hotel* (☎ *055 531 162, Soi Wat Luang*) Rooms with fan & private bathroom 100-120B. The cheaper rooms in this hotel are in the old wooden wing, while the others are found in the newer concrete one.

Siam Hotel (☎ *055 531 376, fax 055 531 974, 185 Thanon Prasat Withi*) Rooms with fan/air-con 200/350B, with fan & TV 250B, with air-con, carpet & TV 500B. The Siam has adequate rooms, all with private bathroom. Although it's basically a truckers' and gem-traders' hotel, local rumour has it that Myanmar intelligence agents hang out at the Siam.

Places to Stay – Mid-Range & Top End
Porn Thep Hotel (☎ *055 532 590, 25/4 Thanon Si Wiang*) Rooms with fan & cold-water bathroom 250B, with air-con & hot-water bathroom 400B, deluxe rooms with air-con, TV & hot-water bathroom 700B. Off Thanon Prasat near the day market, the clean and efficiently run Porn Thep features regular rooms in the rear wing of the hotel,

and a few deluxe rooms in the newer front wing. Secure parking is available.

First Hotel (☎ 055 531 233, fax 055 531 340, 444 Thanon Intharakhiri) Rooms with private bathroom & fan/air-con from 250/350B. This hotel near the police station has rooms that are large and comfortable; all come with TV. Like the Siam, it's favoured by Thai truckers. The hotel is still undergoing renovations, so prices may change.

DK Hotel (☎ 055 531 699, 298/2 Thanon Intharakhiri) Rooms with fan 250B, with air-con 450-800B. Attached to DK Book House, the three-storey DK Hotel offers smallish apartment-style rooms with fan, and larger rooms with air-con. All come with private hot-water bathroom. The rooms tend to vary a lot in quality, so it might be best to look at a few before checking in.

Central Mae Sot Hill Hotel (☎ 055 532 601/8, fax 055 532 600, 100 Thanon Asia; in Bangkok ☎ 025 411 234) Standard rooms 900B, suites from 1200B. This hotel is the most upmarket place in town; it's on the highway to Tak, just outside the town centre. It has a swimming pool, tennis courts, a good restaurant, a disco, a cocktail lounge and a shuttle bus into town. All rooms come with air-con, hot water, fridge, TV, video and telephone.

Places to Eat

Mae Sot has an unusually good selection of places to eat.

Thai-Chinese food centre Dishes 20-40B. Open 8am-4pm daily. Near the Siam Hotel on Thanon Prasat Withi are several choices, including this adjacent food centre. It's fairly rustic and holds several different vendors serving noodles and curry. You can also try the rambling *market* behind the Siam Hotel for cheap Thai takeaway; dishes cost 10B to 20B and it's open 5am to 6pm daily.

Indian-Burmese restaurant Dishes 10-30B. Open 8am-8pm daily. Opposite the mosque, this place (the sign reads 'Tea Shop') has good *rotii kaeng* (Indian-style flatbread with curry), fresh milk, curries and *khâo sawy* (Chinese noodles).

Burmese Muslim teashop Open 8am-7pm daily. On the same side of the street as the Indian-Burmese restaurant, about 50m south, this place does cheap and tasty samosas, curries and naan. A meal of curry, dhal, vegetables, two naan, two plates of rice, two teas and two coffees costs only 70B.

A favourite local snack is *krabawng jaw* (Burmese for 'fried crispy'), a sort of vegetable tempura. The best place to eat it is at the small *vendor stand* 1km east of Mae Sot Guest House on the southern side of Thanon Intharakhiri, where the same family has been supplying Mae Sot residents with 'fried crispy' for many years. You can sit at a small table near the wok and order fresh chunks of squash, pumpkin or papaya fried in egg batter and dipped in a delicious sauce of peanuts, tamarind, molasses and dried chilli. If you don't want to eat it here they'll wrap for takeaway in two portion sizes, costing 5B or 10B. The family fires up the wok around 4.30pm and keeps cooking until 8pm or until they've run out of ingredients.

Another local specialty is *kǔaytǐaw meuang,* a rich bowl of rice noodles covered with sliced pork, greens, peanuts, chilli and green beans very similar to *kǔaytǐaw sùkhǒthai.* Look for *rice-noodle vendors* along Thanon Prasat Withi; the best place is the vendor on the western side of Soi Sapphakan, running north off Thanon Prasat Withi. Dishes cost 20B to 25B, and the hours are erratic.

Kwangtung Restaurant (no English sign) Dishes 30-90B. Open 10am-10pm daily. This is the best Chinese restaurant in town. The kitchen here specialises in Cantonese cooking, but it's a cut above the average. It's around the corner from the Porn Thep Hotel, south of Thanon Prasat Withi.

There are a few *faràng* (Western) restaurants along Thanon Tang Kim Chiang and Thanon Intharakhiri.

Pim Hut (☎ 055 532 818, 415/11-12 Thanon Tang Kim Chiang) Dishes 40-120B. Open 7.30am-8pm daily. The menu here offers decent pizza, steak, Thai and Chinese dishes, ice cream and international breakfasts at moderate prices.

Fah Fah 2 Bakery (☎ *055 532 569, 417/6-7 Thanon Tang Kim Chiang*) Open 7.30am-9pm daily. This brightly lit place has a similar but slightly less expensive menu than the Pim Hut. Like the Pim Hut, the bakery caters to tourists, foreign volunteer workers (working at from nearby refugee camps) and upper-middle-class Thais.

The River (☎ *055 534 593, 626 Thanon Intharakhiri*) Dishes 35-100B. Open 6am-9pm Mon-Sat. This is a cosy place in an old wooden building serving good freshly ground coffee, excellent banana pancakes, Thai and vegetarian dishes, ice cream, fruit shakes and beer. It's also a good place to pick up a map and some information about the area.

Crocodile Tear Dishes 40-80B. Open 11am-midnight daily. The next place west from The River is the Crocodile Tear, serving Thai food but really more of a bar scene, with live Thai and Western music. A bit farther west past Soi Ruam Jai is the friendly *KCB Snack Shop*, and finally, *Bui Fern*, next to the guesthouse of the same name, both open 8am to 9pm daily, and both with the usual mix of Thai and faràng dishes (35B to75B).

A small, *no-name vegetarian restaurant* next to the Um Phang săwngthăew stop offers good, inexpensive Thai vegetarian food (10B to 20B) from around 7am to 7pm, or until the food is sold out.

Khao Mao Khao Fang (☎ *055 533 607, 382 Mu 5, Mae Pa*) Dishes 40-70B. Open 10am-10pm daily. If you're looking for an atmospheric evening out, try this place a little north of town between the Km1 and Km2 markers on the road to Mae Ramat. A Thai botanist designed the open-air restaurant to make it feel as if you're dining in the forest, with lots of common and not-so-common live plants from around Northern Thailand. The Thai cuisine is equally inventive, with such specialities as *yam hèt khon* (spicy salad made with forest mushrooms available in September and October only) and *mŭu khâo mâo* (salad of home-cured sausage, peanuts, rice shoots, lettuce, ginger, lime and chilli).

Shopping

The large *municipal market* in Mae Sot, behind the Siam Hotel, sells some interesting stuff, including Burmese clothing, cheap cigarettes, roses, Indian food, sturdy Burmese blankets and velvet thong slippers from Mandalay.

Getting There & Away

Air THAI flies to Mae Sot from Bangkok (1895B) four times a week, and four times from Chiang Mai (1035B) and Phitsanulok (860B). The THAI office in Mae Sot (☎ 055 531 730) is in the town centre at 76/1 Thanon Prasat Withi.

Bus & Săwngthăew The so-called green bus *(rót meh khĭaw)* leaves at 6am daily from a dirt lot on the southern side of Thanon Intharakhiri, one block west of the post office. The air-con bus departs at 8am. Destinations include Tak (60B air-con), Lampang (86/155B ordinary/air-con), Chiang Mai (115/207B), Chiang Rai (176/317B) and Mae Sai (193/348B). An orange bus to Mae Sot (50B) leaves every day at 2pm, 4pm and 5pm from the Tak bus station.

The more frequent orange-and-white minivans (35B, 1½ hours) along the same route usually arrive a little quicker than the bus. The minivans depart from the roadside in front of the First Hotel in Mae Sot. The trip goes along a beautiful winding road through mountains.

Ordinary buses between Bangkok and Mae Sot (165B) depart from both cities three times each evening. First-class air-con buses run between Bangkok and Mae Sot (302B) five times daily, while 2nd-class air-con buses (232B) have similar departures.

VIP buses (24 seats) to/from Bangkok leave four times daily (460B, about eight hours). Thanjit Tour offers 32-seat VIP buses to Bangkok for only 345B, departing at 10pm. In Mae Sot, Bangkok-bound air-con and VIP buses leave from the northern side of Thanon Intharakhiri just west of the police station; ordinary buses to Bangkok leave from the bus station near the market north of the police station.

There's one bus daily between Mae Sot and Mae Sariang (160B, five to six hours). Săwngthăew to other destinations north of Mae Sot, such as Mae Sarit (66B, 2½ hours), Tha Song Yang (55B, 1½ hours) and Mae Sariang (165B, five to six hours) leave frequently between 6am and noon from the rót meh khĭaw station west of the post office.

Săwngthăew heading to Phop Phra (34B), Waley (40B) and Um Phang (120B, five to six hours) leave hourly between 7am and 3pm.

Myawadi to Mawlamyaing (Myanmar) Theoretically it's possible to cross the river to Myawadi and catch a bus to Mawlamyaing via Kawkareik. Each leg takes about two hours; the Myawadi-Kawkareik stretch can be dicey when fighting between Yangon and KNU troops is in progress; the Kawkareik-Mawlamyaing stretch is generally safe, although the road itself is quite rough. Another way to reach Mawlamyaing is to get off the road at Kyondo and continue by boat along the Gyaing River. At the moment it's not legal to travel beyond Myawadi, but it's quite conceivable that this road will open to foreigners within the next couple of years.

Getting Around
Most of Mae Sot can be seen on foot. Jit Motorcycle, a motorcycle dealer on Thanon Prasat Withi, rents out motorcycles for 160B a day. Make sure you test-ride a bike before renting; some of the machines are in rather poor condition. Cars and vans can be rented for around 1200B a day; ask at any hotel. Motorcycle taxis charge 10B for trips around town.

AROUND MAE SOT
Karen & Burmese Refugee Camps
ค่ายผู้อพยพชาวกะเหรี่ยงและพม่า

A couple of refugee camps have been set up along the eastern bank of Mae Nam Moei in either direction from Mae Sot. Most of the refugees in these camps are Karen fleeing

battles between Burmese and KNU troops across the border. The camps have been around for over a decade but the Thai government has generally kept their existence quiet, fearing the build-up of a huge refugee 'industry' such as the one that developed around the Indo-Chinese camps in eastern Thailand in the 1970s.

Although many Thai and foreign volunteers have come to the refugees' aid, the camps are very much in need of outside assistance. Tourists are no longer permitted to visit the camps, although if you meet a camp volunteer in Mae Sot you might be able to visit by invitation. Donations of clothes and medicines (to be administered by qualified doctors and nurses) may be offered to the camps via No 4 Guest House in Mae Sot.

Waley
บ้านวะเลย์

Thirty-six kilometres from Mae Sot, Rte 1206 splits southwest off Rte 1090 at Ban Saw Oh and terminates 25km south at the border town of Waley, an important smuggling point.

The Burmese side was once one of the two main gateways to Kawthoolei, the Karen nation, but in 1989 the Yangon government ousted the KNU from the area. Until the Thai government cut off all timber trade with Myanmar's military government, teak was the main border trade. Nowadays there's a brisk legal trade in teak furniture instead.

One can visit hill-tribe villages near Ban Chedi Kok and, if invited, the large Mawker refugee camp, both off Rte 1206 on the way to Waley. Opium is cultivated extensively in this area, much to the chagrin of Thailand's authorities, who send rangers in every year to cut down the production. There is a small *hotel* in Phop Phra with basic rooms and shared bath for 60B.

Getting There & Away Săwngthăew to Phop Phra (34B) and Waley (40B) depart frequently between 6am and 6pm from a stop southeast of the mosque in Mae Sot. If you go by motorcycle or car, follow Rte 1090 southeast towards Um Phang and after 36km take Rte 1206 southwest. From this junction it's 25km to Waley; the last 10km of the road is unpaved. Your passport may be checked at a police outpost before Waley.

UM PHANG
อุ้มผาง

Route 1090 goes south from Mae Sot to Um Phang, 150km away. This stretch of road used to be called the 'Death Highway' because of the guerrilla activity in the area that hindered highway development. Those days ended in the 1980s, but lives are still lost because of brake failure or the treacherous turns on this steep, winding road through incredible mountain scenery.

Along the way – short hikes off the highway – are two waterfalls, **Nam Tok Thararak** (26km from Mae Sot) and **Nam Tok Pha Charoen** (41km). Nam Tok Thararak streams over limestone cliffs and calcified rocks with a rough texture that makes climbing the falls easy. It's been made into a park of sorts, with benches right in the stream at the base of the falls for cooling off and a couple of outhouse toilets nearby; on weekends *food vendors* set up here.

The eucalyptus-lined dirt road leaves the highway between Km24 and Km25. A side road at Km48 leads to a group of government-sponsored hill-tribe villages (Karen, Lisu, Hmong, Mien, Lahu). Just beyond Ban Rom Klao 4 (previously Um Piam) – roughly midway between Mae Sot and Um Phang – is a very large **Karen and Burmese refugee camp** and several **Hmong villages**.

Um Phang is an overgrown village populated mostly by Karen people at the junction of Mae Nam Mae Klong (Klong River) and Huay Um Phang (Um Phang River). Many Karen villages in this area are very traditional – elephants are used as much as oxen for farm work. *Yaeng* (elephant saddles) and other tack used for elephant wrangling are a common sight on the verandas of Karen houses outside of town. You'll also see plenty of elephants in other Karen villages throughout the district. The name for the district comes from the Karen word *umpha* (a type of bamboo container in which Karen who were travelling carried their documents to show to Thai border authorities).

An interesting **hike** can be done following the footpaths southeast of the village through rice fields and along Huay Um Phang to a few smaller Karen villages.

At the border where Um Phang district meets Myanmar, near the Thai-Karen villages of Ban Nong Luang and Ban Huay, is

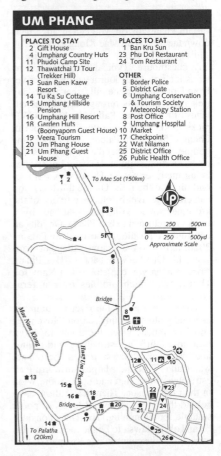

UM PHANG

PLACES TO STAY	PLACES TO EAT
2 Gift House	1 Ban Kru Sun
4 Umphang Country Huts	23 Phu Doi Restaurant
11 Phudoi Camp Site	24 Tom Restaurant
12 Thawatchai TJ Tour (Trekker Hill)	**OTHER**
13 Suan Ruen Kaew Resort	3 Border Police
14 Tu Ka Su Cottage	5 District Gate
15 Umphang Hillside Pension	6 Umphang Conservation & Tourism Society
16 Umphang Hill Resort	7 Meteorology Station
18 Garden Huts (Boonyaporn Guest House)	8 Post Office
19 Veera Tourism	9 Umphang Hospital
20 Um Phang House	10 Market
21 Um Phang Guest House	17 Checkpoint
	22 Wat Nilaman
	25 District Office
	26 Public Health Office

To Mae Sot (150km)

0 250 500m
0 250 500yd
Approximate Scale

Bridge

Mae Nam Klong

Huay Um Phang

Airstrip

Bridge

To Palatha (20km)

a **Karen refugee village**. It's inhabited by over 500 Karen who originally hailed from Htikabler village on the other side of the border.

South of Um Phang, towards Sangkhlaburi in Kanchanaburi Province, **Um Phang Wildlife Sanctuary** links with the Thung Yai Naresuan and Huay Kha Kaeng Reserves as well as Khlong Lan and Mae Wong National Parks to form Thailand's largest wildlife corridor and one of the largest intact natural forests in Southeast Asia.

Nam Tok Thilawsu
น้ำตกทีลอซู

In Um Phang district you can arrange trips down the Mae Nam Mae Klong to Nam Tok Thilawsu and Karen villages – inquire at any guesthouse. Typical three-day excursions include a raft journey along the river from Um Phang to the falls, then a two-day trek from the falls through the Karen villages of **Khotha** and **Palatha**, where a 4WD picks trekkers up and returns them to Um Phang (25km from Palatha by road). Some people prefer to spend two days on the river, the first night at a cave or hot springs along the river before Thilawsu and a second night at the falls. On the third day you can cross the river by elephant to one of the aforementioned villages to be met by a truck and returned to Um Phang. Or you can continue south along the road to Palatha 20km farther to the Hmong village of Kangae Khi. On the way back to Um Phang from Palatha you can stop off at **Nam Tok Thilawjaw**, which tumbles over a fern-covered cliff.

The scenery along the river is stunning, especially after the rainy season (November and December), when the 200m to 400m limestone cliffs are streaming with water and Nam Tok Thilawsu is at its best. This waterfall is Thailand's largest, measuring an estimated 400m high and up to 300m wide in the rainy season. There's a shallow cave behind the falls and several levels of pools suitable for swimming. The Thais consider Nam Tok Thilawsu to be the most beautiful waterfall in the country; it is now part of Um Phang Wildlife Sanctuary, declared a Unesco World Heritage site in 1999.

Between 1 December and 1 June the border police open the rough 47km road from Um Phang to the falls (suitable for 4WD or a skilled dirt-bike rider only). Alternatively, you can follow the main paved road south of Um Phang to the Km19 marker; the walk to the falls is a stiff four hours from here via Mo Phado village. A săwngthăew goes to the Km19 marker from Um Phang once a day; ask for *kii-loh sìp kâo* and expect to pay 15B to 20B per person.

Along the roadside near Palatha, keep an eye out for the beautiful **purple orchid tree** (*Bauhinia variegata*).

Beung Kleung & Letongkhu
เลตองงคุ

From Ban Mae Khlong Mai, a few kilometres east of Um Phang via the highway to Mae Sot, a graded dirt road (Rte 1167) heads southwest along the border to Beung Kleung (sometimes spelt Peung Kleung), a Karen, Burmese, Indo-Burmese, Talaku and Thai trading village where buffalo carts are more common than motorbikes. The picturesque setting among spiky peaks and cliffs is worth the trip even if you go no farther. Impressive **Nam Tok Ekaratcha** is an hour's walk away. Săwngthăew from Um Phang usually make a trip to Beung Kleung once a day, and it's possible to put up at the village clinic or in a private home for a donation of 100B per person. On the way you can stop off at the small, traditional Karen village of **Ban Thiphochi**.

Four hours' walk from here along a rough track (passable by 4WD in the dry season), near the Myanmar border on the banks of Mae Nam Suriya next to Sam Rom mountain, is the culturally singular, 109-house village of Letongkhu (Leh Tawng Khu). The villagers are for the most part Karen in language and dress, but their spiritual beliefs are unique to this area. They will eat only the meat of wild animals and hence do not raise chickens, ducks, pigs or beef cattle. They do, however, keep buffalo, oxen and elephants as work animals.

According to what little anthropological information is available, the villagers belong to the Lagu or Talaku sect, said to represent a form of Buddhism mixed with shamanism and animism. Letongkhu is one of only six such villages in Thailand; there are reportedly around 30 more in Myanmar. Each village has a spiritual and temporal leader called a *pu chaik* (whom the Thais call *reusǐi* – 'rishi' or 'sage') who wears his hair long – usually tied in a topknot – and dresses in white, yellow or brown robes, depending on the subsect.

According to Christian Gooden, author of *Three Pagodas: A Journey Down the Thai Border,* the residents of Letongkhu were chased out of Myanmar in the mid-19th century. The current 48-year-old pu chaik at Letongkhu is the 10th in a line of 'white-thread' priests dating back to residence in Myanmar. The reusǐi's many male disciples also wear their hair in topknots (often tied in cloth) and may wear similar robes. All reusǐi abstain from alcohol and are celibate. The priests live apart from the village in a temple and practise traditional medicine based on herbal healing and ritual magic. Antique elephant tusks are kept as talismans.

An altercation between the Thai border police and another group of reusǐi (said to be a rival sect, known as the 'yellow-threads' for the colour of their robes) over hunting rights resulted in the knifing deaths of five policemen a few years ago. Hence the Thai border police can be a little touchy about outsiders, and there are several checkpoints along the way (as frequently as every 3km in some areas); in fact you need permission from the Border Patrol Police before going to Letongkhu.

At the same time evangelistic Christian missionaries have infiltrated the area and have tried to convert followers of the Talaku sect; this has made the Talaku more sensitive to outside visitation. If you visit Letongkhu, take care not to enter any village structures without permission or invitation. Likewise, do not take photographs without permission. If you treat the villagers with respect, then you shouldn't have a problem.

Opposite Letongkhu on the Myanmar side of the border, the KNU has set up its latest tactical headquarters. Yangon government offensives against the KNU can break out in this area during the dry months of the year, but when this is happening or is likely to happen, Thai military checkpoints will turn all trekkers back. It wouldn't hurt to make a few inquiries in Um Phang first, just to make sure.

Beung Kleung to Sangkhlaburi

Sangkhlaburi (Kanchanaburi Province, Central Thailand) is 90km or four to five days' walk from Beung Kleung. On the way (11km from Beung Kleung), about 250m off the road, is the extensive cave system of **Tham Takube**. From Ban Mae Chan, 35km on the same route, there's a dirt road branching across the border to a **KNU-controlled village**. The route to Sangkhlaburi has several branches; the main one crosses over the border into Myanmar for some distance before crossing back into Thailand. There has been discussion of cutting a newer, more direct road between Um Phang and Sangkhlaburi.

Because of the overall sensitive nature of this border area, and the very real potential for becoming lost, ill or injured, a guide is highly recommended for any sojourn south of Um Phang. You may be able to arrange a guide for this route in either Um Phang or Beung Kleung. Umphang Hill Resort in Um Phang can also arrange a trek but you need to give it a couple of weeks' notice. The best time of year to do the trek is between October and January.

Organised Tours

Several of the guesthouses in Um Phang can arrange trekking and rafting trips in the area. The typical three-night, four-day trip costs from 2000B per person (seven or more people) to 3500B (two people). The price includes rafting, an elephant ride, food and guide service.

Longer treks of up to 12 days may also be available, and there are day trips to Nam Tok Thilawsu as well. It is worth checking to see what kind of rafts are used; most places have switched to rubber, as bamboo rafts can break up in the rough rapids. Choose rubber, unless you are really looking for adventure – like walking to your camp site rather than rafting there.

If you want to book a tour in Um Phang, a good choice is *Umphang Hill Resort* (☎ *055 561 063,* ⓔ *umphanghill@thaimail .com; in Mae Sot* ☎ *055 531 409; in Bangkok* ☎ *025 737 942).* It appears to have the best equipment and trip design. Programs offer basic three- to six-day rafting and hiking trips to Nam Tok Thilawsu and beyond, including one itinerary that takes rafters through 11 different sets of rapids on the Mae Nam Mae Klong. Longer or shorter trips may also be arranged, and elephant riding instead of walking is always an option. *BL Tour* at Um Phang Guest House, *Thawatchai TJ Tour* and most other lodgings in Um Phang (see Places to Stay later) can arrange similar trips.

Companies based in Mae Sot, such as *SP Tour* (☎ *055 531 409)* at SP House, do Um Phang trips for about 1500B to 2000B more per person than local Um Phang agencies. This adds private transport between Mae Sot and Um Phang to the trip, but nothing more. The typical Nam Tok Thilawsu–Palatha trip, for example, costs 4000B to 5000B per person for a four-day trip in which two half-days are spent in transit from Mae Sot.

Places to Stay

Accommodation in Um Phang is plentiful, and the majority of visitors to the area are Thai.

Thawatchai TJ Tour (*Trekker Hill;* ☎ *055 561 090)* Beds 60B. On a hillside near the village centre, this place has accommodation in rustic thatched-roof shelters with shared facilities.

Phudoi Camp Site (☎ *055 561 049, 01 886 8783, fax 055 561 279)* Bungalows 100B per person, tent sites 50B. On another hillside, around the corner from Trekker Hill towards the market, you can pitch your own tent at the camp ground or rent one of four clean wooden bungalows at this well-landscaped place. All bathrooms have hot water. Additional bungalows were under construction when we visited.

Um Phang House (☎ *055 561 073)* Rooms/cottages 150/300B. Owned by the local *kamnan* (precinct officer), Um Phang House offers a few motel-like rooms with private bathroom that sleep up to three, and nicer wood-and-brick cottages with hot water and ceiling fans that sleep up to four (a solo traveller might be able to negotiate the price down a bit). There's a large outdoor restaurant in an open area near the cottages.

Um Phang Guest House (☎ *055 561 021, fax 055 561 322)* Rooms in Thai-style houses 500B, rooms in a cottage 300B, thatched huts 100B. Owned by BL Tour (see Organised Tours earlier), the rooms here are a real bargain since each room or cottage can sleep up to six persons for the same price, but of course they hope you'll take one of their trekking/rafting trips (no hard sell, though, as yet). All rooms have attached private shower and toilet.

Veera Tourism (☎ *055 561 239)* Rooms with private bathroom 100B per person. Farther west toward Huay Um Phang, this place has rooms in a wooden house.

Continuing west, next to Huay Um Phang, are a couple of other guesthouses (often called 'resorts' in typical Thai fashion).

Garden Huts (*Boonyaporn Guest House; Thaphae Resort)* Rooms 300-700B. This place features five levels of accommodation ranging from bamboo huts with shared cold-water bathroom to bungalows with attached hot-water bathroom; most of these rooms will sleep up to four people. The place is run by a nice Thai lady who brews good Thai-grown arabica coffee.

Umphang Hill Resort (☎ *055 561 063, fax 055 561 065,* ⓔ *umphanghill@thaimail .com; in Mae Sot* ☎ *055 531 409; in Bangkok* ☎ *025 737 942)* Wooden bungalows 500B, large wood-and-thatch bungalows with 2 or 3 bathrooms each around 2000B. Exact prices depend on the season. The large bungalows here are usually rented by Thai groups, and can accommodate up to 20 people. When not full, the resort will rent out beds in these bungalows for 50B per person. There are only a few of the solid wooden bungalows; they come with attached hot-water shower, small TV and refrigerator. This is one of the best places in Um Phang to book treks or raft trips.

Tu Ka Su Cottage (☎ 055 561 295, 01 487 1643) 10-person bungalows 1500B. South of the checkpoint and west of Huay Um Phang, this place consists of a set of Japanese-owned, tin-roofed wooden bungalows surrounded by flowers.

Suan Ruen Kaew Resort (☎ 055 561 119) Rooms with private bathroom 100B per person. Farther west of the checkpoint, past Huay Um Phang and on the road to Palatha, this spot has nice cottages as well as rooms in a house overlooking a stream.

Umphang Hillside Pension (☎ 055 561 315) Rooms with private bathroom 80B per person. Owned by a local policeman, this place has rooms that are basic and worn, but the owners are friendly and keep the place clean. Information about the area is posted. Follow a road through Umphang Hill Resort to reach Umphang Hillside Pension.

Umphang Country Huts Rooms 400-700B. Rooms in a wood-and-thatch, two-storey building facing Huay Mae Klong, in a nice hilly setting off the highway before Um Phang, share a common veranda with benches. There's a less-expensive downstairs room with private bathroom and a larger upstairs room which sleeps up to four. Larger, more atmospheric rooms in another two-storey building come with private verandas. Every room has a private cold-water shower. Umphang Country Huts can arrange raft trips; it gets lots of Thai tour groups.

Gift House (☎ 055 561 181) Huts with shared bathroom 80-100B. A short distance out of town towards Mae Sot, this quiet spot has simple timber huts.

By the time you arrive in Um Phang other guesthouses will surely have opened as the area's popularity continues to grow.

Places to Eat

Um Phang has four or five simple noodle and rice shops plus a *morning market* and a small sundries shop.

Tom Restaurant does rice dishes (20B to 40B) and is open 9am to 8pm daily.

Phu Doi Restaurant Dishes 20-40B. Open 8am-10pm daily. On the main street into town, this place has very good food, especially the *phá-naeng* (mild curry) dishes.

There are also rice dishes, noodles, tôm yam and cold beer. Phu Doi has a bilingual menu and seems to be virtually the only place open past 8pm.

Ban Kru Sun Dishes 30-80B. Open 11am-9pm. This is a small indoor-outdoor place just out of town, near Gift House and off the main road. It is owned and operated by a local teacher who is also a composer and performer of Thai folk music inspired by the beauty of the Um Phang area. He usually performs live on weekends, when the pub may be open later. The kitchen serves typical Thai and Northern Thai dishes.

Getting There & Away

Săwngthăew to Um Phang (120B, five to six hours) leave several times a day from Mae Sot, starting around 7am and finishing around 3pm. Săwngthăew usually stop for lunch at windy Ban Rom Klao 4 along the way. In the reverse direction, săwngthăew depart between 7am and 3pm.

If you decide to try to ride a motorcycle from Mae Sot (3½ to four hours), be sure it's one with a strong engine as the road has lots of fairly steep grades. The only petrol pump along the way is in Ban Rom Klao 4, 80km from Mae Sot, so you may want to carry 3L or 4L of extra fuel. The road is barely 1½ lanes wide and is roughly sealed in some spots. The stretch between Ban Rom Klao 4 and Um Phang passes impressive stands of virgin monsoon forest.

MAE SOT TO MAE SARIANG

Route 105 runs north from Mae Sot all the way to Mae Sariang in Mae Hong Son Province. The section of the road north of Tha Song Yang has finally been sealed and public transport is now available all the way to Mae Sariang (226km), passing through Mae Ramat, Mae Sarit, Ban Tha Song Yang and Ban Sop Ngao (Mae Ngao). In Mae Ramat a temple called **Wat Don Kaew**, behind the district office, houses a large Mandalay-style marble Buddha. Other attractions on the way to Mae Sariang include **Nam Tok Mae Kasa**, between the Km13 and Km14 markers, and extensive limestone caverns at **Tham Mae Usu**, at the

Km94 marker near Ban Tha Song Yang. From the highway it's a 2km walk to Tham Mae Usu; note that in the rainy season, when the river running through the cave seals off the mouth, it's closed.

Instead of doing the Myanmar border run in one go, some people elect to spend the night in Mae Sarit (118km from Mae Sot), then start fresh in the morning to get to Ban Tha Song Yang in time for a morning săwngthăew from Ban Tha Song Yang to Mae Sariang.

Săwngthăew to Mae Sarit (66B, 2½ hours) leave hourly between 6am and noon from the market north of the police station in Mae Sot. Mae Sarit to Ban Tha Song Yang costs 23B; from there to Mae Sariang costs 55B (three hours). If you miss the morning săwngthăew from Mae Sarit to Mae Sariang, you can usually arrange to charter a truck for 180B to 220B.

If you decide not to stay overnight in Mae Sarit you can take a direct Mae Sariang săwngthăew from Mae Sot for 165B. These large orange săwngthăew have the same departure times as the Mae Sot–Mae Sarit săwngthăew (five to six hours).

Along the way you'll pass through thick forest, including a few stands of teak, and see Karen villages, the occasional work elephant and a large Thai ranger post.

Places to Stay

Mae Salid Guest House Singles/doubles 70/100B. In Mae Sarit, this guesthouse offers very basic rooms with private toilet and shared shower.

There are no guesthouses in Ban Tha Song Yang but it would probably be easy to arrange a place to stay by inquiring at the main market (where the săwngthăew stop) in this prosperous black-market town.

Mae Hong Son Province

Thailand's northwestern-most province is a crossroads for hill tribes (mostly Karen, with some Hmong, Lisu and Lahu), Shan and Burmese living in and around the Mae Pai valley. Reportedly 75% of Mae Hong Son consists of mountains and forest.

As Mae Hong Son Province is so far from the influence of sea winds and is thickly forested and mountainous, the temperature seldom rises above 40°C and in January can drop to 2°C. The air is often misty with ground fog in the winter and smoke from slash-and-burn agriculture in the hot season (March to June). The best time to visit Mae Hong Son is between November and March when the valleys throughout much of the province are at their most beautiful. During the rainy season (June to October) travel in the province can be difficult because there are few paved roads. During the hot season (March to June), the Mae Pai valley fills with smoke. The only problem with going in the cool season is that the nights are downright cold – you'll need at least one thick sweater and a good pair of socks for mornings and evenings and a sleeping bag or several blankets. If you're caught short, you might consider buying a blanket at a market (the Chinese acrylic blankets are cheap) and cutting a hole in the middle for use as a poncho.

The province has undergone a tourist mini-boom over the last decade, with many resorts opening in the area around the capital. So far, few visitors seem to leave the beaten Mae Hong Son-Soppong-Pai track.

MAE SARIANG & KHUN YUAM
แม่สะเรียง/ขุนยวม

postcode 58110 • pop 7800
Many of the hill-tribe settlements in Mae Hong Son Province are concentrated in the districts and towns of Khun Yuam, Mae La Noi and Mae Sariang, which are good departure points for treks to Hmong, Karen and Shan villages. Of these three small towns, Mae Sariang is the largest and offers the most facilities for use as a base. Khun Yuam is also a good place to start from. Mae Sam Laep, southwest of Mae Sariang on the Myanmar border, can be reached by săwngthăew or motorcycle, and from there

MAE HONG SON PROVINCE

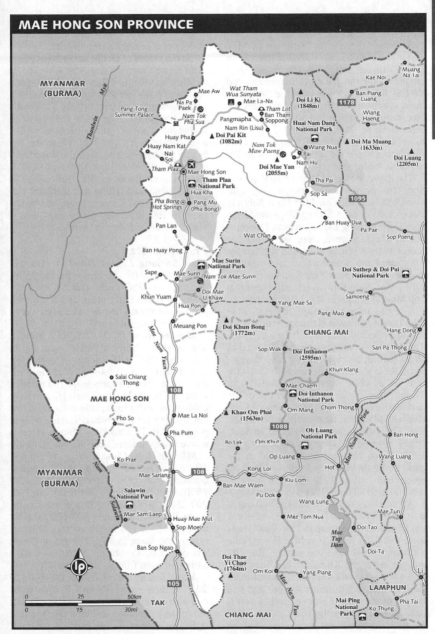

MYANMAR
(BURMA)

Thanlwin

Kae Noi

Muang
Na Tai

Ban Piang
Luang

Wiang
Haeng

1178

Pang Tong
Summer Palace

Mae Aw

Na Pa
Paek

Wat Tham
Wua Sunyata

Mae La-Na

Doi Li Ki
(1848m)

Nam Tok
Pha Sua

Pangmapha

Tham Lot
Ban Tham
Soppong

Huai Nam Dang
National Park

Nam Rin (Lisu)

Huay Pha

Doi Pai Kit
(1082m)

Nam Tok
Maw Paeng

Doi Ma Muang
(1633m)

Huay Nam Kat

Nai
Soi

Wiang Nua

Pai

Doi Luang
(2205m)

Tham Plaa

Mae Hong Son

Nam Hu

Tham Plaa
National Park

Doi Mae Yan
(2055m)

Hua Kha

Tha Pai

Pha Bong
Hot Springs

Pang Mu
(Pha Bong)

Sop Sa

1095

Pan Lan

Wat Chan

Ban Huay Dua

Pa Pae

Sop Poeng

Ban Huay Pong

Sape

Mae Surin
National Park

Mae Surin

Nam Tok Mae Surin

Doi Suthep & Doi Pui
National Park

Khun Yuam

Doi Mae
U Khaw

Yang Mae Sa

Samoeng

Hua Pon

Pang Mao

Hang Dong

Meuang Pon

Doi Khun Bong
(1772m)

CHIANG MAI

Mae Nam Yuan

Sop Wak

Doi Inthanon
(2595m)

San Pa Thong

Salai Chiang
Thong

Khun Klang

108

Mae Chaem

MAE HONG SON

Doi Inthanon
National Park

Chom Thong

Mae Nam Ping

Pho So

Mae La Noi

Khao Om Phai
(1563m)

Om Mang

Ban Hong

Pha Pum

1088

Bo Lek

Om Khut

Ob Luang
National Park

Ko Prae

Mae

Nam

Op Luang

Wang Luang

MYANMAR
(BURMA)

Mae Sariang

108

Kong Loi

Kiu Lom

Hot

Mae Tun

Salawin
National Park

Ban Mae Waen

Pu Dok

Salawin

Mae Sam Laep

Huay Mae Mut

Wang Lung

Mae Tom Nua

Mae Tup
Dam

Doi Tao

Sop Moei

Doi Ta

Ban Sop Ngao

Doi Thae
Yi Chao
(1764m)

Om Koi

Yang Piang

Mae Nam Tun

Li

LAMPHUN

105

TAK

CHIANG MAI

Mai Ping
National Park

Ko Thung

Pha Tai

0   25   50km
0   15   30mi

you may be able to hire boats for journeys along the quite scenic Mae Nam Salawin.

Although there is little to see in Mae Sariang, it's a pleasant riverside town with a small travel scene. Two Burmese/Shan temples, **Wat Jong Sung** (Uthayarom) and **Wat Si Bunruang**, just off Mae Sariang's main street (not far from the Mae Sariang bus station), are worth a visit if you have time. Built in 1896, Wat Jong Sung is the more interesting of the two temples and has slender, Shan-style chedi and wooden monastic buildings.

The Riverside Guest House (see Places to Stay following) can arrange day and overnight boat trips on Mae Nam Salawin that include stops in Karen villages and Mae Sam Laep. During the dry season (November to May), a truck from the Riverside leaves every morning at around 6.30am for Mae Sam Laep, where a boat takes visitors two hours down Mae Nam Salawin (locally called Mae Nam Khong) to a sand beach at **Sop Moei**. The total cost is 110B per person.

You can take a boat upriver from Mae Sam Laep to **Salawin National Park**, a 722-sq-km protected area established in 1994. The boat trip to the park headquarters takes about half an hour. There are no lodgings, but in the dry season you can pitch a *tent* for free on a white-sand beach, called Hat Thaen Kaew, along the river in front of the park offices. There are good views of the river and Myanmar from the park headquarters. The park is heavily forested in teak, Asian redwood and cherrywood. During the 1990s Karen refugees homesteaded in the park, hiring on as labour for illegal logging enterprises, but in 1998 the Thai government ordered all non-Thai residents to leave.

About 36km southeast of Mae Sariang at **Ban Mae Waen** is Pan House, where a guide named T Weerapan (Mr Pan) leads local treks. To get to Ban Mae Waen, take a Chiang Mai–bound bus east on Rte 108 and get out at the Km68 marker. Ban Mae Waen is a 5km walk south along a mountain ridge and (during the rainy season) across a couple of streams. If you're driving you'll need a 4WD when the road is wet. *Pan House* charges 50B per person to spend the

night in a big wooden house. Ban Mae Waen is a mixed Thai/Karen village in the middle of a heavily Karen district.

On the slopes of Doi Mae U Khaw, 25km from Khun Yuam via upgraded Rte 1263, is the Hmong village of **Ban Mae U Khaw** and the 250m **Nam Tok Mae Surin** (50km northeast of Khun Yuam), reportedly Thailand's highest cataract. The area blooms with scenic *bua thawng* (golden lotus; more like a sunflower than a lotus) in November; this is also the best time to view the waterfall.

The North West and Riverside Guest Houses (see Places to Stay following) in Mae Sariang lead **rafting and elephant-riding tours** to local Karen villages and waterfalls for 1000B per day per person – less if you do it all on foot and by truck.

Places to Stay

Mae Sariang *Ekalak Hotel (☎ 053 631 426, 77/2 Rte 108)* Rooms with fan 250B, with air-con 350-450B. Out on Rte 108, rooms here are fairly clean and come with private hot-water showers. The hotel has an attached restaurant as well.

Mitaree Hotel (☎ 053 681 110, Thanon Mae Sariang) Singles/doubles with fan in old wing 120/200B, rooms in new wing with fan/air-con 250/400B. At Mae Sariang's oldest hotel, rooms in the old wooden wing (called the Mitaree Guest House) have cold-water bathrooms, while those in the newer wing have hot water. The old wing is popular with Thai truckers. Mitaree Hotel is conveniently located near the bus station.

Mitaree Hotel (New Mitaree; ☎ 053 681 109, 24 Thanon Wiang Mai) Singles/doubles with cold-water bathroom 120/150B, with fan & hot-water bathroom 190/200-250B, with air-con & hot-water bathroom 300/400B, cottages 600-1200B. Near the post office you'll find another Mitaree, run by the same family. The set of newer wooden 'resort' cottages at the back have sitting areas in front, air-con and TV.

Mae Sariang Guest House (☎ 053 681 203, Thanon Laeng Phanit) Rooms without/with bathroom 80/150B. If you turn left out of the bus station and then take the first right you'll come to this small guesthouse, which is nothing special but OK if everything else is full.

Riverside Guest House (☎ *053 681 188, Thanon Laeng Phanit*) Singles/doubles with shared facilities 80/160B. The efficiently run Riverside boasts a pleasant sitting and dining area overlooking Mae Nam Yuam.

North West Guest House (☎ *053 681 956, fax 053 681 353, Thanon Laeng Phanit*) Singles/doubles with shared bathroom 90/160B. Nearby, on the opposite side of the street from the Riverside and under the same ownership, the North West offers rooms in a large wooden house. The guesthouse also has a separate leaf-thatched cottage across the road facing the river, usually reserved for groups.

See View Guest House (☎ *053 681 556, 149 Thanon Mae Sariang-Mae Sot*) Rowhouse rooms with fan/air-con 200/400B, bungalows 300B. On the western side of Mae Nam Yuam, the row-house rooms here have private hot-water showers, but are located far back from the river. The less attractive, overpriced bungalows are closer to the river. The management says these rates are negotiable in the low season, and

offers free transport to and from the bus station. The open-air Old House restaurant on the premises sometimes features live Thai country music during high season – a plus or minus, depending on your sleeping schedule.

Kamolsorn Hotel (☎ *053 681 204, Thanon Mae Sariang*) Rooms with TV & fan 350B, rooms with air-con without/with TV 450/600B. This newer multistorey place is just south of Thanon Wai Weuksa on Thanon Mae Sariang. All rooms have private bathroom.

Hotel Lotus (*Lotus Guest House;* ☎ *053 681 048, 73/5 Thanon Wiang Mai*) Singles/doubles with fan 120/250B, rooms with air-con 350B. This is an odd little complex in a cul-de-sac with a restaurant, karaoke, massage and barber shop. The rooms are clean and all have private hot-water facilities.

Khun Yuam *Mit Khun Yuam Hotel* (☎ *053 691 057, 61 Thanon Chiang Mai-Mae Hong Son*) Upstairs singles with shared bathroom 150B, 3-bed room with fan & cold-water shower 300B, with air-con & hot-water shower 500B. This hotel is in an old

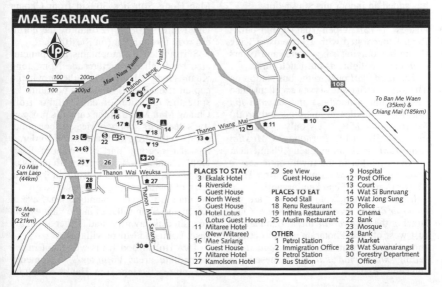

MAE SARIANG

PLACES TO STAY	29 See View	9 Hospital
3 Ekalak Hotel	Guest House	12 Post Office
4 Riverside		13 Court
Guest House	PLACES TO EAT	14 Wat Si Bunruang
5 North West	8 Food Stall	15 Wat Jong Sung
Guest House	18 Renu Restaurant	20 Police
10 Hotel Lotus	19 Inthira Restaurant	21 Cinema
(Lotus Guest House)	25 Muslim Restaurant	22 Bank
11 Mitaree Hotel		23 Bank
(New Mitaree)	OTHER	24 Bank
16 Mae Sariang	1 Petrol Station	26 Market
Guest House	2 Immigration Office	28 Wat Suwanarangsi
17 Mitaree Hotel	6 Petrol Station	30 Forestry Department
27 Kamolsorn Hotel	7 Bus Station	Office

To Ban Me Waen (35km) & Chiang Mai (185km)

To Mae Sam Laep (44km)

To Mae Sot (221km)

wooden building on the main road through the town centre. The rooms with attached shower and toilet are in a newer building towards the back of the property. Watch out for the owner's dog, which has been known to nip a guest or two.

Ban Farang (☎ 053 622 086, 053 691 023, 499 Thanon Ratburana) Dorm beds 50B, row-house rooms with private facilities 200B, new bungalows 250-350B. This clean and friendly place is off the main road towards the northern end of town (look for the signs).

Rustic accommodation is available at the Hmong village of Mae U Khaw, between Khun Yuam and Nam Tok Mae Surin.

Places to Eat

The *Riverside Guest House* on Thanon Laeng Phanit in Mae Sariang has a pleasant *restaurant* area upstairs overlooking the river, serving inexpensive Thai and faràng dishes.

Inthira Restaurant (Thanon Wiang Mai) Dishes 30-75B. Open 10am-10pm daily. Near Thanon Mae Sariang, this place is well known for its batter-fried frogs, although you won't see them on the English menu. It has added an indoor air-con section.

Renu Restaurant (Thanon Wiang Mai) Dishes 30-75B. Open 10am-11pm daily. Renu is decorated with 10 photos of King Bhumibol playing saxophone, and offers such menu delights as nut-hatch curry.

The *food stall* next to the bus station on Thanon Mae Sariang serves excellent khâo sawy (Chinese noodles) and *khanŏm jiin* (meat and noodles in spicy curried broth) for less than 15B – it's only open from morning till early afternoon. A *Muslim restaurant* on Thanon Laeng Phanit near the main market in the town centre serves good curries and khâo mòk kài (the Thai-Muslim version of chicken biryani).

In Khun Yuam, your best bets are the *open-air dining area* at the Mit Khun Yuam Hotel or the cosy *restaurant* at Ban Farang. Just west of Wat Photaram at the southern end of Khun Yuam are several *food stalls* selling khâo man kài (Hainanese-style chicken rice).

Getting There & Around

Ordinary buses to Mae Sariang (78B, four to five hours) leave Chiang Mai's Arcade terminal at 8am, 1.30pm, 3pm and 8pm. First-class air-con buses (140B) depart at 6.30am, 11am and 9pm. From Mae Sariang to Khun Yuam it's another 50B, or to Mae Hong Son 85B (four to five hours). An air-con bus to Mae Hong Son costs 135B but there's no way to reserve a seat – you must wait for the bus from Chiang Mai and hope there's a vacant seat. There's one bus daily between Mae Sot and Mae Sariang (160B, five to six hours).

One săwngthăew goes to Mae Sam Laep on Mae Nam Salawin every morning (70B) or you can charter one for 450B. See the Mae Sot to Mae Sariang section earlier in this chapter for details on săwngthăew between Mae Sot and Mae Sariang.

Destinations anywhere in town are 10B by motorcycle taxi. Next to the petrol station across from the bus station is a small motorcycle rental place.

MAE HONG SON
อ.เมืองแม่ฮ่องสอน

postcode 58000 • pop 7400

Mae Hong Son lies 368km from Chiang Mai by the southern route through Mae Sariang (on Rte 108), or 270km by the northern road through Pai (on Rte 1095).

Surrounded by mountains and punctuated by small but picturesque Nong Jong Kham (Jong Kham Lake), the provincial capital itself is still relatively peaceful despite the intrusion of daily flights from Chiang Mai. Much of the capital's prosperity is due to its supply of rice and consumer goods to the drug lords across the border. It has also become part of Northern Thailand's standard tourist scene, with plenty of guesthouses, hotels and resorts in the area, most of them catering to Thais. The town's population is predominantly Shan. Several Karen and Shan villages in the vicinity can be visited as day trips, and farther afield are Lisu, Lahu and Musoe villages.

Two Hollywood films were shot in the immediate area: *Volunteers,* a comedy-adventure starring Tom Hanks and John

Candy about the Peace Corps; and *Air America,* a Mel Gibson vehicle loosely based on events that occurred during the secret US war in Laos during the 1960s.

Information

Tourist Police Tourist brochures and maps can be picked up at the fledgling tourist police office (☎ 053 611 812, 1155), which is located on Thanon Singhanat Bamrung. Office hours are 8.30am to 9.30pm, but you can call 24 hours a day to report mishaps such as theft or to lodge complaints against guesthouses and trek operators.

Money Foreign-exchange services are available at Bangkok Bank, Thai Farmers Bank and Bank of Ayudhya, all located along Thanon Khunlum Praphat in the centre of town. Bangkok Bank and Thai Farmers Bank have ATMs.

Post & Communications The Mae Hong Son main post office, towards the southern end of Thanon Khunlum Praphat, is open 8.30am to 4.30pm weekdays except holidays. International telephone service is available at the attached CAT office – hours are the same as the post office. All other

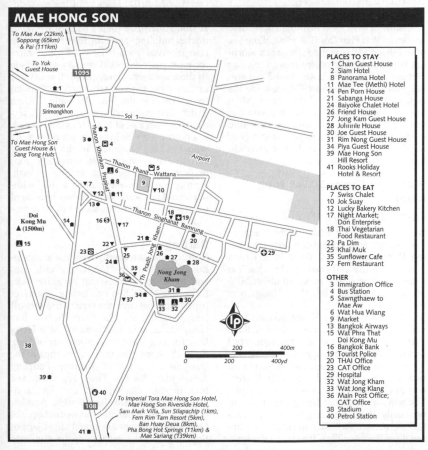

MAE HONG SON

To Mae Aw (22km),
Soppong (65km)
& Pai (111km)

To Yok
Guest House

1095

Thanon
Sirimongkhon

Soi 1

Thanon Khunlum Praphat

To Mae Hong Son
Guest House &
Sang Tong Huts

Thanon Phanit
Wattana

Airport

Doi
Kong Mu
(1500m)

Thanon Singhanat Bamrung

Th Pradit Jong Kham

Nong Jong
Kham

0   200   400m
0   200   400yd

To Imperial Tora Mae Hong Son Hotel,
Mae Hong Son Riverside Hotel,
Sam Mark Villa, Sun Silapachip (1km),
Fern Rim Tarn Resort (5km),
Ban Huay Deua (8km),
Pha Bong Hot Springs (11km) &
Mae Sariang (139km)

108

PLACES TO STAY
1 Chan Guest House
2 Siam Hotel
8 Panorama Hotel
11 Mae Tee (Methi) Hotel
14 Pen Porn House
21 Sabanga House
24 Baiyoke Chalet Hotel
26 Friend House
27 Jong Kam Guest House
28 Johnnie House
30 Joe Guest House
31 Rim Nong Guest House
34 Piya Guest House
39 Mae Hong Son
Hill Resort
41 Rooks Holiday
Hotel & Resort

PLACES TO EAT
7 Swiss Chalet
10 Jok Suay
12 Lucky Bakery Kitchen
17 Night Market;
Don Enterprise
18 Thai Vegetarian
Food Restaurant
22 Pa Dim
25 Khai Muk
35 Sunflower Cafe
37 Fern Restaurant

OTHER
3 Immigration Office
4 Bus Station
5 Sawngthaew to
Mae Aw
6 Wat Hua Wiang
9 Market
13 Bangkok Airways
15 Wat Phra That
Doi Kong Mu
16 Bangkok Bank
19 Tourist Police
20 THAI Office
23 CAT Office
29 Hospital
32 Wat Jong Kham
33 Wat Jong Klang
36 Main Post Office;
CAT Office
38 Stadium
40 Petrol Station

times you can use public phones – there's a Lenso phone (see International Phonecards in the Facts for the Visitor chapter) as well as a Home Country Direct phone outside the entrance to the CAT office. A separate CAT office on Thanon Udom Chow, west of Pa Dim restaurant, also offers international phone service, along with Internet access.

Several places around town, including Sunflower Cafe, provide Internet access by the minute.

Wat Phra That Doi Kong Mu
วัดพระธาตุดอยกองมู

Climb the hill west of town, Doi Kong Mu (1500m), to visit this Shan-built wát, also known as Wat Phai Doi. The view of the sea of fog that collects in the valley each morning is impressive; at other times of the day you get a view of the town. Two Shan stupas, erected in 1860 and 1874, enshrine the ashes of monks from Myanmar's Shan State. Around the back of the wát you can see a tall, slender standing Buddha and catch views west of the ridge. No shorts or miniskirts are permitted in the wát grounds, but you can rent cover-ups.

Wat Jong Kham & Wat Jong Klang
วัดจองคำ/วัดจองกลาง

Next to Nong Jong Kham in the southern part of town are a couple of mildly interesting Burmese-style wát. Wat Jong Kham was built nearly 200 years ago by Thai Yai (Shan) residents, who make up about 50% of the population of Mae Hong Son Province today.

Adjacent Wat Jong Klang houses 100-year-old glass *jataka* (stories of the Buddha's past lives) paintings and has small rooms full of wooden reliefs and figures depicting the *Vessantara* jataka (the popular jataka in which the Bodhisattva develops the Perfection of Giving) – all very Burmese in style. The wíhǎan containing these is open 8am to 6pm daily. Wat Jong Klang has several areas that women are forbidden to enter – not unusual for Burmese/Shan Buddhist temples.

Wat Hua Wiang
วัดหัวเวียง

Although its wooden *bòt* (central sanctuary) is in an advanced state of decay, a famous bronze Buddha in the Mandalay style, called Chao Phlalakhaeng, can be seen in this wát on Thanon Phanit Wattana east of Thanon Khunlum Praphat.

Trekking

Trekking out of Mae Hong Son can be arranged at several guesthouses and travel agencies; *Mae Hong Son Guest House* (☎ 053 612 510) has some of the most dependable and experienced guides. Guides at *Don Enterprise* (in the back of the night market building) and *Sunflower Cafe* have also received good reviews. Typical rates for most treks are 600B per day per person (if there are four or more people), with three to five days the normal duration. Popular routes include the Mae Pai valley, Khun Yuam district and north of Soppong. A six-day trek from east of Mae Hong Son to near Soppong costs 400B per day per person. As with trekking elsewhere in the North, be sure to clarify when a trek starts and stops or you may not get your money's worth. Nearby Karen villages can be visited without a guide by walking two hours outside of town – several guesthouses in town can provide a map.

Rafting

Raft trips on the nearby Mae Pai are gaining in popularity, and the same guesthouses and trekking agencies that organise treks from Mae Hong Son can arrange the river trips. The most common type of trip sets off from Tha Mae Pai (Pai River Pier) in Ban Huay Deua, 8km southwest of Mae Hong Son, for a day-long upriver journey of 5km. From the same pier, down-river trips to the 'longneck' village of Kariang Padaung Kekongdu (Hoi Sen Thao; see the boxed text in this chapter) on the Thailand-Myanmar border are also possible. Another popular raft route runs between Sop Soi (10km northwest of town) and the village of Soppong to the west (not to be confused with the larger Shan trading village of the same name to the east). These day trips typically cost 500B per person if arranged in Ban Huay Deua, or 800B to 1200B if done through a Mae Hong Son agency.

The Mae Pai raft trips can be good fun if the raft holds up – it's not uncommon for rafts to fall apart or sink. The Myanmar trip, which attracts travellers who want to see the Padaung or 'long-necked' people, is a bit of a rip-off and, to some, exploitative – a four-hour trip through unspectacular scenery to see a few Padaung people who have fled to Mae Hong Son to escape an ethnic war in Myanmar. When there is fighting between Shan armies and Yangon troops in the area this trip may not be possible.

Special Events

Wat Jong Klang and Wat Jong Kham are the focal point of the **Poi Sang Long Festival** in March, when young Shan boys are ordained as novice monks during the school holidays in the ceremony known as *bùat lûuk kâew*. Like elsewhere in Thailand, the ordinands are carried on the shoulders of friends or relatives and paraded around the wát under festive parasols, but in the Shan custom the boys are dressed in ornate costumes (rather than simple white robes) and wear flower headdresses and facial makeup. Sometimes they ride on ponies.

Another important local event is the **Jong Para Festival**, held towards the end of the Buddhist Rains Retreat in October (three days before the full moon of the 11th lunar month – so it varies from year to year). The festival begins with local Shan bringing offerings to monks in the temples in a procession marked by the carrying of models of *praasàat* (castle-like shrines) on poles. An important part of the festival is the folk theatre and dance which is performed on the wát grounds, some of it unique to Northwestern Thailand.

During **Loi Krathong** – a national holiday usually celebrated by floating *krà-thong* (small lotus floats) on the nearest pond, lake or river – Mae Hong Son residents launch balloons called *krà-thong sa-wăn* (heavenly krà-thong) from Doi Kong Mu.

Places to Stay – Budget

Guesthouses *Mae Hong Son Guest House* (☎ *053 612 510, 295 Thanon Makasanti)* Longhouse rooms with shared facilities 100-150B, bungalows with private bathroom 250-500B. At a secluded location on the northwestern outskirts of town (about 700m west of Thanon Khunlum Praphat), this was the first guesthouse in town and is still among the most amenable. The guesthouse is a good source of information and inexpensive meals.

Sang Tong Huts (☎ *053 620 680,* e *sangtonghuts@hotmail.com)* Small/large huts 200/1000B. In a pretty setting in the hills nearby, the equally secluded Sang Tong offers recently renovated huts with panoramic views. The smaller huts have shared facilities, while the larger ones are nicely furnished and come with balcony, hot-water shower and fridge. Set dinners are available in the dining area, with menus in English and German.

Chan Guest House (☎ *053 620 432, Thanon Sirimongkhon)* Rooms 150B. Head north from the airport on Thanon Khunlum Praphat; just over a little bridge turn left onto Thanon Sirimongkhon and you'll come to Chan Guest House. It's a large house with a few small but clean rooms with fan and private cold-water shower, plus four common hot-water showers. The high ratio of bathrooms to guest rooms and fairly quiet location are pluses.

Yok Guest House (☎ *053 611 532, 14 Thanon Sirimongkhon)* Rooms with private hot-water bathroom & fan/air-con 250/400B. If you continue northwest along Thanon Sirimongkhon another 300m, past a wát, you'll come to this small, very quiet, family-run place on the right. Yok features nine super-clean rooms around a courtyard parking area.

In the area of Nong Jong Kham are several very pleasant guesthouses.

Jong Kam Guest House (☎ *053 611 150, Thanon Pradit Jong Kham)* Singles/doubles with shared bathroom 100/200B, double with hot-water bathroom 250B. Some of the slightly worn but clean rooms are in a row house, while others are in some newer thatched huts. There's only one hut with fan and attached hot-water shower available.

Friend House (☎ *053 620 119, fax 053 620 060, 20 Thanon Pradit Jong Kham*) Singles & doubles with fan & shared hot-water bathroom 100B, doubles with private bathroom 250B, 4-person room 300B. This guesthouse overlooking the northern side of the lake has large, clean rooms in a teak house. The upstairs rooms have a view of the lake. Friend House also rents out motorcycles.

Johnnie House (*Thanon Pradit Jong Kham*) Singles/doubles with shared bathroom 80/100B, rooms with private hot-water bathroom 120B. Also facing the northern side of Nong Jong Kham, this place offers clean rooms in a wooden row house.

Piya Guest House (☎ *053 611 260, 1/1 Thanon Khunlum Praphat*) Rooms 500B. On the southwestern side of the lake you'll find the Piya built around a garden, with a bar/restaurant in front. All rooms have air-con and private hot-water shower; although Piya is an OK place, it is perhaps a little overpriced for the local market.

Rim Nong Guest House (☎ *053 611 052, 4 Thanon Chamnan Sathit*) Dorm beds 120B, rooms with shared hot-water bathroom 250B, 1 air-con room 500B. This is a friendly place on the southern side of the lake with a little restaurant on the water's edge.

Joe Guest House (☎ *053 612 417*) Rooms with shared bathroom 100B, with private bathroom up to 250B. Across the

'Longnecked' Padaung Villages

Near Mae Hong Son are several Padaung refugee villages where 'longneck' women are a local tourist attraction. The brass ornaments the Padaung women wear around their necks and limbs, which look like separate rings but are actually continuous coils, may weigh up to 22kg (though 5kg is a more common maximum) and stand 30cm in height. The neck coils depress the collarbone and rib cage, making it look as if their necks have been unnaturally stretched. A common myth says that if the coils are removed, the women's necks will fall over from atrophy and they'll die, but the women attach and remove the coils at will with no such problems.

No-one knows for sure how the coil custom got started. One theory says it was conceived to make the women's appearance strange enough that men from other tribes wouldn't pursue them. Another story says it was so tigers wouldn't carry them off by their throats. The Padaung themselves tell an apocryphal story claiming their ancestors were the offspring of a liaison between the wind and a beautiful female dragon, and that the coil-wearing custom pays tribute to their dragon progenitor. The women also wear thin hoops made of cane or lacquered cord gathered in bunches around their knees and calves. As fewer and fewer Padaung women adopt the custom, the coil-wearing tradition is gradually dying out.

As a tourist attraction, the longneck village business is for the most part controlled by the Karenni National Progressive Party (KNPP), a Kayah (Karenni) insurgent group whose reported objective is to establish an independent Kayah state in eastern Myanmar. The Padaung are, in fact, an ethno-linguistic subgroup of the Kayah. Of the 7000 Padaung thought to be residents of Myanmar, around 300 have fled to Thailand as refugees.

The biggest of the Padaung villages is Nai Soi (also known as Nupa Ah), 35km northwest of the provincial capital. Independent interviews with the women have ascertained that they earn around 3000B a month from selling handicrafts and from a small portion of the 250B entrance fee collected from foreigners. On average 1200 tourists a year visit this village (as many as 50 per day in the high season), and the bulk of the entry fees is thought to go to the KNPP. The typical tourist visit consists of extended photography sessions during which the coil-adorned Padaung women pose while weaving, or standing next to visitors. The women tell reporters they aren't bothered by the photography, which they consider to be part of their livelihood. As Nai Soi's Ma Nang was quoted in street, away from the lake, the very basic Joe has rooms with shared facilities in an old teak house; the rooms with private facilities are in a newer section.

Sabanga House (☎ *053 612 280, 14 Thanon Udom Chaonithet)* Rooms 100B. This bamboo row house contains eight rooms that have a mattresses on the floor, fan and shared hot-water shower.

Pen Porn House (☎*/fax 053 611 577, 16/1 Thanon Wat Muay To)* Doubles/4-bed rooms 250/400B. Located in a residential neighbourhood on a slope on the western side of town, this place has clean and spacious rooms in a row house; all of them have fan and private hot-water shower.

Other less-convenient places can be found around Mae Hong Son – the touts at the bus station will be able to direct you there.

Hotels Most of the hotels in Mae Hong Son are along the main north-south road, Thanon Khunlum Praphat.

Siam Hotel (☎ *053 612 148, 23 Thanon Khunlum Praphat)* Singles/doubles with fan 170/250B, rooms with air-con 350B. Next to the bus station, the Siam has rather ordinary and overpriced rooms, recommendable only in a pinch.

Mae Tee Hotel (Methi; ☎ *053 612 141, 053 611 141, 55 Thanon Khunlum Praphat)* 1/2-bed rooms with fan 150/160B, 1/3-bed rooms with air-con 300/400B. Though slightly cheaper than the Siam, this hotel is better.

'Longnecked' Padaung Villages

one of several stories the *Bangkok Post* has run on the Padaung: 'We had nothing in Myanmar. I had to work relentlessly in the rice fields. We miss our homes, but we don't want to go back.'

Other Padaung women may not have been as fortunate. A decade ago a Shan man brought seven longneck women into Thailand and tried to 'sell' them to a resort in Soppong. Thai police arrested the man and freed the women, who immediately went to Nai Soi. One occasionally hears of other such tales, although we have received no confirmed reports of any occurrences in Thailand since 1991. The same thing reportedly goes on in Myanmar as well, particularly in the Shan State around Inle Lake.

Opinions are sharply divided as to the ethics of 'consuming' the Padaung as a tourist attraction. Obviously there's the claim that viewing of the longnecked Padaung in Thailand amounts to crass exploitation, but those who have taken the time to interview these people and learn about their lives have pointed out that this is the best opportunity they have available for making a living under current social conditions in Myanmar and Thailand. One thing seems certain: They are usually in Thailand by choice, having fled a potentially worse fate in Myanmar amid ethnic war. Thai authorities view Nai Soi as a self-sustaining refugee camp.

We see the longneck phenomenon as sitting squarely on the same cline of ethno-tourism as tribal trekking, one of the crasser forms to be sure, but only differing in degree from paying an Akha or a Guatemalan Indian to pose for a photo. Ethically it surely beats paying a trek operator for the privilege of photographing tribal people on a trek when the latter receive nothing.

If you want to see any of the Padaung settlements, you can choose from Hoi Sen Thao (11km west of Mae Hong Son, 20 minutes by boat from the nearby Huay Deua landing), Nai Soi (35km northwest) and Huay Ma Khen Som (about 7km before Mae Aw). Travel agencies in Mae Hong Son arrange tours to these villages for 700B to 800B per person, which means they take in 450B to 550B over the village entry fees to pay for transport and expenses.

If you go to Nai Soi on your own, it's possible to arrange overnight accommodation in the village for 50B per person a night. At the entrance to the village your name, passport number and country of residence will be noted on a payment receipt issued by the 'Karenni Culture Department'. A couple of hundred metres beyond Nai Soi is a large Kayah refugee settlement, also controlled by the KNPP.

Places to Stay – Mid-Range & Top End

Baiyoke Chalet Hotel (☎ 053 611 486, fax 053 611 533, 90 Thanon Khunlum Praphat) Rooms 1330B, including breakfast; low-season rates 40% less. Towards the southern end of town near the post office, the Baiyoke Chalet offers all the typical amenities.

Mountain Inn Hotel (☎ 053 612 284, fax 053 611 309, 112 Thanon Khunlum Praphat) Rooms 800B (500-600B in low season), including breakfast. This large, spread-out hotel features clean, medium-sized air-con singles and doubles with hot water that are set around a courtyard. There are well-kept, nicely landscaped public areas.

Panorama Hotel (☎ 053 611 757, fax 053 611 790, 51 Thanon Khunlum Praphat) Singles/doubles with fan & hot water 400/500B, rooms with air-con, hot water, TV & fridge 800B. The rooms in this multi-storey hotel are simple but clean.

Mae Hong Son Hill Resort (☎/fax 053 612 475, 106/2 Thanon Khunlum Praphat) Rooms with fan/air-con 400/500B. Near the stadium, this is a quiet spot with 22 well-kept bungalows in a semi-garden area.

Rooks Holiday Hotel & Resort (☎ 053 612 324, fax 053 611 524, ℮ rooksgroup@ hotmail.com, 114/5-7 Thanon Khunlum Praphat) Rooms & bungalows 1800-2200B. A bit farther south of the Mae Hong Son Hill Resort, this place represents the top end in town. Facilities include a swimming pool, tennis courts, disco, snooker club, bakery, coffee shop and restaurant.

Out of Town Southwest of town on the river, a few kilometres towards Ban Huay Deua and Ban Tha Pong Daeng, are several 'resorts', which in the Thai sense of the term means any hotel near a rural or semi-rural area.

Imperial Tara Mae Hong Son Hotel (☎ 053 611 021, fax 053 611 252, ℮ taramaehongson@imperialhotels.com, 149 Mu 8, Tambon Pang Mu) Doubles from 2060B. The amenities at this upmarket hotel include a pool, sauna and fitness centre.

Fern Rim Tarn Resort (☎ 053 611 374, fax 053 612 363, ℮ fernresort@ maehongsontourism.net, 64 Mu Bo, Tambon Pha Bong) Bungalows 1250-1500B. About 5km southwest of town via Rte 108 and a turn-off for Ban Hua Nam Mae Sakut, this ecofriendly resort features Shan-style wooden bungalows adjacent to rice paddies. Low-season discounts are readily available, and there are good walks in the vicinity. Regular guests here enjoy the lovely surroundings and peaceful atmosphere, not to mention the pool.

Farther off the highway are a couple more mid-range places worth considering. **Mae Hong Son Riverside Hotel** (☎ 053 611 504, 053 611 406, 165 Mu 3, Ban Huay Toe, Tambon Pha Bong) has doubles from 1150B (discounted to 750B), and **Sam Mork Villa** (☎ 053 611 478, Tambon Pha Bong) has doubles with fan/air-con from 500/800B.

Places to Eat

Mae Hong Son isn't known for its food, but there are a few decent places to eat besides the guesthouses. The **morning market** behind the Mae Tee Hotel is a good place to buy food for trekking. Get there before 8am.

Jok Suay (Soi Niwet Phisan, opposite the municipal market) Dishes 15-20B. Open 5am-9.30am daily. This is the best place in town for jók (rice congee).

Khai Muk (☎ 053 612 092, 23 Thanon Udom Chaonithet) Dishes 25-60B. Open 10am-2pm & 5pm-midnight daily. This outdoor spot is one of the better Thai-Chinese restaurants in town.

Pa Dim (Thanon Khunlum Praphat) Dishes 20-40B. Open 8am-8pm daily. Diagonally opposite Khai Muk, this restaurant features dishes from every region in Thailand; it's popular because of its reasonable prices and good-sized portions.

Fern Restaurant (Thanon Khunlum Praphat) Dishes 40-80B. Open 10am-10pm daily. Although the long-running Fern gets the occasional tour group, the Thai food here is still the best in town. Specialities include chùu-chìi kûng (shrimp in a succulent curry sauce) and hèt hăwm òp sii-íu (mushrooms baked in soy sauce and served with a roasted garlic sauce). The restaurant is south of the post office.

Thai Vegetarian Food Restaurant *(Thanon Singhanat Bamrung)* Dishes 10-30B. Open 9am-3pm. Next to the tourist police office, this simple eatery serves inexpensive vegetarian Thai as well as some nonvegetarian dishes.

Lucky Bakery Kitchen *(Thanon Singhanat Bamrung)* Dishes 40-100B. Open 8am-9pm daily. This bakery is popular for 'cowboy steak' and baked goods.

Swiss Chalet *(☎ 053 612 050)* Dishes 40-80B. Open 7am-1am daily. Next door to the bakery, Swiss Chalet serves cheese fondue, roesti and pasta.

Sunflower Cafe *(Thanon Udom Chaonithet)* Dishes 20-100B. Open 7.30am-9pm daily. This pleasant spot near the post office offers freshly baked whole-wheat breads and cakes, pizzas and coffee, plus information on local trekking. It may be closed in the rainy season.

Getting There & Away

Air THAI flies to Mae Hong Son from Chiang Mai three times daily (690B, 35 minutes). For many people, the time saved flying to Mae Hong Son versus bus travel is worth the extra money. Mae Hong Son's THAI office (☎ 053 611 297, 053 611 194) is at 71 Thanon Singhanat Bamrung.

Bus From Chiang Mai there are two bus routes to Mae Hong Son: the northern route through Pai (100/130B ordinary/air-con, seven hours) and the southern route through Mae Sariang (143/257B, eight hours). The fare as far as Mae Sariang is 78B (140B air-con).

Although it may be longer, the southern route through Mae Sariang is a much more comfortable ride because the bus stops every two hours for a 10- to 15-minute break and larger buses – with large seats – are used. Buses to Mae Hong Son via Mae Sariang leave Chiang Mai's Arcade bus station five times daily between 6.30am and 9pm.

The northern route through Pai, originally built by the Japanese in WWII, is very winding and offers spectacular views from time to time. Because the buses used on this road are smaller they're usually more crowded, and the younger passengers tend to get motion sickness. The Pai bus leaves the Chiang Mai Arcade station four times a day at 7am, 9am, 10.30am and 12.30pm. The 4pm bus only goes as far as Pai.

Buses to from Mai Hong Son to Soppong cost 35B, to Pai 53/74B.

Getting Around

It is pretty easy to walk around most of Mae Hong Son. Motorcycle taxis within town cost from 10B to 20B; to Doi Kong Mu it's 30B one way or 50B return. Motorcycle drivers will also take passengers farther afield but fares out of town are expensive. There are now a few túk-túk in town, charging 20B to 30B per trip.

Several guesthouses rent out bicycles (20B to 30B) and motorcycles (150B for 24 hours). Avis Rent-A-Car (☎ 053 620 457/8) has an office at the Mae Hong Son airport.

AROUND MAE HONG SON
Pha Bong Hot Springs
บ่อน้ำร้อนผาบ่อง

Eleven kilometres south of the capital at the Km256 marker on Rte 108, this public park with hot springs covers 8 râi (0.12 sq km). Facilities include bathing rooms and a couple of simple restaurants.

Mae Aw
แม่ออ

Another day trip you can do from the provincial capital is to Mae Aw, 22km north of Mae Hong Son on a mountain peak at the Myanmar border. Mae Aw is a Chinese KMT settlement, one of the last true KMT outposts in Thailand, although it's not as interesting as Doi Mae Salong or Ban Mai Nong Bua near Doi Ang Khang. There's no feeling of 'wow, this is an exciting place filled with old renegade fighters'; it's just a quiet place with border people going about their own business, but it's an interesting trip.

The town lies along the edge of a large reservoir and the faces and signs are very Chinese. Occasionally there is fighting along the border between the KMT and the Mong Tai Army, formerly led by the infamous opium warlord Khun Sa but now operating as four splinter units under separate leaderships. When this happens, public transport to these areas is usually suspended and you are advised against going without a guide. The modern Thai name for Mae Aw is Ban Rak Thai (Thai-Loving Village).

In the Chinese/Hmong village of Na Pa Paek, 7.3km southwest of Mae Aw, accommodation in thatched huts is available at *Roun Thai Guest House* for 50B per bed (150B with two meals). Two small tea shops set up for tourists serve tea, cola and snacks of dubious sterility. The better of the two is *Mr Huang Yuan Tea & Restaurant*. You can also purchase a slightly unusual souvenir here – a section of bamboo filled with tea labelled 'special blend tea, made by KMT' in English, Thai and Chinese.

From Na Pa Paek a rough dirt road leads southwest to the Hmong village of **Ma Khua Som** (3.5km) and the KMT village of **Pang Ung La** (6km) on the Myanmar border. Pang Ung La also has a *guesthouse*.

Since the sealing of the 22km road to Na Pa Paek, trips to Mae Aw are easier, although it's still a steep, winding route. The final unsealed 7km to Mae Aw can be very troublesome in the wet season.

There are rather irregular săwngthăew (50B to 60B) going back and forth from Mae Hong Son, but it's so unpredictable these days that you're better off getting a group of people together and chartering a săwngthăew. It will cost you 600B to 1300B (depending on whether the drivers have any paid cargo). This option lets you stop and see the sights along the way. Check Thanon Singhanat Bamrung near the telephone office at around 9am to see if there are any săwngthăew going.

The trip takes two hours and passes Shan, Karen and Hmong villages, the Pang Tong Summer Palace and waterfalls. Mae Aw is also included on some day tours operated out of Mae Hong Son.

If you have your own transport, you can stop off at **Nam Tok Pha Sua** on the way to Mae Aw. About 17km north of Rte 1095, turn onto a marked dirt road. The multilevel cataract has water year-round; during the rainy season swimming can be dangerous due to thundering water flow. Facilities include picnic tables and toilets.

Tham Pla National Park
อุทยานแห่งชาติถ้ำปลา

A trip to Mae Aw can be combined with a visit to this recently established national park centred on the animistic Tham Pla (Fish Cave), a water-filled cavern where hundreds of soro brook carp thrive. These fish grow up to 1m in length and are found only in the provinces of Mae Hong Son, Ranong, Chiang Mai, Rayong, Chanthaburi and Kanchanaburi. The fish eat vegetables and insects, although the locals believe them to be vegetarian and feed them only fruit and vegetables (which can be purchased at the park entrance).

You can see the fish through a 2-sq-metre rock hole at the base of an outer wall of the cave. A statue of a Hindu rishi (sage) called Nara, said to protect the holy fish from danger, stands nearby.

A path leads from the park entrance to a suspension bridge that crosses a stream and continues to the cave. The park is a shady, cool place to hang out; picnic tables are available. You can pitch a *tent* for free on the grounds. Last we checked admission to the park was still free, although the recent general increase in national park entry fees may mean the rangers will eventually begin charging. The park is 17km northeast of Mae Hong Son on the northern side of Hwy 1095.

Mae La-Na, Tham Lot & Soppong
แม่ละนา,ถ้ำลอดและสบปอง

It's possible to walk a 20km half-loop all the way from Mae La-Na to Tham Lot and Soppong, staying overnight in Red Lahu villages along the way. Ask for a sketch map at the

Mae Lana Guest House (see Places to Stay later in this section). Experienced riders can accomplish this route on a sturdy dirt bike – but not alone or during the rainy season.

Mae La-Na Between Mae Hong Son and Pai, Rte 1095 winds through an area of forests, mountains, streams, Shan and hill-tribe villages and limestone caves. Some of Mae Hong Son's most beautiful scenery is within a day's walk of the Shan village of Mae La-Na (6km north of Rte 1095 via a half-sealed road), where overnight accommodation is available. From here you can trek to several nearby Red and Black Lahu villages and to a few caves within a 4km to 8km radius.

Local guides will lead visitors to nearby caves for set prices per cave. **Tham Mae La-Na**, 4km from the village, is the largest and most famous – it's threaded by a 12km length of river – and a journey to the cave and through it costs 600B. **Tham Pakarang** (Coral Cave), **Tham Phet** (Diamond Cave), **Tham Khao Taek** (Broken Rice Cave) and **Tham Khai Muk** (Pearl Cave) all feature good wall formations and cost 200B each for guides. Rates are posted at a small *săalaa* (shelter) near a noodle stand and petrol-barrel pumps in the centre of the village; this is also where you may contact the guides during the day. If no-one's at the săalaa when you go there, just mention *thâm* (cave) to someone at the petrol pumps.

Even if you don't go trekking or caving, Mae La-Na can be a peaceful and mildly interesting cul-de-sac to stay for a short while. Beyond a Shan-style temple, a school, some houses and the aforementioned 'downtown' area around the noodle shops and petrol pumps, there's little to see, but the surrounding montane scenery is quite pleasing.

Twenty-seven kilometres west of Pangmapha is a short turn-off for **Wat Tham Wua Sunyata**, a peaceful forest monastery.

The Mae La-Na junction is 55km from Mae Hong Son, 10km from Soppong and 56km from Pai. The village is 6km north of the junction. Infrequent săwngthăew from the highway to the village cost 20B per person – mornings are your best bet.

Tham Lot About 8km north of Soppong is Tham Lot *(pronounced 'thâm lâwt' and also known as 'thâm náam lâwt'; admission 100B; open 8am-5.30pm daily)*, a large limestone cave with a wide stream running through it. Along with Tham Nam Lang farther west, it's one of the longest known caves in mainland Southeast Asia (although some as yet unexplored caves in Southern Thailand may be even longer). It is possible to hike all the way through the cave (approximately 200m) by following the stream, although it requires some wading back and forth. Apart from the main chamber, there are three side-chambers that can be reached by ladders – it takes two to three hours to see the whole thing. Where the stream exits the cave, thousands of bats and swifts leave the cave at dusk.

At the park entrance you must hire a gas lantern and guide for 100B (one guide can lead up to four people) to take you through the caverns; they no longer permit visitors to tour the caves alone. The guide fee includes visits to the first and third caverns; to visit the second cavern you must cross the stream. Raft men waiting inside the cave charge 10B per person per crossing; in the dry season you may be able to wade across. For 100B you can stay on the raft through the third cavern. If you decide to book a Tham Lot day tour from Mae Hong Son, ask if the tour cost includes guide, lamp and raft fees.

Outside the park entrance a row of outdoor *restaurants*, open 9am to 6pm daily, offers basic Thai fare for 15B to 35B.

Soppong Soppong is a small but relatively prosperous market village a couple of hours northwest of Pai and about 70km from Mae Hong Son. Since the paving of Rte 1095, Soppong and Tham Lot have become popular destinations for minivan tours from Mae Hong Son and Chiang Mai.

Close to Soppong are several Shan, Lisu, Karen and Lahu villages that can easily be visited on foot. Inquire at the Jungle Guest

House or Cave Lodge (see Places to Stay following) in Soppong for reliable information. It's important to ask about the current situation at the Myanmar border area, as it's somewhat sensitive due to the opium trade and smuggling.

Soppong has a post office opposite the main market area on the highway.

The rough back road between Soppong and Mae La-Na is popular with mountain bikers and off-highway motorcyclists.

Places to Stay All three places have accommodation options, though most are concentrated in Soppong.

Mae La-Na & Vicinity Sitting on a hill overlooking the village, *Top Hill* offers OK bungalow accommodation with shared facilities for 40B. A little farther below towards the valley bottom, *Mae Lana Guest House* has four large doubles (80B) with

Coffin Caves

A 900-sq-km area of Pangmapha and adjacent districts may contain more caves than any other region in the world. Over 30 of these limestone caverns are known to contain very old wooden coffins carved from solid tree logs. Up to 6m long, the coffins are typically suspended on wooden scaffolds inside the caves and bound with ceremonial tassels (very few of which have been found intact). The coffins – which number in the dozens – are of unknown age and origin, but Thai anthropologists have classified them into at least 14 different design schemes. Pottery remains associated with the sites have also been found.

The local Thais know these burial caves as *thâm phĭi* (spirit caves), or *thâm phĭi maen* (coffin caves). Eight coffin caves that scientists are investigating at the moment remain off limits to the public, but you may be able to find guides in the Pangmapha district willing to tour others. Tham Nam Lang, 30km northwest of Soppong near Ban Nam Khong, is 9km long and said to be one of the largest caves in the world in terms of volume.

mosquito nets, as well as a four-bed dorm (40B per bed). Mae Lana Guest House closes during the rainy season.

At Ban Nam Khong, and run by the same family that owns the Cave Lodge in Tham Lot, the *Wilderness Lodge* has huts for 50B per person. The Rte 108 turn-off for Wilderness Lodge is located 25km west of Pangmapha village.

About 12km north of Mae La-Na in the Black Lahu village of Ban Huay Hea (close to the Myanmar border) is the *Lahu Guest House*, with beds for 50B. Run by a village teacher who speaks English, the lodging is simple and the money goes to a community fund.

Soppong Soppong has developed into an important stop for both day and overnight package tours.

Lemon Hill Guest House Bungalows with hot-water shower 150/200B. Just off the highway, near the bus stop, this guesthouse features nice huts facing the Nam Lan stream and with bougainvillea tumbling over the roofs.

Kemarin Garden Lodge On the opposite side of the road from Lemon Hill Guest House, past the market, a narrow lane leads to this lodge. It was closed when we visited; the owners say they plan to renovate and reopen, but they didn't say when.

Charming Home Single/double huts 120/150B. If you continue along the track another 1km (the last ½km is accessible by foot or bicycle only) and cross a footbridge over a stream you'll come to Charming Home. Two well-designed, well-spaced huts with private shower and toilet sit on a breezy hillside backed by primary forest. There are many birds in this area and you can easily hike to Lisu and Lahu villages nearby.

Jungle Guest House (☎ 053 617 099) Single/double huts with shared hot-water facilities 100/120B, with private bathroom 250/300B. This friendly place is 1km west of Charming Home on the road to Mae Hong Son. The huts are well-designed and the new restaurant overlooking the river serves better fare than most of the other guesthouses in the area. The nearby *Pangmapa Guest House*, northwest of the Jungle Guest House on the same road, is similar.

Soppong River Inn Bungalows with shared hot-water facilities 200B, 1 bungalow with private bathroom 450B. Soppong River Inn is on the opposite side of the road from Jungle Guest House, overlooking the river. It offers Internet services.

T Rex House (☎ 053 617 054, fax 053 617 053) Regular/VIP rooms 350/450B. A Thai woman who speaks English, German and Danish runs T Rex, well off the road in a nice river setting. It features solar water heating and a swimming pool in a tropical garden. Nine A-frame bungalows are available, all with private toilet and hot-water shower. The two VIP rooms are in the main house. Discounts may be available during the rainy season. T Rex rents motorcycles for 200B per day.

Tham Lot Near Tham Lot several guesthouses have come and gone. Royal Forest Department officials have on occasion cracked down on illegal accommodation encroaching on the forest area, although we haven't heard of that happening lately. At the moment there are only two places, both within a few hundred metres of the cave.

Cave Lodge Dorm beds 60B, bungalows with shared bathroom 120-250B, newer 2/4-person bungalows with private bathroom 280/350B. The newer bungalows at this long-running place are more spacious than the older ones. Guided day-hikes are available for a very reasonable 350B, and inflatable kayak trips for 500B.

Lang River Guest House Dorm beds 70B, single/double bungalows 150/200B. This relaxed guesthouse stands on the banks of the stream that runs through the cave, west of the park entrance. It has a large shed-like dormitory back from the river with raised, partitioned sleeping platforms, each fairly wide with a mattress, mosquito net and built-in shelves. The regular bungalows overlook the river, while two nicer bungalows are usually reserved for tour groups. Trekking guides can also be arranged here.

You may also be able to rent a *room* for around 100B a night from villagers at Ban Tham, the village closest to Tham Lot.

On foot it takes about 1½ hours from Soppong along a well-marked, half-sealed road to reach Ban Tham, Cave Lodge and Lang River Guest House. Nowadays there's plenty of vehicular traffic, so you should also be able to hitch a ride fairly easily.

Ban Nam Rin At this Lisu village 10km south of Soppong towards Pai, between the Km132 and Km133 markers, you can stay at *Lisu Lodge* (in Chiang Mai ☎ 053 281 789, fax 053 281 788, ℮ adventures@lisulodge .com) by prior arrangement. Lodging/ecotour/trekking packages start at 1960B per person. The Lisu Lodge no longer accepts walk-ins.

Getting There & Around Buses from Pai to Mae Hong Son stop in Soppong and there are two or three each day in both directions. From Mae Hong Son to Soppong, buses take about 2½ hours (35/46B ordinary/aircon). The trip between Pai and Soppong (25/28B) takes 1½ to two hours.

Motorcycle taxis stationed at the bus stop in Soppong will carry passengers to Tham Lot or the Cave Lodge for 50B per person; private pick-up trucks will take you and up to five other people for 200B. If you have your own wheels, the road from Soppong to Ban Tham is graded until the Km7 marker, after which it's rough dirt all the way to the cave.

PAI

ปาย

postcode 58130 • pop 3000

It first appears that there's not a lot to see in Pai (pronounced like the English word 'bye', not 'pie'), a peaceful crossroads town about halfway between Chiang Mai and Mae Hong Son on Rte 1095. But if you stick around a few days and talk to some of the locals, you may discover some beautiful spots in the surrounding hills.

Most of the town's population are Shan and Thai, but there's also a small but visible Yunnanese Muslim population.

Information

The Krung Thai Bank located on the eastern side of Thanon Rangthiyanon (the main road through town) has an ATM.

Several places around town offer Internet services, including conveniently located Avu Internet Cafe (☎ 053 699 824) on Thanon Rangthiyanon; it's open 8am to 10pm daily.

Wat Phra That Mae Yen

วัดพระธาตุแม่เย็น

This temple sits atop a hill with a good view overlooking the valley. Walk 1km east from the main intersection in town, across the river and through a village, to get to the stairs (a decent climb – 353 steps) that lead to the top. Or take the 400m sealed road that follows a different route to the top.

Tha Pai Hot Springs

บ่อน้ำร้อนท่าปาย

Across the Mae Pai and 8km southeast of town via a paved road is Tha Pai Hot Springs (*admission free; swimming or bathing 50B*). This well-kept local park is 1km from the road. A scenic stream runs

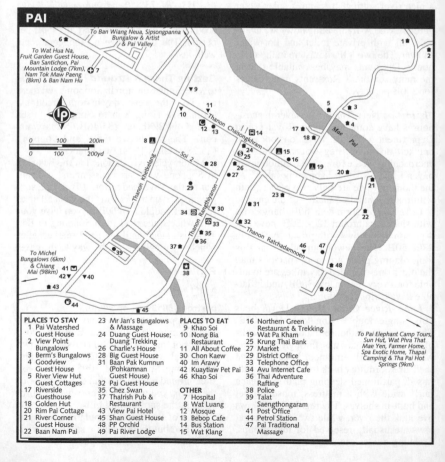

PAI

Scale: 0   100   200m
        0   100   200yd

To Ban Wiang Neua, Sipsongpanna Bungalow & Artist & Pai Valley

To Wat Hua Na, Fruit Garden Guest House, Ban Santichon, Pai Mountain Lodge (7km), Nam Tok Maw Paeng (8km) & Ban Nam Hu

To Michel Bungalows (6km) & Chiang Mai (98km)

To Pai Elephant Camp Tours, Sun Hut, Wat Phra That Mae Yen, Farmer Home, Spa Exotic Home, Thapai Camping & Tha Pai Hot Springs (9km)

Thanon Khettkelang
Thanon Chaisongkhram
Thanon Rangthiyanon
Thanon Ratchadamnoen
Soi 2
Mae Pai

PLACES TO STAY
1 Pai Watershed Guest House
2 View Point Bungalows
3 Berm's Bungalows
4 Goodview Guest House
5 River View Hut Guest Cottages
17 Riverside Guesthouse
18 Golden Hut
20 Rim Pai Cottage
21 River Corner Guest House
22 Baan Nam Pai
23 Mr Jan's Bungalows & Massage
24 Duang Guest House; Duang Trekking
26 Charlie's House
28 Big Guest House
31 Baan Pak Kumnun (Pohkamnan Guest House)
32 Pai Guest House
35 Chez Swan
37 Thalrish Pub & Restaurant
43 View Pai Hotel
45 Shan Guest House
48 PP Orchid
49 Pai River Lodge

PLACES TO EAT
9 Khao Soi
10 Nong Bia Restaurant
11 All About Coffee
30 Chon Kaew
40 Im Arawy
42 Kuaytiaw Pet Pai
46 Khao Soi

OTHER
7 Hospital
8 Wat Luang
12 Mosque
13 Bebop Cafe
14 Bus Station
15 Wat Klang
16 Northern Green Restaurant & Trekking
19 Wat Pa Kham
25 Krung Thai Bank
27 Market
29 District Office
33 Telephone Office
34 Avu Internet Cafe
36 Thai Adventure Rafting
38 Police
39 Talat Saengthongaram
41 Post Office
44 Petrol Station
47 Pai Traditional Massage

through the park; it mixes with the hot springs in places to make pleasant bathing areas. There are also small public bathing houses to which hot spring water is piped.

Trekking

Northwest of town, a **Shan**, a **Lahu** and a **Lisu village**, along with a KMT village called **Ban Santichon** (San Ti Chuen in Yunnanese) and **Nam Tok Maw Paeng**, can all be visited on foot. The Shan, Lisu and KMT villages lie within 4km of Pai, while the Lahu village is near Nam Tok Maw Paeng, another 4km farther from town (8km total).

You can cut the hike in half by taking a Mae Hong Son–bound bus north about 5km and getting off at a signpost for the falls; from the highway it's only 4km (about 2km beyond the Pai Mountain Lodge). A couple of pools at the base of the falls are suitable for swimming – best just after the rainy season, October to early December.

Organised Tours

Any of the guesthouses in town can provide information on local trekking and a few do guided treks for as little as 500B per day if there are no rafts or elephants involved. Among the more established local agencies are *Duang Trekking* and *Northern Green*, both near Duang Guest House and the bus station.

Raft trips on the nearby Mae Pai operate from July to December, sometimes longer in rainy years; September is usually the best month. Most outfits use flimsy bamboo rafts but it's fun anyway if you don't mind getting wet.

Thai Adventure Rafting (☎/fax 053 699 111, ✉ rafting@activethailand.com) leads excellent two-day white-water rafting trips in sturdy rubber rafts from Pai to Mae Hong Son for 1800B per person including food, rafting equipment, camping gear, dry bags and insurance. Along the way rafters visit a waterfall, a fossil reef and hot springs; one night is spent at the company's permanent riverside camp. The main rafting season is July to December; after that the trips aren't normally run. It has offices in Pai (Thanon

Rangthiyanon) and in Chiang Mai (Thanon Charoen Prathet).

Pai Elephant Camp Tours (*Thom's Elephant Camp Tours*; ☎/fax 053 699 286, Thanon Ratdamrong) offers jungle rides year-round at its camp southeast of Pai near the hot springs. The cost is 300B to 550B per person (minimum of two persons) for a one- to three-hour ride that includes a visit to the hot springs. It can also arrange bamboo or rubber rafting trips down the Mae Pai. Combination elephant-trekking and river-rafting tours cost 1000B per person, and include lunch and transport. Other combination tours and treks are available, including overnight stays in hill-tribe villages. Their office is about 20m south of Thanon Rangthiyanon.

Traditional Massage

Pai Traditional Massage (☎ 053 699 121, 68/3 Thanon Sukhaphiban 1; 1/1½-hour massage 150/230B, sauna 50B; open 4.30pm-8.30pm Mon-Fri, 8.30am-8.30pm Sat-Sun) In a house near the river, this place offers very good Northern Thai massage, as well as a sauna where you can steam yourself in *samŭn phrai* (medicinal herbs). The couple that do the massages are graduates of Chiang Mai's Old Medicine Hospital. A three-day massage course is available for 2000B.

Another place in town, called **Mr Jan's Massage** (*Soi Wanchalerm 18*), employs a slightly rougher Shan/Burmese massage technique.

There are several other massage places in town, most of them newer and not as experienced as Pai Traditional Massage and Mr Jan's.

Places to Stay

Duang Guest House (☎ 053 699 101, fax 053 699 581, Thanon Chaisongkhram) Singles with shared bathroom 60-70B, doubles with shared bathroom 120-130B, doubles with private bathroom 200B, 1 room with private bathroom, TV & fridge 400B. This rambling, friendly spot right across from the bus station offers 26 rooms, most with shared facilities, a few with private bathrooms.

WESTERN PROVINCES

Charlie's House (☎ *053 699 039, Thanon Rangthiyanon*) Dorm beds 60B, singles/doubles with shared bathroom 60/100B, rooms with private hot-water shower 200-250B (add 40B for a 3rd person). Two doors southwest of Krung Thai Bank is the clean and secure Charlie's House, with rooms in buildings arranged around a large courtyard. Charlie's is often full during the high season.

Big Guest House (☎ *053 699 080, Soi 2, Thanon Rangthiyanon*) Small single/double A-frame huts 60/100B, larger rooms with shared/private bathroom 120/150B. The rooms with private facilities are a bit nicer than the ones without.

Chez Swan (☎ *053 699 111, Thanon Rangthiyanon*) Rooms 200B. The restaurant of the same name has a row of large rooms behind it, with private hot-water showers and thick mattresses.

Along the Mae Pai in the eastern part of town is a string of quiet bungalow operations.

Pai River Lodge (☎ *01 980 4970*) Older A-frame huts 80B, 2 slightly larger nicer huts 100B. Here you'll find simple huts arranged in a large circle with a dining and lounge area on stilts in the middle. Because of its quiet, scenic location it's often full.

Baan Nam Pai (☎ *01 830 1161*, e baannampai@hotmail.com, *88 Mu 3, Wiang Tai*) Small single/double huts with shared bathroom 80/120B, slightly larger huts 100/150, large huts 120/200. This is a very friendly and well-kept place. All huts have shared shower and toilet facilities; eight new huts under construction will feature private facilities and cost 500B.

PP Orchid (☎ *053 699 159, 80 Mu 3, Wiang Tai*) Single/double bungalows 100/150B. Close to the river, the basic bungalows here sit in a nicely landscaped area.

Pai Guest House (*Wiang Neua*) Singles/doubles with shared bathroom 70/90B, with private bathroom 80/100B. The rooms here are very basic with thin mattresses on the floor.

Mr Jan's Bungalows (☎ *053 699 554, Soi Wanchaloem 18*) Huts with shared bathroom 70B, 2 single/double units with private cold-water shower 150/200B (less in the low season). Part of Mr Jan's Massage, this place has 10 simple bamboo huts set among a large herb garden and fruit trees. All guests have access to facilities where you can bathe with heated, herb-infused water.

Baan Pak Kumnun (*Pohkamnam Guest House;* ☎ *053 699 382, 109 Soi Wanchaloem 18*) Bungalows/row-house rooms 80/120B. Down the soi that's opposite Wat Klang is this newer spot, owned by the *kamnan* (precinct chief) and popular with Thai guests. Separated from the road by a large expanse of grass, all the rooms have shared bathrooms.

Rim Pai Cottage (☎ *053 699 133, 053 235 931, Thanon Chaisongkhram*) Row-house rooms/A-frame huts/bungalow 300/400/600B, including breakfast. Farther north along the river, the upmarket (for Pai) Rim Pai offers clean, quiet A-frames with private bathroom, electricity and mosquito nets, as well as rooms in a row house. One large bungalow is available by the river.

River Corner Guest House (*60 Mu 3, Wiang Tai*) Basic cottages low/high season 120/250B, larger cottage 500/750B. The cottages here are of simple bamboo-and-thatch and have private bathrooms.

Golden Hut (☎ *053 699 949*) Dorm beds 50B, doubles with shared bathroom 100B, separate bungalows with shared hot-water bathroom 120B, singles/doubles/triples with private bathroom 200/250/300B. North of Rim Pai Cottage around a bend in the river, the well-landscaped Golden Hut offers a variety of simple thatched huts on stilts lined up along the river.

Riverside Guest House (☎ *053 699 929*, e the.riverside.guesthouses@gmx.net, *111/1 Mu 3, Wiang Tai*) Single/double bungalows 80/120B. A path continues from Rim Pai along the river to this relaxed spot with simple thatched bungalows scattered around a large area on the river. The Riverside boasts a large kitchen where you're welcome to cook for yourself, and the staff recycles glass and plastic. Live Northern Thai musical ensembles perform here occasionally. Bathroom facilities are shared.

Across the bamboo slat bridge near Golden Hut are a few more guesthouses.

River View Huts (Wiang Tai) Huts with shared/private bathroom 100/150B. The River View offers very simple A-frame huts on stilts.

Goodview Guest House (Wiang Tai) Single/double huts with shared bathroom 80/100B, huts with private bathroom 250B. About 50m from the bridge, Goodview provides simple, basic A-frame huts.

Berm's Bungalows (Wiang Tai) Single/double huts with shared facilities 80/100B. This place is 50m beyond Goodview, and has not-so-well-kept A-frames on stilts.

Pai Watershed Guest House (1 Mu 1, Ban Mae Yen) Singles/doubles with shared bathroom 100/150B. About 500m from the bamboo bridge, the trail begins to climb up to a ridge where you'll find this guesthouse. Good views of the valley, plus quiet surroundings, attract many long-term guests.

View Point Bungalows (Wiang Tai) Singles/doubles with shared bathroom 100/150B. This place is near Pai Watershed and overlooks Pai. There's a good view of the northeastern part of town and terraced rice fields.

Shan Guest House (☎ 053 699 162, Thanon Rangthiyanon) Bungalows 200B. On the southern edge of town, off Thanon Rangthiyanon, the quiet, well-run Shan features solid bungalows with private hot-water showers and comfortable beds. A separate dining and lounging building sits on stilts in the middle of a large pond. Long-term discounts are available.

View Pai Hotel (☎ 053 699 174, Thanon Rangthiyanon) Rooms with fan/air-con 300/500B. Farther south towards Chiang Mai, past the petrol stations, this three-storey hotel is a rather plain place with overpriced rooms.

Blue Mountain Guest Cottages (☎ 053 699 282, Thanon Chaisongkhram) Small huts 50B, larger single/double huts with shared facilities 80/100B, with private shower 100/150B. Towards the western end of Thanon Chaisongkhram, near the hospital, you'll find this place offering several simple, small wooden bungalows and three larger cottages.

Fruit Garden Guest House (30 Mu 5, Wiang Tai) Bungalows 100B. Farther out on Thanon Chaisongkhram, about 50m past Wat Hua Na, is a turn-off onto a narrow 200m dirt road that leads to this guesthouse. Six bamboo bungalows are thinly scattered over hillsides around a stream.

Across Mae Pai, southeast of town, are a number of places to stay along the road that leads to the hot springs.

Farmer Home (☎ 053 699 378, 79 Mu 1, Ban Mae Yen) Bungalows 50-200B. Farmer Home, about 600m east of the river on a hillock, is a nice, friendly spot with a variety of huts.

Sun Hut (☎ 053 699 730, 01 960 6519, 28/1 Ban Mae Yen) Single/double huts & tree house with shared facilities 100/120B, huts with private shower 120-200B. This is a new place with nicely spaced bamboo huts, plus one tree house. The turn-off for Sun Hut comes right before a bridge over a stream, about 200m before the entrance to Wat Phra That Mae Yen.

Farther down this road are a couple of small resorts that take advantage of the local hot springs by piping the mineral-rich water into the facilities.

Spa Exotic Home (☎ 053 699 035, 053 699 145, fax 053 699 462, 86 Mu 2, Tambon Mae Hi) 1-/2-bed bungalows 500/700B, tent sites 100B. The spa features comfortable wooden bungalows with private hot-water shower and large beds. Discounts of 40% are available May to August. On the well-landscaped premises are a nicely designed set of outdoor hot tubs for the use of guests, and a restaurant serving good Thai and Western food.

Thapai Spa Camping (84-84/1 Mu 2, Tambon Mae Hi; in Chiang Mai ☎ 053 218 583, fax 053 219 610) Cottages 600-800B. Next door to Spa Exotic Home, Thapai features 15 wood-and-stone cottages with natural hot mineral-water showers. There's also an outdoor hot-water pool. Visitors may use the mineral baths here for 50B without staying overnight. Herbal sauna and Thai massage are also available at reasonable prices, and you can order drinks or food from the restaurant.

Out of Town *Sipsongpanna Bungalow & Artist Homestay (☎ 053 216 096, 01 769 0142, ℮ sipsongpanna33@hotmail.com, 60 Mu 5, Ban Huang, Wiang Neua)* Bungalows 150B. This is a small but charming collection of wood-and-bamboo bungalows alongside the river, a couple of kilometres north of town in the village of Ban Wiang Neua. The Thai artist-owner has designed the units with lots of deft little touches, such as private but separate toilet/shower facilities for each. There are sitting areas sprinkled throughout the compound, along with a vegetarian cafe and art studio. Thai vegetarian cooking lessons are available.

Pai Mountain Lodge (☎ 053 699 068, Ban Mo Pang) Bungalows 500-600B. This lodge is 7km northwest of Pai near Nam Tok Maw Paeng and several hill-tribe villages. It offers well maintained spacious A-frames with hot-water showers and stone fireplaces which sleep four – good value. A few VIP bungalows are under construction, and will probably cost 1000B per night. In town you can book a room or arrange transport at 89 Thanon Chaisongkhram, near Northern Green Restaurant & Trekking.

Michel Bungalows Row-house rooms with hot-water and fan 250B, bungalows 400B. Rooms are discounted 50B if you stay more than one night. About 6km outside Pai on the road to Chiang Mai, Michel Bungalows features a big pool with a stone filtration system. The bungalows are down a dirt lane about 200m off the main road.

Places to Eat
Nong Bia Restaurant (☎ 053 699 103, Thanon Chaisongkhram) Dishes 20-50B. Open 8am-10pm daily. One of the oldest restaurants in town, Nong Bia serves a good variety of inexpensive Thai and Chinese standards, as well as khâo sawy.

Chon Kaew (Thanon Rangthiyanon) Dishes 50-70B. Open 11am-10pm daily. This is without question the best Thai restaurant in town, as long as you know how to order Thai food. The menu features Bangkok-style specialities such as spicy poached river fish salad and quail stir-fried with curry paste.

ThaIrish Pub & Restaurant (☎ 053 699 149, Thanon Rangthiyanon) Dishes 60-100B, steak 350B. Open 8am-11pm daily. Housed in the historic former Wiang Pai Hotel, once Pai's only commercial accommodation, this cosy restaurant and bar specialises in delicious Thai and Indian food, plus Western breakfasts and the best steak in town.

All About Coffee (Thanon Chaisongkhram) Dishes 40-120B. Open 8.30am-6pm Mon-Sat. This small, slightly artsy spot serves very nice pastries, coffees, teas, fruit drinks and egg breakfasts.

Chez Swan (☎ 053 699 111, Thanon Rangthiyanon) Dishes 45-200B. Open 11am-11pm daily. Good French food – including several cheeses – is available at this nicely decorated place in an old wooden building.

Every evening a row of local *food vendors* sets up in front of the day market. During the day, takeaway food can also be purchased at the larger *Saengthongaram Market* on Thanon Khetkelang. Also on this street you'll find a row of *noodle shops* near the post and telegraph office, including *Kuaytiaw Pet Pai (Pai Duck Noodles)*, just south of the post office; and *Im Arawy*, opposite, which specialises in *khâo râat kaeng* (curry over rice).

Entertainment
Bebop Cafe (Thanon Chaisongkhram) Open 4pm-midnight daily. Several places featuring live music seem to come and go with the seasons, but only this one seems to be a perennial. Simply decorated with Asian hippie gear and blues/jazz posters, the musician-owned Bebop features live blues and rock nightly.

ThaIrish Pub & Restaurant (☎ 053 699 149, Thanon Rangthiyanon) recently took on a house band that plays mostly reggae.

Getting There & Away
Buses (50/80B ordinary/air-con) depart Chiang Mai's Arcade bus station at 8.30am, 11am, noon, 2pm and 4pm daily. The distance is only 134km but the trip takes about four hours due to the steep and winding

road. From Mae Hong Son there are also five buses a day with the same departure times as the buses from Chiang Mai. This winding, 111km stretch takes three to four hours (53/74B). In the other direction, buses depart Pai for Chiang Mai and Mae Hong Son at 8.30am, 10.30am, noon, 2pm and 4pm. Buses from Pai to Soppong cost 25B ordinary, 28B air-con.

Getting Around

All of Pai is accessible on foot. For local excursions you can rent bicycles or motorcycles at several locations around town. A place next door to Duang Guest House rents out bicycles for 50B per day (80B for newer bikes). Motorcycles can be rented at MS Motorcycle Rent just south of Pai Elephant Camp Tours office – 100cc bikes for 150B per 24 hours, larger bikes for 200B. All motorcycle rental places keep your passport as collateral.

Motorcycle taxis can be hired from the taxi stand at the bus stop. Typical fares are 25B to Ban Nam Hu and Ban Wiang Neua, 35B to Nam Hu Lisaw and Nam Hu Jin, and 45B to Tha Pai.

AROUND PAI

Pai can be used as a base for excursions to hill-tribe villages, as described earlier in the Pai section. Farther afield, the area northeast of Pai has so far been little explored. A network of unpaved roads – some little more than footpaths – skirts a mountain ridge and the Mae Taeng valley all the way to the Myanmar border near Wiang Haeng and Ban Piang Haeng, passing several villages along the way. This area can also be visited by road from Chiang Dao in Chiang Mai Province. See the Around Chiang Mai chapter for further detail.

Huay Nam Dang National Park

อุทยานแห่งชาติห้วยน้ำดัง

The main entrance to this 1247-sq-km park (☎ *053 471 699, Mu 5, Tambon Keut Chang, Mae Taeng District, Chiang Mai Province; Thais/foreigners 20/200B*) is found off Rte 1095 between Km65 and Km66, about 37km southeast of Pai on the way to Chiang Mai. The park covers four districts – Pai District in Mae Hong Son Province as well as Mae Taeng, Chiang Dao and Wiang Haeng districts in Chiang Mai Province. Most of the park environs extend along a ridge of the Chiang Dao mountain range, with the highest peak, **Doi Chang**, at 1962m. Much of the park features natural forest cover, including teak, dipterocarp, pine and cedar. Fauna include elephant, gaur, serow and fishing cat.

Two 1.5km nature trails – **Euang Ngoen Nature Trail** and **Chom Doi Nature Trail** – take visitors along labelled pathways. **Nam Phu Pong Deuat** is an area of four or five hot springs that erupt into occasional geysers as high as 2m. The 1.5km **Pong Deuat Nature Trail** leads to the natural springs. Several waterfalls, including **Nam Tok Huay Nam Dang**, **Nam Tok Mae Yen** and **Nam Tok Mae Hat** can be visited within the park area.

HRH Princess Galyani Vadhana, sister of the current Thai king, has a residence here called **Wang Euang Ngoen** (Silver Orchid Palace). There are also several **Lisu villages** within the park.

Park accommodation in group-oriented bungalows is available at a cost of 100B per person. Reservations are handled via the National Park Division, Royal Forest Department (☎ 025 797 223, 025 795 734) in Bangkok.

Language

Learning some Thai is indispensable for travelling in the kingdom; naturally, the more language you pick up, the closer you get to Thailand's culture and people. Foreigners who speak Thai are so rare in Thailand that it doesn't take much to impress most Thais with a few words in their own language.

Your first attempts to speak the language will probably meet with mixed success, but keep trying. When learning new words or phrases, listen closely to the way the Thais themselves use the various tones – you'll catch on quickly. Don't let laughter at your linguistic forays discourage you; this apparent amusement is an expression of appreciation. Thais are among the most supportive people in the world when it comes to foreigners learning their language.

Travellers, both young and old, are particularly urged to make the effort to meet Thai college and university students. Thai students are, by and large, eager to meet visitors from other countries. They will often know some English, so communication is not as difficult as it may be with shop owners, civil servants etc, plus they are generally willing to teach you useful Thai words and phrases.

For a handy pocket-size guide to Thai, get a copy of Lonely Planet's excellent *Thai phrasebook*; it contains a section on basic grammar and a broad selection of useful words and phrases for travel in Thailand.

Many people have reported modest success with *Robertson's Practical English-Thai Dictionary* (Charles E Tuttle Co, Tokyo), which has a phonetic guide to pronunciation with tones and is compact in size. If you have difficulty finding it, write to the publisher at 2-6 Suido 1-chome, Bunkyo-ku, Tokyo, Japan.

More serious learners of the language should get Mary Haas' *Thai-English Student's Dictionary* (Stanford University Press, Stanford, California) and George McFarland's *Thai-English Dictionary* (also Stanford University Press) – the cream of the crop. Both of these require that you know the Thai script. The US State Department's *Thai Reference Grammar* by RB Noss (Foreign Service Institute, Washington, DC, 1964) is good for an in-depth look at Thai syntax.

Other learning texts worth seeking out include:

AUA Language Center Thai Course: Reading & Writing (two volumes) – AUA Language Center (Bangkok), 1979

AUA Language Center Thai Course (three volumes) – AUA Language Center (Bangkok), 1969

Foundations of Thai (two volumes) – by EM Anthony, University of Michigan Press, 1973

A Programmed Course in Reading Thai Syllables – by EM Anthony, University of Hawaii, 1979

Teaching Grammar of Thai – by William Kuo, University of California at Berkeley, 1982

Thai Basic Reader – by Gething & Bilmes, University of Hawaii, 1977

Thai Cultural Reader (two volumes) – by RB Jones, Cornell University, 1969

Thai Reader – by Mary Haas, American Council of Learned Societies, Program in Oriental Languages, 1954

The Thai System of Writing – by Mary Haas, American Council of Learned Societies, Program in Oriental Languages, 1954

A Workbook for Writing Thai – by William Kuo, University of California at Berkeley, 1979

An interactive CD-ROM called *Learning Thai Script* (Allen & Unwin, 1997) is also an excellent resource for teaching yourself to read and write the Thai script.

For information on language courses, see Language under Courses in the Facts for the Visitor chapter.

Dialects

Thailand's official language is Thai as spoken and written in Central Thailand. This dialect has successfully become the lingua franca of all Thai and non-Thai ethnic groups in the kingdom. Of course, native Thai is spoken with differing tonal accents and with slightly differing vocabularies as you move from one part of the country to the next, especially in a north to south direction. But it is the central Thai dialect that is most widely understood.

All Thai dialects are members of the Thai half of the Thai-Kadai family of languages and are closely related to languages spoken in Laos (Lao, Northern Thai, Thai Lü), northern Myanmar (Shan, Northern Thai), north-western Vietnam (Nung, Tho), Assam (Ahom) and pockets of south China (Zhuang, Thai Lü). Modern Thai linguists recognise four basic dialects within Thailand: central Thai (spoken as a first dialect through Central Thailand and throughout the country as a second dialect); Northern-Thai (spoken from Tak Province north to the Myanmar border); north-eastern Thai (north-eastern provinces towards the Lao and Cambodian borders); and southern Thai (from Chumphon Province south to the Malaysian border). Each of these can be further divided into subdialects; north-eastern Thai, for example, has nine regional variations easily distinguished by those who know Thai well. There are also a number of Thai minority dialects such as those spoken by the Phu Thai, Thai Dam, Thai Daeng, Phu Noi, Phuan and other tribal Thai groups, most of whom reside in the North and North-East.

Vocabulary Differences

Like most languages, Thai distinguishes between 'vulgar' and 'polite' vocabulary, so that *thaan*, for example, is a more polite everyday word for 'eat' than *kin*, and *sǐi-sà* for 'head' is more polite than *hǔa*. When given a choice, foreigners are better off learning and using the polite terms since these are less likely to lead to unconscious offence.

A special set of words, collectively called *kham raachaasàp* (royal vocabulary), is set aside for use with Thai royalty within the semantic fields of kinship, body parts, physical and mental actions, clothing and housing. For example, in everyday language Thais use the word *kin* or *thaan* for 'eat', while with reference to the royal family they say *sa-wǒey*. For the most part these terms are used only when speaking to or referring to the king, queen and their children, hence as a foreigner you will have little need to learn them.

Script

The Thai script, a fairly recent development in comparison with the spoken language, consists of 44 consonants (but only 21 separate sounds) and 48 vowel and diphthong possibilities (32 separate signs). Experts disagree as to the exact origins of the script, but it was apparently developed around 800 years ago using Mon and possibly Khmer models, both of which were in turn inspired by south Indian scripts. Like these languages, written Thai proceeds from left to right, though vowel signs may be written before, after, above, below, *or* 'around' (before, after *and* above) consonants, depending on the sign.

Though learning the alphabet is not difficult, the writing system itself is fairly complex, so unless you are planning a lengthy stay in Thailand it should perhaps be foregone in favour of actually learning to speak the language. The names of major places included in this book are given in both Thai and Roman script, so that you can at least 'read' the names of destinations at a pinch, or point to them if necessary.

Tones & Pronunciation

In Thai the meaning of a single syllable may be altered by means of different tones – in standard central Thai there are five: low tone, level or mid tone, falling tone, high tone and rising tone. For example, depending on the tone, the syllable *mai* can mean 'new', 'burn', 'wood', 'not?' or 'not'; ponder the phrase *mái mài mâi mâi mǎi* (New wood doesn't burn, does it?) and you begin to appreciate the importance of tones in spoken Thai. This makes it a rather tricky language to learn at first, especially for those of us unaccustomed to the concept of tones. Even when we 'know' what the correct tone in Thai should be, our tendency to denote emotion, verbal stress, the interrogative etc, through tone modulation often interferes with producing the correct tone. Therefore the first rule in learning to speak Thai is to divorce emotions from your speech, at least until you have learned the Thai way to express them without changing essential tone value.

The following is a visual representation in chart form to show relative tone values:

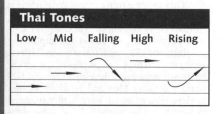

Thai Tones				
Low	Mid	Falling	High	Rising

The following is a brief attempt to explain the tones. The only way to really under-stand the differences is by listening to a native or fluent non-native speaker. The range of all five tones is relative to each speaker's vocal range so there is no fixed 'pitch' intrinsic to the language.

1 The low tone is 'flat' like the mid tone, but pronounced at the relative *bottom* of one's vocal range. It is low, level and with no inflection, eg, *bàat* (baht – the Thai currency).

2 The level or mid tone is pronounced 'flat', at the relative middle of the speaker's vocal range, eg, *dii* (good); no tone mark used.

3 The falling tone is pronounced as if you were emphasising a word, or calling someone's name from afar, eg, *mâi* (no/not).

4 The high tone is usually the most difficult for Westerners. It is pronounced near the relative top of the vocal range, as level as possible, eg, *máa* (horse).

5 The rising tone sounds like the inflection used by English speakers to imply a question – 'Yes?', eg, *săam* (three).

Words in Thai that appear to have more than one syllable are usually compounds made up of two or more word units, each with its own tone. They may be words taken directly from Sanskrit, Pali or English, in which case each syllable must still have its own tone.

The following is a guide to the phonetic system that has been used for the words and phrases included in this chapter (and throughout the rest of the book when tran-scribing directly from Thai). It's based on the Royal Thai General System (RTGS), except that it distinguishes: between short and long vowels (eg, 'i' and 'ii'; 'a' and 'aa'; 'e' and 'eh'; 'o' and 'oh'); between 'o' and 'aw' (both would be 'o' in the RTGS); between 'u' and 'eu' (both would be 'u' in the RTGS); and between 'ch' and 'j' (both would be 'ch' in the RTGS).

Consonants

The majority of consonants correspond closely to their English counterparts. Here are a few exceptions:

k	as the 'k' in 'skin'; similar to 'g' in 'good', but unaspirated (no accom-panying puff of air) and unvoiced
p	as the 'p' in 'stopper', unvoiced and unaspirated (not like the 'p' in 'put'); actually sounds closer to an English 'b', its voiced equivalent
t	as the 't' in 'forty', unaspirated; similar to 'd' but unvoiced
kh	as the 'k' in 'kite'
ph	as the 'p' in 'put' (never as the 'ph' in 'phone')
th	as the 't' in 'tea'
ng	as the 'nging' in 'singing'; can occur as an initial consonant (practise by saying 'singing' without the 'si')
r	similar to the 'r' in 'run' but flapped (tongue touches palate); in everyday speech often pronounced like 'l'

Vowels

i	as the 'i' in 'it'
ii	as the 'ee' in 'feet'
ai	as the 'i' in 'pipe'
aa	as the 'a' in 'father'
a	half as long as **aa**, as the 'a' in 'about'

ae	as the 'a' in 'bat' or 'tab'
e	as the 'e' in 'hen'
eh	as the 'a' in 'hate'
oe	as the 'er' in 'fern' (without the 'r' sound)
u	as the 'u' in 'flute'
uu	as the 'oo' in 'food', longer than **u**
eu	as the 'u' in 'fur'
ao	as the 'ow' in 'now'
aw	as the 'aw' in 'jaw' or 'prawn'
o	as the 'o' in 'bone'
oh	as the 'o' in 'toe'
eua	a combination of **eu** and **a**
ia	as 'ee-ya', or as the 'ie' in French *rien*
ua	as the 'ou' in 'tour'
uay	sounds like 'oo-way'
iu	as the 'ew' in 'yew'
iaw	as the 'io' in 'Rio' or Italian *mio*
aew	like a Cockney pronunciation of the 'ow' in 'now'
ehw	as 'air-ooh'
awy	as the 'oi' in 'coin'

Here are a few extra hints to help you with the alphabetic tangle:

- **ph** is never pronounced as the 'ph' in phone but like the 'p' in 'pound' (the 'h' is added to distinguish this consonant sound from the Thai 'p' which is closer to the English 'b'). This can be seen written as **p**, **ph**, and even **bh**.
- to some people, the Thai **k** sounds closer to the English 'g' than the English 'k'. The standard RTGS chooses to use 'k' to represent this sound to emphasise that it is not a 'voiced' sound, but more a glottal stop.
- there is no 'v' sound in Thai. *Sukhumvit* is pronounced Sukhumwit and *Viang* is really Wiang.
- **l** and **r** are always pronounced as an 'n' when word-final, eg, *Satul* is pronounced as Satun, *Wihar* as Wihan. The exception to this is when 'er' or 'ur' are used to indicate the sound 'oe', as in 'ampher' *(amphoe)*. In the same way 'or' is sometimes used for the sound 'aw', as in 'Porn' *(phawn)*.
- **l** and **r** are often interchanged in speech and this shows up in some transliterations. For example, *naliga* (clock) may

appear as 'nariga' and *râat nâa* (a type of noodle dish) might be rendered 'laat naa' or 'lat na'.

- **u** is often used to represent the short 'a' sound, as in *tam* or *nam*, which may appear as 'tum' and 'num'. It is also used to represent the 'eu' sound, as when *beung* (swamp) is spelt 'bung'.
- phonetically, all Thai words end in a vowel (**a**, **e**, **i**, **o**, **u**), semi-vowel (**w**, **y**), nasal (**m**, **n**, **ng**) or one of three stops (**p**, **t**, **k**). That's it. Words transcribed with 'ch', 'j', 's' or 'd' endings – like Panich, Raj, Chuanpis and Had – should be pronounced as if they end in 't', as in Panit, Rat, Chuanpit and Hat. Likewise 'g' becomes 'k' (Ralug is actually Raluk) and 'b' becomes 'p' (Thab becomes Thap).
- the 'r' in *sri* is always silent, so the word should be pronounced 'sii' (extended 'i' sound, too). Hence 'Sri Racha' really comes out 'Si Racha'.

Transliteration

Writing Thai in Roman script is a perennial problem – no wholly satisfactory system has yet been devised to assure both consistency and readability. The Thai government uses the Royal Thai General System of transcription for official government documents in English and for most highway signs. However, local variations crop up on hotel signs, city street signs, menus and so on in such a way that visitors often become confused. Add to this the fact that even the government system has its flaws. For example, 'o' is used for two very different sounds ('o' and the 'aw' in the Vowels section earlier), as is 'u' (for 'u' and 'eu' earlier). Likewise for 'ch', which is used to represent two different consonant sounds ('ch' and 'j'). The government transcription system also does not distinguish between short and long vowel sounds, which affect the tonal value of every word.

To top it off, many Thai words (especially names of people and place) have Sanskrit and Pali spellings but their actual pronunciation bears little relation to that spelling if Romanised strictly according to the original

Sanskrit/Pali. Thus Nakhon Si Thammarat, if transliterated literally, becomes 'Nagara Sri Dhammaraja'. If you tried to pronounce it using this Pali transcription, very few Thais would be able to understand you.

Generally, names in this book follow the most common practice or, in the case of hotels for example, simply copy their Roman script name, no matter what devious process was used in its transliteration! When this transliteration is markedly different from actual pronunciation, the pronunciation is included (according to the system outlined in this section) in parentheses after the transliteration. Where no Roman model was available, names have been transliterated phonetically, directly from Thai. Of course, this will only be helpful to readers who bother to acquaint themselves with the language – and it's surprising how many people manage to stay for great lengths of time in Thailand without learning a word of Thai.

Problems often arise when a name is transliterated differently, even at the same location. 'Thawi', for example, can be seen as Tavi, Thawee, Thavi, Tavee or various other versions. Outside the International Phonetic Alphabet, there is no 'proper' way to transliterate Thai – only wrong ways. The Thais themselves are incredibly inconsistent in this matter, often using English letters that have no equivalent sound in Thai: Faisal for Phaisan, Bhumibol for Phumiphon, Vanich for Wanit, Vibhavadi for Wiphawadi. Sometimes they even mix literal Sanskrit transcription with Thai pronunciation, as in King Bhumibol (which is pronounced Phumiphon and if transliterated according to the Sanskrit would be Bhumibala).

Here are a few words that are often spelt in a way that encourages native English speakers to mispronounce them:

Common Spelling	Pronunciation	Meaning
bung	beung	pond or swamp
ko or koh	kàw	island
muang	meuang	city
nakhon or nakorn	nákhawn	large city

| raja | usually râatchá if at the beginning of a word, râat at the end of a word | royal |

Greetings & Civilities

When being polite, the speaker ends his or her sentence with khráp (for men) or khâ (for women). It is the gender of the speaker that is being expressed here; it is also the common way to answer 'yes' to a question or show agreement.

Greetings/Hello.
  sa-wàt-dii   สวัสดี
  (khráp/khâ)   (ครับ/ค่ะ)
How are you?
  sa-bai dii rěu?   สบายดีหรือ?
I'm fine.
  sa-bai dii   สบายดี
Thank you.
  khàwp khun   ขอบคุณ
Excuse me.
  khǎw thôht   ขอโทษ

I/me
  phǒm   ผม
  (for men)
  dì-chǎn   ดิฉัน
  (for women)
you
  khun   คุณ
  (for peers)
  thân   ท่าน
  (for elders and people in authority)

What's your name?
  khun chêu àrai?   คุณชื่ออะไร?
My name is ...
  phǒm chêu ...   ผมชื่อ...
  (men)
  dì-chǎn chêu ...   ดิฉันชื่อ...
  (women)

Do you have ...?	
mii ... măi?/	มี...ไหม/
... mii măi?	...มีไหม?
No.	
mâi châi	ไม่ใช่
No?	
măi?/châi măi?	ไหม?/ใช่ไหม?
(I) like ...	
châwp ...	ชอบ...
(I) don't like ...	
mâi châwp ...	ไม่ชอบ...
(I) would like ...	
(+ verb)	
yàak jà ...	อยากจะ...
(I) would like ...	
(+ noun)	
yàak dâi ...	อยากได้...
When?	
mêua-rai?	เมื่อไร?
It doesn't matter.	
mâi pen rai	ไม่เป็นไร
What is this?	
nîi àrai?	นี่อะไร?
go	
pai	ไป
come	
maa	มา

Language Difficulties

I understand.	
khâo jai	เข้าใจ
I don't understand.	
mâi khâo jai	ไม่เข้าใจ
Do you understand?	
khâo jai măi?	เข้าใจไหม?
A little.	
nít nàwy	นิดหน่อย
What do you call	
this in Thai?	
nîi phaasăa thai	นี่ภาษาไทย
rîak wâa àrai?	เรียกว่าอะไร?

Getting Around

I'd like to go ...	
yàak jà pai ...	อยากจะไป...
Where is (the) ...?	
... yùu thîi năi?	...อยู่ที่ไหน?
airport	
sa-năam bin	สนามบิน
bus station	
sa-thăanii khŏn sòng/	สถานีขนส่ง/
baw khăw săw	บขส
bus stop	
pâi rót meh	ป้ายรถเมล์
train station	
sa-thăanii rót fai	สถานีรถไฟ
taxi stand	
thîi jàwt rót	ที่จอดรถแท็กซี่
tháek-sîi	
I'd like a ticket.	
yàak séu tŭa	อยากซื้อตั๋ว
What time will the ...	
leave?	
... jà àwk kìi	...จะออกกี่
mohng ?	โมง?
bus	
rót meh/rót bát	รถเมล์/รถบัส
car	
rót yon	รถยนต์
motorcycle	
rót maw-toe-sai	รถมอเตอร์ไซค์
train	
rót fai	รถไฟ
straight ahead	
trong pai	ตรงไป
left	
sái	ซ้าย
right	
khwăa	ขวา
far/not far/near	
klai/mâi klai/	ไกล/ไม่ไกล/
klâi	ใกล้

Accommodation

hotel
rohng raem โรงแรม
guesthouse
kèt háo เกสต์เฮาส์
Do you have a
room available?
mii hâwng wâang มีห้องว่าง
măi? ไหม?
How much is it
per night?
kheun-lá thâo rai? คืนละเท่าไร?
bathroom
hâwng náam ห้องน้ำ
toilet
hâwng sûam ห้องส้วม
room
hâwng ห้อง
hot
ráwn ร้อน
cold
yen เย็น
bath/shower
àap náam อาบน้ำ
towel
phâa chét tua ผ้าเช็ดตัว

Around Town

Can (I/we) change money here?
lâek ngoen thîi níi dâi măi?
แลกเงินที่นี้ได้ไหม?
What time does it open?
ráan pòet mêua rai?
ร้านเปิดเมื่อไร?
What time does it close?
ráan pìt mêua rai?
ร้านปิดเมื่อไร?

bank
thá-naakhaan ธนาคาร

beach
hàat หาด
market
ta-làat ตลาด
museum
phíphítháphan พิพิธภัณฑ์
post office
praisànii ไปรษณีย์
restaurant
ráan aahăan ร้านอาหาร
tourist office
sămnák ngaan สำนักงาน
thâwng thîaw ท่องเที่ยว

Shopping

How much?
thâo raí? เท่าไร?
too expensive
phaeng pai แพงไป
How much is this?
nîi thâo rai?/ นี่เท่าไร?/
kìi bàat? กี่บาท?
cheap, inexpensive
thùuk ถูก

Geographical features

beach
hàat sai หาดทราย
countryside
chonnábòt ชนบท
island
kàw เกาะ
lake
tháleh sàap ทะเลสาบ
map
phăen thîi แผนที่
mountain/hill
phuu khăo/khăo ภูเขา/เขา
paddy (field)
(thûng) naa (ทุ่ง) นา

Emergencies

I need a doctor.	
tâwng-kaan măw	ต้องการหมอ
Help!	
chûay dûay!	ช่วยด้วย
Stop!	
yùt!	หยุด
Go away!	
pai sí!	ไปซิ
I'm lost.	
chăn lŏng thaang	ฉันหลงทาง

pond	
năwng/beung	หนอง/บึง
river	
mâe náam	แม่น้ำ
sea	
tháleh	ทะเล
town	
meuang	เมือง
track	
thaang	ทาง
village	
(mùu) bâan	(หมู่) บ้าน
waterfall	
náam tòk	น้ำตก

Health

chemist/pharmacy	
ráan khăi yaa	ร้านขายยา
dentist	
măw fan	หมอฟัน
doctor	
măw	หมอ
hospital	
rohng pháyaabaan	โรงพยาบาล
aspirin (pain killer)	
yaa kâe pùat	ยาแก้ปวด
mosquito repellent	
yaa kan yung	ยากันยุง

Please call a doctor.
  ka-rúnaa rîak măw nàwy
  กรุณาเรียกหมอหน่อย

I'm allergic to penicillin.
  pháe yaa phenísinlin
  แพ้ยาเพนิซิลลิน

I'm pregnant.
  tâng khan láew/mii tháwng
  ตั้งครรภ์แล้ว/มีท้อง

It hurts here.
  jèp trong níi
  เจ็บตรงนี้

I feel nauseous.
  rúusèuk khlêun sâi
  รู้สึกคลื่นไส้

I keep vomiting.
  aajian bàwy bàwy
  อาเจียนบ่อยๆ

I feel faint.
  rúusèuk jà pen lom
  รู้สึกจะเป็นลม

I have diarrhoea.
  tháwng rûang
  ท้องร่วง

I have a fever.
  pen khâi
  เป็นไข้

I have a stomachache.
  pùat tháwng
  ปวดท้อง

I have a headache.
  pùat hŭa
  ปวดหัว

I have a toothache.
  pùat fan
  ปวดฟัน

Time, Days & Numbers

What's the time?

kìi mohng láew? กี่โมงแล้ว?

today

wan níi วันนี้

tomorrow

phrûng níi พรุ่งนี้

yesterday

mêua waan เมื่อวาน

Sunday

wan aathít วันอาทิตย์

Monday

wan jan วันจันทร์

Tuesday

wan angkhaan วันอังคาร

Wednesday

wan phút วันพุธ

Thursday

wan phréuhàt วันพฤหัสฯ

Friday

wan sùk วันศุกร์

Saturday

wan săo วันเสาร์

0	*săun*	ศูนย์
1	*nèung*	หนึ่ง
2	*săwng*	สอง
3	*săam*	สาม
4	*sìi*	สี่
5	*hâa*	ห้า
6	*hòk*	หก
7	*jèt*	เจ็ด
8	*pàet*	แปด
9	*kâo*	เก้า
10	*sìp*	สิบ

11	*sìp-èt*	สิบเอ็ด
12	*sìp-săwng*	สิบสอง
13	*sìp-săam*	สิบสาม
20	*yîi-sìp*	ยี่สิบ
21	*yîi-sìp-èt*	ยี่สิบเอ็ด
22	*yîi-sìp-săwng*	ยี่สิบสอง
30	*săam-sìp*	สามสิบ
40	*sìi-sìp*	สี่สิบ
50	*hâa-sìp*	ห้าสิบ
100	*ráwy*	ร้อย
200	*săwng ráwy*	สองร้อย
300	*săam ráwy*	สามร้อย
1000	*phan*	พัน
10,000	*mèun*	หมื่น
100,000	*săen*	แสน
one million	*láan*	ล้าน
one billion	*phan láan*	พันล้าน

FOOD
Ordering

(For 'I' men use *phŏm*; women use *dì-chăn*)

I eat only vegetarian food.

phŏm/dì-chăn kin jeh
ผม/ดิฉันกินเจ

I can't eat pork.

phŏm/dì-chăn mâi kin mŭu
ผม/ดิฉันไม่กินหมู

I can't eat beef.

phŏm/dì-chăn mâi kin néua
ผม/ดิฉันไม่กินเนื้อ

(I) don't like it hot & spicy.

mâi châwp phèt
ไม่ชอบเผ็ด

(I) like it hot & spicy.

châwp phèt
ชอบเผ็ด

(I) can eat Thai food.

kin aahăan thai dâi

กินอาหารไทยได้

What do you have that's special?

mii a-rai phí-sèt?

มีอะไรพิเศษ?

I didn't order this.

níi phŏm/dì-chăn mâi dâi sàng

นี่ผม/ดิฉันไม่ได้สั่ง

Do you have ...?

mii ... măi?

มี ...ไหม?

Food Glossary

The following list gives standard dishes in Thai script with a transliterated pronunciation guide, using the system outlined at the beginning of this chapter.

Soups *(súp)* ซุป

mild soup with vegetables & pork

kaeng jèut

แกงจืด

mild soup with vegetables, pork & bean curd

kaeng jèut tâo-hûu

แกงจืดเต้าหู้

soup with chicken, galanga root & coconut

tôm khàa kài

ต้มข่าไก่

prawn & lemon grass soup with mushrooms

tôm yam kûng

ต้มยำกุ้ง

fish-ball soup

kaeng jèut lûuk chín

แกงจืดลูกชิ้น

rice soup with fish/chicken/shrimp

khâo tôm plaa/kài/kûng

ข้าวต้มปลา/ไก่/กุ้ง

Egg *(khài)* ไข่

hard-boiled egg

khài tôm

ไข่ต้ม

fried egg

khài dao

ไข่ดาว

plain omelette

khài jiaw

ไข่เจียว

omelette with vegetables & pork

khài yát sâi

ไข่ยัดไส้

scrambled egg

khài kuan

ไข่กวน

Noodles *(kŭaytĭaw/* ก๋วยเตี๋ยว/

bà-mìi) บะหมี่

rice noodle soup with vegetables & meat

kŭaytĭaw náam

ก๋วยเตี๋ยวน้ำ

rice noodles with vegetables & meat

kŭaytĭaw hâeng

ก๋วยเตี๋ยวแห้ง

rice noodles with gravy

râat nâa

ราดหน้า

thin rice noodles fried with tofu, vegetables egg & peanuts

phàt thai

ผัดไทย

fried noodles with soy sauce

phàt sii-íu

ผัดซีอิ๊ว

wheat noodles in broth with vegetables & meat

bà-mìi náam

บะหมี่น้ำ

wheat noodles with vegetables & meat
bà-mìi hâeng
บะหมี่แห้ง

Rice *(khâo)* ข้าว

fried rice with pork/chicken/shrimp
khâo phàt mǔu/kài/kûng
ข้าวผัดหมู/ไก่/กุ้ง

boned, sliced Hainan-style chicken with marinated rice
khâo man kài
ข้าวมันไก่

chicken with sauce over rice
khâo nâa kài
ข้าวหน้าไก่

roast duck over rice
khâo nâa pèt
ข้าวหน้าเป็ด

'red' pork with rice
khâo mǔu daeng
ข้าวหมูแดง

curry over rice
khâo kaeng
ข้าวแกง

Curries *(kaeng)* แกง

hot Thai curry with chicken/beef/pork
kaeng phèt kài/néua/mǔu
แกงเผ็ดไก่/เนื้อ/หมู

rich & spicy, Muslim-style curry with chicken/beef & potatoes
kaeng mátsàmàn kài/néua
แกงมัสมั่นไก่/เนื้อ

mild, Indian-style curry with chicken
kaeng kà-rìi kài
แกงกะหรี่ไก่

hot & sour, fish & vegetable ragout
kaeng sôm
แกงส้ม

'green' curry with fish/chicken/beef
kaeng khǐaw-wǎan plaa/kài/néua
แกงเขียวหวานปลา/ไก่/เนื้อ

savoury curry with chicken/beef
phá-naeng kài/néua
พะแนงไก่/เนื้อ

chicken curry with bamboo shoots
kaeng kài nàw mái
แกงไก่หน่อไม้

catfish curry
kaeng plaa dùk
แกงปลาดุก

Seafood *(aahǎan tháleh)* อาหารทะเล

steamed crab
puu nêung
ปูนึ่ง

steamed crab claws
kâam puu nêung
ก้ามปูนึ่ง

shark-fin soup
hǔu cha-lǎam
หูฉลาม

crisp-fried fish
plaa thâwt
ปลาทอด

fried prawns
kûng thâwt
กุ้งทอด

batter-fried prawns
kûng chúp pâeng thâwt
กุ้งชุบแป้งทอด

grilled prawns
kûng phǎo
กุ้งเผา

steamed fish
plaa nêung
ปลานึ่ง

grilled fish
plaa phăo
ปลาเผา

whole fish cooked in ginger,
onions & soy sauce
plaa jĭan
ปลาเจี๋ยน

sweet & sour fish
plaa prîaw wăan
ปลาเปรี้ยวหวาน

cellophane noodles baked with crab
puu òp wún-sên
ปูอบวุ้นเส้น

spicy fried squid
plaa mèuk phàt phèt
ปลาหมึกผัดเผ็ด

roast squid
plaa mèuk yâang
ปลาหมึกย่าง

oysters fried in egg batter
hăwy thâwt
หอยทอด

squid
plaa mèuk
ปลาหมึก

shrimp
kûng
กุ้ง

fish
plaa
ปลา

saltwater eel
plaa lòt
ปลาหลด

spiny lobster
kûng mangkawn
กุ้งมังกร

green mussel
hăwy ma-laeng phûu
หอยแมลงภู่

scallop
hăwy phát
หอยพัด

oyster
hăwy naang rom
หอยนางรม

Miscellaneous

stir-fried mixed vegetables
phàt phàk ruam
ผัดผักรวม

spring rolls
pàw-pía
เปาะเปี๊ยะ

beef in oyster sauce
néua phàt náam-man hăwy
เนื้อผัดน้ำมันหอย

duck soup
pèt tŭn
เป็ดตุ๋น

roast duck
pèt yâang
เป็ดย่าง

fried chicken
kài thâwt
ไก่ทอด

chicken fried in holy basil
kài phàt bai kà-phrao
ไก่ผัดใบกะเพรา

grilled chicken
kài yâang
ไก่ย่าง

chicken fried with chillies
kài phàt phrík
ไก่ผัดพริก

chicken fried with cashews
kài phàt mét má-mûang
ไก่ผัดเม็ดมะม่วง

morning-glory vine fried in garlic, chilli &
bean sauce
phàk bûng fai daeng
ผักบุ้งไฟแดง

skewers of barbecued meat (satay)
sà-té
สะเต๊ะ

noodles with fish curry
kha-nŏm jiin náam yaa
ขนมจีนน้ำยา

prawns fried with chillies
kûng phàt phrík phăo
กุ้งผัดพริกเผา

chicken fried with ginger
kài phàt khĭng
ไก่ผัดขิง

fried wonton
kíaw kràwp
เกี๊ยวกรอบ

cellophane noodle salad
yam wún sên
ยำวุ้นเส้น

spicy chicken or beef salad
lâap kài/néua
ลาบไก่/เนื้อ

hot & sour, grilled beef salad
yam néua
ยำเนื้อ

fried chicken with bean sprouts
kài phàt thùa ngâwk
ไก่ผัดถั่วงอก

fried fish cakes with cucumber sauce
thâwt man plaa
ทอดมันปลา

Northern Thailand Specialities

khae soup
kaeng khae
แกงแค

sour herb soup
kaeng phàk hêuat
แกงผักเฮือด

sour bamboo shoot soup
kaeng hó
แกงโฮะ

spicy pomelo salad
tam sôm oh
ตำส้มโอ

banana palm curry
kaeng yùak
แกงหยวก

jackfruit curry
kaeng kha-nŭn
แกงขนุน

spicy Chiang Mai-style pork sausage
sâi ùa
ไส้อั่ว

fermented pork 'pot' sausage
năem mâw
แหนมหม้อ

bland pork sausage
mŭu yaw
หมูยอ

roast green chilli dip
náam phrík nùm
น้ำพริกหนุ่ม

galangal-chilli dip
náam phrík khàa
น้ำพริกข่า

chilli-pork-tomato dip
náam phrík àwng
น้ำพริกอ่อง

fried pork rinds, usually eaten with *náam phrík nùm*
khâep mǔu
แคบหมู

Shan-Yunnanese curry noodles
khâo sawy
ข้าวซอย

fresh rice noodles with sweet spicy sauce
kha-nǒm jiin náam ngíaw
ขนมจีนน้ำเงี้ยว

rice noodles with peanuts, barbecued pork, ground dried chilli, green beans and bean sprouts
kǔay tǐaw sùkhǒthai
ก๋วยเตี๋ยวสุโขทัย

Vegetables *(phàk)* ผัก

bitter melon
márá-jiin
มะระจีน

brinjal (round eggplant)
má-khǔua pràw
มะเขือเปราะ

cabbage
kà-làm plii
กะหล่ำปลี

cauliflower
dàwk kà-làm
ดอกกะหล่ำ

Chinese radish
hǔa phàk kàat
หัวผักกาด

corn
khâo phôht
ข้าวโพด

cucumber
taeng kwaa
แตงกวา

eggplant
má-khǔua
มะเขือ

garlic
krà-thiam
กระเทียม

lettuce
phàk kàat
ผักกาด

long bean
thùa fàk yao
ถั่วฝักยาว

okra ('ladyfingers')
krà-jíap
กระเจี๊ยบ

onion (bulb)
hǔa hǎwm
หัวหอม

onion (green, 'scallions')
tôn hǎwm
ต้นหอม

peanuts (ground nuts)
tùa lísǒng
ถั่วลิสง

potato
man fa-ràng
มันฝรั่ง

pumpkin
fák thawng
ฟักทอง

taro
phèuak
เผือก

tomato
má-khěua thêt
มะเขือเทศ

Fruit *(phǒn-lá-mái)* ผลไม้
banana – over 20 varieties (year-round)
klûay
กล้วย

coconut (year-round)
má-phráo
มะพร้าว

custard-apple
náwy nàa
น้อยหน่า

durian
thú-rian
ทุเรียน

guava (year-round)
fa-ràng
ฝรั่ง

jackfruit
kha-nǔn
ขนุน

lime (year-round)
má-nao
มะนาว

longan – 'dragon's eyes'; similar to
rambutan (July to October)
lam yai
ลำไย

mandarin orange (year-round)
sôm
ส้ม

mango – several varieties & seasons
má-mûang
มะม่วง

mangosteen
mang-khút
มังคุด

papaya (year-round)
málákaw
มะละกอ

pineapple (year-round)
sàp-pàrót
สับปะรด

pomelo
sôm oh
ส้มโอ

rambeh – small, reddish-brown and apricot-
like (April to May)
má-fai
มะไฟ

rambutan
ngáw
เงาะ

rose-apple – apple-like texture; very fragrant
(April to July)
chom-phûu
ชมพู่

sapodilla – small and oval; sweet but
pungent (July to September)
lá-mút
ละมุด

tamarind – sweet and tart varieties
má-khǎam
มะขาม

watermelon (year-round)
taeng moh
แตงโม

Sweets *(khǎwng wǎan)* ของหวาน
Thai custard
sǎngkha-yǎa
สังขยา

coconut custard
sǎngkha-yǎa má-phráo
สังขยามะพร้าว

sweet shredded egg yolk
fǎwy thawng
ฝอยทอง

egg custard
mâw kaeng
หม้อแกง

banana in coconut milk
klûay bùat chii
กล้วยบวชชี

fried, Indian-style banana
klûay khàek
กล้วยแขก

sweet palm kernels
lûuk taan chêuam
ลูกตาลเชื่อม

Thai jelly with coconut cream
ta-kôh
ตะโก้

sticky rice with coconut cream
khâo nǐaw daeng
ข้าวเหนียวแดง

sticky rice in coconut cream with ripe mango
khâo nǐaw má-mûang
ข้าวเหนียวมะม่วง

DRINKS
Beverages *(khrêuang dèum)* เครื่องดื่ม
plain water
náam plào
น้ำเปล่า

hot water
náam ráwn
น้ำร้อน

boiled water
náam tôm
น้ำต้ม

bottled drinking water
náam khùat
น้ำขวด

cold water
náam yen
น้ำเย็น

ice
náam khǎeng
น้ำแข็ง

soda water
náam soh-daa
น้ำโซดา

orange soda
náam sôm
น้ำส้ม

iced lime juice with sugar
(usually with salt too)
náam má-nao
น้ำมะนาว

no salt (command)
mâi sài kleua
ไม่ใส่เกลือ

plain milk
nom jèut
นมจืด

Chinese tea
chaa jiin
ชาจีน

weak Chinese tea
náam chaa
น้ำชา

iced Thai tea with milk & sugar
chaa yen
ชาเย็น

iced Thai tea with sugar only
chaa dam yen
ชาดำเย็น

no sugar (command)
mâi sài náam-taan
ไม่ใส่น้ำตาล

hot Thai tea with sugar
chaa dam ráwn
ชาดำร้อน

hot Thai tea with milk & sugar
chaa ráwn
ชาร้อน

hot coffee with milk & sugar
kaafae ráwn
กาแฟร้อน

traditional filtered coffee
with milk & sugar
kaafae thǔng
กาแฟถุง

iced coffee with sugar, no milk
oh-líang
โอเลี้ยง

Ovaltine
oh-wantin
โอวันติน

bottle
khùat
ขวด

glass
kâew
แก้ว

Glossary

aahǎan – food

ajahn – *(aajaan)* respectful title for teacher; from Sanskrit term *acharya*

amphoe – district, the next subdivision down from province; also written *amphur*

amphoe meuang – provincial capital

bàat – a unit of weight equal to 15 grams

baht – *(bàat)* the Thai unit of currency

ban – *(bâan)* house or village

bàw náam ráwn – hot springs

bòt – central sanctuary in a Thai temple used for official business of the Order *(sangha)* of monks, such as ordinations; from Pali term *uposatha*

chaa – tea

chao bâan – villager

chao khǎo – literally, mountain people; ie, hill tribes

chedi – (from the Pali *chetiya*) stupa; monument erected to house a Buddha relic

chiang – old Thai for 'city'. There were five chiang of the Lanna-Lan Xang-Xishuangbanna Thai diaspora: Chiang Mai, Chiang Rai, Chiang Thong (the original name for Luang Prabang), Chiang Rung (Yunnan's Jinghong) and Chiang Klang (Nan).

dawn – river islands; also spelt *don*

doi – (Northern Thai) mountain

faràng – Western, a Westerner

hâwng thǎew – shophouses arranged side by side along a city street; rowhouse

hǎw phǐi – spirit shrine in a Buddhist monastery compound

hǎw rá-khang – bell tower

hǎw trai – a *Tripitaka* (Buddhist scripture) hall

hǐn – stone

jão meuang – political office in traditional Thai societies throughout Southeast Asia; literally, principality chief

jataka – (Thai *chaadòk*) stories of the Buddha's previous lives

jiin – Chinese

jiin haw – literally, galloping Chinese; a reference to Muslims of Yunnanese descent

jók – broken-rice congee

kaafae – coffee

kaafae thǔng – filtered coffee

kaalae – X-crossed, carved gables common to traditional rooflines found in Northern Thailand

kàat – Northern Thai term for 'market'

kâew – crystal, jewel, glass or gem

kài yâang – grilled spiced chicken

kamnan – precinct officer, the next higher official after a *phûu yài bâan* (village chief)

kàp klâem – literally, with the bottle; drinking food

kàthoey – male transvestites and transsexuals

khǎn – bowl for holding Northern Thai foods

khǎn tòhk – low, round dining table traditionally found in Northern Thai homes; nowadays this also refers to special dinner shows that feature Northern Thai food and Northern Thai music and dancing

khǎo – hill or mountain

khâo – rice

khâo mòk – spiced rice steamed with chicken, beef or mutton; a Muslim Thai speciality

khâo nêung – literally, steamed rice; the Northern Thai term for *khâo nǐaw*

khâo nǐaw – sticky or glutinous rice, the main form of rice consumed by Northern Thais

khâo sawy – a Shan-Yunnanese dish consisting of flat, squiggly, egg noodles served in a curried broth with small saucers of shallot wedges, sweet-spicy pickled cabbage, lime and a thick red chilli sauce

khâo tôm – boiled rice soup

khon meuang – 'people of the principality', ie, Northern Thais

king-amphoe – subdistrict

klawng – drums

ku – small *chedi* that is partially hollow and open

kŭaytĭaw – rice noodles, often served with a bowl of broth along with meat, chicken or fish, plus various herbs and spices

kŭaytĭaw sùkhŏthai – thin rice-noodles served dry in a bowl with peanuts, barbecued pork, spices, green beans and bean sprouts

kùtì – monastic residence

laai kham – gold stencil patterns on lacquer; common interior wall decorations in Northern Thai temples

lâap – spicy meat or fish salad with mint leaves

lákhon – classical Thai dance-drama

làk meuang – city pillar/phallus

langsat – *(laangsàat)* small, round fruit grown in Thailand

lâo khăo – 'white spirit', an often home-made distilled liquor

lâo thèuan – home-made (ie, illegal) liquor

lék – little, small (in size)

loi (lawy) kràthong – the ceremony celebrated on the full moon at the end of the rainy season

longyi – Burmese sarong

mâe chii – Thai Buddhist nun

mâe náam – river; literally, water mother; in the North often shortened to *mae*

maha that – common name for temples containing Buddha relics; from the Sanskrit-Pali term *mahadhatu*

masjid – *(mátsàyít)* mosque

mátàbà – Indian pancake stuffed with savouries

mát-mìi – technique of tie-dying silk or cotton threads and then weaving them into complex patterns, similar to Indonesian *ikat;* also refers to the patterns themselves

măwn khwăn – wedge-shaped pillow popular in Northern and Northeastern Thailand; literally, axe pillow

meuang – city or principality

meuang kào – old city

mondòp – small square shrine building in a *wát*; from Sanskrit *mandapa*

muay thai – Thai boxing

mùu-bâan – village

mŭu yaw – white pork sausage

náam – water

náam ngíaw – sweet, spicy sauce used in Northern Thai dishes

náam phrík – chilli sauce

náam plaa – fish sauce

náam tòk – waterfall

năem – pickled pork sausage

naga – *(nâak)* a mythical serpent-like being with magical powers

nákhon – city; from the Sanskrit-Pali *nagara;* also spelt *nakhorn*

nĕua – north

ngaan sòp – funeral ceremony

ngaan wát – temple fair

nirvana – (Pali *nibbana,* Thai *níp-phaan*) in Buddhist teachings, the state of enlightenment; escape from the realm of rebirth

noen – hill

noi – *(náwy)* little, small (amount); also spelt *noy*

nok – *(nâwk)* outside; outer

nûat phăen bohraan – traditional Thai massage

paa-thâwng-kŏh – Chinese 'doughnut', a common breakfast food in Thai cities

phâakhamáa – piece of cotton cloth worn as a wraparound by men

phâa mát-mìi – thick cotton or silk fabric woven from tie-dyed threads

phâasîn – wraparound for women

phansăa – 'rains retreat' or Buddhist Lent; a period of three months during the rainy season, traditionally a time of stricter moral observance for monks and lay followers

phĭi – ghost, spirit

phĭi tawng lĕuang – 'spirits of the yellow leaves'; Mabri, the most nomadic of all the tribes in Thailand

phík-sù – a Buddhist monk; from the Sanskrit *bhikshu*, Pali *bhikkhu*

phin – small, three-stringed lute played with a large plectrum

phleng phêua chii-wít – 'songs for life', modern Thai folk music

phrá – an honorific term used for monks, nobility and Buddha images; from the Pali *vara,* meaning 'excellent'

phrá khrêuang – amulets of monks, Buddhas or deities worn around the neck for spiritual protection; also called *phrá phim*
phrá phuum – earth spirits
phrá sàksìt – monk or amulet believed to have spiritual power
phuu khăo – mountain
plaa bèuk – giant Mekong catfish, *Pangasianodon gigas*
plaa ráa – an unpasteurised fermented fish used as an accompaniment for rice in the North; called *háa* in Northern Thailand
prang – *(praang)* Khmer-style tower on temples
prasat – *(praasàat)* any of a number of different kinds of halls or residences with religious or royal significance; from the Sanskrit term *prasada*

râi – an area of land measurement equal to 1600 sq metres
reua hăang yao – longtailed boat
reuan thăew – row house
reusĭi – an ascetic, hermit or sage (Hindi *rishi*)
rotii – round, flat bread, a commonly found street food often sold in Muslim restaurants
rót ka-sèt – farm truck
rót pràp aakàat – air-con vehicle
rót thammádaa – ordinary bus (non air-con) or ordinary train (not rapid or express)
rót tûu – a minivan

săalaa – open-sided, covered meeting hall or resting place; from Portuguese term *sala;* literally, room; also written *sala*
săalaa klaang – provincial offices
saalaapao – Chinese steamed buns with sweet or savoury filling; also written *salabao*
săamláw – three-wheeled pedicab; also written *samlor*
săi kào – old route
săi mài – new route, a reference to bus routes along newer highways
sămnák sŏng – monastic centre
sămnák wípàtsànaa – meditation centre
samsara – in Buddhist teachings, the realm of rebirth and delusion
sa-tàang – Thai unit of currency; 100 *satàang* equals 1 baht; usually written *satang*

săwngthăew – literally, two rows; common name for small pick-up trucks with two benches in the back, used as buses/taxis; also written *songthaew*
sĕhmaa – boundary stones used to consecrate ground used for monastic ordinations; from Sanskrit-Pali term *sima*
sêua máw hâwm – indigo cotton farmer's shirt, a symbol of Northern Thai cultural solidarity
sîn tiin jòk – the highly decorative end pieces for the traditional Northern Thai women's sarong
soi – *(sawy)* lane or small street
sôm-tam – spicy green papaya salad
Songkran – *(sŏngkraan)* Thai New Year water festival, held in mid-April
sŭan aahăan – outdoor restaurant with any bit of foliage nearby; literally, food garden
sùkhăaphíbaan – sanitation district, a political division lower than *thêtsabaan*
sù-săan – cemetery

tâi – south
tambon – precinct, next subdivision below *amphoe;* also written *tambol*
tha – *(thâa)* pier, landing
thâat – Buddhist reliquary stupa
thâat krà-dùuk – bone reliquary, a small stupa containing remains of a Buddhist devotee
Thai Lü – one of the larger tribal Thai ethnic groups in Northern Thailand
thâm – cave
thammájàk – Buddhist wheel of law; from the Pali *dhammachakka*
Thammayutika – one of the two sects of Theravada Buddhism in Thailand; founded by King Rama IV while he was still a monk
thâm reusĭi – hermit cave
thanŏn – street
thêp – angel or divine being; from Sanskrit term deva; also *thewádaa*
thêtsabaan – a division in towns or cities much like 'municipality'
thŭng yaang ànaamai – condom
tràwk – alley; also *trok*
Tripitaka – the collection of Theravada Buddhist scriptures; the Pali Canon
túk-túk – motorised *săamláw*

vipassana – *(wípàtsànaa)* Buddhist insight meditation

wâi – palms-together Thai greeting
wang – palace
wát – temple-monastery; from Pali term *avasa,* meaning monk's dwelling
wáthánátham – culture
wiang – Northern Thai for 'city'
wíhăan – any large hall in a Thai temple, but not the bòt; from Sanskrit term *vihara,* meaning dwelling; also *wihan* or *viharn*

yaa bâa – 'crazy medicine', the popular term for amphetamines
yaa dawng – herbal liquor; also the herbs inserted in *lâo khăo*
yâam – cloth shoulder bag, popular in Northern Thailand

yài – big
yam – spicy and tart Thai-style salad

ACRONYMS
AUA – American University Alumni
CAT – Communications Authority of Thailand
CPT – Communist Party of Thailand
KMT – Kuomintang
KNU – Karen National Union
NGO – Nongovernmental Organisation
PLAT – People's Liberation Army of Thailand
SRT – State Railway of Thailand
TAT – Tourism Authority of Thailand
TOT – Telephone Organization of Thailand
THAI – Thai Airways International

LONELY PLANET

You already know that Lonely Planet produces more than this one guidebook, but you might not be aware of the other products we have on this region. Here is a selection of titles that you may want to check out as well:

Thailand's Islands & Beaches
ISBN 1 74059 063 5
US$16.99 • UK£11.99

Bangkok CitySync
ISBN 1 86450 228 2
US$49.99 • UK£29.99

Hill Tribes phrasebook
ISBN 0 86442 635 6
US$5.95 • UK£3.99

Bangkok
ISBN 1 86450 285 1
US$15.99 • UK£9.99

World Food Thailand
ISBN 1 86450 026 3
US$12.95 • UK£7.99

Thai phrasebook
ISBN 0 86442 658 5
US$6.95 • UK£4.50

Read This First: Asia & India
ISBN 1 86450 049 2
US$14.95 • UK£8.99

Thailand
ISBN 1 86450 251 7
US$24.99 • UK£14.99

South-East Asia on a shoestring
ISBN 1 86450 158 8
US$21.99 • UK£12.99

Thailand, Vietnam, Laos & Cambodia Road Atlas
ISBN 1 86450 102 2
US$14.99 • UK£8.99

Diving & Snorkeling Thailand
ISBN 1 86450 201 0
US$16.99 • UK£10.99

Healthy Travel Asia & India
ISBN 1 86450 051 4
US$5.95 • UK£3.99

Available wherever books are sold

Index

Abbreviations

NP – National Park   HP – Historical Park   NM – National Museum

Text

Boxed Text

MAP LEGEND

CITY ROUTES

Freeway .... Freeway	⊐⊐⊐⊐ ...... Unsealed Road
Highway ...... Primary Road	➤ ...... One Way Street
Road ...... Secondary Road	...... Pedestrian Street
Street .... Street	⊞⊞⊞⊞⊞ ...... Stepped Street
Lane .... Lane	⊃= = ... Tunnel
...... On/Off Ramp	...... Footbridge

REGIONAL ROUTES

.... Freeway
...... Primary Road
...... Secondary Road
.... Minor Road

BOUNDARIES

...... International
...... Provincial
...... Disputed
.... Wall

HYDROGRAPHY

...... River, Creek	...... Lake
...... Canal	⊛ ✛ .... Spring; Waterfalls

TRANSPORT ROUTES & STATIONS

...... Train	...... Walking Trail
...... Underground Train	...... Walking Tour
...... Skytrain	...... Path
...... Ferry	...... Pier or Jetty

AREA FEATURES

...... Building	...... Market	...... Beach	...... Campus
...... Park, Gardens	...... Sports Ground	+ + + ... Cemetery	...... Plaza

POPULATION SYMBOLS

✪ **CAPITAL** .... National Capital	⊙ **CITY** ...... City	● Village	.... Village
◉ **CAPITAL** ...... Provincial Capital	● **Town** ...... Town		...... Urban Area

MAP SYMBOLS

■ ...... Place to Stay	▼ ...... Place to Eat	● ...... Point of Interest

✈ ...... Airport	⊞ ...... Cinema	☪ ▥ ... Mosque, Museum	♫ ...... Shrine (Taoist)
⊡ .. Archaeological Site	◘ ...... Embassy	▨ ...... National Park	⚐ ...... Stupa or Chedi
❾ ⚲ Bank, Bird Sanctuary	▣ ⚑ ...... Fort, Fountain	℗ ⊛ .. Parking, Picnic Area	⊞ ...... Swimming Pool
✪ ...... Border Crossing	♥ ⊕ Golf Course, Hospital	⊙ ⊞ Petrol Station, Police	⊟ ...... Taxi or Tuk-Tuk
▣ ▤ .. Bus Terminal, Stop	➊ ...... Information	▭ ...... Post Office	⊠ ...... Telephone
▢ ▥ ...... Cafe, Camping	▣ ...... Internet Cafe	▢ ...... Pub/Bar	▮ ... Temple (Buddhist)
⌂ ...... Cave	※ ▲ ..Lookout, Mountain	▢ ...... Sawngthaew	▥ ...... Temple (Hindu)
▬ ⛪ ..Cathedral, Church	⚑ ...... Monument	⊗ .... Shopping Centre	▣ ▭ ...... Theatre, Zoo

Note: not all symbols displayed above appear in this book

LONELY PLANET OFFICES

Australia
Locked Bag 1, Footscray, Victoria 3011
☎ 03 8379 8000 fax 03 8379 8111
email: talk2us@lonelyplanet.com.au

USA
150 Linden St, Oakland, CA 94607
☎ 510 893 8555 TOLL FREE: 800 275 8555
fax 510 893 8572
email: info@lonelyplanet.com

UK
10a Spring Place, London NW5 3BH
☎ 020 7428 4800 fax 020 7428 4828
email: go@lonelyplanet.co.uk

France
1 rue du Dahomey, 75011 Paris
☎ 01 55 25 33 00 fax 01 55 25 33 01
email: bip@lonelyplanet.fr
www.lonelyplanet.fr

World Wide Web: www.lonelyplanet.com *or* AOL keyword: lp
Lonely Planet Images: lpi@lonelyplanet.com.au